NINETEENTH-CENTURY AMERICAN LITERATURE

THE OXFORD HANDBOOK OF

NINETEENTH-CENTURY AMERICAN LITERATURE

Edited by
RUSS CASTRONOVO

OXFORD
UNIVERSITY PRESS

OXFORD
UNIVERSITY PRESS

Oxford University Press is a department of the University of Oxford.
It furthers the University's objective of excellence in research, scholarship,
and education by publishing worldwide.

Oxford   New York
Auckland   Cape Town   Dar es Salaam   Hong Kong   Karachi
Kuala Lumpur   Madrid   Melbourne   Mexico City   Nairobi
New Delhi   Shanghai   Taipei   Toronto

With offices in
Argentina   Austria   Brazil   Chile   Czech Republic   France   Greece
Guatemala   Hungary   Italy   Japan   Poland   Portugal   Singapore
South Korea   Switzerland   Thailand   Turkey   Ukraine   Vietnam

Oxford is a registered trade mark of Oxford University Press
in the UK and certain other countries.

Published in the United States of America by
Oxford University Press
198 Madison Avenue, New York, NY 10016

© Oxford University Press 2012

First issued as an Oxford University Press paperback, 2014.

Library of Congress Cataloging-in-Publication Data
The Oxford handbook of nineteenth-century American literature / edited by Russ Castronovo.
p. cm. —(Oxford handbooks)
Includes bibliographical references and index.
ISBN 978-0-19-973043-8 (hardcover : acid-free paper); 978-0-19-935589-1 (paperback)
1. American literature—19th century—History and criticism.
I. Castronovo, Russ, 1965-
PS201.O94 2011
810.9'003—dc23
2011018469

In chapter 11, the poems of Emily Dickinson, edited by Ralph W. Franklin, are reprinted by permission
of the publishers and the Trustees of Amherst College from *The Poems of Emily Dickinson*, edited by Ralph W. Franklin,
Cambridge, Mass.: The Belknap Press of Harvard University Press, Copyright ©1998, 1999 by the President and Fellows
of Harvard College. Copyright ©1951, 1955, 1979, 1983 by the President and Fellows of Harvard College.

Dickinson's letters are reprinted by permission of the publishers from *The Letters of Emily Dickinson*, edited by
Thomas H. Johnson, Cambridge, Mass.: The Belknap Press of Harvard University Press, Copyright ©1958, 1986,
The President and Fellows of Harvard College; 1914, 1924, 1932, 1942 by Martha Dickinson Bianchi; 1952
by Alfred LeeteHampson; 1960 by Mary L. Hampson.

CONTENTS

....

PART II   ZIGZAGS

PART III   IMPACTS

LIST OF CONTRIBUTORS

Jesse Alemán is Associate Professor of English at the University of New Mexico. He edited and reprinted Loreta Janeta Velazquez's 1876 autobiography and coedited (with Shelley Streeby) *Empire and the Literature of Sensation*. He is currently working on *Wars of Rebellion*, a book that places nineteenth-century Hispanic writings about the U.S. Civil War within a context that considers related wars of rebellion in Cuba and Mexico.

Nancy Bentley is Professor of English at the University of Pennsylvania. Her most recent book is *Frantic Panoramas: American Literature and Mass Culture, 1870–1920*, and she is currently completing a book entitled *New World Kinship and the American Novel*.

Colleen Glenney Boggs is Associate Professor of English and Women's and Gender Studies at Dartmouth College. She has published work in *American Literature* and *PMLA*, is the author of *Transnationalism and American Literature: Literary Translation 1773–1892*, and is currently working on a monograph entitled *Animalia Americana: Animal Representations and the Affective Construction of Biopolitical Subjectivity*.

Anna Brickhouse is Associate Professor of English at the University of Virginia. She is author of *Transamerican Literary Relations and the Nineteenth-Century Public Sphere*, which won the Gustave Arlt Award for Best First Book in the Humanities.

Russ Castronovo is Dorothy Draheim Professor of English at the University of Wisconsin-Madison. He is author of three books: *Fathering the Nation: American Genealogies of Slavery and Freedom*; *Necro Citizenship: Death, Eroticism, and the Public Sphere in the Nineteenth-Century United States*; and *Beautiful Democracy: Aesthetics and Anarchy in a Global Era*. He is also editor of *Materializing Democracy: Toward a Revitalized Cultural Politics* (with Dana Nelson) and *States of Emergency: The Object of American Studies* (with Susan Gillman).

James Dawes is Chair and Professor of English at Macalester College, and Founder and Director of the Program in Human Rights and Humanitarianism. He is the author of *That the World May Know: Bearing Witness to Atrocity* and *The Language of War: Literature and Culture in the US from the Civil War through World War II*.

Elizabeth Duquette is an Associate Professor in the English Department at Gettysburg College. She is the author of *Loyal Subjects: Bonds of Nation, Race, and Allegiance in Nineteenth-Century America*.

John Ernest, the Eberly Family Distinguished Professor of American Literature at West Virginia University, is the author or editor of ten books, including *Liberation Historiography: African American Writers and the Challenge of History, 1794–1861*; *Chaotic Justice: Rethinking African American Literary History*; and *A Nation within a Nation: Organizing African American Communities before the Civil War*.

Travis M. Foster is assistant professor of English at The College of Wooster. He is completing a book manuscript on American literary culture and the politics of friendship.

Paul Giles is Challis Professor of English Literature at the University of Sydney, Australia. His books include *The Global Remapping of American Literature*; *Transnationalism in Practice: Essays on American Studies, Literature, and Religion*; *Atlantic Republic: The American Tradition in English Literature*; *Virtual Americas: Transnational Fictions and the Transatlantic Imaginary*; *Transatlantic Insurrections: British Culture and the Formation of American Literature, 1730–1860*; *American Catholic Arts and Fictions: Culture, Ideology, Aesthetics*; and *Hart Crane: The Contexts of The Bridge*. The chapter in this book is part of an Australian Research Council Discovery project entitled "Antipodean America: Australasia, Colonialism, and the Constitution of U.S. Literature."

Susan Gillman is Professor of Literature at the University of California, Santa Cruz. Her books include *Dark Twins: Imposture and Identity in Mark Twain's America* and *Blood Talk: American Race Melodrama and the Culture of the Occult*. She is also coeditor of *States of Emergency: The Object of American Studies* (with Russ Castronovo) and *Next to the Color Line: Gender, Sexuality, and W.E.B. Du Bois* (with Alys Eve Weinbaum).

Paul Gilmore is professor of English at California State University, Long Beach and author of *The Genuine Article: Race, Mass Culture, and American Literary Manhood* and *Aesthetic Materialism: Electricity and American Romanticism*.

Jared Hickman is an Assistant Professor of English at Johns Hopkins University. He has published on theology, democracy, and race in *The New England Quarterly*, *Early American Literature*, and other venues. He is currently working on a book entitled *Black Prometheus: Political Theologies of Atlantic Antislavery*.

Gregory S. Jackson is Associate Vice President for Academic Affairs and Associate Professor of English at Rutgers University. He is the author of *The Word and Its Witness: The Spiritualization of American Realism* and numerous articles on Anglo-American religion and literature.

Maurice S. Lee is an Associate Professor of English at Boston University. He is the author of *Slavery, Philosophy, and American Literature, 1830–1860* and the editor of *The Cambridge Companion to Frederick Douglass*. His most recent book is *Uncertain Chances: Science, Skepticism, and Belief in Nineteenth-Century American Literature*.

Stephanie LeMenager is Associate Professor of English at the University of California, Santa Barbara. Her first book, *Manifest and Other Destinies*, won the 2005 Thomas J. Lyon Award for Best Book in Western American Literary Studies. She is a co-editor of *Environmental Criticism for the Twenty-First Century* and author of several articles and book chapters treating US/American Studies and environmental criticism. She is completing a third book, *This Is Not a Tree: Cultures of Environmentalism in the Twilight of Oil.*

Robert S. Levine is Professor of English and Distinguished Scholar-Teacher at the University of Maryland, College Park, where he is Director of the Center for Literary and Comparative Studies. He is the author of *Conspiracy and Romance*; *Martin Delany, Frederick Douglass, and the Politics of Representative Identity*; and *Dislocating Race and Nation*, and the editor of a number of volumes, including *Hemispheric American Studies* (coedited with Caroline F. Levander). He is the new General Editor of *The Norton Anthology of American Literature.*

Dana D. Nelson is the Gertrude Conway Vanderbilt Professor of English at Vanderbilt University, where she teaches courses on democratic activism and the commons. She is author of three books: *The Word in Black and White: Reading "Race" in American Literature, 1638–1867*; *National Manhood: Capitalist Citizenship and the Imagined Fraternity of White Men*; and *Bad for Democracy: How the Presidency Undermines the Power of the People.* She is also editor of *Materializing Democracy: Toward a Revitalized Cultural Politics* (with Russ Castronovo) She is currently at work on a book that studies alternative democratic cultures in the early US.

Ellen Samuels is Assistant Professor of English and Gender & Women's Studies at the University of Wisconsin at Madison. Her critical writing on disability, race, gender, and American literature has been published in numerous journals and anthologies. She recently completed a book titled *Fantasies of Identification: Disability, Gender, Race*, and is now working on a new book, *Double Meanings: Gendered Representations of Conjoined Twins.*

Shirley Samuels teaches American literature at Cornell University. She has written *Romances of the Republic: Women, the Family, and Violence in the Literature of the Early American Nation* and *Facing America: Iconography and the Civil War.* She has also edited *The Culture of Sentiment: Race, Gender, and Sentimentality in 19th-Century America* and *Companion to American Fiction.* Forthcoming books include the edited *Cambridge Companion to Abraham Lincoln* and *Reading the American Novel, 1780-1865.*

Jeffrey Steele is Professor of English at the University of Wisconsin–Madison. He books include *Transfiguring America: Myth, Ideology, and Mourning in Margaret Fuller's Writing*; *The Essential Margaret Fuller*; and *The Representation of the Self in the American Renaissance.*

Jordan Alexander Stein teaches in the English department of the University of Colorado at Boulder. He coedited a special issue of *Early American Literature* on "Methods for the Study of Religion" (with Justine S. Murison) as well as a forthcoming essay collection on early African American print culture (with Lara Langer Cohen).

Shelley Streeby is Professor of Literature and an affiliate of the Ethnic Studies Department and Gender Studies Program at the University of California, San Diego. She is the author of *American Sensations: Class, Empire, and the Production of Popular Culture*, which received the American Studies Association's 2003 Lora Romero First Book Publication Prize, as well as the forthcoming *Radical Sensations: World Movements, Violence, and Visual Culture* (Duke University Press). She is also coeditor (with Jesse Alemán) of *Empire and the Literature of Sensation: An Anthology of Nineteenth-Century Popular Fiction*.

Elisa Tamarkin is Associate Professor of English at University of California, Berkeley and the author of *Anglophilia: Deference, Devotion, and Antebellum America*. She is currently working on a book titled *Irrelevance*, on the culture of the news and on ideas of relevant and irrelevant knowledge since 1830.

INTRODUCTION: SHIFTS, ZIGZAGS, IMPACTS

RUSS CASTRONOVO

NINETEENTH-CENTURY American literature is not going anywhere. As an eminently convenient rubric for identifying texts, assembling a field of study, and establishing critical patterns, this literary historical designation remains very much a product of its time, defined by its moment and place. A handy one-hundred-year span demarcates recognizable temporal limits. National geography provides different but equally workmanlike coordinates—an author's birthplace, setting, place of publication, and the like—for identifying American literature as American, tautological as that undertaking may be. From such a perspective, one might reasonably expect the field boundaries of nineteenth-century American literature to have been set long ago, perhaps at the end of the last century, and that they are not going to change very much in the coming one.

Fortunately, the boundaries of nineteenth-century American literature are not so ironclad as to limit the field to fiction, poetry, essays, or drama written within the United States between the years 1801 and 1900. There are at least three challenges to such a narrow understanding: (1) the idea of the long nineteenth century; (2) the asymmetry of the United States and America; (3) the expansion of literature beyond traditional genres. In fact, almost all the chapters in this volume expand—or explode—the idea of nineteenth-century American literature along one or more of these axes. In terms of this interlocking trio of new directions, it is not simply that understandings about what this body of literature is and how it functions might change; rather, more profoundly, it is that this seemingly complete tradition is always experiencing changes in shape, definition, and possibility.

The long nineteenth century stretches from 1789 to 1914, bracketed by the French Revolution and the start of World War I. These signposts, as proposed by the historian Eric Hobsbawm, have unmistakable European accents. Nevertheless, they invite musings about what an elongated American version might look like. At one end, the Haitian Revolution (1791–1804), the ratification of the U.S. Constitution (1787), the *Vente de la Louisiane* (the Louisiana Purchase of 1803) and, at the other end, the opening of the Panama Canal (1914), the landing of U.S. Marines in Haiti (1915), the U.S. entry into World War I (1917), the Pan-African Congress of 1919, or even the crash of the U.S. stock market (1929) are all significant arguments for lengthening the nineteenth century from American vantage points that reference but are surely broader than the United States. As readers of this *Oxford Handbook* will discover, an expanded time frame for this literature encompasses James Fenimore Cooper's nineteenth-century historical novels about eighteenth-century settlement and frontier racial warfare just as it includes Toni Morrison's twenty-first-century examination, by way of her commentary on Nathaniel Hawthorne and Herman Melville, of three centuries of slavery in the Americas.

Even more profound—and usefully disruptive—has been critical attention to texts written beyond what was then or is now the sovereign borders of the United States. This turn to transamerican sources from the Caribbean, Canada, Latin America, the Southwest, and the Atlantic hemisphere, including sources not written in English, represents a shift in the thinking about what, after all, makes American literature American. By what "rules" does American literature have to be written in English? The promise as well as the problem of transnational American literature is taken up and debated at several points in this volume. The authors here hardly agree on the overall import or potential of this widened America, what the Cuban poet and patriot José Martí called "nuestra América," but certain it is that this sensibility challenges many of the familiar assumptions regarding the Americanness of American literature.

If this critical geographic axis leads to questions about the Americanness of American literature, a third line of inquiry takes aim at the literariness of the field. Do only familiar genres—the novel, the poem, the essay—count as literature? What places do philosophical reflection (to choose one end of the spectrum) or mass-market journalism and magazine writing (to choose the other end) occupy on the bookshelf of American literature? So, too, more than one of the chapters focus their interpretative energies on nonverbal texts by examining nineteenth-century illustrations, religious-themed board games, and other artifacts of visual and material culture. In thus focusing on the formal as well as contextual attributes that make American writing literary, the trajectory of this *Oxford Handbook*, moving from "Shifts" to "Zigzags" to "Impacts," spurs mediations on the complex role that American literature qua literature plays in our thinking about and acting in the world.

Under this schema, nineteenth-century American literature hardly seems to be a self-evident category. The field is so much more than its name implies. It extends both backward and forward, making a mess of any presumptions about temporal demarcations that seem neatly keyed to a hundred-year time span. Likewise, the field pays little heed to nationalist checkpoints since the idea of America, under which might be classed various histories of and beliefs about liberty, racial identity, religion, art, and humanity, has never been isomorphic to the geopolitical entity of the United States. Finally, American literature hardly looks the same when that looking opens onto visual texts, which, from a more traditional perspective, have often seemed somehow different or less than literary.

For all the ways in which the field can appear new and different, these changes to the time and space of nineteenth-century American literature should not distract us from the fact that literary and other materials can—and regularly do—take shape within familiar rubrics. Spatial and temporal considerations force us to recognize that American literature is necessarily finite, bounded by the very delimitations that the long nineteenth century, the broadened idea of America, and an eye for popular materials all seek to overcome. Writers and texts fall in and out of fashion—how regularly do poets like William Cullen Bryant or Henry Wadsworth Longfellow, the authors of former schoolroom standards, now appear in college courses?—but incremental changes to canons and reading lists only rarely shift the overall shape of the field. When a long-lost nineteenth-century novel by Louisa May Alcott, *The Inheritance*, was unearthed in 1988, it quickly became part of classic American literature (a major publishing house markets the novel as a "classic"), but without substantively impacting the field, for instance, by transforming the ways we read or understand relations among texts. With the exception of remarkable finds such as this one, it is not as if a bevy of freshly discovered novels are going to be added every decade.

The more pressing task has been to raise new questions about familiar texts, to suggest the importance of expanded contexts, indeed, to change how this area of study itself is constructed and used. New critical developments, such as the interest in cultural productions throughout the Americas, have an impact that is more profound than recovering texts once lost to literary history and simply adding them to the tradition. This depth is found in refreshed thinking about such critical nodes as the natural environment, capital and its flows, whiteness and the process of racialization, and print culture and circulation that emerge from transnational and hemispheric realignments of American literature. What's more, this sort of spatial remapping of the field represents but one avenue of transformation. The three sections of this volume register the multiple and competing senses of newness that can enter a field that is seemingly as established, as predictable, in a word, as old as nineteenth-century American literature.

Instead of merely outlining a topic of study such as gender or nation, "Shifts," "Zigzags," and "Impacts" each explores how readers identify and tackle interpretative problems, of how we approach texts that range collectively, as the chapters in this volume do, from recognizable books such as Henry James's *The American* to popular but now obscure artifacts such as Edward Maturin's *Montezuma, the Last of the Aztecs*, from the philosophical abstractions of Ralph Waldo Emerson to the intimately grounded articles featured in the *Ladies' Home Journal*, and from the globetrotting of Washington Irving to the intensely local sensuousness that Henry David Thoreau found in a patch of huckleberries. The contributors to this volume are united in foregrounding issues of method and approach, focusing on how critics and students read, understand, and make use of American literary and cultural texts. "Shifts," "Zigzags," and "Impacts" suggest a range of unfamiliar yet practical coordinates for revising, questioning, and unsettling what we think we know and mean when we take novels, poems, and other discursive and visual artifacts as somehow emblematic or belonging to the body of nineteenth-century American literature. Unlike the predominant patterns for a good deal of history (and historiography), straight lines are downplayed under this tripartite schema. In practical terms, the organizational structure implies that this handbook does not need to be read in sequence from beginning to end. Multiple and varied are the paths that lead through this volume. The three sections highlighted here emphasize the connections as well as contentions that characterize the project as a whole. More than anything, they motivate questions that do not invite a single or easy answer but rather impel continuing investigation and debate. Such questions can be keyed to the individual chapters within each section.

SHIFTS

- **What happens when maps of national literature are shifted onto a cosmopolitan axis?** In responding to this question, Paul Giles looks at Washington Irving within the broad framework of global narratives.
- **How does moving away from aesthetic criteria of unity and toward those of chaos require new approaches to African American literature?** This is the task that John Ernest undertakes in his chapter on William Wells Brown, Martin Delany, and William Grimes in the context of African American literary and cultural theory.
- **By what criteria does a literary work count as an American novel?** Beginning with this fundamental question, Jordan Alexander Stein turns to Melville, who time and again thwarted the conventional expectations for literary narrative.
- **How does an orientation informed by disability studies shift understandings of race?** Mark Twain's entangling of slavery and nonnormative bodies is a good place to begin searching for answers, as Ellen Samuels contends.
- **In what ways does Creole consciousness give fresh accents to accounts of discovery and anticolonial resistance?** For Jesse Alemán, the answer entails an investigation of the role played by Mexican America in the U.S. literary imagination.

- **Why do novels about New World families knock notions of liberal subjectivity off their stable centers?** Abraham Lincoln, Harriet Beecher Stowe, Melville, and James, in Nancy Bentley's explanation, have much to say on the topic of kinship and privacy.
- **How does the expansion of mass-market visual culture shape literary meanings in the nineteenth century?** To answer this question, Shelley Streeby provides a transnational history of the Haymarket bombing and executions.
- **How might American literature be situated in a modern world system of the racialized Atlantic world?** Anna Brickhouse plots a surprising course that ranges from Hawthorne to Toni Morrison, from the seventeenth century to the nineteenth and beyond.

ZIGZAGS

- **How does the "complicated zigzag" of U.S. empire building inflect the relationship between frontier romances and white imperialism?** Robert Levine's answer travels a path, full of unexpected reversals, that moves from Cooper to George Copway, an Ojibwa Indian.
- **How do American writers access social and political phenomena that elude visual perception?** As Jeffrey Steele demonstrates, Lydia Maria Child, George Lippard, Fanny Fern, and other authors who toured, investigated, and ambled around city spaces confronted this challenge posed by urbanization.
- **Why do nineteenth-century views upon human subjectivity repeatedly cross into the terrain of the nonhuman and animals?** In considering this question, Colleen Glenney Boggs offers subtle readings of John Locke, Emily Dickinson, and theorists of what has become known as animal studies.
- **How does archival research change what we think we know about American authors?** Documents left by Hawthorne, Harriet Beecher Stowe, and Hannah Crafts, as Shirley Samuels shows, continue to revise standard assumptions about the American canon and its outliers.
- **What does it mean to say that people in the nineteenth century read religiously?** For Gregory Jackson, the pursuit of this question follows the tortuous pathways depicted in homiletic novels such as Alcott's *Little Women* or Lew Wallace's *Ben-Hur*.
- **How do we draw lines between literature and other forms of discourse?** In examining the interlacing of philosophy and literature during the nineteenth century, Maurice Lee shows why any answer to this challenge must begin with skepticism.

- **How should we evaluate transnational American studies?** Jared Hickman tracks across continents and regions in a chapter that ranges from Thomas Paine to Simón Bolívar and from James to José Vasconcelos.

IMPACTS

- **What impact did authors and readers think that reading had upon the formation of social bonds?** As Travis Foster suggests, answers lie in the rich archive of regionalism found in the *Ladies' Home Journal* and the short stories of Sarah Orne Jewett.
- **How does literature speak to its contemporary situation?** Elisa Tamarkin takes up this question by connecting novels, ranging from George Lippard's popular works to the literary-minded productions authored by Henry James, to the explosion of newspapers and the daily events reported in their pages.
- **How does literature shape minds?** Drawing on Kate Chopin and Charles Brockden Brown in the contexts of neuroscience, Paul Gilmore argues for an approach attuned to the history of mental processes.
- **What are the ethics of using and making examples out of people?** For Elizabeth Duquette, this investigation is best pursued by reading literature, especially the work of William Wells Brown and Douglass, as philosophy.
- **What is the relationship between literary critical practice and human rights?** This profoundly ethical question posed by James Dawes leads to an examination of abolitionism, as it was conceived and practiced by Emerson, Stowe, Douglass, and William Lloyd Garrison.
- **"How do we compare?"** In posing this question, Susan Gillman examines social protest literature authored—and adapted—by Stowe, Helen Hunt Jackson, and José Martí.
- **"What is to be done with nineteenth-century American literature" in an era of global climate change?** In taking up this unsettling question, Stephanie LeMenager turns to Thoreau, John Muir, Walt Whitman, George Perkins Marsh, and other nineteenth-century defenders of Nature.
- **Can nineteenth-century American literature provide lessons for twenty-first-century citizenship?** For Russ Castronovo and Dana Nelson, a consideration of Stowe in conjunction with the actions of John Brown raises some interesting possibilities.

Amid this diversity of texts and topics, these questions share the consistent thread of method and approach. How do we approach the field? How do we recalibrate the coordinates of critical vision? How do we open up new areas of investigation?

It might be said that in the closing decades of the twentieth century, critics put especial pressure on *what* was included in the American literary canon. Beginning in the 1980s, canon deformation altered the landscape of American literature, making a case for the inclusion of texts by women, working-class writers, African Americans, Latino/as, and other ethnic minorities. Important editorial projects, including the Schomburg Library of Nineteenth-Century Black Women Writers, the American Women Writers Series, and Recovering the U.S. Hispanic Literary Heritage, have ensured that literary scholarship and course syllabi no longer look as they once did a generation ago. While this attention to identity categories occasioned sharp debate during the so-called culture wars, the result has been a more nuanced literary history. Attention to race, class, and gender in the 1980s and 1990s—and fortunately this attention has not waned—entails a complex accounting of the intersections among these markers as opposed to a singular focus upon any one of these categories. This ameliorative pattern has continued so that considerations of sexuality, sovereignty, disability, environments, regions (like the Atlantic or the hemisphere), imperialism, and transnationalism have provoked generative debates about topics that were once ignored (such as disability), taken for granted (such as the natural environment), or disavowed (such as the history of imperialism). In the twenty years or so leading up to the close of the twentieth century, notions of *what* constitutes nineteenth-century American literature experienced radical revision, widening the scope of both *American* (to include hemispheric, transnational, and diasporic expressions) and *literature* (to include pamphlets and tracts, journals and diaries, dime novels, oral narratives, theatrical performances, legal decisions, scientific accounts, graphic texts, folk materials, and so on).

These welcome challenges to the component terms of American literature have changed the study of the nineteenth century sometimes so quickly that students and scholars have not always had the chance to evaluate and consider what these changes mean. In other words, in addition to the focus on *what* constitutes the canon of nineteenth-century literature, critical readers must also address the questions of *how* and *why*. Why is it significant that texts ranging from maritime narratives (think of Cooper, Melville, and Poe's contributions to this genre) to slave narratives (think of Frederick Douglass's and Harriet Jacobs's sojourns in England) are now frequently perceived as transnational performances? Why is it significant that Billy Budd's stutter, Roger Chillingworth's hunched back, Magawisca's severed limb in Catharine Maria Sedgwick's *Hope Leslie*, or the broken-down workers in Rebecca Harding Davis's *Life in the Iron Mills* can be recognized as figures of disability? How do John Muir and Whitman encourage new departures in the thinking about the imbrications of humans and the natural world? In other words, surely the point of a transnational reading must be something more than the demonstration that a text is transnational just as readings indebted to disability studies or environmental criticism must offer an interpretative payoff that is more than a thematic hunt for nonnormative bodies or variations on nature as the romantic sublime. Even as the chapters in this volume examine specific works of nineteenth-century literature, they also seek to address the implications about the scope and scale of analysis that they employ. Each takes up methodological implications by assessing the benefits as well as the challenges of expanding contexts, shifting perspectives, and implementing new approaches.

For the contributors to this *Oxford Handbook*, this concern is more than theoretical. It is also intensely practical, inviting attention to *how* readers read, *how* critics critique, and *how* interpreters interpret. In an effort to develop an analysis that resonates beyond any particular novel or poem, the writers here have all explained—some for several paragraphs and others for pages—how to produce a reading. How does one work with letters and archival material? How does one wrest meaning from "boring" novels like Melville's *Mardi*? How might one turn to abolitionist literature and the novels of Stowe for models that connect rhetoric to political action? In exploring these precise questions and others like them, the chapters offer practical insights and hands-on strategies for exploring novels, poems, and other literary creations beyond those that receive explicit discussion. In this way, *The Oxford Handbook to Nineteenth-Century American Literature* truly strives to be a handbook; the project is designed both to examine and advance the state of the field. While the book does register how the field has changed, the bulk of its critical energy is devoted to the ways in which American literary studies are changing.

This collective effort is not a monument to the scholarly accretions of literary history. Starting with this introduction, it both offers a perspective upon lasting and recent developments within American literary criticism and represents a future history of the field. Because this volume prioritizes method, because it is designed not as a compendium or catchall, and because its contributors represent scholars working at the forefront of new and different approaches, it seeks to register what is happening—as opposed to what has happened—in studies of nineteenth-century American literature.

PART I

SHIFTS

CHAPTER 1

ANTIPODEAN AMERICAN GEOGRAPHY: WASHINGTON IRVING'S "GLOBULAR" NARRATIVES

PAUL GILES

WHAT is now known as nineteenth-century "American" literature was in fact predicated upon a shifting, unstable conception of the national domain. It was not until after the war with Mexico in the 1840s that California became part of the United States, and in *Two Years before the Mast* (1840) Boston author Richard Henry Dana writes of "the desolate hills of San Diego" (336) as a foreign country overrun with shiftless Spaniards. Much of the Pacific Northwest was also British territory until the late 1840s, and it was not until the late 1860s that the outcome of the U.S. Civil War served effectively to solder the country into "one nation, indivisible," bringing East and West as well as North and South into the federal shape that has become thoroughly naturalized today. In a postscript to *Two Years before the Mast*, written in 1868, Dana looked back with some bemusement on how in 1836 the coast of California had seemed "remote and almost unknown," whereas a mere thirty years later San Francisco was now an integral part of American life, "the great center of a worldwide commerce" (338). Such retrospective compressions of temporal and spatial perspective have tended to obscure ways in which, during the earlier part of the nineteenth century, the rationale for grounding American literature upon the continental shape of the nation appeared much less self-evident. The purpose of this chapter is to examine how geographical variables enter into the writings of Washington Irving, and how as an author he plays self-consciously with the contours of cultural mapping, taking delight in reversing conventional geospatial trajectories so as to stand familiar cultural assumptions on their head. In this sense, the reflexive nature of Irving's work speaks to a meta-geographical dimension that was common to many American writers in the antebellum period, who were concerned in one way or another with how the national domain might be mapped.

Irving's general skepticism about the efficacy of national narratives does tend to be read more sympathetically today than it was sixty years ago, when F. O. Matthiessen dismissed him as a derivative stylist who "had not desired to pass beyond current models or usage" (30). Nevertheless, the transnational impetus of Irving's writing is normally understood as having worked itself out across a specifically transatlantic axis, a binary model opposing Europe to America, rather than one where oceanic space introduces global crosscurrents. The traditional story recounts his extended residence in Europe between 1815 and 1832, the phenomenal success of *The Sketch Book* (1819–1820), with its account of "the charms of storied and poetical association" in old England (744), followed by several years working for the American diplomatic service in Spain during the late 1820s. Irving's return to the United States in May 1832 is thus thought to herald an attempt to reestablish connections with the land of his birth, a project exemplified in the subsequent publication of various narratives treating America's western territories: *A Tour on the Prairies* (1835), *Astoria* (1836), and *Adventures of Captain Bonneville* (1837). But such a geographical or conceptual antithesis between home and abroad was, for Irving himself, a misleading formulation, and I would argue that traditional questions of Irving's literary nationalism arise from fundamentally inappropriate premises. Instead, his writing was always invested in a quite different conception of what in the *Life and Voyages of Christopher Columbus* he called a "globular" narrative (47), whose ontological conditions of burlesque spoke not to an Earth organized along lines of partition, but rather to one that was always mutating and spinning. In this sense, the upside-down logic of burlesque resonates more with the universalizing idiom of Irving's transgressive narratives than do the hierarchical structures of a merely transatlantic postcolonialism, within whose rubric power relations would be locked into a more linear dialectic. Throughout his writings, Irving thus appropriates the figure of the antipodes in both a geographic and a conceptual sense, to open up flat terrestrial landscapes to the revolution of the globe.

Irving's relation to U.S. cultural politics was never a simple matter, and he shared with Charles Brockden Brown a skepticism toward the spirit of Jeffersonian republicanism that was prevalent in the United States during the first decade of the nineteenth century. From his earliest literary endeavors, Irving's project involves normalizing the burlesque, making the idea of antipodes, in a figurative rather than merely geographical sense, integral to the cultural consciousness of the nation. *Tales of a Traveller* (1824) mentions sardonically the notion of "a voyage to improvement to Botany Bay" (1:50), the penal colony established in Australia by the British in 1788, but what interests Irving more than the prospect of transpacific displacement are situations in which disparate categories are inverted or superimposed upon each other. Rather than the hegemonic claims of imperialism or the authoritarian aspects of penal transportation, Irving's imagination responds to structures of bouleversement where the respectable and the off-limits are creatively confused, as in an early piece he wrote in 1807 for the journal *Salmagundi*:

> [N]ow this is what I like; and I intend in my present tour to digress as often and as long as I please. If, therefore, I choose to make a hop, skip, and jump to China, or New-Holland, or Terra Incognita, or Communipaw, I can produce a host of examples to justify me even in books that have been praised by the english reviewers, whose *fiat* being all that is necessary to give books a currency in this country, I am determined, as soon as I finish my edition of travels in seventy-five volumes, to transmit it forthwith to them for judgment. If these transatlantic censors praise it, I have no fear of its success in this country, where *their* approbation gives, like the tower stamp, a fictitious value, and makes tinsel and wampum pass current for classick gold. (223)

This passage is interesting not only for Irving's metaphorical appropriation of "New-Holland, or Terra Incognita," but also for his vituperative stance toward "English reviewers," whom he casts as "transatlantic censors," since in this upside-down world their critical "approbation" is a sure indication that any given book will be unsuccessful in America. A few lines later, Irving's persona Jeremy Cockloft starts speculating on "the first peopling of America," citing various fictitious authorities

> to prove that America was first of all peopled either by the antipodeans, or the cornish miners, who, he [Linkum Fidelius] maintains, might easily have made a subterraneous passage to this country, particularly the antipodeans, who, he asserts, can get along under ground, as fast as moles—quere, which of these is in the right, or are they all wrong?—For my part, I dont see why America had not as good a right to be peopled at first, as any little contemptible country of Europe, or Asia; and I am determined to write a book at my first leisure, to prove that Noah was born here—and that so far is America from being indebted to any other country for inhabitants, that they were every one of them peopled by colonies from her! (224–225)

Again, Irving deploys the conceptual axis of the antipodes to reverse domestic assumptions by suggesting that America is not, as in standard political rhetoric of the time, a "New World" but one as old as Noah. By citing a biblical provenance for America and so ratcheting up exceptionalist fantasies to an absurdly comic level, Irving effectively hollows out the kind of imperialist ambitions that, in this Jeffersonian era, liked to regard the new United States as the fountain and crucible of a new world order.

Noah also makes an appearance in Irving's first extended work, *A History of New York, from the Beginning of the World to the End of the Dutch Dynasty* (1809). This is a burlesque account of the world which offers to rewrite American history according to structural principles of "perverseness" (389) and contradiction, with Irving's narrator, Diedrich Knickerbocker, speculating that when Noah "portioned out his estate among his children," giving Asia to Shem, Africa to Ham, and Europe to Japhet, he must have looked upon America "as mere wild unsettled land" and thus "said nothing about it" (401). Irving's *History* starts out in chapter 1 with a spherical image, as Knickerbocker suggests the world "has the form of an orange, being an oblate spheroid, curiously flattened at opposite parts, for the insertion of two imaginary poles, which are supposed to penetrate and unite at the centre; thus forming an axis on which the mighty orange turns with a regular diurnal revolution" (385). Such contemplation of polar opposites produces a ripple effect in thinking about time and history, with the spherical motion of the Earth anticipating Irving's ontological pattern of burlesque in *A History of New York*, where the linear teleology of progressivist history is displaced into cyclic forms that fold back recursively upon themselves as the narrative develops.

The idiosyncratic genius of Irving's *History*, then, involves abjuring the rational, positivistic premises of history. He argues, for example, that nothing is more conducive to the growth of a great empire than "calamity": "Paris rises in importance, by the plots and massacres, which have ended in the exaltation of the illustrious Napoleon—and even the mighty London itself, has skulked through the records of time, celebrated for nothing of moment, excepting the Plague, the great fire, and Guy Faux's gunpowder plot!" (683). This reconstitution of history as a form of structural paradox is given a specific American resonance when Knickerbocker claims that the activities of Peter Stuyvesant, governor of New York, induced Lord Baltimore to persuade the British cabinet to subdue "the whole province of New Netherlands," thus serving politically to consolidate "hitherto scattered colonies" and helping to spark off the American Revolution (722). Irving's premise is that history works itself out contrariwise, and this systematic inversion of cause and effect is given a geographical dimension in chapter 4:

> Speaking of the islands of Solomon, New Guinea, and New Holland, the profound father Charlevoix observes, "in fine, all these countries are peopled, and *it is possible*, some have been so *by accident*. Now if it could have happened in that manner, why might it not have been at the *same time*, and by the *same means*, with *the other* parts of the globe?" This ingenious mode of deducing certain conclusions from possible premises, is an improvement in syllogistic skill, and proves the good father superior even to Archimedes, for he can turn the world without any thing to rest his lever upon. (410–411)

Irving here slyly mocks Charlevoix, the medieval churchman who claimed that the "inhabitants of both hemispheres are certainly the descendants of the same father" (411). Charlevoix was seeking in this way to overcome the traditional theological objection to the idea of antipodes, which was that people unbeknownst to each other in different parts of the world could not all have been descended from Adam in the Garden of Eden. Irving lampoons the syllogistic efforts of Charlevoix to reduce diffuse earthly matter to narrow theological doctrine, to "turn the world without any thing to rest his lever upon"; but he also suggests that such upside-down logic, tracing causes back from desired outcomes rather than the other way around, is characteristic of philosophical thought in general. Countermanding Enlightenment principles of free rational inquiry, Irving ironically salutes Charlevoix for exposing the elements of wish fulfillment that, so he believes, underpin the antipodean structure of human reasoning in general.

Irving thus invokes New Holland in this passage to address the condition of what he calls "this outlandish planet" (420), whose constant rotations defy any attempt to impose rationalistic systems upon it. Rather than being based upon logical or liberal premises, *A History of New York* is organized thematically around processes of reciprocal interaction, with Knickerbocker for example debating "whether it was most probable we should first discover and civilize the moon, or the moon discover and civilize our globe" (420–421): again, by disestablishing any conventional First Cause, Irving represents apparent opposites as mutually constitutive. All of this is related specifically to American cultural politics, with *A History of New York* mocking the legalistic ambitions of Thomas Jefferson in its portrayal of "William the Testy" (513), and Robert A. Ferguson describing it as "the first American book to question directly the civic vision of the Founding Fathers" (158). But this critique of Anglo-American hegemony through the focus of the *History* on the prevalence in New York of a Dutch American legacy merges into both an epistemological play with perspective—there is much discussion of "telescopes" and other ocular devices here (522)—and also a more general disquisition on the global processes of colonization. Irving refers to New York here as "Nieuw Nederlandts" (440), writing of how a Dutch nobleman's estate was located "some where in Terra Incognita" (442), and this implicitly links the Dutch colony in America with "New Holland" on the other side of the globe. The first European explorers of Australia in the seventeenth century were Dutch, with Joan Blaeu in 1645 first giving the continent the name "Nova Hollandia" (Schilder 103). The term "New Holland" was used familiarly in the Netherlands to refer to Australia until the end of the nineteenth century, even though after 1788 the British understood it only to refer to that part of the continent not yet annexed to New South Wales. Although Irving's book does not develop this analogy, it evokes geographical dislocation—"the islands of Solomon, New Guinea, and New Holland" (410)—as a corollary to the alternative historical topographies adduced here. Walt Whitman accused Irving in *A History of New York* of perpetrating merely a "shallow burlesque, full of clown's wit" (Roth 12); but, as Richard Grant White wrote in a theoretical piece "The Age of Burlesque" for the August 1869 issue of *Galaxy*, burlesque should not be seen as a synonym for "wicked, disgusting, or hateful" but as a strategy for conveying the "monstrously incongruous and unnatural." White went on to describe how the "system" of burlesque involves "a defiance of system" (Allen 136–137), and this is exactly what we find in Irving's work, which forces into juxtaposition a conventional category and its shadow self: Yankee America and Dutch America, Nieuw Nederlandts and New Holland. Through this kind of disarming proximity, Diedrich Knickerbocker subversively mirrors alternate categories in the light of each other and thus sets the globe spinning in disorienting directions.

Although *A History of New York* was a commercial success, this was only a pale harbinger of the general acclaim directed ten years later toward *The Sketch Book of Geoffrey Crayon, Gent.* (1819–1820), the book which established Irving's reputation and gave him financial independence. But, though it now enjoys the reputation of being a genteel portrait of English manners, *The Sketch Book* is actually predicated upon the same burlesque premises as *A History of New York*. From the start, in "The Author's Account of Himself," he invokes the idea of "terra incognita," saying he "was astonished to find how vast a globe I inhabited" (743); and this sense of disorientation is reinforced in the following chapter, "The Voyage," where Crayon describes how "[t]he vast space of waters, that separates the hemispheres is like a blank page in existence" (746). In this way, the Atlantic crossing functions for Irving as a kind of metaphysical rupture: rather than allowing for a gradual change of social scenery, the ocean's blankness finds Irving's persona "sent adrift upon a doubtful world" (746). When he sees a "distant sail" on the ocean, Geoffrey Crayon contemplates the forces of contingency that have "brought the ends of the earth into communion" (747); and some sense of the conventional social fabric always being haunted by a vast uncharted space always hovers over the book's subsequent invocation of Europe's "storied and poetical association" (744). *The Sketch Book* is thus deliberately framed perspectively—Crayon says, "I might fill a volume with the reveries of a sea voyage, for with me it is almost a continual reverie—but it is time to get to shore" (750)—and this partially suppressed metaphysical dimension helps to ensure his representations of England's "hearty old holyday customs" (914) are refracted through an estranged vantage point.

Such estrangement represents, as it were, the Byronic side of Irving, the exponent of romantic irony whose work approaches native customs through a rigorous strategy of intellectual alienation. Irving shared a London publisher (John Murray) with Byron, and the London publication of *The Sketch Book* in 1820 followed hard upon the heels of Byron's *Don Juan* in 1819, another huge popular success for Murray; indeed, when he was in London Irving spent some time with Murray looking over Byron's letters from Venice, and he later considered writing a life of Byron himself.[1] In this sense, the more common association of Irving with literary figures of the previous generation such as Oliver Goldsmith is misleading. This parallelism, suggested by William Hazlitt in 1825, was later echoed by Herman Melville in his essay "Hawthorne and His Mosses," which, without mentioning Irving by name, refers disparagingly to "smooth pleasing authors" in America who "but furnish an appendix to Goldsmith" (248). However, in his short essay "Lord Byron" (1814) Irving wrote admiringly not of the English poet's smoothness but his edginess, how his work "benefited by the caustic of criticism" emerging from conventional society; and Irving's own remarks in the "Rural Life in England" chapter of *The Sketch Book* on the illusions of pastoral "harmony" carry with them a Byronic punch which seeks to disrupt the picturesque nature of this apparently idyllic setting:

> The man of refinement, therefore, finds nothing revolting in an intercourse
> with the lower orders in rural life, as he does when he casually mingles with the

> lower orders of cities. He lays aside his distance and reserve, and is glad to wave
> the distinctions of rank, and to enter into the honest heartfelt enjoyments of
> common life. Indeed the very amusements of the country bring men more and
> more together; and the sound of hound and horn blend all feelings into harmony.
> I believe this is one great reason why the nobility and gentry are more popular
> among the inferior orders in England than they are in any other country; and
> why the latter have endured so many excessive pressures and extremities, without
> repining more generally at the unequal distribution of fortune and privilege. (799)

Despite its agreeable formulations, which are skillfully designed not to give offense, the last words of this paragraph—addressing the "excessive pressures and extremities" of the "lower orders," and the "unequal distribution of fortune and privilege" in British society—serve clearly to unmask the structural inequities that Irving finds epitomized in this sentimental scene.

Like Byron, therefore, Irving fuses romance and irony together in a deliberately double-edged discourse. The very instability and duplicity of this rhetoric has been a source of discomfort for some traditional American critics, who have been advocates for a kind of sturdy independence supposedly characteristic of the American spirit, where authors should say what they mean and mean what they say. But such unilateralism was never part of Irving's style; instead, *The Sketch Book* cultivates the alien aspects of what its final chapter, "L'Envoy," calls "a strange land" (1090). This kind of strangeness is not confined merely to the landscapes of England, but is endemic to Irving's burlesque world more generally. In "The Legend of Sleepy Hollow," set again in Dutch New York, schoolmaster Ichabod Crane enjoys frightening "the old Dutch wives" of the village "with speculations upon comets and shooting stars, and with the alarming fact that the world did absolutely turn round, and that they were half the time topsy-turvy!" (1064–1065). Later in the story, Crane himself becomes an object of bouleversement when Brom Bones and his "gang of rough riders,.,broke into the school house at night, in spite of its formidable fastenings of withe and window stakes, and turned everything topsy-turvy" (1071). Just as Crayon's American sensibility surreptitiously inverts English customs, so Brom Bones's Dutch ancestry upends Crane's devotion to "his invaluable author, Cotton Mather" (1080) and to the orthodoxies of Puritan New England. Irving's creative imagination, in other words, is attached compulsively to situations where an established world is liable to be turned upside down.

While *The Sketch Book* is still quite widely read, and its two most famous stories—"Rip Van Winkle" and "The Legend of Sleepy Hollow"—have been heavily anthologized, Irving's *Life and Voyages of Christopher Columbus* (1828) has now generally fallen off the literary map. This contemporary neglect contrasts oddly with the book's visibility throughout the nineteenth century, when it was, as William H. Shurr observes, a "publishing phenomenon" (237), going through 175 editions in Europe and America and being translated into twelve languages by that century's end. Irving himself labored long and hard over this work, writing to Thomas Wentworth Storrow when he was serving as a diplomat in Spain of the "heavy and

"misleading and mischievous nonsense," since, said Morison, the issue in question was not the "sphericity of the globe," which was widely accepted by the 1480s, but rather "the width of the ocean" (1:117). Jeffrey Burton Russell in 1991 also accused Irving of using his sources "carelessly" (54) and trying to fool people with his "literary game" (52), particularly in the way he tends to conflate the medieval idea of a flat earth with a geocentric conception of the universe that Copernicus, also in the teeth of papal opposition, subsequently helped to unravel. In his description of the Council of Salamanca, Irving mentions how Copernicus "was then in existence, whose solar system should reverse the grand theory of Ptolemy, which stationed the earth in the centre of the universe" (52); but Irving neglects to mention that Copernicus, although born in 1473 and so "in existence" when the Council of Salamanca took place in 1487, was only a child at that time and did not publish his controversial work *On the Revolution of the Celestial Spheres* until significantly later, in 1543. Yet to indict Irving for these sometimes misleading historical slants is fundamentally to misapprehend the nature of his literary achievement. Irving's goal is not so much chronological accuracy but a revisionist account of the historical process that underscores its compulsive elements of buffoonery and misprision, and this is why he chooses to highlight the link with Copernicus, so as to emphasize the more transgressive aspects of Columbus's enterprise. Like other nineteenth-century American historians such as Francis Parkman and George Bancroft, Irving is more interested in the "spirit" that informs history than in its sequence; but for him this spirit expresses itself not so much in nationalistic as in burlesque or antipodean terms. After Columbus's first voyages to America, Irving recounts how Peter Martyr, a Spanish historian and chaplain to the court of Ferdinand and Isabella, wrote to his friend Pomponius Laetus "certifying to you the hitherto hidden world of the antipodes" (163); and it is such an exposure of this "hitherto hidden" antipodes that attracts Irving to Columbus and that links *Life and Voyages* with the author's earlier works. Irving here also makes merry with papal bulls issued in May 1493, decreeing that all possessions west of a line one hundred leagues to the west of the Azores were to belong to Spain and all land to the east to Portugal: "It seems never to have occurred to the pontiff," remarks Irving wryly, "that by pushing their opposite careers of discovery, they might some day or other come again in collision, and renew the question of territorial right at the antipodes" (169). Again, the geography of the "globular" earth, turning upon an antipodean axis, serves to trump the flatter designs of papal orthodoxy.

Much twentieth-century criticism of the *Life and Voyages of Columbus* attempted simply to accommodate it to the demands of literary nationalism, with James W. Tuttleton in 1974 linking the book to the Emersonian conception that all history is biography. Such approaches, however, represent a woeful simplification of Irving's art, since the transcendentalist notion of embodying what Tuttleton calls "providential design" in the person of one individual ("Romance" 19) is worlds away from Irving's understanding of the necessary disjunction between pioneering heroism and the contradictory nature of cultural progress. Similarly, Shurr's description of the narrative as a "mirror into the disappointed soul of Columbus himself" (239), which again takes the book to be the history of an individual rather than a history of the world, is highly reductive. Rather than reading Irving as an Emerson man-qué, or Columbus as a Thoreauvian wanderer who somehow lost his bearings, it would be more productive to think of the *Life and Voyages* as structured formally around a burlesque consciousness where the "hidden" nature of the antipodes, both geographic and metaphorical, is brought systematically to light. In the introduction to his sequel *Voyages and Discoveries of the Companions of Columbus* (1831), Irving describes how the Genoese mariner's last voyage "was made for the express pur-pose" of discovering a strait in South America that would enable him to make his way from the Atlantic into the "Southern Ocean" (3), and of how Columbus died on the threshold of discovering the Pacific; he also writes here of how Vasco Núñez de Balboa's subsequent "discovery of the Pacific Ocean forms one of the most beautiful and striking incidents in the history of the New World" (5). *Life and Voyages* starts with an enigmatic treatment of transatlantic commerce, suggesting that perhaps "there existed an intercourse between the opposite shores of the Atlantic" in ancient times (9), and some sense of the great unknown always lurks around the edges of these books' maritime charts, as on the island of Marigalante, in the Antilles, where Columbus puzzles over the washed-up sternpost of a vessel, wondering whether it was a "fragment of some European ship which had drifted across the Atlantic" (186). In this sense, Irving uses both the transatlantic and transpacific not to reify binary oppositions between continental land masses, but to interrogate the principles of identity upon which such cultural formations have been grounded. He thus deploys a "globular" consciousness to disrupt and disorient the rigid, legalistic orthodoxies of the known world.

After his return from Europe to the United States in 1832, Irving published in quick succession three narratives that center upon the American West: *A Tour on the Prairies* (1835), *Astoria: or Anecdotes of an Enterprize Beyond the Rocky Mountains* (1836), and *The Adventures of Captain Bonneville* (1837). These are often attributed to a desire on Irving's part to reestablish his nationalist credentials after, in William L. Hedges's presumptuous phrase, "remaining abroad too long" (5); but in all of these works it is noticeable how Irving's West takes on a hybrid or global quality rather than simply remaining the open frontier of American legend. In *A Tour on the Prairies*, for instance, the narrator notes how the way rays of the sun shine through trees on the prairie reminds him "of the effect of sunshine among the stained windows and clustering columns of a Gothic cathedral" (33). This is exactly the kind of image disliked by nationalist critics of Irving who argue that, rather than being a traveler receptive to what John Francis McDermott called "the actual West" of the 1830s (66), Irving falls into the stance of a "self-conscious literary man" (50). But such metaphorical cross-dressing is endemic to Irving's purposes: he consistently compares the prairie to the ocean, saying that a "clump of trees" seen in the distance reminds him of glimpsing "a ship at sea" (82), while the prairie dogs are said anthropomorphically to convene "in noisy assemblage" to discuss the "dig-nity of the republic" (147). By superimposing different categories upon each other in this way—trees and cathedrals, prairie and ocean, human and animal—Irving confounds traditional oppositions, disturbing the whole conception of what the American frontier might mean, while reorienting the western country as a landscape where many different cultural formations intersect. As Stephanie LeMenager has observed, the "sea and West exist in charged, dialectical tension in nineteenth-century U.S. literatures," and by transposing the rhetoric of Manifest Destiny and "agrarian empire" (17) into a more amorphous metaphorical conceit of the ocean, Irving implicitly casts shadows over the theme of imperial westering. The American exploration of the West, like Columbus's exploration of the Atlantic, is subject to many more misconstructions and forms of creative confusion than millennial typologies of the New World customarily allowed for.

Irving's *Astoria* again represents the American West in disjointed and multidirectional terms, opening out what the author calls his "widely excursive narrative" (589) to many different historical and geographical trajectories. He chronicles here the development of "the North West Coast of America" in the wake of "that renowned but unfortunate discoverer, Captain Cook," whose explorations helped to bring "the watery wastes of the Pacific" into a U.S. commercial orbit (199). He also describes the territorial claims to the Pacific Northwest of the British and the Native Americans, as well as the interests of New York magnates such as John Jacob Astor. By deliberately alternating the narrative focus of *Astoria* between the Pacific Ocean and the Rocky Mountains, between "the Maritime part of this enterprize" and "the adventurous band to whom was entrusted the land expedition" (279), Irving effectively highlights the transpacific as well as transcontinental aspects of Astoria's desirable location. Just as the Americans sought to encompass the Pacific coast within their domain in order to fulfill the agenda of Manifest Destiny, so the British wished to hold on to this territory, and in particular its West Coast ports, to preserve their profitable fur trade with China and other Pacific nations. By chronicling these cross-purposes, Irving's structural irony balances off the claims of U.S. nationalism against a recognition of the many different ways in which this landscape can be approached and apportioned. Again the prairies are systematically compared to oceans, and in *Astoria* this sense of oceanic displacement is developed further, with Irving describing how geologists suppose the "Great American desert" of the West once "formed the ancient floor of the ocean, countless ages since, when its primeval waves beat against the granite bases of the Rocky Mountains" (358). By introducing this kind of archaeological echo, Irving exposes the country to a deterritorializing impulse where the equation between territory and nation appears arbitrary. LeMenager has described *Astoria* as articulating "a postwestern theory of nationhood in which the nation-form was conceived as improvisatory" (99); but this might equally be understood as a prewestern theory of nationhood, under whose geological shadow the utopian myths of the American West are revealed as contingent and mutable constructions. It is true that Irving always publicly defended U.S. rights to its western frontier, writing in "The 'Empire of the West'" (1840) of America's "indefeasible right to the Oregon territory" (135), and acting in 1846 in a diplomatic capacity to assist the U.S. minister to London, Louis McLane, with negotiations over the disputed Pacific Northwest boundaries: "I still hope the matter may be settled by negotiation," Irving wrote to his nephew in December 1845; "but, should England provoke a war upon the question as it stands, I am clearly of opinion that we have the right on our side, and that the world will ultimately think so" (*Letters* 3:1041). But whereas Irving the political diplomat sought to advance U.S. national interests, Irving the cultural historian was more prone to problematizing them, and the aesthetic impact of his western narratives derives not from proselytizing inclinations but from a chameleonic capacity to face in many different directions.

In this sense, Irving's comment in an 1832 journal entry about how in western landscapes "the world is turned upside down" speaks not only to his sense of how these landscapes confound conventional social hierarchies, but also to the tenuous nature of the epistemological parameters that uphold them. Irving's journal expresses surprise at how not only "Half breeds" but also "dogs & cats" appear to rule the roost in western establishments, so that "the Slave" becomes "the master—the master the slave" (*Journals* 5:97). Such a state of inversion, though, is entirely commensurate with Irving's wider representation of the American West as a cultural and political landscape always susceptible to reversal. *The Adventures of Captain Bonneville* again reconceptualizes the West in multidirectional terms, describing how rivers flowing from the Rocky Mountains "find their way to the opposite waves of the Atlantic and the Pacific" (664), and reconfiguring the country's geographical locations within a more expansive framework, as it portrays Bonneville standing on the "dividing ridge" of the Rockies, "which Indians regard as the crest of the world; and on each side of which, the landscape may be said to decline to the two cardinal oceans of the globe" (790). This is a splendid image of global fluidity, one that fits with Irving's observations here on the "Italian effect" of the Californian climate (880), as well as with his remarks on how the arid spaces of the American Southwest rival "the deserts of Asia and Africa in sterility" (875). By metaphorically conflating different parts of the globe, Irving not only defamiliarizes American domestic landscapes—so that the Rocky Mountains are seen as "almost a terra incognita to the American trapper" (636)—but also reimagines U.S. cultural identity in terms of a constitutional hybridity, as he observes how horses are regarded by veterans of the mountains as having "almost human intellect" (946) and also how the Kansas chief White Plume is dressed with "whimsical incongruity," being "grand officer at top, and ragged Indian at bottom" (647). Such "incongruity," which Irving explicitly associates in his introduction to *Captain Bonneville* with the literary influence of Laurence Sterne's *Tristram Shandy*, also enables him to project backward and forward in time, describing the current state of California as "almost a terra incognita," while simultaneously anticipating how, with its natural wealth and resources, California will ultimately become the basis of "a powerful and prosperous empire" (882).[2]

Irving's idiom of romantic irony thus dislocates the American West into various alternative dimensions, whose forms of structural alienation expose the country to the specters of many different times and places. In an 1835 review of *A Tour on the Prairies*, James Hall expressed his astonishment at the notion of such a cultivated figure as "Irving on the prairies," saying "[t]he very idea has a novelty about it" (Antelyes 45). But it was, of course, the deliberate cultivation of such incongruities, the transposition and exchange of apparently antithetical qualities, that always formed the basis of Irving's art. Wai Chee Dimock has written of how in his writings on Muslim Spain Irving sought to remap the contours of American literature "against the coordinates of hemispheric Islam" (47), and *The Alhambra* (1832) presents Spanish landscapes in something like a trompe l'oeil fashion, with Irving intent upon depicting the country's hybrid character, "half Spanish half Oriental" (723), and also ways in which it partakes "of the savage and solitary character of Africa" (725). By deliberately bringing different cultural and temporal zones into juxtaposition, Irving invests his picturesque scenes with an elusive quality, where contemporary conditions are always susceptible to being reversed.

In this sense, the old image of Irving as merely offering his fellow Americans what Perry Miller called "a welcome interlude from the strenuousness of prosperity" (378), or of his narratives as exemplifying a case of arrested psychological development, seems hardly less than absurd. Indeed, there is probably no other major nineteenth-century American writer whose work has been so short-changed by the nationalist assumptions that came to regard the embodiment of U.S. cultural identity as a natural good in itself.[3] Yet the more recent critical positioning of Irving in terms of postcolonial thematics is also restrictive in the way it highlights how Irving's texts negotiate with traditional European cultures, particularly those of Britain and Spain, rather than also considering how they deliberately realign themselves in relation to a welter of global affairs. The primary interest of Irving, as with his hero Columbus, was in exploration, in juxtaposing familiar territory with terra incognita, and thus in rotating the known world upon its axis. Consequently, the burlesque mode for Irving was not simply a form of comic demystification or despoilment but a way of restoring sphericity to flat terrain, of demonstrating how the world appears differently once its "globular" nature is recognized. Columbus himself has a cameo role in *The Alhambra*, with the narrator describing how it was in the walls of Santa Fe that "Columbus was called back by the heroic queen, and…the treaty was concluded which led to the discovery of the Western World" (801), and all of Irving's writing bears witness to a latent potential for standing the world on its head. This global spin explains the wider significance of Irving's appropriation of the antipodes, which he presents not so much as a geographical phenomenon, but as a figurative analogy to his notion of a world turned upside down. As an author dedicated to the art of burlesque, Irving disperses the exceptionalist spirit of American transcendentalism across a wider agglomeration of worldly matter, and his global narratives thrive on the discrepancies inherent within these inverse dynamics.

NOTES

1 On Murray's relationships with Byron and Irving, see McClary 7–35.
2 Irving's introduction to *Captain Bonneville* compares the book's hero to Corporal Trim, a character in *Tristram Shandy* (631).
3 For a treatment of the "infantile" qualities of Irving's writing, see, for example, Pajak 128.

BIBLIOGRAPHY

Allen, Robert C. *Horrible Prettiness: Burlesque and American Culture*. Chapel Hill: University of North Carolina Press, 1991.

Antelyes, Peter. *Tales of Adventurous Enterprise: Irving and the Poetics of Western Expansion*. New York: Columbia University Press, 1990.

Dana, Richard Henry Jr. *Two Years before the Mast: A Personal Narrative*. Ed. John Seelye and Wes Davis. New York: New American Library, 2009.

Dimock, Wai Chee. "Hemispheric Islam: Continents and Centuries for American Literature." *American Literary History* 21.1 (2009): 28–52.

Ferguson, Robert A. *Law and Letters in American Culture*. Cambridge, MA: Harvard University Press, 1984.

Hazlett, John D. "Literary Nationalism and Ambivalence in Washington Irving's The Life and Voyages of Christopher Columbus." *American Literature* 55.4 (December 1983): 560–575.

Hedges, William F. Introduction. *The Old and New World Romanticism of Washington Irving*. Ed. Stanley Brodwin. New York: Greenwood Press, 1986. 1–9.

Irving, Washington. *The Adventures of Captain Bonneville*. 1837. Irving, *Three Western Narratives* 617–956.

——. *The Alhambra*. 1832. *Bracebridge Hall, Tales of a Traveller, The Alhambra*. New York: Library of America, 1991. 719–1050.

——. *Astoria: or Anecdotes of an Enterprize Beyond the Rocky Mountains*. 1836. Irving, *Three Western Narratives* 163–616.

——. "The 'Empire of the West.'" 1840. Irving, *Miscellaneous Writings, 1803–1859*. 135–137.

——. *A History of New York, from the Beginning of the World to the End of the Dutch Dynasty*. 1809. Irving, *History, Tales and Sketches* 363–729.

——. *History, Tales and Sketches*. New York: Library of America, 1983.

——. *Journals and Notebooks*. Vol. 5:1832–1859. *Complete Works*. Vol. 5. Ed. Sue Fields Ross. Boston: Twayne, 1986.

——. *Letters*. Vol. 3:1839–1845. *Complete Works*. Vol. 25. Ed. Ralph W. Aderman, Herbert L. Kleinfeld, and Jenifer S. Banks. Boston: Twayne, 1982.

——. *Letters*. Vol. 4:1846–1859. *Complete Works*. Vol. 26. Ed. Ralph W. Aderman, Herbert L. Kleinfeld, and Jenifer S. Banks. Boston: Twayne, 1982.

——. *Letters of Jonathan Oldstyle, Gent*. 1802–1803. Irving, *History, Tales and Sketches* 1–43.

——. *The Life and Voyages of Christopher Columbus*. 1828. *Complete Works*. Vol. 11. Ed. John Harmon McElroy. Boston: Twayne, 1981.

——. "Lord Byron." 1814. Irving, *Miscellaneous Writings, 1803–1859*. 114–117.

——. *Miscellaneous Writings, 1803–1859: Complete Works*. Vol. 28. Ed. Wayne R. Kime. Boston: Twayne, 1981.

——. *Salmagundi; or The Whim-Whams and Opinions of Launcelot Longstaff. Esq., & Others*. 1807–1808. Irving, *History, Tales and Sketches* 45–361.

——. *The Sketch Book of Geoffrey Crayon, Gent*. 1819–1820. Irving, *History, Tales and Sketches* 731–1091.

——. *Tales of a Traveller, by Geoffrey Crayon, Gent*. 2 vols. London, 1824.

——. *Three Western Narratives*. New York: Library of America, 2004.

——. *A Tour on the Prairies*. 1835. Irving, *Three Western Narratives* 1–162.

——. *Voyages and Discoveries of the Companions of Columbus*. 1831. *Complete Works*. Vol. 12. Ed. James W. Tuttleton. Boston: Twayne, 1986.

Leary, Lewis. *Washington Irving.* Minneapolis: University of Minnesota Press, 1963.

LeMenager, Stephanie. *Manifest and Other Destinies: Territorial Fictions of the Nineteenth-Century United States.* Lincoln: University of Nebraska Press, 2004.

Matthiessen, F. O. *American Renaissance: Art and Expression in the Age of Emerson and Whitman.* New York: Oxford University Press, 1941.

McClary, Ben Harris, ed. *Washington Irving and the House of Murray: Geoffrey Crayon Charms the British, 1817–1856.* Knoxville: University of Tennessee Press, 1969.

McDermott, John Francis, ed. *The Western Journals of Washington Irving.* Norman: University of Oklahoma Press, 1944.

McElroy, John Harmon. Introduction. *Life and Voyages of Christopher Columbus.* By Washington Irving. xvii–xcvii.

Melville, Herman. "Hawthorne and His Mosses." 1850. *The Piazza Tales and Other Prose Pieces, 1839–1860.* Ed. Harrison Hayford et al. Evanston, IL: Northwestern University Press, Newberry Library, 1987. 239–253.

Miller, Perry. Afterword. *The Sketch Book.* By Washington Irving. New York: New American Library, 1961. 371–378.

Morison, Samuel Eliot. *Admiral of the Ocean Sea: A Life of Christopher Columbus.* 2 vols. Boston: Little, Brown, 1942.

Pajak, Edward F. "Washington Irving's Ichabod Crane: American Narcissus." *American Imago* 38.1 (1981): 127–135.

Roth, Martin. *Comedy and America: The Lost World of Washington Irving.* Port Washington, NY: Kennikat Press, 1976.

Russell, Jeffrey Burton. *Inventing the Flat Earth: Columbus and Modern Historians.* New York: Praeger, 1991.

Schilder, Günter. "New Holland: The Dutch Discoveries." *Terra Australis to Australia.* Ed. Glyndwr Williams and Alan Frost. Melbourne: Oxford University Press-Australian Academy of the Humanities, 1988. 82–115.

Shurr, William H. "Irving and Whitman: Re-Historicizing the Figure of Columbus in Nineteenth-Century America." *American Transcendental Quarterly* NS 6.4 (December 1992): 237–250.

Sterne, Laurence. *The Life and Opinions of Tristram Shandy, Gentleman.* 1759–1767. Ed. Graham Petrie. London: Penguin, 1967.

Tuttleton, James W. Introduction. *Voyages and Discoveries of the Companions of Columbus.* By Washington Irving. xvii–lv.

———. "The Romance of History: Irving's *Companions of Columbus.*" *American Transcendental Quarterly* 24.1 (Fall 1974): 18–24.

Williams, Stanley T., ed. *Washington Irving and the Storrows: Letters from England and the Continent, 1821–1828.* Cambridge, MA: Harvard University Press, 1923.

CHAPTER 2

THE ART OF CHAOS: COMMUNITY AND AFRICAN AMERICAN LITERARY TRADITIONS

JOHN ERNEST

In his preface to Frederick Douglass's *My Bondage and My Freedom*, James McCune Smith, one of the leading African American intellectuals of his day, asserts that "if the volume now presented to the public were a mere work of ART, the history of its misfortune might be written in two very simple words—TOO LATE" (105). Instead, Smith added, the public "is not invited to a work of ART, but to a work of FACTS—Facts, terrible and almost incredible, it may be—yet FACTS, nevertheless" (105). Smith clearly thought that "a mere work of art" was inconsequential compared to Douglass's attempt to convey the terrible and incredible truths related to the system of slavery and the racist culture that he encountered after his successful escape to the North. *My Bondage and My Freedom*, Smith suggests, was a book with work to do, work that in some ways put it at odds with the then current ideals of aesthetical achievement. Smith's dismissal of aesthetics as a significant concern in Douglass's autobiography has been the judgment as well of many readers ever since—concerning not just *My Bondage and My Freedom* but nearly all of nineteenth-century African American literature, though with the change that the facts that Douglass and others wrote about seem now less relevant, less pressing. As Frances Smith Foster put it in 1994, a judgment that remains sadly relevant today: "While it is customary now for survey courses to include one or two early works, they are generally given as evidence of a few extraordinary individuals' ability to read and write or as examples of abolitionist protest literature. The common interpretation is that in either case, they wrote primarily for white folks and that, as in the idea of the dog who walks on two legs, the wonder is not what or how well they wrote but that they wrote at all. Early African American literature, we continue to believe, is more valuable as artifact than artistry" (xx). Virtually all of nineteenth-century African American literature has similarly made the transition from fact to artifact over time, with some works celebrated as important first steps toward the artistic achievements of the turn of the century and the full flowering of the Harlem Renaissance in the early twentieth century.

As we enter—and we are still only entering—a time when more scholars and students are reading nineteenth-century African American literature, our challenge is to account for a broad and complex tradition, and not just for the work of a few extraordinary individuals. One might say that our old challenge was to actually *read* nineteenth-century African American literature, beyond the work of Douglass and a very few others, and the new challenge is to think about *how to read* not just a few texts but a literary tradition, and how to determine an aesthetic ideal that might both guide and follow from those readings. What has kept scholars from searching for such methods and ideals is exactly what Foster addresses—the assumption that this is a body of literature produced by writers who could manage, by and large, only a rough account of their lives or world. This is a literature characterized by digressions, fragmented narratives, apparent didacticism, and frequent resorts to sentimental conventions—a body of work with all the markings of postmodern literature, but in a period that few acknowledge to be characterized by the conditions of the postmodern age (focusing on the white Euro-American calendar of history), joined with the markings of literary conventions popular in the nineteenth century but hardly sophisticated enough to rise to the level of serious literature. Add to this a certain roughness that speaks of educational limitations or of the challenges of writing against the press of time, and many scholars have been quick to conclude that African Americans of the nineteenth century, and especially before the Civil War, were simply unprepared to be literary artists. Accordingly, African American literary history of this time is often taken to be a rather self-evident tradition—a collection of works published by African American writers, with a rough literary veil obscuring the real work of political protest and activism.

Consider, for example, William Wells Brown's *Clotel or The President's Daughter: A Narrative of Slave Life in the United States* (1853). In this work—which some critics call a novel and some a fictional narrative, and for which some critics look for other terms entirely to identify—scholars have been so frustrated by the presence of so many sources and plots in one text that they have had trouble seeing the one in the many, a unified artistic achievement greater than the sum of its parts. Vernon Loggins complained in 1931 that "the great weakness of *Clotel* is that enough material for a dozen novels is crowded into its two hundred and forty-five pages" (166); by 1970, Arthur Davis had reduced the number of potential novels in *Clotel* to five, asserting that Brown "tried to cram too many things into one work: antislavery lectures and verse; enough situations to supply at least five novels; newspaper accounts, some pertinent, others flagrant digressions; minstrel jokes and sketches; and every slavery anecdote he considered even remotely pertinent" (xv). Putting the best light on this wealth of material, J. Noel Heermance noted in 1969 that "[w]hat we finally have in *Clotel*...is not so much an artistic novel as a loosely structured skeleton of a plot on which the author can hang true and vivid anecdotes, stories, advertisements and Virginia legislature speeches." *Clotel*, Heermance concludes, is "not a work of sculptured unity resting on American soil," but rather "a nineteenth century 'deus ex machina' mobile, propitiously hanging from the sky" (164–165). More recently, even readers who find great value in Brown's fictional narrative often feel compelled to add that *Clotel* is not, after all, very good as a novel. But what if we were to consider *Clotel* not as an anomaly but as a representative or even foundational text, not as a work that fails to meet the usual standards for gauging aesthetic value but one that actually embodies and sets those standards? What if we approach *Clotel*, in short, not as if Brown struggled to meet the literary standards of his day but as if he knew exactly what he was doing?

If we approach *Clotel* in this way, we might well find ourselves thinking differently about nineteenth-century African American literature as a whole. That is, instead of taking *Clotel* as a work of African American literature simply because its author was African American, and instead of thinking of Brown's subject in this narrative as being the self-evident concerns of antislavery and antiracist protest, we might view *Clotel* as an entrance into the challenge of thinking about *how we read* nineteenth-century African American literature and how we read as well the world that African American writers represented in the nineteenth century. Central to that challenge is the task of questioning the neatly coherent "black community" at the center of this history—an oppressed community devoted to addressing familiar sociopolitical concerns, such as slavery and racism. To understand the complex world of African American literature, in other words, we need to understand the complex world of African American history and culture, and we must look for our understanding of this literary tradition within a complexly unstable and polycentric cultural collective. We must approach African American literary study as a process that requires attention to the cultural and even institutional settings in which readings were and are discussed, disseminated, and applied to individual and collective life, and we must build into our readings an active awareness of the nature and the limits of the claims one can ground in a reading of any text or group of texts by African American writers. In this way, we can come to appreciate the relation between works of facts and works of art—that is, we can reenvision the attempt to represent the absurd facts of African American life as itself an aesthetic achievement, an achievement in which familiar but resituated literary conventions, frequent digressions, and fragmented narrative lines are exactly to the point.

Questions about how to identify or locate an imagined African American community and history are central to Brown's approach to *Clotel*, which begins with Brown's third-person narration of his own life in slave communities and ends eventually in a cosmopolitan, transatlantic community. The narrative involves the imagined experiences of the enslaved daughter of Thomas Jefferson, and enters into its opening chapter with commentary on the "fearful increase of half whites, most of whose fathers are slaveowners, and their mothers slaves" (81). This is a story, in other words, of an African American community forged through violent contradictions, a collective defined legally and socially as both part of and distinct from the larger community of white Americans. At its most basic, generic level, in fact, *Clotel* calls attention to the intricate relationship between the construction of subjectivity and the representation of black life in a slaveholding, white supremacist nation. It is significant that Brown never identifies *Clotel* as a novel; rather, he presents the work as the product of two narratives working in productive tension with one another—the main narrative indicated by the book's title, *Clotel; or, The President's Daughter: A Narrative of Slave Life in the United States*, and the third-person account of Brown's own life, "Narrative of the Life and Escape of William Wells Brown" that precedes the main narrative. In effect, the book is a lesson in both standpoint theory and systemic analysis as approaches to the contingencies (local, national, and international) of social identity. The opening narrative is the story of the boy and man shaped by life as an African American, and former slave, in the United States, and the second is the account of U.S. history available only through the perspective shaped by that experience. It would not be too much to say, then, that Brown's central project operates in the space between the two narratives, somewhere between the man in the nation and the nation in the man. It is this highly dynamic and unstable relation between nation and subjectivity that made racial designations significant—indeed, defining—dynamics of nineteenth-century American life, and it is here that the designation "African American," in its nineteenth-century variants, was both encountered as a legal and social imposition by white America and forged as a declaration of collective identity and cultural independence by black America.

Operating in that unstable interstice, what we know as African American literature did not emerge from a stable entity that can be termed the African American population or community. To a great extent, scholarly and popular references to an African American past engage in a convenient fiction, the assumption of a conceptually coherent community. Throughout the early national period, such a community simply didn't exist, though the grounds and need for such a community were strongly recognized by black leaders and writers. Long after Africans were brought to the United States by force—people of different regions, often speaking different languages and shaped by different religious beliefs and cultural practices—African Americans remained scattered and fragmented geographically and culturally, both in terms of the conditions under which they lived and in terms of the possibilities they could reasonably entertain. Hosea Easton, an influential minister and community activist, stated in 1837 that African Americans "belong to no people, race, or nation; subjects of no government—citizens of no country—scattered surplus remnants of two races, and of different nations—severed into individuality—rendered a mass of broken fragments, thrown to and fro, by the boisterous passions of this and other ungodly nations" (37). Martin Robison Delany, one of the most accomplished black leaders of his time, referred to the imagined African American community in 1852 as "a *broken people*" (*The Condition* 209). As is emphasized even by the anguished and sometimes contentious disagreements over what name to use to identify this group—African, Negro, Colored, Anglo-African, and the like—this was a collective defined in part by a dominant culture and in part by their own variously organized efforts to understand themselves as a self-defining community.

The confusion about how to identify the community was inevitable, given the absurd dynamics of racial classification in the nineteenth century. Over time and generations, the color line separating black and white Americans became harder to draw as mixed-race individuals increasingly populated all of the nation's regions. But such racial mixing did little to shift the nation's emphasis on white privilege, leading instead to an increasingly complicated legal and social landscape. White people were kidnapped and held in slavery; enslaved people escaped from slavery by presenting themselves as white; and numerous juries faced court cases in which the central issue was to decide whether someone was white or black. Increasingly, that is, many people found themselves living on a very unstable color line, and racial identity—in the courts and elsewhere—was often determined not simply by ancestry but by social affiliations: the people one knew, the places one went, the life one lived. Such racial mixing often complicated African American development as well, as many found their achievements ascribed to "their white blood," making even some African Americans examples of white claims to superior ancestry and civilization. Certainly, many shared Delany's view that "we are not identical with the Anglo-Saxon," and were sympathetic to Delany's argument that "we have…inherent traits, attributes, so to speak, and native characteristics, peculiar to our race, whether pure or mixed blood" ("Political" 334–335)—but any attempt to identify the nature and force of those native characteristics involved one in the absurdities of U.S. racial culture.

As Brown's approach to *Clotel* suggests, the various forces that shaped black life in America complicated even the most seemingly straightforward of literary endeavors—for example, relating the story of one's life. How could one tell the story of one's life through straight autobiographical narration? How does one give a realistic account of one's life, one's character, one's nature in an absurd social environment? One needed to account for the fictions, the absurdities, of the U.S. racial order as being the primary forces shaping one's life. One needed to represent the fictions of the larger culture in order to get at the realities of one's life. Consider, for example, Harriet E. Wilson's *Our Nig; or, Sketches from the Life of a Free Black, in a Two-Story White House, North, Showing That Slavery's Shadows Fall Even There*, by "*Our Nig*," a book about life in New Hampshire published in 1859. In her approach to this book, based on her own experiences, Wilson gives readers reason to question whether *Our Nig* is to be identified as a work of autobiography or as a work of fiction. Taking our cue from Brown, though, instead of resolving such questions we might rather note that the text itself blends the two genres. In other words, this is not merely a matter of deciding, through research, whether this book is an autobiography or a novel, but rather of noting the narrator's own shifting focus and voices throughout the text. Chapters narrated in the third person are headed by chapter titles that identify this as another episode in the life of the writer of this narrative—so that chapters about Frado's experience carry titles that refer to "my mother" or "my father," and the chapter about Frado's entrance into the Bellmont household is headed by the title "A New Home for Me" (5, 14, 24). The narrative tells of the experiences of its protagonist Frado, quite clearly Wilson's representative in this story; but Wilson never allows us to view Frado as simply a character in a work of fiction, nor does she allow us to view Frado simply as a thin veil covering an act of self-representation. This is, in other words, a book about the need to turn to fictional representations in order to construct an autobiography. Ironically appropriating the racist designation "Our Nig" as her title of authorship, Wilson identifies the heart of her story in a dynamic similar to that which Brown announces through the interaction of his narrative of his own life, told in the third person, and his narrative of slave life in the United States.

Such interactions were a regular and arguably inevitable presence in the work of African American writers throughout the nineteenth century. While many white writers of the time found it possible to write histories, tell stories, craft poems, or fashion autobiographical accounts without mentioning anyone but other white people, African Americans found it virtually impossible to tell their stories—historical, autobiographical, or fictional—without somehow accounting for the pressing presence of white people, the effects of the system of slavery, or the absurd machinations of systemic racial control. Such double bindings—the nation that shapes the individual, and the individual who is either lost in the process or uniquely capable of seeing and critiquing the nation—are perhaps most dramatically represented by William Grimes in his autobiography, first published in 1825 and then expanded in the 1855 narrative *Life of William Grimes, The Runaway Slave, Brought Down to the Present Time, Written by Himself*. In this text, readers find themselves engaged with a narrator who establishes a remarkable relationship with the page, with his own authorship, and with readers, a relationship brought to a dramatic point in the provocative concluding statement of the 1825 portion of the narrative: "If it were not for the stripes on my back which were made while I was a slave, I would in my will leave my skin as a legacy to the government, desiring that it might be taken off and made into parchment, and then bind the constitution of glorious, happy and *free* America. Let the skin of an American slave bind the charter of American liberty!" (103). Grimes's application of an intensely personal story to an understanding of national character is a particularly striking but not unusual example of the ways in which African American writers addressed the relation between the individual in the nation and the nation in the individual that we encounter in *Clotel* and *Our Nig*.

But are such texts best understood as approaches representative of an African American literary tradition or are they best understood as stories from and about the history and culture of a white supremacist, slaveholding nation? As William Andrews observes of Grimes's narrative, "The *Life* is not so much a representation of Grimes's past as it is the record of his psyche in the act of reviving and revenging itself on its past. To open Grimes's book is to open the wounds of the ex-slave's body and mind, for the book is the man's psychic body manifested in language. The violation of many literary proprieties in the *Life* testifies to the violation of the act of recall by unrepressed affects associated with the memories of his life" (79). The intensely personal nature of Grimes's experience leads, if we follow Andrews on this, to an understanding of the relation between a racialized subjectivity and a literary approach—but it might be difficult to consider "the violation of many literary proprieties" as a literary achievement, let alone the makings of a broader literary tradition. Is there a literary tradition to be found in this scattered gathering of writers devoted to representing the unrepressed affects of acts of violation? Small wonder, then, that so many look for and find only two-legged dogs, and that approaches to nineteenth-century African American literature focus on the wonder of written testimonies, albeit testimonies better taken as artifacts than as art. What constitutes a coherent collective under such conditions, something that might encourage us to talk of an established and/or developing African American literary tradition?

Increasingly, scholars attentive to the activist roots of black studies are arguing for the need to move beyond the usual working assumptions about a homogeneous or otherwise settled African American community and are examining the terms by which this "community" might be understood. Eddie Glaude, for example, recognizes that central to any work devoted to the lives and rights of this imagined community must be the attempt to theorize both African American history and the concepts of agency, moral responsibility, identity, and community that have been shaped by that history. Glaude appropriately looks for an approach that does not rely on essentialist notions of black identity, on the one hand, or, on the other, that does not theorize black history, experience, and identity beyond the reach of both recognition and relevant social action. "How we think about black identity," Glaude argues, "how we imagine black history, and how we conceive of black agency can be rendered in ways that escape bad racial reasoning—reasoning that assumes a tendentious unity among African Americans simply because they are black, or that short-circuits imaginative responses to problems confronting *actual* black people" (x). Glaude is of course responding to numerous approaches to African American history, identity, and community that rely on quasi-biological assumptions, noting that "black history, for some, constitutes a reservoir of meaning that predetermines our orientation to problems, irrespective of their particulars, and black agency is imagined from the start as bound up with an emancipatory politics. When identity is determined by way of reference to a fixed racial self, the complexity of African American life is denied. Moreover, the actual moral dilemmas African Americans face are reduced to a crude racial calculus in which the answers are somehow genetically or culturally encoded" (8–9). The challenge, in effect, is to conceptualize black history and black communities in ways that force us beyond our usual habits of association and thought.

But how might we imagine African American history and identity on other terms? Literature is our best guide here, for in their writings, those of African heritage themselves studied the ideological terms and cultural dynamics by which they were forcibly affiliated and by which they might negotiate a more positive collective self-image. Indeed, the value of African American literature is that its complexity belies the simplified concepts of collective identity that so often prevail, now as in the nineteenth century, in public discourse on race and community. The problem is that such identity politics often guide our readings of African American literature, transforming complexity into the safe harbors of familiar racial designations and assumptions, a problem that scholars have long struggled to correct. W. Lawrence Hogue, for example, grants that "most, if not all, African Americans have racism, Otherization, and devaluation in common" (3). But Hogue observes as well that common conditions are no guarantees of a common or singular identity, for—"due to class, skin color, geographical location, education, and other sets of conditions— they experience them differently, and they consequently develop/devise different methods, communities, and cosmologies, or have different sets of conditions, for defining and representing their social reality" (3). For Hogue, the challenge is to "examine and discuss African Americans in terms of their own distinctions and traditions, to engage the polyvalent nature of African American literature, history, and criticism" (2).

Such an approach, of course, constitutes a significant change not only in how we understand African Americans but also in how we understand the implicit sense of collective mission usually associated with this collective—the "African American sociopolitical mission of racial uplift, the classic African American historical eman-cipatory narrative, and the canon of African American literature with all their exclu-sions and systematized hierarchies" (Hogue 2). Through the years, of course, African Americans have been not only associated with such missions but also defined by them—to the extent that a challenge to the usual protocols of collective identifica-tion can be seen as an act that undermines both the integrity of the community and the importance of such efforts to address injustices in American history and culture. In his attempt to reconceptualize such dynamics, to "arrive at a language and a theoretical concept that can envision differences," Hogue proposes "the idea of polycentrism, the principle of advocating the existence of independent centers of power within a singular political, cultural, or economic system" (2–3). Polycentrism, Hogue notes, allows one to "envision/construct a reading of American/African American life in which relations have many dynamic cultural, historical, critical, and literary locations, many possible vantage points, rather than a center/norm and peripheries" (4). With such changes, of course, would come changes in understand-ings of African American activism—including a reenvisionment of "the canon of African American literature with all their exclusions and systematized hierarchies."

Of course, Hogue's overview here is deceptive, for just as we need to account for multiple "centers of power," so we need to account for the fact that, in the nineteenth century and beyond, these centers have not been wholly independent of one another. From the late eighteenth century to the Civil War, African Americans gathered in many associations designed to promote education, provide financial security, dis-seminate information, popularize antislavery sentiment, protect fragile privileges while arguing for full civil rights, worship freely, and promote stable communities in the face of harsh restrictions, prejudices, and outright oppression. The most basic of these organizations were mutual benefit organizations, associations designed in part to provide insurance against financial loss in times of personal and family crisis, including funding for funerals and, in some cases, access to cemeteries in a time of segregated burials. But such associations both encouraged and overlapped with other organizations, including the formation of African American fraternal organizations, literary societies, churches and religious denominations, schools, and black-run and black-oriented periodicals and publishing venues. Some of these organizations were interracial, and others were devoted specifically to claiming pride in an African heritage and piecing together an African American history capable of encouraging a politically unified community. Many organizations were short-lived, but many others lasted through the years, often communicating with one another to form a web of relations that stretched across the nation, north and south, east and west. Interaction among these organizations was significant, as people moved from place to place and started new ventures related to those they had been involved with in the past, or organized new extensions—new lodges, for example, or churches—of existing organizations. The overwhelming majority of texts produced by African Americans in the nineteenth century were written in association with, presented at, or otherwise inspired or promoted by these organizations—especially religious, fraternal, and journalistic organizations and, frequently, some combination of the three—and that dynamic literary network is one of the central, though still relatively ignored, aspects of nineteenth-century African American literary history.

So, accounting for its polycentric and dynamic nature, we return to that problematic concept, the African American community. Instead of treating that community as a self-evident and settled fact, however, we are now in the position to think of it as a process, an entity both as stable and as constantly changing as a river. But how might we trace the currents of that river? By what terms can this community be known? The answer is that, like a river, the contours and currents of this community are defined by its dynamic interactions with its environment, the social, legal, and economic world that both gives shape to and is shaped by the developing course of the community. That is, the blended self-consciousness and self-awareness that follows from the individual but interrelated cultural positions of the community's citizens, joined with the unavoidable necessity of addressing issues of race, social justice, and cultural incoherence, are the most prominent characteristics of anything that might be termed the African American community. This is, in short, a community defined less by what Glaude terms "bad racial reasoning" than by what Saidiya Hartman terms "the networks of affiliation enacted in performance"—the community developed in response to the bad racial reasoning of the dominant culture. Indeed, this imagined but fragmented community, *enacted in performance*, constituted the defining framework in which most nineteenth-century African American political activism (including literary activism) functioned. Accordingly, the African American literary tradition is better understood as process than as product—a process that often involves a complex intertextual engagement with the dynamics of the environment within which the author performs.

Frederick Douglass, for example, never had the luxury of approaching writing as something separate from his activist labors or from his position as a public representative of an oppressed community. A list of Douglass's major writings would certainly include his autobiographical narratives, his novella "The Heroic Slave," and a few of his best-known speeches—but ultimately what defined Douglass as a writer was the need to address specific concerns as they arose; the need to represent a cause that was variously ignored, misrepresented, or rejected; and the need to continually engage in the shifting cultural politics of a white supremacist nation. Douglass's career and achievements as a writer, in other words, are best represented by his indefatigable labor in producing newspaper articles, his ability to meet virtually every public occasion with the right words, the necessity of his attendance and the inevitability of his representative role on such occasions, and the pervasive presence of racial science and racist laws that not only defined the occasion for his words but also connected him to communities unrepresented by any image of a generalized American. Nor was Douglass exceptional in this regard, for the overwhelming majority of nineteenth-century African American texts include either responses to white representations of black character, strategically embedded excerpts from white-authored texts, pointed interpretations of everything from legislative documents to scientific treatises to newspaper articles published by and for white America, or simply stories designed to counter influential white-authored fiction (for example, Martin R. Delany's *Blake, or The Huts of America; A Tale of the Mississippi Valley, the Southern United States, and Cuba*, written in part to counter Harriet Beecher Stowe's representation of slave life in *Uncle Tom's Cabin*). That process, I suggest, does not lend itself to either a linear process or a concept of aesthetics that involves balanced structure, generic integrity, or resolution. Rather, the literary art that emerged from African American writers corresponded to the absurd contradictions and falsely founded "truths" that African Americans encountered in American social life.

The world that African Americans experienced, I suggest, was a world characterized by the elements of what scientists and sociologists call chaotic design—a world apparently chaotic that actually operates under certain principles of order. Specifically, it is productive to think about African American literary art as a mode of representation both devoted to and characterized by fractal patterns—a Mandelbrot set, in which, as the poet Alice Fulton has usefully explained, "each part of a fractal form replicates the form of the entire structure. Increasing detail is revealed with increasing magnification, and each smaller part looks like the entire structure, turned around or tilted a bit" (55). African Americans might have been scattered both geographically and ideologically, but they encountered similar patterns in the shaping forces of their lives, the legal and social restrictions they encountered, and the networks by which they were able to recognize and *enact* themselves as a functioning community—a "nation within a nation," as Delany put it. A central figure in the science of chaos, Benoit Mandelbrot developed fractal geometry in his attempt to account for those "mathematical structures," as F. J. Dyson explains, discovered through the years "that did not fit the patterns of Euclid and Newton" and that accordingly challenged established models of order and measurement (qtd. in Mandelbrot 3). Many mathematical problems had led to seemingly inexplicable patterns, forms sometimes referred to as freakish or monstrous (Gleick 102–103). Recognizing that much of the natural world might be described in the same terms, Mandelbrot begins his seminal book *The Fractal Geometry of Nature* with a simple question: "Why is geometry often described as 'cold' and 'dry'?"; and he answers: "One reason lies in its inability to describe the shape of a cloud, a mountain, a coastline, or a tree. Clouds are not spheres, mountains are not cones, coastlines are not circles, and bark is not smooth, nor does lightning travel in a straight line" (1). Mandelbrot successfully applied fractal geometry to the irregular forms that characterize the natural, biological, and social worlds, from "pulmonary and vascular trees to real botanical trees, trees that need to capture sun and resist wind, with fractal branches and fractal leaves" (Gleick 110). Indeed, fractal geometry, and chaos theory more broadly, have been applied to a still wider field of concerns, accounting not just for natural forms but also for the arrangements and technologies of social systems, ranging from economic practices to literary dynamics.

As a targeted group living in an absurd culture defined by monstrous structures of systemic racial distinctions, African Americans knew something about the limitations of the ideal forms we use to describe our world, including the concepts of aesthetics we use to evaluate literary achievement. We are, as Glaude has observed, "historically conditioned organisms transacting with environments" (83), and at the center of these complex interactions remains the difficult reality of African American experience—that "African Americans were forced to create themselves amid the absurdity of a nation committed, at once, to freedom and unfreedom" (48). "Theirs was a blue note," Glaude observes, "an unstable chord that called attention to the unbridled chaos at the heart of American democracy" (48). That unstable chord is one of the distinguishing features of nineteenth-century African American literature. Negotiating with chaos, the communities "enacted in performance" are well represented in a performative body of literature that marks the transformation of the objects of racial chaos into its savvy students. The representation of nineteenth-century African American life, that is, required attention to the force of the various laws that both restricted and inspired not only approaches to resistance and community organization but also concepts of individual independence and agency. Indeed, orations, essays, treatises, pamphlets, and newspaper publications are central to nineteenth-century African American literary history because it was through such forums that African American writers responded to misrepresentations, appealed legal injustices, promoted social reform, established the contours of a history marginalized by the dominant culture, and worked to foster concepts of collective identity and agency. These various concerns, and the social contexts in which they were conceptualized and acted upon, become fundamental presences in nineteenth-century African American aesthetics, but always with what one might call a fractal turn.

Let us return, then, to Brown's significantly uncategorizable *Clotel*, this novel that doesn't quite work like a novel, this fictional narrative devoted to representing a world of experience, or, as Ann duCille has put it, this work of "unreal estate," by which she means "a fictive realm of the fantastic and coincidental, not the farfetched or the fanciful or 'magical realism' but an ideologically charged space, created by drawing together a variety of discursive fields—including 'the real' and 'the romantic,' the simple and the sensational, the allegorical and the historical—usually for decidedly political purposes'" (18). As I have noted, Brown has been criticized for trying "to cram too many things into one work"—and, indeed, a lot is crammed in. Brown draws heavily, for example, and usually verbatim, from a short story by white activist Lydia Maria Child and white abolitionist Theodore Dwight Weld's *American Slavery As It Is* (1839), the latter of which is itself a compendium of documents, testimonies, and advertisements drawn from the South. Brown draws as well from a wealth of other books, newspaper articles, and personal experience, including the stories drawn from his own life and that of other fugitive slaves. He pulls from his own publications, reprinting (and sometimes recontextualizing significantly) passages that he had published before. Brown, in short, doesn't simply represent a world, he represents a world of representations—various and sometimes conflicting documents that represent the world of forces, both well intentioned and otherwise, that reminded African Americans constantly that they had no choice but to negotiate a white supremacist world, as well as new iterations of stories that Brown had told before (and that he would tell again in his dramatic revisions of *Clotel* later in his career) that give an improvisational performance on a chaotic stage, including the intertextual dynamics by which that world maintained the illusion of philosophical stability.

Indeed, one could approach *Clotel* by virtually any chapter and productively read the work as a whole through the framework provided by that chapter—with each chapter, each story, replicating, as with fractals, "the form of the entire structure." Certainly, Brown's opening chapter, "The Negro Sale," sets up the work as a whole, both in its description of a slave auction and in its commentary on the instability of marriage under the system of slavery—with marriage as an institution that Brown identifies as "the foundation of all civilisation and culture" (83). Every main story line in the chapters that follow examine the consequences of this instability. But one could also enter the novel by way of chapter 2, "Going to the South," in which we witness a disastrous race between two steamboats, significantly called the *Patriot* and the *Columbia*, in which the competitive drive leads to an explosion and loss of life, while on the steamboats slave owners lose their property, even their slaves, in card games. Or one could follow the hunt in the third chapter, "The Negro Chase," or the thirteenth chapter, "A Slave Hunting Parson," among other instances—and one might productively consider Brown's description of a fox hunt in a later version of *Clotel* (now *Clotelle*). One might follow "A Ride in a Stage-Coach," chapter 22, in which Clotel passes as a Southern gentleman (Brown's appropriation of the true story of his antislavery colleague Ellen Craft, mixed somewhat with Stowe's story of George Harris in *Uncle Tom's Cabin*), and connect that incident with other cases of mistaken identity in the book, including the enslavement of a free German woman and a story about someone taking Daniel Webster to be a black man. In these and many other chapters, Brown follows certain dynamic patterns of American culture set in motion by the operations of the system of slavery and by the systemic racism both encouraged and required by that system. The unity of *Clotel* is less a matter of narrative design than of narrative performance, a way of seeing past a contradictory and chaotic world to the recurring patterns beneath the surface of things, a perspective Brown has mastered through his education as one of the chief products of that chaotic culture, an American slave.

In this way, *Clotel* offers readers a good entrance into the complexly intertextual (and therefore nonlinear, or at least non-Euclidian) process of nineteenth-century African American literary history. In spite of the simple stories we sometimes tell about nineteenth-century African American literature, this is a body of literature that contains and responds to a world of complexity. Indeed, the chaotic processes of racial history have everything to do with those features of nineteenth-century African American literature most frequently observed, features often spoken of disparagingly. But if we recognize the ways in which these and other writers worked to represent a chaotic world, then we can see the value of the fragmented narratives, the sudden narrative shifts, the often unexplained juxtapositions, the generic complexity, and the frequently unstable or elusive narrative perspectives so common to nineteenth-century African American narratives, fiction, histories, and other texts. Sociologist Frederick Turner has said of chaos theory that "the power of the new science may be precisely that it offers intelligible ways of obtaining deterministic systems out of randomness, randomness out of deterministic systems, space out of mathematical logic, irreversible time out of reversible space, scientific method out of scientific content, living systems out of nonliving matter, and human freedom out of biocultural necessity" (xii). Historically, African Americans have demonstrated a rich understanding of this power, including the ability to recognize that apparently random acts of racism operated within a deterministic social system, and then to draw from that system for improvisational performances in both life and art, and even to create living systems against all odds—singing, as James Weldon Johnson put it, "a race from wood and stone to Christ" (Johnson 65).

Crafting fractal representations of a fractal world, African Americans have in the process crafted an understanding of aesthetics that challenges our usual assumptions. In his work, Mandelbrot discusses his own challenge in training himself to recognize the need for and operations of fractal geometry. "One had to create an intuition from scratch," he notes, for "intuition as it was trained by the usual tools—the hand, the pencil, and the ruler—found these shapes quite monstrous and pathological. The old intuition was misleading." Concerning the images that would be computer generated by his innovative mathematical formulas, he observes, "The first pictures were to me quite a surprise; then I would recognize some pictures from previous pictures, and so on." Nineteenth-century African American literature operates in much the same way—and those who read only a relative handful of texts are not in a position to see, at the intuitive level and beyond, the patterns that emerge, the pictures that we recognize from previous pictures. This is a body of literature that is as beautiful and accomplished as one's blood veins, the branches of a tree, or the veins in a leaf—branching out to capture the slanted light of a complex world, designed to suggest beyond what can be said, calculated to represent a world in which history is stranger than fiction and fictions are taken to be settled truths. When we take the fractal measure of the works that together constitute a tradition of literature enacted in performance, linked by the priorities of improvisational negotiations, and devoted to representing a chaotic world, we will come to an understanding of the difference between artifact and art, a new understanding of aesthetics, and a significantly different understanding of American literary and cultural history.

BIBLIOGRAPHY

Andrews, William L. *To Tell a Free Story: The First Century of Afro-American Autobiography, 1760–1865.* Urbana: University of Illinois Press, 1986.

Brown, William Wells. *Clotel; or, The President's Daughter: A Narrative of Slave Life in the United States.* Ed. Robert S. Levine. Boston: Bedford/St. Martin's, 2000.

———. *Clotelle; or, The Colored Heroine. A Tale of the Southern States.* Boston: Lee and Shephard, 1867.

Davis, Arthur. Introduction. *Clotel; or, The President's Daughter: A Narrative of Slave Life in United States.* By William Wells Brown. New York: Collier Books, 1970. vii–xvi.

Delany, Martin R. *Blake, or The Huts of America; A Tale of the Mississippi Valley, the Southern United States, and Cuba.* Boston: Beacon Press, 1970.

———. *The Condition, Elevation, Emigration, and Destiny of the Colored People of United States.* 1852. New York: Arno Press and the *New York Times,* 1968.

———. "Political Destiny of the Colored Race on the American Continent." *Two Biographies of African-American Women.* Ed. William L. Andrews. New York: Oxford University Press, 1991. 327–367.

Douglass, Frederick. *My Bondage and My Freedom. Frederick Douglass: Autobiographies.* Ed. Henry Louis Gates Jr. New York: Library of America, 1994.

duCille, Ann. *The Coupling Convention: Sex, Text, and Tradition in Black Women's Fiction.* New York: Oxford University Press, 1993.

Easton, Hosea. *A Treatise on the Intellectual Character, and Civil and Political Condition of the Colored People of the U. States; and the Prejudice Exercised Towards Them: With a Sermon on the Duty of the Church to Them.* 1837. New York: Arno Press and the *New York Times,* 1969.

Foster, Frances Smith. Introduction. *"Minnie's Sacrifice," "Sowing and Reaping," "Trial and Triumph": Three Rediscovered Novels by Frances E. W. Harper.* Ed. Frances Smith Foster. Boston: Beacon, 1994. xi–xxxvii.

Fulton, Alice. *Feeling as a Foreign Language: The Good Strangeness of Poetry.* Saint Paul, MN: Graywolf Press, 1999.

Glaude, Eddie S. Jr. *In a Shade of Blue: Pragmatism and the Politics of Black America.* Chicago: University of Chicago Press, 2007.

Gleick, James. *Chaos: Making a New Science.* New York: Penguin, 1987.

Grimes, William. *Life of William Grimes, the Runaway Slave.* Ed. William L. Andrews and Regina E. Mason. Oxford: Oxford University Press, 2008.

Hartman, Saidiya V. *Scenes of Subjection: Terror, Slavery, and Self-Making in Nineteenth-Century America*. New York: Oxford University Press, 1997.

Heermance, J. Noel. *William Wells Brown and Clotelle: A Portrait of the Artist in the First Negro Novel*. Hamden, CT: Archon Books, 1969.

Hogue, W. Lawrence. *The African American Male, Writing, and Difference: A Polycentric Approach to African American Literature, Criticism, and History*. Albany: State University of New York Press, 2003.

Johnson, James Weldon. "O Black and Unknown Bards." *The Vintage Book of African American Poetry: 200 Years of Vision, Struggle, Power, Beauty, and Triumph from 50 Outstanding Poets*. Ed. Michael S. Harper and Anthony Walton. New York: Vintage Books, 2000. 64–65.

Loggins, Vernon. *The Negro Author: His Development in America*. New York: Columbia University Press, 1931.

Mandelbrot, Benoit B. *The Fractal Geometry of Nature*. San Francisco: W. H. Freeman, 1982.

Smith, James McCune. Introduction. *My Bondage and My Freedom*. By Frederick Douglass. *Frederick Douglass: Autobiographies*. Ed. Henry Louis Gates Jr. New York: Library of America, 1994. 125–137.

Stowe, Harriet Beecher. *Uncle Tom's Cabin; or, Life among the Lowly*. 1852. New York: Vintage Books/The Library of America, 1991.

Turner, Frederick. "Foreword: Chaos and Social Science." *Chaos, Complexity, and Sociology: Myths, Models, and Theories*. Ed. Raymond A. Eve, Sara Horsfall, and Mary E. Lee. Thousand Oaks, CA: Sage, 1997. xi–xxvii.

Weld, Theodore Dwight. *American Slavery As It Is: Testimony of A Thousand Witnesses*. 1839. New York: Arno Press and the *New York Times*, 1968.

Wilson, Harriet E. *Our Nig; or, Sketches from the Life of a Free Black, in a Two-Story White House, North. Showing That Slavery's Shadows Fall Even There*. By "Our Nig." New York: Penguin, 2005.

CHAPTER 3

ARE "AMERICAN NOVELS" NOVELS? *MARDI* AND THE PROBLEM OF BORING BOOKS

JORDAN ALEXANDER STEIN

STUDIES of the novel are usually premised on the assumption that there is such a thing as "the novel." The purpose of the present chapter is to investigate what can happen when this assumption about genre is instead treated as a critical problem. To be sure, generic categories like "the novel" (and, indeed, "American novel") are useful ways of organizing and differentiating among texts, and the advantage of such categorical thinking is that it allows scholars to work deductively, positing categories and collecting examples that verify the categorical ideal. Necessarily, however, this kind of deductive work carries with it normative generic standards, so that, for example, many texts might count as novels, but some can be shown to be better examples because they more closely comply with an abstract sense of the genre. This chapter contends that the problem attendant upon such categorical thinking is that it seems inevitably unable to explain generic outliers as anything other than bad examples, poor relations, failed attempts. Taking Herman Melville's *Mardi and a Voyage Thither* (1849) as its principal case study, this chapter will demonstrate that in order to make sense of "bad" novels—to understand them as something other than a failure to generically conform—one might be well served to suspend the categories required for deductive conclusions.[1] Bad novels prove good for revealing the limits of the category "novel" itself. Accordingly, this chapter argues that to call *Mardi* (or any text) "a novel" is already to put it into a context for interpretation. To demonstrate these points, this chapter will historicize generic claims about American novels (which depend, as we will see, on thematic as much as formal properties), as well as critical responses to *Mardi*, in lieu of trying to historicize that novel itself. Rather than putting texts into context, the aim of the following pages is to put contexts into context.

I.

The term "novel" was hardly new by the time it caught on. In the English language, the use of "novel" to refer to a long narrative in prose dates to the eighteenth century, through the end of which period it was often (though unevenly) a synonym for "history" (as in Henry Fielding's *History of the Adventures of Joseph Andrews* [1742]), "memoir" (as in John Cleland's *Memoirs of a Woman of Pleasure* [1749]), and even "poetry" (in the case of Anna Seward's *Louisa: A Poetical Novel, in Four Epistles* [1792]). Yet the connotations of nonfiction suggested by synonyms like "history" or "memoir" gradually ebbed away during the nineteenth century, and "novel" conclusively became a term for "fiction" by that century's close. Such connotative changes to the word are due in part to material changes in the artifact: nineteenth-century novels were subject to manufacturing technologies that made printing cheaper (allowing for both greater access and greater profits) and to an expanding commercial book market that helped to make reading fiction a refined and respectable habit. "Novel," by the late nineteenth century, came to connote not only "fiction," but "literature."[1]

Quite in spite of its slow consolidation, the novel became a dominant literary form in both Britain and the United States by the last third of the nineteenth century. Yet, if around 1870 commentators in the United States afforded the novel a principal status in American literature, their predecessors had given that pride of place to other literary forms. When Melville famously took up the mantle of the Young America movement in 1850, for example, he did so by asking readers of the *New York Literary World* to "Believe me, my friends, that Shakespeares are this day being born on the banks of the Ohio" (*Piazza* 245). By 1872, those fabled Shakespeares would have been young women and men, poised to make their generation's mark, when Thomas Sargent Perry unceremoniously demoted the vocation of the bard, telling readers of the *North American Review* that there could be an "American Shakespeare" with "good Presidents and a proper tariff" but still "the public, detecting the great differences between the society of Europe and that of this country, cried aloud for the novel that should do for us what Fielding had already, and Thackeray has since, done for England" (368). The idea of the great American novel was a critical obsession of the 1870s and 1880s, in part, perhaps, because during this period a truly national book market was for the first time possible. As Lawrence Buell writes, "The literary nationalism that had run strong in US criticism since the Revolutionary era and had intensified during the antebellum years was an indispensable precondition, but not until the late 1860s was a self-conscious discourse of the (or even 'a') great American novel possible" (135).[3] Though surely the precondition of a literary nationalism and the realization of national networks for production and distribution were requisite elements for the appearance of a self-identified American literature, there is nevertheless no necessary reason why this literature (or its critical apparatus) would privilege the novel to a degree that previous generations had not.

To understand why the American novel became so central to accounts of American literature, we can return to Perry's above-cited commentary. Americans, it seems, wanted great novels in order to compete with Britons, who already had them. Further circumstantial evidence for this nationalist motive becomes apparent inasmuch as calls for the great American novel intensified contemporaneously with the centennial of 1876 and the outpouring of literary histories of the United States, beginning with Moses Coit Tyler's in 1878. As Claudia Stokes nicely summarizes, these "literary histories seemed poised to aid both the realists and their opponents in their respective positions toward the literary past" (28). Additionally, one of the concomitant historical projects of the last quarter of the nineteenth century was the invention of the American novel's tradition. In 1894, for example, Arthur W. Brayley's journal, the *Bostonian*, serially reprinted William Hill Brown's *The Power of Sympathy* (1789) "with considerable fanfare and specifically to celebrate the first American novel," according to Cathy N. Davidson, despite the fact that *The Power of Sympathy* was not the first novel written in the United States, nor published there, nor written about America, nor by an American (85). Brayley's apparent disregard for meaningful criteria by which "first-ness" could be accurately measured seems born of a desire to swell the category of American novels with examples and antecedents.[4]

The perdurability of this desire for origin has obscured the paradox by which the case for the American novel's distinctiveness was built on evaluative criteria that were developed with reference to the British novel. In the British case, Victorian critics increasingly evaluated novels on a combination of formal merits and narrative thematics.[5] By the 1950s, influential studies such as those by Ian Watt and Lionel Trilling had helped to standardize the criteria by which "good" novels were understood to privilege realism as their dominant mode and to organize their narratives around memorable characters who live in (and, Trilling emphasized, often take a critical stance toward) thick social worlds. According to this understanding, the novel was first and foremost a narrative form. As Watt made the point, "the novel's realism does not reside in the kind of life it presents, but in the way it presents it" (11). Though character was considered a significant element of that form, character mattered most as a vehicle for the thematics of bourgeois individualism, with which the novel form was often shown to be ideologically complicit.

While these criteria enabled adequate generic claims about the novels of Samuel Richardson (a favorite example of Watt's) or Jane Austen (a favorite example of

Trilling's), the same criteria made little sense of fiction written in the United States before the Civil War. Indeed, as American literature gradually became a subject for university study in the United States (emerging in the early twentieth century out of belles lettres and popular U.S. history), this understanding of the novel as a genre strained the critical acumen of young Americanist scholars attempting to produce a coherent account of the American novel as such. Ultimately, scholars solved this problem by embracing the generic aberrations of the American novel from the British as a means of explaining what was distinctively "American" about it. As early as 1921, in the first academic monograph devoted to the American novel, Carl Van Doren described his subject as "a record of the national imagination as exhibited in the progress of native fiction" (vii). What this example already implies became more explicit as the twentieth century wore on: critical accounts of the American novel privileged themes over form and character, and prized national thematics above all. By the 1950s, literary critics had established two thematically driven generic strains for the American novel that dominated criticism for the second half of the century: the romance and the sentimental novel.

On the one hand, the romance tradition rejected the (already elastic) criteria of novelistic realism in favor of an even more elastic symbolic structure of writing, one whose appearance was not circumscribed to fictional prose narratives. According to Richard Chase, in a paradigmatic account, "Being less committed to the immediate rendition of reality than the novel, the romance will more freely veer toward mythic, allegorical, and symbolistic forms" (13). Likewise, in the words of Joel Porte, "American romance is characterized by a need self-consciously to define its own aims, so that 'romance' becomes frequently [...] theme as well as the form of these authors' works" (x). The thematic content of American romance, argued Perry Miller, was a "serious effort to put the meaning of America, of life in America, into the one form that seemed providentially given, through the exemplum of Scott, for expressing the deepest passions of the continent" (245). As a literary form, the value of the romance designation was its capaciousness and, thereby, its ability to coordinate the generic diversity (and putative thematic consistency) of American narratives into a categorical whole. By the 1980s and 1990s, as literary scholarship generally turned toward more historical questions, the diversity of narratives that fell under the sign of "romance" was recast as a problem of the 1840s and 1850s. Michael Davitt Bell and Christopher Looby, for example, respectively historicized and problematized "romance" and the many meanings it had for nineteenth-century authors. That there was no master theory of "romance" was, for all these accounts, always part of the point—though the expansiveness of the term sat uncomfortably with the fact that examples of American romance cohered around a highly contracted canon of overwhelmingly male, mostly mid-nineteenth-century authors including Melville, but also James Fenimore Cooper, Nathaniel Hawthorne, and Henry James (whose designation of novels, in the preface to *The Tragic Muse* [1890], as "loose baggy monsters" frequently earned him an authoritative citation in these discussions).

On the other hand, the sentimental novel in the United States had long been seen as a more feminine, more frivolous, and less distinctively American genre.

Herbert Ross Brown's *The Sentimental Novel in America* (1940) treats this tradition as the "light reading" of "our ancestors" (3)—"our" meaning "American," though the book acknowledges the transatlantic circulation of sentimental fiction. Subsequent studies, however, dropped transatlantic considerations in favor of feminine ones. Helen Waite Papashvily's *All the Happy Endings* (1956), for example, tracks the "almost, if not quite, forgotten" popular sentimental novels whose "crumbling pages reveal the dream world of women" (xiv, xv). This gendered problematic was taken up a generation later by Ann Douglas's *The Feminization of American Culture* (1977), a study that remains one of the most archivally rich recoveries of nineteenth-century sentimental writings by women, while at the same time being one of the most pessimistic accounts of the critical merits of that writing. On the later point, however, the sentimental novel was powerfully defended by Philip Fisher and Jane Tompkins in separate 1985 books, both arguing that sentimental writing should be estimated in terms of the "cultural work" it performs. Fisher eschewed the dura-bility of a capacious category like "romance," arguing instead that "cultural acts" such as *Uncle Tom's Cabin* "by their very success made themselves obsolete, and perhaps even a hindrance, once their cultural work was complete" (7). More pro-grammatically still, Tompkins argued that "novels and stories should be studied not because they manage to escape the limitations of their particular time and place, but because they offer powerful examples of the way a culture thinks about itself, articulating and proposing solutions for problems that shape a particular historical moment" (xi). Sentimental fiction mattered not because it was productive of great American novels, but because it was productive of America itself. In the decade and a half following these studies scholars including Gillian Brown, Lora Romero, Elizabeth Barnes, Glenn Hendler, and Kristin Boudreau argued for the interdepen-dence of supposedly separate masculine and feminine spheres of American writing and social life, leading toward the recognition of what Shirley Samuels dubbed a "culture of sentiment."

In sum, the curious legacy of late nineteenth century calls for the great American novel is that they begot two critical traditions for the American novel, neither of which is ultimately or consistently an account of the novel at all. Far more significant to critics over the last century is the national, rather than the formal, dimension of the "American novel." By the 1990s, the romance construc-tion (of major thematic questions about America, as engaged by major authors) was losing ground to sentimental construction (of historically situated claims about politics and genres, as supported by the recovery of forgotten or popular writers). Yet despite this general opposition, it is crucial to see that both the romance and sentimental traditions took as their project a descriptive account of national American literature. Accordingly, both traditions erred on the side of generality in their self-definitions in order to compensate for an American literature that, these capacious definitions notwithstanding, seems never to have been a uniform phenomenon. Consequently, the same authors and texts often served as examples of both traditions. In the case of Melville's writings, *Moby-Dick* (1851) was taken as a quintessential romance, while *Pierre* (1852) and *Billy*

Budd (c. 1890; pub. 1924) served as important dialectical turns in the sentimental tradition.

Despite the interpretive versatility thereby ascribed to Melville's corpus, however, *Mardi* remained generally unread and undiscussed—in no small part because it fit into neither tradition. Such a conclusion, at least, would follow from what I have been suggesting so far: the traditions and categories—in short, the contexts—that critics developed for the American novel (very much including the generic ascription, "novel") significantly shaped the ways that texts were read. In spite of the capaciousness of these critical contexts, *Mardi* had apparently little to offer them. And though Melville did describe *Mardi* in a letter to John Murray as "a *real* romance" "with a meaning too," this fateful pronouncement seems to have consigned critical discussions of *Mardi* to the place of a footnote in Melville's authorial development, as a supposed trial run for his major romance, *Moby-Dick* (*Correspondence* 106). Indeed, critics of the American novel typically prefaced any more elaborate discussion of *Mardi* with an apology. For Van Doren, *Mardi* was "one of the strangest, maddest books ever composed by an American" (71), and, fifty years later, Edwin Haviland Miller predicted that "[t]here will probably never be a satisfactory interpretation of *Mardi*" (149). Even a deft reading by Richard H. Brodhead began with the concession that "[e]very unkind thing that has been said about *Mardi* is more or less true" (29). The strangeness, the madness, and the uninterpretability of *Mardi* were (as these critical assessments already suggest) always treated as problems with the work itself, and never problems with the categories by which *Mardi* was being assessed. Yet I'm arguing that the means by which *Mardi*'s status as a problem text comes so close to being self-evident is itself a problem worthy of interpretation. As we shall see, however, the burden of my argument is that few texts have ever seemed to readers as self-evidently problematic as *Mardi*.

II.

Early reviews of *Mardi* present a study in readerly befuddlement. Upon *Mardi*'s publication in 1849, the *London Weekly Chronicle* reported that "[w]e have turned the book over, like a dog might a jellyfish, without being able to make it out, for the life of us," while the *London Literary Gazette* despaired that "[w]e never saw a book so like a kaleidoscope" (Higgins and Parker 205, 196). One of the most recurrent objections within the reviews is to *Mardi*'s style. Among the more generous readings, the *New Orleans Commercial Bulletin* called *Mardi* "a regular Mardi-gras of a novel, to judge from the richness of its prose" (Higgins and Parker 225). But more often reviews claimed, as for example did the *London Athenaeum*, that "[o]n opening this strange book, the reader will be at once struck by the affectation of its style, in which are mingled many madnesses" (Higgins and Parker 193). Less generous still was the *London Examiner*, describing a book in which "[a] heap of fanciful speculations, vivid descriptions, satirical insinuations, and allegorical typifications, are flung together with little order or connexion" (Higgins and Parker 197). Indeed, nearly all the book's favorable reviews appear to be puffs, including a lengthy and delicately equivocal review in *Bentley's Miscellany* (that is, written under the auspices of Melville's London publisher), three mentions in the *New York Literary World* (at least two of which were penned by Melville's friend and literary associate Evert Duyckinck), and a review by N. P. Willis in the *New York Home Journal* (the details of which are so thin and so misleading that one wonders if Willis read *Mardi* before reviewing it).[6] The generally negative assessments by reviewers were confirmed by sales figures, and in December 1853 Harper and Brothers, Melville's New York publisher, recorded only 2,544 copies of *Mardi* sold to date, compared to 6,328 of Melville's previous book, *Omoo* (1847), and 4,316 of Melville's next book, *Redburn* (1849) (*Correspondence* 250).

To make matters worse, Melville got it all wrong when, mindful of these reviews, he wrote in 1849 to reassure his father-in-law, Lemuel Shaw, that "Time, which is the solver of all riddles, will solve 'Mardi' " (*Correspondence* 130). Indeed, not only have critics in the twentieth century largely continued to dismiss *Mardi*, as we have seen, but they have done so on terms that are uncannily resonant with those of the nineteenth-century reviewers. For example, Robert K. Martin excluded *Mardi* from his important study of homosexuality in Melville's sea novels on the grounds that *Mardi* is "hopelessly prolix" (3). Samuel Otter likewise excluded *Mardi* from his major account of discourse and ideology because "verbosity in *Mardi* serves merely as self-display or pedantry or excess for the sake of excess, rather than also serving as an object of analysis" (6). Geoffrey Sanborn's study of cannibalism and signification somewhat more sanguinely proposes that *Mardi's* "only organizational principle seems to be the idea of escape" (*Sign* 122). And Brian Higgins and Hershel Parker rehearse the conventional account of *Mardi's* place in Melville's career when they observe that "[f]rom delighting his readers with racy anecdotes of South Sea vagabondizing, Melville had shifted to delighting himself with a multiplicity of learned allusions and recondite speculations" (xiii). A small number of critics have more thoughtfully engaged *Mardi* according to a range of theoretical orientations, from Brodhead's formal one, to Neal Tolchin's psychoanalytic one, to Wai Chee Dimock's new historicist one, to John Evelev's material cultural one; yet despite such theoretical diversity, these studies treat the book consistently and almost exclusively in the context of Melville's biography and career. It is a true testament to the readerly difficulty of *Mardi* that any work by an author as much studied as Melville could be so rarely and so narrowly read.[7]

Taken collectively, the initial reviewers and the contemporary critics imply that *Mardi* is a paradigmatically difficult read, and it is as such that *Mardi* can offer an unusually succinct glimpse of the properties that make a text inaccessible to readers. Despite a near consensus to the contrary, however, objections to *Mardi's* style do not account for the text's difficulty. The prolixity, pedantry, and reconditeness by which readers dismiss *Mardi* are hardly the burden of that text alone—a point that comes into relief when we recall that critics studying the American novel conventionally take *Mardi* as Melville's rehearsal for *Moby-Dick*. While even *Moby-Dick*'s admirers will admit that this text is, in its turn, prolix, pedantic, and recondite, those aspects of readerly difficultly do not consign *Moby-Dick* to anything near the obscurity that *Mardi* faces. (Length is also not the issue; *Mardi* clocks in at just over 15,000 fewer words that *Moby-Dick*.) Furthermore, while complaints about *Mardi*'s style are applicable to Melville's other writings, it is also the case that *Mardi*'s chief offense is not, properly speaking, stylistic. To be sure, *Mardi* includes some maddening sentences—for example, the narrator's description of Bishop Berkeley as "extremely matter-of-fact in all matters touching matter itself" (63) or one character's pronouncement that "the mystery of mysteries is still a mystery" (389). Yet what makes these sentences maddening is not precisely style—at least not if "style" denotes emphasis on the formal features of language. These sentences are maddening more as a result of their semantic than their stylistic expression. Moreover, while both sentences produce a kind of semantic collapse, they do so by means of contrasting formal or stylistic techniques. The first sentence uses three different meanings for the word "matter" in close succession, whereas the second sentence uses the same meaning for the word "mystery" three times consecutively. In the first sentence, this proliferation of meaning occurs in the predication of the sentence; in the second, the deployment of the same word freights the subject. Readers committed to the idea that *Mardi*'s style is consistently poor, in other words, will be hard-pressed to demonstrate that its style is in fact consistent.

But if *Mardi*'s style is not easily characterized by any consistent features, we have already seen that the effects of that so-called style on readers nevertheless is. The manifold objections to the text's "style" over the last 160 years generate a collective euphemism for a singular truth: *Mardi* is a boring book. Yet the point I wish to establish is that the impressive consistency by which *Mardi* has dulled its readers is itself remarkably interesting. At the risk of courting paradox, I propose that *Mardi* is interesting for its ability to demonstrate the limits of Interest Itself, and, more specifically, the limits of interest in novel reading.

These limits begin to be legible, for instance, in the maddening sentences quoted above. I have suggested that both sentences veer toward non-sense, though they do so according to different formal strategies. What is equally worth noticing, however, is that both constructions play with nouns while keeping verbs as simple forms of "to be." Both, in other words, take the form of what in logic is called the law of identity, according to which the condition of being is that things are equal to themselves (classically demonstrated: a = a). Despite taking the form of an identity principle, however, these constructions render identity absurd by suggesting, respectively, that matter is equal to the several things which count as itself, while mystery is only equal to the unknown thing which counts as itself. However, an absurd account of identity is not the only consequence of these propositions. In addition, the act of logically proposing itself becomes absurd—for there is hardly any point to building a container for something that can never be contained. *Mardi* manages to complicate identity in such a way as to frustrate nearly any reader's attempt to make sense of those complications, by presenting the permutations of identity as exceeding the proposition of identity. These sentences, then, are uninteresting in the most basic sense: there is nothing about them in which one could plausibly have a stake. What makes these sentences uninteresting—and, by extension, what makes *Mardi* a boring book—is that they describe phenomena in such a way that the cognitive attention readers bring to the act of reading is entirely beside the point. Colloquially put, *Mardi* doesn't need you.

Historically speaking, however, the phenomenology of novel reading is exactly the inverse: novels offer readers interest—often bordering on pleasurable self-indulgence. The form of readerly interest partial to the novel is usually called identification, a term that, de facto, emphasizes the relation between readers and characters. Though a full history of reading for identification far exceeds the scope of the present chapter, the relationship between character and identification requires some explication. Specifically, it should be observed that early novels offered a much greater range of protagonists than novels came to offer by the end of the eighteenth century. As Deidre Lynch and others have shown, novels such as Charles Johnstone's *Chrysal, or, The Adventures of a Guinea* (1760) or Thomas Bridges's *The Adventures of a Bank-Note* (1770) pursued novelistic formulae without human characters. The disappearance of these so-called "it-narratives" by the end of the eighteenth century, and the coincident proliferation in the novel of characters capable of psychological mimesis, indicates how (if not precisely why) reading for identification ascended in the nineteenth century as a dominant mode of novel reading.[8]

Mardi cannot be called an "it-narrative," because it does follow the perspective of a human character. However, that perspective is hardly the organizing principle of the narrative. During the first approximately forty chapters, *Mardi*'s unnamed narrator registers discontent with his Pacific whaling voyage, partners with a fellow sailor named Jarl, jumps ship, and seeks adventure. He and Jarl team up with two Hawaiians, Annatoo and Samoa, and together they encounter and rescue a beautiful maiden named Yillah. For about twenty more chapters, our narrator stays with Yillah on the archipelago of Mardi as a guest of King Media, where he assumes the name of the local god Taji, and where Jarl, Annatoo, and Samoa are unceremoniously dispatched by plot and characters alike. When Yillah mysteriously disappears without a trace around chapter 64, Taji pursues her from island to island for 125 additional chapters, through to the book's final sentence, in the company of the king and his faithful servants, the chronicler Mohi and the philosopher Babbalanja. It is Babbalanja's wild and logorrheic speculations that dominate narrative attention in the second half of the book, and they appear to do so at the expense of our nominal main character. Taji recedes almost entirely from this half of the narrative, such that his words are not quoted in dialogue, his actions are only described when they are part of the group (e.g., "pursuers and pursued flew on" [654]), and at points his existence is mentioned in the third-person (e.g., "Of Taji, Bello sought to know…" [477]). As even this brief summary will suggest, *Mardi*'s characters thwart readerly identification in multiple ways. The apparently universally boring effect of this denial of characterological points for identification, coupled with the commercial nonviability of *Mardi*, together create a powerful counterexample in the history of the phenomenology of novel reading. By 1849, it seems, a text that denies readers the opportunity for identification is not a readable book.[9]

But if *Mardi* may therefore always have been a boring book, we have previously seen that only by the early twentieth century did it become a bad novel. Thus far, this chapter has been arguing that extratextual phenomena, such as the reader response to, or the generic identity of, a text, might best be understood as contexts, inasmuch as they significantly but subtly mediate the range of interpretive possibility for a given text. However, as we have seen from the examples of the reader response to *Mardi* and the critical provenance of the category "American novel," these contexts can (and often do) mediate interpretive possibility in discrepant ways. The case of *Mardi* furthermore suggests that though amateur readers (who read for identification) and literary critics (who read for themes) espouse different criteria by which to value literary works, these differences do not preclude the possibility that each camp might value (or, in the case of *Mardi*, reject) the same books in the same way, albeit for different reasons. Indeed, insofar as a given text might thematize any social (or political or national or, in broad terms, contextual) issue as though it were a matter of characterological experience, readers and professionals may well be drawn to the same passages, even if the claims they make on those passages are in the pursuit of different ends. Though this chapter has so far presented the problems that readers have had with *Mardi* as problems of interpretive context that have been displaced onto that text, what remains to be seen in the final section is, precisely, what kinds of alternative contexts for interpretation *Mardi* might itself propose.

III.

If *Mardi* thwarts the interpretive contexts to which professional critics and amateur readers have variously tried to assimilate it, then one promising alternative in the effort to wrestle sense out of *Mardi* would be to attempt an interpretation of the text more squarely on its own terms. The problem with this alternative, however, is the extent to which it makes clear that *Mardi* determinedly refuses the very idea of interpretive contexts, at least as critics conventionally conceive them. For the field of American literary studies, "context" typically refers to the historical or political circumstances of a text's production or reception. However, the *Oxford English Dictionary* defines the term far more broadly, as "the weaving together of words and sentences," the construction of speech as well as the composition of literature. As I will elaborate, it is in this second, broader sense that *Mardi* seems most engaged with the idea of context. For now, however, it is important to recognize the challenges this broader definition of "context" creates for literary interpretation. Where contextually minded literary critics often build interpretations using circumstances external to the text, the *OED* definition reminds us that a text's very words are the contexts for one another. In this sense, "context" presents a kind of Archimedean problem, where it would be possible to put a text into context only if one could conclusively determine what part of the text wasn't already a context.

While this sense of "context" is perhaps more technical than conventional, it is nonetheless the one in which *Mardi* revels. Unable or uninterested to occupy an Archimedean vantage, *Mardi* uses the relations between words and sentences to explode meaning, rather than to construct it. Accordingly, the reader who experiences semantic confusion in chapter 124, upon learning that "the mystery of mysteries is still a mystery" (389), gains no additional exposition or clarity on this point by chapter 195. *Mardi's* sentences proffer context for neither their own local semantics nor for a cumulative sense of narrative development. If anything, *Mardi* seems invested in exploring how long one can engage with a suspended meaning and still not know what it means.

In addition to exploring this exploded sense of context semantically, *Mardi* reduplicates it thematically. Accordingly, *Mardi's* characters—who would be, as we have seen, the points that anchor readerly identification in a novel—have an impressively difficult time locating even themselves. Consider, for instance, Babbalanja's account of himself in chapter 143:

> [T]hough I have now been upon terms of close companionship with myself for nigh five hundred moons, I have not yet been able to decide who or what I am. To you, perhaps, I seem Babbalanja; but to myself, I seem not myself. All I am sure of, is a sort of prickly sensation all over me, which they call life; and, occasionally, a headache or a queer conceit admonishes me, that there is something astir in my attic. But how know I, that these sensations are identical with myself? For aught I know, I may be somebody else. At any rate, I keep an eye on myself, as I would on a stranger. There is something going on in me, that is independent of me. Many a time, have I willed to do one thing, and another has been done. I will not say by myself, for I was not consulted about it; it was done instinctively. My most virtuous thoughts are not born of my musings, but spring up in me, like bright fancies to the poet; unsought, spontaneous. Whence they come I know not. (456)

The discrepancies between sensation and perception, between will and action, between conscious and unconscious thought lead Babbalanja to be radically suspicious of the categories into which he might collect his experiences of himself *as his own experiences*. It is important to note that Babbalanja is here *both* immanently attuned to the phenomenology of his own sense perception ("To you, perhaps, I seem Babbalanja; but to myself, I seem not myself") and objectively calibrated to view himself from the outside ("I keep an eye on myself, as I would on a stranger"). Leaving aside the implausibility of either position, the fact that Babbalanja is presented as simultaneously occupying both suggests that this passage provides a critique of neither. Instead, what is being critiqued is the categorical integrity of identity itself. Neither from a position of pure immanence nor from a position of pure objectivity (nor from their overlap) can Babbalanja contextualize himself. And having thus ruled out this rather comprehensive set of options, it becomes difficult to imagine what a stable context could look like according to *Mardi*. (Likewise, it becomes difficult to imagine that on its own terms *Mardi* could be boring or, for that matter, interesting.)

We have seen that for twentieth-century critics constructing a self-conscious tradition for the American novel, *Mardi* failed to cohere with the thematic concerns that made American novels *American*; whereas, for nineteenth-century readers invested in the pleasures of identification, *Mardi* failed to cohere with the phenomenology of reading that made American novels *novels*. To both positions, Babbalanja's extensive meditation on identity offers an implicit skepticism, by which the contexts and criteria for identity and category are themselves held in reflexive suspension. Though *Mardi* seems hardly to be an American novel by any conventional means of classification, an aggressive suspension of meaning, pitched at the level of classification, turns out to be the project of that text. Put differently, that *Mardi* fails to be an American novel is perhaps the clearest measure of its success, at least on the text's own terms.

Many readers of *Mardi* have freely admitted that this text is an exception to nearly any generic rule, and so to suggest, as the present chapter has, that *Mardi* gives the lie to the category "American novel" may seem to risk exaggeration. However, it would not be an exaggeration to say that fiction written and consumed in the United States prior to the Civil War does a comparatively poor job of realizing the generic integrity and possibility of "the novel" as it came to be retrospectively classified in the early twentieth century than does early nineteenth-century British fiction, on the order of Jane Austen, or later nineteenth-century U.S. fiction, on the order of W. D. Howells. (Indeed, one of the most popularly reprinted novelists in the antebellum United States, Charles Dickens, is often considered as the author of some of the "flattest" characters in Victorian fiction.[10]) What looks from the vantage of twentieth-century novel criticism like the relative crudeness of antebellum novels and characters looks instead from the vantage of the present chapter like the strong possibility that the project of these texts lies elsewhere than in the domains of genre and psychology by which the category "novel" slowly cohered. From this perspective, *Mardi* differs in degree but not in kind from many texts that have been considered foundational to the study of the American novel—for instance, *Moby-Dick*.

Directing its critique of context and category toward character and identity is, as I previously suggested, arguably one of *Mardi's* most alienating aspects, because doing so leaves readers with neither the pleasures of identification nor the sense that anything could be at stake in their reading. Yet the alienating effects of *Mardi's* critiques are hardly alien to Melville's corpus. Critics including Leo Bersani, Geoffrey Sanborn, and Sharon Cameron have powerfully and influentially suggested that more traditionally celebrated American novels like *Moby-Dick* and *Billy Budd* display versions of the critique of identity we have seen in *Mardi*. In Bersani's reading of *Moby-Dick* "Melville's characters have no sexual subjectivity at all" and so, "psychologically, there is nothing at stake" (146). On Sanborn's account, the relationship between Ishmael and Queequeg "presents us with a way of being alone in which we are nonetheless together and a way of being together in which we are no longer ourselves" ("Whence" 251). And for Cameron "*Billy Budd* is a drama in which the category of character is more radically distributed by the fact that the features which apply to characters (who represent individuals and types) also apply to elements that lie outside the characterological" (*Impersonality* 182). Though these brief quotations admittedly do not capture the complexity of each critic's arguments, their juxtaposition here should nonetheless make clear that one does not have to dust off an unread copy of *Mardi* in order to generate *Mardi*-esque claims about American literature. As Cameron observed thirty years ago in her celebrated reading of *Moby-Dick*, "we normalize the novel at the risk of failing to comprehend it" (*Corporeal* 15). My argument in the present chapter is that recognizing the full implications of this possibility for the study of "the America novel" goes a long way toward reclaiming the value of *Mardi* as something other than a bad book.

And yet however much the radical phenomenology of identity posed by Babbalanja in the passage quoted above mirrors some of this chapter's larger claims for a more reflexive understanding of context, my conclusion will nonetheless not be to advocate for *Mardi*'s method. For one, *Mardi* turns reflexivity into an unending quest. Such an endless program is not advisable for scholarship, as most scholars do hope eventually to arrive at some conclusions about the evidence with which they work, however necessarily provisional those conclusions inevitably will be. The difference between responsible reflection and infinite regress is worth trying to maintain. All the same, one of the most significant—and portable—consequences of *Mardi*'s conception of identity is that it locates the problem with a claim like "*Mardi* is a novel" not only in the proper noun and the analytic category, but equally in the verb "to be." From the perspective of *Mardi*'s critique of identity, things are different from themselves in a way that makes them fit uneasily into the categories of which they might otherwise be members. Moreover, the syntactic equation of a linking verb does nothing to acknowledge this problem of fit. Following *Mardi*'s logic, then, this chapter's governing question—are "American novels" novels?—has been poorly proposed. More properly, the inquiry ought to be, how, when, or why are "American novels" novels?; and, indeed, it has been to these questions that the foregoing has offered some provisional answers.

NOTES

This essay is much improved for having been presented to the Americanist Research Group at Cornell; for having been discussed with Rachel Buurma; and for having been read by Russ Castronovo.
1   For a historical account of deduction, see Poovey.
2   On fiction see Gallagher; and McKeon; on literature see McGurl.
3   See also H. Brown, "Great." On the slow materialization of networks for national print distribution, see Loughran.
4   There have never been reliable criteria by which the American novel's origin could be measured. In addition to Davidson's study, see those by Spengemann; Armstrong and Tennenhouse; Dillon; and Rezek.
5   See Graham; and Stang.
6   On the puffing system, see Charvat 168–189; and Cohen.

7 A small number of studies have approached the difficulty of reading *Mardi* as a historical problem, variously taking the text as incongruous with mid-century reading practices (Person), ideologies (Weinstein) or genres (Post-Lauria). All of these studies display optimism in the elucidating powers of historical contexts. Though two extended studies from the postwar period attempted to take *Mardi* more seriously, they yield ineffectual results. Merrell R. Davis's *Melville's* Mardi: *A Chartless Voyage* (1952) consists entirely of plot summary and biographical "whodunit," while Maxine Moore's *That Lonely Game* (1975) offers an imaginative but pointedly inconclusive mapping of *Mardi*. While these extended studies are admirable for their perseverance, both leave real questions about whether *Mardi* can sustain extended study.

8 The "it-narrative" did, however, experience a brief and abortive revival in 1843 with James Fenimore Cooper's *Autobiography of a Pocket-Handkerchief.*

9 For a reading of *Moby-Dick* along these lines, see Eckel.

10 The charge of "flatness" in Dickens's characters dates at least to E. M. Forster's *Aspects of the Novel* (1921). For relevant accounts of characterological complexity in Dickens, see Stout; and Woloch. On Dickens in relation to antebellum print culture, see McGill 109–140; Claybaugh 52–84; and Hack.

BIBLIOGRAPHY

Armstrong, Nancy, and Leonard Tennenhouse. "The American Origins of the English Novel." *American Literary History* 4.3 (1992): 386–410.

Barnes, Elizabeth. *States of Sympathy: Seduction and Democracy in the American Novel.* New York: Columbia University Press, 1997.

Bell, Michael Davitt. *The Development of American Romance: The Sacrifice of Relation.* Chicago: University of Chicago Press, 1980.

Bersani, Leo. *The Culture of Redemption.* Cambridge, MA: Harvard University Press, 1990.

Boudreau, Kristin. *Sympathy in American Literature: American Sentiments from Jefferson to the Jameses.* Tallahassee: University of Florida Press, 2002.

Brodhead, Richard H. "*Mardi*: Creating the Creative." 1978. Reprinted in *Herman Melville: A Collection of Critical Essays.* Ed. Myra Jehlen. Englewood Cliffs, NJ: Prentice Hall, 1994. 27–39.

Brown, Gillian. *Domestic Individualism: Imagining Self in Nineteenth-Century America.* Berkeley, CA: University of California Press, 1990.

Brown, Herbert Ross. "The Great American Novel." *American Literature* 7.1 (1935): 1–14.

———. *The Sentimental Novel in America 1789–1860.* Durham, NC: Duke University Press, 1940.

Buell, Lawrence. "The Unkillable Dream of the Great American Novel: *Moby-Dick* as Test Case." *American Literary History* 20.1 (2008): 132–155.

Cameron, Sharon. *The Corporeal Self: Allegories of the Body in Melville and Hawthorne.* Baltimore: Johns Hopkins University Press, 1981.

———. *Impersonality: Seven Essays.* Chicago: University of Chicago Press, 2007.

Charvat, William. *The Profession of Authorship in America 1800–1870.* Ed. Matthew J. Bruccoli. 1968. New York: Columbia University Press, 1992.

Chase, Richard. *The American Novel and Its Tradition.* Garden City, NY: Doubleday Anchor, 1957.

Claybaugh, Amanda. *The Novel of Purpose: Literature and Social Reform in the Anglo-American World*. Ithaca, NY: Cornell University Press, 2007.

Cohen, Lara Langer. "Democratic Representations: Puffery and the Antebellum Print Explosion." *American Literature* 79.4 (2007): 643–672.

Davidson, Cathy N. *The Revolution and the Word: The Rise of the Novel in America*. New York: Oxford University Press, 1986.

Davis, Merrell R. *Melville's* Mardi: *A Chartless Voyage*. New Haven, CT: Yale University Press, 1952.

Dillon, Elizabeth Maddock. "The Original American Novel, or, the American Origin of the Novel." *A Companion to the Eighteenth-Century English Novel and Culture*. Ed. Paula R. Backscheider and Catherine Ingrassia. Malden, MA: Blackwell, 2005. 235–260.

Dimock, Wai Chee. *Empire for Liberty: Melville and the Poetics of Individualism*. Princeton, NJ: Princeton University Press, 1991.

Douglas, Ann. *The Feminization of American Culture*. 1977. New York: Noonday, 1998.

Eckel, Leslie. "Reading with Wonder: Encounters with *Moby-Dick*." *Common-place* 10.2 (January 2010). http://www.common-place.org/vol-10/no-02/reading/.

Evelev, John. *Tolerable Entertainment: Herman Melville and Professionalism in Antebellum New York*. Amherst: University of Massachusetts Press, 2006.

Fisher, Philip. *Hard Facts: Setting and Form in the American Novel*. New York: Oxford University Press, 1985.

Gallagher, Catherine. "The Rise of Fictionality." *The Novel, Volume I: History, Geography, and Culture*. Ed. Franco Moretti. Princeton, NJ: Princeton University Press, 2006. 336–363.

Graham, Kenneth. *English Criticism of the Novel, 1865–1900*. Oxford: Clarendon Press, 1965.

Hack, Daniel. "Close Reading at a Distance: The African Americanization of *Bleak House*." *Critical Inquiry* 34.4 (2008): 731–743.

Hendler, Glenn. *Public Sentiments: Structures of Feeling in Nineteenth-Century American Literature*. Chapel Hill: University of North Carolina Press, 2001.

Higgins, Brian, and Hershel Parker, eds. *Herman Melville: The Contemporary Reviews*. Cambridge: Cambridge University Press, 1995.

Looby, Christopher. "George Thompson's 'Romance of the Real': Transgression and Taboo in American Sensation Fiction." *American Literature* 65.4 (1993): 651–672.

Loughran, Trish. *The Republic in Print: Print Culture in the Age of U.S. Nation Building, 1770–1870*. New York: Columbia University Press, 2007.

Lynch, Deidre Shauna. *The Economy of Character: Novels, Market Culture, and the Business of Inner Meaning*. Chicago: University of Chicago Press, 1998.

Martin, Robert K. *Hero, Captain, and Stranger: Male Friendship, Social Critique, and Literary Form in the Sea Novels of Herman Melville*. Chapel Hill: University of North Carolina Press, 1986.

McGill, Meredith L. *American Literature and the Culture of Reprinting, 1834–1853*. Philadelphia: University of Pennsylvania Press, 2003.

McGurl, Mark. *The Novel Art: Elevations of American Fiction after Henry James*. Princeton, NJ: Princeton University Press, 2001.

McKeon, Michael. *The Origins of the English Novel, 1600–1740*. Baltimore: Johns Hopkins University Press, 1987.

Melville, Herman. *Correspondence*. Ed. Lynn Horth. *The Writings of Herman Melville*. Vol. 14. Ed. Harrison Hayford et al. Evanston, IL: Northwestern University Press and the Newberry Library, 1993.

———. *Mardi and a Voyage Thither. The Writings of Herman Melville.* Vol. 3. Ed. Harrison
Hayford et al. Evanston, IL: Northwestern University Press and the Newberry Library,
1970.

———. *The Piazza Tales and Other Prose Pieces 1839–1860. The Writings of Herman
Melville.* Vol. 9. Ed. Harrison Hayford et al. Evanston, IL: Northwestern University
Press and the Newberry Library, 1987.

Miller, Edwin Haviland. *Melville.* New York: George Braziller, 1975.

Miller, Perry. "The Romance and the Novel." *Nature's Nation.* Cambridge, MA: The Belknap
Press of Harvard University Press, 1967. 241–278.

Moore, Maxine. *That Lonely Game: Melville,* Mardi, *and the Almanac.* Columbia:
University of Missouri Press, 1975.

Otter, Samuel. *Melville's Anatomies.* Berkeley and Los Angeles: University of California
Press, 1999.

Papashvily, Helen Waite. *All the Happy Endings: A Study of the Domestic Novel in America,
the Women Who Wrote It, the Women Who Read It, in the Nineteenth Century.* New
York: Harper and Brothers, 1956.

Perry, T[homas]. S[argent]. "American Novels." *North American Review* 115.237 (1872):
366–379.

Person, Leland S. Jr. "*Mardi* and the Reviewers: The Irony of (Mis)reading." *Melville Society
Extracts* 72 (1988): 3–5.

Poovey, Mary. *A History of the Modern Fact: Problems of Knowledge in the Sciences of
Wealth and Society.* Chicago: University of Chicago Press, 2000.

Porte, Joel. *The Romance in America: Studies in Cooper, Poe, Hawthorne, Melville, and
James.* Middletown, CT: Wesleyan University Press, 1969.

Post-Lauria, Sheila. *Correspondent Colorings: Melville in the Marketplace.* Amherst:
University of Massachusetts Press, 1996.

Rezek, Joseph. *Tales from Elsewhere: Fiction at a Proximate Distance in the Anglophone
Atlantic, 1800–1850.* PhD Thesis, UCLA, 2009.

Romero, Lora. *Home Fronts: Domesticity and Its Critics in the Antebellum United States.*
Durham, NC: Duke University Press, 1997.

Samuels, Shirley, ed. *The Culture of Sentiment: Race, Gender, and Sentimentality in
Nineteenth-Century America.* New York: Oxford University Press, 1992.

Sanborn, Geoffrey. *The Sign of the Cannibal: Melville and the Making of the Postcolonial
Reader.* Durham, NC: Duke University Press, 1998.

———. "Whence Come You, Queequeg?" *American Literature* 72.2 (2005): 227–257.

Spengemann, William C. "The Earliest American Novel: Aphra Behn's *Oroonoko.*"
Nineteenth-Century Fiction 38.4 (1984). 384–414.

Stang, Richard. *The Theory of the Novel in England, 1850–1870.* London: Routledge and
Paul, 1959.

Stokes, Claudia. *Writers in Retrospect: The Rise of American Literary History, 1875–1910.*
Chapel Hill: University of North Carolina Press, 2006.

Stout, Daniel. "Nothing Personal: Decapitations of Character in *A Tale of Two Cities.*"
Novel: A Forum on Fiction 41.1 (2007): 29–52.

Tolchin, Neal L. *Mourning, Gender, and Creativity in the Art of Herman Melville.* New
Haven, CT: Yale University Press, 1988.

Tompkins, Jane. *Sensational Designs: The Cultural Work of American Fiction 1790–1860.*
New York: Oxford University Press, 1985.

Trilling, Lionel. "Manners, Morals, and the Novel." 1948. Reprinted in *The Liberal
Imagination.* New York: Viking, 1950.

Van Doren, Carl. *The American Novel.* New York: Macmillan, 1921.

Watt, Ian. *The Rise of the Novel: Studies in Defoe, Richardson, and Fielding.* London: Chatto and Windus, 1957.

Weinstein, Cindy. "The Calm before the Storm: Laboring through *Mardi.*" *American Literature* 65.2 (1993): 239–253.

Woloch, Alex. *The One vs. the Many: Minor Characters and the Space of the Protagonist in the Novel.* Princeton, NJ: Princeton University Press, 2003.

CHAPTER 4

READING RACE THROUGH DISABILITY: SLAVERY AND AGENCY IN MARK TWAIN'S *PUDD'NHEAD WILSON* AND "THOSE EXTRAORDINARY TWINS"

ELLEN SAMUELS

IN her 1992 monograph *Playing in the Dark*, Toni Morrison made a radical intervention into American literary studies by suggesting that racialized representations pervade the entirety of our national literature. Since that time, a similar argument has been made by scholars in the emerging field of disability studies, which approaches disability as an embodied social identity much like race, gender, or sexuality. This chapter employs both critical race and disability analysis to argue for a mutually constitutive relationship between these categories of representation in nineteenth-century American literature. Such an approach does not merely include disability as an additive component to an existing analysis, but much like Morrison's original intervention, provides an entirely new lens for understanding both literature and the social world in which it was produced. To read race and disability as mutually constitutive is crucial for a full understanding of how these social categories intersected in nineteenth-century America such that they can never be fully disentangled, either as representation or as material and legal realities.

To read race and disability as culturally inseparable becomes particularly intriguing when considered in relation to Mark Twain's controversial final novel, *Pudd'nhead Wilson*, and its accompanying short story, "Those Extraordinary Twins," which are structured around the mutually supportive tropes of conjoined twins and racial ambiguity. While most critical interpretations of Twain's work have focused upon racial representation, such interpretations are necessarily incomplete without an integrated analysis which takes account of how physically different or "extraordinary" bodies are deployed within the text to ground its depictions of race. This dynamic takes place within a larger context of social anxieties regarding the shifting and constructed nature of racial identity and corresponding attempts to reground social identity versus the fixed physical body which is represented by conjoinment and other forms of physical difference and disability.

Disability Studies and American Literature

Disability studies provides an innovative and provocative framework for understanding works of literature both within and outside the canon. While disability has long been framed as a matter of individual misfortune and medical intervention, this relatively new field of inquiry conceives of disability as "a socially driven relation to the body that became relatively organized in the eighteenth and nineteenth centuries" (Davis, *Enforcing* 3). In nineteenth-century America, disability took on new social significance with the emergence of entitlement programs for war veterans, specialized schools, and a general shift toward institutionalization and state management of disability. With this shift, legal and medical discourses became concerned with defining and validating those disabilities that qualified for state recognition and support, a dynamic that intersected with concurrent anxieties regarding racial identity and slave status. Such anxieties, heightened by the "visible, progressive 'whitening' of the slave body throughout the century" (Wiegman 47), centered on the failure to read blackness as clearly marked upon the body. Since both blackness and slave status increasingly had to be inferred or projected through a variety of discursive claims about racial difference, a focus upon the disabled body emerged as a contrasting example of the "true" biological difference.

Literary explorations of this phenomenon, such as Twain's novel, often invoke physical disability as a marker to signify "real" physical difference, against which claims of racial embodiment may be exposed as constructions. Critical responses to such works have continued this dynamic by reading disability metaphorically, as symbolizing another identity or meaning, rather than paying critical attention to disability as a category of representation and meaning in itself. Such metaphorical analyses resemble those of an earlier generation that read representations of blackness and enslavement in works by Twain, Faulkner, and other white American authors as metaphors for larger "universal" human concerns such as mortality, individualism, and coming of age. Disability studies scholars instead highlight the necessity for an analysis that takes into account the disabled bodies, both real and representational, that appear regularly in works of classic American fiction. Such an analysis, for example, would read Captain Ahab's missing leg in Herman Melville's *Moby-Dick* not merely as an emblem of his damaged nature, or even the wounded nature of the nation itself, but also in relation to amputees' vivid presence in nineteenth-century America, as both wars and industrial accidents produced increasing numbers of visibly disabled citizens in the public sphere, as well as heightened public discourse regarding the appropriate social response to such figures.

Disability studies, then, seeks to reframe our historical and critical understandings of major works of literature by restoring the submerged or misunderstood component of nonnormative bodies. As Rosemarie Garland-Thomson observes:

> Cultural and literary criticism has generally overlooked the…perceptions of corporeal otherness we think of variously as "monstrosity," "mutilation," "deformation," "crippledness," or "physical disability." Yet the physically extraordinary figure these terms describe is as essential to the cultural project of American self-making as the varied throng of gendered, racial, ethnic, and sexual figures of otherness that support the privileged norm. (*Extraordinary* 5)

Recent disability studies works in the field of nineteenth-century American literature have examined such topics as the prominence of disabled figures in the novels of Herman Melville, bodily dismemberment in stories by Edgar Allan Poe, blindness and benevolence in sentimental novels by Maria Cummins and Harriet Beecher Stowe, the ideal of physical perfection in the poetry of Walt Whitman, the Duboisian "hearing line" in works by deaf and hearing authors, and the use of disability masquerades in fugitive slave narratives (see Otter and Mitchell, Warne, Klages, Garland-Thomson, Scholnick, Krentz, Samuels).

The increasing presence of disability studies in the field of literary criticism has raised the question of how to understand the complex interactions between cultural representations of disability and the "figures of otherness" described by Garland-Thomson. Until quite recently, very few literary scholars had "addresse[d] the ways in which the categories of race/ethnicity and disability are used to constitute one another" (James and Wu 4). This is an important issue for American literature, in which it is often difficult to disentangle representations of disability from their racial contexts, or vice versa. In part, this entanglement has been historically produced, as "attitudes to disabilities in the West also evolved in response to interactions with other races. The colonial encounter and the series of migrations that it triggered in its wake served to displace the discourse of disability onto a discourse of otherness that was correlated to racial difference" (Quayson 10).

To explore the relationship between race and disability is not simply a matter of adding disability to the mix of identities under analysis. Representations of disability often serve a uniquely supplementary function in literature, entering a text in order to anchor a particular symbolic purpose, yet remaining unacknowledged or examined for their own particularity. Such a function can be understood through Jacques Derrida's concept of the supplement, as that which is added to an apparently complete text but is actually necessary to its meaning, "the not-seen that opens and limits visibility" (Derrida 163). David T. Mitchell and Sharon L. Snyder call this dynamic "narrative prosthesis," as the introduction of a disabled character may prosthetically enable the narrative to move forward (*Narrative Prosthesis*), yet remain an artificial device, "permitting dominant social norms to be written on the body of a person who is politely asked to step offstage once the metaphoric exchange has been made" (Davidson 1). When we consider how narrative prosthesis operates in a text that explores both racial and bodily difference, we are confronted with questions such as: How is disability being used to supplement racial meanings? Is race also being used to supplement disability? And finally, is the prosthetic relationship inevitable, or through a text's exploration of ambiguous and intersectional bodily relations, is a more free play of meanings possible? The remainder of this chapter will explore these questions in relation to Twain's 1894 novel and short story, as well as the critical responses to them.

READING THE CONJOINED TEXT

Pudd'nhead Wilson and "Those Extraordinary Twins" overflow with representations of racial identities and physical disabilities, of which the first term has received considerable critical attention, while the second has garnered almost none. To bring a disability analysis to Twain's novel, however, is not to displace or elide race, but rather to fully explore the meanings of race as it exists inextricably entwined with disability. My analysis examines both the novel and its critical interpretations in order to demonstrate the supplementary function of disability in constructing Twain's elaborate and multivalenced exploration of race, identity, agency, and nationhood. My argument has three related points, all of which are new to critical interpretations of the novel: (1) that Twain's portrayal of conjoined twinning uses disability to disconnect race from the physical body, (2) that fingerprinting, a main trope of the novel, is metonymically as well as historically linked to physical disability, and (3) that disabled characters in the novel are key to understanding its racial meanings. In each of these points, I explore how both Twain and his critics have attempted to unmoor race from disability, to show its mutability and constructed nature, and how disability has returned to haunt the text in various forms.

In *Pudd'nhead Wilson*, Twain's protagonist, lawyer David "Pudd'nhead" Wilson, solves a murder and a case of identity-switching through his "fad" of taking finger-prints from the residents of the town of Dawson's Landing, which he demonstrates dramatically during the climactic trial that closes the novel. Wilson discovers that Tom Driscoll, heir of one of the town's foremost white families, was switched in infancy by his nurse Roxy for her own enslaved son, Chambers. The spurious "Tom" eventually murders his guardian, leaving on the weapon a fingerprint, which Wilson is able to identify. Wilson then exposes Roxy's deception by comparing infant and adult fingerprints.

Any discussion of Twain's novel necessitates consideration of its complicated textual background. The novel now known as *Pudd'nhead Wilson* began, in 1892, as a short story about a pair of conjoined ("Siamese") twins (*PW* ix). Also set in the town of Dawson's Landing, this original comic tale told of the townspeople's awed reaction to the twins, who had two heads, four arms, two legs, and one torso. However, the original subplot of racial switching grew and took over the tale until it was necessary to separate them out in what Twain famously referred to as a "liter-ary Caesarean operation" ("ET" 119). The result was the current novel, *Pudd'nhead Wilson*, and a concurrently published, raggedly edited compilation of the excised material, known as "Those Extraordinary Twins."[1] (For clarity, I will refer to these two works as "the novel"—*Pudd'nhead Wilson*—and "the story"—"Those Extraordinary Twins"—although the textual history is somewhat more generically complicated.) In the revised novel, the twins, Angelo and Luigi, still exist as very minor characters, but they are no longer conjoined. However, in a textual move that has been read as both careless and intriguing, "ghostly remnants" of the twin's original conjoinment remain in the novel (Fredricks 484): the twins speak at one point of having been exhibited in a circus, and later are referred to derogatorily as "side-show riff-raff" and "dime museum freaks" (*PW* 28, 83; see also Parker; Wu, "On the Concept"; Gillman and Robinson).

Thus any reading of disability in *Pudd'nhead Wilson* must also include con-sideration of "Those Extraordinary Twins," and of the intertexuality between the two works, for "the image of the tangled twins represents an origin for the text of *Pudd'nhead Wilson*—an origin that, despite the attempts of the author, stub-bornly refuses to be erased" (Fredricks 486). When we consider that Twain wrote the conjoined twins material first, as the foundation so to speak, and constructed the eventual text of the novel atop that foundation, we can see how considerations of disability become crucial to reading the novel's mediations of bodies, texts, and power. This is true both in analyzing the novel itself, and in responding to the body of criticism it has produced. Many critics have read the novel as critiquing the social construction of race, what Twain calls the "fiction of law and custom" (*PW* 9) that makes Roxy and her son "black" although they appear white, and several have pointed out that Twain also portrays gender as highly constructed and con-tingent (see Jehlen, Morris, and Gillman, *Dark.*). Disability, however, has remained an apparently fixed and naturalized category that resists—and thus enables—other supposed bodily identities like race and gender to be exposed as constructions.

One way to understand this dynamic is through the deployment of terms such as "freak," "monster," and "unnatural." In the world of Twain's novel—and in the critical responses to it—race slavery perverts human relations and character to an extent that can only be represented by comparisons to disability, the ultimate state of un-nature: put simply, slavery is monstrous; the twins are an actual *monster*, functioning, in Michel Foucault's terms, as "the principle of intelligibility" of all other forms of abnormality (56). This abnormality makes itself felt at the cultural level of the novel, which reverses proslavery rhetorical and legal assertions that racial mixing was itself "abominable," "unnatural," and "monstrous" (Gillman, *Dark* 82–83; Sundquist, "Mark" 66). As "monsters," the twins are placed outside the realm of signification, as reflectors rather than producers of meaning. This process, described by David Hevey as "enfreakment" (335), has been integral to Western cultural definitions of the "human," and more specifically, to nineteenth-century American definitions of the citizen-subject.

Writing of the hugely popular freak shows in the United States from the mid-century through the early 1900s, Garland-Thomson argues that the display of freaks served to fashion the "self-governed, iterable subject of democracy—the American cultural self…at a time when modernization rendered the meaning of bodily differences and vulnerabilities increasingly unstable and threatening" (*Freakery* 10–11). The American subjects of Twain's story struggle with problems of identity, autonomy, and will—problems that are represented through race but mediated through a process of enfreakment, which at once submerges and solidifies the disabled presence in the text. Critical responses to *Pudd'nhead* have generally mirrored and extended this process. Critics such as Forrest Robinson, Myra Jehlen, Nancy Fredricks, and Eric Sundquist repeatedly refer to aspects of the novel and story as "unnatural," "freakish," and "monstrously deformed" (Robinson 35; Jehlen 110, 108; Fredricks 493). Tom Driscoll, for example, is described as both an "unnatural" and "monstrous" son to Roxy, since even after learning she is his mother, he contemplates selling her down the river. These critics also use terms of enfreakment to describe the system of racial slavery, and Sundquist extends the metaphor to include the 1896 *Plessy v. Ferguson* decision, in which "the Court left equal protection, like Twain's mulatto, and even more, like his Siamese twins, monstrously lodged in two bodies, neither of which had full responsibility for its legal or moral guarantee" ("Mark" 56).

I wish to emphasize that Twain himself never actually describes Tom Driscoll or slavery as "monstrous" or "unnatural"; these critics are not adopting the language of the novel, but rather are transcribing its submerged meanings, meanings which are driven by the haunting presence of the freakish bodies imperfectly excised from the novel's racial narrative. In other words, while these critics accurately perceive the racial metaphorics of Twain's monstrous bodies, they do not pay heed to the actualities of those bodies, their material and historical particularities. Yet such particularities are both meaningful and provocative in the resonance they add to critical understandings of Twain's explorations of race, agency, and American selfhood.

We can begin by exploring the historical sources of Twain's portrayal of his original, conjoined twins, Angelo and Luigi. In 1869, Twain published a humorous sketch about Chang and Eng Bunker (fig. 4.1), "Personal Habits of the Siamese Twins," as well as a lesser-known piece about another famous pair of conjoined twins, Millie and Christine McKoy, which appeared in the *Buffalo Herald* (fig 4.2; Gillman, *Dark* 58; see also Cox 14). However, when embarking on his tale, Twain did not base Angelo and Luigi upon either Chang and Eng or the McKoys, but upon the Italian brothers, Giacomo and Giovanni Tocci (Fredricks 486, Gillman 58–60). Twain refers to the Toccis in his essay which connects the novel and the story:

> I had seen a picture of a youthful Italian "freak"—or "freaks"—which was—or
> which were—on exhibition in our cities—a combination consisting of two heads
> and four arms joined to a single body and a single pair of legs—and I thought
> I would write an extravagantly fantastic little story with this freak of nature for
> hero—or heroes. ("ET" 119)

The differences between these twins' bodily configurations is important: while Chang and Eng Bunker had two distinct and "normally" configured bodies merely connected by a band of tissue, the Tocci brothers' bodily configuration presented a far more challenging blurring of boundaries of body and self, for they shared a single set of legs and lower torso, only dividing midchest into separate upper bodies (see figure 4.1).

On the choice of the Toccis as Twain's model, Susan Gillman observes that "the crucial distinction is the shared body, which heightens the dilemma of whether the twins should be accorded individual or collective status" (*Dark* 60).

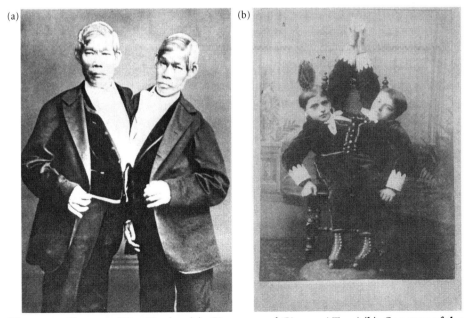

Figure 4.1 Chang and Eng Bunker (a). Giacomo and Giovanni Tocci (b). Courtesy of the North Carolina Office of Archives and History, Raleigh, North Carolina.

Figure 4.2 Millie and Christine McKoy. Courtesy of the North Carolina
Office of Archives and History, Raleigh, North Carolina.

Eric Sundquist similarly suggests that the "more physiologically apt Tocci brothers were an even better model" for signifying the doubling of Tom and Chambers, as well as Tom's dual racial status as mulatto ("Mark" 67). Gillman's and Sundquist's observations are certainly valid, yet leave a great deal unexplored regarding the question of bodily configuration with regard to both the twins' historical model and fictional presentation. I would like to highlight three largely unexplored issues here: (1) the choice of the Toccis versus Chang and Eng or other contemporaneous models, (2) the differences between Luigi and Angelo and the Toccis, and (3) the critical reception (or elision) of these differences. I will briefly explore each issue with a view toward demonstrating how the depiction of the twins crucially engages with issues of racial identification through the trope of the immutable (disabled) body.

The choice of the Toccis over Chang and Eng, Millie and Christine, or other conjoined twins of Twain's era certainly points to a desire to signify a more profoundly merged and ambiguous bodily condition than that of two bodies merely connected, as in Chang and Eng's case (Millie and Christine, while more extensively joined than Chang and Eng, had discrete torsos, arms, and two sets of legs. See figure 4.2 above). In his earlier sketch, Twain had played upon the recent strife of his "conjoined" nation by humorously (and falsely) claiming that Chang and Eng fought on opposite sides during the Civil War, took each other prisoner, and were then exchanged since an army court could not determine "which one was properly the captor and which the captive" ("Personal" 297). This scene foreshadows a farcical trial in "Those Extraordinary Twins" in which Luigi and Angelo are acquitted of kicking Tom Driscoll since the court cannot determine which of them was controlling the legs, as well as the story's denouement, in which both twins are hanged for Luigi's crime ("ET" 146–148). However, bodily configuration produces an important difference: while Chang and Eng are *inseparable*, Luigi and Angelo are *indistinguishable*. In other words, the rhetorical and practical dilemma for Chang and Eng is that one twin's movements mirror the other's. In the case of Twain's fictional twins, however, the twins' actions are not mirrored but merged: in the extended comic scene of the twins' trial, Wilson challenges witness and court alike to tell the difference between a kick by Luigi and one by Angelo.

Susan Gillman and Eric Sundquist both suggest that the merged twins' bodies better represent the racial entanglement of Twain's America, a claim which my argument does not contradict but rather strengthens through nuance. In 1869, Twain used the connected bodies of Chang and Eng Bunker to sketch the absurdity of a nation recently divided against itself; in 1892, he chose the merged bodies of the Tocci brothers to explore the dilemma of a postbellum nation attempting to reimagine itself as a unified, indivisible whole entering a new century.[2] Yet he sent his twins to the antebellum South, to the world of the slavocracy, whose dark doings gradually transformed his tale of bodily confusion into one of racial contention, entangling his narrative to a point where he had to take an authoritative surgeon's scalpel to separate his conjoined tale.

I would suggest that Chang and Eng's bodies might be read to signify the *imagined* slavocracy, in which black and white, slave and master, inhabit distinct but intimately connected worlds: neither can survive without the other, but each stays in its socially and physically demarcated arena, and separation—if contemplated—involves a quick and authoritative snip of the connecting ligature. Luigi and Angelo's merged bodies, however, metaphorically enact the *reality* of antebellum America—the races merged through decades of rape and sexual intermingling and the crumbling distinction between black slave and white master upheld by elaborate and increasingly threadbare social and legal fictions based upon bodily configuration in name only. Such fictions crucially turned upon vehement claims that racial differences were based in nature: "Only a theory rooted in nature could systematically explain the anomaly of slavery existing in a republic founded on a radical commitment to liberty, equality, and natural rights" (Roberts 186, see also Jordan 216–234). Thus Twain's choice of the Tocci brothers as his model logically connects to his seemingly irresistible need to explore the slaveholding world of his boyhood in terms at once more grisly and complex than those of *Huck Finn*. In this context, making the twins Italian rather than Asian, like Chang and Eng, or African American, like Millie and Christine, foregrounds his troubling of the category of whiteness, which is the true race "problem" at the heart of his tale.

Such a claim is bolstered by the significant changes that Twain *did* choose to enact upon his twins, changes that largely cluster around issues of agency and monstrosity. In the first place, Twain made his twins even more "freakish" in configuration than the Toccis by placing two arms on each of their outside shoulders, a configuration not only inaccurate but physiologically impossible (see figure 4.3). In fact, parapagus (joined at the pelvic region) twins either have one arm on each outside shoulder and one on the inside shoulder (like the Toccis) or one on each outside shoulder while the inside shoulders are merged, like contemporary twins Abigail and Brittany Hensel (Dreger 28–29).

Placing two arms on each shoulder allows Twain to exaggerate the enfreakment of the twins through the townspeople's reactions to them, as in their landlady Aunt Patsy's first horrified impression of a "wormy squirming of arms in the air" ("ET" 126), and through descriptions of the twins as nonhuman objects, such as a "tarantula" ("ET" 127), a "philopena" [double-kerneled nut] ("ET" 125)," a "pair of scissors" ("ET" 145), and "one of those pocket knives with a multiplicity of blades" ("ET" 130).

As a result of the placement of the twins' arms, Aunt Patsy is mystified by the question of the twins' agency, as evinced by her internal monologue at the breakfast table:

"Now that hand is going to take that coffee to—no, it's gone to the other mouth; I can't understand it; and now here is the dark-complected hand with a potatoe

Figure 4.3 Original 1894 illustration by C. H. Warren and F. M. Senior.
Courtesy of the Mark Twain Project, University of California.

[*sic*] on its fork, I'll see what goes with it—there, the light-complected head's got it, as sure as I live!" ("ET" 131)

This confusion is figured racially as well, as a matter of "dark-complected" hands feeding "light-complected" heads, a depiction that hardly needs glossing in the context of race slavery. Aunt Patsy's confusion is mediated through the enfreakment of the twins, their unnaturalness standing in for the supposed normalcy of the other "dark" hands feeding "light" mouths at this table: the hands of the enslaved woman, Nancy, who is serving the food during this scene. Here we see how exaggerating the twins' monstrosity serves Twain's racial critique of the slave system, while simultaneously undermining it by separating "normal" and "abnormal" problems of agency. If agency, and by extension control of the body's actions, lies at the heart of the system of slavery, it is vital to note that it is virtually impossible to represent problems of physical agency without referencing disability. A consideration of the particularities of disability representation, then, enables us to appreciate the particular aspects of enslavement being represented, and in Twain's case, ironically critiqued. If the novel turns upon Tom Driscoll's deceptive duality, in which, "his second (slave) self is internal but also unwilled, an unwanted identity imposed by society's racial classification" (Gillmann *Dark* 71–72), the story mirrors that duality through the ambiguous agency of the twins.

The second alteration performed by Twain, also predicated on agency, is the invention of another historically and physiologically inaccurate feature: the "switching" of control of the twins' legs, which plays a key role in the story's plot. Angelo explains that "by a mysterious law of our being, each of us has utter and indisputable control of our [legs] a week at a time, turn and turn about" ("ET" 139).[3] This alternation, said to occur precisely each Saturday at midnight, is presented as the solution to the dilemma of merged agency, in which the twins would be immobilized by the need to agree:

> We should always be arguing and fussing and disputing over the merest trifles.
> We should lose worlds of time, for we couldn't go down stairs or up, couldn't go
> to bed, couldn't rise, couldn't wash, couldn't dress, couldn't stand up, couldn't sit
> down, couldn't even cross our legs without calling a meeting first, and explaining
> the case, and passing resolutions, and getting consent. ("ET" 138)

This comically ironic description bypasses the fact that the conjoined twins upon whom Luigi and Angelo were modeled did not have the problems so eloquently imagined by Twain, a fact of which Twain must surely have been aware through his encounters with them. While many real-life conjoined twins make agreements as to which twin will make decisions on certain days, these are voluntary arrangements, not an actual physiological mechanism (Dreger 40). Yet Twain chose to create such a mechanism for his twins, substituting for a socially constructed, negotiated, and discursive solution one which is involuntary, physically based, and supposedly "natural."

As a result, Twain is able to predicate his plot upon the mystery of the twins' agency, a mystery founded in their unreadable, inseparable body. From the "who

Figure 4.4 Original 1894 illustrations by C. H. Warren and F. M. Senior.
Courtesy the Mark Twain Project, University of California.

is kicking?" trial to the final solution of hanging both twins to keep Angelo out of town meetings, the plot of "Those Extraordinary Twins" turns upon the impossibility of determining "who" is acting through the twins' shared body (see figure 4.4). This impossibility is presented both ironically and straightforwardly as a social threat. The judge who presides over the "kicking" trial melodramatically proclaims that the acquittal of the twins sets

> adrift, unadmonished, in this community, two men endowed with an awful and mysterious gift, a hidden and grisly power for evil—a power by which each in his turn may commit crime after crime of the most heinous character, and no man be able to tell which is the guilty and which the innocent part in any case of them all. Look to your homes—look to your property—look to your lives—for you have need! ("ET" 154)

The justice's impassioned warning, which echoes antebellum white fears of slave rebellions, ironically describes not the twins but their symbolic corollary in the novel, Tom Driscoll, whose racial identity is "hidden," and who proceeds to commit "crime after crime," all the while secure that he cannot be found out due to both his many disguises and his "innocent" status as a white gentleman. After murdering his uncle, for example, Tom reflects complacently that "[a]ll the detectives on earth couldn't trace me now; there's not a vestige of a clew left in the world" (*PW* 95).

Wilson's ability to pin the crime on Tom through fingerprinting suggests that the solution to the problem of agency presented by the conjoined twins is a new definition of identity as rooted in the normative body. I agree with Katherine Rowe that "the Siamese [*sic*] twins represent the nightmare of a legal apparatus unable to make their physiology testify for them," but not with her conclusion that the "extraordinary, radical uniqueness of their body" precludes the usefulness of fingerprints to determine their agency (193). Rather, I would suggest that the twins' body stands in for the "extraordinary, radical uniqueness" now discoverable in *all* bodies through their fingerprints, as well as demonstrating the problems of agency inherent in that technology. Thus I will move now to the second point of my argument, the metonymic and historical connection between physical disability and fingerprinting which is then used, ironically, to disconnect racial difference from the physical body.

READING THE NATAL AUTOGRAPH

During the climactic murder trial in *Pudd'nhead Wilson*, the character of Pudd'nhead Wilson makes a famous speech about fingerprints:

> Every human being carries with him from his cradle to his grave certain physical marks which do not change their character, and by which he can always be identified—and that without shade of doubt or question. These marks are his signature, his physiological autograph, so to speak, and this autograph cannot be counterfeited, nor can he disguise it or hide it away, nor can it become illegible by the wear and the mutations of time. This signature is not his face—age can change that beyond recognition; it is not his hair, for that can fall out; it is not his height, for duplicates of that exist; it is not his form, for duplicates of that exist, also, whereas this signature is each man's very own—there is no duplicate of it among the swarming populations of the globe! (*PW* 108)

This ringing endorsement of the infallibility of fingerprints as marks of embodied, "natural" identity is frequently cited and reproduced not only in literary criticism, but also in forensic textbooks and histories, and has even been cited in actual court decisions to support the reliability of fingerprint evidence (Beavan ix; Rowe 233 n. 51).

Yet only a greatly oversimplified and selective reading of Twain's novel can render it as a wholesale endorsement of fingerprinting technology or the ideology of identification that it represents. Instead, Twain's "complicated and contradictory attitudes toward fingerprinting" reflect his ambivalence about "systems of knowledge…that create fixed boundaries and thereby control human beings" (Gillman, *Dark* 80). Certainly the primary system of knowledge challenged by Twain is the ideology of absolute and natural racial difference, which he exposes through the device of the switched babies, legally defined as "white and free" or "black and enslaved," but physically identical with their "blue eyes and flaxen curls" (*PW* 9).

Yet Twain's deployment of fingerprinting as trope and plot device through which to explore race is crucially mediated through the evocation of physical disability, which stands for the *truly* absolute bodily difference. This connection becomes clear when we consider Twain's first use of the plot device of a bloody thumbprint, in his 1881 *Life on the Mississippi.* In the brief tale, "A Thumb-print and What Came of It," the narrator tracks down and identifies two murderers—one, painstakingly, through his thumbprint; the other, immediately, through the fact he is missing his thumb. The implication that this physical disability—the missing finger—is semantically and practically equivalent to the textual mark of the fingerprint introduces the connection of disability to fingerprinting through their signification of a fixed and legible physical identity.

Literary historian Ann Wigger confirmed in 1957 that Twain had learned about fingerprinting by reading Sir Francis Galton's 1892 work *FingerPrints,* and many critics have commented on the relationship between Galton's racial biases and Twain's novel (Wigger 518; Chinn 65–67; Gillman 88–89; Cox 19; Gillman 91; Rowe 180; Rogin 78–80; Sundquist, "Mark" 63). What has not yet been explored is how the connection between race and fingerprinting is mediated in the novel, other than through our knowledge of Galton's racialist, eugenic agenda. I suggest that disability functions as a necessary supplement in this significatory process, representing the "natural" physical body against which race may be shown as a construct, exposed as such by the technology of fingerprinting which, like disability, is rooted in "nature" and the body's immutability: "The immediacy of fingerprinting suggests the 'naturalness' of symbolic forms in general, forms upon which the society depends" (Fredricks 496).

It is well established that Galton first sought to use fingerprints, not primarily to identify individuals or criminals, but to prove the natural, physiological superiority of the white race. Indeed, Galton's racist agenda affected his scientific method, as we see when he writes that, having compared fingerprints from English, Welsh, Basque, Hebrew, and different groups of "Negro" peoples, he finds that "no very marked characteristic distinguished the races" (*FP* 195), but then continues in the very same breath that: "Still, whether it be from pure fancy on my part . . . or from some real peculiarity, the general aspect of the Negro print strikes me as characteristic. The width of the ridges seems more uniform, their intervals more regular, and their courses more parallel than with us. In short, they give an idea of greater simplicity" (*FP* 196). Twain's choice of fingerprinting as the arbiter of both personal and racial identity in his novel, then, has justly received a great deal of critical attention and analysis (see Chinn 66–67; Cole 77, 99; Gillman, *Dark* 91; Rowe 180; Rogin 78–80; Sundquist, "Mark" 63). Yet discussions of Galton's eugenic agenda rarely acknowledge that disability was an equally crucial concern.[4] Galton not only made a point of comparing fingerprints from people of different races, but also collected prints from the "lowest" and "worst" "idiots" in London (*FP* 19, 197). As in the case of his racial comparisons, Galton was disappointed, for he found "prints of eminent thinkers and of eminent statesmen that can be matched by those of congenital idiots" (*FP* 197).

Disturbingly, despite Galton's failure to demonstrate differences in the fingerprints of racial groups or people with disabilities, attempts to do so still crop up periodically in the field of forensic science. Harold Cummins's 1943 work, *Fingerprints, Palms, and Soles,* makes claims of discernible patterns in the fingerprints of different racial groups, schizophrenics, and epileptics (Cole 114). Cummins's work is cited in a 1987 article in the trade journal *Identification News*, whose author, FBI fingerprint specialist Donald F. McBride, devotes a paragraph to a study on "Mongoloids"—referring to people with Down syndrome, a group who in Galton's day would have been referred to as "Mongolian idiots," and who very likely comprised a large number of the "idiots" he printed at the Darenth Asylum (McBride 1).

At the time of Galton's writing, British physicians distinguished between three levels of mental deficiency—idiots, imbeciles, and the feeble-minded—and Dr. John Langdon H. Down had already popularized the term "Mongolian idiot" in medical circles (Jackson 168). Whether or not the widely read Galton was familiar with Down's "Observations on the Ethnic Classification of Idiots," published in 1866, he is certain to have encountered such racialized classifications in his visits to the Darenth Asylum in the late 1880s and early 1890s. Thus we may uncover the submerged enmeshment of race and disability in Galton's work and work toward an integrated analysis of their later representations. Such an analysis allows us to see that Galton did not just happen to fingerprint nonwhite people and "idiots," but that the two groups were integrally merged for both his peers and his followers. As Mark Jackson observes, "[M]edical constructions of idiocy were not merely derived from debates about racial inferiority and the origins of racial difference but were also a principal ingredient of those debates" (172).

Thus, when we move to Twain's literary representations of fingerprinting, we can see even more clearly the impossibility of separating race from disability. Here is where the metonymic importance of the conjoined twins to mediate this connection becomes apparent. If by "drawing connections between fingerprinting and the economics of possession expressed in race slavery, Twain shows their paradoxical dependence on a pervasive loss of self-control" (Rowe 180), he most clearly depicts this dilemma of self-control through the twins' extraordinary body and its social effects.

The twins' symbolic function as signifiers of bodily immutability—fingerprinting—and bodily immobility—slavery—can be read through their contaminating influence upon the nondisabled characters they encounter. Angelo and Luigi's presence produces multiple impairments as they move through the town of Dawson's Landing, leaving in their wake a slew of characters described as "paralyzed," "petrified and staring," "tottering," "tongue-tied and dazed," "silent," "unconscious," "faint," and "blind" ("ET" 124–125, 131–134). Even "the city government stood still, with its hands tied" once one of the twins was elected as alderman while the other was excluded ("ET" 169). This effect is parallel to that which Sarah Chinn sees produced by the evidence of his fingerprints upon Tom Driscoll during the novel's climactic trial: "In the moment of revelation...Tom is rendered mute and immobile....These prints speak for themselves, removed from his body and erasing Tom as a speaking subject" (Chinn 51). Indeed, from the moment of Wilson's identification of him, Tom never speaks in the novel again; in our last glimpse of him, he "made some impotent movements with his white lips, then slid limp and lifeless to the floor" (*PW* 113).

Here we see again a symbolic and causative corollary between the effect of encountering the freakishly disabled body and the effect of encountering the bodily authority of fingerprints. Both produce muteness and immobility in the subjects they encounter, signifying the location of identity in the fixed, involuntary body. The translation of this effect from the story to the novel suggests that Twain's efforts to excavate disability from the novel by removing the conjoined twins material and to focus instead on race produced a kind of palimpsestic haunting that rewrote disability insistently into his revised text, including his treatment of race. We can see this dynamic most clearly when we consider the two African American characters with disabilities who appear in the novel: the bellringer and Roxy. I will move now to the final point of my argument, examining these characters to demonstrate the incompleteness of a critical framework that fails to theorize disability as a meaningful and constructed identity.

The Haunting Presence of Disability

Thus far, my discussion of disability has centered upon the extraordinary figures of the conjoined twins. But there are two notable characters in *Pudd'nead Wilson* who have more commonplace physical debilities, and not coincidentally, both are African American. The bellringer appears in the novel's fifth chapter, when the young people of Dawson's Landing, fed up with Tom Driscoll's eastern finery and airs, arrange a prank so that Tom is followed by an "old deformed negro bellringer straddling along in his wake tricked out in a flamboyant curtain-calico exaggeration of his finery, and imitating his fancy eastern graces as well as he could" (*PW* 24).

This figure, which literally "shadows" Tom, obviously represents another instance of ironic doubling in the novel, which suggests, in Eric Lott's words, "that Tom's whiteness is itself an act, a suggestion that is truer than either the bellringer or Tom can know, since Tom's identity is precisely a black man's whiteface performance" (Lott 145). In this context, some critics have read the bellringer's disabled status metaphorically, as symbolizing Tom's " 'deformed' black nature" (Berkson 314). Linda Morris suggests, however, that "to assume the joke is somehow on Tom because he is 'really' black but does not know it misses the point. Lott's notion that Tom's whiteness is itself a performance comes much closer to the mark; nonetheless, his analysis stops with this observation, thereby missing the opportunity to investigate the convergence of a racialized *and* gendered performance" (43–44). Morris argues instead that the scene is an example of Bakhtinian carnivalesque, "with the most lowly member of the community, the deformed Negro bellringer, dressed in clothing intended to mock a member of the town's most privileged class" (43–44). As in this excerpt, Morris's essay centers upon the use of clothing to anchor Twain's unsettling of race and gender identities, and as far as it goes, her argument is compelling. However, even she seems aware that there is a missing term in her equation, as she poses a final unanswered question in her discussion of the bellringer: "We might wonder why this scene has such a haunting quality about it" (43). Myra Jehlen similarly characterizes the bellringer scene as semantically mysterious: "It is unclear just what is being satirized" (110).

These critical reactions highlight the necessity of theorizing the representation of disability, not merely as an additive component, but as a key to a text's range of meanings, including its raced, gendered, and classed meanings. I would suggest that the "haunting" quality of the scene not only indicates the hidden "truth" of Tom's race, but also the anchoring of that racial/personal identity in the fixed physical body, here as elsewhere signified by the physically disabled body. Furthermore, the bellringer's shadowing of Tom evokes the "ghostly remnants" of the conjoined twins found elsewhere in the novel, suggesting that removing that "deformed" body from the text has left semiotic gaps that necessarily evoked another similarly marked body. We are never told the nature of the bellringer's "deformity"; our only textual clue is that his manner of walking is described as "straddling along" (PW 24). Thus, we are left to visualize his bodily appearance by drawing upon an imaginary realm already aggressively haunted by the image of the imperfectly excised "monstrous" body of the twins. This connection is further reinforced by the fact that, in the novel, the bellringer scene immediately precedes the first appearance of the (separated) twins (PW 27).

Another symbolic corollary to the bellringer is marked by his costuming in "flamboyant curtain calico," the same material donned earlier by Roxy, Tom's enslaved mother, just before switching the babies. Roxy comically dons her "new Sunday gown—a cheap curtain-calico thing, a conflagration of gaudy colors and fantastic figures," as a preparation for drowning herself and her baby to avoid being sold down the river (PW 13). But when she completes her toilette by switching the babies' clothing, she realizes their physical resemblance and so conceives the plan of making the switch permanent. By doing so, she inscribes the mirroring relationship already represented by the two babies in their wagon, "one at each end and facing each other," an image which also evokes the split-mirror twinning of the conjoined Luigi and Angelo (PW 8). Yet the physical exchangeability of Tom and Chambers is contradicted by their legal and social distinction, and so Roxy's actions produce a representational double, a "shadow," which later returns to haunt Tom in the form of the disabled bellringer, the figure of bodily irreducibility.

Thus far, these dynamics demonstrate the supplementary role played by disability in constructing racial and gender performativity. However, in Twain's novel, it becomes clear that the reverse dynamic is true as well—namely, that evoking disability also necessarily evokes race, particularly in the nineteenth-century American context of scientific racism. This dynamic is apparent in Twain's depiction of the twins, who in the novel are strangely colorless characters stripped of their freakish connection as well as their racial duality: "One was a little fairer than the other, but otherwise they were exact duplicates" (*PW* 27). Ironically, while "regular" twins can be either similar or dissimilar, conjoined twins, formed from the incomplete division of a fertilized egg, are always necessarily identical. Yet, in the original conjoined versions in "Those Extraordinary Twins," Luigi is "dark-skinned" ("ET" 125), while Angelo is "blonde" with a "fresh complexion" ("ET" 126). Their different coloring is reflected in their cravats, "a delicate pink in the case of the blonde brother, a violent scarlet in the case of the brunette" ("ET" 127). The racialization of this color contrast is clear in an earlier version's sentence which Twain later deleted, in which Luigi pleads with Angelo: "Be humane, be generous—don't carry me in there before all those people in this heart-breaking costume which offends against every canon of harmony in color and will make everybody think we have been brought up among African savages" (*PW* 184). The "violent scarlet" of Angelo's cravat clearly evokes Roxy's flamboyant dress, which included a shawl of "a blazing red complexion" (*PW* 13). Furthermore, the twins' costume produces a sartorial equivalent of miscegenation, since "as a combination they broke all the laws of taste known to civilization. Nothing more fiendish and irreconcilable than those shrieking and blaspheming colors could have been contrived" ("ET" 127). Thus we see how Twain's exploration of the paradox of individuality and duality embodied by the conjoined twins was inevitably represented in terms of racial difference and racial anxiety. We are then left with my original question: is a more free play of meanings possible?

We can explore this question by examining the semantic connection between the twins, the bellringer, and Roxy. It would seem that Roxy's final appearance in Twain's novel reinforces the power of fingerprinting to establish "indisputable racial difference" (Rogin 85). The free play of race, and its haunting echo in disability, which has circulated throughout the novel, is brought to a crashing halt in the climactic trial scene when the secret knowledge that gave Roxy power is usurped by the white lawyer's technological mastery. Indeed, once Wilson has revealed Tom's true identity through fingerprints, Roxy loses her strength: she "[flings] herself upon her knees, cover[s] her face with her apron, and out through her sobs the words [struggle]—'De Lord have mercy on me, po' misable sinner dat I is!'" (113). Yet a full reading of Roxy's character reveals a more complex dynamic at work.

It is virtually unnoted by critics that Roxy becomes disabled in the course of the novel, and that her disability plays a key role in the unfolding of the plot. Roxy is "crippled" by "rheumatism in her arms" after working for eight years of freedom as a chambermaid on a steamboat (*PW* 22, 33). Roxy refuses to beg as she believes that a lifetime of hard work merits a disability pension. Tom Driscoll doesn't agree, and his refusal seals Tom's fate, for Roxy has the power of her knowledge of his true identity. Morris's observation that "this moment represents the most powerful embodiment of [Roxy's] strength" demonstrates a possible reason for the critical silence about Roxy's disability status (46–47). It is politically as well as semantically difficult to reconcile "powerful embodiment" with the usual understanding of disability as the ultimate in power*less* embodiment. Thus, like Morris's, even critical analyses explicitly focused on the character of Roxy emphasize her "force and shrewdness," her "courage," her strong will and "calculating mind," and never get around to mentioning that she has a disability (Jehlen 109; Porter 125).

This is not to say that I disagree with these characterizations of Roxy, for I believe that it is possible to be strong, shrewd, *and* disabled. Rather, I am suggesting that it is not incidental but crucial that Roxy is disabled, and that her return to play a pivotal and powerful role in the plot is driven by her disability status. Indeed, in the moment in the text when Roxy is most powerful, she manipulates the power of marked bodies to reverse the master-slave relationship. While before becoming disabled, Roxy despaired that "she could prove nothing" about Tom's true identity, and raged at herself for "not providing herself with a witness," *after* she becomes disabled, she easily persuades Tom of the untruth that "all dis is down in writin,' en it's in safe hands, too" (*PW* 22; 41). The novel presents no explanation for this change; but I contend that Roxy's physical disability, even as it produces her as the object of identification, also enables her to see beyond the fictionality of objectification, to see that identification can be discursively manipulated. Thus, the ending of the novel, which leaves the reader with a feeling of uneasy satisfaction at the unmasking and subsequent enslavement of Tom, may also be seen as a foreclosing of the possibilities of greater freedom briefly glimpsed through Roxy's exercise of power. Such freedom is portrayed as residing in the manipulable relation between body and text, identity and proof, which so powerfully shaped understandings of disability and racial difference in nineteenth-century America.

Developing an intersectional analysis of race and disability, then, provides innovative new understandings of major works in American literature. Just as this chapter has examined how disability and race supplement one another in Twain's work, we may consider how Frederick Douglass's representation of his emergence from slavery relies upon the idea of an "upright" and "able" body, how Walt Whitman's expansive vision of a multiethnic society shifts from his antebellum celebration of physical perfection to his postwar incorporation of the fragmented body/nation; how abolitionist appeals to Northern readers draw emotive power from portrayals of broken and suffering bodies, while pro-slavery rhetoricians insist that slavery is the only "natural" state for African Americans and that freedom will "cripple" them. We may begin to notice literary figures whose disabilities have been overlooked, metaphorized, or misread, and to examine how their representations productively intersect with questions of race, gender, nationality, and citizenship. And when we consider what the character of Roxy shows us about the power of disability representation to both disrupt and resolve a narrative, we have a critical lens to trace this narrative dynamic through other characters, from Chillingworth in *The Scarlet Letter*, to Ahab in *Moby-Dick*, to Deborah in *Life in the Iron Mills*, and beyond. Through such full and nuanced considerations of disability representation, we crucially expand our understanding of American literature and the social world in which it was produced.

NOTES

1 The complete textual history of the work(s) is quite complicated. The two original 1892 manuscripts, the Berg manuscript, which is titled "Those Extraordinary Twins," and the longer Morgan manuscript, titled "Pudd'nhead Wilson," both precede Twain's decision to split the twins' story from the longer tale. After the "Caesarean operation," the *Pudd'nhead Wilson* section was serialized in the *Century Magazine*, beginning in December 1893, and was published in book form in 1894 in the United States and simultaneously in England. The American edition also included the excised twins material, which Twain sold for an additional $1,500 (*PW* 173–181).

2 Cynthia Wu cogently argues that "the rendering of the Bunkers' anatomy…into a metaphor" and the "invocation of readily recognizable racial stereotypes about the Asian mind" are used by Twain in "Personal Habits" to depict "the seeming paradox of national unity with which many white Americans struggled during the latter part of the nineteenth century" ("Siamese Twins" 39).

3 Twain inconsistently describes this process as conferring control of the twins' "body" ("ET" 127, 138, 139) or of their "legs" (139, 140, 143, 149–153, 155, 158, 167). However, the twins are consistently portrayed as having individual control of their upper bodies, so that it becomes clear that only the legs are meant, even when Twain refers to the "body."

4 Lennard Davis indeed incorporates Galton's development of fingerprinting into his valuable discussion of the emergence of normalcy in the nineteenth century, but does not address the role of disability in Galton's actual studies of fingerprinting (*Enforcing* 32).

BIBLIOGRAPHY

Beavan, Colin. *Fingerprints: The Origins of Crime Detection and the Murder Case that Launched Forensic Science*. New York: Hyperion, 2001.

Berkson, Dorothy. "Mark Twain's Two-Headed Novel: Racial Symbolism and Social Realism in Pudd'nhead Wilson." *Studies in American Humor* 3.4 (1984): 309–320.

Chinn, Sarah E. "A Show of Hands: Establishing Identity in Mark Twain's *The Tragedy of Pudd'nhead Wilson*." *Nineteenth-Century Studies* 13 (1999): 48–82.

Cole, Simon A. *Suspect Identities: A History of Fingerprinting and Criminal Identification*. Cambridge, MA: Harvard University Press, 2001.

Cox, James. "Pudd'nhead Wilson Revisited." Gillman and Robinson 1–21.

Davidson, Michael. *Concerto for the Left Hand: Disability and the Defamiliar Body*. Ann Arbor: University of Michigan Press, 2008.

Davis, Lennard J. "Crips Strike Back: The Rise of Disability Studies." *American Literary History* 11.3 (Fall 1999): 500–512.

———. *Enforcing Normalcy: Disability, Deafness, and the Body*. New York: Verso, 1995.

———. Introduction. *The Disability Studies Reader*. New York: Routledge, 1997. 1–6.

Derrida, Jacques. *Of Grammatology*. 1976. Trans. Gayatri Chakravarty Spivak. Baltimore: Johns Hopkins University Press, 1997.

Dreger, Alice Domurat. *One of Us: Conjoined Twins and the Future of Normal*. Cambridge, MA: Harvard University Press, 2004.

Foucault, Michel. *Abnormal: Lectures at the Collège de France, 1974–1975*. 1999. Trans. Graham Burchell. Ed. Calerio Marchetti and Antonella Salomoni. New York: Picador, 2003.

Fredricks, Nancy. "Twain's Indelible Twins." *Nineteenth-Century Literature* 43.4 (March
    1989): 484–499.
Galton, Francis. *Finger Prints*. London: Macmillan, 1892.
———. "Identification by Finger-Tips." *Nineteenth Century* 30 (August 1891): 303–311.
Garland-Thomson, Rosemarie. *Extraordinary Bodies: Figuring Physical Disability in
    American Culture and Literature*. New York: Columbia University Press, 1997.
———. Introduction. *Freakery: Cultural Spectacles of the Extraordinary Body*. New York:
    New York University Press, 1996. 1–19.
Gillman, Susan K. *Dark Twins: Imposture and Identity in Mark Twain's America*. Chicago:
    University of Chicago Press, 1989.
Gillman, Susan K., and Forrest G. Robinson, eds. *Mark Twain's Pudd'nhead Wilson: Race,
    Conflict, and Culture*. Durham, NC: Duke University Press, 1990.
Hevey, David. "The Enfreakment of Photography." Davis, *Disability Studies Reader* 332–347.
Jackson, Mark. "Changing Depictions of Disease: Race, Representation, and the History
    of 'Mongolism.' " *Race, Science, and Medicine, 1700–1960*. Ed. Waltraud Ernst and
    Bernard Harris. New York: Routledge, 1999. 167–188.
James, Jennifer C., and Cynthia Wu, eds. "Editors' Introduction: Race, Ethnicity, Disability,
    and Literature: Intersections and Interventions." *MELUS: Journal for the Study of the
    Multi-Ethnic Literature of the United States* 31.3 (Fall 2006): 3–13.
Jehlen, Myra. "The Ties That Bind: Race and Sex in *Pudd'nhead Wilson*." Gillman and
    Robinson 105–120.
Jordan, Winthrop D. *White over Black: American Attitudes toward the Negro, 1550–1812*.
    Baltimore: Penguin, 1968.
Klages, Mary. *Woeful Afflictions: Disability and Sentimentality in Victorian America*.
    Philadelphia: University of Pennsylvania Press, 1999.
Krentz, Christopher. *Writing Deafness: The Hearing Line in Nineteenth-Century American
    Literature*. Chapel Hill: University of North Carolina Press, 2007.
Linton, Simi. *Claiming Disability: Knowledge and Identity*. New York: New York University
    Press, 1998.
Lott, Eric. *Love and Theft: Blackface Minstrelsy and the American Working Class*. New York:
    Oxford University Press, 1995
McBride, Donald F. "Disease Inheritance and Race Determination by Fingerprints."
    Identification News (August 1987). http://www.scafo.org/library/110203.html.
Mitchell, David T., and Sharon L. Snyder, eds. Introduction. *The Body and Physical
    Difference: Discourses of Disability*. Ann Arbor: University of Michigan Press, 1997. 1–31.
———. "Masquerades of Impairment: Charity as a Confidence Game." *Leviathan* 8.1
    (March 2006): 35–60.
———. *Narrative Prosthesis: Disability and the Dependencies of Discourse*. Ann Arbor:
    University of Michigan Press, 2000.
Morris, Linda A. "Beneath the Veil: Clothing, Race, and Gender in Twain's *Pudd'nhead
    Wilson*." *Studies in American Fiction* 27.1 (Spring 1999): 37–52.
Morrison, Toni. *Playing in the Dark: Whiteness and the Literary Imagination*. New York:
    Random House, 1992.
Moss, Robert. "Tracing Mark Twain's Intentions: The Retreat from Issues of Race in
    Pudd'nhead Wilson." *American Literary History* 30.2 (Winter 1998): 43–55.
Otter, Samuel, and David T. Mitchell, eds. *Leviathan: A Journal of Melville Studies* 8.1
    (March 2006).
Parker, Hershel. *Flawed Texts and Verbal Icons: Literary Authority and American Fiction*.
    Chicago: Northwestern University Press, 1996.

Porter, Carolyn. "Roxana's Plot." Gillman and Robinson 121–136.

Quayson, Ato. *Aesthetic Nervousness: Disability and the Crisis of Representation.* New York: Columbia University Press, 2007.

Roberts, Dorothy E. "The Genetic Tie." *Critical Race Theory: The Cutting Edge.* 2nd ed. Ed. Richard Delgado and Jean Stefanic. Philadelphia: Temple University Press, 2000. 186–189.

Robinson, Forrest G. "The Sense of Disorder in *Pudd'nhead Wilson.*" Gillman and Robinson 22–45.

Rogin, Michael. "Frances Galton and Mark Twain: The Natal Autograph in *Pudd'nhead Wilson.*" Gillman and Robinson 73–85.

Rowe, Katherine. *Dead Hands: Fictions of Agency, Renaissance to Modern.* Stanford, CA: Stanford University Press, 1999.

Samuels, Ellen. "A Complication of Complaints: Untangling Disability, Race, and Gender in William and Ellen Craft's *Running a Thousand Miles for Freedom.*" *MELUS: Journal for the Study of the Multi-Ethnic Literature of the United States* 31.3 (Fall 2006): 15–47.

Scholnick, Robert J. "'How Dare a Sick Man or an Obedient Man Write Poems?' Whitman and the Dis-ease of the Perfect Body." *Disability Studies: Enabling the Humanities.* Ed. Sharon L. Snyder, Brenda Jo Brueggemann, and Rosemarie Garland-Thomson. New York: MLA Press, 2002. 248–259.

Snyder, Sharon L., Brenda Jo Brueggemann, and Rosemarie Garland-Thomson. "Introduction: Integrating Disability into Teaching and Scholarship." *Disability Studies: Enabling the Humanities.* New York: MLA Press, 2002. 1–12.

Sundquist, Eric J. "Mark Twain and Homer Plessy." Gillman and Robinson 46–72.

———. *To Wake the Nations: Race in the Making of American Literature.* Cambridge, MA: Harvard University Press, 1993.

Thomas, Ronald R. "The Fingerprint of the Foreigner: Colonizing the Criminal Body in 1890s Detective Fiction and Criminal Anthropology." *ELH* 61.3 (Autumn 1994): 655–683.

Twain, Mark. "Personal Habits of the Siamese Twins." *Mark Twain's Sketches: Selected and Revised by the Author.* London: Routledge, 1872. 299-304.

———. *Pudd'nhead Wilson and "Those Extraordinary Twins."* 1894. New York: Norton, 1980.

———. "A Thumb-print and What Came of It." *Life on the Mississippi.* 1881. Oxford: Oxford University Press, 1990.

Warne, Vanessa. "'If You Should Ever Want an Arm': Disability and Dependency in Edgar Allan Poe's 'The Man That Was Used Up.'" *Atenea* 25.1 (2005): 95–105.

Whitley, John S. "*Pudd'nhead Wilson*: Mark Twain and the Limits of Detection." *Journal of American Studies* 21.1 (1987): 55–70.

Wiegman, Robyn. *American Anatomies: Theorizing Race and Gender.* Durham, NC: Duke University Press, 1995.

Wigger, Ann P. "The Source of Fingerprint Material in Mark Twain's *Pudd'nhead Wilson.*" *American Literature* 28.4 (January 1957): 517–520.

Wu, Cynthia. "On the Concept of the Flawed Text: Hershel Parker, Mark Twain, and Literary Teratology." Modern Language Association conference, 2002.

———. "The Siamese Twins in Late Nineteenth-Century Narratives of Conflict and Reconciliation." *American Literature* 80.1 (2008): 29–55.

CHAPTER 5

....

THE INVENTION OF
MEXICAN AMERICA

....

JESSE ALEMÁN

Invenīre

In memoriam, Hector A. Torres

As the work of Edmundo O'Gorman, Enrique Dussel, and Walter Mignolo teaches us, America was not discovered; it was invented. European nation-states involved in the modern project of exploration and expansion construed the western hemisphere in a georacial cartography that explained its existence—its discovery—in the prevailing Eurocentric mapping of the world. Even the name America, Mignolo reminds us (3), must be understood in the context of Eurocentricism—not so much because the landmass was named after Amerigo Vespucci as because the German cartographer Martin Waldseemüeller feminized Amerigo's Latinized name, Americus, to make it consistent with the names of the other continents: Asia, Africa, and Europa. America rhymed. "The fault that lies at the root of the entire history of the idea of the discovery of America," O'Gorman explains, "consists in assuming that the lump of cosmic matter which we now know as the American continent has always been that, when actually it only became that when such a meaning was given to it" (42). For O'Gorman, Columbus did not discover America, because discovery implies that the thing being discovered must be known, and Columbus never knew that he landed on a landmass unknown to Europeans; he thought he hit the Indies (73). Instead, America came into being as an idea through a process of historical production that situated the western hemisphere within Europe's colonial imagination.

My project reconsiders Mexican America along similar axes of hemispheric discovery and invention by combining the politics of U.S. ethnic studies with the historical scope and vision of hemispheric American studies—two fields that meet tenuously in recent scholarship because hemispheric studies requires a trans-American view that exceeds the United States' national borders. Yet, hemispheric studies provides the language for two paradigms of knowledge about nineteenth-century Mexican America. In the first case, we can understand the "invention of Mexican America" along the lines of "discovery," as nineteenth-century Anglo-American writers discovered Mexico's antiquity and appropriated it as the United States' own national narrative. In the second case, invention foregrounds how those people ostensibly being discovered are agents of inventing themselves and their own idea of America. Whereas O'Gorman concludes, "Not only was America invented and not discovered,...but it was invented in the image of its inventor" (140), hemispheric studies pushes us to consider multiple reinventions of America. Indeed, the impulse to reinvent the idea of America occurs especially at moments of social and political rupture that trouble what it means to be American in the first place, and in the nineteenth century, the United States' relation to the rest of the hemisphere afforded Mexicans living in the United States a transnational context for imagining themselves against the colonial logic of discovery.

Hemispheric studies isn't new to nineteenth-century American literary history; it wasn't even new in the nineteenth century as culture makers from the upper and lower Canadas to the early Republic of Colombia contemplated, contested, and celebrated the common history of the Americas. It has been as vexed as the hemisphere itself in terms of defining its scope and borders and has undergone a variety of permutations, including the pan-Americanism of the late nineteenth century; the borderlands and inter-Americanism of Herbert Bolton; Latin American and intra-American studies; and areas such as transnational, trans-American, border, New World, and Global South studies. In all cases, the work of hemispheric studies is comparative, although questions about the nature and practice of comparison continue to challenge the field. Does trans-American scholarship ineluctably take the United States as the point of origin for any comparison? Do the methods of comparison lead to a one-way notion of transnationalism mapped to and from the United States? As Claudia Sadowski-Smith and Claire Fox put it, "In the face of the hemisphere's vast inequalities and different disciplinary configurations, any call for transnational scholarly dialogue or assumptions of inter-American unity threatens to replicate the long history of US imperialism in the hemisphere" (7).

For Mexican American studies, hemispheric work is doubly vexed because scholarship often focuses on the regional formations of identity—in California, Texas, or New Mexico—that occur in response to the United States' uneven distribution of power following the 1848 Treaty of Guadalupe Hidalgo. Mexican America in this regard is a regional identity formed against a national one, but such a model forecloses the transnational exchanges that linked nineteenth-century Mexican Americans to the rest of the Americas. Not until recently has hemispheric studies appeared on the scene to complicate and complement Mexican American literary history. José David Saldívar's *Dialectics of Our America* returned to the question of a "common" American sentiment and found one in José Martí's oppositional writings, and Kirsten Silva-Gruesz's *Ambassadors of Culture* demonstrates how hispanophone writings can redefine canonical nineteenth-century American literary history to remap what we think we know about U.S. literary culture, Mexican America, and the tangled genealogies they share with each other and the rest of the Americas.

We might even say that the payoff of hemispheric studies is the way it foregrounds the pervasiveness of empire in the Americas, putting the lie to U.S. exceptionalism by linking disparate indigenous, diasporic, and creole experiences. As Caroline Levander puts it, hemispheric studies "divides nations along new axes" (449) to rewrite American literary history more broadly in terms of depth and scope. We can understand "American" to encompass the Americas and its cultural, literary, linguistic, and historical diversity, or we can rethink the degree to which U.S. literature owes its emergence to hemispheric history. Both are revisionist models that challenge a nationalist paradigm of literary history, and for Mexican America, hemispheric studies reconceptualizes the notion of national belonging altogether, delinking it from the nation-state (i.e., Mexico or the United States) and situating it instead within what David Luis-Brown describes as "hemispheric citizenship," which "expand[s] the 'self' in self-determination beyond the borders of the nation, turning a transnationalism against imperialism" (26).

Thus, I present the notion of invention rather than discovery as a productive distinction for Mexican America. "'Discovery' is the dominant, imperial version of what happened," Walter Mignolo argues, "while 'invention' opens the window of possibility for decolonizing knowledge. That is, if 'discovery' is an imperial interpretation, 'invention' is not just a different interpretation but a move to decolonize imperial knowledge" (32–33). *Invenīre*, to come upon, not only signifies to discover, create, or produce by mental activity, as O'Gorman explained; it also means to plan or to plot, which suggests that at some point the word incorporated its implied context—to come upon something being planned or plotted; perhaps something subversive. In part, this explains why Mignolo sees the potential for decoloniality in invention, and José Rabasa sees in it "the possibility of reversing the centrality of European history...by underscoring the endurance of Amerindians" (7). Invention encompasses the colonial idea of discovery and resistance to it, making it a contested process of imagining history, citizenship, and national belonging. Oppressive and potentially subversive, invention is a duplicitous idea especially apt for understanding how "the categories of subaltern and imperialist, particularly in the American hemisphere, are not mutually exclusive, but often overlaid" (Karem 96).

What follows, then, is a mapping of Mexican America that charts its discovery in nineteenth-century Anglo-American historical romances about the conquest of Mexico and its anticolonial reinvention in contemporaneous Mexican American writings. During what I call the Age of Discovery, U.S. writers appropriated the hemispheric history of the Americas to fashion a distinct "American" literature separate from British and European traditions. In response, U.S. hispanophone writers appropriated the revolutionary discourses of hemispheric citizenship to imagine their own sense of belonging within the Americas. Colonialism and resistance to it thus constitute what I term the invention of Mexican America, but as with the western hemisphere itself, Mexican America sometimes suffers from the contradictions of its own creole consciousness as it redraws the map of the hemisphere in ways that trouble but also transform nineteenth-century American and Mexican American literary histories.

THE AGE OF DISCOVERY

It is well known in U.S. literary history that the Americas in general and Mexico in particular provided a "usable past," as Lois Parkinson Zamora calls it, during the late eighteenth and early nineteenth centuries—the Age of Revolutions, as it is known in hemispheric studies. As Eric Wertheimer's *Imagined Empires* demonstrates, the idea of the Americas has always been formative to the U.S. literary imagination, even as the real-historical relations between the so-called Saxon and Latin hemispheres have been more distant. That is the point. The Americas served as an idea, an invention in the image of its maker that proved foundational to the emergence of a U.S. literary culture distinct from England and Europe. "In a flourish of Columbian thinking," Wertheimer explains, postcolonial Anglo-Americans "contemplated the precedents and possibilities of 'American civilization,' pre-discovery and postcolonial. A certain form of exceptionalism believed America was a nation without precedent; but there was a vital tradition that saw exemplars in the New World" (2–3). When U.S. writers discovered the hemispheric history of the Americas, they used it to produce a creole literary culture that, like the Monroe Doctrine, imagined isolation from the Old World by claiming ownership of the new one. It is a literature of dis-identification, though, as U.S. writers embraced the hemisphere's antiquity but not its racial diversity. The Americas became Anglo-American.

William H. Prescott's *History of the Conquest of Mexico* (1843), for instance, is an ambivalent historical allegory that wrestles with championing the proto-American Aztec civilization against the ruthlessness of the Spanish conquest. However, as the history progresses, and the Aztecs mount their rebellion more successfully, the narrative turns away from its romantic republicanism and becomes gothic as indigenous peoples retaliate against their white oppressors. Here Prescott's anti-Spanish critique buckles, for he cannot bring himself to align young America with the antiquity of Aztec Mexico after all. Rather, his narrative is indicative of the ambivalence of the Black Legend in Anglo-American cultural production. As Anna Brickhouse explains, "The Black Legend provided a powerful historiographical device within Anglo American accounts of the Conquest and narratives of US exceptionalism: its implicit denigration of the contemporary Spanish Americas conveniently gave rhetorical support to a variety of US political positions toward Latin America, while its privileging of ancient Latin American indigenous civilizations highlighted the alleged barbarism of contemporary North American Indians and helped to justify nineteenth-century US Indian policy" (75).

If we think of Prescott's *History* as a hemispheric palimpsest, its significance becomes even more layered in a way that can best be seen mapped out (see figure 5.1).

The historical narrative is ostensibly about Spain's conquest of Mexico in which the Aztecs stand in as early hemispheric "Americans" who succumb to the violence of empire. Thus, on the top horizontal plane, Aztecs and "Americans" share the same latitude, while in longitude, they are in opposition to the Spaniards. But the history of Mexico's conquest is the first map of the hemisphere. The 1843 narrative is also about the United States as a new nation rapidly becoming neocolonial after its successful revolution against England, which is why "Americans" share the same longitude but differ in degree and kind. The top "American" is a hemispheric subject; the bottom one references a national subject of the United States. At the same time, Spaniards and Americans share the bottom latitude because, while Prescott's narrative would like to imagine a difference between the two, the book's historical context reveals the United States to be repeating Spain's hemispheric history. Prescott underscores this point by drawing a distinction between Aztecs of the romantic past and present-day Indians in Mexico and the United States: "Enough has been said, however, to show that the Aztec and Tezcucan races were advanced in civilization very far beyond the wandering tribes of North America" (44).

Prescott's palimpsest extends into the future too as it presages the United States' conquest of Mexico five years after *History*'s publication. The narrative serves as a hemispheric harbinger as "Americans" reenact the Spanish history of the invasion and occupation of Mexico. In this repetition, Indians, Aztecs, and Mexicans suffer a fate that links them on a layered map of conquests. "In their entirety," Brickhouse explains, "Prescott's volumes exemplify the historical and conceptual gap separating the hemispheric sensibilities of the 1820s from those of the mid-century" (80). Prescott's *History* ushers in a new age of discovery, so to speak, as its historical

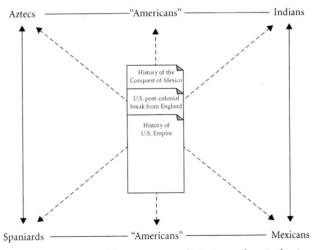

Figure 5.1 *Prescott's History of the Conquest of Mexico as hemispheric palimpsest.*

and geographical information proved so important to the U.S. military that every navy ship held a copy of Prescott's book (Johannsen 150), while the romance of conquest fanned the flames of officers and volunteers as they marched their way to Mexico City, many excited to be "following in the footsteps of Cortes," as the popular saying went (245). A little over a decade after Prescott's *History*, Herman Melville would capture the haunting legacy of conquest the United States inherited from Spain with the simple phrase, "*Seguid vuestro jefe*," chalked underneath Aranda's bones (49).

The United States' early national period, then, might best be renamed as an Age of Discovery during which Anglo-American writers "discovered" the history of the Americas in order to remake the hemisphere in their own republican image. It is not so much the postcolonial break with England that defines American literature, as has been the understanding in American literary history. Anglo-America rediscovered the New World following its break from the old one and imagined a national literary history filled with indigenous republicans, protorevolutionary Incans, and a hemispheric history of anticolonialism. Reviewing Edward Maturin's 1845 *Montezuma: The Last of the Aztecs*, for instance, an anonymous writer for the *American Whig Review* proclaimed Maturin "has done what we wish our American authors were more in the habit of doing—he has introduced his readers to what should be claimed by appropriation, as an exclusively American field—for in a Literary sense, at least, 'The whole boundless continent is now ours.' The legendary and historical wealth of this entire hemisphere should be made ours by the bloodless conquest of the Pen" (224). Of course, as U.S. literary culture used the indigenous history of the Americas, it waged real forms of dispossession and displacement of indigenous peoples through a form of Manifest Destiny that appropriated Mexico's cultural history as quickly as it did Mexico's property.

Alongside Prescott's work, there is a body of hemispheric American historical romances that, as "foundational fictions" of the United States' discovery of Mexican America (Sommer 6), smooth out the uneven ideological rifts of expansionism, class division, and slavery. We're already familiar with the way the historical romance genre imagined Native America into oblivion in Lydia Maria Child's *Hobomok*, Catharine Maria Sedgwick's *Hope Leslie*, and James Fenimore Cooper's *The Last of the Mohicans*. But unlike so-called frontier romances, which imagine the rebirth of Anglo-America sans the past, hemispheric American histories mine the past to discover the New World origins of the United States. This excavation uncovers the "hauntology," to borrow from Derrida (10), of empire in the Americas that gives new, gothic meanings to the idea of "inter-Americanism." I don't mean "inter" as a prefix but as a transitive verb denoting burial to highlight the idea that our national periodizations and categories repress—bury—the presence of an other America already at the heart of our national formation and literary history (Alemán 79). That is, the Age of Discovery reminds us that American literary history once belonged to the Americas rather than just to the country that appropriated the name of the entire western hemisphere.

The preface to Robert Montgomery Bird's *Calavar; or, The Knight of the Conquest* (1834) stages the moment when Mexico's ancient history becomes Anglo-America's: An American wandering Mexico inherits a multivolume manuscript of Mexico's history from a mad priest, who charges the American to translate and publish the document in the United States. The American "shaved, therefore, and he cut, he amputated and he compressed; and he felt the joy of an editor, when exercising the hydraulic press of the mind. . . . He expunged as much of the philosophy as he could" to produce a historical romance about Mexico fit for the United States' "intellectual dyspepsia" (xxvii–iii). Ironically, narratives like Bird's *Calavar* and his follow-up, *The Infidel*, as well as Joseph Holt Ingraham's *Montezuma, the Serf (1845)* and the *Montezuma: The Last of the Aztecs* (1845) fed the United States' "intellectual dyspepsia" with gothic romance structures, impossible plot twists, maidens in drag, and, in the case of Maturin's *Montezuma*, a politically zealous dwarf. Written by an Irish national who corresponded with Prescott, *Montezuma* is a grotesque mock epic that marks the transition from the romantic discovery of Mexico's antiquity to the sensationalism associated with the U.S.-Mexico War. "Indeed, it is not hard to see how Anglo-American fascination with the Spanish Conquest held the seeds of U.S. imperialism," Brickhouse writes (44), and it is equally interesting to see how that colonial transition changes the narration of Mexico's past. For Maturin, neither Cortés nor Montezuma is a grand epic character that battles for the right over Mexico, as they are in Prescott; rather, the narrative's main character is an Aztec dwarf, a member of Montezuma's court who attempts to uphold Aztec patriotism and valor against the overwhelming odds of the Spanish conquest, internecine conflict between the Aztecs and the Tlaxcalans, and traitorous Aztec priests. By 1845, perhaps the dwarf is also symbolic of a Mexican body politic that cannot keep at bay the overwhelming invasion of U.S. forces.

The era of the United States' discovery of Mexico's antiquity culminated with the de jure invention of Mexican America in 1848, when the Treaty of Guadalupe Hidalgo ended the U.S.-Mexico War and recognized the Mexicans living in Mexico's far northern frontier as U.S. citizens—of sorts. This is the moment that Chicano/a and American studies scholars mark as the origin of Mexican America, as the treaty granted citizenship rights to the Mexicans living in the annexed territory while Anglo-American social, cultural, and legal practices accorded the new citizens with second-class status at best. As John-Michael Rivera puts it, the treaty "is the first document to deal with both the question of U.S. democracy's capacity to expand into the west and to establish, in natural rights theory, the newly constituted political subject known as the 'Mexican American' " (66). The inclusion of Mexican America wasn't an uncontested battle. The United States appeased its appetite for all of Mexico by settling for its sparsely populated northern frontier, which contained too many mixed-race subjects for the likes of South Carolina senator John C. Calhoun, who proclaimed in his January 4, 1848, resolution opposing the war and its outcome: "To incorporate Mexico, would be the very first instance of the kind of incorporating an Indian race; for more than half of the Mexicans are Indians, and the other is composed chiefly of mixed tribes. I protest against such a union as that! Ours, sir, is the Government of a white race. The greatest misfortunes of Spanish America are to be traced to the fatal error of placing these colored races on an equality with the white race" (16–17).

There's much to make of Calhoun's statement in terms of Mexican America's racial status as "off-white," as Laura Gómez calls it (83–84), but neither the treaty nor the debates surrounding it created Mexican Americans, as Gómez has it in *Manifest Destinies*. For Gómez, "the U.S. colonization of northern Mexico should be understood as the moment in which Mexican Americans first became constituted as a racial group" (17). Thus, she maintains that U.S. law "played [an important role] in the creation of Mexican Americans as racial group" (40). The problems here are twofold and both related to the lessons that hemispheric studies can teach us. First, Gómez overlooks how Mexican Americans were already hemispheric rather than regional subjects who had lived through two different forms of colonialisms in the Americas before the U.S.-Mexico War (the Spanish conquest and Mexican neocolonialism). Even Calhoun's logic invokes a hemispheric sensibility, as he understands the ostensible instability of Spanish America as a result of racial equality between indigenous, mixed-race, and white subjects—the latter of which is the most important concession as it recognizes a white population in Spanish America in the first place. Second, Gómez's lack of hemispheric vision leads her to attribute to Anglo-America sole power to create Mexican Americans into a racial group that did not exist prior to 1848. But what were these very same people before their discovery under U.S. colonization? As Calhoun mentions, they maintained a racial identity within the Spanish and Mexican caste systems that had everything to do with how they negotiated their way into whiteness after 1848, when Anglo-American racial codes displaced Spanish American cultural practices. Gómez reproduces the problem of discovery iterated earlier: she argues that Anglo-America and its legal systems created the Mexican American race but overlooks how Mexican Americans reinvented their racial status after 1848 to fit into a new hemispheric colonial regime, just as they did throughout the Spanish colonial and Mexican independence periods.

The difference here is agency in identity formation, which John-Michael Rivera underscores in his understanding of how stories constitute what he calls the "emergence of Mexican America." "By telling their stories," Rivera argues, Mexicans "enter the public sphere and transform the very contours of democratic culture that had affected their constitution in the United States as personae non gratae" (2). Despite the second-class status the treaty bestowed on Mexicans in the United States, storytelling gives them agency in their articulation of U.S. citizenship. "Although Anglo-Americans played a part in the racial constitution of the political people now ethnically defined as 'Hispanic,'" Rivera explains, "the first Mexicans to engage the public spheres in the United States *reinvented* their racial and political ontology and therefore refashioned the contours of Mexican peoplehood" (19; emphasis added). I underscore the idea of "reinvention" here to distinguish it from Rivera's notion of the "emergence" of Mexican America, for "reinvention" is neither as organic nor as seamless as "emergence" suggests. Reinvention is uneven, contradictory, and perhaps even a reproduction of a previous formulation but with a difference. It is the embodiment of creole double consciousness that rejects the colonial logic of discovery through a strategic identity formation that spans competing forms of colonialisms, imperialisms, and empires across the Americas.

THE INVENTION OF MEXICAN AMERICA

If discovery is one side of invention, resistance to being discovered is another. Invention in this regard is duplicitous—it is colonial and anticolonial insofar as it can mean to "come upon" something being "planned or plotted." What I have been calling the Age of Discovery, then, ushered the invention of Mexican America, as U.S. hispanophone writers appropriated discourses of republican independence to resist the double threat Spain and the United States posed as uncanny figurations of empire in the Americas. Once again, the historical romance gets pressed into service, but this time as an anticolonial genre used to situate Mexican America within a larger hemispheric citizenship that, on the one hand, critiques colonial power and, on the other, risks the danger of reproducing it.

Let me begin with *Xicoténcatl*, the 1826 historical romance that was penned in Spanish and published in Philadelphia. Its authorship remains anonymous, but Luis Leal and Rodolfo Cortina attribute it to Cuban-born Catholic priest Felix Varela, citing similarities in content, style, and syntax found in Varela's body of published writings (xvi). Varela's stance on Cuban and Latin American independence from Spain and the abolition of slavery in Cuba landed him in the United States as an exiled priest who lived in Philadelphia when *Xicoténcatl* was published before he moved to New York. While the book's publication history coincides with Valera's record of print production in the United States, some skepticism still surrounds the book's authorship, leading Brickhouse to speculate that the book might have been coauthored by exiled Cuban poet José María Heredia and Vicente Rocafuerte, a writer, diplomat, and Cuban exile whose republican sensibilities make him a cosmopolitan hemispheric citizen (53–55). Either way, the book's authorship is important for the recovery of hispanophone writings in the United States and for understanding the hemispheric palimpsest the narrative maps.

Xicoténcatl is a short, six-chapter historical romance that narrates the fall of the Tlaxcalan republic after it allies with Hernán Cortés's army against the Aztecs. Known for its long, successful resistance to the Aztec empire, the "confederated republic" of Tlaxcala is in the midst of an internal struggle for power between Magiscatzin and Xicoténcatl the Elder and his eponymous son, Xicoténcatl, the indigenous republic's general (8). Hernán Cortés exploits the Tlaxcalan rift to put Magiscatzin in power and oust the elder Xicoténcatl from the senate, while forcing the younger one to ally his republican army with Cortés's small band of Spanish conquistadores. Their confederation of mutual interests against the Aztecs binds their alliance, but as the historical romance has it, Cortés is also invested in keeping Teutila, Xicoténcatl's Indian maiden, captive to enjoy the pleasure of threatening her with rape or forced prostitution to coerce the Tlaxcalan general's submission. There is no romance at the end the narrative: Cortés falsely accuses Xicoténcatl of treason and has him executed; Teutila attempts to assassinate Cortés and poisons herself in the process; Magiscatzin dies in moral anguish; and the independent Tlaxcalan republic is left in shambles on the eve of Cortés's reconquest of the Aztec empire after the famous *noche triste*, when the Aztecs ousted the Spaniards and their allies.

Xicoténcatl is ostensibly an allegory for the instability of the newly independent Mexican nation-state. Having gained its independence from Spain in 1821, Mexico struggled with defining its system of governance. Agustín de Iturbide, the criollo who helped to force Spain's capitulation, proclaimed himself Augustín I, emperor of Mexico, but within three years, a revolt against Iturbide led to the creation and adoption of the 1824 republican constitution, based in part on the United States' constitution as a model. The conflicts between liberal criollos and conservative clerics, though, fostered and fueled Mexico's political and economic instability throughout most of the mid-nineteenth century—a danger that the narrator of *Xicoténcatl* laments: "When internal divisions destroy the unity of a people, they inevitably become the victims of their enemies, and more so if the practitioners of political shrewdness and craftiness are able to take advantage of that discord" (79). What threatens Mexico in the narrative is not the Spanish monarchy, as most scholars see Cortés and his men, but the duplicity of the United States as both a model republic and an emergent empire. With the 1823 Monroe Doctrine freshly announced, *Xicoténcatl* narrates a new menace to Mexico, a new conquest strangely familiar to the fall of the Aztec empire. U.S. imperialism across the Americas, rather than European monarchy, compromises the stability of American republics.

Thus, the narrative imagines a trans-American consolidation that can be read as a layered historical allegory. Faced with the fall of the Tlaxcalan republic and the conquest of the Aztec empire, Xicoténcatl and Teutile, a general in Moctezuma's army and uncle of the "American maiden" Teuitla, broker a marriage plot between Xicoténcatl and Teutila that would unite indigenous forces against Cortés after the fall of the Aztec empire:

> The two generals reached an accord, moved by their great desire to save their country from all the evils that threatened it, and they agreed that, for the moment, the most prudent thing to do was to allow Hernán Cortés to continue toward Mexico, where he should destroy the prestige in which a fanatical people held their tyrant's majesty via the insults and degradation that he would undoubtedly suffer in his impotence; that Xicoténcatl would appear with his troops at a place favored by the circumstances; that Teutile would spare no sacrifice to cooperate with him in his magnificent enterprise; and that, once the foreigners had been defeated, Mexicans and Tlaxcalans would create a solid peace, ensured by reform, so generally desired and so necessary in the Mexican Empire. (84)

Reminiscent of a modern-day coup plaguing postindependent Mexico, the plan enacts the covert insurgency at the heart of inventing Mexican America. It is an alliance between what the narrative terms "Mexicans" (i.e., subjects of the Aztec empire) and the Tlaxcalans, whom the narrative calls "Americans." The confederacy between the Mexicans and the Americans collapses the animosity between the two warring groups and brokers peace with the Zocotlans and Cholulans as a way to "save their country," as the narrator puts it. But up until now, there has been no single "country" in the narrative. There has been the Tlaxcalan republic, Mexico, and "the nations of Zocotlan and Cholula" (85). The indigenous alliance, then, is nothing short of an invention of Mexican America crafted to check Cortés's conquest of the Americas after the fall of the Aztec empire. This last part is important because the indigenous insurgency is not just opposed to Cortés's plans but also invested in bringing republican reform backed by military might to the "Mexican empire" after the fall of "their tyrant's majesty," literally meaning Montezuma but also suggesting the vestiges of Spanish monarchy in Cuba and the Americas (84). We should see the Mexican-American consolidation in the narrative as an articulation of the anonymous author's criollo double consciousness that stakes an anti-imperial position against two colonial powers: the Spanish empire, figured in the narrative as the declining Aztec empire, and U.S. imperialism, an emergent threat that Hernán Cortés embodies in the text.

That the indigenous alliance fails is not as telling as that it was imagined in the first place. Indeed, with *Xicoténcatl*, the power of hemispheric citizenship stretches from the content of the novel to the context of the narrative's authorship. Within the narrative itself, the invention of Mexican America appears an anti-imperialist coalition across different indigenous nation-states for the sake of an indeterminate "country." But we can also read this coalition as an allegory of the text's anonymous authorship and the transnational possibilities it raises as a hispanophone text penned and published in the United States but linked to the independence movements in Cuba and Mexico. If Varela penned the text, for instance, then the narrative links Cuba's fledgling independence movements in the 1820s and 1830s to Mexico's postindependence turmoil and sees them as equally susceptible to the duplicity of the United States as a model republic and emergent empire. What's more, if Brickhouse is right to surmise that Heredia and Rocafuerte coauthored the book, then we can understand *Xicoténcatl* as a cautionary tale warning all of the Americas against allying with the United States when it comes to gaining national independence, a point made more pressing when we recall that the novel was published the same year as the Congress of Panama, when Simón Bolívar convened leaders of Latin American countries to present a more unified front against Spain but were reluctant to include the United States in the proceedings (Brickhouse 44).

Xicoténcatl challenges national boundaries to map Mexican America more broadly across the hemisphere and, in the process, pushes us to rethink how we account for U.S. ethnic identity formation. Indeed, the entire nineteenth-century hispanophone world pressures contemporary constructions of Mexican America as a regionally specific identity category linked only to the United States. Just the opposite: Mexicans in the United States imagined themselves within a larger notion of America exactly because of their second-class status in the so-called model republic. Take, for instance, Francisco P. Ramírez's editorials for the *El Clamor Público*, a Los Angeles, California, Spanish-language newspaper that circulated between 1855 and 1859. "But here in this fabulous country," Ramírez writes in 1855, "he who robs and assassinates the most is he who enjoys freedom. Certain people have no kind of freedom—this freedom, we say, is that which the courts deny to all individuals of color. To buy a man for money, to hang or burn him alive arbitrarily, is another great liberty which any individual has here, according to his likes. This happens in the United States, where slavery is tolerated, where the most vile despotism reins unchecked—in the middle of a nation that they call the 'Model Republic.' " (110). We would not be wrong to read Ramírez's argument as an oppositional stance against U.S. empire that articulates a nascent Chicano critique of Mexican America's second-class citizenship. As Rivera argues, "Ramírez's comments suggest that Mexicans are democracy's representative 'other' precisely because of the racial logic of U.S. democracy and its desire to incorporate minorities according to asymmetrical relations" (12–13). However, reading the passage hemispherically underscores how Ramírez's invention of Mexican America also invokes a discourse about race and citizenship familiar to antislavery and anticolonial movements in the United States and the Americas.

Linking slavery in the United States to the lynch violence that plagued Mexicans across California, Ramírez extends Mexican America across the Southwest and into the U.S. South. Admitted as a free state, California tempered its antislavery status by electing one pro- and one antislavery senator to represent the state in Congress. Such a compromise, Ramírez infers, enslaves California to slave interests even if it does not literally allow slavery in the state, an argument that Ralph Waldo Emerson, Henry David Thoreau, and Frederick Douglass also maintained in response to the 1850 Fugitive Slave Law. Similarly, Mexicans are enslaved to an unfair legal system and mob violence that target people of color. Ramírez draws on the discourse of slavery to imagine a symbolic link between enslaved blacks and disenfranchised Mexicans after the U.S.-Mexico War. His critique of the "Model Republic" recalls the problem the United States posed to the rest of the Americas as both an ostensible model of republicanism and a new world empire. Even though Ramírez's editorial questions two pieces of California legislation directed against Mexicans—the Sunday law and the so-called Greaser vagrancy act—he draws on a discourse of hemispheric citizenship that situates Mexican America within a transnational opposition to slavery and imperialism across the Americas.

But the invention of Mexican America is not always revolutionary. The work of María Amparo Ruiz de Burton, considered the first Mexican American author to publish two novels in English, shores up the reactionary retrenchment of creole consciousness that plagued most of nineteenth-century independence movements across the hemisphere. Born in La Paz, Baja California, Mexico, Ruiz de Burton married the captain of the invading U.S. Army during the U.S.-Mexico War and lived a life embattled over land, money, and legal trouble. She penned two historical romances, *Who Would Have Thought It?* (1872), published by Philadelphia's J. B. Lippincott, and *The Squatter and the Don* (1885), published in California. While the latter has garnered critical praise for its critique of Anglo-America, monopoly capitalism, and the displacement of California's landed Mexican class, the former offers a troubling invention of Mexican America that remaps the hemisphere to situate elite, landed Mexican Americans within a free white citizenship more European than American after all.

Who Would Have Thought It? recounts the story of Lola Medina, who is born in Indian captivity, raised in New England by the Norvals, and eventually reunited with her father in Mexico, where she stays with her Yankee lover, Julian Norval. While Lola comes of age, Mrs. Norval, the republican mother who treats Lola miserably, plots to exploit Lola's wealth, and eventually succumbs to brain fever. The novel has several important backdrops, including the U.S. Civil War, Mexico's War of Reform, the subsequent occupation by the Hapsburg emperor Maximilian, and the history of Indian raids plaguing Mexico's far northern frontier and the United States' newly acquired southwestern territory. Far from being plot twists, the backdrops draw a map that eventually traces the lineage of Ruiz de Burton's Mexican America to Austria. Recall that Lola Medina's father and grandfather are figured at first as two liberal Mexican republicans who fight off the tripartite invasion of England, France, and Spain. However, when the French stay to occupy Mexico by seating the Austrian prince Maximilian, the two republicans sing a different tune:

> "This is rather too much of a dilemma for me, I must say," Don Luis Medina
> observed. "Whilst the question is of repelling the French, or any other nation
> that comes to Mexico as a hostile invader, I shall not hesitate in giving my all in
> defense of our country. But, though I am Mexican at heart as well as by adoption,
> I shall find it too difficult to make up my mind to fight against an Austrian prince,
> and above all Prince Maximilian. My Austrian blood rebels against fighting him."
> (196–197)

There are several telling details here. First, the scene, and the entire novel in fact, make no mention of ousted liberal, republican Mexican president Benito Juárez. "His indigenous roots and dark skin may very well be at the heart of this displacement," José Aranda explains (72). Second, the brief episode condenses a complex colonial moment for Mexico and the United States. The tripartite invasion and Maximilian's subsequent rule put the Monroe Doctrine to the test because the United States was too occupied with its own internecine war to intervene on behalf of its "sister republic," but the scene also presages the problems political liberalism will pose for Mexico in relation to the United States' economic, territorial, and military expansion after their civil wars and into the twentieth century. Third is how the scene reimagines the tension between liberal republicanism and Austrian monarchy as a filial rebellion—"My Austrian blood rebels against fighting him." Here is where Ruiz de Burton's narrative is inventing Mexican America to situate it within the context of Napoleon III's invention of Latin America. Napoleon's grand scheme for a "Latin" race worked to check the growing U.S. influence on the hemisphere by encouraging elite criollos to see their Spanish language and Catholicism as common cultural ties that linked them more to Europe than the United States. So, as if to answer the Reverend Hackwell's incredulous question, "Who ever heard of a blue-eyed Mexican?" (253), Ruiz de Burton imagines Mexican America within a Latin America governed by French rule and embodied by the most blue-eyed Mexican of them all, the emperor Maximilian.

Ruiz de Burton's novel wages a war against second-class citizenship for Mexicans residing in the United States and against liberal, republican citizenship in Mexico embodied by Juárez and his dark skin. Neither befits her Enlightenment notion of Mexican America's "latinidad," so the narrative redraws the Americas altogether to critique the United States and imagine a new transnational citizenship for elite hemispheric whites. Thus, the novel represents the U.S. Northeast and the Southwest as *terra pericolosa*, dangerous or barbarous lands under the Union's hypocritical republicanism and Mexico's inability to govern itself. In contrast, the genteel white culture that Isaac Sprig experiences in a Confederate prison camp is reminiscent of the hacienda culture he enjoys in Mexico, in much the same way that France and Maximilian supported the Confederacy's cause, even if both never officially recognized the Confederate States of America. These two remappings converge on the plot's point of origin: Dona Theresa de Medina's abduction and Lola's subsequent birth into Indian captivity:

> Isaac inquired for the hacienda mentioned in the manuscript as being situated in the northern part of Sonora, and was told that it had not been visited by its owners since 1846, when a fearful calamity had befallen the family there, and the hacienda, though a most beautiful place, was now left in the care of a major-domo, who lived and grew rich there, but who had to keep the hacienda as a besieged fortress, with a garrison always on the alert because the government of Mexico, *being a free and independent government*, lets its Indians live as they please, and its more civilized citizens take care of themselves as best they may. (194)

The problem all along has been Mexico's attempt at an independent, liberal form of republicanism that recognizes Indian citizenship rights. It is thus significant that, upon arriving in Mexico City, Isaac stays at the Iturbide Hotel, for Iturbide's short reign as emperor after Mexico's 1821 independence checked the liberal reform that fueled Mexico's break from Spain in the first place. The passage directs a double rejection of Benito Juárez, who embodies both the "free and independent government" and Mexico's Indians that the narrator laments as the cause of the moral and social collapse of the besieged de Almenara hacienda. Indians are the problem and not the solution in Ruiz de Burton's Mexican America, where elite, landed Mexicans like her imagine their seamless transition into U.S. citizenship at the expense of blacks and Indians. Contra to Ramírez's Mexican America, in which blacks and Mexicans share the same enslaved fate, or even the indigenous, anti-imperial Mexican America imagined in *Xicoténcatl*, Ruiz de Burton's hemispheric citizenship is extended only to free whites. To be sure, the Anglos are a bit crass for her, but as both of her narratives emphasize, there are a couple of upstanding ones, especially handsome men, worthy of the fair hand of a Mexican maiden.

With Ruiz de Burton we are thus reminded that the invention of Mexican America is not simply an anti-imperial counterbalance to Anglo-America's discovery of all things Mexican. Yes, the invention of Mexican America is oppositional to dispossession and displacement, real and symbolic; it is a socially subversive act, to recall *invenīre* as a strategic, collective event. The invention of Mexican America occurs as an argument against discovery, but it can also reproduce the unevenness that has plagued the development of the Americas. Ruiz de Burton's novel shores up the idea that Mexicans are neither Indians nor black but part of a hemispheric white citizenship that extends across the Confederate South to the Austrian empire in Mexico long after Maximilian's reign ended with his 1867 execution. Such a hemispheric vision should trouble any notion that sees the invention of Mexican America as only an anticolonial response to the United States. At the same time, we should read in it the complexity of the Americas as a site of layered colonialisms, overlapping geographies, and the contradiction of a creole double consciousness inventing itself over and over again to avoid discovery.

BIBLIOGRAPHY

Anonymous. "Montezuma: The Last of the Aztecs." *American Whig Review* 3.2 (February 1846): 223–224.

Anonymous. *Xicoténcatl: An Anonymous Historical Novel about the Events Leading up to the Conquest of the Aztec Empire.* Trans. Guillermo I. Castillo-Feliú. Austin: University of Texas Press, 1999.

Alemán, Jesse. "The Other Country: Mexico, the United States, and the Gothic History of Conquest." *Hemispheric American Studies.* Ed. Caroline F. Levander and Robert S. Levine. New Brunswick, NJ: Rutgers University Press, 2008. 75–95.

Aranda, José F. Jr. "Breaking All the Rules: María Amparo Ruiz de Burton Writes a Civil War Novel." *Recovering the U.S. Hispanic Literary Heritage.* Vol. 3. Ed. María Herrera-Sobek and Virginia Sánchez Korrol. Houston: Arte Público Press, 2000. 61–73.

Bird, Robert Montgomery. *Calavar; or, The Knight of the Conquest: A Romance of Mexico.* Philadelphia: Carey, Lea, and Blanchard, 1834.

Brickhouse, Anna. *Transamerican Literary Relations and the Nineteenth-Century Public Sphere.* New York: Cambridge University Press, 2004.

Calhoun, John C. "Conquest of Mexico." *The Anti-Imperialist Reader.* Vol. 1. Ed. Philip S. Foner and Richard C. Winchester. New York: Holmes and Meier, 1984. 14–19.

Derrida, Jacques. *Specters of Marx: The State of the Debt, The Work of Mourning, and the New International.* Trans. Peggy Kamuf. New York: Routledge, 1994.

Dussel, Enrique. *The Invention of the Americas: Eclipse of "The Other" and the Myth of Modernity.* Trans. Michael D. Barber. New York: Continuum, 1995.

Gómez, Laura. *Manifest Destinies: The Making of the Mexican American Race.* New York: New York University Press, 2007.

Ingraham, J. H. (Joseph Holt). *Montezuma: The Serf, or The Revolt of the Mexitili.* Boston: H. L. Williams, 1845.

Johannsen, Robert W. *To the Halls of the Montezumas: The Mexican War in the American Imagination.* New York: Oxford University Press, 1985.

Karem, Jeff. "On the Advantages and Disadvantages of Postcolonial Theory for Pan-American Study." *New Centennial Review* 1.3 (2001): 87–116.

Leal, Luis, and Rodolfo J. Cortina. "Introduccíon." *Jicoténcal.* By Félix Varela. Ed. Luis Leal and Rodolfo J. Cortina. Houston: Arte Público Press, 1995. vii–xli.

Levander, Caroline. "Reinventing American Literary History." *American Literary History* 20 (2008): 449–456.

Luis-Brown, David. *Waves of Decolonization: Discourses of Race and Hemispheric Citizenship in Cuba, Mexico, and the United States.* Durham, NC: Duke University Press, 2008.

Maturin, Edward. *Montezuma: The Last of the Aztecs: A Romance.* New York: Paine and Burgess, 1845.

Melville, Herman. "Benito Cereno." 1855. *The Piazza Tales and Other Prose Pieces, 1839–1860.* Ed. Harrison Hayford et al. Evanston, IL, and Chicago: Northwestern University Press and Newberry Library, 1987. 46–117.

Mignolo, Walter. *The Idea of Latin America.* Malden, MA: Blackwell, 2005.

O'Gorman, Edmundo. *The Invention of America: An Inquiry into the Historical Nature of the New World and Its Meaning.* Bloomington: Indiana University Press, 1961.

Prescott, William H. *History of the Conquest of Mexico.* 1843. New York: Modern Library, 2001.

Rabasa, José. *Inventing America: Spanish Historiography and the Formation of Eurocentrism.* Norman: University of Oklahoma Press, 1993.

Ramírez, Francisco P. "Editorials." *Herencia: The Anthology of Hispanic Literature of the United States.* Ed. Nicolás Kanellos et al. Oxford: Oxford University Press, 2002. 109–111.

Rivera, John-Michael. *The Emergence of Mexican America: Recovering Stories of Mexican Peoplehood in U.S. Culture.* New York: New York University Press, 2007.

Ruiz de Burton, María Amparo. *Who Would Have Thought It?* 1872. Ed. Rosaura Sánchez and Beatrice Pita. Houston: Arte Público, 1995.

Sadowski-Smith, Claudia, and Claire F. Fox. "Theorizing the Hemipshere: Inter-Americas Work at the Intersection of American, Canadian, and Latin American Studies." *Comparative American Studies* 21.1 (2005): 5–37.

Saldívar, José David. *The Dialectics of Our America: Genealogy, Cultural Critique, and Literary History.* Durham, NC: Duke University Press, 1991.

Silva-Gruesz, Kirsten. *Ambassadors of Culture: The Transamerican Origins of Latino Writing.* Princeton, NJ: Princeton University Press, 2002.

Sommer, Doris. *Foundational Fictions: The National Romances of Latin America.* Berkeley: University of California Press, 1991.

Wertheimer, Eric. *Imagined Empires: Incas, Aztecs, and the New World of American Literature, 1771–1876.* New York: Cambridge University Press, 1999.

Zamora, Lois Parkinson. "The Usable Past: The Idea of History in Modern U.S. and Latin American Fiction." *Do the Americas Have a Common Literature?* Ed. Gustavo Pérez Firmat. Durham, NC: Duke University Press, 1990. 7–41.

CHAPTER 6

CREOLE KINSHIP: PRIVACY AND THE NOVEL IN THE NEW WORLD

NANCY BENTLEY

As European states began colonizing the New World, many political and literary writers became preoccupied with questions of kinship. American plantations were cultivating not just tobacco and sugar, not just domesticated animals, but generations of human "stock" as well. What did the emergence of these Creoles—the peoples born and raised in the colonies—mean for the fate of families and nations? A survey of texts imagining the "Americanization" of kinship would make for long and lively reading. It might begin with Henry Neville's utopian narrative *The Isle of Pines* (1668), in which an English trader, shipwrecked on an uncharted island, eventually populates the island through a form of colonial polygamy with two maidservants, his patron's daughter ("Sarah English"), and his own black slave, only to have this paradise of sanctioned sexual liberty lapse within two generations into a warring society of "whoredoms, incests and adultery" (201). A glimpse of the same dystopian possibility appears in Shelley's *Frankenstein* (1818), in which the "vast wilds of South America" (120) are at once the monster's only hope for life with a domestic companion and Dr. Frankenstein's terrified vision of a site with the potential for propagating a whole race of aberrant creatures like his monster, a "filthy mass that moved and talked" (117).

As these examples begin to suggest, a certain strain of modern thought has long associated the New World with the threat of a transformative disorder in human kinship, a disorder that could invade and remake the sphere of domestic relations that are a fundamental feature of the modern social imaginary. Even as the New World fostered real and imaginary schemes of utopia, it also gave rise to the counterpart concept of a kinship dystopia—an "incest nation."[1] There is more than a whiff of hysteria in such stories. But it would be a mistake to dismiss the Americanization of kinship as a figment of overheated imaginations. With the advent of settler states, a distinct family system in the Americas became not just a source of transatlantic political reflection but also a new demographic reality. In this chapter I take seriously the idea of a terrain of New World kinship and argue that these distinct familial conditions hold important consequences for understanding the Anglophone novel in the United States. But the demographic reality of New World kinship still brings attendant interpretative puzzles. Now as then, stories about families seem to hold significance for understanding larger political structures like the nation; but what is the proper critical method for understanding the relation of kinship and the state?

Given the importance of the domestic household for modern politics, it is not surprising that allegories of the state are often conjured out of stories of kinship. And such allegories are not just a vehicle for political reflection; they have also provided a keystone for literary interpretation, especially for analysis of the novel. By identifying a homologous relation between the nation and the novel, literary scholars have been able to investigate political dimensions of the domain of private experience—the matters of love and betrayal, vocation and adventure, affect and internal thought—that make up the novel's traditional subject matter. But the gain in scholarly insight has also introduced the risk of interpretive error. Modern states wish to identify themselves with the domestic family; but are domestic novels really allegories of the state? Reading them as such has become a favorite hermeneutic for criticism of the novel. But when we read novels allegorically, I contend, we may get things only half right.

While there are important historical reasons why novels seem saturated by macropolitical significance, to understand novels *as* national or imperial allegories is to occlude precisely what is most political about them, namely, the immanent authority the genre locates *within* private lives. In this chapter I pursue two related claims. I argue in the first instance that the political origins of the novel are the source of the genre's ability to conduct experiments in imagining subjectivity, the space of interior thought and feeling. The novelistic subject is born of the bourgeois invention of private life, a zone of political liberty defined in relation to, yet existing apart from, the positive power of the nation-state. But far from locating stable signifiers of national identity, subjectivity in the novel follows from dialectical discoveries that uncover increasingly deeper, mutating versions of familial privacy—religious conscience, aesthetic consciousness, the sexual unconscious— each of which can afford a different way of registering (or refuting or ignoring) the claims of the nation and national history. Secondly, to understand the particular contours of these subjectivities as they emerge in American novels, I argue, we have to look to what demographers call the Creole American family, a form of kinship that is not a conjugal household but a system, descended from New World slavery and colonialism, linking different kinds of licit and illicit families. There *is* no national home; there is only a mix of family forms whose very differences bespeak the volatile political history of a settler society.

Fears of an "incest nation" in the New World remind us that kinship is never merely private; the fate of families, as much as the strength of armies or the health of governments, seem to offer an index of a national future. But as the "incest nation" trope comes close to confessing, as a language for the nation kinship is an unstable, even incoherent kind of signifier that erodes or erases as much as it conceptualizes. This lack of stable fit, however, is actually a boon for the novel, a resource for writing beyond and against the stories preferred by the state. In its career in the New World, the novel emerges not from a dialectic of public and private alone but from a dynamic historical nexus that joins the civil categories of public and private to the category of colonial privation.

THE DIALECTICS OF PRIVACY

In a moment of national crisis, Lincoln invoked the fundamental trope that envisions the polity as a family writ large: "A house divided against itself cannot stand" (426). To many scholars, familial language like Lincoln's has seemed crucial to American republican politics, a metaphorical vocabulary for articulating the necessity of independence from a parent country and, later, for defining the bonds of belonging in the "new political family" established by the founding fathers.[2] Jay Fliegelman identified the filial trope as the "quintessential motif" of the rhetoric of the revolution, while later scholars point to sexual and familial symbolics as a key idiom of U.S. nationhood, a metanarrative that evinces a "shared reliance upon family metaphors to allegorize the nation" (Castronovo 5).[3] There is no question but that family affiliation has long been a crucial political signifier. In fact, one way to define the elusive epoch we call modernity would be to say that it begins when Europe's monarchs, under pressure from the rising middle classes, are compelled to rationalize monarchical authority in the familial terms so important to their bourgeois subjects. Drawing on a medieval tradition of similitude, Sir Robert Filmer's patriarchalist theory posited an analogy between the state and the family that sought to give the monarch the same natural superiority over his subjects that the male head possesses over his household. "Care in superiors, and fear in inferiors, cause a godly government both private and public, in family, church and commonwealth" (qtd. in McKeon 113). Patriarchal theory argued for an essential continuity between the state and the "little commonwealth" of the family; the two were greater and lesser incarnations of the same unchanging order of "godly government." Familial terms could therefore discover in kingship the authority already inherent in nature and natural law. As James I declared, "I am the Husband, and the whole Isle is my lawfull Wife" (qtd. in McKeon 114). But this solution also introduced trouble: monarchists could not dictate the way the terms of the analogy would be deployed by others, and the family-state analogy opened the door to alternative interpretations of "godly government." Sovereign magistrates, like fathers, ruled by nature. But if fathers were the "chief rulers" of families, were they not thereby political sovereigns after a fashion as well?

For Richard Hooker, the authority possessed by fathers was crucial in its own right, so much so that the father's private power was the central reason why the public power of the monarch could not be absolute: "To fathers within their private families nature has given a supreme power," he writes, and because a kingdom is made up of a multitude of such families, there is no single sovereign who could properly claim to be their natural head. It is therefore "impossible that any should have complet lawfull power but by consent of men" (qtd. in McKeon 113). Through this path of reasoning, the father's private role as head of a family emerges with new and far-reaching political implications. A crucial dialectical shift has occurred: kinship is not just an available signifier that could illuminate the political; it has become the signified, the entity that could itself be illuminated by the signifier of sovereign power—with results that could not be predicted in advance. Is the king like a father? Perhaps he is. But the notion of a fatherly king suggests the image of a kingly father, a figure who possesses a new kind of household sovereignty that will eventually carry the name of privacy.

While critics of the king wished to demystify the patriarchalist analogy, then, they did not mean to sever altogether the political linkage between fathers and magistrates, and between private and public domains. Thomas Paine and John Adams, for instance, would make the analogy serve the cause of revolution, arguing that when a king behaves like a cruel and "unnatural" parent, nature itself supports the right for private subjects to reject his authority. In this way the analogy could be redeployed to find new political implications lodged *within* the realm of the private. It is no coincidence that Locke's definitive treatise on the sovereignty of consent took Filmer's analogy as its point of departure. "The Power of a Magistrate over a Subject, may be distinguished from that of a Father over his Children, a Master over his Servant, a Husband over his Wife, and a Lord over his Slave" (286). Even as it recognizes a formal similitude, Locke's crucial distinction between the power of kings and of fathers eventually gives rise to the structural opposition between a depersonalized state and the private subjects who authorize that state by way of their consent. In the Lockean model, the consent of the private subject not only gives legitimacy to the positive power of the state, it also marks the negative liberty of the individual subject ("a just and reasonable liberty") to exercise a freedom of thought, conscience, and family governance apart from state control.

The private realm of households, in other words, is not only and always private. Under the pressure of analysis, the "little commonwealth" of the private household could be further subdivided into its own versions of public and private domains, creating an "empire of the father" where male heads enjoy the positive power that comes with autonomy from the state and where, as we'll see, the private subjects of *this* empire—wives, children, servants—will begin to stake out their own claims on the negative liberties that are articulated in and through the private. The modern domain of the private, in other words, is no longer a fixed entity or a static category;

it is a dialectical concept that can replicate new versions of the public-private distinction within an existing terrain of the private, creating another *order* of authority (the quasi-public governance of the father) and autonomy (the private liberty of wives and children) one level down. The genre of the novel is born of this dialectical turning and carries within itself the same power of conceptual mutation, allowing the changing notion of the private to become the vehicle of new articulations of dependence and independence, of belonging and autonomy.

Rather than leading readers back to the undifferentiated mysteries of God's unchanging order, then, these deployments of the family-state analogy generated new concepts of liberty and new distributions of sovereignty. But crucially, this regime of privacy also retained and redefined the *absence* of liberty that was slavery. The emergence of private family would also open a new space of modern political *privation*, the abject condition of the slave who, although she lives and works for the larger private household, is understood according to Locke's schema to have the status of a captive of war, bereft of any claim to the privileges of the private sphere.[4] As many scholars of American slavery have come to emphasize, slavery was not a premodern relic destined to wither in the modern state. Rather, New World colonies and republics became modern nations as slave states, founded on and enriched by slave power.

But, by the same token, slavery—no less than modern privacy—was never safe from the mutations possible in modern political thought. As a dialectical pairing, the relational terms of private and public would become an index of political struggle and open historical change, including the struggle over the status of the slave. For instance, although neither Filmer nor Locke could have anticipated it (and both would have deplored it), before long the momentum acquired by the modern concept of the private would license an African American bondsman to write a novel depicting the enslaved family members of a head of state, Thomas Jefferson. William Wells Brown's *Clotel; or, the President's Daughter* (1853) was an effort not to allegorize the nation but rather to dialectically reverse the political current of the family-state analogy by making the head of state a mere signifier of the sovereignty denied to the lives of African American slaves. Within the precincts of Brown's novel, slaves' lives matter; the name of a president is only a pointed symbol of the liberty denied them. (Indeed, Jefferson never makes an appearance in the novel.) Private lives in *Clotel* actually uncover what is obscured by the allegory of a national home, namely, the colonial kinship system that subtends the life of the state.

The Novel and the Domestication of Knowledge

Just as the private-public dyad became a path of political struggle, the same dialectic would also generate new literary forms, the novel chief among them—but it would also thereby generate a new kind of political signification unique to novelistic form. In his magisterial history of early modern divisions of knowledge, *The Secret History of Domesticity*, McKeon closely traces the way a confluence of related factors—Protestant conscience, private property, an emergent empiricism, the power of print to publicize ordinary experience, the conjugal family—lent a new epistemological weight to the lowly stuff of the senses and the lives of ordinary subjects. Gradually recognized as separable from traditional truths handed down from above, these areas of private experience provided the grounds for what McKeon calls the modern "domestication" of knowledge: a rethinking and testing of the great mysteries of sages and the arcane secrets of princes and priests by means of "the little, the proximate, the local, the familiar, or the native" (326). As tools for reflecting and arguing, these modes of domestication opened the way through which familiar objects, common situations, and ordinary family life acquired a new ability to discover larger meaning.

This epistemological shift meant a political promotion for fiction. The materials of fiction afforded eighteenth-century authors a veiled language for political analysis and polemics, and in new genres like the secret history (Aphra Behn's *Love-Letters*) and the modern political allegory (Jonathan Swift's *Tale of a Tub*), fictional characters were enlisted to represent actual persons and events from a higher political plane—to signify coded condemnations of the French court, for instance, or Tory justifications for Charles's ministers or policies. But, as with the family-state analogy, another turn of the dialectical screw would reverse the direction of the analysis, transforming this fictional domestication of politics into the politics of domestic fiction. With the emergence of the novel proper, the repertoire of the local, the familiar, and the common no longer served merely as figural signs pointing beyond themselves to a higher level of political significance. Instead, in the novel, the private domain sheds its allegorical function and the experience of common lives and ordinary events become important in their own right, a site of both epistemological discoveries and small-scale (but now foundational) governance. If Gulliver's adventures as a sailor ultimately refer to actual court intrigues or Royal Society disputes, Robinson Crusoe's adventures matter in their own right, as a fictional illumination of lives like his own (and Gulliver's)—sailors, traders, their wives and children.

The novel, in other words, opens a different order of signification. The figures in novels—fathers, wives, picaros, seducers and their victims—are not metaphoric but rather metonymic, private figures meant to refer to the sphere of the domestic household or the open-road adventures of private persons. But why does this shift to referents of private life matter? After all, I have been arguing that the distinction between these two kinds of signifiers, allegorical and metonymic, is really a dialectical relation that makes them rhetorically similar; the signs that give life to novels are a *domesticated* version of the "higher" things signified in political allegories, bringing the same concerns of sovereignty, courtly conduct, and state-approved knowledge to the lower plane of ordinary private life. Hence the overtones of national allegory that critics, and even contemporary readers, have so frequently discerned in domestic novels. (John Adams's gloss on Richardson in the wake of revolution—"The people are Clarissa"—is a well-known case in point [Fliegelman 89]).

As I hope to demonstrate, however, a great deal is at stake in the different kind of political signification made possible in the genre of the novel, for as a narration of private persons novels are able to uncover and explore a history of settler kinship that is illegible to national narrative.

Returning to Lincoln's invocation of the family-state analogy can begin to clarify how and why the distinction between public allegory and private story matters. When Lincoln asks the members of a fractious polity to see themselves as a single "house," he relies on an ingrained practice of conceiving the nation-state as the seat or home of a natural political family, a national "people" and not just a scattered collection of colonial subjects who one day found themselves under the dominion of new political masters. Condensing an allegory of political birth into a single trope, Lincoln's invocation of a "house" makes the nation-state a single coherent entity, one presumed to have an organic life and ethical meaning from the moment it can be so conceived. When Lincoln holds up the image of a national "house," in other words, he is "seeing like a state," the phrase that James C. Scott has invented to describe the cognitive habits that underwrite the modern state's imperative to make a society appear clearly bounded, continuous, and legible to its powers of statecraft.

If Lincoln is seeing like a state, he is also here speaking *as* a state, as the human voice of an otherwise mute collective sovereignty. But we can contrast that kind of speech with what issued from a recurring challenge Lincoln faced during his campaigns for office, a challenge that forced him to speak as a domestic subject—in effect as a private father and husband. Confronted with charges from his opponents that he was a radical who favored miscegenation, Lincoln fashioned a slyly effective comeback: "I protest, now and forever, against the counterfeit logic which presumes that because I do not want a negro woman for a slave, I do necessarily want her for a wife" (454–455). Clearly the issue of interracial sex or marriage was highly charged politically. But because miscegenation pertained to private families as such, the topic actually made starkly clear that the United States in fact could *not* be conceived as a metaphoric house—even a divided house—because the very figure had no stable referent. Just what was a family in the New World? Was it a household that operated on the virtues of white rule, giving protection and proper employment to the black servants and laborers who assisted the white family? Or (as Lincoln's riposte implied) was it a household untainted by forced servitude and the black concubinage that was practiced on Southern plantations and Caribbean islands?

Indeed, intensifying transatlantic debates about family reform had exposed the particular difficulties faced by former colonial possessions like the United States in identifying a national family form. From metropolitan centers like London and Paris, New World colonies and settler states were often condemned for possessing the deviant family and sexual mores thought to characterize these slave societies and their Creole cultures. Reformers decried the "ruinous tastes of the colonies" where "everyone had their mulatresse" and where the most debased were even known to take a slave for a legal wife. As reformers saw it, the conditions of war endemic to colonization and slavery had infected the sacred precincts of the family, producing "multiform incests, polygamy, and adultery" (qtd. in Berman 89, 50, 44). Residents in the European metropole were thus able to disavow and indict kinship practices that Europeans themselves had originally instigated.

Those who lived in settler states, of course, could not so easily dodge these difficulties. The figure of the political family retained its appeal, as Lincoln's "house divided" speech attests. But, as soon as one dropped down from the allegorical to the metonymic level, picturing a private household could only *disable* the figure of a national house. Any discussion or narrative of private American homes would now discover a domain of irreducibly different family kinds, particulars inassimilable to a single whole. As a settler state created out of the domestication of colonial slavery, the United States could not take part in the transatlantic reformation of family life without recognizing itself as a creole society, a society where even men like Lincoln were answerable to the question of whether they preferred black women as slaves or as wives.

What was troublesome for a symbolics of the state, however, was a boon for the polemical novel. Writing at the metonymic level of private homes, novelists could exploit the irreducible diversity of households to make invidious comparisons among the different types of families coexisting in a settler state. Harriet Beecher Stowe would produce the most famous example of the fictional conjunction of irreconcilable private homes. Readers of *Uncle Tom's Cabin* are asked to recognize the legal ties and interstate trade that linked conjugal households to a variety of slaveholding families, ranging from benevolently "mild" to violently despotic but all highly destructive to private lives. In perhaps the most damning of these links, the free state of Vermont produces the sadistic slave owner Simon Legree, a rapist and torturer who "learned his trade well among the pirates of the West Indies" (437). To focus on private families, Stowe insists, is actually to expose the ongoing trafficking of persons, the Atlantic commerce within which U.S. national liberty and state independence are finally irrelevant.

Antislavery reformers like Stowe were not the only ones to employ fiction in this way, however. Apologists for slavery also used the novel to point up the differences among distinct kinds of private homes. In *The Planter's Northern Bride*, for instance, Caroline Lee Hentz indicts the "prejudice and intolerance" (281) bred in fanatical Northern homes, the source of a tyrannical will to drive slaves from the homes of their "sympathizing" masters and mistresses. This homegrown despotism, Hentz insists, is destructive of true American "liberties and rights" (407).

Within the precincts of the novel, private families and ordinary lives matter most. If exposing conflicts among settler-state households belied the state's claim to be an "edifice of liberty" (Lincoln 28), then so much the worse for the state. Because novels give greatest epistemological weight to all things private, these narratives are not an allegory of the nation as a house (divided or otherwise) but the revelation of an enduring colonial culture, a culture where domestic love has a damning proximity to sexual domination and where household sovereignty turns out to be ruinously close to rule by force. As conceived in novels, that is, American homes belong to a colonial system that permits even the Caribbean torture techniques of white male sadists (Stowe); they are vulnerable to an "indomitable will" (281) that an oppressive state can impose on private homes (Hentz); and they partake of a "war spirit" (73) that pervades American institutions both public and private (G. Brown). As seen through the lens of the novel, the United States is not conceivable as a house at all. It is instead something closer to the inverse of a national home—an "incest nation" of private persons who continue the troubling creole kinship begun by New World planters and settlers.

These antebellum novels, then, acquire political insight at the expense of the ethical state. But systemic political critique is really only a side effect of the novel's investment in private lives and families. More powerfully, the novel's jurisdiction over the domain of the private allows novels to discover ethical subjectivity in sites furthest from public purview: in inner lives and the protected recesses of conscience. Despite their lack of political standing, unlikely subjects such as women, youths, and slaves can acquire a position of high authority—an authority, in fact, derived precisely from their distance from political power. One of the heroine's of Brown's *Clotel*, Georgiana Peck, gives a succinct formulation of this paradox: "I will not be unjust because the state is" (155). As an eighteen-year-old woman, Georgiana has no political standing. And even in her own home, she is subject to the governance of her father, a kind enough parent but a "cruel master" to his slaves. But, through the optics of the novel, the private family is revealed to contain a second-order privacy, a deeper zone of private feeling and understanding where a daughter can hold greater knowledge and moral vision than her father: "whether it was admitted by the father, or not," the narrator observes, "she was his superior and his teacher" (131).

The negative liberty of private life—the freedom of one's religious conscience and solitary reflections to remain untouched by public power or even paternal rule—thus allows the novel to represent and explore the virtual spaces of interior feeling, thought, and mood, the psychic landscape that McKeon calls "the secret precincts of the self" (148). And it is here that the epistemology of privacy gives the novel its most potent political illumination. In William Wells Brown's words, the novel enjoys power to uncover "a thousand wrongs and woes" that "never see the light" (199), giving a place on the pages of a novel to what is unseen or ignored by precincts such as the newspaper, the pulpit, and the courtroom. Ethical subjectivity is discovered in the free interior spaces (heart, mind, conscience) where power has no sway. Abjuring the actual for the virtual, fiction can acquire access to what Brown in *Clotel* calls the "innermost depths" (58) of human experience.

And yet, as I will argue next, the very capacity to imagine new depths of subjectivity that makes the novel so powerful for political reform also makes the category of the private unstable and subject to mutation. Because the private family has its own secondary zone of privacy, it can uncover invisible spaces of interiority; but if this interior theater allows ethical subjects to be seen and heard, it can also give away secrets that some would wish to keep hidden ("a human soul," Stowe intones, "is an awful ghostly, unquiet possession, for a bad man to have" [491]). What is more, the novel can even discover aspects of selfhood that subjects themselves do not know and never will; private consciousness can give way to the murky depths of the unconscious. The results, I contend, are finally corrosive to the very premise of the family-state analogy: the idea that natural bonds—and not rule by force—have made a new kind of polity with new human liberties. Through its dialectics of privacy, the epistemology of the novel is capable of discerning what underlies the private family in a slaveholding settler state, namely, the conditions of war that are the occluded legacy of a colonial history. To tell the story of this legacy, in tones comic as well as tragic, will be the special office of the novel in the Americas.

Ethical Subjects and Sexual Secrets: The Case of Melville's *Pierre*

A short story by Lydia Maria Child, "Slavery's Pleasant Homes," shows with particular clarity the way domestic fiction can claim the epistemological resources necessary to tell the true history of settler kinship. The story initially mimics proslavery discourse by introducing a scene of shared household joy in which the slaves of a Georgia plantation celebrate the marriage of their young master to the daughter of a New Orleans planter. As the story goes forward, however, Child splits her narrative in two. After Frederic Dalcho, the young planter, is killed, the public account narrated by newspapers is contrasted with the story's own inside account uncovered through the privileged epistemology of fiction. Announcing a "Fiend-like Murder," the Georgia papers report that the assault on the planter was committed by "one of his slaves," an atrocity for which the unnamed "black demon" was summarily tried and hanged. The Northern papers reprint the same account, adding the dire admonition that "these are the black-hearted monsters, which abolition philanthropy would let loose upon our brethren of the South" (242). Addressing their readers as national "brethren," these public reports tell a story of domestic outrage: a peaceful home was suddenly ruptured by the violence of a lawless fiend.

These public reports, in other words, exercise the prerogative of "seeing like a state": they borrow the axiomatic knowledge that the private home bespeaks the ethical identity of a family-like nation, and they represent the state's execution of the slave as a restoration of the rule of law necessary to restore and protect the peace ("hanging was too good for him" [242]). With its fealty to the private, however, Child's fictional portrait reveals what the state cannot or will not see: this household has existed from the beginning in a state of war, not domestic peace. Frederic was indeed killed by his slave, a man named George (who is also Frederic's half brother). But George killed Frederic because that master had repeatedly raped and tortured George's common-law wife. George also confesses the act rather than let another suspect die in his place—and does so even though that suspect, a thieving slave named Mars, had also stalked and menaced George's wife. For homes like these, domestic fiction reveals a category mistake: this household is not a product of law, it is a theater of war—captivity, violent enmity, torture and rape, desperate valor.

Child's conclusion underscores the absence of any record of George's true motives and acts: "Not one [newspaper] recorded the heroism that would not purchase life by another's death, though [Mars] was his enemy" (242). But Child's story, of course, has recorded exactly that missing truth—truth that proves this home is in fact an armed camp organized around force and privation, not consensual law and mutual love. The resources of fiction do the work of revision. Omniscient narration reveals household secrets: with its air of certainty, the preterite tense of the third-person narrator is able to locate the precise relay point between domestic love and predatory desire. When Frederic noticed George exchanging affectionate looks with Rosa, the sight of "mutual, happy love," the narrator informs us, actually incited the master's lust and enmity: "it kindled in him an unholy fire" (239). Similarly, the resource of first-person narration allows Child to introduce the speech of an ethical black subject ("Mars is innocent. I murdered [the master]—for he killed my wife" [242]), whereas the public newspapers recognize only a black brute, one who lacks a name let alone the ability to speak as an ethical subject. Fiction possesses potent weapons: third-person narration and first-person speech usurp from the male head and his political "brethren" the right to supervise the space of the household. Fiction can thus disclose predatory sexual desires and discover new ethical subjects that belie the state's wish to find its own ethical image in the little commonwealth of the family.

For any purpose of reform, Child's fictional portrait—she calls it a "faithful sketch"—is an advance over public discourse. Her willingness to paint a black slave's killing of a white man as valorous, in fact, was remarkably audacious for its time. But in the process of exposing sexual violence behind the front of "pleasant homes," Child also gives new life to some of the colonial categories she means to critique. The epistemology of Child's reform fiction discovers the impossible truth that a black slave can be "a man of nobler soul than any of them all" [242]. His nobility emerges in contrast to degeneracy of a white slaveholder who is discovered to be a vicious libertine, no better than the French and British Creoles who turned their plantations into "one vast brothel" (qtd. in Berman 44). But the proof of George's ethical subjectivity is also his difference from the slave Mars, a "cunning enemy" (242) who is precisely the kind of innate black predator the newspapers presume has killed the Georgia planter. Reform American families, and you will rid the nation of colonial despots like Frederic—but what of black brutes like Mars? In Child's story, Mars is the colonial remainder who can have no place in civil society, public or private. A cunning mulatto, he is the irredeemable product of a system of creole kinship; he can be neither erased nor reformed.

As his name suggests, the survival of Mars will thus mean an enduring threat of war, and if families are to be protected the United States would still require spaces of privation. Plantations will be abolished but, as historians have recently shown, reformist energies helped build and expand a new postbellum prison system in which conditions of armed surveillance and forced labor undo the integration of captivity and kinship that was the colonial plantation. Henceforth American families and American captives would be located in separate sites: enclosed conjugal homes and state-run prisons. Even abolitionist fiction, therefore, carries within itself the colonial legacy it means to combat, and the same novelistic vision that uncovers ethical subjectivity in the abject slave can also conceive a new class of enemy—the slave turned perpetual criminal.[5]

Despite their aim to reform the disparate families of an "incest nation," once novelists like Child, Brown, and Stowe use domestic fiction to uncover an inside picture of creole kinship, the contours of the American novel are changed in profound and permanent ways. Exploring the Americanization of kinship becomes one of the most innovative projects of novelists from Twain and Faulkner to Marquez and Morrison, authors who use the novel's powers of interior sight to trace the enduring entanglements of privacy and violent privation in New World subjects. Because these novelists have written chiefly about the U.S. South and the Caribbean basin, their portraits have focused most closely on what demographer Goren Therborn calls the triangular family system of New World kinship, the relations that connect "white, non-white and mixed" kin groups, "each very different, but each crucially shaped by the other(s)" (34). But it is not just novels about Southern territories that show the imprint of the Americanization of kinship. With its close but unsettling ties to reform fiction, Melville's novel *Pierre; or, the Ambiguities* anticipates the experiments of those later novelists in tracing distinctive features of the New World family. Most strikingly, Melville shows the strange but compelling results that can occur when the ethical subject of reform fiction—the "nobler soul" Child separates from the "unholy fire" of the corrupt patriarch—is transformed into alternative versions of private subjectivity.

Imitation is not always a form of flattery. When Melville writes his curious, sometimes torturous domestic novel, he betrays contempt for the "countless tribes of common dramas" (169) he is also attempting to join. But, in one respect at least, Melville's reason for taking up the genre of the domestic novel closely parallels the aims of reformers like Brown and Child. With the genre's power to exercise what Melville's narrator calls "remorseless insight" (11), *Pierre* undertakes a corrosive examination of what looks like the charmed household of the Glendinning family of rural Massachusetts. What it finds there is something closer to warfare than family amity, uncovering sexual exploits and filial rebellion, and terminating in murder and imprisonment.

These revelations will dissolve in acid the initial portrait of the Glendinning family, which expressly defines itself as a national household. Pierre is of "double revolutionary descent" (27), his great-grandfather and grandfather having fought different combinations of "Indians, Tories, and Regulars" on the very "aboriginal" land that would become the Glendinning estate (10). Through this history, the nation's martial "Glory" is transmuted into family "Grace," and the young Pierre lives and breathes the national as the very atmosphere of private life. The family-state analogy itself has been privatized, internalized as a form of lived consciousness. But while this allegory is an existential foundation for Pierre's sense of self ("the illuminated scroll of his life" [11]), for readers the story's allegorical resonances only sound like noise. For one thing, as Eric Sundquist puts it, "no one can fail to be struck by *Pierre*'s insanely pastoralized opening" (150). The images of rural felicity and family devotion are so overwrought that the sphere of private life is immediately and weirdly derealized. And when the narrator begins to portray the "lover-like adoration" (22) between Pierre and his widowed mother (whom he calls "sister"), there is no mistaking that the life at Saddle Meadows is fraught by unstable semiotics, a risky slippage among private terms and relations. The declaration that "much that goes into the deliciousness of a wife, already lies in the sister" (12) is just one example of the odd cast of Glendinning family wisdom.

In time even Pierre asks what is wrong with this picture. And when he discovers (or thinks he discovers) that his father, now deceased, had sired a daughter with a woman from the Saddle Meadows village, he rejects both public and private frameworks as meaningful contexts for his life: "Pierre hath no paternity, and no past" (235). After Pierre loses the allegorical structure that had made his life a "sweetly-writ manuscript" (11), it is as if metonymic signifiers fly apart and reattach at will, driven by invisible forces that now rule the private sphere. Pierre disavows his dead father, casts off his mother, seeks out his half sister Isabel, and becomes her lover. By the time the novel crash-lands with Pierre's murder of a male cousin, he has reinvented the conjugal family by collecting a household that consists of Isabel (joined to him in a "secret marriage" [238]), his former fiancée Lucy (claiming "some indirect cousinship" [361]), and a bewildered servant Delly, all living with Pierre in dreary rooms in the city. Undercutting the very notion of a national house, Melville creates a domestic novel governed by what Gillian Brown aptly dubs an "aesthetics of incest" (152).

Yet, even though *Pierre* comes to display a "wreckage of family relations" (Weinstein 161), the novel's familial and sexual relations still present an uncannily accurate portrait of enduring New World kinship patterns. Newly critical of a family history he once revered, Pierre now views his father's authority as a power he used to exploit the weak. That power, in other words, begins to look like what Therborn calls the "rigidification of patriarchy" characteristic of New World societies, where "male sexual predation became almost institutionalized among the white rulers" (35). By finding a sexual partner in the town adjoining the ancestral manor (a woman who may or may not have consented to provide sex and bear his "dark" child, we can't know), Pierre's father exercises the customary rights of the colonial American planter. Indeed, with the discovery of the father's anonymous mistress and unacknowledged child, the fact that Pierre's grandfather was a slave master begins to take on new resonance. The slave master's sexual rights somehow seem to obtain even in the absence of actual slaveholding. This enduring influence of white sexual mastery, according to Therborn, is also part of the demographic picture of New World kinship: by providing subaltern men with a model "from above" of how to define and seize "the prize of masculine prowess" (35), the New World planter institutionalized habits of sexual conquest and male rivalry that would make violence an enduring feature of the American kinship system. Melville, too, finds mimetic violence in his portrait of kinship: though highly melodramatic, the gunshot murder that ends Pierre's story ("spatterings of his own kindred blood were upon the pavement" [417]) actually captures a certain grim statistical realism regarding domestic patterns in American settler societies.

   Like the reformers, Pierre sets himself in opposition to the kind of patriarchal privilege he discovers at Saddle Meadows. Also like reformers, his critique will be based in a "larger interior development" (10) in Pierre's way of thinking and feeling, a new capacity for ethical sight. But even as he rejects the authority of the sanctified Glendinning household and vows to cast off all "kith and kin" (109), Pierre still unwittingly follows the contours of the creole kinship system. He does so when he improvises an extralegal household of a type that functions in tandem with the normative white household, a type with traits that include (according to Therborn's demographics) "active, little-controlled sexuality," "informal, unstable unions," forms of improvised "polygamy," and, soon enough for Pierre's female household, "male absenteeism" (36). Melville's contemporaries—or the few who read *Pierre*, anyway—were outraged at the novel's portrait of sex and family, claiming it struck at "the very foundations of society."[6] In truth, Melville's domestic novel describes what actually *is* the foundation of his society: a systemic conjunction of distinct family kinds, formed in relation to one another in the wake of colonial settlement. In Therborn's description, "The patrilineal, patriarchal, ritually formal white family had its opposite in the loose, matrilineal informality of coloured Creoles" (36), and the male sexual privileges and female purity of the one inform and rely on the sexual practices of the other. The son of a white planter, Pierre has merely re-created a family life as it were on the other side of the creole color line.

   Now as then, this swerve in Pierre's story is startling. After he learns his father's secrets, Pierre has the reformer's zeal to renounce sexual exploitation and power; but his determination to follow a nobler path somehow leads him to his fate as a kind of sexual antihero. Even Melville seems uncertain about whether his character is a sexual martyr or a self-deluded satyr. It is one of the strangest turns in American literary history; but it is also one of the most prescient. For, with its willful compression of modes of literary reform and rebellion, *Pierre* not only shows a wide-lens picture of the creole family system, it also provides a dramatic window on the way the genre would innovate forms for articulating New World subjectivity and would in turn be shaped by the Americanization of kinship.

   Pierre's remarkable sexual career is born of the negative liberty of private conscience, the free interiority that distinguishes the ethical subject. The son's "deeper" (393) spiritual sight reveals the sins of the father. The reformist impulse to unveil truth thus gives Melville the narrative resources necessary to locate illicit sexuality on the one hand and ethical subjectivity on the other. As in Child's story, third-person narration in *Pierre* allows readers to learn about the sexual errancy of a powerful planter. Meanwhile, the first-person speech of Pierre gives expression to an ethical subjectivity that emerges from the depths of private reflection and feeling: "I will gospelize the world anew" (319). And, like many a young "enthusiast" (198), Pierre's commitment to pursuing truth is of a piece with his effort to become an author; he will undertake to turn ethical subjectivity into literary expression.

A parallel vehicle of truth-telling, aesthetic consciousness emerges from the same space of private family feeling.

But it is precisely at this point that Melville's novel begins its bizarre transmutation. As the novel unfolds, the narrator's "remorseless" revelations spare no one—not libertine fathers or haughty mothers, not obsequious pastors, not philistine publishers and, above all, not Pierre, the ethical subject. When Pierre follows the "cause of his heart" (198), he thinks he is pursuing a life of high ideals. The narrator, however, knows better. Unfailingly, every time Pierre takes a principled stand (leaving Saddle Meadows) or commits some noble action (rescuing Isabel, taking in Lucy), the narrator darkly glosses the act as leading him one step closer to delusion and ruin. Even more significant, the narrator teaches the reader to mistrust Pierre's innermost feelings. The deep "interior development" expressed in his wish to both reclaim Isabel and achieve literary profundity is really something else altogether: beneath every instance of ethical expression the reader comes to discern other "nameless" and "latent" feelings that will drive Pierre to re-create a new version of the creole planter "phallocracy" (Therborn 310) he had so fervently rejected. Through the knowing scrutiny of the narrator, Pierre's first-person ethical speech becomes unwitting self-betrayal, uncovering what the narrator calls the "universal lurking insincerity of even the purest written thoughts" (393).

Rather than separate illicit sexuality from ethical interiority, Melville's novel locates them in the same subject. The collapse of this fundamental reform distinction marks *Pierre* as a postreform novel: there is no going back to an epistemology of secure ethical feeling. The results will color aesthetic feeling as well: when the narrator points to "unfathomable cravings" (355) that Pierre pours into his effort to write a great book, we realize that *literary* subjectivity is as saturated by desire and unconscious meaning as ethical interiority is. Indeed, it now seems that aesthetic consciousness *is* the form of subjectivity that is born when the ethical has merged with the sexual, both turning out to belong to the same interior region of profound "ambiguities." And this discovery, of course, is problematic for Melville's narrator, not just for Pierre. Although the narrator is the knowing subject who uncovers this region of Pierre's ambiguous desire and "presentiments," the revelation will also implicate the narrator's own aesthetic practice: as critics never fail to point out, as much as the narrator castigates Pierre he also betrays a close sense of sympathetic identification with him, making the two frequently indistinguishable on the page and therefore making the narrator's project of truth-telling as problematic as Pierre's.[7]

The resulting sense of nihilistic collapse has led many to see Melville's novel as a failure, if a momentous one. Even the strongest champions of *Pierre* acknowledge the novel's self-cannibalizing nature, the way its own revelations about Pierre's revelations lead to a kind of formal implosion. But from another angle, the collapse of first-person subjectivity with third-person knowledge is a crucial formal achievement. In *Pierre*, precisely *because* he merges first-person and third-person narration, Melville brings to the domestic novel and its explorations of privacy the powerful narrative instrument of free indirect discourse ("Into Pierre's awe-stricken, childish soul, there entered a kindred, though still more nebulous conceit" [71]). This form of speech—unique to literary discourse—allows the more knowing perspective of a narrator to articulate the feelings and wordless perceptions of a character, allowing third-person narration to give a distinctive style to a character's psychic life by throwing into relief the limits of his or her first-person comprehension. Free indirect discourse thus enables a striking kind of double vision, alerting the reader to the existence of meaning that remains out of reach for subjects themselves but that is still somehow located within the depths of their own subjectivity.

Some four decades later, Freud will famously name this psychic terrain the unconscious, defining it as part of the ahistorical structure of the human psyche. But as novels like *Pierre* show us, even before Freud there is already under way a literary effort to illuminate the secret precincts of subjectivity. The novel is a chief vehicle of this effort at excavating subjectivity; but it is a form that sees traces of history in interior lives, not just ahistorical structures. The unruly, catastrophic discoveries unearthed by the free indirect discourse in *Pierre* may offer little more than confusion if read as national narrative. But as an inside picture of dialectical change, Pierre's layered private consciousness illuminates a historical unconscious, made manifest in the dialectical turns that give changing conceptual shape to what will count as New World liberty and dependence, love and coercion. As the sovereignty of the state is transformed into the ethical privacy and epistemological revelations of the novel, Pierre in his idealism imagines a clean break from the exploitation endemic to New World history, only to have the precincts of his heart become an unforeseen mapping of new patterns of male rule, sexual desire, and dreams of freedom.

Is the free indirect discourse of the novel, then, our richest history of the New World private subject, her transformation over time and her dependence on and struggle with shaping events? The history told in novels is invented, of course. But a deeper, more objective historical change is registered in the novel's formal turns and mutations—registered, that is, in precisely the kinds of conceptual shifts excluded in advance from the closed form of allegory. The free indirect discourse Melville introduces into the American domestic novel becomes the basis for the daring literary experiments of later novelists who chronicle New World lives. Henry James's mastery of this technique in literary realism, for instance, will allow him to write his own examination of postbellum American kinship as part of an unfolding history of subjectivity. In *The Bostonians* (1886), free indirect discourse will discover in Basil Ransom's private desires for Verena Tarrant a newly sublimated version of the racialized power of the Southern planter, while the narrator's canny insight into the fusion of ethical and sexual feeling will produce one of the most open portraits to date of same-sex desire in Olive Chancellor's own love for Verena. Later the modernist mutations of free indirect discourse pioneered by William Faulkner will turn the terrain of American creole kinship into a landmark development in world literature. In the combustible racial consciousness of the orphaned Joe Christmas, unable to know whether or not he is black, or in the living speech of a dead mother being taken for burial by her husband and children, Faulkner's experimental language discovers new sites of enunciation for the history of the Americanization of kinship. Against the singular story told again and again by national allegory, the epistemology of the novel uncovers multiple mutations of an ongoing history at once traumatic, creative, and generative.

NOTES

1 Brian Connolly discusses the efforts of white U.S. writers to depict African peoples as an "incestuous nation." Black populations in the New World thus posed the prospect of a disordered sexual presence within the state ("In all the southern regions it is thus"). At the same time, antislavery writers on both sides of the Atlantic associated creole societies as a whole with "multiform incests."

2 The trope of a "new political family" was used by Roger Taney in an especially telling way in his Dred Scott opinion. *Dred Scott v. Sanford*, 60 U.S. 702 (1856), 700.

3 Critics exploring transnational writing in more recent scholarship have also assumed that familial themes and tropes allegorize the macropolitical designs of colonizing states. In her study of the rise of the Anglophone novel in Atlantic modernity, for instance, Laura Doyle argues that any expression of the "genealogical idea" (6), whether it appears in early modern political debates or in the family plot of a Virginia Woolf novel, rehearses an enduring political allegory of the "racialization of freedom" (3) in the modern nation-state.

4 See chapter 4 ("Of Slavery") and chapter 16 ("Of Conquest") of Locke's *Second Treatise*.

5 Recent scholarship on the continuities between slavery and the U.S. prison system includes Dayan, Wacquant, and Smith.

6 Review in the *American Whig Review*, quoted in Weinstein 173.

7 Weinstein puts it this way: "The narrator wildly vacillates between cudgeling Pierre for his naiveté and sympathizing with his suffering. Sometimes the distance between Pierre and the narrator is absolutely clear; other times the two seem to collapse into each other" (167). My reading of *Pierre* is indebted to Weinstein's keen analysis of the novel's freighted language of kinship.

BIBLIOGRAPHY

Berman, Caroline Vellenga. *Creole Crossings: Domestic Fiction and the Reform of Colonial Slavery*. Ithaca, NY: Cornell University Press, 2006.

Brown, Gillian. *Domestic Individualism: Imagining Self in Nineteenth-Century America*. Berkeley: University of California Press, 1990.

Brown, William Wells. *Clotel; or, the President's Daughter*. New York: Bedford/St. Martin's, 2000.

Castronovo, Russ. *Fathering the Nation: American Genealogies of Slavery and Freedom*. Berkeley: University of California Press, 1996.

Child, Maria Lydia. "Slavery's Pleasant Homes." *A Lydia Maria Child Reader*. Ed. Carolyn L. Karcher. Durham, NC: Duke University Press, 1997. 238–242.

Connolly, Brian. "'This insidious enormity': The Theology of Incest in the Early Republic." Unpublished paper. McNeil Center for Early American Studies, October 17, 2007.

Dayan, Colin. "Legal Slaves and Civil Bodies." *Materializing Democracy*. Ed. Russ Castronovo and Dana D. Nelson. Durham, NC: Duke University Press, 2002. 53–94.

Doyle, Laura. *Freedom's Empire: Race and the Rise of the Novel in Atlantic Modernity, 1640–1940*. Durham, NC: Duke University Press, 2008.

Fliegelman, Jay. *Prodigals and Pilgrims: The American Revolution against Patriarchal Authority, 1750–1800*. Cambridge: Cambridge University Press, 1982.

Hentz, Caroline Lee. *The Planter's Northern Bride*. Chapel Hill: University of North Carolina Press, 1970.

Lincoln, Abraham. *Speeches and Writings, 1832–1858*. Ed. Don E. Fehrenbacher. New York: Library of America, 1989.

Locke, John. *Two Treatises of Government*. Ed. Peter Laslett. 2nd ed. Cambridge: Cambridge University Press, 1967.

McKeon, Michael. *The Secret History of Domesticity: Public, Private, and the Division of Knowledge*. Baltimore: Johns Hopkins University Press, 2005.

Melville, Herman. *Pierre; or, The Ambiguities*. Pierre, Israel Potter, The Confidence-Man, Tales & Billy Budd. Ed. Harrison Hayford. New York: Library of America, 1984. 1–421.

Neville, Henry. *The Isle of Pines*. Three Early Modern Utopias. Ed. Susan Bruce. Oxford: Oxford University Press, 1999. 187–212.

Scott, James C. *Seeing Like a State*. New Haven, CT: Yale University Press, 1998.

Shelley, Mary. *Frankenstein or The Modern Prometheus*. Oxford: Oxford University Press, 2009.

Smith, Caleb. *The Prison and the American Imagination*. New Haven, CT: Yale University Press, 2009.

Stowe, Harriet Beecher. *Uncle Tom's Cabin*. Three Novels. Ed. Kathryn Kish Sklar. New York: Library of America, 1982. 1–520.

Sundquist, Eric. *Home as Found: Authority and Genealogy in Nineteenth-Century American Literature*. Baltimore: Johns Hopkins University Press, 1979.

Therborn, Goren. *Between Sex and Power: Family in the World, 1900–2000*. London: Routledge, 2004.

Wacquant, Loic. "From Slavery to Mass Incarceration: Rethinking the 'Race Question' in the US." *New Left Review* 13 (2002): 41–60.

Weinstein, Cindy. *Family, Kinship, and Sympathy in Nineteenth-Century American Literature*. Cambridge: Cambridge University Press, 2004.

CHAPTER 7

LOOKING AT STATE VIOLENCE: LUCY PARSONS, JOSÉ MARTÍ, AND HAYMARKET

SHELLEY STREEBY

IN this chapter, I suggest that literary and cultural meanings in the late nineteenth century were crucially mediated and shaped by the expansion of the pictorial marketplace and the transformation of visual culture. In the wake of the removal of state-sponsored executions from public spaces, an emergent mass visual culture promised access to such forbidden scenes of punishment, while the state and the police tried to use new visual technologies and cultural forms to turn Haymarket into a spectacle, enforce their own interpretations, and regulate the responses of viewers and readers. José Martí and Lucy E. Parsons intervened in late nineteenth-century practices of looking by reenvisioning iconic sentimental and sensational Haymarket scenes and raising questions about violence, the visual, and state power that connect world movements across space and time. Comparing Martí's and Parson's interventions in visual culture thereby opens up transnational, anarchical literary histories and adaptations, transformations, and displacements of sentimentalism and sensationalism that diverge from the tracks of the U.S. literary canon and liberal nationalism.

Many scholars of Martí's years in the United States have suggested that Haymarket coincided with a larger transformation in his thinking: I build on this work by emphasizing how he responded to a changing visual culture and new mass-produced images of Haymarket. Although in an earlier piece Martí harshly criticized the anarchists and defended the state, he wrote a very different article in the wake of the November 11, 1887, executions of four of the anarchists, who were found guilty of inciting the violence at Haymarket Square that led to the death of a police officer on May 4, 1886. Several other people also died and many more were severely injured as a result of the blast of a bomb as well as the bullets that the police fired into the crowd and, accidentally, at each other. Although the bomb thrower's identity was never determined, the state claimed that the anarchists were part of a conspiracy to "excite the people, or classes of the people" to "sedition, tumult and riot" in order to "overthrow the existing order of society and to bring about a social revolution by force." As part of that conspiracy, it charged, the anarchists, in their speeches, newspaper writings, pamphlets, and broadsides used "incendiary," sensational language to provoke the murder of the police. Although Martí initially supported the state, after the executions he adapted and altered discourses of sentiment and sensation in order to reimagine iconic Haymarket scenes and mobilize sympathy for the anarchists.

Martí's chronicles, which were written for the Buenos Aires newspaper *La Nación*, reached readers in Argentina, Mexico, Cuba, the United States, and other parts of the Americas, for whom debates about violence and the state in visions of future revolutionary and anticolonial transformation were both relevant and pressing. By the late 1880s, as Benedict Anderson has observed, globe-stretching and nation-linking networks connected anarchists in many different parts of the world, notably including Cuba, Mexico, the Philippines, Spain, the United States, China, France, England, and Japan, and anarchism had become "the dominant element in the self-consciously internationalist radical Left" (2). As a writer for a Spanish-language newspaper with a transnational circulation, Martí participated in just such a network, but as an anticolonial, revolutionary nationalist, he was alarmed by anarchist objections to the nation-state, although he ambivalently admired their passion for social justice and sympathized with their desire to change the world. Martí's anxieties about working-class violence and his commitment to the ideal of a utopian, fraternal, and anticolonial nation shaped his perspective on "la guerra social" (331) in Chicago, despite his outrage at the police violence and the legal injustice that followed. Even so, Martí's chronicle of the "escenas extraordinarias" (331) in Chicago suggests the global significance of the Haymarket drama, as he called it, as well as the challenges posed by anarchist world movements to nations and nationalisms at the end of a long century of anticolonial wars and nation and empire building in the Americas.

In representing Haymarket as a global drama to a world audience, Martí's chronicles also respond to significant transformations in visual culture. He repeatedly refers to or reenvisions in words the images of Haymarket scenes that were disseminated by means of new technologies such as the telegraph and the camera and in illustrations based on photographs and eyewitness sketches. Scenes of the speeches and bombing at Haymarket, the trial, the anarchists' imprisonment, the visits made by family and friends, their final hours and execution, along with the massive public funeral that followed, were graphically illustrated in lithographs, cabinet cards, cartoons, albums, mass-circulation daily newspapers, weekly illustrated papers, pamphlets, and books. Many of Martí's elaborately rendered *escenas* suggestively evoke the most iconic images of the conflict, including line drawings of the explosion of the bomb at Haymarket Square, photographs of the anarchists, and illustrations of the suicide in his prison cell of the youngest of the anarchists, Louis Lingg, a German immigrant youth who, Martí marveled, wanted to "desventrar la ley inglesa/eviscerate English law" and did not even speak English! (347). Martí was not alone in reworking such visual material, for the anarchists and their allies also struggled to make use of newly ubiquitous images by reproducing and reimagining iconic ones. The struggle over the meaning of Haymarket, then, was also a struggle over the images of state violence and anarchist world movements that circulated in the popular press and through the transnational networks of which Anderson writes.

Martí's modernist newspaper chronicle recasts a wide range of such popular images and narratives of the Haymarket drama: he responds to the events of the day by assimilating, revising, and stylizing the representations of an emergent mass visual culture. As Julio Ramos suggests, the Latin American chronicler at the fin de siècle struggled to "dominate in the very process of representation" a "conjunction of materials, tied to journalism."[1] In this way, Martí seeks to "overwrite" (107) inscriptions of U.S. newspapers, anarchist literature and culture, and other sources with his own interpretation of the events. But although Martí cites anarchist literature as he criticizes the state's case and the representations of Haymarket purveyed in mass culture, he ultimately draws back in horror from the anarchists' denial of the patria, for he remained committed to the ideal of the nation and to republican institutions even as he was forced to confront the question of whether violence against the state was necessary in anticolonial contexts.

Twenty-five years after Martí wrote his chronicle, Lucy E. Parsons self-published a memorial edition of the *Famous Speeches* of the Haymarket anarchists that gave a prominent place to an illustration of the gallows scene, one of the most widely reproduced of the scenes associated with Haymarket. During this era, Parsons was one of the founding members of the Industrial Workers of the World (IWW), the "one big" U.S. union that organized immigrants and women, and one whose official publication declared that workers had "no country" and frequently criticized the sentiment of patriotism. Parsons also made speeches and raised money for Mexican anarchists who were imprisoned in the United States, such as Enrique and Ricardo Flores Magón, two of the leaders of the revolutionary Partido Liberal Mexicano, a transnational movement that initially helped to overthrow Porfirio Díaz and eventually tried to push the Mexican Revolution in a more anarchist, rather than liberal reformist, direction.

In his second Haymarket chronicle Martí referred to her as "la mestiza Lucy Parsons" and declared that her tempestuous eloquence and heroic efforts to wrest the bodies of the anarchists from the gallows amazed him. She may have been a former slave and was described in the popular press as a "mulatto" [*sic*] although she claimed to be solely of Mexican and Indian descent. She played an active role in the events surrounding Haymarket, for she was an important organizer, writer, and orator as well as the wife of Albert Parsons, one of the leaders of the Chicago branch of the International Working People's Association (IWPA) and the editor of the anarchist newspaper *The Alarm*, who was hung along with three of the other Chicago anarchists. In the years after the executions, she continued to write, speak, and organize, and compiled the *Life of Albert R. Parsons* (1889; 1903) as well as the *Famous Speeches* of the Haymarket anarchists, which went through many editions and translations and traveled all over the world. This last text was eventually illustrated with a few prominent images, most notably an illustration of the gallows scene that Parsons instructed her reader to "look at" while swearing "in your heart" to work for the overthrow of the "accursed system" that was responsible for the "awful murder of our comrades."

In bringing Lucy Parsons and José Martí together, I combine insights from nineteenth-century visual culture studies with methodologies in literary studies that look below, above, and beyond the nation and the state, unsettling both as the primary horizons of analysis. As Martí scholar Laura Lomas suggests, much of the recent revisionary American studies work on transnational literature in the Americas has focused on "the multilingual and deterritorialized routes and roots of Latino or trans-American writing in the work of mainly light-skinned Creole elites of early to mid-nineteenth-century Cuba." By the 1880s, in the wake of "truncated wars of independence and after the gradual abolition of slavery began," the "numbers of islanders and other Latino Americans in multiracial barrios, especially Florida, swelled to the thousands" (Lomas 1). Many were anarchists who questioned what they saw as the narrowness of the idea of national independence championed by the previous generation of exiles and émigrés as well as by wealthy businessmen prominent in the independence movement of their own time (Ronning, Poyo). Martí's perspective on Haymarket, which betrays anxieties about anarchism as a rival worldview as well as sympathy for the Chicago anarchists, was thus shaped by his complex relationships with Cuban anarchists and by debates over state power, violence, direct action, and political reform within and around the independence movement.

For Haymarket was an epochal event that provoked responses not only in Chicago and the United States but also in Cuba, Mexico, Spain, Russia, Germany, England, and other places where anarchism flourished. And despite his ambivalence about the Chicago anarchists, Martí, like Lucy Parsons, was part of a larger transnational world of migrants, writers, and organizers at odds with or openly critical of states and state power, including anticolonial revolutionists, socialists, and anarchists. In the United States, many anarchists, like most of the men on trial at Haymarket, were immigrants. Lucy Parsons and her husband Albert were both born in the United States, but they cast their lot with the German immigrant workers who led the Chicago labor movement when they joined the IWPA, whose Pittsburgh Manifesto insisted that "political structures (States), which are completely in the hands of the propertied, have no other purpose than the upholding of the present order of exploitation." As a woman of color whose marriage was not recognized by the state and who may well have been a former slave who was thereby legally classified as property, it is not surprising that Lucy Parsons had a strong critique of the state, legal institutions, and the limits of political reform. In the early twentieth century, during the Mexican and Russian Revolutions and World War I, Haymarket continued to be remembered by others who imagined alternatives to state power and who were punished by states for doing so, including the Flores Magón brothers, Emma Goldman, and Alexander Berkman, all of whom were targeted by federal immigration, citizenship, sedition, and obscenity laws.

The changing meanings of the Haymarket archive in transnational contexts suggest that debates about state violence and state power responded to what Joshua Brown has called the "vast expansion of the pictorial marketplace" (8) in this era. Recent work in nineteenth-century visual culture studies, especially American studies scholarship on violence, photography, and discourses of sentiment and sensation, is helpful in making these connections. Some of this work emphasizes how the visual cultures of sentiment and sensation make evidence of violence disappear: in *Tender Violence*, Laura Wexler traces "the constitutive sentimental functions of the innocent eye" in white women's photographs that erase "the violence of colonial encounters in the very act of portraying them" (7) as she argues for the connections between literary sentimentalism and a broader visual culture of sentiment at the end of the nineteenth century. But if sentimental literature and visual culture may hide evidence of the violence of white supremacy and imperialism, showing that violence can cause other problems, as scholars such as Saidiya Hartman, Shawn Michelle Smith, and Jacqueline Goldsby suggest. These theorists of literature and visual culture warn that the spectacles of death and suffering in sentimental and sensational representations of violence may reproduce or extend that violence.

In what follows, I argue for the importance of new forms of sentimental and sensational visual culture in struggles over Haymarket, violence, and the mass-mediated spectacle of state power. Sentimental and sensational images of the dead and wounded bodies of the police were used to mobilize public sentiment against the anarchists, while newspapers and illustrated magazines tried to turn the imprisonment, execution, and funeral of the anarchists into a spectacle. On the other hand, the anarchists and their allies disrupted the spectacle by critically commenting on such scenes as well as by reproducing them, along with other images of the anarchists' trial and punishment, as evidence of unjust state violence. In the decades after Haymarket, writers and artists would reproduce and critically reframe many of these very Haymarket icons in order to inspire participation in the great "world movements" of the era. Although it is often said that the fallout from the Haymarket tragedy was a huge setback for the labor movement and that alternative voices were quickly overwhelmed by dominant media, Haymarket's long afterlife looks different if we widen our perspective to trace its reemergence as a powerful image in the decades to come throughout the world.

THE SCAFFOLD AS BATTLEGROUND:
HAYMARKET AND VISUAL CULTURE

A key source that Martí used and that he sought to "overwrite" in his Haymarket chronicle was the New York *Evening Sun*, one of the mass-circulation daily newspapers of the period. An evening edition of the *Sun* began to appear just before the executions took place, filled with news that the paper boasted came over "our own private wire from the jail." In this way, the *Sun* purveyed a glimpse of that which was out of bounds to the crowd: the execution of white criminals. Although witnessing the execution scene in person was proscribed for all but a few, the *Sun* promised access to readers, claiming it was "the first time in the journalistic history of the world" that the telegraph, or "electric current had been introduced right into the very corridor of death itself, for the purpose of chronicling the final movements" of the anarchists. The men were imprisoned in a "cage" that "was so located that every movement...could be discerned," while the "finger of the operator" made the "click, click" of the "telegraph instrument" echo through the corridor of the prison. As the operator watched the men walk to the gallows, the paper reported, their white linen shrouds "rubbed against the wires of the outside of the cage" and before they ascended the stairs, "the fact that the final moment was at hand was flashing over the United Press wires in all directions." The operator "sat motionless, his eyes riveted" on the sentry box where the executioner awaited the signal, heard the crack on the chisel that severed the rope, pressed his finger on the key, "and even before the bodies had fallen in the full length of their ropes it was known in tens and hundreds of cities throughout the country that the sentence of the law had been fulfilled." Never before, the *Sun* writer commented, "had realism in the distribution of news been more graphically illustrated, and never before had the echo of the hammer and chisel of the executioner been flashed over the wires to the outer world."

This "graphically illustrated" realism, spurred by the telegraph and new mass-circulation daily newspapers, partly responded to the incomplete withdrawal of scenes of state-sponsored execution from U.S. public spaces in the nineteenth century. As Foucault's analysis would lead us to expect, in Chicago in November of 1887 the machinery of state executions was "placed inside prison walls and made inaccessible to the public by blocking the streets leading to the prison" (15). Chicago police captain Michael Schaack reported in his mammoth, illustrated *Anarchy and Anarchists* (1889) that on the morning of the executions three hundred police were deployed "to preserve order and keep away from the immediate vicinity of the building all persons not having proper credentials or not properly vouched for" (643). As the time of the execution neared, the crowd pushed to get closer to the scene as "the streets beyond the ropes became crowded with people of all grades and descriptions" but they were "all kept moving by policemen scattered along the thoroughfares...so that no groups might gather and under the excitement of the moment precipitate a row or a riot" (644). Schaack even observed that Lucy Parsons "dressed in mourning and accompanied by her two children, presented herself at the ropes and demanded admittance to see her husband, 'murdered by law,' " but instead police took her to the police station and "detained" her "until after the execution" (644). All of these measures would seem to confirm Foucault's claim that by the 1840s the "punishment" of (white) criminals became "the most hidden part of the penal process" (9) and that execution scenes were increasingly removed from public view.

Such scenes were hidden, Foucault suggests, in order to prevent "the intervention of the people in the spectacle of the executions," as sometimes happened in these "ambiguous rituals," which risked evoking a longer history of "struggles and confrontations" and thereby becoming a "battleground around the crime, its punishment, and its memory" (67). But the punishment of the Haymarket anarchists was not really hidden, even though it took place behind prison walls and even though police kept the crowd away from the scene. After all, the men were placed in cages where their every movement was visible to the journalists who visited the prison in order to cover the unfolding story; the telegraph was even brought inside the prison to chronicle the "final movements" of the men to the "outer world." While the telegraph, newspapers, books, and images mediated the "visible intensity" of the Haymarket executions in new and different ways, scenes of their punishment were also disseminated to wide networks of people and thereby became a battleground of competing meanings and memories in U.S. mass culture and all over the world.

Although Jeffory Clymer persuasively argues that mass cultural representations of the Haymarket executions provided a political spectacle that served the dominant social, political, and symbolic order, Haymarket scenes, as well as the anarchists' life stories, speeches in court, and final words circulated in multiple cultural forms and languages, often creating new conversations and affiliations as they were translated into new contexts, especially in Spain, Italy, and throughout much of Latin America. Martí's Haymarket chronicle exemplifies how the circulation of Haymarket scenes in transnational contexts could generate new meanings that clashed with those of the dominant U.S. order, for his engagement with mass-circulation newspapers and the ubiquitous images of an emergent mass culture provoked him to ask unsettling questions about attributions of crime and criminality and the role of violence in maintaining state power.

Often, Martí drew on discourses of sentiment, sensation, and melodrama to raise such questions. Isn't it criminal, Martí asks, for "la república" to take advantage of a crime that was born as much from its own crimes as from the criminals' "fanatismo/fanaticism" (334)? Here the "republic"—the United States—becomes the villain, a tyrant that makes the accused anarchists into "víctimas del terror social/ victims of social terror" (334) within a melodramatic narrative that exposes injustice, recognizes injured victims, and upsets or inverts social hierarchies.[2] A sentimental and melodramatic crime narrative runs through Martí's recasting of the Haymarket drama as one in which a "wrathful nation" fights the efforts of a benevolent lawyer, a young girl ("una niña") who has fallen in love with one of the anarchists, and an "Indian and Spanish mestiza, who is the wife of another" (334) to seize the anarchists' bodies from the gallows. The lawyer was Captain William Black, who defended the anarchists in court and delivered a eulogy in which he compared their execution to the hanging of Jesus and insisted that the men were moved to act by a gracious tenderness of heart. The "young girl" was Nina Van Zandt, the daughter of a rich Chicago chemist, who became enamored of August Spies, whom she thought had a "good face" (Spies i) when she attended the trial and whom she married by proxy before he was executed. Their cross-class romance became a media sensation (see figure 7.1) as well as a source of fascination for Martí, who found the girl's loyal

Figure 7.1 Nina Van Zandt, August Spies, and Cook County Jail Interior on cover of *Frank Leslie's Illustrated Newspaper*, October 1, 1887. Courtesy of Dunn Library, Simpson College.

misery moving and implied that Spies was too cold, too busy redeeming mankind, to love her properly. Finally, the "Indian and Spanish mestiza" was Lucy Parsons, who became a fantasy figure of racial mixture for Martí, who, unlike the U.S. popular press, accepted her own account of her racial genealogy, one that was almost certainly altered to shield her from the racism of those around her.

Martí's vision of Parsons as an impassioned mestiza whose heart responds to the suffering of the abject classes is saturated with keywords of sentiment and sensation. Recent work on Martí by Lomas, David Luis Brown, Gillman, and others helps us to see him as a "sentimental man" (Chapman and Hendler) and to understand his sentimentalism as part of a broader transnational cultural matrix, one that is inseparable from what Anderson calls "the universalist currents of liberalism and republicanism" that nourished the "Spanish American nationalist independence movements" (2). Throughout the Americas, melodramatic stories of national race romance, with their villains, heroes, and virtuous victims, provided a grammar for nineteenth-century nation building and anticolonial struggles. Such narratives modeled relationships among classes, races, and nations for readers, and Martí's translation of the Haymarket events into a cross-class and cross-racial romantic melodrama is one sign among many of his engagement with transnational literary and visual cultures of sentiment and sensation, as is his focus on bodies in pain and corpses in order to narrate injustices. In what follows, I suggest that Martí's rendering of the trial, the gallows scene, and the anarchists' funeral opens up questions about state power and state violence that are not put to rest by his anxiety over the anarchists' rejection of the *patria* and their emotional synergy with tumultuous multitudes. In this sense, despite his discomfort with the anarchists' critiques of patriotism and their rejection of the state form, the chronicle resembles accounts in anarchist newspapers, pamphlets, speeches, and other literature that also return to iconic Haymarket scenes in order to overturn the interpretations that circulated in an emergent mass culture.

Many of these iconic Haymarket scenes appeared in *Frank Leslie's Illustrated Newspaper* which "set the standard for representing the news" (Joshua Brown 8) in the nineteenth-century United States and was the most popular of all the illustrated papers that contributed to the expansion of the pictorial marketplace. Although *Leslie's* did not cover the trial, the paper prominently featured many large, eye-catching illustrations of scenes of the anarchists in prison, their final days, the execution, and the funeral. These illustrations emphasized the power of the law, the state, the police, and the prison to contain and control the threat posed by the anarchists, who refused to recognize the authority of those institutions. The day after the executions, *Leslie's* published a full-page picture of the gallows, over the captions "the shadow of death" and "preparations for the execution of the condemned anarchists." This illustration is yet another example of how *Leslie's*, like the *Sun*, tried to appeal to readers by offering views of scenes that were increasingly being removed from public sight: the execution of white criminals. But while the production of a degree of sentimental sympathy for the men in the wake of the spectacle of their punishment often involved emphasizing their whiteness, Albert Parsons's marriage to Lucy associated him with people of color. In other words, whiteness is not only a solution but also a problem in sentimental and sensational Haymarket literature and visual culture, which raise questions about the boundaries of whiteness and the relationship of the anarchists to that category. In the same issue of *Leslie's*, a cover illustration depicted an "affecting interview between Parsons and his little daughter" in which Lucy is rendered a slightly whitened, almost ghostly presence in the background, drawn in lighter shades of ink and difficult to see behind prison bars. This drawing was part of a tripartite cover (see figure 7.2) that also featured a picture of Samuel Fielden,

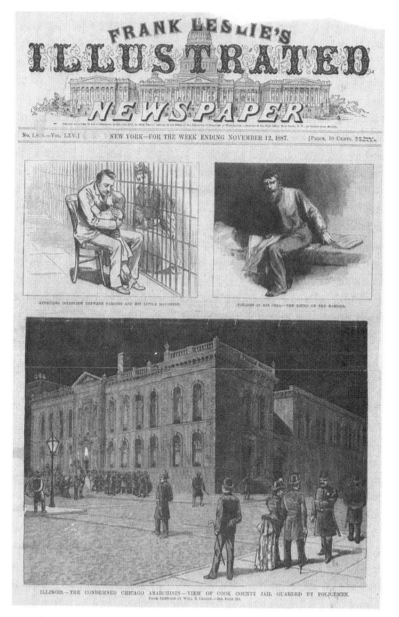

Figure 7.2 "Affecting Interview" and execution day scenes on cover of *Frank Leslie's Illustrated Newspaper*, November 12, 1887. Courtesy of Dunn Library, Simpson College.

one of the anarchists whose death sentence was commuted to life imprisonment after he appealed to the governor for clemency, as well as a larger one of the prison guarded by police. It is notable that the two anarchists who were singled out for a measure of sympathy were of English descent: Fielden was an English immigrant while Parsons was a native-born Southerner. Along with their Anglo-Saxon whiteness, their easy eloquence in their native language provoked admiring responses from many readers of their speeches and testimony. The sentimentality on display in *Leslie's* seemed to require ghosting Lucy, however, whose presence is written out of the picture's caption even as her face is whitened and made a part of the blurry background. The viewer is positioned inside the cell with Parsons and the child, looking out at Lucy: along with the prison bars, then, the color line also divides the space, further whitening those on the inside.

But if the production of sentimentality about the executions depended on whitening the anarchists and foregrounding the family, it also relied on properly regulating the feelings provoked by the spectacle of their death. In an issue published the week after the executions, *Leslie's* claimed that the "whole country participated" in "the conflicting feelings of awe, pity, and a stern satisfaction at the final operation of justice inspired by the executions" as it continued to focus on "the doom of anarchy" ("Chicago Anarchists," 219). The issue's most striking feature was a three-part pictorial narrative of the execution day (see figure 7.3): a drawing of Parsons defiantly singing in his cell, another of the "march to the scaffold" of the white-clad anarchists, whose white faces also stand out in contrast with the black clothing worn by the guards, and finally, a picture of the executioner "drawing the caps over the prisoners' faces" as the hooded men stand before the gallows with ropes tied around their necks, along with several witnesses, including at least two rows of observers. The space is represented as a theater in which the anarchists stand on an elevated stage before the gaze of an array of spectators.

Martí lingers on many of these iconic scenes but he alters or elaborates on them and thereby changes their meanings. He retells, for instance, the sentimental story of the final visits from the families the night before the execution, remarking especially on "las mujeres sublimes/the sublime women" (350) and emphasizing the stark contrast in the way Nina and Lucy are treated by officials: while Nina passes easily by the prison guards, who hold their hands out to her respectfully, Lucy is prevented from seeing her husband. Like *Leslie's* and the *Sun*, Martí extensively narrates the story of the anarchists' last night in their cells, and even remarks that the final strokes of the carpenter's hammer were audible above "el golpeo incesante del telégrafo que el *Sun* de Nueva York tenía en el mismo corredor etablecido/the chatter of the telegraph that the *New York Sun* set up in the same corridor" (351). Martí follows the men as they walk to the gallows and as the head of each is covered with a "mortaja blanca/ white shroud" that resembles the "túnica de los catecúmenos cristianos/tunic of neophyte Christians" while down below the "concurrencia/audience" sits in rows in front of the scaffold "como en un teatro!"/as if in a theater!" (354).

Figure 7.3 *Frank Leslie's Illustrated Newspaper*, November 19, 1887: 216. Courtesy of
Dunn Library, Simpson College.

While whiteness subtly shadows *Leslie's* pictorial narrative, in Martí's chronicle
it enables a comparison that turns the men into martyrs devoted to a sacred
cause and associates the punishing state with imperial Rome. Martí vividly
imagines the body, face, and voice of each of the men in ways that resonate
with anarchist literature that tried to disrupt the execution as spectacle, and he
records the final words of each, which were reported in the papers and would
be echoed around the world for decades to come. In giving the men a voice and

by drawing on sentimental discourses to give them faces and bodies, Martí reimagines the execution scene as something other than a "satisfying" spectacle of state power. Both the *Sun* and Martí also emphasized the "horror" of the scene, since all but Parsons died slowly and painfully of strangulation. Martí narrates how each responded to the giving way of the trap door, concluding with Spies' protracted "danza espantable/terrible dance" of death, ending with his broken neck and head facing forward, saluting the "espectadores/spectators" (355). In this way, Martí draws on sentimental, sensational, and melodramatic modalities to foreground forms of state violence hidden from all but a chosen audience of witnesses.

After revising the execution scene, Martí ends his chronicle with an account of the funeral rites that is also saturated with keywords and signifiers of sentimentalism and that privileges cultural memories of the meaning of the execution rather than the execution itself as a spectacle of state power.[3] He lingers on the funeral scene, a privileged locus of sentimentality, and on the display of the bruised corpses, the caskets containing the bodies, and the parade of workers' associations that marched mournfully that day. Twenty-five thousand "almas amigas/friendly souls," Martí writes, listened to Black declare in his eulogy that the men were not criminals but instead resembled Christ, a comparison that *Leslie's* characterized as "somewhat blasphemous" and that Martí emphasizes through translated quotation.

Finally, Martí imagines a voice emerging as the men are lowered into their graves, an angry voice that accuses the workers of Chicago of allowing five of their noblest friends to be executed. Here, Martí's swerve away from what can be seen and shown, this "gesturing with flourishes to what it cannot represent in the mode of a photographic reproduction or copy" breaks with "the dominant ideology of realism in the United States in the 1880s," by "pushing available forms of representation," such as journalism, "to their limit" (Lomas 24). The spectral voice that Martí imagines suggests that the crowd may still participate in what Foucault calls the "small but innumerable disturbances around the scaffold" (60) that took place before state-sponsored executions were removed from public spaces. But the possibility of overturning the ritual of state violence is quickly set aside, as the defense attorney consoles the unquiet soul and the crowd quietly returns to their homes. Martí concludes with a translated quotation from the next morning's edition of the *Arbeiter-Zeitung*, the German-language workers' newspaper Spies edited, advising its readers to be wise as serpents and harmless as doves, for although they had lost the battle, they would "veremos al fin el mundo ordenado conforme a la justicia/see a just world order in the end" (356). At the end, then, republican institutions, though damaged, still survive: the lawyer comforts the man, thereby quieting his reproachful voice, and the next morning the workers' voice, the newspaper, is not suppressed, but instead appears in the public sphere to counsel caution and peaceful waiting for a just world order "al fin," whenever that may come.

Lucy Parsons, Race, and the Visual Cultures of Sentiment and Sensation

Like Martí, Lucy Parsons adapted and transformed discourses of sentiment and sensation as she intervened in late nineteenth-century practices of looking and tried to "pintar al mundo el horror" (348) of the unhappy classes in her oratory, newspaper writings, and the books she edited, including *The Life of Albert R. Parsons*, which she published at her own expense in 1889. In this book there is no picture of the gallows scene, though Parsons returns to other iconic Haymarket scenes that Martí, illustrated newspapers, and new mass-circulation daily newspapers reproduced and reenvisioned. The book compiles diverse kinds of writings loosely organized around the life and writings of Parsons, the Haymarket riot, and the trial, imprisonment, execution, and funeral of the men, and it includes many different voices and cultural forms, ranging from speeches and newspaper editorials to interviews and letters.

Instead of picturing the gallows scene or the funeral, the illustrations that frame the 1889 edition depict Albert in the honorific, sentimental mode of the portrait rather than the repressive one of the mug shot (Sekula) and imagine him as a sentimental husband and father. The engraving of Albert that serves as the frontispiece circulated (and still does) widely, reaching viewers all over the world in a variety of forms. Engraved portraits in this era were "governed by conventions developed by commercial photography during the 1840s" (74) according to Joshua Brown, and despite "their transmogrification into a different medium, the engravings preserved the approved qualities of the emulatory photographs" (74) that presented idealized faces. The engraving of Albert's head and shoulders offers such an idealized, white face: it is not a frontal image or profile, as criminal mug shots often were; instead, he looks off in the distance, rather than directly at the viewer. Instead of representing Albert through physiognomic and phrenological codes associated with criminal types, this engraving adapts classical, racialized codes of portraiture borrowed from commercial photography to suggest that he is an intelligent individual with a complex interiority. With its oval framing, the portrait resembles those that families placed on their walls or in other places within the home during this era.

In the 1889 edition, Lucy included engravings of daughter Lulu and son Albert Jr. as well as a reproduction of the last letter Albert wrote to their children before he died, which he begins by noting the tears that blot their names as he writes. The sentimental tropes of family ties and separation suggested by these illustrations were fundamentally transformed in the second edition that Lucy published in 1903, however, for she removed the illustrations of the couple's children, though she kept the reproduction of the letter. Perhaps the pictures were painful reminders of what Lucy had lost: Lulu died two years after Albert was executed, and in 1899 she asked a judge to commit her son to a hospital for the insane, where he would die in 1919. The alteration also, however, deemphasizes Albert's role as husband and father and thereby makes the visual focus less on sentimental domesticity and more on the two Parsons' roles in the public world.

Lucy altered her own image as well when she replaced the engraving of her head and shoulders with a photograph that became part of the frontispiece (see figure 7.4). Versions of both of these images circulated widely, both at the time and in the years that followed. The engraving in the 1889 edition is similar to one that appeared in 1886 in the Chicago newspaper *Knights of Labor*, which sympathized with the anarchists, as well as one in George McClean's "profusely illustrated" 1888 screed, *The Rise and Fall of Anarchy in America*, a defense of the police and the state. This engraving does not rely on the harsh physiognomic codes and the ethnic and racial typing that Brown argues were reinvigorated during the Haymarket era. In an excerpt from the newspaper *Women's World* that Lucy placed in an appendix, the writer, Helen Wilmans, denounced the many images that did rely on such codes and typing when she charged that "[d]istorted and outrageous pictures, purporting to be portraits of these men, appeared; wherever a socialist is represented in print the head of a baboon is given him." Wilmans's comment that "Mrs. Parsons was represented in the dailies with the face of a negro and the retreating forehead of a monkey" (281) also starkly reveals how Lucy's race became an issue during the Haymarket crisis.

As we have seen, the production of a measure of mass cultural sentimentality in behalf of the anarchists in *Frank Leslie's Illustrated Newspaper* depended on whitening the men as well as Lucy. In antianarchist texts such as Schaack's *Anarchy and Anarchists*, however, Lucy was described as a "mulatto" [*sic*]. Schaack questioned what he reported as Lucy's claim that "she is of Mexican extraction with no negro

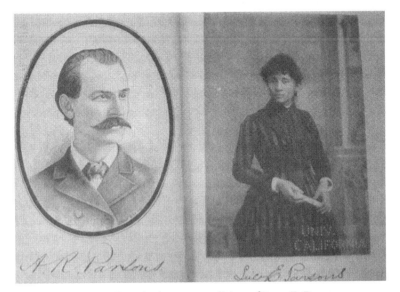

Figure 7.4 Frontispiece, 1903 edition of Lucy E. Parsons,
The Life of Albert R. Parsons.

blood in her veins," boasting of his own ability to accurately read physiognomic codes and insisting that "her swarthy complexion and distinctively negro features do not bear out her assertions" (167). These remarks accompanied an illustration of Lucy that a caption claimed was based on a photograph. Despite key differences, it resembles the photograph of Lucy that was substituted for the engraving in the 1903 edition of *The Life of Albert R. Parsons*. She appears to be wearing the same elegant, striped dress and jewelry in both texts, and in both her hair is curly and dark and she looks at the viewer, though not in the directly head-on way typical of criminal mug shots. Schaack's illustration isolates her shoulders and head, which is tilted slightly upward at an angle as she regards the viewer, while the photograph shows more of her body and captures a more level and cooler, rather than melancholy, gaze. The photograph also provides her with a setting: she stands holding a scroll in front of what looks like an elegant public space but is probably a backdrop in a photographer's studio. The scroll emphasizes her roles as a writer and public speaker and, implicitly, as a leader of movements. Schaack's text, on the other hand, removes both scroll and setting as it claims physiognomic racial knowledge that is partly based on photographic evidence.

In the 1889 edition, the issue of Lucy's race is raised at least twice: in the *Women's World* article and in a brief autobiography narrated in the first person, in which Albert recalled his first meeting with the "charming young Spanish-Indian maiden who, three years later, would become his wife" (9). In the 1903 edition, Lucy added further testimony from Albert's brother, William, who in a newspaper interview made a point of noting his own family's "pilgrim-father parentage" as he characterized Lucy as a "Mexican lady of youth, beauty, and genius" whom Albert married in 1871 in Austin, Texas, "where miscegenation is a crime." William's insistence that Lucy was of Mexican descent responds to Schaack and others who claimed that she was "mulatto": he even adds that her "Spanish and Aztec blood were then never questioned" (3), making it clear that in the wake of Haymarket, questions about her race and "blood" were indeed often raised as a way of "blackening" the anarchists.

Although the testimony of the Parsons brothers and the *Women's World* editor marked Lucy as Mexican and Indian in response to claims that she was a "negro" or a "mulatto," the 1903 edition, especially, emphasizes how she was treated differently than the white families of the other accused anarchists. This racialized difference emerges especially as Lucy returns to an iconic scene that both *Leslie's* and Martí also reenvision: the final meeting between Albert Parsons and his family. While the illustrated newspapers raved about Nina Van Zandt's beauty and Martí reported that the prison guards held out their hands respectfully to her as she left the jail after her final visit the night before the executions, in a chapter entitled "Arrest of Mrs. Parsons and Children," Lucy's friend Lizzie Holmes tells a very different story about Lucy's experiences with the police. Lucy was not allowed to see Albert that night and was told to return early the next day, which she did, bringing her children along with her to seek "a last sad interview" (249). Instead, they were arrested, strip-searched, and confined in cells until the executions were over. There are also other key differences among the three versions of this scene in *Leslie's*, Martí's, and

Lucy Parson's texts. *Leslie's*, as I have suggested, focused on the "affecting interview between Parsons and his little daughter," ignoring Lucy in the caption and both whitening her and relegating her to the background, on the other side of prison bars, in a sentimental cover illustration. The "Arrest" chapter, on the other hand, foregrounds questions of looking and power as it describes how the police sent Lucy from one corner to another near the closely guarded jail, suggesting each time that perhaps at the next she might be admitted. According to Holmes, Lucy "besought the officers" to allow the children, at least, "one last look that the image of that noble father might dwell forever in their heart of hearts," but they denied her the consolation of "the sacred rite of a last goodbye" (250). The *Leslie's* cover illustration therefore depicts a scene that, if it took place at all, happened days before the executions, and thereby provides a sentimental closure that did not actually occur. In showing this scene, it hides the "shameful deeds" done "in the name of law and order," that "passed almost unnoticed" in the "veil" of "gloom, so dense that the close of the century will scarcely see it lightened" (249). Holmes perhaps alludes to the sentimental displacements of such Haymarket pictures when, in her account of Lucy's arrest, she inquires, in a direct address to the reader, "Who can picture her agony?" (250).

In representing the execution, Holmes and Parsons suggest, such Haymarket pictures made some scenes disappear even as they made others visible. In these ways, the representational strategies of the illustrated papers and the mass-circulation dailies converged with those of the police and the state: "Thus it was," Holmes charged, "that while organized authority was judicially murdering the husband and strangling 'the voice of the people,' the wife and children were locked up in a dungeon, that no unpleasant scene might mar the smoothness of the proceedings" (252–253). Instead of reproducing pictures of the gallows scene in the two editions of *The Life of Albert R. Parsons*, Lucy Parsons used both words and pictures to make visible what was obscured by the mass-circulation dailies and the illustrated press in ways that challenged the claims to smooth transparency of a "graphically illustrated realism."

Holmes and Parsons focus on what the sentimental pictures and "the extras of Friday, Nov. 11" hide, partly, like Martí, by themselves drawing on discourses of sentiment and sensation. Parsons adapts the moral polarities of melodrama, typified by villains, heroes, and victims, to stage other scenes of the recognition of virtue and the upheaval and inversion of social hierarchies. In an author's note near the beginning of the 1889 edition, Parsons announces her intention to show not only that her husband was no "aider, nor abettor, nor counselor of crime in any sense," but also that "the proud State of Illinois murdered him under the guise of law and order" (viii). In Lucy's melodrama of crime and punishment the state is the villain and Albert is a victim whose exemplary virtue is made manifest in scenes of sacrifice and suffering such as "Parsons' self-surrender," as William Black called it. In a letter, the defense lawyer wrote admiringly of Albert's voluntary surrender to the court: when "prompted by his own sense of right and of loyalty to his comrades in labor, from a place of absolute security" he submitted himself to the imprisonment from which he was liberated on the scaffold" (102). In an 1887 lithograph of this scene entitled "Surrender of Parsons," Black and Parsons are rendered tiny figures at the bar of justice, while the cavernous courtroom, with rows and rows of spectators as in a theater, looms large, dwarfing them in scale: in this illustration, Parson's surrender is noble, but the majesty and sheer massiveness of the institutions of the law dominate the scene.

In her own representations of the imprisonment and execution scenes in the *Life*, rather than "vindicating the law," Lucy Parsons charges the law, the courts, and the state with injustice. Echoing Martí, she argued that, instead of being a model republic, "with this atrocious, five-fold murder, America stands today in the vanguard as the most bloodthirsty of all the despotisms of so-called civilized Governments," despotic because the state "erected a scaffold and attempted to murder thought" (210). But instead of showing a picture of the scaffold or the "murder," the rest of her illustrations situate Albert's life within social movements, emphasize his ingenuity in eluding detectives and his selfless virtue in turning himself in, and document his activities while imprisoned. The only "gallows picture" (222) that Lucy reproduced was an account of the "final scenes copied from the city press" (210), which identified Albert as "the one American" among the anarchists as it narrated, in a classic sentimental move, his transcendence of his body and his "transfiguration" (222). While Lucy isolates this sentimental scene, she does so in order to contest mass-cultural efforts to affirm the verdict and sentimentalize the state.

Many of the other extracts, especially in the 1903 edition, make the state the villain in a melodrama of crime and punishment that recalls the popular crime literature of which Foucault writes. Parsons reproduced, for instance, the last words of the men, including Albert's final truncated sentences, before "the officers of the State performed their mission by strangling both speakers and speech" (247). Lizzie Holmes's piece also echoes this emphasis on the state's "strangling" of "the voice of the people," and adds the judgment: "Only in the State where dying men are forbidden to speak a few last words can such a scene be possible" (253). Such extracts resonate with the multiform and transnational, sentimental and sensational literature on crime and punishment that Foucault suggests registered a long history of struggles around the scaffold over state power.

While Lucy did not include a gallows picture in either of the two editions of *The Life of Albert R. Parsons*, in 1912 she finally added one to the Twenty-Fifth Anniversary Souvenir edition of her compilation of the anarchists' courtroom speeches. The engraving of the gallows scene (see figure 7.5) appeared on the second page of this text, following an ad for Albert's *Life* on the inside cover and a first page featuring engraved portraits of all of the men, including the oval portrait of Albert that appears in the mediated autobiography. The gallows scene is a full-page engraving that resembles *Leslie's* "Vindication of the Law" illustration, but with key differences: the dominating figure of the prison guard in the foreground of *Leslie's* picture disappears and the space seems even more like a theater, with a higher ceiling and more vertical space. In an adaptation that reveals much about the creative and promiscuous circulation of images among different cultural and political agents and

Figure 7.5 Scaffold Scene in Lucy Parsons, *Eleventh of November Memorial
Edition of the Famous Speeches of Our Martyrs* (1910).

movements at the turn of the long nineteenth century, the very same picture, just
cropped a little differently, occupies a full page in Schaack's *Anarchy and Anarchists*,
where he used it to illustrate the "tragedy" (644) of the execution, witnessed by
"two hundred spectators" (646), in ways that are at times at odds with his stated
purpose of helping the Assistant State's Attorney "vindicate" the "outcome" as a "vic-
tory for outraged law" (vi). The viewer's eye is drawn to the white shrouds of the
men in the center, whose faces are not hooded. Instead, the men who are about to

die look out at the audience, returning the gaze. Schaack even calls attention, like Martí, to the different "looks," "glances," and "gazes" of each of the doomed men as they "faced the spectators," whose "every eye was centered on the spot whence the Anarchists would first be seen" (646). On the other hand, a quarter of a century later, on the opposite page from the almost identical illustration in her memorial edition, Parsons instructed readers to "[r]ead the poem; then look at the gallows scene," and then "in looking upon the awful murder of our comrades, swear within your own heart never to cease your work until this accursed system of capitalism is overthrown." In doing so, she tried to guide her readers' practices of looking, so that when they viewed the gallows scene, they would see state violence in concert with capitalism rather than the vindication of the law or a spectacle of state power. While Parsons's appeal to the reader's heart is a sentimental one, she calls for action rather than voyeuristic withdrawal into the spectacle or even the watchful waiting Martí's narrator advises.

Indeed, the poem that Parsons chooses models, in the process of its composition, the very breaking with the spectacle and embrace of action that she hopes to teach her readers. She frames the poem by claiming that one of the spectators of the execution scene wrote it and then gave it to Captain Black, who read it at the funeral. Extracting the poem from Black's eulogy and making it part of the frontispiece, Parsons emphasizes the anonymous poet's exemplary response; rather than being mesmerized by the spectacle of state power, he is moved to write a poetic elegy that situates the execution scene within a long history of "the gallows old disgraced" by state "tyranny." Like Martí, the poet envisions the men "[w]earing their robes of white / As saints or martyrs might," and looking back, as they did in the picture, at the spectators as they "faced" the "world" in "conscious right." Like Martí also, he sentimentally wonders how to "judge a heart" whose "throbbing valves" were torn asunder by witnessing "wrong and suffering." Ultimately, however, the poem represents the anarchists' struggle against the state as a struggle for justice rather than affirming the resilience of republican institutions, as Martí's ending does.

But despite their different conclusions, the poet, Martí, and Lucy Parsons all use discourses of sentiment, sensation, and melodrama to insist that looking at the gallows scene means understanding that, in Black's words, "the ruthless taking of human life under the forms and by the machinery of the law is a dagger thrust into the heart of justice." While Martí still hoped republican institutions and the "machinery of law" might prevail in a truly just state, Parsons and the anarchists believed that state power was intrinsically violent. Visual culture became a site of struggle for all of these writers, as well as the world movements of which they were part, precisely because all of them challenged the state's efforts to use new forms of media and visual culture to both withdraw and intensify spectacles of violence, punishment, and the vindication of the law. In looking above, below, and beyond the nation and the state, then, we also need to attend to practices of looking and to struggles over the transformation of sentimental and sensational visual cultures at the end of the long nineteenth century.

NOTES

1 My understanding of Martí's chronicles has been greatly enhanced by Ramos's work and by my conversations with John Blanco, who translated Ramos's *Desencuentros de la modernidad en América Latina* into English and who generously shared his notes on Martí, Haymarket, and anarchism with me. See also Belnap and Fernández; David Luis Brown; Ferrer; Lomas; and Rotker.

2 Like film scholar Linda Williams, I analyze the sentimental and sensational not as discrete genres, but rather in their "more general and pervasive operation" as modes that cut across genres, where they sometimes converge and overlap.

3 For a rich analysis of Haymarket elegies and their references to Christian eschatology and gallows scenes, see Boudreau 67–104.

BIBLIOGRAPHY

"The Anarchist Funerals." *New York Evening Sun*, November 12, 1887.

Anderson, Benedict. *Under Three Flags: Anarchism and the Anti-Colonial Imagination*. New York: Verso, 2002.

Belnap, Jeffrey, and Raúl Fernández. *José Martí's "Our America": From National to Hemispheric Cultural Studies*. Durham, NC: Duke University Press, 1998.

Boudreau, Kristin. *The Spectacle of Death: Populist Literary Responses to American Capital Cases*. New York: Prometheus Books, 2006.

Brooks, Peter. *The Melodramatic Imagination: Balzac, Henry James, Melodrama, and the Mode of Excess*. New Haven, CT: Yale University Press, 1995.

Brown, David Luis. *Waves of Decolonization: Discourses of Race and Hemispheric Citizenship in Cuba, Mexico, and the United States*. Durham, NC: Duke University Press, 2008.

Brown, Joshua. *Beyond the Lines: Pictorial Reporting, Everyday Life, and the Crisis of Gilded Age America*. Berkeley: University of California Press, 2002.

Chapman, Mary, and Glenn Hendler. *Sentimental Men: Masculinity and the Politics of Affect in American Culture*. Berkeley: University of California Press, 1999.

"Chicago Anarchists." *Frank Leslie's Illustrated Newspaper*, November 19, 1997: 219.

Clymer, Jeffory. *America's Culture of Terrorism: Violence, Capitalism, and the Written Word*. Chapel Hill: University of North Carolina Press, 2002.

Ferrer, Ada. *Insurgent Cuba: Race, Nation, and Revolution, 1868–1898*. Chapel Hill: University of North Carolina Press, 1999.

Foucault, Michel. *Discipline and Punish: The Birth of the Prison*. 2nd edition. Translated by Alan Sheridan. New York: Vintage Books, 1995.

Gaines, Jane. *Fire and Desire: Mixed Race Movies in the Silent Era*. Chicago: University of Chicago Press, 2001.

Gillman, Susan. "The Epistemology of Slave Conspiracy." *Modern Fiction Studies* 49.1 (Spring 2003): 101–123.

Goldsby, Jacqueline. *A Spectacular Secret: Lynching in American Life and Literature*. Chicago: University of Chicago Press, 2006.

Hartman, Saidiya. *Scenes of Subjection: Terror, Slavery, and Self-Making in Nineteenth-Century America*. New York: Oxford University Press, 1997.

Illinois v. August Spies et al. trial transcript no. 1, Court's instructions to the jury on behalf of the people, August 19, 1886. Chicago Historical Society Haymarket Digital

Collection. http://www.chicagohs.org/hadc/transcript/volume0/000-050/O001-010. htm. Accessed May 30, 2010.

Lazo, Rodrigo. *Writing to Cuba: Filibustering and Cuban Exiles in the United States.* Chapel Hill: University of North Carolina Press, 2005.

Lomas, Laura. *Translating Empire: Jose Martí, Migrant Latino Subjectivities, and American Modernities.* Durham, NC: Duke University Press, 2009.

Martí, Jose. *Obras Completas.* Vol. 11: *En Las Estados Unidos.* La Habana: Editorial de Ciencias Sociales, 1975.

Parsons, Lucy. *Life of Albert R. Parsons: With Brief History of the Labor Movement in America.* Chicago: Lucy E. Parsons, 1889; 1903.

———. *Twenty-Fifth Anniversary Eleventh of November Memorial Edition of the Famous Speeches of Our Martyrs.* Chicago: Lucy E. Parsons, 1913.

Poyo, Gerald. *With All and for the Good of All: The Emergence of Popular Nationalism in the Cuban Communities of the United States, 1848–1898.* Durham, NC: Duke University Press, 1989.

Ramos, Julio. *Divergent Modernities: Culture and Politics in Nineteenth-Century Latin America.* Trans. John Blanco. Durham, NC: Duke University Press, 2001.

Ronning, C. Neale. *Jose Martí and the Émigré Colony in Key West: Leadership and State Formation.* New York: Praeger, 1990.

Rotker, Susana. *The American Chronicles of Jose Marti: Journalism and Modernity in Spanish America.* Hanover, NH: Dartmouth University Press, 2000.

Schaack, Michael J. *Anarchy and Anarchists: A History of the Red Terror and the Social Revolution in America and Europe.* Chicago: F. J. Schulte and Company, 1889.

Sekula, Alan. "The Body and the Archive." *The Contest of Meaning: Critical Histories of Photography.* Ed. R. Bolton. Cambridge, MA: MIT Press, 1992.

Smith, Carl. *Urban Disorder and the Shape of Belief.* Chicago: University of Chicago Press, 1995.

Smith, Shawn Michelle. *Photography on the Color Line: W. E. B. Du Bois, Race, and Visual Culture.* Durham, NC: Duke University Press, 2004.

Spies, August. *August Spies' Auto-Biography; His Speech in Court, and General Notes.* Chicago: Nina Van Zandt, 1887.

Sturken, Marita, and Lisa Cartwright. *Practices of Looking: An Introduction to Visual Culture.* New York: Oxford University Press, 2004.

Wexler, Laura. *Tender Violence: Domestic Visions in an Age of U.S. Imperialism.* Chapel Hill: University of North Carolina Press, 2000.

Williams, Linda. *Playing the Race Card: Melodramas of Black and White from Uncle Tom to O. J. Simpson.* Princeton, NJ: Princeton University Press, 2001.

CHAPTER 8

TRANSATLANTIC VS. HEMISPHERIC: TONI MORRISON'S LONG NINETEENTH CENTURY

ANNA BRICKHOUSE

READERS may well wonder why a chapter on Toni Morrison's *A Mercy*, published in the twenty-first century and set in the seventeenth, belongs in a volume of studies on nineteenth-century American literature. Let me cut to the chase, then, by announcing the end point up front: I will be arguing that Morrison's 2008 novel meditates powerfully on nineteenth-century American literary history, and how we have read and misread it. The first methodological impulse behind this argument is fairly straightforward: I am working from the assumption that literature develops its own theories about the interpretive modes of those who read it, and therefore that traditional periodization need not limit how we think about literary history—indeed, that we unnecessarily limit ourselves and the texts we study if we assume an exclusive relation between a work and the narrow temporal slice in which it is produced, in which it is first received or, for that matter, in which it is set. According to this logic, Morrison's novel can speak as productively to the topic of "nineteenth-century American literature" as can a novel by Cooper, Hawthorne, Stowe, or Melville. As the scare quotes are meant to suggest, a second assumption at work here involves the phrase "American literature" as an always vexed metonymy for the tradition of belles lettres in the United States—a phrase that now holds an arguably tenuous relationship to the actual territory demarcated by U.S. national bound-aries. In this regard too Morrison's *A Mercy* addresses the topic of this volume—nineteenth-century *American* literature—as well as its troubled parameters in the wake of the so-called transnational turn in (U.S.-) American studies. In fact, the novel's seventeenth-century setting—a geo-temporal expanse that encompasses not just the Anglo-American colonies but Europe's relation to Africa and the early modern Americas—critically frames the problems and possibilities of nineteenth-century "American literature" and the critical tradition that we have inherited from it. As I will argue here, *A Mercy*'s meta-historiographical project, which explores the racialized Atlantic world of a particular seventeenth-century colonial American moment, lays the theoretical foundation for the novel's related meta-literary project: a reconceptualizing of nineteenth-century (U.S.-) American writing as a national literary geography that both naturalizes and sometimes actively renders invisible the early modern world system from which it can never quite imaginatively separate. To put this another way, *A Mercy*'s seventeenth-century historical context registers a compelling argument about nineteenth-century American literature—and, most important, how it continues to shape our own practices of reading. Ultimately, the novel stages a series of critical insights into the disciplinary moment of the early twenty-first century, allowing us to acknowledge and to reevaluate the distinct and often competing transatlantic and hemispheric trajectories our field has developed for comprehending the long nineteenth century of the American literary past.

The Geography of Critical Priority: or, Should the Land Be an Afterthought?

In an eerie scene midway through *A Mercy*, the ailing character Rebekka, an English indentured servant turned tobacco bride, recalls what she terms the "life of water" revealed during her transatlantic journey from London to Virginia (Morrison 73). In a brief flashback that occurs as she hallucinates from smallpox and the strong possibility of her own death, Rebekka remembers talking to the sea and promis-ing to "keep [its] secrets": "that you own the globe," as she says to the ocean, "and [that] land is an afterthought to entertain you; that the world beneath you is both graveyard and heaven" (73). In this curious antagonism between the oceanic and the territorial, Rebekka experiences the vertigo of a deep conceptual shift: that the water came first, that territoriality is mere "afterthought" to the metaphysical pri-macy and conceptual priority of the ocean; that the land is "own[ed]" by, subsumed by the sea—both "graveyard" of the Middle Passage and, in a philosophical involu-tion of the Christian telos, the position of "heaven." In this alternative cosmology, the land does not take center stage, does not enlighten or instruct; the role of the land is rather to "entertain" with its anthropocentric narrative, its unfolding drama of human dwelling.

But let's rephrase Rebekka's Atlantic-borne observation as a question—and turn briefly from Morrison's novel to the critical tension that this scene evokes: *Does* the ocean own the globe? *Is* land merely an afterthought, or should it be? From the point of view of transatlantic studies, the answer may well be yes: as Kate Flint puts it in a 2009 review essay in *American Literary History,* land is "the potentially tillable, fertile territory of individual nation-states"—and thus, of course, an inevitably compromised unit of analysis, against which we may pit "the fluid, mutable, dangerous oceanic, the Atlantic...the body of water that both unites and divides": "an undulating surface"; the "space of translation and transformation, rather than of straightforward transmission"; "international territory, un-ownable" (Flint 324–334). Proponents of hemispheric studies will argue that their approach shares much of this analytic pliability. In lieu of undulating water, sedimentation and overlap become the recurrent metaphors for this subfield that takes as its organizing frame the landmass of North, Central, and South America and the proximate islands. Its practitioners advertise (to quote some work in this vein) "an emphasis on taking account of overlapping and sedimented histories," on addressing "intricately intertwined geographies," on parsing "overlapping, mutually inflecting fields" (Levander and Levine 3, 5).

Critics have warned of the perils that inhere in each mode. On the hemispheric side of things lies the possibility of reinscribing U.S. imperialism as academic formation, a version of American studies emanating outward from its U.S., usually English-department center and into the inquiry fields of other (often less funded) disciplines (Jay, McClellan, and Fox). Second (and less convincing, to me, at least), there is the ostensible risk of what Paul Giles has called "hemispheric partiality," the risk of "replacing nationalist essentialism predicated upon state autonomy with a geographical essentialism predicated on physical contiguity" (649). As Giles certainly knows, the problem of "geographical essentialism"   even if one were to agree upon its supposed urgency—is hardly an intellectual failing of hemispheric studies alone: the term "transatlantic" bespeaks its own geographical centricity. Moreover, despite (or perhaps because of) the celebrated fluidity of the Atlantic, the field originated with, and has sometimes tended toward, a narrowly conceived crossing between England and northeastern Anglo-America—and has thus required the correctives of Gilroy's "Black Atlantic," Roach's "circum-Atlantic," Ian Baucom's "specters of the Atlantic," to name just a few of the concepts that have redressed transatlanticism for both its elision of Africa and its Anglophone exceptionalism, and that, as Roach puts it, emphasized "the centrality of the diasporic and genocidal histories of Africa and the Americas, North and South" (4).

Proponents of both transatlantic and hemispheric studies have embraced expansion as a potential way out of their respective impasses. Baucom, for example, proposes redefining Atlantic for these purposes as "[n]ot...a delimited territory," not "determinate"; instead, he advocates an "expansion...that seeks to enlarge the temporal, canonic, geographic, and linguistic boundaries of an Atlanticist discourse" ("Introduction," 6). Similarly, Wai Chee Dimock posits "hemispheric studies" as "any research protocol that goes beyond a single nation, that requires more than one continent for an adequate archive": "a way to rethink the contours of the planet, looking East and West as well as North and South, the better to multiply the platforms on which alternate worlds might emerge" ("Hemispheric Islam," 32). Baucom and Dimock make use of a similar grammatical loophole to build their respective cases for an expanded transatlantic and hemispheric studies: Baucom articulates "transatlantic" as "a formulation...in which the Atlantic functions not as a noun or a proper name but as an adjectival qualifier of now" '("Introduction," 8); Dimock (following Diana Taylor) proposes using the term "hemisphere" not as "a substantive noun, indicating a fixed pair of continents," but as "a conjuring verb—at once 'animative' and 'performative'—that invites us to reconnect the world's landscapes" ("Hemispheric Islam," 32). Defined in such ways, each of the two terms—transatlantic and hemispheric—would thus encompass the perspective of the other in its multidirectional analytic. Both terms would presumably gesture toward other geographic axes as well, moving ever outward to the fulsomeness of planetarity. But why stop there? Why risk a *geo*centric view and yet another exceptionalism, when we could—to quote Poe's *Eureka*—undertake the "Universe" itself, "using the word in its most comprehensive and only legitimate acceptation [as] the utmost conceivable expanse of space, with all things spiritual and material, that can be imagined to exist within the compass of that expanse" (8)? In this spirit, Jennifer Greeson reads Poe's "Universe of Stars" as a satiric stand-in for nineteenth-century U.S. expansionism (159–168); following her, we might take Poe's words as a cautionary note vis-à-vis both transatlantic and hemispheric approaches as well as, for that matter, any form of transnational American studies that ventures too close to the forbidden fruits of synthesis and totality. As Harry Harootunian puts it, "by appealing to enlarged, singular spatial categories—currently the global and empire dominate our agendas—the arena of social action has broadened and displaced other kinds of causality traditionally employed to account for social phenomena" (24).

My own inclination, nevertheless, would be to retain both the transatlantic and the hemispheric models within our literary-critical practices. The different geographical axes of "transatlantic" and "hemispheric," and the disparate but overlapping cuts of the map attending each, introduce separate (if also overlapping) theoretical insights and archives of knowledge to which, often, we would not otherwise have access. This, at least, we know: how one maps and bounds the territorial or oceanic dimensions of the investigation gives significant shape to its findings. It also seems to account, directly or indirectly, for the particular limitations associated with the critical trajectories attaching to each cartographic lens. In the transatlantic approach, we may detect a certain reactiveness in the continual return, however inventive, to the American cultural relation to England (is it imitative?—competitive?—belated?—influential?—deferential?); in the hemispheric approach, we may find a certain aggressive predictability of the U.S. imperialism narrative, despite the forcefulness of its necessity. This is why, in my view, we should also retain the generative grammatical loopholes, however expansionist, registered by Baucom and Dimock. The blind spots of each approach lie precisely in the insistence on the primacy and the necessary boundedness of one's respective cut of the map; there is a critical advantage, on the other hand, in always holding that cut in tension with what has been sliced away. Without dispensing with either the transatlantic or hemispheric lens, we can acknowledge a world system—as well as a global/local dialectic—in which each takes part: we can continue to embrace *both* geo-critical trajectories, that is, and still acknowledge—to adapt Fernand Braudel adapting Marc Bloch—"there is no 'transatlantic' or 'hemispheric' history; there is a world history" (20, *The Identity of France*; see also Wallerstein and Mignolo). Moreover, the idea that these critical modes are or need be mutually exclusive is just as misleading as the idea that we must choose definitively between diachronic and synchronic readings of the past, between the *longue durée* or the thick description, as if the one necessarily precludes the other. We open ourselves to more nimble conceptions of space and time, I think, once we dispense with what are ultimately false choices.[1]

THE COMPETING GEOGRAPHIES OF COLONIAL AMERICAN HISTORY: OR, SHOULD WE "REMOVE RACE FROM SLAVERY"?

With its territorial-oceanic tensions, Morrison's *A Mercy* provides an illuminating perspective on one such false choice—a choice that produces, as the novel suggests, insidious disavowal in one form or another. To understand the full extent of the novel's contribution in this regard, we need first to look closely at its metahistoriographical project; for, like much of Morrison's recent work, *A Mercy* enlists a number of critical conversations about contemporary historical imagining.[2] Most explicit is Morrison's attempt to "remove race from slavery," as she put it in early interviews about *A Mercy*, in exploring the colonial American past—a project that entails creating a doubled perspective upon slavery in both its transatlantic and its hemispheric historical dimensions (Norris). The novel develops its transatlantic perspective upon slavery, as Morrison herself has acknowledged, largely out of research presented in the 2008 study *White Cargo: The Forgotten History of Britain's White Slaves in America*, by Don Jordan and Michael Walsh. As its subtitle suggests, *White Cargo* addresses the history of Anglo-American traffic in indentured British servants, deploying a self-conscious transatlantic critical frame to argue against the long-standing nationalist "creation myth" of America: that "free men and women . . . created a democratic and egalitarian model society more or less from scratch," only to see it marred by the onset of African chattel slavery (16).

Following *White Cargo*'s historiographical impulse, Morrison's novel meditates on the variety of free, enslaved, and indentured forms of labor intertwining with each other across colonial America. The central character is Florens, separated from her enslaved African mother at the age of eight, when their owner gives her away as his payment on a defaulted loan. The lender, Florens's new owner, is an English immigrant and failed farmer named Jacob, whose land is unsuccessfully worked by a varied range of enslaved, indentured, and free laborers: Florens and two other female slaves, indigenous Lina and mixed-race Sorrow; Jacob's wife Rebekka, also purchased, but in this case as a form of "white cargo" from England in exchange for tobacco; a free black man known only by the name of his profession as "the blacksmith"; and two British indentured servants named Scully and Willard Bond.

The novel's transatlantic historical vision, which allows readers to follow its characters through their memories back and forth between colonial America and seventeenth-century England, shores up *White Cargo*'s most general argument: that enslaved and indentured forms of labor were largely indistinguishable—indeed, that we could more accurately conceive of both groups as slaves, whether African or British.[3] Working from this premise, Morrison's novel parses a historical turning point explored in *White Cargo*'s fourteenth chapter, when America's "white slaves" began separating from other enslaved groups along rigidly calcified racial lines after a specific moment of colonial violence (205–212). Morrison describes this shift near the beginning of her nonlinear narrative:

> Half a dozen years ago an army of blacks, natives, whites, mulattoes—freedmen, slaves, and indentured—had waged war against local gentry led by members of that very class. When that "people's war" lost its hopes to the hangman, the work it had done—which included the slaughter of opposing tribes and running the Carolinas off their land—spawned a thicket of new laws authorizing chaos in defense of order. By eliminating manumissions, gatherings, travel and bearing arms for black people only; by granting license to any white to kill any black for any reason; by compensating owners for a slave's maiming or death, they separated and protected all whites from all others forever. (10)

The novel thus announces as its point of critical departure the historical tipping point enacted by the 1676 series of uprisings in colonial Virginia known as Bacon's Rebellion. More specifically, Morrison concerns herself with the eruption of social contradictions signaled by the rebellion and their subsequent containment through what Theodore Allen famously called "the invention of the white race" (239)—or, in the novel's phrase, "a hammer wielded in the interests of the gentry's profits" (10). Morrison's listing of the particular "new laws" designed to distinguish "all whites from all others forever" suggests her own investment in dismantling the historical narrative of "innate racism" advanced by Winthrop Jordan, and refuted via the work of Allen and other historians demonstrating the legal institution of white privilege first encoded in the "Act Concerning Servants and Slaves."[4]

But if the novel's transatlantic perspective allows Morrison to "remove race from slavery"—and thus to see both the forgotten British "white cargo" traded into colonial America and the nature of American un-freedom just before race was "invented"—its concurrent hemispheric perspective critically intervenes into the historiography of this "invention of whiteness," as Allen and others have theorized it. Specifically, *A Mercy* imaginatively investigates the emergence of a white colonial identity not as a proto-national enterprise or peculiarly *American* ideology, but as an international mode of production that in turn lays the foundations for a trans-national and racialized system of capitalism. From its hemispheric vantage, that is, *A Mercy* witnesses the twinned birth of whiteness and a capitalist world system in the arc of Jacob's ineluctable transformation, over the course of the novel's second chapter, from failing farmer and local lender into an overseas investor. This trans-formation culminates in a Virginia tavern when Jacob gets a particular lesson in economics from a more seasoned investor, who spells out in no uncertain terms what we might call the spatiotemporal logic of hemispheric investment: that "[a] month [is] the time…from [a Barbados sugar] mill to Boston," that in a month, "a man can turn fifty pounds into five times as much." Telling "mesmerizing tales" of "exotic places" in the wider Americas, where birthrates ensure an ever-expanding supply of labor in "a stew of mulattoes, creoles, zambos, mestizos, lobos, chinos, coyotes," the investor assures Jacob that the outcome of hemispheric finance is guar-anteed: "Each and every month five times the investment. For certain" (30–31).

What the novel makes clear from this hemispheric perspective upon its invest-ment plot is that the so-called invention of whiteness cannot be fully understood within a national framework or along an East-West, Anglo-American axis. The outcome of the overseas investment plot for Scully and Bond, Jacob's two white indentured servants, makes this clear. By the end of the novel they have profited from Jacob's investment in Barbados and, pondering the money they are now being paid for the first time, the narrator observes, "Perhaps the wages were not as much as the blacksmith's, but for Scully and…Bond it was enough to imagine a future" (156). The connotations of the name "Bond" thus broaden over the course of the novel from the original seventeenth-century conflation of enslaved and indentured or *bond labor* to the *interest-yielding bond* of emergent racial identity that will soar in value with the passing of the next two centuries. In the transnational racial econ-omy adumbrated at the novel's close, the scant amount the two white servants earn may indeed be "enough to imagine a future"—but it is not the peculiarly American "wages of whiteness," to use David Roediger's phrase, they are being paid. What Willard's last name articulates is instead something more like a *domestic bond*—a bond whose potential interest-bearing value is always dependent upon an interna-tional division of labor, upon that ever-fluctuating distance between Barbados and Boston, margin and center, periphery and core.

The Transatlantic Frontier of Nineteenth-Century American Literature: East-West or "Afric and Much More"?

It is from this vantage of a racialized world system that Morrison's novel sheds light on the ultimately false choice between transatlantic and hemispheric—a choice we have in some sense unwittingly inherited from nineteenth-century American literature and its attendant critical tradition. Morrison's exploration of this false inheritance is, at least for the purposes of this volume, the novel's most compelling contribution: to reconceptualize *literary* history by exploring how nineteenth-century literary formulations of national geography work to naturalize, overwrite, or disguise the very uneven developments and concomitant racial identities that *A Mercy* engages head-on.

From its outset, the novel produces a sense of geographic disorientation both at the formal level (we have no idea where we are when the narration begins, only glancing references by the sixth page to "wild plums," "wicked Virginians," and "Mary's Land") and at the thematic and historical levels (a key journey in the novel is Jacob's trip from Virginia to Maryland, but it takes him *southward*—seventeenth-century Virginia reached from the Chesapeake Bay to Massachusetts, but skipping over the royal colony of Mary's Land, or Maryland). This disorientation begins to work on a more conceptual level when the novel starts to trouble the neat symbolic abstractions that have often been mapped onto the nineteenth-century landscapes of canonical U.S. literary history. For example, the central protagonist Florens also undertakes a journey, this one with a familiar psycho-geographical itinerary—an itinerary that moves along the horizontal axis of the transatlantic. Traveling alone, Florens goes west, encounters Indians, and along the way exhibits a newfound self-reliance and ability to commune with nature. This familiar westerly trajectory is, of course, the imaginative terrain of nineteenth-century novelists, poets, and critics of the American frontier, from the narratives of James Fenimore Cooper to the historiography of Frederick Jackson Turner, and from the poems of William Cullen Bryant to the essays of Ralph Waldo Emerson, that venerable "meeting point between savagery and civilization" that not only coincides with the East-West axis of the transatlantic but purports to establish a transatlantic difference par excellence: American exceptionalism itself (Turner 3).

To travel into the West was, as Turner put it, "[l]ittle by little [to] transform the wilderness":

> but the outcome is not the old Europe, not simply the development of Germanic germs....The fact is, that here is a new product that is American. At first, the frontier was the Atlantic coast. It was the frontier of Europe in a very real sense. Moving westward, the frontier became more and more American....Thus the advance of the frontier has meant a steady movement away from the influence of Europe....(4)

But what begins as Florens's mythic journey westward—a distinctly nineteenth-century American literary trajectory that might have taken her into sovereign selfhood and, ultimately, U.S. statehood—derails violently when she wanders into a misplaced patch of Puritans straight out of Hawthorne.[5] Bent on ferreting out witchcraft, the Puritans take one look at Florens and demand a full-scale examination of her naked form in a scene of subjection in which she must perform her own hypervisibility, to use Saidiya Hartman's term, before their collective gaze (22).

When they pronounce her the product of Hawthorne's diabolical apotheosis, the "Black Man," Morrison's Puritans remind readers of the elided historical geography underpinning the abstract figure of theological terror we find in Hawthorne's demonic Black Man—a geography realized when one of the Puritans describes Florens as "Afric[,] Afric and much more" (111). The narrative similarly strips away the metaphysical guise of their efforts to condemn an accused witch, a young Puritan woman, when she explains to her mother that "it is the pasture they crave" (109)—not, in other words, a rigorous Calvinist fear of the "blackness of darkness" that drives them, as the tradition running from Herman Melville to Harry Levin would have it, but rather greed for the land itself and its means of production.[6]

At the same time, in a pointed reversal of the semiotics of the *Scarlet Letter* (1850), the Puritans take away from Florens what she calls "the letter"—the text of ownership that has authorized her to travel—and the metaphysical itinerary of her westward journey toward freedom implodes into the stark plotline of her reduction from social being to nonentity: "I am a thing apart," she says. "With the letter I belong and am lawful. Without it I am a weak calf abandoned by the herd…a minion with no telltale signs but a darkness I am born with.…Is this dying mine alone?" (115). The question implies a particular argument about the object of literary history and its geographical constitution: the literary landscape of Hawthorne's Puritans is not an empty space; it is also, unmistakably, the site of Florens's social death in which racial blackness overlaps with the Puritans' sense of moral blackness.[7] To read Hawthorne through this scene in her own novel, Morrison suggests, is not just to recognize the shadowy figure of the Africanist presence in the text, as she has encouraged us to do in her more directly literary-critical work, but instead to see how the space of Puritan Boston itself might be reconceived as the space of a western frontier, of "Afric, Afric and much more"—of a present that is simultaneously the past as well as the future.[8] Morrison thus points us toward a practice of reading that attends to literature's particular ability to show the palimpsestic quality of both space and time: to walk, as it were, into this scene in Morrison's novel is to move across a temporally ambiguous textual landscape with a sense of both foreshadowing and déjà vu, a sense that we are, at once, both here and there—in a seventeenth-century western frontier in the Virginia that is north of Maryland, in the seventeenth-century Puritan environs of Boston, in a seventeenth-century Afric Angola figured by the Puritans.[9] The scene's complex intercalation of nature and frontier, both within and in excess of a definitive region, thus deepens and widens the geo-temporality of nineteenth-century American romanticism, from Emerson's woods to Bryant's prairies and Hawthorne's untamed forests.[10]

It is hardly surprising, then, that when Florens arrives at her western destination—the house of the free blacksmith, with whom she is in love—she finds (contrary to the transatlantic logic of the American frontier) that it is she, not the land, who is, in the blacksmith's words, "nothing but wilderness" (141). The violent scene of their final conversation concerns the safety of a child—a son whom the blacksmith has adopted, and whom Florens has physically attacked because she perceives him as a threat, a rival for the love of the blacksmith, just as her younger brother was long ago, in her eyes, a rival for their mother's affections. Florens's conversation with the blacksmith embeds a disagreement about the significance of freedom and the future of a child, and as such it distinctly recalls a remarkably similar scene from the American literary past—a scene from Harriet Beecher Stowe's *Uncle Tom's Cabin* (1852, 26–31) that, restaged in Morrison's novel, shifts the geographic axis of the text from east-west to north-south, or from transatlantic to hemispheric.

Transatlantic Innocence and/as Hemispheric Disavowal

In Stowe's novel, Eliza and George Harris—like Florens and the blacksmith—argue about the meaning of slavery and its consequences for their son Harry (who corresponds to the blacksmith's adopted boy). While Stowe's Eliza accepts her enslavement as the duty of a good Christian, George pronounces himself "a man as much as [his master] is" and sets out north to secure the future freedom of their child who may be sold, at any moment, to "nobody knows who" (27, 30). Reprising and contorting this famous scene from the beginning of *Uncle Tom's Cabin*, Morrison's novel figures instead the blacksmith's devastating rejection of Florens: "[Y]ou are a slave...your head is empty and your body is wild...Own yourself, woman, and leave us be. You could have killed this child...as I live and breathe, [you are] a slave by choice" (141). The blacksmith's rebuke seems directed not simply at Florens but at Stowe and her representation of obedient Eliza who—like Florens—has been quasi-adopted by her owners. Even Stowe's George concedes, speaking to and about Eliza, "they have brought you up like a child, fed you, clothed you, indulged you, and taught you, so that you have a good education; that is some reason why they should claim you" (28). The blacksmith, however, rejects this logic as well as the sentimental closure potentially promised by Florens's journey to find him.

For it is ultimately a logic of geographic disavowal upon which George's concession—and Stowe's novel as a whole—lays its claim to moral authority. Eliza's benevolent enslavement in Kentucky partakes of the larger northern-inclined trajectory of her life: born in New Orleans, she is bought and "brought...up" to Kentucky by Mr. Shelby, who saves her from the Louisiana and indeed Caribbean fate of her mother, Cassy: concubinage and degradation at the hands of Simon Legree, who has "learned his trade well...in the West Indies" (496, 427). Eliza's life journey is thus ever northward into new regional spheres of increasing moral legitimacy, from her salvation from New Orleans to her god-fearing but still partially flawed home in Kentucky to her eventual refuge in an Ohio Quaker settlement without slaves. Like Eliza's trajectory, the novel as a whole moves along a North-South axis and consistently deploys the greater, hemispheric South as a disavowed foil for the moral heart of the nation, New England. As Stowe's narrator rhapsodically observes:

> Whoever has travelled in the New England States will remember, in some cool
> village, the large farmhouse, with its clean-swept grassy yard...and remember the
> air of order and stillness, of perpetuity and unchanging repose....Nothing lost,
> or out of order; not a picket loose in the fence, not a particle of litter in the turfy
> yard....Within, he will remember wide, clean rooms, where nothing ever seems
> to be doing or going to be done....There are no servants in the house....(187)

Against this New England ideal lies the Gothic Caribbean: the Marquis-de-Sade Louisiana plantation of Simon Legree; the West Indian marriage of master and slave that allows George's sister to reconstruct herself as the "French lady," Madame de Thoux; and, in the background, the "San Domingo hour"—the Haitian Revolution—overshadowing the novel as a whole (494, 315). And though Eliza, George, and their extended family will never experience Miss Ophelia's beloved Vermont or any other New England state—rushed as they are to francophone Montreal and, ultimately, off the North-South axis altogether, to France and then Liberia—the hemispheric geography of Stowe's novel is what makes possible the ostensible moral innocence of its northern pastoral.

Morrison's novel, committed to interrupting the simplistic symbolic directionality of the American literary past, sends Florens on a different sort of journey. She now goes not north or west, but back east to return to slavery, somewhere in the Virginia "North," in what is now New York. In a dark nod to Eliza's celebrated barefoot flight to freedom on a "raft of ice," "her stockings cut from her feet" (79), Florens notes that she too "ha[s] no shoes" as she watches "an ice floe cut away from the riverbank in deep winter" (158). But where Eliza's flight charts the moral geography of the nation—from the lawless, slaveholding, racially mixed, francophone, hemispheric South into the virtuous, orderly, domestic, and utterly Anglo-American North—Florens's journey tracks and retracks across a map of nineteenth-century literary nationhood exploring the ideological contours of its transatlantic and hemispheric landscapes. Such moments in Morrison's text do not merely mark allusions to a prior textual landscape, in other words. Rather, they point to a deeper intervention into the structural relations between geography and literary history that account for our readerly disorientation as we move south, north, west, and east with a narrative that refuses to allow us an omniscient view of the landscape from above. At the same time, the shifting and unsettling cardinal axes of Morrison's narrative remind us that the fixed symbolic coordinates of Stowe's and Hawthorne's novels are neither natural nor inevitable. In this sense, *A Mercy* invites a practice of reading that draws theoretical sustenance from literature's capacity for figuring the complexity of time and space while also holding that generative capacity in tension with the spaces of literary production itself: juxtaposing the simultaneously seventeenth- and nineteenth-century Boston world of Hawthorne's historical imagination as well as the northeastern publishing center that marketed both his novel and Stowe's; and, finally, the relation of *this* center to those sites it constitutes as peripheral—including the sugar mill in Barbados where, in Morrison's twenty-first-century novel, seventeenth-century Jacob Vaark has made his investments. Ultimately, the geographical dislocations of *A Mercy* suggest a defining pattern of both nineteenth-century American literature and, to some degree, of our own misreading of it: specifically, how transatlantic models of literary history have enabled a concomitant literary history of hemispheric disavowal. Crucial here is the novel's early elaboration of Jacob as a figure of transatlantic-immigrant innocence. We first see Jacob traveling through a primeval "[f]og, Atlantic and reeking of plant life," and soon learn that he is a "ratty orphan, making a place out of no place, a temperate living from raw life" (9). Jacob, it seems, is walking into Morrison's novel right off the pages of R. W. B. Lewis's *American Adam*, bounding forth from the New World garden in self-made glory. In Lewis's famous description, the American Adam is "the hero of a new adventure: an individual emancipated from history, happily bereft of ancestry, untouched and undefiled by the usual inheritances of family and race, an individual standing alone, self-reliant and self propelling, ready to confront whatever awaited him with the aid of his own unique and inherent resources" (5)—or, as Morrison's narrator puts it, "Breathing the air of a world so new, almost alarming in rawness and temptation, never failed to invigorate him ... the warm gold of the bay ... forests untouched since Noah, shorelines beautiful enough to bring tears, wild food for the taking" (11).

Radiating the hallmark optimism and good will of American characterology (as well as the literary impulse to Adamic "invention"), Jacob "wave[s] to the sloopmen" and stops "to free the bloody hindleg of a young raccoon stuck in a tree break" (9, 11). Philosophically inclined toward both natural rights and pragmatism, he understands that in this world of competing imperial land claims, it is the "natives, to whom it all belonged," and he pays "scant attention to old or new names of towns or forts": "In his own geography, he [is] moving from Algonquin to Sesquehanna via Chesapeake on through Lenape" (12–13). In other words, like the Adamic Leatherstocking, Jacob apprehends the landscape within a native rather than a European framework—a trait which, as in Cooper's portrait of Natty Bumppo, also a follower of the Lenape, clearly bespeaks a kind of cartographic innocence vis-à-vis the aggressions of colonialism.[11] But as the novel makes clear, when Jacob arrives at his destination, his state of transatlantic innocence entails a structure of hemispheric disavowal—just as in Stowe—that projects the worst violence of colonialism and its offspring in plantation culture onto a morally suspect geography that he imagines as cordoned off from his own new world. The site of this foil to Jacob's American Eden turns out to be a plantation called *Jublio*, owned by a Portuguese slave trader, Senhor D'Ortega, who has defaulted on a loan from Jacob after the loss of his ship and its human cargo.[12] The symbolism of the names winks broadly at the reader with what Jacob, referring to the sensibility of the entire province, calls "the lax, flashy cunning of the Papists" (14): *Jublio* signals the time of Jubilee, the consecrated fiftieth year in which, according to the instructions in Leviticus, liberty shall be proclaimed throughout the land to all its inhabitants, when slaves are freed and debts are forgiven (Leviticus 25:11–54). Jubilee, of course, has a long tradition in U.S. cultural history as an expression for and reference to freedom from slavery; as the name of a Portuguese slave trader's plantation, *Jublio* evokes the linguistic hybridity of the Americas, a phonetic variation of the Latin *jubilo*, as well as a convergence of the Portuguese *júbilo* or joy and *jubleu* or jubilee. As a form of Jubilee, *Jublio* thus articulates a dark, heavily Catholic irony that is entirely lost on innocent, Protestant Jacob, who has arrived, of course, to collect on a defaulted loan: there is no liberation in sight for D'Ortega's slaves.[13]

The name D'Ortega, as well, resonates with hemispheric allusions during the ensuing scene of cultural clash whose contradictions Jacob sums up with a simple rhetorical question: "A trader asked to dine with a gentleman?" (14). One is a middle-class Anglophone merchant-lender, the other a landowning, Iberian aristocrat; and their seething antipathy for each other recalls the famous critique of another Ortega, the Spanish philosopher José Ortega y Gasset, who famously characterized the early twentieth century by the rise of an insidious mass culture, exemplified by the commercialism and bland homogeneity of the modern United States, which had its roots precisely in the kind of democratic, Anglo-merchant sensibility represented by Jacob.[14] Ortega's philosophy and his concept of *razón historico* has proved extraordinarily influential among Latin American intellectuals, from Octavio Paz to critics of twenty-first-century neoliberalism (Garrido 142–155). It has found particular resonance among those writers who wish to pit an elite, honor-bound, aesthetically inclined, historical-minded, melancholic culture against a coldly pragmatic, progress-oriented, future-facing, endlessly optimistic, and ultimately barbaric cultural wasteland to the north. For Paz, Morrison's fellow Nobel laureate, Ortega's legacy in Latin American thought simply could not be overestimated, for his ideas were "instruments, weapons, mental objects which we use … not for the purpose of knowing ourselves or contemplating essences but to clear a way through our circumstances, to dialogue with the world, with our past and our fellow men" (102, also cited in Zamora 30). For Morrison to summon Ortega's name in the context of this meeting between the English immigrant Jacob and a Portuguese plantation owner is thus to reorient the novel's Anglo-American transatlantic framework along an Iberian-hemispheric axis.

While the philosopher Ortega warned against an ongoing sinking of Western culture to its lowest common denominators in commercialism and mediocrity, an imminent "revolt of the masses," to quote the title of his best-known work, the plantation world of D'Ortega leaves Morrison's Jacob unsettled for quite different reasons that are nevertheless signaled by the shared name of its owner and the modern author: "surrounded by a passel of slaves," Jacob hears in their foreboding silence "an avalanche at an unseen distance" (22). A portent of slave revolution and a self-made Anglo-American in a vexed encounter with an inscrutable Latin slave-trader: Morrison's novel nods unmistakably here to Herman Melville—perhaps, of all nineteenth-century American writers, the most ironic and self-knowing author to represent the psychology of hemispheric disavowal. Drawing on Melville, Morrison lifts off her transatlantic protagonist what has until now been the mask of Cooper's Natty Bumpo, a veil of cartographic innocence. Underneath, we find a narrative point of view uncannily like that of Melville's Captain Delano as he considers his Iberian interlocutor in *Benito Cereno* (1855). As Morrison's narrator observes,

D'Ortega's strut as they had walked the property disgusted [Jacob]. Moreover, he
believed the set of that jaw, the drooping lids, hid something soft, as if his hands,
accustomed to reins, whips, and lace had never held a plow or axed a tree. There
was something beyond Catholic in him, something corrupt and overripe. (23)

As their confrontation moves threateningly toward potential violence, we might as
well be on board the *San Dominick* watching the face-off between a corrupt Iberian
colonial order and a self-reliant Anglo-American: when D'Ortega's

hand move[s] to his hip...Jacob's eyes follow...as the ringed fingers
curl...around a scabbard. Would he? Would this curdled, arrogant fop really
assault his creditor, murder him and, claiming self-defense, prerogative, rid
himself of both debt and social insult even though it would mean complete
financial disaster, considering that his coffers were as empty as his scabbard? The
soft fingers fumbled for the absent haft...Out here in the wilderness dependent
on paid guards nowhere in sight...[Jacob] felt like laughing. Where else but in
this disorganized world would such an encounter be possible? Where else could
rank tremble before courage? Jacob turned away, letting his exposed, unarmed
back convey his scorn. (25)

Or, in Melville's words: "I to be murdered here at the ends of the earth...by a horrible Spaniard?—Too nonsensical to think of! Who would murder Amasa Delano?
His conscience is clean" (77). But Delano's belief in his own clean conscience is,
of course, a central problem of Melville's novella, which gradually gives the lie to
the protagonist's smug sense of his own "republican impartiality" and "democratic
conclusion" vis-à-vis his Latin American interlocutor.[15] As a kind of palimpsest for
the *Jublio* scene in *A Mercy*, Melville's text warns readers to look more closely at
Morrison's Jacob, who leaves the Portuguese plantation with a plan to profit from
the wider hemisphere without risking its perceived corruptions, and without having
to forfeit the cartographic innocence of the transatlantic immigrant.

Morrison's description of D'Ortega, filtered through Jacob's perspective, echoes
numerous passages from Melville, who hints at Benito Cereno's perversion, from
Delano's point of view: the Spaniard has a "constitutional" "debility...bodily and
mental"; a "mind...unstrung if not still more seriously affected"; a "distempered
spirit...lodged...in as distempered a frame" (52). Like Jacob, Delano is as much
offended by Benito Cereno's "aristocracy"—"proud as he was moody [the Spaniard]
condescended to no personal mandate" in a "manner [that] conveyed a sort of sour
and gloomy disdain, which he seemed at no pains to disguise" (53)—as he *purports*
to be by his slave owning, as when Delano notes "the cringing submission to their
master of all the ship's underlings, mostly blacks; as if by the least inadvertence they
feared to draw down his despotic displeasure" (78). Like Jacob, Delano continually
notices the minute, textured details of Benito Cereno's genteel appearance—"The
Spaniard wore a loose Chili jacket of dark velvet, white small clothes and stockings,
with silver buckles...a slender sword, silver mounted, hung from a knot in his sash"
(57)—and sees them as out of place in Anglo terrain: "[T]here seemed something so
incongruous in the Spaniard's apparel as almost to suggest the image of an invalid

courtier tottering about London streets in the time of the plague" (58). Delano, like Jacob, ponders a series of questions, narrated in free indirect discourse, about his Iberian interlocutor as he entertains the Spaniard as a potential threat to his safety: "Why was the Spaniard, so superfluously punctilious at times, now heedless of common propriety [leaving] all…eclipsed in sinister muteness and gloom…? Did this imply one brief, repentant relenting at the final moment, from some iniquitous plot? Or was the Spaniard less hardened than the Jew, who refrained not from supping at the board of him whom the same night he meant to betray? What imported all these day-long enigmas and contradictions, except they were intended to mystify, preliminary to some stealthy blow?" (96). And like Jacob—who notes the "empty…scabbard" of his host—Delano too will finally dismiss the potential threat posed by Cereno by casting his Latin counterpart as impotent: as the narrator observes, "[T]hat silver-mounted sword, apparent symbol of despotic command, was not, indeed, a sword, but the ghost of one. The scabbard, artificially stiffened, was empty" (116).

In Morrison's long nineteenth century of hemispheric disavowals, Jacob returns to his "Virginia" home with a new, Sutpen-esque perspective on the process of self-gentrification. Like Faulkner's mythic sire, who "didn't remember how he got to Haiti" but returned as the father of mixed-race Charles Bon (205), Jacob too comes home with a dark child—Florens, exchanged as the payment for D'Ortega's defaulted debt—and a plan "as sweet as sugar": dreaming of "a grand house of many rooms," a house the size of *Jublio*, Jacob will build his own *Sutpen's Hundred* but ruin his life and the lives of his makeshift, illegitimate family in the process (35). As in Faulkner's novel, Jacob will ardently desire but will leave behind no living heir, and his great monument, "the grandest house in the whole region," will be visited by a "shadow" after his death, and then finally set aflame and destroyed by fire (143). Sutpen figures a kind of hemispheric alibi for slavery's corruption of (U.S.-) American innocence: his trajectory from Appalachian ignorance to Caribbean experience—"he went to the West Indies" is Quentin's simple explanation (191)—stands in for a host of nineteenth-century literary predecessors seduced by a hemispheric South, from Cooper's Colonel Munro to Stowe's Simon Legree.[16] Like all of them, Jacob too will be corrupted by his traffic with the hemisphere, his body consumed by smallpox, most likely contracted in Barbados.[17]

But the point here is not to establish Morrison's influences or their more muscular cousin, Revision. Rather, it is to show how *A Mercy*, with its powerful and acute nineteenth-century literary-historical imagination, explores and lays bare this broad literary structure of disavowal that depends upon a hemispheric landscape lying safely beyond U.S. borders: whether, as in Captain Delano's case, off the coast of Chile, or in Sutpen's Haiti, or in Colonel Munro's "islands of the West Indies" (Cooper, *Last of the Mohicans* 180) or in the pirate-infested waters where Legree learns the sadistic depredations of a Caribbean-style slavery that makes the Kentucky Shelbys look like kind godparents to their "servants." Through its odd literary overlaps and uncanny, not-quite allusions, its sense of textual déjà vu, Morrison's novel powers the machinery of hemispheric disavowal only to lodge a wrench in its works: its scene of Anglo-Iberian encounter takes place, after all, not in Brazil or Barbados, Haiti or the West Indies—but in Maryland. Thus, when Jacob, suffering the heat as he nears *Jublio*, observes that "he might as well have been in Barbados," his statement is true in more than one register (11): for though he sees himself as a world apart from D'Ortega, Jacob has in fact bought his first slave, the Native American Lina, long before he enters the Iberian world of *Jublio*. The point, then, is not that *Jublio* changes Jacob, catalyzing his transition from transatlantic-immigrant innocence to hemispheric corruption and experience—but rather that *Jublio* enables Jacob to forget and to disavow what has been there all along.

A *Mercy*, then, is showing us why transatlantic and hemispheric models of American studies cannot be advanced in isolation, as primary, without risking one form of disavowal or another. Perhaps the tension *between* the transatlantic and hemispheric models even offers a certain methodological potential of its own—a potential that reminds me, oddly enough, of what we are taught about swimming safely in the Atlantic Ocean. Know where you're swimming, so to speak, and recognize the riptides of the particular approach you've engaged; when you feel yourself pulled out too far in the transatlantic direction to keep swimming productively, don't try to head back along the same line: swerve a little, and swim parallel to the shoreline. In other words, cultivate a feel for the dialectical pull between the one approach and the other, not in order to synthesize the two, but in order to make use of their different intellectual currents as needed. The metaphor is flawed, of course, since the undertow doesn't really pull in two perpendicular directions; the point is that knowing one's critical inclination, as well as that of the text, and then occasionally working against it can yield unexpected and often fruitful results.

To mix metaphors a bit (and in the spirit of Morrison's novel), when we also, simultaneously, step away from this mode of reading the text suspiciously, against its grain, we may discover that it embeds its own theorization of an interpretive mode, whether transatlantic, hemispheric, or a productive antagonism between the two. In *A Mercy*, near the very end of Florens's first-person narrative, we learn that Florens has been writing rather than speaking her narrative all along, etching it into the walls of a room. Florens has been writing for the blacksmith, but a memory interrupts the flow of her story:

> Suddenly I am remembering. You won't read my telling. You read the world but not the letters of talk. You don't know how to.... There is no more room in this room. These words cover the floor.... I am near the door and at the closing now. These careful words, closed up and wide open, will talk to themselves. Round and round, side to side, bottom to top, top to bottom all across the room. Or...perhaps no. Perhaps the words need the air that is out in the world. Need to fly up, then fall, fall like ash over acres of primrose and mallow...beyond the eternal hemlocks...and flavor the soil of the earth. (160–161)

The passage turns on its head the venerable tradition of equating literacy with freedom in the black literary tradition, for it is the enslaved Florens who writes and the free blacksmith who cannot read the "letters of talk." We realize at this late point in the novel that we have not been reading what Henry Louis Gates once called a "speakerly text," whose rhetorical figures have worked to create the "illusion of oral narration" in Florens's narrative (96). Rather, we have been reading a *critique of the concept of the speakerly itself*: a writing narrator who announces that her "letters of talk" will not call into existence a speaking self, will not, in Maurice Wallace's words, "personate" or embody "living speech" (802, 796). They will talk not to human readers but only to themselves. The narrator in Morrison's 1992 novel *Jazz* was the book itself, the embodiment of Gates's trope of the Talking Book—and thus also of both the Western fetishization of print and what Wallace, drawing on Fred Moten, has called the "break" between what writing aspires to do and what its formal disabilities prevent it from doing, which are also, paradoxically, its enabling conditions (180). Here in *A Mercy* we have not a talking book but a room of speaking words about to burn, a written but unlasting textuality, that is emplotted as both a turning point in the novel and a revelation for Florens.

It is this revelation that allows Florens in the book's final chapter to hear (or to re-create) the lost voice of what she calls "a minha mãe"—translated literally from Portuguese, "a my-mother," a syntactical elision carried over from a language she no longer remembers, and always fraught with the trauma of her perceived abandonment by this figure.[18] In the novel's last pages, the lost mother's voice finally returns to explain that the abandonment was, as in *Beloved*, an act of both resistance and mercy: "Oh Florens," she says, "My love. Hear a tua mae" (167). The novel's final line registers the complex multilingual structure of its closing scene, which is rendered in English, but as a translation from either Portuguese or the mother's Angolan language or a mixture of the two. The Portuguese phrase "a tua mae" has entered into the English and shaped its content. But it shapes the narrative at the syntactical level as well: "hear a tua mae" follows the grammatical structure of Portuguese, in which the article "a" ("the") precedes the second-person possessive and its noun. not "A minha mãe begs no" as in Florens's syntactical elision for her memory of the maternal figure who pleads to keep her son but rejects her daughter (7), but "hear your mother": *ouve a tua mae*.[19]

To hear or overhear the lost mother, to hear or overhear the words talking not to readers but to themselves, requires an alternative conception of the textual condition, envisioned in Morrison's novel not as linear, moving from first page to last, but as architectural, three-dimensional, and to some extent extra- or posthuman: not even requiring a human presence or reader. But this room of words will last only until the house is set afire, allowing the words to fly up and out in the world, and then fall with the ash back to the earth. Both hermetically enclosed and autonomous and yet ultimately tied to the planet and its soil, Florens's narrative figures forth the textual condition as apocalyptic, tenuous, contingent, on the verge of destruction— but not merely in the politico-linguistic, Baudrillardian sense that "even signs must burn" (163), nor in the Derridian metonym of "the cinder" as that which "recall[s] at the delicate, charred bottom of itself only non-being or non-presence" (39). For Florens's "writing on the wall[s]" does more: it prophecies the end of empire, from the Book of Daniel through Morrison's own historical moment, and its tenuous nonrepresentationalism is less generically deconstructive than it is melancholically shadowed by languages no longer remembered, from the Angolan mother's tongue to the Portuguese spoken at *Jublio*.[20] The directionality of this haunted text, this room of words, is in the end neither transatlantic nor hemispheric, but "[r]ound and round, side to side, bottom to top, top to bottom." Florens's description of her writing might be said to embody the reflexive possibilities of our discipline at their most sobering and generative: for the purview of this room of words is neither transatlantic nor hemispheric, neither global nor local, but the enclosed space of a shrinking room, a room running out of room, a room about to be gone. And yet the writing on the wall is nevertheless abiding like the "eternal hemlocks," for it flavors the soil of the earth. If nothing else, this paradoxical image serves to miniaturize our disciplinary project as but one part of a much greater interlocution: one narrow span of the wall in a room that is about to be burned, rendering the fate of our own words as both destruction and survival, words that can do far less than we want, but perhaps more than we imagine.

NOTES

1 I refer here to Braudel's concept of the *longue durée* as elaborated in "Histoire et sciences sociales: La longue durée"; and to Geertz's concept of "thick description" as the *longue durée*'s New Historicist opposing term. For an exemplary study that self-consciously refuses to choose between transatlantic and hemispheric, organizing itself instead around two "spatial dialectics," see Bauer. At the same time, a number of scholars have proposed alternative space-time models around which literary history might be studied and theorized; see e.g., Gillman, "Otra vez Caliban"; Castronovo and Dimock, "Planetary Time."

2 See Morrison's trilogy: *Beloved* (1987), *Jazz* (1992), and *Paradise* (1999). On "historiographic metafiction" more generally, see Hutcheon, especially chapter 7.

3 As Morrison puts it in the NPR interview, "The only difference between African slaves and European or British slaves was that the latter could run away and melt into the population." See Norris.

4 See Jordan, chapter 2, "Unthinking Decision: Enslavement of Negroes in America to 1700," 44–98. Allen's work elaborates on Edmund S. Morgan's *American Slavery, American Freedom*.

5 See especially *The Scarlet Letter* and "Young Goodman Brown."

6 The "Black Man" in the woods, or Satan, figures prominently in *The Scarlet Letter* (and in Puritan belief). The phrase "blackness of darkness" comes from Melville's 1850 essay, "Hawthorne and His Mosses," where it is linked to a "Calvinistic sense of Innate Depravity and Original Sin" (1159). Melville later uses the same phrase in *Moby-Dick* (chapter 2, "The Carpet-Bag," and chapter 96, "The Try-Works") 10 and 423. On the ostensible theological and philosophical rigorousness of this sense of blackness, see especially Levin.

7 On the idea of "social death," see Patterson's classic study.

8 See Morrison's *Playing in the Dark* 5–6.

9 On the "spatiotemporal relationship," see Harootunian; his essay is cited and discussed by Gillman in "Otra Vez."

10 See especially Emerson's *Nature* (10), Bryant's "The Prairies" (1832), and chapter 16 of *The Scarlet Letter*.

11 Cooper's Leatherstocking novels include *The Last of the Mohicans* (1826), *The Pioneers* (1823), *The Prairie* (1827), *The Pathfinder* (1840), and *The Deerslayer* (1841). "Leatherstocking" is the name given to the character Natty Bumppo by the English; like Morrison's Jacob, Natty Bumppo prides himself on his ethical comportment vis-à-vis the land, its animals, and its native inhabitants—which sets him apart from the European characters and marks him out as "American."

12 The novel's description of D'Ortega's loss distinctly evokes a phenomenon theorized in Baucom's *Specters of the Atlantic*, which addresses precisely the kind of "econometric logic" evinced in Morrison's scene, as it emerges in a similar historical episode from the next century (5), by which time England had worked out a series of insurance policies that both contained the "high risk" of the international slave trade and fostered its expansion: the notorious 1781 case of the slave ship *Zong*, whose owners decided, after losing 60 of their slaves to disease (ship fever, as Jacob calls it), that they stood to make more profit from their venture by drowning 133 of their living (but sickly and therefore potentially "unsalable") slaves in order to collect on their cargo insurance policy. Jacob's recounting of his client's loss—the chained slaves who drowned with the sinking of the ship—links the history of the Atlantic slave trade indelibly with the graveyard of the sea and the "vanishing but not vanished, drowning but not transformed, lost but repeating bod[ies]" that Baucom describes as central to "black Atlantic narrative, aesthetic, and commemorative practices" and their collective project of what he calls a "hauntological rethinking of justice" (68). Indeed, in the "hauntological" project of Morrison's novel, we find not only a "phantom ship", but also a ghostly girl named Sorrow, a lone survivor discovered on the foundered vessel. Described by her discoverer as "A bit mongrelized" (120), Sorrow is the literal product of a slave ship: she knows her father was called "Captain," but her mother remains nameless, and "her memories of the ship, the only home she ever knew, seemed as stolen as its cargo" (117). And in this world of human cargo, Sorrow has witnessed some unspecified tragedy of the sea that is also a crime: "all people were gone or drowned...if any unmurdered [had] escaped she didn't know" (117). Sorrow is, in other words, a veritable "specter of the Atlantic," in Baucom's phrase, as if she had walked off the pages of his groundbreaking transatlantic study.

13 Jubilee appears in texts ranging from Henry Clay Work's Civil War song "Kingdom Coming," which cites the Latin *jubilo* to the 1966 historical novel *Jubilee* by Margaret Walker to Ward Moore's uncanny 1953 novel of counterfactual history *Bring the Jubilee*, which envisions a hemispheric, confederate South stretching from the original southern confederate states through the southern tip of Argentina and Chile, and vastly overpowering a geographically diminished United States that is in perpetual economic decline.

14 Ortega y Gasset's most popular formulation of mass culture can be found in *La rebelión de las masas* (1930), translated as *The Revolt of the Masses*.

15 The first phrase is from *The Piazza Tales* (80); Melville used the second phrase in the version that appeared in *Putnam's* (360).

16 On Faulkner's novel, and the "US South's relation to the West Indies," see John T. Matthews. Cooper's Colonel Munro appears in *The Last of the Mohicans*, where he famously confesses to being seduced by the "luxurious people" of the West Indies, and fathering a child (the character Cora) with the mixed-race daughter of a plantation owner (180).

17 The shipping circuit running between the West Indies and Boston was made famous for transporting smallpox after the April 1721 outbreak of an epidemic brought in by a ship from Barbados. Though this particular epidemic postdates Jacob's death, it intertwines with the larger literary history to which Morrison responds in *A Mercy* because Cotton Mather was at the center of the famous inoculation controversy that ensued. See Creighton.

18 Filtered though Florens's consciousness in free indirect discourse, the narrative voice refers to Florens's mother as "the *minha mãe*" throughout the novel, apparently following Portuguese grammar, in which an article precedes the second-person possessive.

19 That both words and syntax bear the traces of another language in this narrative—we might adapt Gates's term and call it a *multilingual speakerly text*—elicited damning, faint praise from John Updike, whose last published piece of writing was his review of *A Mercy* for the November 2008 issue of the *New Yorker*. Backhandedly describing the narrative voices of Florens and her mother as characterized by "a compressed, anti-grammatical diction unlike any recorded patois," Updike argued in his essay for the novel's unsuccessful "depiction of people," most particularly its black characters. Conceding in one grand gesture that Morrison's oeuvre takes up a "noble and necessary fictional project," he then deflates his own estimation by describing that project as the work of "exposing the infamies of slavery and the hardships of being African-American." *A Mercy* is merely "another installment" in the larger Morrison series about these "hardships," Updike charges, and her "betranced pessimism saps her plots of the urgency that hope imparts to human adventures." But the most telling criticism Updike levels is his charge that Morrison is under "the pernicious influence of William Faulkner," or, as he puts it later in the review, that she is once again working "in line with the celebrated Faulknerian dictum that the past is not past." Morrison's appropriation of Faulkner to open up the potentials of history and voice has been much remarked, as Updike surely knew. His comments thus exemplify the perennially vexed conception of literary relations that Morrison's image of a "talking room" so powerfully recasts in offering an alternative structure for textuality.

20 In the *Book of Daniel*, Daniel correctly interprets the handwriting on the wall as a prophecy of the end of the Babylonian empire (Daniel 5:1–32).

BIBLIOGRAPHY

Allen, Theodore William. *The Invention of the White Race*. 2 vols. New York: Verso, 1994.

Bales, Kevin. *Understanding Global Slavery: A Reader*. Berkeley: University of California Press, 2005.

Baucom, Ian. "Introduction: Atlantic Genealogies." *South Atlantic Quarterly* 100 (2001): 61–82.

———. *Specters of the Atlantic: Finance Capital, Slavery, and the Philosophy of History*. Durham, NC: Duke University Press, 2005.

Baudrillard, Jean. "Toward a Critique of the Political Economy of the Sign." *For a Critique of the Political Economy of the Sign*. New York: Telos Press, 1981.

Bauer, Ralph. *The Cultural Geography of Colonial American Literatures: Empire Travel Modernity*. Cambridge: Cambridge University Press, 2003; paperback 2008.

Braudel, Fernand. *Grammaires des Civilisations*. Paris: Flammarion, 2008.

———. "Histoire et sciences sociales: La longue durée." *Réseaux* 5.27 (1987): 7–37.

———. *The Identity of France: History and Environment*. Vol. 1. New York: Harper Collins, 1990.

Castronovo, Russ. "American Literature Internationale." *ESQ: A Journal of the American Renaissance. Special Issue: American Literary Globalism* 50 (2005): 59–93.

Cooper, James Fenimore. *The Deerslayer*. Oxford: Oxford University Press, 1993.

———. *The Last of the Mohicans*. New York: Oxford University Press, 2009.

———. *The Pathfinder*. Oxford: Oxford University Press, 1993.

———. *The Pioneers*. Oxford: Oxford University Press, 1999.

———. *The Prairie*. Oxford: Oxford University Press, 1999.

Creighton, Charles. *A History of Epidemics in Britain*. Cambridge: Cambridge University Press, 1891.

Derrida, Jacques. *Cinders*. Lincoln: University of Nebraska Press, 1991.

Dimock, Wai Chee. "Hemispheric Islam: Continents and Centuries for American Literature." *American Literary History* 21 (2009): 28–52.

———. "Planetary Time and Global Translation: 'Context' in Literary Studies." *Common Knowledge* 9.3 (Fall 2003): 488–507.

Faulkner, William. *Absalom, Absalom! The Corrected Text*. New York: Vintage, 1990.

Flint, Kate. "Transatlantic Currents." *American Literary History* 21 (2009): 324–334.

Fox, Claire. "Comparative Literary Studies of the Americas." *American Literature* 76 (2004): 871–886.

Garrido, Manuel. "Ortega y Gasset's Heritage in Latin America." *A Companion to Latin American Philosophy*. Ed. Susana Nuccetelli et al. Boston: Blackwell, 2010. 142–155.

Gates, Henry Louis. *The Signifying Monkey: A Theory of Afro-American Literary Criticism*. New York: Oxford University Press, 1989.

Geertz, Clifford. "Thick Description: Toward an Interpretive Theory of Culture." *The Interpretation of Cultures*. New York: Basic Books, 1973. 3–32..

Giles, Paul. "Commentary: Hemispheric Partiality." *American Literary History* 18 (2006): 648–655.

Gillman, Susan. "The New, Newest Thing: Have American Studies Gone Imperial?" *American Literary History* 17 (2005): 196–214.

———. "Otra vez Caliban/Encore Caliban: Adaptation, Translation, Americas Studies." *American Literary History* 20 (Spring/Summer 2008): 187–209.

Gilroy, Paul. *The Black Atlantic: Modernity and Double-Consciousness*. Cambridge, MA: Harvard University Press, 1995.

Greeson, Jennifer. *Our South: Region, World, and the Rise of a National Literature*. Cambridge, MA: Harvard University Press, 2010.

Harootunian, Harry. "Some Thoughts on Comparability and the Space-Time Problem." *boundary* Boundary 2 32 (2005): 23–52.

Hartman, Saidiya. *Scenes of Subjection: Terror, Slavery, and Self-Making in Nineteenth-Century America*. New York: Oxford University Press, 1997.

Hawthorne, Nathaniel. *Nathaniel Hawthorne: Collected Novels: Fanshawe, The Scarlet Letter, The House of Seven Gables, The Blithedale Romance, The Marble Faun*. New York: Library of America, 1983.

———. "Young Goodman Brown." *Nathaniel Hawthorne: Tales and Sketches*. New York: Library of America, 1982. 276–289.

Hutcheon, Linda. *A Poetics of Postmodernism: History, Theory, Fiction*. New York: Routledge, 1988.

Jay, Paul. "Locating Disciplinary Change: The Afterlives of Area and International Studies in the Age of Globalization." *American Literary History* 18 (Spring 2006): 175–189.

Jordan, Don, and Michael Walsh. *White Cargo: The Forgotten History of Britain's White Slaves in America.* New York: New York University Press, 2008.

Jordan, Winthrop D. *White over Black: American Attitudes toward the Negro, 1550–1812.* Chapel Hill: University of North Carolina Press, 1968.

Levander, Caroline, and Robert Levine. "Introduction: Essays beyond the Nation." *Hemispheric American Studies.* New Brunswick, NJ: Rutgers University Press, 2008.

Levin, Harry. *The Power of Blackness: Hawthorne, Poe, Melville.* New York: Knopf, 1958.

Lewis, R. W. B. *The American Adam: Innocence, Tragedy, and Tradition in the Nineteenth Century.* Chicago: University of Chicago Press, 1955.

Matthews, John T. "Recalling the West Indies: from Yoknawpatawpha to Haiti and Back." *American Literary History* (16) 2004: 238–262.

McClellan, Sophia. "Inter-American Studies or Imperial American Studies?" *Comparative American Studies* 3.4 (2005): 393–413.

Melville, Herman. *Benito Cereno, The Piazza Tales and Other Prose Pieces, 1839–1860.* Chicago: Northwestern University Press, 1987.

———. *Benito Cereno, Putnam's Monthly Magazine of American Literature, Science and Art.* 6.34 (October 1855): 353–367.

———. "Hawthorne and His Mosses." *The Piazza Tales: and Other Prose Pieces, 1839–1860.* Chicago: Northwestern University Press, 1987. 239–253.

———. *Moby-Dick, or the White Whale.* Ed. Hayford et al. Chicago: Northwestern University Press/Newberry Library, 1988.

Mignolo, Walter. *Local Histories/Global Designs: Coloniality, Subaltern Knowledges* and *Border Thinking.* Princeton, NJ: Princeton University Press, 2000.

Moore, Ward. *Bring the Jubilee.* New York: Ballantine Books, 1953.

Morgan, Edmund S. *American Slavery, American Freedom: The Ordeal of Colonial Virginia.* New York: Norton, 1975.

Morrison, Toni. *Beloved.* New York: Knopf, 1987.

———. *Jazz.* New York: Knopf, 1992.

———. *A Mercy.* New York: Knopf, 2008.

———. *Paradise.* New York: Knopf, 1999.

———. *Playing in the Dark: Whiteness and the Literary Imagination.* New York: Vintage, 1992.

Moten, Fred. *In the Break: The Aesthetics of the Black Radical Tradition.* Minneapolis: University of Minnesota Press, 2003.

Norris, Michelle. "Toni Morrison Finds 'A Mercy' in Servitude." NPR interview, October 27, 2008. http://www.npr.org/templates/story/story.php?storyId=95961382.

Ortega y Gasset, José. *The Revolt of the Masses.* New York: Norton, 1932.

Patterson, Orlando. *Slavery and Social Death: A Comparative Study.* Cambridge, MA: Harvard University Press, 1982.

Paz, Octavio. "El cómo y el para qué: José Ortega y Gasset." *Hombres en su siglo.* Barcelona: Seix Barral, 1984, 97–110.

Poe, Edgar Allan. *Eureka, Edgar Allan Poe: Poetry and Tales.* New York: Library of America, 1984.

Roach, Joseph. *Cities of the Dead: Circum-Atlantic Performance.* New York: Columbia University Press, 1996.

Roediger, David. *The Wages of Whiteness: Race and the Making of the American Working Class.* London: Verso Books, 1999.

Stowe, Harriet Beecher. *Uncle Tom's Cabin, or, Life among the Lowly.* New York: Library of
     America, 1982.

Taylor, Diana. "Remapping Genre through Performance: From American to *Hemispheric*
     Studies." *PMLA* 122 (2007): 1416–1430.

Turner, Frederick Jackson. *The Frontier in American History.* New York: Henry Holt, 1920.

Updike, John. "Dreamy Wilderness: Unmastered Women in Colonial Virginia." *New
     Yorker*, November 2008.

Walker, Margaret. *Jubilee.* New York: Houghton Mifflin, 1996.

Wallace, Maurice. "Print, Prosthesis, (Im)Personation: Morrison's Jazz and the Limits of
     Literary History." *American Literary History* 20 (2008): 794–806.

Wallerstein, Immanuel. World-Systems Analysis: An Introduction. Durham, NC: Duke
     University Press, 2004.

Work, Henry Clay. "Kingdom Coming." *American Poetry, The Nineteenth Century.* Vol. 2.
     Ed. John Hollander. New York: Library of America, 1993. 33.

Zamora, Lois Parkinson. *The Usable Past: The Imagination of History in Recent Fiction of
     the Americas.* Cambridge: Cambridge University Press, 1997.

PART II

ZIGZAGS

CHAPTER 9

TEMPORALITY, RACE, AND EMPIRE IN COOPER'S *THE DEERSLAYER*: THE BEGINNING OF THE END

ROBERT S. LEVINE

THE *Deerslayer* (1841) both begins and ends the five novels of Cooper's Leatherstocking series (1823–1841). In terms of the chronological temporality of the novels, *The Deerslayer* is the first, set in the early 1740s, when Natty Bumppo is in his mid-twenties, and *The Prairie* (1827) is the last, culminating in Natty's death over sixty years later at the time of the Louisiana Purchase. But in terms of Cooper's actual composition of the series, *The Deerslayer* comes last. The first, *The Pioneers* (1823), portrays Natty during the 1790s at the New York settlement of Templeton (Cooper's fictionalized version of Cooperstown); *The Last of the Mohicans* (1826) moves Natty back in time to 1757 during the height of the Seven Years' War; and then, after projecting Natty forward to the early 1800s in *The Prairie*, Cooper moves him back in time to the Seven Years' War in *The Pathfinder* (1840), which is set a few years after *The Last of the Mohicans*. Finally, Cooper moves two decades further back, setting *The Deerslayer* in a still naturally pristine midstate New York. D. H. Lawrence declared that Cooper's five Leatherstocking novels constitute a "lovely myth" (54) of America, steadily moving Natty "from old age to golden youth" (60). But in fact, over the approximately twenty-year composition period of the series, Cooper moved forward and backward in a jagged, uneven fashion very different from the steady regression evoked by Lawrence (see Axelrad). Still, the ending of the Leatherstocking series does take us to the beginning, and that beginning, I will be arguing in this chapter, provides a clarifying and revisionary ending to the series. My reading of *The Deerslayer* addresses the complicated temporality of the Leatherstocking series in relation to the chronology of its composition history, raising questions about the less complicated temporality informing current discussions of Cooper as a writer who allegedly used the series to champion white U.S. empire.

Arguments about Cooper's implication in U.S. empire building, particularly the project of Indian Removal, tend to deploy overdetermined critical strategies of temporal juxtaposition and homology that take as a given that literary history and the history of expansionism can best be understood, not as a complicated zigzag within a deep and uneven time frame, but as a simple (and symbiotic) chronological unfolding. Although Cooper throughout his career was fascinated with echoes, repetitions, progress, and regression, and although antebellum culture itself was marked by "heterogeneous temporal modes" (Allen 4), there has been a flattening of temporal thinking in most considerations of the Leatherstocking series. As a number of critics have elaborated, Cooper wrote the series during a period in which the future of the Indians in the United States was debated by white political leaders (the 1820s), Indian Removal was adopted as law (1830), and the Cherokees of Georgia were pushed west in the infamous Trail of Tears (1838–1839), resulting in the deaths of thousands, especially women and children. For some critics, the simple juxtaposition of historical atrocity and novel writing is enough to indict Cooper. Joshua David Bellin ominously notes that "Cooper's *Last of the Mohicans* appeared two years after James Monroe presented a formal plan of Indian removal to Congress and four years before Andrew Jackson signed act into law" (158), with the clear implication that Cooper's novel lent support to those efforts simply by virtue of temporal overlap (see also Rosenwald 20–47). Philip Fisher similarly builds a case against Cooper through overlap, remarking that "Cooper writes *The Deerslayer* in 1840 at the moment of the conclusion of Jacksonian Indian Removal" (36)—as if this fact makes *The Deerslayer* complicit in what Fisher terms "the inevitable extermination of the American Indian" (35). (Fisher never considers that a novel concluding with whites' massacre of Indian women and children might be raising questions about a providentially inscribed "inevitable extinction.") In a study focusing on the first three novels of the Leatherstocking series, Theresa Strouth Gaul asserts that there was "collusion between literary policy and national polity during the period immediately preceding the passage of the Indian Removal act of 1830" (159). However, the only evidence Gaul offers for collusion between Cooper and the makers of public policy is once again temporal overlap, focusing on suggestive homologies (structural resemblances) between juridical and literary "modes of race representation" (160) in the Supreme Court's 1823 ruling on *Johnson v. McIntosh*, which dispossessed Indians of land, and Cooper's 1823 *The Pioneers* (see also Cheyfitz and Sheckel).

Reading through conventional interpretations of *The Pioneers, The Last of the Mohicans*, and the other novels of the Leatherstocking series, one might be surprised to learn that Cooper did not work for the U.S. government's Bureau of Indian Affairs and that he had virtually nothing to say about the Jacksonian policy of Indian removal. I have been unable to find *anyone* writing during the 1823–1841 period (critic or political leader) who draws connections between the Leatherstocking novels and Indian removal. In fact, most commentators on the series complained that Cooper's portrayals of Indians were too positive (see Dekker and McWilliams's comprehensive collection of contemporary reviews and essays). And yet over the past two decades it has become a tenet of U.S. literary studies that Cooper's Leatherstocking series supported and enabled Indian removal, gloried in an emerging white U.S. empire, and trafficked in essentialist notions of race (for sharp dissents from the orthodoxy, see Franklin, Mann, and Rans). My point isn't that Cooper was a progressive reformer who actively worked for Indian rights, but that the connections that most commentators insist upon between cultural context and Cooper's novels have become rigidified to the point where we are virtually unable to see conflict and critique in the Leatherstocking series. It is almost as if we need Cooper forever fixed as our "demon of the continent" (to signify on Bellin) so we don't have to read him anymore. I want to suggest that within the constraints of his somewhat typically nineteenth-century vision of the Indians, Cooper raises significant questions about Indian policy and, in a larger sense, about the nature of white empire on the North American continent. At the very least, there is much in the Leatherstocking series that voices clear opposition to whites' racist violence against the Indians.

Cooper is nowhere clearer in his critique of white racist violence and the course of white empire in the region that would become the northern United States than in the concluding novel of the Leatherstocking series, the 1041 *The Deerslayer*, which can be taken as Cooper's critical commentary on the whole series. In this last-written but temporally first novel of the series, Cooper provides new ways of thinking about the earlier novels published in the Leatherstocking series. Reading the four earlier novels through the lens of *The Deerslayer* can be a transformative experience, as Cooper in this novel revises and more clearly articulates his vision of race and empire in the Americas, leaving readers with a feeling of revulsion at the "rise" of a white empire based on untenable notions of racial differences and violence. In *The Deerslayer*, binaries between good and bad Indians, and Indians and whites, are exposed as fictions, and Indians and women emerge as the most prescient critics of the violence identified with colonizing Euro-Americans. In this, his most feminist novel, Cooper builds to an antipatriarchal and antiracist critique of a nascent U.S. empire. That critique fundamentally alters our reading of the earlier novels, and of the Leatherstocking series itself.

Arguably, it is precisely because *The Deerslayer* represents an act of authorial (re)interpretation of the Leatherstocking series that Cooper in 1841, and again in 1850, made an effort to enjoin readers to read *The Deerslayer* first. In a letter of January 31, 1841, to his publisher Richard Bentley, Cooper declares that "[t]he order of the books, as regards time, will be, this book [*The Deerslayer*], Mohicans, Pathfinder, Pioneers, Prairie" (*Letters and Journals* 4:112); and in his prefaces to *The Deerslayer* and the Leatherstocking series, he underscores the importance of reading the novels in that order. He writes in the 1841 preface to *The Deerslayer* that this is "the last in execution, though the first in the order of perusal" (1); and he remarks in the 1850 preface to the five novels of the Leatherstocking series that "[t] aking the life of the Leather-Stocking as a guide, 'The Deerslayer' should have been the opening book" (5). Cooper is most insistent on the order in which the novels should be read in the 1850 preface to *The Deerslayer*: "'The Deerslayer' is properly the first in the order of reading, though the last in that of publication" (11). (All of these prefaces are collected in the State University of New York Press edition of *The Deerslayer*.) There are complicated issues of temporality here, for readers remain free to read the novels in any order they choose. Moreover, as Geoffrey Rans points out in his excellent study of the Leatherstocking series, there are also fascinating temporal issues raised by reading the novels in their order of publication, for each earlier novel, he argues, is immanent in the novel to come. *The Last of the Mohicans*, for instance, published shortly after *The Pioneers*, contains within its scene of 1757 what we know from *The Pioneers* will happen by the 1790s. (Thus, to take an obvious example, Natty and Chingachgook cannot be killed in *The Last of the Mohicans* because we already know they will live into the 1790s.) Given Rans's emphasis on compositional temporalities, *The Pioneers* (the first published novel) remains key to his interpretation of Leatherstocking: "Whatever attraction the sequence read in chronological order possesses, *The Pioneers* is the controlling determinant simply because as the first written it prescribes certain unalterable conditions" (55). True, *The Pioneers* establishes unalterable conditions of plot, but there remains the alterable space of social, cultural, and historical thematics, particularly given the importance of unresolved conflict to all of the novels. The series presents an unfolding, often highly conflicted, conversation on race and empire, and Cooper's late comments on the series suggest that he wants us to begin that conversation with *The Deerslayer*. In this way, oddly enough, Cooper seeks to alter our understanding of the conversation to come in the four novels written before this one.

Much of the talk and action in the Leatherstocking series focuses on the "rise" of a white U.S. empire in North America, and in *The Deerslayer*, as in all of the novels, Cooper's approach to this large topic is profoundly historical. Inspired by D. H. Lawrence's mythic reading of the novel, H. Daniel Peck asserts that *The Deerslayer* is set in "a time *before* history" (159), and William P. Kelly similarly proclaims that the novel is set at a moment of "timelessness consistent with the force of myth" (168). And yet Cooper explicitly states that the novel is set "between the years 1740 and 1745" (16), not too long after the end of "a time of peace between England and France" (146). This is the historical moment that we know will culminate in the Seven Years' War, which Cooper will take up (or, depending on one's temporal point of view, had already taken up) in *The Last of the Mohicans* and *The Pathfinder*, and it is a time of historical conflict that is absolutely crucial to an understanding of U.S. history in a global context. As historian Thomas Bender notes, "The struggle between England and France...for the riches of empire was played out on a global scale between 1689 and 1815" (62). Gregory H. Nobles reminds us that within that same time frame, from around 1689 to 1783, "[t]he struggle for control of North America embroiled European governments and their American colonists in a series of wide-scale wars" (63). In the coda-like conclusion of *The Deerslayer*, which jumps forward fifteen years, Cooper places the action in relation to *The Last of the Mohicans* and *The Pathfinder* with a proleptic limning of Natty and Chingachgook's role in the ongoing wars between England and France as depicted in previously published novels: "A peace had intervened, and it was on the eve of another and still more important war, when he [Natty Bumppo] and his constant friend, Chingachgook, were hastening to the forts to join their allies [the British]" (546). The conclusion thus underscores the importance of the contention for empire in the entire series. *The Deerslayer* focuses on one particular moment in the global and hemispheric war for empire, and in many respects offers "prefatory" guidance to how we might understand that war in the already written Leatherstocking novels that follow.

Key to the contention for empire depicted in *The Deerslayer* is, to borrow Philip Fisher's term, a "hard fact": both the French and the English have offered bounties for scalps of their enemies (Indians and whites). For many critics, the overarching suggestion of the five Leatherstocking novels is that "civilized" whites are different from "savage" Indians; and that within the progressive design of the series, whites should therefore naturally ascend to power while the Indians, lamentably, should "vanish" (see Dekker). But Cooper's presentation of Europeans' promotion of scalping raises questions about such differences, and even about Natty's oft-stated claim, here and elsewhere in the series, that scalping constitutes one of the Indian's racial "gifts."

In a key scene in *The Last of the Mohicans*, for instance, Chingachgook scalps a friendly French sentry, and Natty defends the action because it is an Indian who did the scalping: "'Twould have been a cruel and an unhuman act for a white-skin; but 'tis the gift and natur of an Indian" (138). Critics have generally regarded Natty's interpretation of that moment as Cooper's. Consider how John P. McWilliams uses the depiction of scalping in the 1826 *Mohicans* to shape an interpretation of the 1841 *Deerslayer*. He writes (correctly, I think) that the "entire narrative of *The Deerslayer* rests upon two laws enacted by the colonial authorities. The French army in Canada has passed a law paying bounty for the scalps of all Englishmen and Delawares. The English army along the Hudson has passed a law paying bounty for the scalps of all Frenchmen and Hurons." But he also asserts that "[t]he white Christians have sunk to legalizing Indian codes of vengeance" (278). The scalping laws do play a crucial role in the action of *The Deerslayer*, but have the white Christians really "sunk," and is scalping truly crucial to "Indian codes of vengeance"? Moreover, are Indians really more "vengeful" than whites? McWilliams further argues that "the frontiersman becomes an Indian, while the Indian resembles an honorable white" (280). This is precisely how Natty understands such reversals in *The Deerslayer*, but the question remains as to whether Natty's views are portrayed uncritically by

Cooper. In short, we need to ask if there are crucial differences between whites and Indians, if Indians more "naturally" turn to scalping and vengeance, and if a white acting cruelly and sadistically has turned against his "gifts"? These crucial questions inform *The Deerslayer*. McWilliams's readings work with stereotypes that may have had greater force in the novels published during the 1820s, but which Cooper in 1841, particularly in a scene in which Indians scalp *only* because of the white bounty, suggests are fictions, with the clear sense (in his repeated injunctions that we should be reading *The Deerslayer* first) of attempting a temporal revision of the presentation of race or "gifts" in the earlier novels.

Before turning to race, a few words on the plot of *The Deerslayer*, a novel that Mark Twain singled out for its unintentionally comic improbabilities. In this, the longest novel of the Leatherstocking series, Natty Bumppo is helping his friend, the Delaware Chingachgook, to rescue his beloved Wah-ta!-Wah, or Hist-oh!-Hist (usually called Hist), who had been kidnapped by a renegade Delaware into a Huron (Iroquois) tribe residing by Glimmerglass (Cooper's fictionalized name for Otsego Lake). At the novel's opening, Natty is accompanying Henry March, known as Hurry Harry, who is in love with Judith Hutter, one of the two daughters of Thomas Hutter, a former pirate who basically claims Glimmerglass and the immediately surrounding lands as his property. There are ambiguities about whether Hutter is actually the father of Judith and her sister, the feebleminded Hetty; and there are rumors that the beautiful and boldly assertive Judith had earlier been seduced by a British army officer. Hutter has recently "buried" his wife in Glimmerglass, and one suspects that a buried family history will eventually come to surface. Crucial to the unfolding action is the historical fact that the English and French are in conflict, and that conflict drives the action, which focuses on efforts to liberate Hist from the Hurons, and the Hurons' own efforts to fight off the whites (particularly Hurry and Hutter) who want their scalps for the reward money. There are repeated scenes of captivity and escape. Cooper details Judith's growing love for Natty and her increasing revulsion at Hurry, and clearly the author has a soft spot for Hetty, whose mental slowness doesn't stop her from evincing a Christian love for the Iroquois. Viewed in relation to the Leatherstocking series, this novel has a key role in depicting what many regard as a mythic aspect of the series: Natty's emergence as a killer (see Person "Historical Paradoxes" and Slotkin). In a great early chapter, Cooper shows how Natty comes to kill his first Indian—an act of self-defense in which Natty lovingly comforts the man he was forced to shoot. By killing, the Deerslayer becomes the Hawkeye of the fictions that chronologically follow. But despite scenes of intense action amidst the sublime beauty of the wilderness and Glimmerglass, the bulk of the novel consists of conversations on topics central to the Leatherstocking series—religion, war, marriage, law, the seeming course of history, and race.

Race, of course, is essential to Natty's conception of himself in all five novels of the series, for the man who has spent years with the Delaware Indians regularly finds it necessary to assert his identity as a pure white. But in *The Deerslayer*, Natty is not the only character affirming the importance of whiteness. Dana D. Nelson describes Hurry Harry as "the spokesperson for racial purity" (139), and in that respect he has to some extent taken over this function from Natty, who in *The Last of the Mohicans* in particular repeatedly asserts versions of "I am genuine white" (31) with "no cross in my veins" (183). In *The Deerslayer*, we are compelled to read Natty's race-thinking much more critically, for his insistence on his pure whiteness becomes inextricably linked with Hurry's virulent and violent racism. As the narrator remarks, "Hurry was one of those theorists who believed in the inferiority of all of the human race, who were not white" (59). Hurry baldly lays out his vision of racial hierarchy: "White is the highest colour, and therefore the best man; black comes next, and is put to live in the neighborhood of the white man...; and red comes last, which shows that those that made 'em never expected an Indian to be accounted as more than half human" (49–50). Hurry's racial views are repeatedly enlisted as justifications for his violence, for he regards all Indians as "animals, with nothing human about 'em" (60). Whereas Natty declares that it is "onlawful to take the life of man, except in open and ginerous warfare" (22), Harry along with Hutter view the frontier as in a perpetual state of war that perpetually legitimates whites' violence against the Indian, a vision that obscures the historical specificity of their actions. As Hutter explains, "We...must do to our enemies as our enemies would do to us" (91).

Given that whites have instituted the scalping bounties, and given that Harry and Hutter are presented as violent racists who are willing to kill Indian women and children for pay, how seriously are we meant to take Natty's repeated assertions of racial difference, or what Natty calls "nat'ral gifts" (34)? The idea of grounding "gifts" or racial characteristics in nature would suggest an ideology that emphasizes biology over culture, and an ideology, at least as elaborated by Natty in *The Last of the Mohicans* and *The Deerslayer*, which is in many ways consistent with the romantic racialism circulating in the antebellum United States. As Alexander Kinmont and other romantic racialists of the period would have it, different blood contributes to different behaviors among different races, and those differences, viewed in Natty Bumppo fashion as gifts derived from blood, are not necessarily bad. For instance both Kinmont and Harriet Beecher Stowe saw blacks as "natural" Christians because of the way their blood supposedly made them more domestic and attached to the land (see Fredrickson 97–129). Praising blacks as "naturally and originally distinct" from less religious whites, Kinmont wrote in his 1839 *Twelve Lectures on the Natural History of Man* that it was all for the good that "each peculiar race of men should occupy those limits, which have been assigned" by what he terms "an express law of nature" (qtd. Fredrickson 104). In *The Last of the Mohicans* and other of the Leatherstocking novels, there are suggestions that Indians' "gifts" for life in the wilderness make them unsuitable for a rising civilization and that they should therefore "occupy those limits" of the ever-vanishing forests. But in *The Deerslayer* the appeal to biology (or blood) soon comes to seem incoherent, merely serving the interests of racists who appear anything but civilized. That incoherence has much to do with Cooper's sly importing of the racial terms of the 1840s into a novel of the 1740s that in crucial respects looks forward to the "rise" of white empire in the 1840s.

Again, the matter of bounty is crucial to the novel's troubling of the concept of racial gifts. Natty initially speaks about racial gifts in relation to a providentially ordered nature, stating that "it's sinful to withstand nat'ral gifts" (34). But in his response to the British and French offer of bounties for scalps, Natty, while insisting that his gifts will keep him from scalping, begins to loosen his hold on such appeals to nature, becoming a critic of white culture from the perspective of the Indians: "Even the Indians, themselves, cry shame on it [white scalping for pay], seeing it's ag'in a white man's gifts....I will maintain that tradition, and use, and colour, and laws, make such a difference in races as to amount to gifts" (50). Looking forward (or backward) to *The Pioneers*, which builds to a focus on the problematics of Judge Temple's laws, Natty makes the radical declaration that laws running "ag'in the laws of God...ought not to be obeyed" (51), a declaration that in *The Deerslayer* links him with the Indians. At the very least, he insists that he will refrain from scalping, even as he is implicated with Hurry as a defender of Hutter's dwelling, boat, and putative daughters. He asserts that he will "cling[] to colour to the last, even though the King's Majesty, his governors, and all his councils, both at home and in the colonies, forget from what they come, and where they hope to go" (125). According to this critique, both the French and English have gone "red." But before we naturalize such stereotypes or gifts, it is worth noting that the narrator regularly belittles "Deerslayer's innocent vanity on the subject of colour" (123), remarking rather bluntly that Natty's ideas of "gifts" are ultimately based on "prejudice": "This tyrant of the human mind...had made some impression on even the just propensities of this individual" (49). The narrator's critique of Natty's concept of racial gifts becomes more pronounced over the course of the novel, as does Natty's confusion on his favorite topic. By focusing on Natty's confusion about ideas that can be linked both to the 1740s and to the romantic racialism of the antebellum period, Cooper destabilizes notions of race, which the novel (and overall series) suggests were always unstable in the culture anyway.

Relatively early in the novel, Natty announces that "[r]evenge is an Injin gift, and forgiveness a white man's" (89). But over the next several hundred pages, whites are extraordinarily vengeful and Indians regularly display an ability to forgive. After Hutter and Harry are ransomed from the Hurons for elephant chess pieces, the narrator notes that the white men's "humility partook of the rancor of revenge" (254). Harry's vengeful feelings in particular lead to the random killing of an Indian woman, which I will discuss in more detail below. Hutter is eventually scalped by the Hurons, but he had already been mortally wounded by the chief Rivenoak, who kills in self-defense, and Cooper makes clear that he is scalped not because scalping is an Indian gift, but because it is difficult for three Iroquois not to pursue "the usual trophy" (355) in order to be paid by the French. Hurry's response to the scalping is to castigate Natty for trying to stop him and Hutter from killing for profit: "I heartily wish old Hutter and I had scalped every creatur' in their camp" (404).

Faced with such overwhelming evidence that whites can be just as vengeful and cruel as Indians, which is to say faced with evidence that stereotypes about white/Indian differences simply do not work, Natty is forced to rethink his concept of gifts. Although Natty in *The Deerslayer* initially conceives of "gifts" in relation to nature (or blood), there is always some tension between blood and culture in his remarks on the subject (see Tomc). By the end of the novel, Natty, who has seen whites exhibiting vengeance in "savage" ways and who has wrestled with the historical reality that the English and French have been promoting scalping, offers one final disquisition on "gifts" in which the main emphasis is now placed on culture. He elaborates his views to Hetty and Judith in the manner of a schoolmaster who has finally come to understand the subject he is teaching: "A natur'," he explains, "is the creatur' itself; its wishes, wants, idees, and feelin's, as all are born in him.... Now, gifts come of sarcumstances. Thus, if you put a man in a town, he gets town gifts; in a settlement, settlement gifts; in a forest, gifts of the woods.... Still, the creatur' is the same at the bottom; just as a man who is clad in regimentals is the same as the man that is clad in skins" (439). Here is a fundamental rejection of the romantic racialism of the early to mid-nineteenth century and a rejection as well of the racialism that at times can seem to inform the Leatherstocking series. The collapsing of men in regimentals with men in skins also raises questions about conventional progressive readings of the series, pointing us toward the darker Thomas Cole–like cyclical vision implicit in the images of the mounds in *The Prairie* as burial grounds of former civilizations.

To underscore my argument about the revisionary temporality of the Leatherstocking series: here we have Natty's "final" reflections on "gifts" in the final novel of the series, but in a novel that, when read in the chronological order that Cooper advises, actually initiates the debate on "gifts" and race. One could say that Natty changes his views later in the chronological time of the series, or can seem less complex in his views (that is what we might argue if Cooper wrote the Leatherstocking novels in chronological order over chronological time); or, as I am suggesting, one could say that Natty's reflections on "gifts" in this final novel work to revise our understanding of the discussions to come in the four earlier novels. Viewed in this light, one of Cooper's great contributions as a historical novelist to a philosophy of history is the a-chronological temporal revisionism of the Leatherstocking series, which unfixes connections between time and space in order to emphasize repetition over progress, even as he shows that such temporal revisionism does allow for possibilities of new knowledge and cultural change.

Nowhere is the revisionary force of Natty's rethinking more apparent than in the way he connects his new ideas about gifts to a revised view of heaven. Again, what's interesting here in terms of temporality is that Natty is rethinking notions in a 1841 novel (set in the early 1740s) that had initially been set forth in an 1826 novel (set in 1757). At the conclusion of *The Last of the Mohicans*, the Delaware young women's mourning song about Uncas and Cora dwelling together in heaven disturbs Natty. The narrator writes: "But when they spoke of the future prospects of Cora and Uncas, he shook his head, like one who knew the error of their simple creed, and resuming his reclining attitude, he maintained it until the ceremony—if that might be called a ceremony, in which feeling was so deeply imbued—was finished. Happily for the self-command of Heyward and Munro, they knew not the meaning of the wild sounds they heard" (344). The narrator seems to be aligned with Natty in rejecting the notion of an interracial heaven, though there are ambiguities. We can't be absolutely certain about why Natty shakes his head, and the use of the word "Happily" could be meant to underscore the prejudices of both Cora's admirer and her father, rather than to convey solidarity with such prejudices. That Natty in the closing paragraphs of *Mohicans* is holding hands with Chingachgook and vowing to stay by his side in the wilderness also seems at odds with his views. Would Natty think it a good thing to be separated from Chingachgook in heaven?

Apparently not, for in *The Deerslayer* he has a change of mind on the subject. In the same discussion of "gifts" and "natur'" that comes late in the novel, Natty also talks to Hetty and Judith about heaven: "The Delaware, here, and Hist, believe in happy hunting grounds, and have ideas befitting their notions and gifts, as red skins, but we who are of white blood hold altogether to a different opinion" (436). In certain respects, Natty at this moment seems to share the beliefs of his older self in the earlier *Mohicans*. But then he has an insight, and years before facing the conundrum of *Mohicans*, he conceives of a way for him and Chingachgook to stay together even after death do they part: "Still, I rather conclude our heaven is their land of spirits, and that the path which leads to it will be travelled by all colours alike. 'Tis onpossible for the wicked to enter on it, I will allow, but fri'nds can scarce be separated, though they are not of the same race on 'arth" (436). Viewed from this perspective, the Delaware women at the end of *The Last of the Mohicans* got things right. Having reformulated his views while speaking to Hetty and Judith, Natty then conveys the happy news to Chingachgook and, as in *The Last of the Mohicans*, they "warmly" (457) hold hands. Cooper gives the last word on the subject to Chingachgook himself: "The Delawares believe that good men and brave warriors will hunt together in the same pleasant woods" (456).

Despite Chingachgook's emphasis on men, *The Deerslayer* suggests that women like Hetty and Hist will also be part of a racially inclusive heaven. That the "fallen" Judith is depicted as a victim of seduction makes her a good candidate as well. But to move from heaven back to earth: Cooper's troubling of the notion of "gifts" has important consequences for how we might think about the rise of white empire. Given that Natty never quite achieves clarity on the matter of race, it is not surprising that the women characters emerge as the most prescient critics of Anglo-American empire in particular, which throughout the novel works its will through racism and patriarchal violation. Cooper's valuing of the critical perspectives of Judith, Hetty, and Hist is made clear not only in the text itself, but in his January 31, 1841, letter to his publisher, when he suggests as possible titles for his novel "Judith and Esther; or, the Girls of Glimmerglass"; or "Wah!-Ta-Wah!, or, Hist!-Oh!-Hist!" (*Letters and Journals* 4:112; on the importance of women to the Leatherstocking series, see Baym). Hurry and Hutter's violence, as I have been emphasizing, is regularly directed at Indian women and children. As Hutter proclaims about the bounty: "If there's women, there's children, and big and little have scalps; the Colony pays for all alike" (87). Hurry goes on to justify their plans to scalp women and children as an act of revenge, and it is Judith, not Natty, who poses the most compelling challenge to his world view: "is it religion to say that one *bad* turn deserves another" (87). Her frustrations and anger build over the course of the novel. As she remarks shortly after the two men go in pursuit of scalps: "I get warm, when I think of all the wrong that men do" (137). The religious Hetty poses a similar challenge to the violence of Hurry and Hutter, and the English more generally, through sentimental appeals to the heart and Bible, and Cooper honors the moral clarity of her vision. Still, he leaves it to Judith and Hist to articulate the sharpest critiques of white imperial culture. In certain respects, then, they become model readers of the five novels of the Leatherstocking series.

Hist's role as a critic of the violence, racism, and hypocrisy undergirding white empire (which is to say, as a critic of the course of empire depicted in the series when read in the chronological order of plot) is of particular importance. When Hurry and Hutter are being held by the Iroquois, Hetty, who is honored by the Indians for her spirituality, is allowed to visit, and she asks Hist to tell the Iroquois the truth of the matter: "Tell them, first, that father and Hurry came here with an intention to take as many scalps as they could, for the wicked governor and the province have offered money for scalps, whether of warriors, or women, men or children" (190). Hist's phrasing here suggests that Hurry and Hutter cannot be understood apart from the British colonizers; and as Hetty attempts to teach Hist about the Bible, it is Hist, and the eavesdropping Iroquois chief Rivenoak, who point to the limits, indeed the evils, of those who use the Bible to legitimate conquest. Rivenoak wonders why Bible-reading whites, who are "ordered to *give* double to him that asks only for one thing," decide instead to "*take* double from the poor Indian who ask for *no* thing" (194). When Hetty starts crying from confusion, Hist, who had expressed a caustic rage that a Bible calling for love "is the law by which my white brethren professes to live" (194), now attempts to comfort Hetty with her own form of racial egalitarianism: "Why you so trouble? You no make he book, if he be wrong, and you no make he pale face if he wicked. There wicked red man, and wicked white man—no colour all good—no colour all wicked" (195). Still, as the novel develops, it can seem that wickedness falls mainly on the side of the whites, and that it is Hetty, Hist, and Judith who call white men to account. After Hutter is scalped by Indians who want the reward money, both Hetty and Judith take note of the poetic justice. As Judith pointedly remarks to Hurry: "His skin and hair have been torn from his head to gain money from the governor of Canada, as you would have torn theirs from the heads of the Hurons, to gain money from the governor of York" (362).

Though Hutter is killed by the Hurons, it is Hurry who commits the most despicable act of the novel, wantonly killing an Indian woman in revenge for having been held prisoner. Shortly after being ransomed from captivity, Hurry returns with a gun, demonstrating that revenge knows no color, and shoots randomly into the Indian settlement. Cooper describes the scene: "The crack of a rifle succeeded, and then followed the roll of the echo along the eastern mountains. Almost at the same moment, a piercing female cry arose in the air in a prolonged shriek. The awful stillness that succeeded was, if possible, more appalling than the fierce and sudden interruption of the deep silence of midnight" (317). When *The Deerslayer* is read as the first of the Leatherstocking series, this "act of unthinking cruelty" (321), as the narrator terms it, stands behind all of the novels to come, and it is an act that, at the very least, makes it difficult to read the series as about the "natural" ascent of white men to power in the North American continent. This is the first of two major assaults by white men on the Iroquois, both of which result in the killing of women, and the wantonness and cruelty of both assaults help to illuminate the Indian anger that we see in the novels to come. There is something haunting about the woman's scream and subsequent silence, and the description of the dying woman (who had been shot shortly after meeting with her lover) only adds to our sense of outrage: "[S]he was in the agonies of death, while the blood that trickled from her bared bosom betrayed the nature of the injury she had received" (317–318). Her body tells the story of violation, and while Natty can barely say a word, it is Hist who mounts the most telling challenge to Hurry's evil action: "What for you shoot?...How you feel, your wife killed?...Why you so wicked, great pale-face?" (322).

The novel builds to a horrific scene of violence, indeed of wickedness, which vindicates both Hist's and Judith's critiques of English colonial forces. The critic Eric Cheyfitz, basing his reading of the Leatherstocking series on *The Pioneers*, the first novel published in the series, writes that "the 'good' Indians must fight on the side of the 'good guys,' who, in Cooper's story of the development of the United States, which is the overriding story of the Tales, are necessarily the English and their descendants" (120). But in *The Deerslayer*, the revisionary first novel of the series, distinctions between "good" and "bad" Indian, Delaware and Iroquois, have broken down. The Iroquois chief Rivenoak is one of the most exemplary Indian characters in all of Cooper's fiction, a democratic leader who has risen to power in his tribe "purely by the force of talents, [and] sagacity" (489), while it is the Delaware Briarthorn, who kidnapped Hist and for a while managed to pass as Iroquois, who contributes to the novel's overall violence. More important with respect to Cheyfitz's argument, while the Iroquois and Delaware are presented as exemplars of democratic practice—"it is well known that little which could be called monarchical, or despotic entered into the politics of the North American tribes" (489)—the English, who serve the King, emerge as monarchical and self-satisfied killers (in the manner of Hurry Harry), thus raising all sorts of questions about the Tales' "overriding story."

In the novel's final dramatic scene, the red-faced British Captain Warley, who has been presented as Judith's probable seducer and whose redness links him with stereotypes of Indian savagery, arrives at Glimmerglass as the "rescuer" of Natty and his compatriots, guided by the racist, hate-filled Hurry. Warley's English troops, Hurry, and Natty himself subsequently participate in a battle that involves the indiscriminate killing of Indian women and children by the troops' phallicized bayonets. There is nothing heroic or admirable about these killers wearing "the scarlet of the King's livery" (521). Natty uses his gun to kill his enemies, but mostly the final battle is about the bayonet: "[T]he shrieks, groans, and denunciations that usually accompany the use of the bayonet followed. That terrible and deadly weapon was glutted in vengeance. The scene that succeeded was one of those, of which so many have occurred in our own times, in which neither age nor sex forms an exemption to the lot of a savage warfare" (522). The reference to "our own times" points to outrages in Cooper's contemporary moment, suggesting that he may have been haunted by the news of the deaths of Indian women and children on the Trail of Tears. In his account of the aftermath of the massacre, Cooper is scathing in his portrayal of Warley. Like Hurry, this "hard featured, red faced, man" (524) betrays no concern about the deaths of the Indians. Hetty is dying from a bullet wound (from an inadvertent shot from the Hurons or Natty, or perhaps the British soldiers), and she is joined in death by the numerous Huron women and children who had been stabbed by the British: "The Sumach, all the elderly women, and some of the Huron girls, had fallen by a bayonet" (526).

In a novel that has at its center women's outrage at Hurry's wanton killing of an Indian woman, there is unambiguous critique of English brutality, which can be viewed on a continuum leading to the "rise" of the U.S. nation as depicted in *The Pioneers* and *The Prairie*. If there is a hero at the conclusion of the novel, it is Rivenoak, who maintains his self-command to the very end: "That he mourned the loss of his tribe, is certain; still he did it in a manner that best became a warrior and a chief" (526). Cooper is often criticized for supposedly confusing extinction with extermination, but there is no ambiguity here. Rivenoak's tribe has been decimated by the bayonets of troops linked to a British seducer. Judith's outraged declaration the day after the massacre resonates as a feminist critique that aligns her with Hist's outrage at Hurry and his murderous compatriots, and in certain ways announces an end to the Leatherstocking series: "I wish never to hear of marks, or rifles, or soldiers, or *men*, again" (530; Cooper's emphasis).

But we hear just a bit more about men in the novel's unsettling concluding chapters. Natty, who has accepted Judith's gift of Killdeer (the magnificent rifle found in Hutter's trunk), and is now Hawkeye and not Deerslayer, proclaims that he will be joining forces with Warley and his successors in order to keep the French from the land claimed by England. Cooper's vision is apparently progressive, as he presents both this battle and the Seven Years' War to come (previewed in the jump forward to the 1750s in the final chapter) as essential to the emergence of an American empire. It is accurate to say with Philip Fisher that over the course of the novel Natty has become a killer; but it would also be accurate to say that from beginning to end Cooper seems at a distance from this killer. When Natty after accepting Judith's gift of Killdeer declares that he will now "become King of the Woods" (390), it is difficult not to cringe at the language of empire linking him with the king of England. While Natty looks forward to a continent cleared of the French and their Indian allies, Cooper at the conclusion of the novel offers an image of inevitable decline, remarking about postmassacre Glimmerglass that the beautiful lake will always be there while humans will come and go: "The frightful event of the preceding evening had left no impression on the placid sheet" (523). But the "placid sheet" contains numerous dead bodies, as do the mounds in *The Prairies*, which Cooper here "anticipates" and enriches through his imaging of Glimmerglass itself as a burial ground. The eternal natural beauty of Glimmerglass is reinvoked in the closing semihopeful sentences of the novel: "We live in a world of transgressions and selfishness, and no pictures that represent us otherwise can be true, though, happily, for human nature, gleamings of that pure spirit in whose likeness man has been fashioned, are to be seen relieving its deformities, and mitigating if not excusing its crimes" (548). How apt that the final word of the Leatherstocking series is "crimes."

With the emphasis on crimes, Cooper provides new ways of thinking about what is implicit in the earlier-published Leatherstocking novels that chronologically follow *The Deerslayer*. The death of Chingachgook in *The Pioneers*, Tamamund's and Magua's sharp critiques of the English in *The Last of the Mohicans*, the mounds of *The Prairies*, the violence of the French and the Indians in both *The Last of the Mohicans* and *The Pathfinder*, all resonate very differently in light of the revisionary implications of the final novel of the series, which really does point to the end. It is difficult, for instance, to make significant distinctions between the Iroquois' slaughtering of English women and children at the midpoint of *The Last of the Mohicans* and the English troops' slaughtering of Iroquois women and children at the end of *The Deerslayer*. If anything, the violent ending of *The Deerslayer* asks readers to regard the Iroquois violence in *The Last of the Mohican* as having been prompted by the earlier crimes of the "lawless empire" (45) of the English invaders.

Near the end of his life, as he was preparing the 1850 prefaces which would urge readers to begin the Leatherstocking series with *The Deerslayer*, Cooper became close friends with George Copway, an Ojibwa Indian also known as Kah-ge-ga-gah-bowh, whose autobiography, *The Life, History and Travels of Kah-ge-ga-gah-bowh (George Copway)* (1847), republished as *The Life, Letters and Speeches of Kah-ge-ga-gah-bowh, or G. Copway* (1850), went into multiple editions and became a best seller. Copway was a Methodist convert who in the late 1840s emerged as an influential writer on Indian affairs, arguing in particular against federal efforts to relocate (or remove) the Ojibwa from Michigan and Wisconsin to Minnesota. While lecturing in New York against removal, he met Cooper, and the two became friends. Although Americanists tend to regard Cooper as a writer whose Leatherstocking novels deviously lent ideological support for Indian removal, Copway saw him as a writer whose works spoke to Indian grievances and ennobled rather than belittled Indians. In all likelihood Copway had read *The Deerslayer*, and if so, it is not surprising that he would see Cooper as that rare white writer who gave voice to Indians' resistance to white empire. After spending time with Cooper at Cooperstown, Copway wrote him in 1850: "Of all the writers of our dear native land, you have done more justice to our down trodden race than any other author.... By your books the noble traits of the savage have been presented in their true light" (qtd. Cooper, *Letters and Journals* 6:275). In a letter of June 1851, Copway wrote Cooper asking for a contribution to a new journal, *Copway's American Indian*, which, he told Cooper, would be "a channel of information for the American people and to the Indian Race of all such things which will tend to give [both] a better idea of each other" (275). Cooper contributed a letter to the first of twelve issues published between July 10 and September 27, 1851, and Copway would write an appreciative essay on Cooper in the July 19 issue and an admiring obituary in the issue of September 20. Cooper's letter to Copway of June 17, 1851, shows why Copway was such an admirer and friend. "Certainly I should take great interest in the success of a journal like that you have mentioned," Cooper writes. "The red man has a high claim to have his cause defended, and I trust you will be able to do much in his behalf" (274–275). Though he remarks that sickness will make it difficult for him to offer a substantial contribution, Cooper concludes his letter by underscoring their friendship: "I hope you may find leisure to make your promised visit and that we may expect the pleasure of seeing you again at my house" (275).

A James Fenimore Cooper who believes that the "cause" of the Indians should be "defended"; a Cooper who works closely with an Indian activist; a Cooper who regards Indians as alive and well in the United States and not on the verge of extinction; a Cooper who numbers among his closest friends at the close of his life an Ojibwa Indian—this is not the Cooper of current American literary studies. It is time that we reread the Leatherstocking novels by beginning with the end.

BIBLIOGRAPHY

Allen, Thomas M. *A Republic in Time: Temporality and Social Imagination in Nineteenth-Century America*. Chapel Hill: University of North Carolina Press, 2008.

Axelrad, Allen M. "The Shock of Recognition: Twain and Lawrence Read Cooper." *Reading Cooper, Teaching Cooper*. Ed. Jeffrey Walker. New York: AMS Press, 2007. 46–75.

Baym, Nina. "The Women of Cooper's Leatherstocking Tales." *American Quarterly* 23 (1971): 696–709.

Bellin, Joshua David. *The Demon of the Continent: Indians and the Shaping of American Literature*. Philadelphia: University of Pennsylvania Press, 2001.

Bender, Thomas. *A Nation among Nations: America's Place in World History*. New York: Hill and Wang, 2006.

Cheyfitz, Eric. "Savage Law: The Plot against American Indians in *Johnson and Graham's Lessee v. M'Intotsh* and *The Pioneers*." *Cultures of United States Imperialism*. Ed. Amy Kaplan and Donald E. Pease. Durham, NC. Duke University Press, 1993. 109–128.

Cooper, James Fenimore. *The Deerslayer; or, The First War Path*. 1841. Ed. James Franklin Beard et al. Albany: State University of New York Press, 1987.

———. *The Last of the Mohicans: A Narrative of 1757*. 1826. Ed. James Franklin Beard et al. Albany: State University of New York Press, 1983.

———. *Letters and Journals*. 6 vols. Ed. James Franklin Beard. Cambridge, MA: Harvard University Press, 1960–1968.

Dekker, George. *The American Historical Romance*. Cambridge: Cambridge University Press, 1987.

Dekker, George, and John P. McWilliams. *Fenimore Cooper: The Critical Heritage*. London: Routledge and Keegan Paul, 1973.

Fisher, Philip. *Hard Facts: Setting and Form in the American Novel*. New York: Oxford University Press, 1985.

Franklin, Wayne. *James Fenimore Cooper: The Early Years*. New Haven, CT: Yale University Press, 2007.

Fredrickson, George M. *The Black Image in the White Mind: The Debate on Afro-American Character and Destiny, 1817–1914*. New York: Harper and Row, 1971.

Gaul, Theresa Strouth. "Romance and the 'Genuine Indian': Cooper's Politics of Genre." *ESQ* 48 (2002): 159–186.

Kelly, William P. *Plotting America's Past: Fenimore Cooper and the Leatherstocking Tales.*
    Carbondale: University of Southern Illinois Press, 1983.
Lawrence, D. H. *Studies in Classic American Literature.* 1923. New York: Viking Press, 1972.
Mann, Barbara Alice. "Race Traitor: Cooper, His Critics, and Nineteenth-Century Literary
    Politics." Person, *A Historical Guide to James Fenimore Cooper* 155–185.
McWilliams, John P. Jr. *Political Justice in a Republic: James Fenimore Cooper's America.*
    Berkeley: University of California Press, 1972.
Nelson, Dana D. "Cooper's Leatherstocking Conversations: Identity, Friendship, and
    Democracy in the New Nation." Person, *A Historical Guide to James Fenimore Cooper*
    123–154.
Nobles, Gregory H. *American Frontiers: Cultural Encounters and Continental Conquest.*
    New York: Hill and Wang, 1997.
Peck, H. Daniel. *A World by Itself: The Pastoral Moment in Cooper's Fiction.* New Haven,
    CT: Yale University Press, 1977.
Person, Leland S., ed. *A Historical Guide to James Fenimore Cooper.* New York: Oxford
    University Press, 2007.
———. "The Historical Paradoxes of Manhood in Cooper's *The Deerslayer.*" *Novel:
    A Forum on Fiction* 32 (1998): 76–98.
Rans, Geoffrey. *Cooper's Leather-Stocking Novels: A Secular Reading.* Chapel Hill: University
    of North Carolina Press, 1991.
Rosenwald, Lawrence Alan. *Multilingual America: Language and the Making of American
    Literature.* New York: Cambridge University Press, 2008.
Sheckel, Susan. "'In the Land of His Fathers': Cooper, Land Rights, and the Legitimation
    of American National Identity." *James Fenimore Cooper: New Historical and Literary
    Contexts.* Ed. W. M. Verhoeven. Amsterdam: Rodopi, 1993. 89–103.
Slotkin, Richard. *Regeneration through Violence: The Mythology of the American Frontier,
    1600–1860.* Middletown, CT: Wesleyan University Press, 1973.
Tomc, Sandra. "'Clothes upon Sticks': James Fenimore Cooper and the Flat Frontier." *Texas
    Studies in Literature and Language* 51 (2009): 142–178.
Twain, Mark. "Fenimore Cooper's Literary Offenses." *North American Review* 161 (July
    1895): 1–12.

CHAPTER 10

THE VISIBLE AND INVISIBLE CITY: ANTEBELLUM WRITERS AND URBAN SPACE

JEFFREY STEELE

1

THERE remain huge gaps in American literary history. In their analyses of the nineteenth century, literary scholars have tended to focus their attention on nature writing. The powerful influence of British romanticism—as well as the impact of writers such as Cooper, Thoreau, Dickinson, and Twain—has made this development inevitable. Despite the ongoing significance of urban writing in American literature, nature writing and—most recently—ecocriticism have long remained dominant focal points for the study and teaching of nineteenth-century American literature. The pastoralism of novelists such as James Fenimore Cooper, as well as the nature and travel writing of transcendentalists such as Henry David Thoreau and Margaret Fuller, have given an air of inevitability to critical methodologies that highlight the natural landscape and literary responses to it. Setting a critical agenda that has persisted for decades, works such as Henry Nash Smith's *Virgin Land: The American West as Symbol and Myth* (1950) and Leo Marx's *The Machine in the Garden: Technology and the Pastoral Ideal in America* (1964) encouraged in-depth critical attention to nineteenth-century nature writing. Despite the importance of urban writers such as Edgar Allan Poe, George Lippard, and Fanny Fern, nineteenth-century urban writing has not yet been systematically examined as a coherent field of study with its own set of literary strategies and concerns. Particularly interesting are the cases of Walt Whitman and Herman Melville, who are often aligned with nature writing, yet who also made important contributions to the representation of the city. Works such as *Song of Myself* and *Pierre* contain both rural and urban scenes. While there exist numerous critical paradigms clarifying their interest in natural landscapes, it is time to consider how American writers conceptualized their experiences of urban space as well.

When one begins to examine nineteenth-century urban writing as a distinct field of study, different literary strategies and styles of reading are necessary. As Michel de Certeau argues in his influential essay "Walking in the City," a vast portion of urban life exists "below the threshold at which visibility begins" (93). As a result, texts that attempt to make "the complexity of the city readable" through "totalizing" discourses of "panoptic power" (95) are incomplete. In contrast to reading the city (or urban writing) as a continuous plane of experience, de Certeau stresses the invisible and discontinuous aspects of a lived space that can only be adequately represented through a narrative "order" that is "torn open by ellipses, drifts, and leaks of meaning" (107). Such observation suggests that urban environments may be best represented by literary forms that value discontinuity over continuity (such as plot) and that such works need to be processed through acts of what Peter Stallybrass has termed "discontinuous reading." Stallybrass and his followers begin with the medieval system of bookmarking passages, so that a reader could jump back and forth from one position in a text to another in a reading "practice of discontinuity" (46). Crossing the Atlantic, Matthew Brown locates in early New England "discontinuous reading habits of random access and cross-referencing" (62). Confronted with a complex urban environment crisscrossed by a welter of competing messages and political agendas, nineteenth-century urban dwellers learned early on the advantages of discontinuous writing and reading. In the face of class conflicts, social divisions, and mystified spatialities, the literature of continuity worked less well than the vignette, the urban "slice" (George Foster), the letter (Lydia Maria Child), the newspaper columns (Margaret Fuller, Fanny Fern, Whitman), or collages of fictional scenes (George Lippard, Fern). Rather than reading the city as a continuous spatial and textual field, antebellum urban writers constructed composite works that require readers to negotiate competing viewpoints, as they navigate the fault lines and divisions marking the city.

While nature writing often involves vast, panoramic vistas and dramatic movement through visible landscapes, in the nineteenth-century city, such sightlines and mobility were often blocked. Although pictorial modes such as the sublime and the picturesque were transposed to urban settings, literary emphasis fell more on the occlusion of vision than on its satisfaction. But despite the fascination of many city writers with urban mysteries and political divisions, much of the critical discussion of urban writing has attempted to maintain the emphasis upon the visual.

From this perspective, what matters most is what can be *seen*. Until recently, three models have shaped much of the analysis of nineteenth-century urban writing. One approach conceptualizes the city as "landscape" that can be approached through analogy with models developed to analyze nature writing. The second builds upon Walter Benjamin's influential discussion of the flaneur—the urban rambler who recorded his impression of what is characterized as the urban "panorama." The third, the "sunshine-and-shadow" tradition, focuses upon opposed urban realms of wealth and poverty, virtue and vice. For the most part, these critical modes tend to be descriptive, focusing upon the visible sights of the city, whether parks, streets, or slums. But in addition to representing the city as a collection of sights, many urban writers stressed as well what could *not* be seen. Instead of lingering over visible spaces, they represented the urban landscape as a site of "spatial trauma" that opens up what I term "the question of the surface." In their works, the city becomes a place where freedom of movement and perception are blocked by hidden forces, visible only in their secondary effects. But before turning to a discussion of the way spatiality is troubled in nineteenth-century urban writing, let me briefly sketch the critical viewpoints that represent the city as a collection of visible locales.

There are striking historical reasons for viewing the city as a landscape analogous to nature. In 1831 the consecration of Mount Auburn Cemetery in Cambridge, Massachusetts, inaugurated the garden cemetery movement in this country—one of the primary inspirations for urban landscape design. The creation of Central Park in Manhattan—dating back to the 1858 acceptance of Frederick Law Olmsted's plan—solidified the culture of urban parks. Recently, proponents of ecocriticism have continued the city-as-natural-landscape tradition by analyzing the development of green spaces within urban environments (Bennett and Teague). We might identify this naturalization of the city as an early stage in the urban imagination— one that blends a romantic nostalgia for nature with a longing to maintain natural rhythms even in the midst of the urban environment. As Walter Benjamin observes in his *Arcades Project*, "the old Romantic sentiment for landscape dissolves and a new Romantic conception emerges—of landscape that seems, rather, to be a city-scape" (420). In the middle of the nineteenth century, Benjamin continues, the novels of James Fenimore Cooper deeply influenced writers who grappled with urban settings. For example, Eugène Sue, the author of the widely read *Les Mystères de Paris* (1842–1843), wrote near the beginning of his famous novel that: "It is our intent to bring before the eyes of the reader some of the episodes in the lives of various other barbarians, no less removed from the civilized world than the tribes so well portrayed by Cooper" (cited Benjamin 441). Following narrative traditions that were set in nature, urban writers began "tranpos[ing] the inhabitants of the prairie to a Parisian setting," at the same time that they saw "the big city as mysterious as the forests of the New World" (Benjamin 441). Such "transposition[s] of…setting" (Benjamin 439) reinforced representations of urban environments as landscapes that could be explored and narrated.

One of the effects of the nature-writing model of urban literature was the ready appropriation of modes of perception that had originally developed in relation to natural landscapes. The "picturesque," especially, was widely adapted as a category that highlighted the pleasing, pictorial, or irregular qualities of urban scenes (Bramen). But although many urban writers described "picturesque" moments in their encounters with the city, most of them moved beyond the mere celebration of pleasing moments of visual perception. As a number of scholars have noted, the picturesque—along with the touristic perspective aligned with it—tends to foreclose political analysis, which is submerged beneath the viewer's concern with his or her own visual pleasure. When viewed objects or people are placed outside of the domains of "social change" or "history," the objects of picturesque awareness become "exotic, apolitical 'others' " (Bailey 231, 233). As Ellen Strain argues, the "trope of picturesqueness" positions spectators as "procurers of images" who are not "immersed" in the spaces they are viewing (89). This was the viewpoint of many early visitors to New York, such as Frances Trollope, who in 1832 praised the beauty of the city's harbor and surrounding "landscape." "Various and lovely are the objects which meet the eye on every side," Trollope gushed, as she bemoaned her inability to communicate the various glories of "the scene" (16). Looking from the outside in, Trollope—like many nineteenth-century visitors to New York—measured her impressions against a preexisting category of visual perception, derived from landscape painting.

A cautionary example of the "naturalist" approach to urban writing is found in Arnold Goldsmith's *The Modern Urban American Novel: Nature as "Interior Structure."* Arguing that "Nature continues to be one of the richest sources for the creative imagination," Goldsmith's study has "three areas of focus": (1) "scenes set in parks, on rivers or lakes, or on green belts," (2) specific characters' "love of nature," and (3) "the use of nature sympathetically to reflect or reinforce the mood of a particular character or scene" (Goldsmith 10–12). But by defining "nature" as a universal environmental context, citing with approval Emerson's conception of nature as "essences unchanged by man: space, the air, the river, the leaf" (9), Goldsmith is unable to consider whether a pastoral model of "nature" may not be a universal epistemological category but rather an urban myth with its own ideological charge. While they nourished pastoral reveries, the green spaces of the city often formed part of a *constructed* urban space in which dreams of nature disguised existing social conditions. Exploring the connection between such conditions and emerging conceptions of nature, Henri Lefebvre has suggested that the concept of "nature" itself was an urban invention. There is "no city, no urban space" Lefebvre argues in *The Urban Revolution*, "without a garden or park, without the simulation of nature"—"a utopia of nature…against which urban reality can situate and perceive itself" (26). What threatens to be obscured in the nostalgia for nature is the recognition that the "urban revolution," as it unfolded, created "another nature…that is *different* from the initial nature" (108, emphasis added). Mediating the experiences of city dwellers, this "second nature" composed of "stone and metal" (25) led to the creation of different modes of dwelling and different imaginative structures. Despite the attraction of pastoral images, it eventually becomes self-defeating to view urban spaces solely through a mode of vision attuned to vistas of prairies and forests. If the vision of the city as nature forms one end of a continuum of urban perception, at the other end, one can conceptualize the city as a "second nature" with its own unique modes of experience, dwelling, and perception.

In the effort to characterize literary responses to this "second nature," a number of critics have utilized a second model of urban writing by analyzing nineteenth-century urban spaces in terms of an aesthetics of visibility centered on panorama, spectacle, and the observations of the flaneur. Orienting themselves in terms of a dynamic of the spectator/spectacle, both Dana Brand (in *The Spectator and the City in Nineteenth-Century American Literature*) and Deborah Nord (in *Walking the Victorian Streets: Women, Representation, and the City*) focus upon the visual mastery of urban observers who located themselves in "panoramic spaces" (Brand) and the "urban panorama" (Nord). When we recall that the nineteenth-century panorama was a *continuously* unrolling painting, often hundreds of feet long, we can begin to recognize the ways that a panoramic model of urban spectatorship privileges visual continuity and mimetic accuracy at the expense of other aspects of urban experience. According to Brand, the texts of American urban writers grew out of their interest in the "perpetually changing spectacle" (4) of the urban "pan-orama" (52)—a literary investment in spectatorship that dated back to eighteenth-century urban essayists and which was imported to the United States by writers such as Fanny Fern's brother, Nathaniel Parker Willis (67). Given the social prohibitions against middle-class women walking city streets alone, it should not surprise us that Brand's portrait of antebellum urban writing is entirely male. (This is a gender imbalance that Nord addresses in her book, as she discusses the struggle of female observers or flaneuses to achieve visual authority.) Neither Lydia Maria Child nor Margaret Fuller, who both created alternatives to the flaneurial model of observation, is mentioned in Brand's book. This is a particularly striking omission, given his assertion that: "After 1840, no one writing in the New York press seems to have had any doubt about the suitability of New York as a venue for the flaneur" (73). Prominent historians have also succumbed to the lure of the flaneur. In their monumental study *Gotham: A History of New York City to 1898*, Edwin Burrows and Mike Wallace highlight the profusion of "street narratives by middle-class walkers," a mode of writing based upon the European tradition of the flaneur (692).

In new penny dailies such as the *New York Sun*, *Herald*, and *Tribune*, descriptions of city streets (such as the fashionable Broadway) amused readers, who delighted in measuring their daily perceptions against the impressions of strolling journalists. Perhaps the most famous American practitioner of this mode of urban observation was Nathaniel Parker Willis, who also penned numerous accounts of his travels abroad. "[F]laneurism," Burrows and Wallace observe, "made Willis New York's first successful professional 'magazinist' " (692). In texts such as "Daguerrotypes of the Present" and *Hurry-Graphs*, Willis presented an impressionistic overview of the urban panorama. His essay "Open-Air Musings in the City" provides an excellent example of his style. Opening with a description of all the urban types that strolled down Broadway and past his office window, Willis then depicts himself walking the city's streets and visiting its picturesque locales. In the process, he clearly segregates

the denizens of Broadway into carefully circumscribed temporal and social categories: "*Eight in the morning*" is a time of "clerks," "seam-stresses and schoolmis-
tresses"; from "*Nine and after*" until "*Five and after*," he records a few merchants
and a wide range of "gentlemen" and "ladies"; finally, at "*Half-past six and after*," he
sees "Business-men" and ladies departing for home. Only then, at the end of the day,
the "unfortunate *outlaws* of charity and pity" come out, along with "sailors, row-
dies, country-people, and strangers" (227–232, emphasis added). This remarkable
catalogue virtually cleanses New York's most famous street of any disruptive social
presence during the day, even though—as Eric Homberger observes in *Scenes from
the Life of a City*—"contemporaries reluctantly acknowledged" that "it was impossible to walk through the city without seeing beggars, malnourished children, and
the many distressing manifestations of poverty and unemployment" (37). Willis's
characterization of prostitutes as "outlaws of charity and pity" vividly suggests the
essentially conservative aspect of flaneurial observation. Recording urban impressions, he lingers over the visually appealing (such as the fashionable ladies prom-
enading up and down Broadway), but he doesn't challenge preexisting social or
moral categories.

At times, Willis's essay reads like a literary equivalent of nineteenth-century
genre painting. Describing the waterfront, for example, he describes the "heavy fog,"
the sails of ships enclosed in "melo-dramatic" mist, and a "horizon...completely
concealed with the spread of canvas" (239). Watching the crew of ships at their daily
tasks, he records "a strangely-mixed *picture*," commenting in passing on the way
the ships' "spars and lines" are "drawn in clear tracery" upon the sky (241, emphasis added). Willis's commitment throughout his essay is to a visual impressionism,
a vantage point reinforced by the "*sliding panorama*" he sees outside his carriage
window (247, emphasis added). But by dramatizing himself as an urban "spectator"
registering "evanescent impressions," a writer like Willis is limited by what his eyes
can see. Rather than evaluating his experience through a moral, spiritual, or political framework of understanding, he is reduced to registering "traces of that which
is fleeting, or struck out like phosphorus from the sea by irregular chance." It is not
surprising, in consequence, that Willis concludes his sketch by lamenting all of the
"ephemeral" experiences that he cannot record, "soundings...too deep for ordinary
life to fathom" (252). As he comes close to intuiting, what is lost in Willis's "panoramic" analyses are other dimensions of the flaneur, who was not only an urban
observer but also (according to David Frisby) a detective, collector of impressions,
archaeologist, and producer of texts (35–38). Confronting the discontinuities and
complexities of the city, this figure (often interpreted as a model of the modern
urban self) actively constructed patterns of meaning in the face of potential chaos.
Nineteenth-century urban reality was not simply an unbroken plane of *visible* experience that "unrolled" panoramically in front of an observer, but contained other
elements that were difficult—if not impossible—to process in visual terms.

Critics have highlighted a third mode of nineteenth-century city writing—
the "sunshine-and-shadow" tradition associated with urban exposés and mysteries. According to Burrows and Wallace, this "perceptual mode" was pioneered by

Sue's *The Mysteries of Paris* and Charles Dickens's stark portraits of London, texts
that stressed the schism between "two shadowy and corrupt worlds, one of the
criminal underground, the other of a decadent elite" (697). Urban writers adapted
the "sunshine-and-shadow" tradition by emphasizing the coexistence of opposed
urban realms, divided by class divisions and demarcated by specific geographical
boundaries. In his 1842 volume, *American Notes*, for example, Dickens recorded
his impressions of New York, as he contrasted "bustling" Broadway (90) with the
squalor of the notorious Five Points slum with its "underground chambers" of "vice
and misery" (101). Despite her profound commitment to social reform, Lydia Maria
Child opened the first of her *Letters from New York* in 1841 by distinguishing the
city's "magnificence and mud, finery and filth, diamonds and dirt," "Wealth" and
Poverty" (25). It is striking that the private diary of the patrician businessman Philip
Hone (one of the most important sources of information on antebellum New York)
also fell easily into the rhetoric of contrasting worlds, suggesting the widespread
influence of the "sunshine-and-shadow tradition." Writing on the "State of Society"
in 1840s New York, Hone observed "Two extremes": one the one hand, "costly
luxury in living, expensive establishments, and improvident waste"; on the other,
"squalid misery and hopeless destitution" (Hone 785). "Sunshine-and-shadow"
writers depicted a city in which "the center no longer held" (Burrows and Wallace
697). Instead of locating patterns of interclass affiliation or even communication,
they represented the wealthy and the poor living on opposite sides of an inseparable
divide. As in the traditions of urban landscape writing and of flaneurial observation, they toured a city defined in terms of concrete geographical locales (some
of them subterranean) that could be visited and *described*. Yet despite their commitment to uncovering and making visible the "mysteries" of the city, writers who
confronted urban shadows eventually demonstrate the insufficiency of any model
of urban writing based solely upon the observation of visible phenomena.

When one moves beyond descriptive modes of critical analysis, it becomes
apparent that nineteenth-century writers were interested both in recording *the
sights* of the city and also in measuring the *limits of urban vision*. As a result, they
supplemented vision with other modes of perception, representing urban experience through multiple organs of perception: the heart (associated with sentimental
narratives), the soul (linked to the discourses of Christianity, transcendentalism,
and utopian socialism), the imagination (popularized by gothic and sensational fiction), and memory (located in discourses of history). Their multifaceted texts led
readers beyond visible spaces in order to reveal the fault lines fracturing society and
to construct mental maps that might help them navigate the complexities of the
evolving city. In the process, they demonstrated that the representation of urban
experience necessitates multiple planes of perception that intersect each other and
sometimes set up patterns of interference and disturbance. In the sixth of her *Letters
from New York*, for example, Child discusses the way her visit to the Crosby Street
synagogue shattered her preconceptions and "unfettered" her mind from "narrow
prejudice." Expecting to find only ancient dress and ritual, she was initially shocked
by the intrusion of contemporary material culture: a "common" English bowl and a

"common black hat." This intermingling of the present and the past, Child reflected, "broke the illusion completely" (25). Throughout her volume, one of her primary goals is to shatter such illusions, freeing her readers from the ideological inertia that chains her readers to "the despotic sway of custom and public opinion" (177). Instead, she asserts the importance of perceiving a "two-fold world" in which the traces of the past can be perceived in the present and in which everyday realities can be balanced against imagined alternatives. What results from this multiple layering of perception is a sense of urban space that gains both spatial depth and temporal complexity. Instead of resembling a flat surface, the city—in Child's writing—dissolves into a series of lingering afterimages that destabilize the apparent solidity of the urban panorama. Exploiting "discontinuities in perception" (Resina 12), she draws attention to the way urban experience is built up through the juxtaposition of discrete moments in time.

II

This sense of troubled space and time becomes especially vivid in the texts of many urban writers. Instead of depicting urban space as a panorama unrolling before his readers' eyes, Poe represents the city as a torn and discontinuous terrain that often blocks immediate perception. As a result, it takes powers of extraordinary deduction, exhibited for example by Poe's detective Dupin in "The Mystery of Marie Roget," to piece together a workable "map" of the city from a variety of planes that are separated from each other in space and time (for example, memory, observation, and journalistic accounts). Similarly, Poe's "The Man of the Crowd" confronts the dilemma of encountering an individual who personifies an urban space that is illegible, unable to be understood within the narrator's preexisting categories of perception. No matter how closely he follows or observes this enigmatic man of the crowd, the narrator cannot plumb the mysterious depths of his being—an encounter that convinces him that: "There are some secrets which do not permit themselves to be told" (506). In similar fashion, George Lippard's urban novels—*Quaker City*, *Empire City*, and *New York: Its Upper Ten and Lower Million*—also explored the unrecorded depths of urban experience. Working like a psychoanalyst probing the depths of urban corruption and crime, Lippard used both gothic and sensationalist modes in an attempt to reveal urban secrets that can only be partially uncovered. Such texts remind us that the idea of the city as a continuous and visible spatial field—a "spectacle"—is an illusion that sutures social and political divisions (Debord 19, 46).

In order to analyze the complex texture of such urban writing, I turn to Marxian and postmodern geographers, who argue that the metropolis is not a visible plane of immediately perceivable phenomena, but rather a site of spatial discontinuity, obstructed views, and invisibility. For example, Edward Soja argues in *Postmodern*

Geographies that the conception of space "only as a collection of things" accessible through "sensory-based perception" (122) obscures awareness of the hidden structures shaping social behavior by creating, instead, a "mystified spatiality, hidden from critical view under thick veils of illusion and ideology" (50). Maintaining the illusion that urban reality is a seamless plane of perceivable phenomena, critics who focus only on the visible spaces of the city obscure the "uneven development" of capitalism (67). Any awareness of society's social fragmentation sinks beneath the homogenizing framework of a continuously unfolding urban perception (128). According to Soja, this habit of mind dates back to René Descartes's conception of visible reality as an observable field, a *res extensa*, available to a detached observer. The two-dimensional mirror/veil of Cartesian space projects an illusory plane of consistency in which the fault lines of repressed social concerns have become invisible. In the process, exclusive focus on the visible world "reifies space, inducing a myopia that sees only a superficial materiality, concretized forms susceptible to little but measurement and phenomenal description: fixed, dead, and undialectical: the Cartesian cartography of spatial science" (7). This geographical misrecognition constructs a "mystified spatiality" (50) that "hides things from us" (61), covering over the stress points and fractures of social conflict. Believing that one walks through an untroubled urban space of "fixed" objects spread out before one's gaze, one fails to perceive suppressed zones of conflict. To the extent that they are forgotten, such sites of spatial trauma are passed over; an "illusion of opaqueness" reinforces the sense that the sights of the city are part of a "collection of things" (122) that have no real tie to forgotten events or invisible social causes.

Mystifying social and political divisions, the panoramic model of Cartesian space unselfconsciously induces what Henri Lefebvre characterizes as the "absolute" model of "abstract space" that has become the dominant model of spatiality in capitalist societies (*Production* 49–50). This viewpoint, Lefebvre argues,

> fragments space and cuts it up into pieces. It enumerates the things, the various objects, that space contains.... Thus, instead of uncovering the social relationships (including class relationships) that are latent in spaces,...we fall into the trap of treating space as space "in itself," as space as such. We come to think in terms of spatiality, and so to fetishize space in a way reminiscent of the old fetishism of commodities. (89–90)

Resisting a fetishism of space that keeps hidden from view economic and social differences, many urban writers focused upon the social, ideological, and textual *production* of urban space. Rather than privileging visuality, they explored aspects of the city that were invisible, discontinuous, and not immediately perceivable in visual terms. In the city, Anthony Vidler has observed, "the invisible is as much an obstacle to the new social order as the visible" (240). As numerous antebellum urban writers recognized, the invisible was also *part* of the social order. Not only were many aspects of the city hidden; but more important, the complexity of urban experience required more than visual recording. Effective urban analysis necessitated the measuring of urban sights against evaluative frameworks that supplemented what the eyes could see. Only in this way could one focus "a politics of resistance" that reveals the ways in which space was "colonized and commodified, bought and sold, created and torn down, used and abused, speculated on and fought over" (Merrifield 173).

As one moves beyond the visible facades of the city, the conception of urban space transforms radically. In the process, one starts to attend to the links between urban geographies, psychological "spaces," and the textual terrains created out of them. Building on the insights of poststructuralist theorists who raised "the question of the subject," one challenges the assumption that consciousness or visual perception is an unbroken surface. Just as the "plane" of consciousness is not a smooth unbroken space, urban space cannot be represented as a seamless terrain extending continuously (like Descartes's *res extensa*) in front of viewers. This awareness troubles urban perception and opens up what I term "the question of the surface." The psychic surface itself, according to contemporary psychoanalysts, is not an unbroken plane. Punctured by blindspots or "holes," consciousness sutures separate impressions into the illusion of continuity (for example, visual continuity). Rather than viewing urban experience as a complicated weaving that contains distortions and tears, one seems to move through a seamless fabric without gaps or holes. The opening page of Lydia Maria Child's *Letters from New York* reminds readers of the expense of such cultural repression: what looks like the facade of an imposing building is really the home of a slave trader, whose occupation is unknown to many New Yorkers. At such moments, Child highlights the social and political discontinuities of urban reality. To use the terminology of the psychoanalyst Serge Leclaire, an original "hole" in the cultural fabric has been "filled...imperfectly by a 'patch' " (cited in Wilden 98). Child's goal (like that of many nineteenth-century urban writers) is to draw attention to that repair, revealing areas of repressed social conflict that have been imperfectly covered over. By showing her readers that the city in actuality contains ruptures and divisions, she overturns the illusion that urban (or psychic) reality is a seamless plane. Troubling the naive realism that equates urban experience with visible, panoramic space, she makes readers aware of the invisible, "blank" spaces that also form part of the fabric of urban experience.

But as George Lippard illustrates in his city novels, urban space is not just discontinuous but also folded. In his fiction, the city is a dangerous and unseen field of hidden economic and political interests. Without the capacity to perceive the "gothic" folds, fissures, and fault lines of such a world, his readers—Lippard insists—will perpetuate the structures of exploitation that keep them victimized. Instead of representing the city as a two-dimensional plane of streets that can be traversed and described (the flaneur's perspective), Lippard imagines urban space as a realm that folds inward in complicated layers of intrigue, desire, and power. The geographical models of Gilles Deleuze help to illuminate Lippard's conception of "folded space." Departing from Renaissance perspective and the spatial grid of René Descartes, Deleuze portrays spatiality, not as a two-dimensional plane or map, but rather a texture that can be folded infinitely inward, in layer upon layer (Rajchman, *Constructions*). Reconfiguring the model of spatial structure, Deleuze envisions a world of increasing complication and multiplicity, in which different layers are "folded" into each other—a remarkably apt characterization of both the urban environment imagined by George Lippard and the complicated texture of his fiction. In Lippard's writing, the city's hidden spaces—even though they may be invisible—maintain a powerful magnetic pull warping daily life. At the same time, his two New York novels, *The Empire City* and *New York: Its Upper Ten and Lower Million*, take on an uncanny, folded quality as they create a narrative double exposure. The second book, *New York*, uses the same cast of characters, the same thematic structures, and the same resolution as the first. But while the plot of *New York* covers basically the same narrative territory as *The Empire City*, it overlaps the earlier novel by including the backstories of characters that the reader has met before. There seems room for an unlimited number of complications, as narrative fold is placed within narrative fold. In this composite work, Lippard pioneers a new model of urban narrative—one that travels through a space that is "folded" both thematically and structurally.

As the example of Lippard reminds us, the analysis of urban writing needs to take into account both the representation of spatiality and the literary structures used to depict the city. By ignoring the gaps and folds in urban perception, one forecloses awareness of the *textuality* of the city. Identifying with the observations of the flaneur, whose travels constitute a moving field of vision, the critic becomes a traveling eye (I) wedded to a phenomenological model of urban perception. But by conflating urban experience with a visual field, one obscures the nonmimetic aspects of urban existence and writing—the existential and textual "folds" that resist visual representation. By stressing such "mimetic logic," founded upon visual obser- vation, the reader loses contact with any critical narrative that might be "non-linear, a narrative of folds and counter-folds or regressions" (Cohen 6). One such coun- ternarrative, according to Tom Cohen, is that of "Benjaminian 'shock' "—the sub- visual experience of disjunction and disturbance that disrupts instituted structures of perception and meaning and makes perceptible "the 'site' or place…from which the very protocols of perception, value or decision are…prescribed" (17, 100). To understand the cultural work of nineteenth-century urban writing, it becomes nec- essary to cultivate this sense of "shock" by examining the ways in which the *texts* of nineteenth-century urban writers registered their awareness of the *discontinuous* spaces of the city. In order to perceive that the city was both a geographical terrain and a *textual* space, one needs to become sensitized to nonvisual and nonmimetic facets of urban writing.

Something as simple as the layout of newspaper columns, David Henkin observes, had an important effect on readers. Like real estate, "newspapers…consisted, ulti- mately and entirely, of…divisible and exchangeable units of space." This represen- tation of "quantifiable space" mirrored the class divisions emerging in the different sectors of the city, as well as in the psychological divisions alienating urban inhab- itants from each other and from parts of themselves (28). Reading and writing the city, many urban writers reflected such divisions by working in discontinuous tex- tual modes that helped to reproduce their experience of urban discontinuities. Rather than creating lengthy narratives, they often utilized short forms—such as the "letter," the familiar essay, the newspaper column, the episodic chapter—that in combination created a disjunctive sense of urban awareness. In order to understand this important aspect of nineteenth-century urban writing, a history of antebellum journalistic practices needs to be completed. Many of the most important writers—Child, Fuller, Willis, Poe, Fern, Foster, Lippard, and Whitman—were journalists or editors. As they confronted the task of recording their sense of the city, they invented or popularized new literary forms. For example, George Foster's 1849 volume *New York in Slices, by an Experienced Carver* utilized a series of vignettes, sampling different aspects of urban experience, that took the place of a sustained narrative. Faced with the impossibility of recording the whole of the metropolis, Foster created slices of life that seemed more comprehensive than lengthy plotlines that imposed more limited perspectives. This style of writing was reflected in Foster's next book, *New York by Gas-Light*, as well as in the urban novels of George Lippard, Fanny Fern, and Herman Melville, which strung together assemblages of disconnected scenes on multiple narrative threads.

The evolution of Melville's writing provides an especially interesting example of the way urban discontinuity influenced literary structure. "Before his move to New York," Andrew Delbanco observes, "Melville's prose had stayed pretty much within the limits of conventional narrative; but as he immersed himself in the city, his books became eclectic miscellanies, with innumerable tangents spoking out from the spine of the story" (118–119). In New York, Delbanco continues, Melville encountered a complex textual world of jumbled messages: "a circulating collection of newspapers, leaflets, business cards, broadsides, tabloids, placards, magazines, banners, hired men walking the streets in sandwich boards, signs affixed to carriages" (119). Such a jumble of messages resembles the disconnected notes and observations recorded in Walter Benjamin's *Arcades Project* and suggests a methodology akin to Benjamin's "dialectical images." Articulating discrete moments of perception divided by both space and time, Benjamin shatters epistemological complacency by bringing "together in a flash" a new form—a "constellation" that suddenly emerges into awareness (462). Rather than maintaining the ideological "dream" (464) of the past, his writing enacts a "moment of awakening" (486). In the works of many urban writers, the construction of parallel scenes and dialogic strategies of citation have a similar function: breaking the epistemological illusion that one is following the traveling perception of a single individual strolling the streets of the city. In place of a single point of view, one encounters multiple perspectives placed in stark contrast to each other—a structure that suggests the coexistence of multiple viewpoints and ways of inhabiting the city.

III

Reinforcing a sense of discontinuity and fracture, a number of historical factors confronted nineteenth-century writers with an urban environment whose complexity exceeded anything tackled to date in American literature. In *The Urban Revolution*, Henri Lefebvre has argued that such complexity is an essential aspect of the urban phenomenon, which "astonishes us by its scale; its complexity surpass[ing] the tools of our understanding and the instruments of practical activity" (45). Specific historical factors contributed to this complexity during the antebellum period. While the Panic of 1837 (the country's first economic depression) had consolidated the power of New York's financial institutions, it also destabilized the class structure of the city, creating a sense of existential vertigo. At the same time, processes of industrialization and urban reform were transforming an urban landscape that required continually revised points of geographical and personal orientation. Simultaneously, swelling waves of European immigration (combined with a growing black population) effected striking demographic changes that tested the political values of middle-class urban dwellers. The consolidation of the Five Points slum, combined with the emergence of an urban criminal class, necessitated the creation of new penal and reform institutions. As nineteenth-century New York was marked by growing economic, social, and political discontinuities, geographical divisions were solidified in the city; the fashionable sidewalks of Broadway contrasted with the cellars of Five Points, the open spaces of Gramercy Park with the high walls of the Tombs (the city's jail). While the antebellum period as a whole has been remembered as a time of social reorientation and geographical transformation, these processes were accelerated in New York City—the event horizon where cultural changes and literary responses first occurred.

Nineteenth-century writers' growing awareness of urban discontinuity necessitated the development of new literary forms that often centered on a dynamic of visibility and invisibility. Although antebellum urban writers continued at times to rely on an aesthetics of visibility (located, for example, in the urban picturesque), they were also faced with the need to deal with the discontinuities and opacities of urban space. Instead of perceiving an unbroken plane of urban phenomena, they located themselves in an urban terrain marked by temporal overlays, geographical disconnection, and social breaks. Any "locale," Dear and Flusty argue, "is . . . a complex amalgam of past, present, and newly forming archaeologies that coexist simultaneously in the landscape" (3). In antebellum America, men and women, whites and blacks existed in different (while, at times, overlapping) social spaces and experienced different tempos of citizenship. As we know from the reluctance of some women writers to visit the notorious Five Points neighborhood or to visit newly constructed prisons without chaperones, their spatial mobility and, hence, their urban imaginaries differed from those of male contemporaries. At the same time, most New York writers bore witness to the uneven and broken terrains in which many nineteenth-century urban dwellers existed. The poor, recent immigrants, streetwalkers, and the institutionalized all inhabited urban spaces that were cut off from the fashionable thoroughfares and the upper-class neighborhoods springing up on the northern border of Manhattan. Confronting the discontinuous spaces of the modern metropolis, many writers moved beyond spectatorial observation—which objectified the persons and places visible in an urban panorama—to include aspects of urban experience that were invisible.

For example, when Lydia Maria Child and Margaret Fuller moved from small towns in New England to New York City, they were forced to recognize that the constructed space of the city—with its walls, cellars, and obscure alleys—was much more complicated than that found in smaller communities, which seemed much more open and accessible. The political schisms and complex power structures of the city demanded modes of interpretation that supplemented the perception of visible spaces with interpretive frameworks transcending vision. In order to bring urban values and ideologies into awareness, they needed to double perspectives, measuring visible phenomena against either a plane of abstraction or images of alternative social structures. Bringing into play a level of critical abstraction, Child and Fuller, as well as many other urban journalists, resorted to patterns of citation and critique that necessarily transcended the visual. In order to "overcome the blindness of the everyday" (141), as Anthony Vidler describes the process, other authors resorted to "the rapid sketch or the framed vignette" (141). For example, the essays of George Foster and Fanny Fern created "slices" of urban life that sampled the complex terrains of the city, often bringing unseen areas of urban life into focus. Urban fiction writers also found that their representations of the city could not rest on what could be immediately perceived with the senses. Adapting the European mode of the urban mystery as well as familiar gothic geographies, Lippard and Melville depicted a city in which spaces, political structures, and individual motives were frequently hidden. All of these writers struggled to bring within the sphere of public attention individuals who had literally become invisible, falling like Bartleby or Lippard's villains beneath the "threshold of respectability" into the hidden realm of society's invisible others.

The issue of invisibility is particularly important when we consider the case of women writers, since critical attention has focused primarily on male urban writers. Melville, Poe, Whitman, and the members of the "Young America" movement have been part of the city visible to literary scholars. There even exists a specialized study of Melville's urban writing, entitled *Melville's City* (Kelley). Although Eliza Richards has examined the female poets in Poe's New York circle, many of the most important literary and social networks of antebellum women writers in New York remain largely invisible and unstudied. An important part of this story involves the shift of cultural and literary gravity from New England to New York City. Before the Civil War, numerous women writers made the decision to move to the site where a critical mass of writers and intellectuals were simultaneously addressing the country's most pressing social issues: slavery, prostitution, prison reform, physical and mental disabilities, capital punishment, woman's rights, immigration, and urban crime. During the 1830s and 1840s, many of the country's leading women writers moved to New York: for example, Catharine Sedgwick, author of the best-selling novel *Hope Leslie*; Caroline Kirkland, author of *A New Home, Who'll Follow?*, an influential account of the settlement of Michigan; Eliza Farnham, the author of *Life in Prairie Land*; and Fanny Fern, who would become the country's most popular newspaper columnist. Many of these women became actively involved in antebellum social reform, especially prison reform. In addition, their paths crossed in New York literary salons and newspaper offices. The omission of women from studies of American urban writing is astounding when one considers that Poe's influential series of essays entitled "The Literati of New York" included Anna Mowatt, Anne Stephens, Mary Gove, Margaret Fuller, Caroline Kirkland, Emma Embury, Fanny Osgood, Elizabeth Bogart, Catharine Sedgwick, Anne Lynch, and Mary Hewitt. As we are beginning to see, such writers formed an active—indeed, essential—part of the New York literary scene, and many of them wrote about the city.

There have been deeper-seated reasons for the exclusion of women from nineteenth-century American urban studies. The paradigm of the strolling flaneur was difficult to reconcile with traditions of *female* writing, especially given the powerful social prohibitions against middle-class women walking the city's streets alone (Nord, Parsons). For example, when Lydia Maria Child visited many parts of New York, including the Five Points slum, she was usually accompanied by a male chaperone. In addition, it has been all too easy for critics to replicate unconsciously the nineteenth-century ideology of "separate spheres," which projected an image of male workers aggressively struggling in the capitalist marketplace while their women stayed at home to create a "pastoral" refuge that lay "outside" harsh urban realities (Boydston). Frequently viewed as a part of "nature," antebellum women were imaginatively located in an ontological realm that cultivated their "natural"—not urban—qualities. Margaret Homans, for example, has discussed the ways in which male Romantic writers identified "matter and otherness as female and subjectivity as male" (19). The ensuing objectification of women, as Deborah Nord persuasively argues, meant that female urban writers had to struggle "to escape the status of spectacle and become a spectator" (12).

The cultural assumption that women formed part of a "nature," beyond the vicissitudes of urban existence, carried a particular irony for women writers like Child and Fuller who were committed to social reform. For many of the social ills plaguing the city (for example, prostitution) had resulted from the belief that women outside of the sanctuary of the home had sacrificed male protection and were fair game for sexual and economic exploitation. There seems to have been the widespread assumption among men that women did not really belong in the city, except for brief excursions for shopping or genteel amusement. What is particularly disconcerting is the recognition that this bias has been shared by many critics of nineteenth-century urban writing, who act as if female urban dwellers and writers were not part of their subject. Fanny Fern's 1855 novel *Ruth Hall* provides a particularly instructive analysis of the social expense of relegating women to the realm of visual consumption, cutting them off from literary production. Throughout the novel, Ruth's family and acquaintances attempt to define her value in terms of their "admiration." In their eyes, the visible performance of beauty and proper feminine decorum embodies female being. But in contrast to a tyranny of the visible that encodes the gender ideology of American society in structures of spectacle, Fern demonstrates the existence of other, nonvisible patterns of valuation. Some of these are linked to a sentimentalized discourse of political sympathy; others to ironic structures of social critique. But in both cases, Fern argues that the interpretive patterns applied to women need to be shifted from objectifying discourses of visual consumption. Strikingly, Fern's novel is structured as a series of brief, discontinuous vignettes that rapidly shift from one urban terrain to another. At the same time, the novel's complicated structure balances scenes of visual display against multiple registers that transcend the visual.

Although the moral register and corresponding structures of feeling are different, similar arguments could be made about George Thompson's *City Crimes* or George Lippard's *Quaker City*. Such works challenge readers to move beyond the well-lit streets and parlors of the city into terrains that challenge the illusion that the fabric of urban experience is continuous and visible. For all of these writers, the city was a complicated text whose recesses, gaps, and folds mirrored the complex structure of the psyche. In the city, they found, new patterns of perception, writing, and motivation were necessary. As these writers realized, new literary forms needed to be invented, in order to communicate the discontinuous spaces of the city. As the nineteenth-century city evolved, the entire texture of everyday life changed along with it. While some scholars have linked this cultural change to a "crisis of representation" (Homberger 20), a more positive critical view links this shift in awareness to the development of new forms of literary representation. Pioneering new structures of literary attention, a number of antebellum urban writers showed their readers vast areas of life that had hitherto been invisible. In the process, they learned how to record their experience of an unexplored American phenomenon—the metropolis.

BIBLIOGRAPHY

Bailey, Brigitte. "Representing Italy: Fuller, History Painting, and the Popular Press." *Margaret Fuller's Cultural Critique: Her Age and Legacy.* Ed. Fritz Fleischmann. New York: Peter Lang, 2000. 229–248.

Benjamin, Walter. *The Arcades Project.* Trans. Howard Eiland and Kevin McLaughlin. Cambridge, MA: Harvard University Press, 1999.

Bennett, Michael, and David W. Teague, eds. *The Nature of Cities: Ecocriticism and Urban Environments.* Tucson: University of Arizona Press, 1999.

Boydston, Jeanne. *Home and Work: Housework, Wages, and the Ideology of Labor in the Early Republic.* Oxford: Oxford University Press, 1990.

Bramen, Carrie Terado. "The Urban Picturesque and the Spectacle of Americanization." *American Quarterly* 52.3 (September 2000): 444–477.

Brand, Dana. *The Spectator and the City in Nineteenth-Century American Literature.* Cambridge: Cambridge University Press, 1991.

Brown, Matthew P. *The Pilgrim and the Bee: Reading Rituals and Book Culture in Early New England.* Philadelphia: University of Pennsylvania Press, 2007.

Burrows, Edwin, and Mike Wallace. *Gotham: A History of New York to 1898.* New York: Oxford University Press, 1999.

Child, Lydia Maria. *Letters from New York.* Ed. Bruce Mills. Athens: University of Georgia Press, 1998.

Cohen, Tom. *Ideology and Inscription.* Cambridge: Cambridge University Press, 1998.

Dear, Michael, and Steven Flusty. Introduction. *The Spaces of Postmodernity: Readings in Human Geography.* Ed. Dear and Flusty. New York: Wiley-Blackwell, 2002. 1–12.

Debord, Guy. *The Society of the Spectacle.* Trans. Donald Nicholson-Smith. New York: Zone Books, 1995.

de Certeau, Michel. "Walking in the City." *The Practice of Everyday Life.* Trans. Steven Rendall. Berkeley: University of California Press, 1984.

Delbanco, Andrew. *Melville: His World and Work.* New York: Vintage Books, 2006.

Deleuze, Gilles. "The Fold–Leibniz and the Baroque." Trans. Tim Conley. *Architectural Design* 63.2 (1993): 17–21.

Dickens, Charles. "New York." *American Notes for General Circulation.* 1842. London: Penguin Books, 2000.

Fern, Fanny. *Ruth Hall & Other Writings.* Ed. Joyce Warren. New Brunswick, NJ: Rutgers University Press, 1986.

Foster, George. *New York by Gas-Light.* 1850. Ed. Struart M. Blumin. Berkeley: University of California Press, 1990.

———. *New York in Slices.* New York: W. F. Burgess, 1850.

Frisby, David. *Cityscapes of Modernity: Critical Explorations.* Oxford: Blackwell/Polity, 2001.

Goldsmith, Arnold L. *The Modern American Urban Novel: Nature as "Interior Structure."* Detroit, MI: Wayne State University Press, 1991.

Henkin, David. *City Reading: Written Words and Public Spaces in Antebellum New York.* New York: Columbia University Press, 1998.

Homans, Margaret. *Women Writers and Poetic Identity: Dorothy Wordsworth, Emily Bronte, and Emily Dickinson.* Princeton, NJ: Princeton University Press, 1980.

Homberger, Eric. *Scenes from the Life of a City: Corruption and Conscience in Old New York.* New Haven, CT: Yale University Press, 1994.

Hone, Philip. *The Diary of Philip Hone 1828–1851.* Ed. Allan Nevins. New York: Dodd, Mead, 1936.

Kelley, Wyn. *Melville's City: Literary and Urban Form in Nineteenth-Century New York.* Cambridge: Cambridge University Press, 1996.

Lefebvre, Henri. *The Production of Space.* Trans. Donald Nicholson-Smith. Oxford: Blackwell, 1991.

———. *The Urban Revolution.* Trans. Robert Bononno. Minneapolis: University of Minnesota Press, 2003.

Lippard, George. *Empire City.* 1850. Freeport, NY: Books for Libraries Press, 1969.

———. *New York: Its Upper Ten and Lower Million.* 1853. New York: Irvington Publishers, 1993.

Marx, Leo. *The Machine in the Garden: Technology and the Pastoral Ideal in America.* London: Oxford University Press, 1964.

Merrifield, Andy. "Henri Lefebvre: A Socialist in Space." *Thinking Space.* Ed. Mike Crang and Nigel Thrift. London: Routledge, 2000. 167–182.

Nord, Deborah Epstein. *Walking the Victorian Streets: Women, Representation and the City.* Ithaca, NY: Cornell University Press, 1995.

Parsons, Deborah L. *Streetwalking the Metropolis: Women, the City and Modernity.* Oxford: Oxford University Press, 2000.

Poe, Edgar Allan. "The Man of the Crowd." *Collected Works of Edgar Allan Poe: Tales and Sketches 1831–1842.* Ed. Thomas Olive Mabbott. Cambridge, MA: Harvard University Press, 1978. 505–518.

Rajchman, John. "Folding." *Constructions.* Cambridge, MA: MIT Press, 1998.

———. "Out of the Fold." *Architectural Design* 63.2 (1993): 61–63.

Resina, Joan Ramon. "The Concept of After-Image and the Scopic Apprehension of the City." *After-Images of the City.* Ed. Joan Ramon Resina and Dieter Ingenschay. Ithaca, NY: Cornell University Press, 2003. 1–22.

Richards, Eliza. *Gender and the Poetics of Reception in Poe's Circle.* Cambridge: Cambridge University Press, 2004.

Smith, Henry Nash. *Virgin Land: The American West as Symbol and Myth.* New York: Vintage, 1950.

Soja, Edward W. *Postmodern Geographies: The Reassertion of Space in Critical Social Theory.* London: Verso, 1989.

Stallybrass, Peter. "Books and Scrolls: Navigating the Bible." *Books and Readers in Early Modern England: Material Studies.* Ed. Jennifer Andersen and Elizabeth Sauer. Philadelphia: University of Pennsylvania Press, 2001. 42–79.

Strain, Ellen. *Public Places, Private Journeys: Ethnography, Entertainment, and the Tourist Gaze.* New Brunswick, NJ: Rutgers University Press, 2003.

Trollope, Frances. *Domestic Manners of the Americans.* Excerpt in *Writing New York: A Literary Anthology.* Ed. Phillip Lopate. New York: Library of America, 1998.

Vidler, Anthony. "Reading the City: The Urban Book from Mercier to Mitterand." *PMLA* 122.1 (January 2007): 235–251.

Wilden, Anthony. Notes to Jacques Lacan. *The Language of the Self: The Function of Psychoanalysis.* Trans. and ed. Anthony Wilden. New York: Dell, 1968.

Willis, Nathaniel Parker. "Open-Air Musings in the City." *Rural Letters and Other Records of Thought at Leisure.* Auburn, NY: Alden and Beardsley, 1856. 227–252.

CHAPTER 11

ANIMALS AND THE FORMATION OF LIBERAL SUBJECTIVITY IN NINETEENTH-CENTURY AMERICAN LITERATURE

COLLEEN GLENNEY BOGGS

IN 1950, Lionel Trilling published a collection of his essays under the title *The Liberal Imagination*. In two essays that frame his reflections on topics ranging across nineteenth- and twentieth-century literature, Trilling outlines his definition of liberalism as well as his understanding of the role literary criticism plays in bringing that liberalism to fruition. For Trilling, liberalism's potential and its shortfalls hinge on its ability to engage both ideas and emotions (or sentiments, which he uses as a synonym), and to keep both in dynamic relation to one another. For models of how such balance might work, he repeatedly turns to examples of nineteenth-century writers for whom the stakes of balancing ideas and emotions—and of engaging with literature—were political (xi). By politics, Trilling means the "wide sense of the word," that is, "the politics of culture, the organization of human life toward some end or other, toward the modification of sentiments, which is to say the quality of human life" (xi). Although this statement echoes the scope and vagueness of his earlier claim that liberalism is "a large tendency rather than a concise body of doctrine" (x–xi), it also makes a programmatic claim about literary criticism itself, namely that its domain is properly the political, where the political is understood as emerging at the intersection of emotions and ideas.

Trilling's assessment of the political has met—as has the larger postwar discourse celebrating liberalism—with a wide range of appropriations and dismissals over the years since the volume's publication.[1] Without positing a causal relationship between Trilling's work and later scholarly developments, we might nevertheless read his remarks on the role of the emotions and their connections to politics as a prescient commentary on the engagement that the scholarly field of nineteenth-century American literary studies has with figuring out how sentiment, emotion, intimacy, and affect produce and unravel subjects, liberal and otherwise. The methodologies of this enterprise have been eclectically borrowed from feminism, gender studies, queer studies, poststructuralism, new historicism, and cultural studies, but scholars have recently begun to identify this field of inquiry as its own theoretical school, and to speak of *The Affective Turn* in American literary studies, as the title of a 2007 book proclaims.

Writing in the foreword to the volume, Michael Hardt argues that "affects refer equally to the body and the mind" and place reason and passion "together on a continuum." Consequently, affect studies produce "a new ontology of the human or, rather, an ontology of the human that is constantly open and renewed" (x). Hardt's comment begs the question of what anchors that new ontology in relation to "the human." While his claim echoes Trilling's emphasis on the role that emotions play for the construction of "the nature of the human mind" (xiv), "the organization of human life" (xi), and "the quality of human life" (xi), Hardt's concluding reference to a new ontology opens a space for inquiry that presses us beyond the explicitly humanist framework of liberal subject formation outlined by Trilling.

It is that ontological openness that I want to explore in order to understand how the affective relationship between human beings and animals founds and confounds the parameters of liberal subject formation. Beginning with an overview of what affect studies might teach us about nonhuman ontologies, I then situate key concerns of this current scholarly undertaking in relation to the historical "origins" of liberal humanism in John Locke's educational philosophy. Tracing the impact of his pedagogy on American literature, I demonstrate how liberal subject formation emerges from the relationship with animals. That relationship plays a key role in the development of literacy that is the very staple of liberal subjectivity. As I demonstrate in a case study of Emily Dickinson, animals literally disrupt and figuratively challenge the parameters of representation on which liberal subjectivity is founded.

Although many scholars working in affect theory remain dedicated to an explicitly humanist enterprise, the logical outcome of their work opens the possibility for thinking about subjectivity in a more expansive register than one limited to existing notions of the human. In *Feeling in Theory* (2001), Rei Terada argues that we need to rethink emotion as "nonsubjective." She explains that emotion is often cast "as a basis for naturalized social or moral consensus," but draws our attention to the fact that "such a gesture depends on an even more fundamental one that casts emotion as proof of the human subject" (4). She takes issue with affect theory's willingness to grant that "even nonsubjects have affects" (6), only to then distinguish emotions as the realm of the human. Terada rejects this differentiation, and rewrites the critical nomenclature of affect theory so that it includes not only the psychological experiences of human beings but also the physiological sensations of all living creatures. Terada's reconceptualization usefully eliminates one of the many binaries that results from the dichotomy between "the human" and "the animal," namely the dichotomy between emotion and affect.

Their conflation hinges on the fact that for Terada, "emotion is an interpretive act" (17): "our emotions emerge only through acts of interpretation and identification by means of which we feel *for others*. . . . We are not ourselves without representations that mediate us, and it is through those representations that emotions get felt" (21). By refusing to specify that those "others" must always already be human, Terada opens the terrain that nineteenth-century literature tried to negotiate in imagining how affective bonds with animals had a constitutive effect on subjectivity. While this attention to the representational and the linguistic might seem to return us to the domain of the human, I want to suggest that it instead presents us with the possibility for reading the relationship with animals as integral to structures of a reconfigured subjectivity. Christopher Peterson has formulated the question at which we arrive this way: "How might our relationship to the 'radical alterity' of nonhuman animals contest, instead of simply reaffirm, our normative conceptions of intimacy? What might the alterity of nonhuman animals have to teach us about the alterity of those human animals with whom we imagine the most intimate kinship?" (354). I want to explore the affective relationship between human beings and animals, and examine how that relationship is worked out in literary representations.

LOCKE, ANIMALS, AND THE FORMATION
OF AMERICAN LITERATURE

These relationships are central to the text—and especially the reception of the text—credited with founding our understanding of liberal subject formation, namely John Locke's *Some Thoughts concerning Education* (1693). The text has variously been recognized as inaugurating the fields of pedagogy, child psychology, children's literature, the sentimental novel, and American literature as such; it was "probably even more widely read and circulated than the *Two Treatises of Government*," and "served in its various popularized forms as perhaps the most significant text of the Anglo-American Enlightenment."[2] Responding to a friend's request for advice on how to rear his son, Locke eschewed physical punishment and made affect central to a pedagogy that accounted equally for children's bodily and mental well-being. What interests me here is the special status he affords animals in the didactic enterprise of enabling children to develop their capacities: the affective relationship to animals forms the nexus between the body and mind that is requisite for liberal subject formation. But it also challenges the very parameters of that subject formation.

At first glance, Locke's reflections seem to distinguish human beings as rational creatures from other beings who are driven by appetites and emotions. Locke not only emphasizes the importance of teaching children how to moderate and control their emotions but also advocates modeling such control in disciplining them: "When I say therefore, that they [children] must be *treated as Rational Creatures*, I mean that you should make them sensible by the Mildness of your Carriage, and the Composure even in your Correction of them, that what you do is reasonable in you, and useful and necessary for them" (181). Locke defines children as "Rational Creatures" who recognize "what is reasonable" in their parents, and who in turn come to act reasonably by the example set for them. However, this emphasis on reason depends on the ability to make children "sensible" to the kinds of emotions their parents exercise when they demonstrate "mildness" and "composure" in their reactions. Children's ability to learn from their parents hinges on their ability to develop a kind of empathy with their parents: they recognize their own ability to reason in seeing what is "reasonable in" their parents, and in turn reflect that reasonableness back on themselves by recognizing it in utilitarian terms, as what is "useful and necessary for them." In the encounter with their parents, they come to recognize their own interests, and to develop a sense of themselves as interest-bearing subjects. That recognition of their interests precedes their entry into full legal personhood, and their social recognition as legal subjects.

Although children learn from watching their parents' reasonable behavior, their mode of education is practical, not abstract. Locke insisted that in all aspects of learning, "Children are *not* to be *taught by Rules*, which will be always slipping out of their Memories. What you think necessary for them to do, settle in them by an indispensible Practice, as often as the Occasion returns; and if it be possible, make Occasions" (158). For Locke, learning occurred experientially, not in the abstract. Eschewing abstract "rules," he argues that memory formation occurs through practice and repetition. This practical education depends on children's experience of other people's actions, but also involves guiding their own actions. Locke set up an analogy by which parents' treatment of their children mirrors children's treatment of animals; this analogy functions as a literal chain of creaturely hierarchy by which the more powerful exercise control over the less powerful, and, as I will explain more fully, as a chain of metaphoric substitutions by which each component of the chain represents the other.

At stake in these carefully calibrated relationships is children's initiation into proper modes of governance. Pointing out that "[c]hildren love *Liberty*;.... I now tell you, they love something more; and that is *Dominion*: And this is the first Original of most vicious Habits, that are ordinary and natural" (207), Locke infuses his reflections with a political vocabulary, in which the desirable "love" of liberty fights against an undesirable affect, and that is the "love" of "*Dominion*." Insisting that affects differ qualitatively, Locke also indicates that his key pedagogical strategy— practice—can produce results conducive or adverse to good social order. In using the explicitly biblical language of "dominion" and an invocation of "Original" sin ("vicious Habits"), Locke is working out what role "natural" inclinations play in forming children's political desires. For Locke, the "natural" is the *product* of habits, not their *origin*.

The relationship with animals is crucial to the process of redirecting children's love for "dominion" into a proper love of "*Liberty*" (207) that hinges on the mutual recognition of subjects' interests. In his advocacy of humane practices, Locke initially focuses on human beings themselves, not on their animal victims. He explains that "the Custom of Tormenting and Killing of Beasts, will, by Degrees, harden their [children's] Minds even towards Men; and they who delight in the Suffering and Destruction of inferiour Creatures, will not be apt to be very compassionate, or benign to those of their own kind. Our Practice takes Notice of this in the Exclusion of *Butchers* from Juries of Life and Death" (226). Locke argues that humane conduct to animals ensures that human beings treat each other with compassion. He suggests that children who become habituated to taking "delight" in the "Suffering and Destruction" of animals lose their capacity to be "compassionate" and "benign." In repeatedly exercising one kind of affect, they lose the ability to engage in the bonds of sympathy that underlie civic society: like butchers, they become unfit to enter into the juridical process which is based on a balance between reason and compassion. Even though Locke's emphasis lies on the way human beings treat each other, his argument depends on the substitution of animals for human beings: being cruel to animals results in being cruel to other human beings; the two are not separate from one another, but on the contrary, they lie on a continuum. The ability to identify affectively with other human beings, and to enter into social and legal relations with them, depends on an ability to exercise proper compassion to animals.

Kindness to animals produces "good Nature" in children. That good nature expresses itself not only in reasoned relationships, but in emotional and physical ones: Locke emphasizes that the children should be "tender"—that is, feeling, loving, caring—to all "sensible" creatures, that is, to all beings who have the capacity for physical and emotional feeling. Locke spells this out when he reproaches children for putting "any thing in Pain, that is capable of it" (226). At this point in his reflections, animals are no longer simply stand-ins for human beings; their own capacity for feeling has become important. Yet a recognition of that importance stands at odds with social conventions, which Locke critiques in comments that pave the way for anticruelty and animal welfare activism. For Locke, the enjoyment of another creature's pain is "a foreign and introduced Disposition, an Habit borrowed from Custom and Conversation. People teach Children to strike, and laugh, when they hurt, or see harm come to others…By these Steps unnatural Cruelty is planted in us; and what Humanity abhors. Custom reconciles and recommends to us, by laying it in the way to Honours. Thus, by Fashion and Opinion, that comes to be a Pleasure, which in it self neither is, nor can be any. This ought

carefully to be watched, and early remedied, so as to settle and cherish the contrary, and more natural Temper of Benignity and *Compassion* in the room of it"
(226–227). Pitting "Humanity" against "Custom," Locke comes close to abandoning his own precept that nature is the product and not the origin of education; he
entertains the notion that human beings are innately good, and that cruelty is the
"unnatural" result of habits "planted in us." Yet Locke retreats from this approach
by casting the "natural" as a comparative term: he advocates establishing a "more
natural Temper" in children that runs contrary to social habits and returns children to a sense of "benignity." The relationship with animals has the capacity to
"instill Sentiments of Humanity, and to keep them lively in young Folks" (227).
Humanity itself has here become a "sentiment," and one that hinges on compassion for animals. Far from functioning as an ontological category, humanity is
the product of an educational process that relies on the relationship to animals to
elicit and direct emotions; the liberal subject emerges through its properly affective engagement with animals.

Locke's work produces two connected strands in its writing on animals: it
engages with the corporeal relationship between human beings and animals, and
it inscribes that relationship at and as the very core of representation. Turning to
the topic of how children learn to read, Locke suggests that adults ought "to teach
Children the *Alphabet* by playing" (256). Once that basic literacy has been accomplished, adults should provide a child with "some easy pleasant Book suited to his
Capacity," for which Locke has a specific recommendation: "I think *Aesop's Fables*
the best, which being Stories apt to delight and entertain a Child, and yet afford useful Reflections to a grown Man" (259). Locke's recommendation takes on an even
more specific tone when he suggests that

> if his *Aesop has Pictures* in it, it will entertain him much the better, and encourage
> him to read, when it carries the increase of Knowledge with it. For such visible
> Objects Children hear talked of in vain, and without any satisfaction, whilst they
> have no Ideas of them; those Ideas being not to be had from Sounds; but from the
> Things themselves, or their Pictures. And therefore I think, as soon as he begins
> to spell, as many Pictures of Animals should be got him, as can be found, with the
> printed names to them, which at the same time will invite him to read, and afford
> him Matter of Enquiry. (259)

Animals come to occupy a central position in the child's—and by extension the
man's—literacy. Children are not able to translate "sounds" into a connection with
"ideas"; they arrive at those ideas through a relationship to "Things themselves, or
their Pictures." Things and pictures take on an interchangeable relationship that
makes animals figuratively *and* literally present for children as they develop their
literacy skills.

These claims establish two important trajectories for the engagement with
animals subsequent to Locke: first, they call into question the distinction between
human beings and animals, and increasingly, animals themselves become subjects. Instead of seeing animals as a vehicle for human relationships, the animals

themselves begin to matter in their own right. Second, they give rise to a new set of writing and reading practices. As scholars such as Karen Sánchez-Eppler have pointed out, sentimentalism makes "reading...a bodily act" (26–27). Reading becomes an act of encountering the bodies of others, and of needing to come to terms with their proximity and alterity. This encounter with the animal's body challenges us to expand our understanding of how "sentimentalism links the capacity of individuals to feel deeply (often, to suffer) to an essential, shared humanity."[3] What happens when sentimentalism does not automatically link back to humanity but instead creates connections with animals that press us beyond the human and humanist pale?

This question is far from peripheral to our understanding of nineteenth-century literature. As Gillian Brown and others have documented, "Americans knew Locke's ideas not only from these books, but also, and more profoundly, from the popular pedagogical modes and texts inspired by Locke's thought. Whether or not they knew Locke's writings, early Americans assimilated Lockean liberalism as they grew up" (4). In Locke's writing, the relationship between human beings and animals provides a model for initiating and integrating children into the social fabric as liberal subjects. But in the hands of a writer such as Emily Dickinson, the relationship to animals also provides modes for resisting social orders and for imagining alternative subjectivities. In the final section of this chapter, I want to situate Dickinson's work in the context of the nineteenth-century engagement with Lockean notions of subject formation. Dickinson's case is interesting to me because she successfully channels a larger social discourse, and in the process questions its assumptions and methodologies. Specifically, she reevaluates the relationship between physical bodies and abstract representation, and is particularly attentive to the role that gender plays in the formation of subjectivity. Demonstrating a link between the social construction of species and the social construction of gender, Dickinson explores how relationships to animals can unsettle both, and can generate alternative forms of representation.

EMILY DICKINSON AND THE DISCONTENTS OF LIBERAL SUBJECTIVITY

> Carlo died—
> E. Dickinson
> Would you instruct me now?
> (Johnson II. 449)

In 1866, Emily Dickinson ended a lapse of eighteen months in her correspondence with Colonel Thomas Wentworth Higginson by sending him three lines that connect the major concerns of her work: death, subjectivity, and the conditions of knowledge.

When Higginson later published these lines among "Emily Dickinson's Letters," he explained that the poet would on occasion include "an announcement of some event, vast to her small sphere as this," the death of her dog who had been her companion for sixteen years (450). In feminizing and privatizing Dickinson's loss and measuring it biographically by the "small sphere" of her life, Higginson sets aside this particular poet's ability to "wade grief" (Franklin 312) and situates Dickinson's letter within the sentimental culture of pet-keeping that had transfigured a predominantly agricultural practice ("pet" initially referred to a lamb) into a staple of genteel domesticity and bourgeois subjectivity.[4] Far from participating uncritically in the roles and relationships Higginson projects onto her, Dickinson interrogates the formation and gendering of sentimental subjectivity (see also Dillon; Blackwood) by placing "Carlo died" in relation to the other two lines, that is, the signature and the call for instruction. "E. Dickinson" refers ambiguously to Emily or to her father Edward Dickinson (see also Holland 146). The signature pluralizes the subject; it doubles and ultimately obscures "E.'s" gender. This ambiguous subject hinges on the animal's death as a scene of pedagogy: it stands in the liminal space between the announcement of Carlo's death and the request: "Would you instruct me now?"

It is easy to overlook this question's relevance and its bearing on Carlo's death, since the call for instruction is a constant refrain in Dickinson's correspondence with Higginson. If we trace that refrain, it becomes apparent that Dickinson consistently links the scene of pedagogy with the formation of subjectivity via the trope of the animal. In her introductory letter to Higginson, she asked him "to say if my Verse is alive?... Should you think it breathed—and had you the leisure to tell me, I should feel quick gratitude" (Johnson II. 403). Dickinson portrays a liveness that animates her poetry, and whose breathing produces the poet's own affective "quick[ening]." She more fully develops these connections when she responds to Higginson's request for a self-description:

> You ask of my Companions Hills—Sir—and the Sundown—and a Dog—large as myself, that my Father bought me—They are better than Beings—because they know—but do not tell—and the noise in the Pool, at Noon—excels my Piano. (Johnson II. 404)

This composite portrait blends the animate and the inanimate, the object with the subject, to unhinge their epistemological meanings and ontological differentiation. But what exactly is the surplus that makes her "Companions... better than Beings"? In using the term "companion," Dickinson draws on the same vocabulary that informs Donna Haraway's reading of human beings and dogs as "companion species" that stand "in obligatory, constitutive, historical, protean relationship" to one another (12). Like Haraway, who argues that animals "are not about oneself... They are not a projection" (12), Dickinson abandons the normative reference to human subjectivity by making the dog "better than Beings" and placing "Beings'" implied adjective, "human," under erasure.

That erasure should also give us pause from mapping Dickinson too readily in relation to Haraway and the growing number of feminist scholars (Donovan and

Adams) who believe animal studies in general and "dog writing" in particular "to be a branch of feminist theory" (3). Dickinson's terse prose cautions us about patriarchy's vested interest in sentimentalizing women's relationship with animals (Ortner), and in making the way women perform their gender contingent on the way they perform their species. That contingency is exemplified in Thomas Wentworth Higginson's 1887 article on "Women and Men: Children and Animals," where he insists that "the care given by the young girl [to her pet] was simply the anticipated tenderness of a mother for her child" (530). As with Locke's metaphors, casting the girl's relationship to the dog as analogous to the mother's relationship with her child infantilizes women (they are like girls), anthropomorphizes animals (pets are like children), and animalizes children (children are like pets).

Early reviews picked up on Dickinson's interest in using infantilization as a strategy for exploring these oddly mutable subject positions; they described Dickinson's poetry as showing "the insight of the civilized adult combined with the simplicity of the savage child" (Bates). In describing the dog as something that "my Father bought me," Dickinson casts herself in the role of her parent's child, that is, in the role of the subject to be formed by Lockean education. She draws attention to the objectifying structures that underlie the sentimental association of women and animals by pointing to Carlo's status as a commodity and gift. Her double reference to "myself" and "me" inscribes Dickinson's subjectivity in this act of gift giving, and places her in the precarious position that women share with fetish objects and anthropomorphized subjects (Sedgwick): by dropping the pronoun "for" and by establishing a simile between the "dog" and "myself," Dickinson allows for the double possibility that Carlo or "me" were the objects her father "bought me." With this odd slippage between the dog and the daughter, the gift and the recipient, she suggests that women, children, and animals mediate the relationship between the object and the subject; they establish the boundaries along which human subject formation in distinction from nature becomes possible.

In staging her relationship to her dog, Dickinson performs and undercuts these differentiations. Although her relationship with the dog her father bought her infantilizes Dickinson, Carlo allows her small stature to appear "large."[5] By drawing on the animal as a trope-reversing trope, Dickinson deconstructs the very processes and parameters of gendered subject formation. The name "Carlo" signifies upon the central role that dogs play in the literary construction of subjectivity. Dickinson named Carlo after two literary characters, St. John River's dog in *Jane Eyre* (Capps 95) and Ik Marvell's dog in *Reveries of a Bachelor* (Eberwein 41, 192). The name Carlo is then not only a referent for a real dog, but also a referent for the fictional representation of animals.

Fictional representations of animals have been popular in English-language literature since the Middle Ages: Caxton published his translation of Aesop's *Fables* in 1484, and Locke's suggestion that this was the "only Book almost" (298) suited to children's education speaks to the work's popularity. Moreover, Locke's recommendation itself initiated an interest in integrating animal characters into the children's literature that emerged as a new genre in response to his writings. Locke's reflections on animals' didactic importance fundamentally changed pedagogical strategies for educating children to become liberal subjects. In the late eighteenth century, animals began to take on a central function *as animals* in the instruction of children. Even fables were enlisted in this new endeavor, as the subtitle of Sarah Trimmer's vastly popular *Fabulous Histories* (1786) illustrates: the book was *designed for the instruction of children respecting their treatment of animals.* In fact, animals played an increasingly important role not just in moral education, but in children's initiation into language itself—as the example of *Aesop's Fables in French: With a Description of Fifty Animals Mentioned Therein and a French and English Dictionary of the Words Contained in the Work* indicates.

Emily Dickinson's Carlo participated in this educational reform. In 1863, Emily Dickinson's uncle by marriage, Asa Bullard, published a book entitled *Dog Stories* that prominently featured a dog named Carlo. As the secretary and general agent of the Massachusetts Sabbath School Society, Bullard edited the *Sabbath School Visitor*, to which Edward Dickinson subscribed for his children beginning in 1837 (Habegger), and Bullard numbered among the relatives Dickinson knew best (Longsworth 28), since she stayed with him and her aunt Lucretia when she visited Boston for eye surgery. In sketches that restage the constant warfare between his dog-loving niece Emily and her cat-loving sister Lavinia (see: "Our Kitty and Carlo," Bullard 11–13), Bullard depicts scenes that amount to Christian allegory: in his portrayal of Carlo, the "Faithful Dog" (Bullard 25–27) cannot be lured away by temptation to abandon his master's charge. In Bullard's account of "Little Charlie and Fido," the dog "appears to *know* about as much as *some* boys; and he is a great deal more ready than some are to do a favor, and more thankful for any act of kindness shown him" (Bullard 7–10). Indeed, dogs come to stand in for knowledge itself when Bullard describes how Carlo eventually clears a ditch because his master's voice has encouraged him: "Many children find their school duties hard to accomplish. Let the *kind* word of encouragement be given, and many of them, like the little dog Carlo, will surmount the difficulty and find their future course a joyous one" (64). Animals inhabit the same didactic position as the texts that represent them, and serve as mediators for liberal subjectivity: Bullard's admonition ties the "*kind* word" and animals to each other, as jointly enabling scholarly accomplishments; it promises that the pursuit of learning will find "joyous" fulfillment in a "future course."

What situates Bullard's book in a larger context of nineteenth-century children's literature is that it does not just portray the animals' behavior as exemplary; it uses animals to teach children kindness, and draws on versification to do so:

> I'll never hurt my little dog,
> But stroke and pat his head;
> I like to see him wag his tail,
> I like to see him fed.
> The coward wretch whose hand and heart
> Can bear to torture aught below,
> Is ever first to quail and start

> From slightest pain or equal foe.
> (Bullard 59–60)

These stories operate on the basis of what I will call didactic ontology, by which I mean the practice of teaching children how to be human by teaching them how to be humane. Animals take on a double role in this didactic literature: one, animals stand in for children—their behavior models for the child how to behave. Two, they are important as animals whose vulnerability and exposure to potential cruelty teaches children to be kind. Children relate to these animals through a double sense of identification and separation: because the animal is like them, they are asked to extend kindness, but the kindness they extend makes them human stewards of animals and marks their separation from them. Animals remain the trace of children's own presocial being, and become the supplement to liberal subjectivity. This relationship depends on the use of simile; in the passage I quoted above, Bullard writes that children should be aided in their school work by the "*kind* word of encouragement," which will allow "many of them, like the little dog Carlo" to "surmount the difficulty" (Bullard 64). Whereas metaphor (as I discuss below) conflates the two positions that ontology wants to separate, the human and the animal, simile keeps them recognizably separate: it gestures at a *tertium comparationis*, a third entity that enables the comparison while maintaining the differentiation between the entities that are being compared. In this case, that third entity is the "*kind* word," which functions not only to encourage children but also to inscribe them in a linguistic structure that separates them from animals: it integrates them into the pedagogical setting and disciplines them into fulfilling their "school duties."

Dickinson reinvents this use of simile by making language itself the locus of an animal presence that does not separate but integrates human beings and animals. Dickinson's portrayal of her dog as "better than [human] Beings" echoes a key assertion of this literature, that the virtues of animals reflect on the moral shortcomings of human beings. But Dickinson undercuts that lesson by dropping "human" and confounding the very parameters of didactic ontology where the human is the teleological outcome. Her insistence that her companions "know—but do not tell" indicates her resistance to the animal's didactic interpretation. Dickinson silences the pedagogical voice, and instead gives play to "the noise in the Pool, at Noon" which functions as a form of knowledge that does not express itself in telling, that is in human language, but in a musical mode of expression that "excels my Piano" in that, as "noise," it is an experiential and disordered form of natural expression (Jonson II. 404).

Dickinson stages and suspends the child's entry into an adult symbolic order that turns animals into dead metaphors by disavowing and historicizing their presence. Using the same metric form and rhyme pattern as Bullard, Dickinson performs a formal parody of this kind of animal writing in a poem from 1871:

> A little Dog that wags his tail
> And knows no other joy

Of such a little Dog am I
Reminded by a Boy
Who gambols all the living Day
Without an earthly cause
Because he is a little Boy
I honestly suppose—
The Cat that in the Corner dwells
Her martial Day forgot
The Mouse but a Tradition now
Of her desireless Lot
Another class remind me
Who neither please nor play
But not to make a 'bit of noise'
Beseech each little Boy—
(Franklin 1236)

Dickinson begins the poem sounding like the didactic literature she is imitating: she suggests that the boy is like the dog, but the moral lesson we expect to follow— that such likeness obliges him to a kindness that ultimately separates him from the dog—is missing. Indeed, if we look closely, the dog is not a stand-in for the boy, but on the contrary, the boy is a stand-in for the dog in Dickinson's reversal of the trope. Dickinson's boy is allowed to inhabit a relationship to the dog that resists their didactic separation from one another. This resistance to didactic separation deepens when we contextualize this poem with its private circulation. In letters to her family, Dickinson habitually referred to herself as a boy—for instance when she wrote to her nephew Ned: "Mother told me, when I was a boy, that I must turn over a new leaf. I call that the foliage admonition. Shall I commend it to you?" (Bianchi 37). Turning an admonition into a question, Dickinson here as in the poem undercuts the didactic message "another class" wants to impart. Indeed, that resistance to "admonition" is a theme throughout her correspondence with Ned. In the letter that included an abridged version of this poem, Dickinson offset its purported didacticism by adding a postscript: "P.S.—Grandma characteristically hopes Neddy will be a good boy. Obtuse ambition of Grandma's!" (Bianchi 37). Far from reprimanding the boy, she allies herself with him against those adults who would silence him. Unlike the cat's dead "Tradition" of a "martial Day" that stands in opposition to the boy's "living Day," the boy is free to "know no other joy" than the expression of his own pleasure.

But in being asked "not to make a 'bit of noise,' " the boy is soon deprived of the ability to participate in "the noise in the Pool, at Noon," that is, in the natural forms of expression that provide an alternative discourse to the language of pedagogy. Dickinson resists the didactic separation of children from animals; it is in their connection with one another that the possibility for poetic expression lies. Yet even in a poem like this one, that possibility is always deferred. Being "reminded" links memory to admonition. In portraying the little boy, the "I" of liberal subjectivity can be "reminded" of the "little Dog," but is already part of the didactic structures that prohibit the subject's participation in that undifferentiated relationship between the boy and the dog.

Whereas her parodic poem identifies this problem, Dickinson reaches in other works for a "Phraseless Melody" (Franklin 334) by reshaping her relationship to language, that is, by making poetry itself animate. Animals mark the liveness in Dickinson's work of a natural language beyond social silencing:

> Many a phrase has the English language—
> I have heard but one—
> Low as the laughter of the Cricket,
> Loud, as the Thunder's Tongue—
> Murmuring, like old Caspian Choirs,
> When the Tide's a'lull—
> Saying itself in new inflection—
> Like a Whippowil—
> Breaking in bright Orthography
> On my simple sleep—
> Thundering it's Prospective—
> Till I stir, and weep—
> Not for the Sorrow, done me—
> But the push of Joy—
> Say it again, Saxon!
> Hush—Only to me!
> (Franklin 333)

Bullard maintained a differentiation between human beings and animals by using simile to establish a third entity, language, as the basis of comparison and distinction, Dickinson here makes language itself the locus for relating animal and human subjectivity. The "one" phrase withheld is figured in relation to "the laughter of the Cricket" and the "new inflection" of the "Whippowil." This utterance takes on the shape of "Orthography" in Dickinson's "simple sleep." Akira Lippit's work is useful for reading this poem: through an interpretation of Freud's dreamwork, Lippit locates "a kind of originary topography shared by human beings and animals," in which "the animal becomes intertwined with the trope, serving as its vehicle and substance" (1112). Lippit coins the term "animetaphor" to describe the animal as both "an exemplary metaphor" and an "originary metaphor," and argues that animals function "as the unconscious of language, of *logos*" (1113). Following Jacques Derrida, Lippit argues that *logos* "is engendered by a *zoon*, and can never entirely efface the traces of its origin. The genealogy of language ... returns to a place outside of *logos*. The animal brings to language something that is not a part of language and remains within language as a foreign presence" (1113). The animal thus takes on the role of "a vital metaphor, that enters the world from a place outside of language," a "figure that is metamorphic rather than metaphoric" (1117-1118). Key to Dickinson's imagining of this metamorphic figure is her odd enjambment: "Like a Whippowil—Breaking in bright Orthography" brings the "new inflection" of the phrase in conjunction with "the branch of knowledge which deals with letters and their combination to represent sounds and words" (Oxford English Dictionary). Dickinson is literalizing one of Higginson's odder suggestions, that "kittens…about the house supply the smaller punctuation in the book of life; their little frisks and leaps and pats are the commas and semicolons and dashes, while the big dog puts in the colons and the periods" (Higginson, "Women and Men: Children and Animals"). Dickinson locates animal presence in orthography, in writing itself.

To achieve a vital poetry, beyond the parameters of animal metaphors, Emily Dickinson deconstructs liberal subjectivity by alphabetizing her poetry. "Carlo" participated in the nineteenth-century vogue of animal alphabets, that is, of alphabets that linked a letter with an image, and with rhymed text to initiate children into literacy. In *The Picture Alphabet* (1879) by "Cousin Daisy," the picture (see figure 11.1) of a scruffy

Figure 11.1 From *The Picture Alphabet* (1879) by "Cousin Daisy."
Courtesy of the American Antiquarian Society.

CARLO.

C stands for Carlo,

　　Looking through the bars,

Down into the dreary street,

　　'Neath the twinkling stars.

Figure 11.2 From *The Picture Alphabet* (1879) by "Cousin Daisy."
Courtesy of the American Antiquarian Society.

dog looking through bars is accompanied by the rhyme (see figure 11.2): "C stands for Carlo, / Looking through the bars, / Down into the dreary street, / 'Neath the twinkling stars." This kind of animal alphabet participated in and circumvented the structures of liberal subjectivity. As Patricia Crain has documented, "by the beginning of the nineteenth century, alphabetization supplants rhetorical training, not only as a mode of communication but as a primary structuring of subjectivity" (5). Alphabets function as an "androgyne, moving back and forth between text and image" (7), and complicate the relationship between textual and physical representation. The extensive use of animals in these alphabets also indicates "that there are two kinds of utterances: a natural, irresistible, autonomic kind, which we share with the animals—an exhale, a cry of a baby, the communication between working man and working beast; and an artificial, learned kind—that of alphabetic, educated speech, which we draw from the animals, but which distinguishes us from them."[6] Dickinson aims to recapture that former utterance, that noise, in her use of animal orthography.

The animation of orthography reshapes the relationship between writing and subject formation. "Carlo" is an anomaly in Dickinson's references to animals in that he is one of only three named animals (Carlo, Chanticleer, Pussy). Even those animals are not named individually but generically; they participate in the larger animal orthography of Dickinson's poetic enterprise. In fact, the sheer range and number of animals Dickinson mentions in her poems is astonishing: by my count, she lists over seventy different animals, and names at least one animal in 20 percent of her poems. In creating an animal orthography, Dickinson then strains beyond metaphor, to an animetaphor that gives poetry itself an extrasocial liveness, as one of her most famous poems illustrates:

> I heard a Fly buzz—when I died—
> The Stillness in the Room
> Was like the Stillness in the Air—
> Between the Heaves of Storm—
> The Eyes around—had wrung them dry—
> And Breaths were gathering firm
> For that last Onset—when the King
> Be witnessed—in the Room—
> I willed my Keepsakes—Signed away
> What portion of me be
> Assignable—and then it was
> There interposed a Fly—
> With Blue—uncertain—stumbling Buzz—
> Between the light—and me—
> And then the Windows failed—and then
> I could not see to see—(Franklin 591)

Having "signed away" that "portion of me" that is "Assignable," Dickinson relinquishes the scene of domestic confinement in the "room" and the social "witnessing" to harness the "Breaths" for her own postliberal subjectivity. The subject's death enables an animation of the poem itself: incessant buzzing and alliterative sounds invoke the impersonal fly whose intervention in the first line separates the "I" of liberal subjectivity from an undefined "I" that gains animation from the scene of death. Animals allow Dickinson to play one kind of death against another. The death of liberal subjectivity is the scene of an imagined overturning of the animal's figurative death, and an entry into a poetic liveness.

Dickinson's letter to Higginson stages such an animal orthography:

> Carlo died—
> E. Dickinson
> Would you instruct me now?
> (Johnson II. 449)

Starting with C for Carlo, moving to D for Died, and to E for a signature, she replicates in her lines the progression of the alphabet. Adding another D for Dickinson, she also symbolizes the rhyme scheme of the poems associated, as Bullard's verses illustrated, with children's education into a relationship with animals: CDED. Her concluding question to Higginson, whom she admired as a naturalist (Asahina), ironizes the didactic lessons that animals impart: she has, indeed, been well instructed. The fact that "Carlo died" then poses a threat and opens up a possibility for Dickinson's enterprise. As Higginson put it, "[A] dog is itself a liberal education, with its example of fidelity, unwearied activity, cheerful sympathy, and love stronger than death" (530). In staging her carefully learnt lessons of animal pedagogy, Dickinson portrays Carlo as a figure for liberal education. But she also takes his literal death to explore Higginson's promise, that the dog exceeds the parameters of liberal subject formation, and provides a figure of liveness beyond social formation. The danger here is that this development naturalizes social formations; in turning to representation, Dickinson offsets the reemergence of ontology with an emphasis on orthography. Carlo's literal death opens the possibility for his orthographic liveness; through Carlo, "E. Dickinson's" subjectivity can again become an open-ended question.

CONCLUSION

I have been tracing an arc that links the ontological questions posed by current affect theory to Lockean origins and subsequent intellectual receptions of liberal subject formation. Affect theory and liberalism each open a space for radical alterity. But they too easily foreclose that space by reinscribing affect in an ontologically defined frame that distinguishes between the human and its animal others. At stake in that foreclosure is the production of a particular notion of subjectivity, as one marked by an individuality independent of others and clearly demarcated by the separation of reasoning from embodiment. Looking at animals gives us a different account of the subject—as relational and contingent on an alterity that cannot easily be reinscribed in the registers of either abstract rationality or embodied affectivity. Because that alterity is both physical *and* representational, it enables us to recognize that reading is a bodily act, and that the body is a readerly act. These two modes of meaning-making are contingent on but not reducible to each other; they function as one another's excess and *différance*. In the process, they unhinge the naturalizing discourse of ontology, and point to ontology itself as a construct that emerges relationally. Through the literal and figurative presence of animals, we come to see a fundamental relationality that points to the contingencies of our being. It is in that relationality that new possibilities for subjectivity and poetry emerge.

NOTES

1 Trilling's work has been claimed by neoconservatives and dismissed by scholars eager to move beyond "the age of heroic criticism"; he has been faulted for being a naive "believer

in Matthew Arnold's ideal of 'disinterestedness,'" and for his exclusion of women from literature and criticism; see Kimmage; Menand; Delbanco; and Heilbrun.

2 Jerome Huyler has documented that Locke's educational writings were "well advertised" in America by the middle of the eighteenth century, with *Thoughts concerning Education*, itself reprinted more than nineteen times before 1761" (201).

3 Dillon, "Sentimental Aesthetics."

4 See Mason; Grier; Kete; Ritvo; Thomas.

5 Carlo was a Newfoundland dog; the breed is said to be particularly intelligent—see Watson.

6 See Crain 36.

BIBLIOGRAPHY

Aesop. *Aesop's Fables in French: With a Description of Fifty Animals Mentioned Therein and a French and English Dictionary of the Words Contained in the Work.* Philadelphia: Lindsay and Blakiston, 1852.

Asahina, Midori. "'Fascination' Is Absolute of Clime': Reading Emily Dickinson's Correspondence with Higginson as Naturalist." *Emily Dickinson Journal* 14.2 (2005): 103–119.

Bates, Arlo. "Books and Authors." *Boston Sunday Courier* 96 (1890): 2.

Bianchi, Martha Dickinson. "Selections from the Unpublished Letters of Emily Dickinson to Her Brother's Family; Chosen and Arranged by Her Niece Martha Dickinson Bianchi." *Atlantic Monthly*, January 1915, 35–42.

Blackwood, Sarah. "'Inner Brand': Emily Dickinson, Portraiture, and the Narrative of Liberal Interiority." *Emily Dickinson Journal* 14.2 (2005): 48–59.

Boggs, Colleen Glenney. "Emily Dickinson's Animal Pedagogies." *PMLA* 124.2 (2009): 533–541.

Brown, Gillian. *The Consent of the Governed: The Lockean Legacy in Early American Culture.* Cambridge, MA: Harvard University Press, 2001.

Bullard, Asa. *Dog Stories, His Sunnybank Stories.* Boston: Lee and Shepard, 1863.

Capps, Jack L. *Emily Dickinson's Reading 1836–1886.* Cambridge, MA: Harvard University Press, 1966.

Crain, Patricia. *The Story of A: The Alphabetization of America from the New England Primer to the Scarlet Letter.* Stanford, CA: Stanford University Press, 2000.

Cvetkovich, Ann. *Mixed Feeling: Feminism, Mass Culture, and Victorian Sensationalism.* New Brunswick, NJ: Rutgers University Press, 1992.

Daisy, Cousin. *The Picture Alphabet.* Philadelphia: J. B. Lippincott, 1879.

Davidson, Jenny. *Breeding: A Partial History of the Eighteenth Century.* New York: Columbia University Press, 2009.

Delbanco, Andrew. "Night Vision." *New York Review of Books* 481 (2001): 38.

Derrida, Jacques. "And Say the Animal Responded?" *Zoontologies: The Question of the Animal.* Ed. Cary Wolfe. Minneapolis and London: University of Minnesota Press, 2003.

Dillon, Elizabeth Maddock. *The Gender of Freedom: Fictions of Liberalism and the Literary Public Sphere.* Stanford, CA: Stanford University Press, 2004.

———. "Sentimental Aesthetics." *American Literature* 76.3 (2004): 495–523.

Donovan, Josephine, and Carol J. Adams, eds. *Beyond Animal Rights: A Feminist Caring Ethic for the Treatment of Animals.* New York: Continuum, 1996.

Eberwein, Jane Donahue. *An Emily Dickinson Encyclopedia*. Westport, CT: Greenwood Press, 1998.

Fliegelman, Jay. *Prodigals and Pilgrims: The American Revolution against Patriarchal Authority, 1750–1800*. Cambridge: Cambridge University Press, 1982.

Franklin, R.W., ed. *The Poems of Emily Dickinson: Reading Edition*. Cambridge, MA: Belknap Press of Harvard University Press, 1998.

Gates, Henry Louis. *The Signifying Monkey: A Theory of African-American Literary Criticism*. New York: Oxford University Press, 1988.

Grier, Katherine. *Pets in America: A History*. Chapel Hill: University of North Carolina Press, 2006.

Habegger, Alfred. "Evangelicalism and Its Discontents: Hannah Porter Versus Emily Dickinson." *New England Quarterly* 70.3 (1997): 386–414.

Haraway, Donna. *The Companion Species Manifesto: Dogs, People, and Significant Otherness*. Chicago: Prickly Paradigm Press, 2003.

Hardt, Michael. "Foreword: What Affects Are Good For." *The Affective Turn: Theorizing the Social*. Ed. Patricia Ticineto Clough and Jean Halley. Durham, NC: Duke University Press, 2007. ix–xiii.

Heilbrun, Carolyn G. "Men Were the Only Models I Had." *Chronicle of Higher Education* 48.7 (2001): B7–B11.

Higginson, Thomas Wentworth. "Emily Dickinson's Letters." *Atlantic Monthly*, October 1891, 444–456.

———. "Women and Men: Children and Animals." *Harper's Bazaar*, July 30, 1887, 530.

Holland, Jeanne. "Scraps, Stamps, and Cutouts: Emily Dickinson's Domestic Technologies of Publication." *Cultural Artifacts and the Production of Meaning: The Page, the Image, and the Body*. Ed. Margaret J. M. Ezell and Katherine O'Brien O'Keeffe. Ann Arbor: University of Michigan Press, 1994. 139–181.

Huyler, Jerome. *Locke in America: The Moral Philosophy of the Founding Era*. Kansas City: University of Kansas Press, 1995.

Johnson, Thomas H., ed. *The Letters of Emily Dickinson*. 3 vols. Vol. 2. Cambridge, MA: Belknap Press of Harvard University Press, 1958.

Kete, Kathleen. *The Beast in the Boudoir: Petkeeping in Nineteenth-Century Paris*. Berkeley: University of California Press, 1994.

Kimmage, Michael. "Lionel Trilling's the Middle of the Journey and the Complicated Origins of the Neo-Conservative Movement." *Shofar: An Interdisciplinary Journal of Jewish Studies* 21.3 (2003): 48–63.

Lippit, Akira Mizuta. "Magnetic Animal: Derrida, Wildlife, Animetaphor." *MLN* 113.5 (1998): 1111–1125.

Locke, John. *The Educational Writings of John Locke: A Critical Edition with Introduction and Notes*. Ed. James L. Axtell. Cambridge: Cambridge University Press, 1968.

Longsworth, Polly. *The World of Emily Dickinson*. New York: Norton, 1990.

Mason, Jennifer. *Civilized Creatures: Urban Animals. Sentimental Culture, and American Literature, 1850–1900*. Ed. Harriet Ritvo. Animals, History, Culture. Baltimore: Johns Hopkins University Press, 2005.

Menand, Louis. "Regrets Only: Lionel Trilling and His Discontents." *New Yorker*, September 29, 2008.

Ortner, Sherry. "Is Female to Male as Nature Is to Culture?" *Woman, Culture, and Society*. Ed. Michelle Zimbalist Rosaldo and Louise Lamphere. Stanford, CA: Stanford University Press, 1974. 67–87.

Peterson, Christopher. "Of Canines and Queers: Review of Melancholia's Dog: Reflections on Our Animal Kinship." *GLQ* 15.2 (2009): 352–354.

Ritvo, Harriet. "Pride and Pedigree: The Evolution of the Victorian Dog Fancy." *Victorian Studies* 29.2 (1986): 227–253.

Sánchez-Eppler, Karen. *Touching Liberty: Abolition, Feminism, and the Politics of the Body.* Berkeley: University of California Press, 1993.

Sedgwick, Eve Kosofsky. *Between Men: English Literature and Male Homosocial Desire.* New York: Columbia University Press, 1985.

Terada, Rei. *Feeling in Theory: Emotion after the "Death of the Subject."* Cambridge, MA: Harvard University Press, 2001.

Thomas, Keith. *Man and the Natural World: A History of the Modern Sensibility.* New York: Pantheon Books, 1983.

Trilling, Lionel. *The Liberal Imagination: Essays on Literature and Society.* New York: Viking Press, 1950.

Trimmer, Sarah. *Fabulous Histories: Designed for the Instruction of Children Respecting Their Treatment of Animals.* London: Printed for T. Longman and G. G. J. and J. Robinson and J. Johnson, 1786. microform.

Watson, J. S. (John Selby). *Reasoning Power in Animals.* London: Reeve, 1867.

CHAPTER 12

ARCHIVES OF PUBLISHING AND GENDER: HISTORICAL CODES IN LITERARY ANALYSIS

SHIRLEY SAMUELS

HAWTHORNE HOLDS A PEN

What does it mean for an author to hold a pen in the nineteenth-century United States? What if that author is Nathaniel Hawthorne and he writes a letter to his editor insisting that no pen has ever satisfied him? Does this evidence of the tactility of his writerly practices teach a twenty-first-century reader how to interpret other aspects of Hawthorne's writing? These questions are the preoccupations of a practitioner who reads for history as well as for the event horizon of the language on a page, whether in print or in an archive. Without hesitation or necessary provocation, I would assert that my investment in historical research is at once extremely personal, insofar as an allegiance to feminism must necessarily be personal, and bound up with the disciplinary imperatives of archival research. Since the purpose of this chapter is at once to explicate some possibilities that arise from the practices of archival research and to suggest what these practices make possible in the interpretation of literature, what follows will look at the opportunities as well as the difficulties of historical research by beginning with crucial details from the dusty archives of authors and editors exchanging letters in the nineteenth-century United States.

The imperatives of historical research range from the persuasion that if I am sitting in a library holding a letter said to have been written by Nathaniel Hawthorne, I assume that he was present, or at least in the room, when the letter was produced. He may not have written it—many nineteenth-century authors, including Hawthorne, dictated to an amanuensis. But one value of primary historical research resides nevertheless in the conviction that I may locate in such a letter a detail that will affect prior understandings. And indeed in one such letter, Hawthorne asserts that the rage he feels toward women writers is such that he would prefer to see them threatened with mutilation if they dared to write: "*All* women, as authors, are feeble and tiresome. I wish they were forbidden to write, on pain of having their faces deeply scarified with an oyster shell."[1]

Such a comment, and the image of women authors with bleeding faces that it conveys, is horrifying enough. And Hawthorne's words deserve the scathing critical commentary they have already received.[2] Keep in mind that Hawthorne writes these words the same year that he publishes *The Blithedale Romance*, with its deeply conflicted understanding of Zenobia, a vibrant and doomed woman "rebelling against her sex," set in ambivalent contrast to the timid Priscilla. Yet the same letter ends with a passage not usually quoted in which Hawthorne inquires of his correspondent, the editor and publisher James T. Fields, if he knows where in the world Portugal might be located. What sort of a country is it, what is its government? This inquiry, presumably a response to thinking about a possible diplomatic posting, suggests that Hawthorne has not thoroughly situated himself, that he is more than a little adrift in a world of popular women authors, a lack of clarity about geography, and uncertain career prospects.

Subsequent letters suggest that Hawthorne has slowly begun to lose his grip on how to write. Literally, he loses his grip on the pen. A decade later, Hawthorne writes Fields at great length with excuses for not delivering his promised next book (*The Dolliver Romance*) and claims that no one could ever have suffered as much as he has from the material difficulty of holding a pen. In a long passage on trying to find the right pen, Hawthorne explains that he has tried glass, steel, gold, and "gutta percha" (an early form of rubber) before complaining that "Nobody ever suffered more from pens than I have" (December 9, 1863; FI 5079). After another year, he declares himself to be at the end of writing (in a letter written shortly before his death): "I shall never publish [crossed out] finish it. Yet it is not quite pleasant for an author to announce himself, or to be announced, as finally broken down as to his literary faculty." In this letter, Hawthorne spends four pages writing about excuses that could be made to the public. These increasingly elaborate excuses perform a story all by themselves. Yet his litany begins, "Say to the public what you think best, and as little as possible." One excuse proffered early on includes this line: "Mr. Hawthorne's brain is addled at last." Finally he asserts, "I cannot finish it, unless a great change comes over me; and if I make too great an effort to do so, it will be my death" (February 25, 1864; FI 2317). This sentence literally presages an exhaustion that becomes mortal, as this is one of Hawthorne's last letters.

Does the poignancy of Hawthorne's deterioration excuse the virulent threats he earlier made against the faces of women writers? Not at all. Can we read in Hawthorne's excoriating of himself an ordinary rage against the success of women writers combined with a form of self-directed violence? Certainly. Yet the advantages of reading through a cache of such letters together must be that answers become more intricately embedded in the historical circumstances that produce easily quoted extracts. The material conditions of writing—as suggestive as the details about holding a pen might be—produce an author whose relation to the labor of words is tactile as well as political. At the risk of becoming lost in the maze of this historical knowledge, let me continue.

Previous inquiries into Hawthorne's relation to history have included examinations of his location in the present as well as of his inquiries into Puritan history.[3] Although Hawthorne may always be best known for his inquiries into and explications of Puritan identity in novels such as *The Scarlet Letter*, he also commented on contemporary political events, especially in his campaign biography of Franklin Pierce, and his fraught account of Abraham Lincoln in "Chiefly about War Matters," first published in the *Atlantic Monthly* in 1862. The latter essay was modified after an exchange of letters with James T. Fields, the editor of the *Atlantic Monthly* and also Hawthorne's publisher (with the firm Ticknor and Fields).

To read these letters for the purpose of explicating the political position of Nathaniel Hawthorne in the fraught political time of the Civil War still rouses a great deal of critical attention. For example, James Bense produces an account of "Hawthorne's Intention in 'Chiefly About War Matters,'" deriving his title from the concept that the work of critics is to recover the author's intentions. I realize that I may have entered inadvertently into such a controversy in my desire to read the letters that Hawthorne exchanges with his publisher as a way of illuminating his political ambivalence. Yet, and always, I would like to leave room for the opposing interpretations of Hawthorne's willed perversity and his obstinate loyalty to proslavery friends. In this essay Bense asserts, tellingly, that "[i]f Hawthorne had altered his text only as a concession to Fields's conditions for publishing it, the surviving version would seem to nullify Hawthorne's original intention."[4] In this view, the letters that Hawthorne writes about the anger he feels about being asked to modify his language produce the critical sense of an essay eviscerated by editorial corrections. Because Bense relies on the published accounts of the affair, mainly the recollections published by Fields years later, the excerpts from Hawthorne's letters that were chosen for publication, and the footnote notations (subsequently attributed to Hawthorne) in the original appearance in the *Atlantic Monthly*, he draws this conclusion. Had he been able to read the letters from Fields as part of the original correspondence concerning the matter, his own historical interpretation might have been rather different.

There is, of course, a temporal reason for the difference between the letters Fields wrote and his later account of the exchange. Emotions recollected in tranquility are always changed. The heat of the letters burns through the handwritten pages. Hawthorne is angry. Fields mollifies, but will not relent. The exchange reflects the anxiety of wartime patriotism. Yet even there, as I suggested, the critic brings her sense of propaganda to bear. When Fields argues that he shows disrespect to refer to the president as "Abe," Hawthorne retorts somewhat petulantly, "The whole description of the interview with Uncle Abe, and his personal appearance must be omitted, since I do not find it possible to alter them, and in so doing, I think you omit the only part of the article really worth publishing. Upon my honor, it seems to me to have a historical value, but let it go. I have altered and transferred one of the notes, so as to indicate to the unfortunate public that here it loses something very nice" (May 23, 1862; FI 2287).

What Fields says to spur this angry retort can be found in the archive. When he asks Hawthorne to alter his essay on "War Matters" for the *Atlantic Monthly*, Fields makes a very rare use of a plural "we" as he refers to the position of the firm "Ticknor and Fields": "Ticknor and I both think it will be politic to alter yr phrase, with reference to the President, to leave out the description of his awkwardness + [*sic*] general uncouth aspect. England is reading the magz. now + will gloat over the monkey figure of 'Uncle Abe' as he appears in yr paper." Fields goes on to urge that Hawthorne "not speak of the President as *Uncle Abe* but wd call him the President in every instance where he is mentioned." Again, "Pray you ameliorate your description of the President" (May 21, 1862; FI 2120). The idea that "England" is watching produces an acute anxiety in a time of war as well as potentially arousing economic worries for a publisher who needs to keep on good terms with an English public, and the assumed vigilance of England changes the tone of the remarks. That anxiety about an English audience "gloating" over the "monkey figure" that Hawthorne conveys does not suggest undue censorship nor an unawareness of the function of satire, but a shrewd metering of how much political propaganda might be allowed.

That Hawthorne was close to Ticknor as well as to Fields might be suggested by his last letter to Fields, concerned mainly with his worries over Ticknor's health. Ticknor died with Hawthorne at his side; Hawthorne died shortly afterward with Franklin Pierce at his side. The very intimacy that he enjoyed with both his editors and with a former president once his roommate may indicate why Hawthorne thought it acceptable to engage in a caricature of a sitting president. And yet that Fields thought it necessary to reprimand him for presenting a president as a "monkey figure" alludes at once to the racialist understanding of Lincoln's origins (that is, to a prevailing rumor that he was not entirely "white") and to the pejorative associations between sympathy for those held in slavery and their origins in Africa; the combination produces Hawthorne's insults as conceived in a fantasy of the United States invaded from within by nonhuman forces. Whether "scarified" women writers or a "monkey" president may be blamed for the paralysis that leaves him unable to hold his pen, the letters reveal a writer whose last works exist as fragments in the throes of ideological fragmentation.

Through invoking a well-known controversy about one of the best-known writers of the nineteenth-century United States in a moment of political panic, this chapter proposes to think about some of the reasons why such historical codes make a difference to literary critics. These codes include abstractions such as iconography as well as the minutiae derived from historical research. In proposing that these are historical codes, I suggest, of course, that they are there to be interpreted and deciphered as much as to be deployed. The pleasure of literary analysis may thus be necessarily embedded in the deciphering of a historical context. To examine the historical codes of literature does not mean, if it ever did, that the critic assumes a univalent concept of national identity. Nor does it suggest that static concepts of history or the nation prevail in historical fiction. Such fiction may, on the contrary, display competing polemical agendas. If, like history, forms of criticism can be read as propaganda, perhaps, indeed, producing critics who can read their objects of inquiry in terms of propaganda, does this suggest that the means, function, and significance of scholarship become tainted by its ends? The suggestion that propaganda invades the practices of either fiction or scholarship arouses the anxiety at the heart of historical inquiry and methods. Once it is a given that there is no "pure" historical research, a claim enhanced long ago in the assertion that each generation must produce its own history, then the objects as well as the aims of history also become something for each generation to examine.[5] The association with propaganda forces literature into a conjunction with national concerns even as such concerns are put on dramatic display by wartime patriotism, an important, and often overlooked, historical code in figuring out the affiliations and attention to composition in Hawthorne's writing.

READING LETTERS

The women writers that Hawthorne excoriates were also published by James Fields, both in his role as editor of *The Atlantic Monthly* and in his editorial capacity with Ticknor and Fields. Since first James and then Annie Fields saved this voluminous correspondence, extending over decades, several possibilities emerge for using historical codes in an examination of literary production. The women writers who address Fields do so in a haze of domestic matters, personal appeals, and pleas for money. The popular writer known as Grace Greenwood, for instance, writes to him on "a little matter of business." She proposes, somewhat timidly, "As yet, significantly enough, we have not exchanged a word on pecuniary matters, but I know that all must be well. Still I would like to know whether the publication is to profit me at all before I think of getting up anything else in the book line. In other words, I wish to know how much I am to receive on a copy." That she has no concept of a percentage of her royalties does not entirely suggest her indifference to money: "I made a purchase of a small farm last year, for which I am to pay in installments" (January 4, 1850; FI 1765). The labor of writing that will result in the payment of royalties becomes, at least implicitly, transmuted into payments for land.

While some writers focus on royalties, others obsess about how editors and printers will manage style. Harriet Beecher Stowe announces happily to James

Fields that she has no idea how to punctuate: "My printers always inform me that I know nothing of punctuation & I give thanks that I have no responsibility for any of its absurdities! Further than beginning my sentences with a capital I go not—" (August 16, 1867; FI 4027). Concentrating on style first, Stowe then writes to Annie Fields, the wife of her editor, and asks if there might be any money due her. Then she has to think about the legal restrictions on publication within the United States. Since Canada provides the same legal access as England for copyright protection, Stowe is contemplating a journey north of the border at the same time as she prepares her final revisions. She pleads to have the publication of her book delayed; the late winter weather makes it too cold to travel to Canada, but she must physically be there when her book is published in England in order to protect copyright.

As she struggles to complete a promised book, Stowe becomes more personal and her later explanations include the plea that she cannot finish the book in time because her children need her to write letters to them instead of writing fiction. In a story that recurs in telling historical stories about women writers, Stowe explains that her novel is inevitably delayed because at present she can only write letters to her children: "To them in their needs I *must* write *chapters* which would otherwise go into my novel" (July 27, 1868; FI 4030). The writing of fiction becomes a mutating process that includes international travel, chapters that become personal letters, and struggles with punctuation.

The aim for a literary critic who conducts such historical research into letters must be to illuminate the text in question as much as to enjoy biographical flourishes. Stowe, for instance, happily asks for space to develop plots for her novel in progress, *Oldtown Folks*: "To play off my characters as much as I want to I *want room*—& I have so many of them that I want to show off & I can have any amount of fun with them." Making the landscape of the book into a playful space in which characters can engage each other as well as the author, Stowe's comment has the elbow-stretching effects that permeate the letter of Rebecca Harding Davis who, addressing Fields as the editor of the *Atlantic Monthly* after he has published *Life in the Iron Mills*, asks plaintively: "If I write for you again, would it be any different if the story was longer than the last? I felt cramped, and we of the west like room—you know." The sense of space that pervades Stowe's fiction appears here as geographic territory that might be associated as easily with Davis's West Virginia as with Stowe's still western city of Cincinnati.

Like Hawthorne, and around the same time, Stowe heads for Washington, D.C., to catch sight of Lincoln. Her aims are rather different, however. She writes to James Fields to announce that "I am going to Washington…to satisfy myself that I may refer to the Emancipation Proclamation as a reality and a substance not to fizzle out at the little end of the horn as I should be sorry to call the attention of my sisters in Europe to any such important conclusion.…I start for Washington tomorrow morning—& mean to have a talk with 'Father Abraham' himself among others" (November 13, 1862; FI 4012). Looking over her shoulder at her "sisters" in Europe, Stowe asserts a responsibility to transatlantic relations as she travels to see the president to assure herself of the political realities associated with the abolition of slavery. Respecting her political sympathies, perhaps, Fields does not mention her tone of intimacy with the president, even as he must have noticed that her familiar address to the president echoes one of the most popular Civil War recruitment ballads, known as "We Are Coming Father Abraham!" Stowe's politics, grounded in the decade-old success of *Uncle Tom's Cabin* (1852), assure her a sympathetic audience where Hawthorne risks his political neck.

The sense of glee and pleasure that pervades Stowe's letters even as she assumes familiarity with the president contrasts with Hawthorne's grim sense in his letters to Fields that he cannot go on, that he has forgotten how to write. Indeed he writes as if he is dying, or preparing to die, long before his swift decline. Stowe is fond of Hawthorne, and she expresses her affection in letters to Fields, but she is also capable of her own rather incoherent rage. When she finds out that Hawthorne has not only written a campaign biography of the presidential candidate Franklin Pierce (his roommate at Bowdoin College), but also praised him in his book of travel essays, *Our Old Home*, she sputters: "So tell me if our friend Hawthorne praises that arch traitor Pierce in his preface and your loyal firm publishes it—I never read the preface & have not yet seen the book but they say so here and I can scarcely believe it of you—if I can of him—I regret that I went to see him last summer—what! 'patronise such a traitor to our faces!'— can scarce believe it—" (November 3, 1863; FI 4016). Again, even as she assaults the loyalty of the publishing firm of Ticknor and Fields, Stowe saves her wrath for Hawthorne's prefatory dedication to *Our Old Home*, his forlorn attachment to English landscapes.

In his explanatory preface to this dedication, dated July 1, 1863, Hawthorne notes that his writing in the volume "meddle[s] with no matters of policy or government." As he wards off writing about the war whose effects reach Concord, Massachusetts, as well as other parts of the country, Hawthorne protests that his ability to write fiction has disappeared. By this account, "The Present, the Immediate, the Actual, has proved too potent for me. It takes away not only my scanty faculty, but even my desire for imaginative composition, and leaves me sadly content to scatter a thousand peaceful fantasies upon the hurricane that is sweeping us all along with it, possibly, into a Limbo where our nation and its polity may be as literally the fragments of a shattered dream as my unwritten Romance." Referring more than once to an "abortive project," Hawthorne alludes to war as a corollary to writing and to birth at once. The "hurricane" has shattered fantasies of national cohesion as well as the writer's dream of giving birth to a romance.

The treachery Stowe finds in Hawthorne's dedication concerns Pierce's support of slavery. By writing a campaign biography, Hawthorne implicates himself in the proslavery cause. All his associations, social and literary, become tainted. Yet the rage Stowe feels dissipates after Hawthorne's death. When she proposes to Fields to write an essay about literary style, she wants to begin with Hawthorne. In her letter about writing a "style" essay called "Learning to Write," Stowe proclaims, "In the first number, under the head, How best to study to form a style, I shall instance Hawthorne as a model, & speak of his Note Book as something which every young author, aspiring to write, should study" (December 24, 1868; FI 4031). That is, the raw material for Hawthorne's writing, published posthumously, becomes the source material for how to have a literary source. The production of such raw material as an archive of Hawthorne's transcribed responses to everyday life persists as a model for the historical analysis of literary production.

Hawthorne appears as another kind of model for a different writer who appeals to Fields. Eager to find the funding that will enable him to marry the writer we now know as Elizabeth Stoddard, perhaps not coincidentally a cousin of Hawthorne's, Richard Henry Stoddard writes:

> By the by—do you think Hawthorne would do anything for me in the way of an office under Pierce? I would like to have his influence, for he must have some, to get any small office for myself. I swear to you, James, I feel like cutting my throat half the time, with utter misery, and despair, poverty and other nuisances. My heart is feeding on itself. If I could only see any way in the future, any hope for me I would do anything, work like hell, but I cant; my heart is heavier than lead. An office in the Custom House with $1000 or so a year would make me a fine noble man, would make me what I am not, and never can be as I am; were I in Hawthorne's place and he in mine, I would help him if I could. Tell me whether you think I should do wrong to ask him. (November 16, 1852; FI 3869)

In this letter, an appeal to an influential commercial house of publishing becomes an excruciatingly personal appeal to use influence free of political motivation and dedicated simply to an extension of the assumption that access to the office in the Custom House leads to success as a writer.

The very excitations of this letter, its alternations between suicidal despair and romantic longing, might become bound up with a reading of Hawthorne's declarations in the "Custom House" preface to *The Scarlet Letter* of a relationship among despair, commerce, and the will to write. Although he does not make the association in writing to Fields, Stoddard must have known that Hawthorne's job at the Custom House was part of what enabled his marriage to Sophia Peabody (it began, of course, with the promise of utopian living recalled in *The Blithedale Romance*). At the same time, it is not clear that Stoddard has read the Custom House preface carefully enough to notice that this particular commercial venture also produced a torpor that Hawthorne claimed to find antithetical to writing. Parenthetically, Stoddard was to attain that job at the New York Custom House and could thereby afford to marry Elizabeth Stoddard, whose novel *The Morgesons* has remained as a literary legacy while Richard Stoddard has been forgotten. In Elizabeth Stoddard's novel, as I will discuss, the associations between romantic longing and suicidal despair drive the narrator as well as its Byronic heroes into phenomenal conjunctions of commerce and desire. Herman Melville's later job at the New York Custom House may also be an imitative model. As with Hawthorne's position at the Custom House in Salem, politics will intervene. Richard Stoddard is fired from his job at the Custom House in New York in 1870 (for being a Democrat).

Hawthorne's job at the Custom House also engages him in a fictitious form of self-murder when the political climate changes: "[M]y own head was the first to roll."[6] Yet only that form of fictitious death, a death achieved through political attachment to the "wrong party," will release him into authorship. For Stoddard to wish himself into "Hawthorne's place" may thus be to wish for commercial comfort but also literary death. This excursion into the historical analysis of patronage and influence allows readers to engage literary history through the discovery of commercial stories as well as personal stories that seek to make room for writing. The letters that reveal the conditions for writing in the nineteenth-century United States can sometimes only be found in the archive of commercial exchange. The relations among letters that reveal the commercial basis for writing (such as the purchase of land or the ability to marry) and letters that ask for room within the fictions that the author wants to produce lead to a further inquiry into what we can find in the archive.

READING DUST

Attending to the archive in her short book of essays, *Dust: The Archive and Cultural History*, Carolyn Steedman notes, of course, that Jacques Derrida's *Archive Fever* delineates the difficulties inherent either in entering or exiting an archive.[7] In her preface to *Dust*, Steedman notes, "Dust is the immutable, obdurate set of beliefs about the material world, past and present, inherited from the 19th century...and Dust is the joke" (ix). Steedman presents her case for inhaling the dust of the archive as potentially deadly. Bringing a Derridean move to bear on the lessons of the master, Steedman proposes "to concentrate on what Derrida did not say, on that which was not the focus of his attention." She notes that the original printed French text includes a preface omitted in the English translation that emphasized how much he addresses the question of "archives du mal," including state secrets and civil war (8). This discovery of evil becomes something other than a fever.

Derrida compares these difficulties to a "fever" or malady, but there are many ways in which his proposed archive does not function as a conventional archive and Steedman proposes to read Derrida in deconstructive terms, that is, to look at what he does not notice as much as what he does. In Steedman's reading of Derrida's reading (and misreading) of the fever in the stacks, the very dust of the archive becomes what's inhaled and exhaled. Breathing in the fragments of pages and mingling them with the archivist's own breath, the researcher reaches an at once ideal and horrifying location vis-à-vis the relation of her body to fragments of history. Her dust joins that of the pages she has taken in with the eye and with the nostrils, inhaling ideas that simultaneously mingle with her brain and her lungs. (Speaking personally, since I love reading old books but am also allergic to them, the dust of the archive simply makes me sneeze.)

One danger Steedman notes is the literal poison that leather-bound books found in the archive might convey, bearing the residue of anthrax spores associated with the leather-binding trade in previous centuries. Steedman's attention to the history of the labor of print recalls her attention to the labors of her mother, a weaver's daughter, in her earlier work, *Landscape for a Good Woman: A Story of Two Lives.* In this autobiographical work, she tells her mother's story as well as her own as she looks at the transformation of class origins in a past that carries with it a residue of shame, and a resistance to elite concepts of historiography. In such lives, as she notes, "the central interpretative devices of the culture don't quite work" (1). That is, through a personal account of origins, Steedman reaches toward her own life as an archival source for assumptions about history and class consciousness even as she finds in the small and incomplete scraps of this life a disciplinary imperative about the forms of history to use as archival sources.

The congruence and incongruence of preparing a discussion of historical codes in literary analysis is that the dust of the archive includes scraps of history, the ephemera that Steedman notes can be at once inescapably functional and misleading. Why does one scrap, one letter, one theater playbill, one café menu, survive and not another? The impulse to save and preserve the debris of daily life in order to reconstruct that day in some improbable future motivates librarians to hold onto miscellany as well as literary manuscripts, discarded comic books, and first editions. What principle of selection then enables the researcher to reconstruct a context for literary production that enhances rather than distracts from interpretation?

As Steedman notes, Derrida insists that readers note the order in which data might be provided. Derrida's work was composed for a 1994 conference: "Memory: The Question of the Archives." The archive, as Derrida said then, is "in the order of commencement as well as in the order of commandment." He suggests that there must be attention to the process of the archive; its insistence on historical memory must be interpreted as produced with a timetable as well as through the critic's attention to the gatekeepers of record. Michel Foucault similarly comments that the archive does not exist simply as "the institutions [that] make it possible to record and preserve those discourses one wishes to keep in circulation" (128), noting particularly the history of the establishment of the Library of Congress in 1800. Rather, Foucault argues for the ways that particular discursive systems make it possible to describe something in an archive.

A looming example in the literary history of the United States continues to be the Civil War. University courses that treat U.S. literature and history offered during the past fifty years have retained a static positioning whereby antebellum and postbellum stay stubbornly opposed. The presuppositions are innumerable. There was only ever *one* war for the citizens of the United States? No writers wrote *during* that war? The nearly 150 years since the war's conclusion can be "covered" in one semester's teaching? In the introduction to the edited volume *States of Emergency: The Object of American Studies,* the editors assert that terms like "antebellum" and "postbellum," "in marking units of space or geopolitical divisions suggests their overlap, in a kind of asymmetrical equivalence."[8] The failure of equivalence that students and scholars face in the twenty-first century is to understand how to acknowledge the dramatic temporal asymmetry of events since 1865. For now, I will propose the difficult solution of considering the "long nineteenth century" as a unit.

Although the Civil War dominated the lives of millions of people over thousands of miles of territory for far more than the four years of bloody battles, many significant writers seem to have ignored it, or simply left town. Mark Twain high-tailed it to California (later to write *Roughing It*), Nathaniel Hawthorne headed to Liverpool and Italy (where *The Marble Faun* determined that expatriate life and artistry belonged together), and Emily Dickinson appears to have gone to her room (though her poems breathe the conversations that reached her about the world's events). There were writers who put literary energy into politics on both sides of the conflict. Lydia Maria Child, Harriet Beecher Stowe, and Maria Amparo Ruiz de Burton threw their writing energies into the fire of patriotism. John William de Forest and Thomas Wentworth Higginson were on the front lines for the Union, later writing about it in *Miss Ravenel's Conversion from Secession to Loyalty* and *Army Life in a Black Regiment*. Louisa May Alcott and Walt Whitman served in military hospitals in Washington, D.C., and found literary inspiration as well as physical exhaustion there, writing "The Brothers" and *Drum Taps*. William Gilmore Simms stayed in the South to write his novels and literary criticism. Augusta Evans wrote *Macaria* and became herself heroic in her romanticization of the lost cause of the Confederacy. Sidney Lanier went to fight for the Confederate Army and caught the tuberculosis that killed him, though not before he wrote his own novel of masculine ideals, *Tiger Lily*. As I will discuss in a moment, Elizabeth Stoddard seems to have focused on writing about her New England girlhood. And Hannah Crafts seems to have focused on escaping from slavery.

When looking for the Civil War in the archive, what does the researcher find? Letters and diaries from soldiers who could not know if they would survive the next battle occupy many feet of shelves in libraries and historical societies. I do not propose to settle the matter of how to interpret the war as an archive, presumptuously asserting here that it cannot be settled. Rather, I wish to note how deeply either its absence or presence becomes felt in a reading of documents, images, and literary works produced from the 1850s through the 1890s. In its absence, the war haunts the reading of a novel like Hawthorne's *The Marble Faun*, written in Italy as the war began to heat up. What are those three lost Americans doing in Rome, we might ask, even as we admire how sculptors like Edmonia Lewis, Harriet Hosmer, and Hiram Powers used Italian quarries and stone masons to produce stunning works such as *Forever Free* (1867), *Zenobia in Chains* (1859), or *The Greek Slave* (1844) that allude to the struggles over slavery while transmuting the conflict into a classical ideal.

According to Steedman, Derrida presents the "desire for the archive" as the desire to "possess that moment of origin" (3). In contrast, Steedman finds that "the practice of history, in its modern mode, is just one long exercise of the deep satisfaction of finding things" (10). The small things that a literary critic or historian finds might tell incoherent stories, perhaps about particular desires for a new house or for connections with children, as in the letters from Harriet Beecher Stowe when she describes her necessary intervals between writing fiction. Or perhaps the things to be found are rather larger, as in the lanky height of the president of the United States. The very height of the president, the ungainly reach of his body, and his homely face serve as a paradigm for political loyalty, reminding us perhaps of the paradigms that resist final interpretation. In recalling this detail, I want to suggest that the dust of the archive and the activity of the reader must always be commingled even as the reader of history must have theory as an interpretive dilemma. Citing Foucault's work on the paradigm as a symptom of power, Giorgio Agamben discusses how he has taken his examples in previous work as "paradigms," there "to constitute and make intelligible a broader historical-problematic context."[9]

In the case of the Civil War, this desire for a relation between narrative and event may appear as a desire to possess a moment of transition between premodern and modern knowledge in the United States. By this narrative, premodern attachments to jingoistic nationalism in literature give way to the ironic detachments of naturalism, in what will finally become the triumphs of lyricism and the modern novel. The problems, again, are multiple. Yet the sheer satisfaction of "finding things" in the archives of the literatures of the United States, from the dusty penciled notes of Civil War soldiers to the ink-stained letters to a prominent American editor, dominates this practice of determining historical codes in literary analysis.

ARCHIVE THEORY

What happens with the process of "finding things" when what you find in the archive can be called a novel? Is there a historical code, or a concept, or an archive theory, to suggest how to move through a contradiction of forces and methods in declaring an identity for what you find? It once seemed that the archive's contents lay inert, latent in significance, waiting for the theory that would transmute its dust to gold. In the meantime, by this view, theory posits itself into significance through the mobility of signifying practices that do not always rely on an object. For archival research and theoretical methods to engage in a mutually productive gaze, we must also consider the relationship between historically based concepts of identity and theoretically produced modes of declaring that identity. One crucial example of the formative power of the critical gaze exists in the repeated controversies over how to determine the relation of a narrative to a declared identity as a novel—of whatever genre—and, further, how to determine the identity of an author.

The extraordinary discoveries of Henry Louis Gates Jr. include the publication of the nineteenth century's earliest fiction by African American women, Harriet Wilson's *Our Nig* and Hannah Crafts's *The Bondwoman's Narrative*. In the case of *Our Nig*, the extended research of P. Gabrielle Foreman established another, more elaborate, set of commercial schemes for the author Hattie Wilson than that established in the novel's original republication. In the case of *The Bondwoman's Narrative*, the publication of Gates and Robbins's *In Search of Hannah Crafts* displays not only the work of historians and literary scholars, but also the work of a sleuth into nineteenth-century paper and penmanship. The volume reproduces signatures and elaborates on influences, from *Uncle Tom's Cabin* to *Jane Eyre*, that affect the style of Hannah Crafts. At issue throughout may be the role of the archive in determining reading practices. What can a reader assume from these editorial practices? How does the recovery of a text affect a reader's understanding of it as literature?

The politics of the recovery movement have their antecedents in the virulent controversies associated with so-called slave narratives in the antebellum period. Forced to acquire influential white patrons to attest to their own identity as authors, writers such as Frederick Douglass and Harriet Jacobs appeared behind the words of other, whiter, authors. The suggestion that Lydia Maria Child was the actual author of *Incidents in the Life of a Slave Girl* persisted far in to the twentieth century. It took extensive inquiry into archives for Jean Fagan Yellin to assert that Harriet Jacobs had an identity beyond the pseudonym of Linda Brent.

Through attention to the archive, the pieces of dusty paper that make up the manuscript of *The Bondwoman's Narrative* became identified as a novel by Hannah Crafts. The insistence on the relation between these handwritten pages and the form of the novel stems from the insistent sense that one can read as a novel pages that at once seemed close to autobiography and that had remained in manuscript, having never been read by a contemporary audience let alone presented as a manuscript under submission to an editor and publisher, a process of submission made repeatedly visible in the letters to James Fields. To read the pages as a novel is to experience the vivid sense that the narrator herself is not sure what the boundary is between the data of abolitionist history, the inheritance of melodramatic phrasing from novels such as Charles Dickens's *Bleak House*, and a life that was in precarious straits.

To take such historical residue in another direction, a direction that makes the archive into a resistant set of tools for a historical moment, I would like to turn to details from Elizabeth's Stoddard's *The Morgesons*, a novel that seems so thoroughly out of the time and place of its production in 1862 that to call it a war novel seems at once to violate its attachment to the Byronic heroism of its antecedents in *Wuthering Heights* and *Jane Eyre* and to insist on overlooking its frequently postmodern vocabulary. What makes *The Morgesons* a war novel? In its attention to the relation between commodities and longing, the novel presents details about the archive as about empire—the objects that collect dust in the home represent what's been collected in circling the globe. The conflicts between the sisters Veronica and Cassandra are also bound up with the shipping business that makes the family fortune. Associations with Hawthorne appear because of the relation of *The House of the Seven Gables* to the house that the Morgesons inhabit as well as to the scenes that are placed in "Belem," an obvious allusion to Salem.

To read through the lens of a romantic tradition is to find this novel suffused with the legacies of *Jane Eyre* and *Wuthering Heights*.[10] The repressed child turns out to have the starring role; a frustrated child will find final satisfaction through a romantic liaison with a damaged hero with a penetrating gaze. The satisfaction that the heroine finds in *Jane Eyre*'s famous resolution ("Reader, I married him") is notoriously tainted by the death of the "madwoman in the attic" whose prior marriage to the hero has left him lonely but also ineradicably damaged. The sense of damage that permeates *Wuthering Heights* becomes graphically figured by the terrifying dream that Cathy Lincote has about having her wrist drawn through a broken window so that the shards of glass leave her bleeding. In *The Morgesons*, this tension is literally enacted through the medium of a runaway horse, leaving Cassandra Morgeson's face scarred. Challenged by Desmond Somers to reveal the origin of her scars, she replies that she has gained them "in battle." That the battle is one of love rather than the Civil War, however, does not so much deplete the possibility for reading this as a novel about war as encourage readers to seek to understand domestic battles as more powerful than a far-off drumbeat. The story of Elizabeth Drew Stoddard includes the information that she had six brothers, none of whom seem to have been fictionalized in the novel, and that one died fighting in Civil War battles in 1862, the year of the novel's publication.

Unlike the resolution for the characters in either *Jane Eyre* or *Wuthering Heights*, the novel takes the central characters past the threshold of marriage. At the end of *The Morgesons*, the two sisters have married brothers, Ben and Desmond Somers. Limping out of a family damaged by expectations of wealth and class privilege, both brothers have become alcoholics. Desmond has taken himself off on a European tour version of going cold turkey and has achieved enough sobriety to return and acknowledge his history as well as his attachment to Cassandra. His brother, and his brother's wife, Cassandra's sister Veronica, are not so lucky. Their baby, appearing in the final pages of the novel, is suspiciously weak and exhibits a vacant stare, suggesting a genetic lassitude, or worse. After their sojourns, the sisters are once again living in the parental home by the sea, near the graves of their family as well as the unmarked graves of sailors whose loss goes unremarked when the family ships go down. The ocean contains lives lost in the slave trade as well, an equivalently unremarked source of wealth that remains loudly present in the context of the Civil War.

Domestic violence, mostly between the sisters, joins with the tutelary violence at once of the classroom and of the home turned into the space where history is learned. In its overturning of narrative expectations, the novel shows violence in the classroom to proceed from the stormy passions of Cassandra Morgeson. When her mother is insulted by a classmate, Cassandra slams a seesaw like a weapon into the girl's head and almost kills her. The turbulent emotional contacts that power the actions of *The Morgesons* include prominently the tense attraction that Cassandra feels for her opaque sister Veronica. Veronica's room looks inland, away from the sea as she finds the sight of the ocean too intense. Her room contains a form of a camera obscura, a pinhole access to light that enters in a filtered manner.

Siblings struggle within their homes as though they were struggling for air, as though there were not only insufficient emotional material to be shared but also not even enough oxygen to breathe. The youngest baby in the household of Desmond and Ben Somers is repeatedly heard to be coughing. Gradually the narrator explains that the brothers wait for this youngest sibling to die in order to release their inheritance. Phenomenally unnatural family attachments continue when Cassandra's father remarries after her mother's death. Choosing to marry the widow of the cousin Cassandra had been obsessed with, Charles, who died after the fatal carriage ride behind a runaway horse, her father presents the choice in part as a way to protect property, denying the implication of incest. Property and inheritance within the novel are thoroughly contaminated by shipping, imperial trading practices, and violent longing. To choose to read this longing backward through violence reminds us of the economic stresses of the Civil War and also suggests the unseen drama of the women escaping slavery together, the friends and sisters of *The Bondwoman's Narrative*.

In the twenty-first-century publication of *The Bondwoman's Narrative*, the story of escape and recapture includes many details of the surrounding environment as well as domestic interiors, keeping the attention of the reader on a similar sense of the landscape that *The Morgesons* provides in noting what it is to look out of the windows of a house with longing. Some of the effect of the attention to landscape appears in the traces of transcription in this narrative's publication where the editor has chosen to show the process of revision by retaining a first draft. For example, the edition reproduces crossed-out words such as these: "At the usual time I went to the room of my mistress The still still night very quiet and beautiful and." In revising her manuscript, the author has replaced the words as follows: "The still still night on the dusty roads and over the quiet woods over the gardens."[11] The description of the night—and of the loneliness she feels as she contemplates leaving what has been her home—occupies the next two paragraphs until she says, "Silently I went to the room of my mistress, and as silently entered."

The delay that the revision inserts here mimics the delay to come as the two women, both running away from the likelihood that they will be sold as slaves, will spend the summer in the nameless woods not far from this home, waiting, as it turns out, to be captured and returned to the system of imprisonment and slavery from which they sought release. The woman who has "passed" as her mistress will die when confronted with imminent sale, an aneurysm rupturing as though her brain cannot contain the knowledge of slavery. The narrator will find herself in a carriage behind a runaway horse like the runaway horse that drives Cassandra Morgeson and her lover to destruction. The traces of the archive remain in this twenty-first-century publication through the careful attention to the misspelled words and rewritten phrases of the manuscript as well as through the appended account of a material culture detective who examines the paper and the ink used in order to declare that this narrative was, indeed, written in the 1860s.

To return to my opening question, what does it mean for an author to hold a pen in the nineteenth-century United States? If the author is Nathaniel Hawthorne? If the author is Hannah Crafts? We are assured by the detailed exegesis of the researchers who examined her pages that she used iron gall ink, that she had a pen-knife, and that she used a needle and thread to sew together the pages that she had so painstakingly produced. These labors, domestic and literary, perform a tactility of writing that needs to be understood in relation to the other nineteenth-century literary labors of writing to editors and balancing royalties against the purchase of land. They indicate that the struggle of women in the narrative ascribed to Hannah Crafts is to survive the denunciations of skin color and the oppression of slavery in a narrative written around the same year as both *The Marble Faun* and *The Morgesons*, that each exists as part of an archive bound by the temporality of the Civil War, and finally that we must use historical codes to bring such literary analysis to life.

NOTES

1   This letter is from Nathaniel Hawthorne to his publisher James Fields, December 11, 1852. Often reproduced in discussions of Hawthorne and misogyny, the original of this letter is in the so-called Fields collection at the Huntington Library in Pasadena, California, with the reference number FI 2290. Subsequent letters from the Fields collection will be included in parentheses in this essay with the call number.
2   See, for instance, the introduction to Idol and Ponder.
3   See, for example, Colacurcio; and Berlant.
4   Bense. See also the forthcoming essay by Murison.
5   The classic formulation of this idea is in Collingwood.
6   "Custom House" preface to *The Scarlet Letter*.
7   Steedman, *Dust*. Further quotations will be indicated by parentheses. Derrida 9; Foucault 128–129.
8   Castronovo and Gillman 5.
9   Agamben 9. See also Burton.
10 See, for example, Penner 131–151. See also, Zagarell 284–307; Weir 427–439; and Matlock 278–302.
11 Crafts 51. See also Gates and Robbins.

BIBLIOGRAPHY

Agamben, Giorgio. *The Signature of All Things: On Method*. Trans. Luca D'Isanto with Kevin Attell. New York: Zone, 2009.

Alcott, Louisa May. "The Brothers." *Atlantic Monthly*, November 1863, 584–595.

Bense, James. "Hawthorne's Intention in 'Chiefly About War Matters.' " *American Literature* 61.2 (1989): 200–214.

Berlant, Lauren. *The Anatomy of National Fantasy, Hawthorne, Utopia, and Everyday Life*. Chicago: University of Chicago Press, 1985.

Brontë, Charlotte. *Jane Eyre*. London: Smith, Elder, 1847.

Brontë, Emily. *Wuthering Heights*. London: Thomas Cautley Newby, 1847.

Burton, Antoinette, ed. *Archive Stories: Facts, Fictions, and the Writing of History*. Durham, NC: Duke University Press, 2005.

Castronovo, Russ, and Susan Gillman, eds. *States of Emergency: The Object of American Studies*. Chapel Hill: University of North Carolina Press, 2009.

Colacurcio, Michael. *The Province of Piety: Moral History in Hawthorne's Early Tales*. Cambridge, MA: Harvard University Press, 1984.

Collingwood, R. G. *The Idea of History*. Oxford: Clarendon, 1946.

Crafts, Hannah. *The Bondwoman's Narrative, A Novel*. Ed. Henry Louis Gates Jr. New York: Warner Books, 2002.

Davis, Rebecca Harding. "Life in the Iron-Mills." *Atlantic Monthly*, April 1861, 430–451.

de Forest, John William. *Miss Ravenel's Conversion from Secession to Loyalty*. New York: Harper and Brothers, 1867.

Derrida, Jacques. *Archive Fever*. Trans. Eric Prenowitz. Chicago: University of Chicago Press, 1996.

Dickens, Charles. *Bleak House*. London: Bradbury and Evans, 1853.

Evans, Augusta. *Macaria*. Richmond, VA: West and Johnson, 1863.

James Thomas Fields Collection. The Huntington Library, San Marino, CA.

Foucault, Michel. *The Archaeology of Knowledge*. Trans. A. M. Sheridan Smith. New York: Pantheon, 1972.

Gates, Henry Louis Jr., and Hollis Robbins, eds. *In Search of Hannah Crafts: Critical Essays on The Bondwoman's Narrative*. New York: Basic Books, 2004.

Hawthorne, Nathaniel. *The Blithedale Romance*. Boston: Ticknor, Reed, and Fields, 1852.

———. "Chiefly about War Matters." *Atlantic Monthly*, July 1862, 43–62.

———. *The Dolliver Romance*. Boston: J. R. Osgood, 1876.

———. *The House of Seven Gables*. Boston: Ticknor and Fields, 1851.

———. *Life of Franklin Pierce*. Boston: Ticknor, Reed, and Fields, 1852.

———. *The Marble Faun*. Boston: Ticknor and Fields, 1860.

———. *Our Old Home*. Boston: Ticknor and Fields, 1863.

———. *The Scarlet Letter*. Boston: Ticknor, Reed, and Fields, 1850.

Higginson, Thomas Wentworth. *Army Life in a Black Regiment*. Boston: Fields, Osgood, 1870.

Hosmer, Harriet. *Zenobia in Chains*. 1859. Marble. The Huntington Library, San Marino, CA.

Idol, John, and Melissa Ponder, eds. *Hawthorne and Women: Engendering and Expanding the Hawthorne Tradition*. Boston: University of Massachusetts Press, 1999.

Jacobs, Harriet. *Incidents in the Life of a Slave Girl*. Ed. Lydia Maria Child. Boston, 1861.

Lanier, Sidney. *Tiger Lilies*. New York: Hurd and Houghton, 1867.

Matlock, James. "Hawthorne and Elizabeth Barstow Stoddard." *New England Quarterly* 50 (1977): 278–302.

McPherson, C. B. *The Political Theory of Possessive Individualism: Hobbes to Locke* [1962]. Oxford University Press, 2011.

Murison, Justine. "Union Loyalty, Political Physiology, and Nathaniel Hawthorne's 'Chiefly About War Matters.' " Forthcoming.

Penner, Louise. "Domesticity and Self-Possession in *The Morgesons* and *Jane Eyre*." *Studies in American Fiction* 27 (1999): 131–151.

Powers, Hiram. *The Greek Slave*. 1844. Marble. Newark Museum, Newark, New Jersey.

Steedman, Carolyn. *Dust: The Archive and Cultural History*. Piscataway, NJ: Rutgers University Press, 2002.

———. *Landscape for a Good Woman: A Story of Two Lives*. London: Virago, 1986.

Stoddard, Elizabeth. *The Morgesons*. New York: Carleton, 1862.

Stowe, Harriet Beecher. *Oldtown Folks*. Boston: Fields, Osgood, 1869.
———. *Uncle Tom's Cabin*. Boston: John P. Jewett. 1852.
Twain, Mark. *Roughing It*. Hartford, CT: American Publishing, 1872.
Weir, Sybil. "*The Morgesons*: A Neglected Feminist Bildungsroman." *New England Quarterly* 49 (1976): 427–439.
Whitman, Walt. *Drum-Taps*. New York, 1865.
Zagarell, Sandra. "'Strenuous Artistry': Elizabeth Stoddard's *The Morgesons*." *The Cambridge Companion to Nineteenth-Century American Women's Writing*. Ed. Dale Bauer and Philip Gould. New York: Cambridge University Press, 2001. 284–307.

CHAPTER 13

THE NOVEL AS BOARD GAME: HOMILETIC IDENTIFICATION AND FORMS OF INTERACTIVE NARRATIVE

GREGORY S. JACKSON

THE first chapter of Louisa May Alcott's *Little Women* (1868) introduces readers to the game of "playing pilgrims," the novel's central plot paradigm and the homiletic paradigm around which the March sisters organize their spiritual development. After their mother gives each of the sisters a copy of John Bunyan's *Pilgrim's Progress*, she encourages them to think about their daily life as though they were accompanying Christian, Bunyan's protagonist, on his journey from the City of Destruction to the Celestial City.[1] Over the course of a year, the sisters come to identify closely with Christian's spiritual struggles, identifying his foes with the moral snares that thwart their own spiritual progress. While the game encourages a level of imaginative play, it also deepens the sisters' sense of spirituality as a journey by which one meets and conquers personal faults. It reveals to each how her own personal story parallels a timeless journey emplotted both in the scriptures and through a host of homiletic works such as Bunyan's allegory. By 1875 Alcott's readers could embrace *Little Women's* implicit call to take up Christian's cross and follow the redemptive path to the Celestial City in the McLoughlin Brothers new *Pilgrim's Progress* board game.

In the board game, as in the March sisters' game of playing pilgrim, players assumed the role of Christian and journey from the City of Destruction to the Celestial City, encountering all the perils that encumber Bunyan's protagonist. While the McLoughlin Brothers edition was the first commercial board game to use Bunyan's title, it had a popular antebellum precursor. In the 1830s, Anne Abbott, daughter of a Congregational minister and member of a family of influential New England ministers, designed the American version of the board game the *Mansion of Happiness*, in which players moved their game tokens along sixty-six squares, advancing toward the Celestial City, figured as the Mansion of Happiness. Structured as spiritual journeys these games and others like them are updated versions of devotional paradigms that date back to medieval heuristic narratives.

The board game makes visible the temporal steps toward redemption in modern American Protestantism, what I refer to as "narrative incrementalism." While narrative incrementalism has a long history in Christian practices, stretching back to the Patristic tradition and moving through a range of medieval devotional guides, to the late-medieval journal, and tradition of Puritan life writing, it became an increasingly important theory and practice for Protestants confronting a modern world. Emerging with the homiletic novel as another innovative pedagogy meant to address the nineteenth-century attempt to adapt scientific empiricism to religious belief—what E. Brooks Holifield calls "evidential Christianity"—board games such as *Pilgrim's Progress* and the Parker Brothers 1923 *Journey to Bethlehem* illustrate the hermeneutic strategies and reading epistemology that made the homiletic novel the most significant popular nineteenth-century American religious genre.[2] Much in the way the March sisters superimposed Christian's pilgrimage across the progress of their own lives, players and readers were to imagine how their daily challenges—the struggles between spirit and flesh that impeded salvific progress—were universal to all Christian pilgrimages through time. Each point is an imaginative space freighted with sacred meaning, a palimpsest of temporally layered action to which each player adds his or her own personal imprint. Such connections tacitly ask players to consider their own connection to typology: where would they meet their own trials of faith, where would they meet their Goliath as Jo met her Apollyon, be tested like Abraham as Meg at her Vanity Fair, or, like Job, be judged for pride and pass, as Amy did, through the Valley of Humiliation?

The religious board game can thus help us distinguish the homiletic novel from its more secular counterpart and the divergent reading practices each fostered. While criticism has largely overlooked the distinctions between these reading practices, the anachronistic typological mode that evangelical readers brought to the homiletic novel is conceptualized through the board game's interactive template. That is, the religious board game's logic of participatory engagement outlines a largely anachronistic epistemic capacity to enter into and imaginatively interact inside the frame of an allegorical text. By foregrounding this distinct hermeneutic principle—an interactive engagement as a kind of sustained characterological impersonation that we might think of as readerly self-textualization—board games such as *Pilgrim's Progress* conceptually illustrate how an incremental template helped readers of the homiletic novel understand their lived experience through typological frames that rendered scripture newly relevant.

Playing religious board games highlights four interconnected hermeneutic principles that still comprise homiletic reading practice: (1) homiletic reading is predicated on readers' capacity to identify with and participate in protagonists' spiritual struggles; (2) this identification in turn strengthens readers' ability to see themselves living in and outside time, garnering the capacity to see themselves as historical subjects with transhistorical agency; (3) the bifurcation of time enables them to recognize a transcendent spiritual reality behind the world's material referents; and (4) counter to modern notions of homogeneous empty time, the homiletic novel teaches the faithful to experience lives as unfolding in prescribed stages of spiritual development. By recovering this hermeneutic process we can understand the significance homiletic novels such as Joseph Ingraham's *The Prince of the House of David* (1855), Louisa May Alcott's *Little Women*, and Lew Wallace's *Ben-Hur* (1880) had for literally hundreds of thousands of American readers. Finally, the success that many homiletic novels enjoyed among religious and secular communities highlights the degree to which allegedly anachronistic allegorical modes of understanding temporal and material details and events continue to structure supposedly secular reading practices.

NARRATIVE INCREMENTALISM AND RELIGIOUS ALLEGORY

Homiletic literature has generally hewed close to the line between the literary and the performative, between the descriptive and the visual, between instruction and exemplarity, characteristics brought into relief by the religious board game. Falling squarely in this tradition of interactive devotional practices, Bunyan's *Pilgrim's Progress* had, in America, since the early eighteenth century lent itself to a range of alternative devotional forms, from foldout tracts and catechisms for the young, to popular children's games and heuristic paradigms for adults. Readers follow Christian—Bunyan's everyman pilgrim—as he journeys from the City of Destruction to the Celestial City. As the protagonist's name suggests, readers are meant to identify with Christian's struggle as he faces temptation, doubt, fear, and real spiritual peril on the road to salvation. Like a roll-and-move board game, the narrative visualizes Christian's incremental progress in steps. Among the many stations of his progress, he passes through the wicket gate, slips into the slough of despond, climbs the Hill of Difficulty and Mount Calvary, rests at the Arbor and Palace Beautiful, passes through the Valley of the Shadow of Death, is captivated by Vanity Fair and captured by the Giant Despair. Like the modern *Game of Life* and its structural precursor *Journey to Bethlehem*, Bunyan's allegory heightens the sense of incrementalism by highlighting topographical or architectural sites—through which the road to the cross passes—where Christian rests or is spiritually enlightened, where he morally stumbles or is held captive by a spiritual foe. In this way, Bunyan's allegory creates a highly visual moral cartography that emphasizes how the Christian journey is at once incremental and accumulative. If spiritual maturation is a slow, difficult process, salvation is the sum of all the steps of that process.

Bunyan's allegory builds on medieval Christianity's and Protestantism's devotional technologies that, like the nineteenth-century board game and homiletic novel, were part narrative, part performative, visually conceptual and discursively descriptive. In the colonial American context, this tradition gave rise to new forms such as New World catechisms and the captivity narrative. By the mid-nineteenth century, however, new homiletic forms had overtaken not just these genres but also the sermon in popularity and relevancy to a life increasingly distant from the primitive agrarian, martial, and maritime context of biblical parables and homilies. As the board game reflected a shift in interactive pedagogy from the church to the home, the pew to the parlor, so the novel marked the emphasis on individual experience as a route to knowledge in a post-Lockean world. Like earlier forms—and in ways parallel to parlor board games—homiletic novels encouraged self-reflection and self-narrativization through an incremental framework. One strategy the homiletic novel used to emphasize incrementalism was through serialization. This worked one of two ways: religious novels were often serialized in periodicals; and themes and the lives of characters were serialized across a novel series. In both cases, the homiletic novel resisted the narrative closure associated with its more secular counterpart. Publishing in increments paced and deferred the novel's narrative closure, encouraging readers to engage with the moral action of the plot in a sustained way that gestured at real time, even as it reminded them that spiritual growth was a process concluded only in death.

The internationally renowned Kansas minister and best-selling novelist Charles Sheldon, for example, delivered chapters of his many novels as "sermon stories" to his weekly congregation and then sent these chapters off for publication in the *Advocate*, a national Congregational weekly. Doing so, he encouraged his local congregants and congregations across the nation to discuss the moral issues the novel raised, articulating choices each character faced in ensuing installments. Sheldon's own congregation's weekly encounters with his sermon stories allowed them to engage with characters' moral development in stages, enabling them to see and intervene in plot revisions as Sheldon drafted the ensuing chapters. In so doing, they modeled a national hermeneutic practice as readers of the serialized installments were similarly invited to assume the role of protagonist in the ongoing serialized plots, prompted by Sheldon's larger invocation of a subjunctive frame that asked each reader to consider literally what Jesus would do were he present. This frame would emerge in 1896 as a template for the enormously popular spiritual-reform movement that took as its credo, "What Would Jesus Do?" Sheldon's stated objective was to engage the young in moral conversations about the plots and actions of his characters, often writing open-ended plot threads as homiletic exercises that encouraged young Christians to imagine alternative story resolutions from a Christ-centered perspective. In this way, when serialized the homiletic novel fostered discussion and engagement, encouraging readers to ask, in the subjunctive mood that underscored Sheldon's homiletic pedagogy, what *should* I do were I in this character's situation?[3]

Another way the homiletic authors deferred narrative closure to foster readerly identification in characters' incremental spiritual development was by publishing novel series. Many homiletic novels followed the spiritual maturation of a young protagonist. Between 1867 and 1905, Martha Finley, for instance, wrote twenty-eight novels about one of the most beloved nineteenth-century protagonists, Elsie Dinsmore. Similar to the occult development of Harry Potter in J. K. Rowling's twenty-first-century series, young readers followed the spiritual trajectory of Elsie's life, emblematized in the putative stages of a nineteenth-century woman's life: *Elsie's Childhood*; *Elsie's Girlhood*; *Elsie's Womanhood*; *Elsie's Motherhood*; *Elsie's Widowhood*; and the like. Beginning with the initial novel, readers literally grew up with Elsie. Hardly just the sentimental fare the series has been labeled, each novel, like the squares of a board game, marks out the incremental stages of the Christian's journey from birth to death, a pilgrimage through the world from Paul's naked "babe in Christ," to his martial Christian decked out in the whole armor of God. As a child Elsie endures her mother's death, her father's assaults on her faith, the death of her childhood sweetheart, an attempted abduction and rape—and still later an attempted murder. As with a board game such as *Life*, these novels, taken together, ask readers to envision the totality of life measured out in emotionally and spiritually significant stages. At the same time, they leave open the question of how the reader would respond in the various circumstances each novel poses. Even the late novels about Elsie as widow and grandmother illustrate the open-endedness built into a plot serially unfolding, revealing how the progress of life is ever contingent. In the preface to *Elsie's Widowhood*, Finley professed to have written against her own desire at the request of readers to "show how the love of Christ in the heart can make life happy even under sore bereavement":

> And since trouble, trial and affliction are the lot of all in the world of sin and sorrow, what greater kindness could I do you, dear reader, than to show you where to go for relief and consolation? That this little book may teach the sweet lesson to many a tried and burdened soul, is the earnest prayer of your friend, the Author.

While homiletic novels no longer generated characters as allegorically open as Bunyan's Christian, they nonetheless worked to create characters with whom readers could identify, by setting up a temporal framework in which all believers follow a similarly incrementalized journey along the path to salvation.

BIFURCATED TIME AND THE NEW
PROTESTANT CURRICULUM

Historians of the novel have cited Bunyan's allegory as an important precursor to the novel's individual and national focus, to its attention to interlacing dialogue and description and its thematization of the individual identity challenged by narrativized events.[4] In failing to attend to the religious novel, however, such histories miss the extent to which the individualizing incrementalism of these texts necessitated a demarcation of time at odds with Walter Benjamin's frequently cited notion of the novel's (and modernity's) empty homogeneous time. In *Little Women*, for example, the March mother's challenge to use Bunyan's allegory as a guide for self-improvement "before Father comes home" (11) frames her daughters' trials in two temporal registers through its double allusion to Reverend March's absence to serve in war and to Christ's return before the Judgment. As such, Alcott's novel, like Bunyan's allegory, focuses on progress incrementally unfolding, offering young readers a heuristic that accounts as much for moral missteps as it does for spiritual advancement.[5]

The double allusion to their father's return sets up a dual time frame essential to incremental thinking. At the same time, the March sisters' game of playing pilgrims evinces one way that space—architecture and topography—helped concretize the invisible world behind the material. Descriptions of salvific progress have, since Augustine popularized the pattern as a heuristic, drawn on spatial metaphors for meaning as in the *Pilgrim's Progress* board game, which features the "Slough of Despond," "Mount Calvary," "Palace Beautiful," "Doubting Castle," "Hill of Difficulty," "Hill of Caution," "Mount Mammon," "the Land of Vain Glory," "Valley of Humiliation," and "the Valley of the Shadow of Death." Taking the persona of pilgrim allows each sister to immerse herself in the work's narrative structure. So for the sisters, the road to the cross and from the cross to the Celestial City passes through the locus of their childhood village, and from there to each new location as they leave home to work or study, to marry, raise families, travel, and retire. Each sister struggles against her own version of Christian's spiritual foes, from Jo's Apollyon and Beth's Valley of the Shadow of Death, to Meg's Vanity Fair and Amy's Valley of Humiliation.

As with the *Pilgrim's Progress* board game, playing pilgrim is a game intended to assist all players succeed, requiring them to identify intensely with their role in the progress, as they travel parallel paths to the same end. Although Christian board games such as *Mansion of Happiness* and *Pilgrim's Progress* foster a level of competition, they subordinate that competition to the games' social purpose. Even when one player reaches the end goal, the game continues, much as the March sisters progress at different paces, not to become *the* champion, but to become, as they do in turn, "heroines" in their own personal progresses. Similarly, like the modern *Game of Life, Journey to Bethlehem* is a spin-and-move game in which players assume either the role of shepherd or wise man and sojourn along winding paths through the ancient Holy Lands to the City of David in the historic time of Christ's birth. As with all the games, the player's journey unfolds incrementally. The shepherds advance along one route, and the Magi another. Likewise, in the *Pilgrim's Progress* board game, when players land on squares signifying important events in the redemptive process, they advance accordingly. When they land on squares signifying spiritual failure, land in the Slough of Despond or Doubting Castle, for example, the space instructs them either to move back to earlier points on the pilgrimage path or sit out a turn. In these games, the organizing narrative of *Pilgrim's Progress* is a journey with a point of origination and destination. In *Life*, that journey, with its various detours, suggests that one's path, if not altogether self-determined, depends on the individual's volition. In *Journey to Bethlehem* players similarly choose an alter identity and one of two primary paths leading to the same goal. While responding to a parallel, nineteenth-century theological shift away from predestinarianism, the narrative teleology of the *Pilgrim's Progress* and *Journey to Bethlehem* games, unlike the road of material success represented in the game *Life*, has not been shorn of its traditional Protestant eschatology.

Religious board games are narrative no less than discursive forms, and their narratives reflect a conventional Protestant teleology. Their spatial organization heightens specific expectations about Christian struggle, redemption, and salvation. Like the homiletic novel, the board game has a closed narrative structure in that it has an end. Yet the game's heuristic purpose and the theological and epistemic conventions of the pilgrimage allegory deny finality. As a template for teaching players how to measure out and narrate the otherwise ineffable nature of spiritual growth, the game is meant to be played repeatedly. Since Augustine's journey in *City of God*, heuristics have sought to engrain a structure of living that envisions day-to-day life within a pattern of spiritual journey that accounted for different modes of time, both historical and eschatological. In *City of God*, Augustine figures this life as a preparatory journey, a dry run for the authentic life to come when one arrives at God's city, or, failing, falls into eternal darkness. From this Augustinian background, Reformation Protestants inherited a focus on two temporal registers: eternal time— timelessness outside of time—and time as history, sequentially marked by events, the time archived in memory.

Following in this tradition, nineteenth-century evangelicals viewed the world as no more real than a virtual game; it simply served to train the redeemed much as modern video games might virtually prepare students today in workforce experience. Yet by the nineteenth century, after more than two centuries in which empiricism and science's material epistemology had come to privilege experience as the foundation of knowledge formation and in the wake of modernity's increasing emphasis on the individual as an economic and political free agent, the material world came increasingly to be perceived as detached from the enchanted context of biblical history. For medieval and early modern Christians, who had a weak sense of anachronism, seeing the world in the double register of the eternal and the temporal had its challenges, but by the nineteenth century, that challenge had become an epistemic hurdle to the biblical literalism at the core of evangelical faith and thus to the Bible's relevancy for the individual's life. In an age skeptical of direct access to the divine, in which rational assaults on the biblical miracles drove an ever-widening wedge between High Church and revival-oriented denominations (a rift exacerbated by the spread of a biblical historicism known as the higher criticism), the details of the material world no longer so readily yielded spiritual meaning, and sacred events and devotional practices—birth, baptism, communion, graveyard visits—that had once served as portals into the spiritual realm began to lose their capacity to open the spiritual world even for the faithful.

Religious board games were part of a larger interdenominational religious curriculum that attempted to overcome this difficulty by familiarizing the young with biblical history, making the memory a storehouse of historical detail and making geographic sites the mnemonic referent of typological connections between the Old and New Testaments. In this context, *Journey to Bethlehem* instilled a sense of first-century geography, enhancing the reality of a virtual experience of those who undertook the pilgrimage—as either Magi or Shepherds—following the Star of David. While the Wise Men depart from the ancient Roman city of Gerasa, Jordan, the Shepherds begin the game from the labyrinthine region of Edrei in the Roman province of Syria. Each route passes through biblical settings that provide a mental exercise in biblical typology through which Old Testament sites are made doubly significant by New Testament events. Bethlehem is both the City of David where a future king once herded sheep and the birthplace of Christ, the itinerant king. Where young players might only recognize the spaces as markers of progress in the game, as they matured, the catechism of biblical topography was meant to strengthen their capacity to engage the game as a template for comprehending their own spiritual journeys. Likewise, the March sisters recall how as little children they had once played pilgrims in the family home, racing from the cellar to the attic, from the City of Destruction toward the Celestial City with their "burdens" on their backs. At a more advanced stage of development, they play pilgrim again, but this time, their mother instructs, "suppose you play again, not in play, but in earnest" (10). The seeming paradoxes here—"play again" but "not in play"; "play… but in earnest"—like Marme's own confession to still playing the role of pilgrim in her own life, were logical progressions to those skilled in experiencing the world through the *imitatio Christi* as patterns of typological replication that during the Christian's spiritual journey moved ever closer to authenticity by the individual's gradual subsumation into the body of Christ. Marme's "play in earnest" bespeaks the degree to which, in the Augustinian tradition, readers attuned to the world-as-training-simulation would have seen even the most seemingly sanctified life as a dress rehearsal for *the* life beyond.

In developing a player's ability to make typological connections between the Old and New Testaments at geographic points, *Journey to Bethlehem* demonstrates the continuation of what Sally Promey calls the Puritan's "analogical imagination," which augmented the novel's capacity to train the religious in making typological connections, to see how their own lives played out in patterns of sacred history.[6] As mnemonic cues of sacred history's recurring cycles, the board's sites work to weaken young players' sense of anachronism. Similarly, the March sisters' various trials are localized in history—in the novel's temporal frame, from Christmas Eve 1861 to Christmas Day 1862—and simultaneously occur outside time, in moments of redemption, and in their attempt to imitate Christ, or, in typological patterns, to struggle against the enemies of Bunyan's Christian. Far into their pilgrimages the Marches continue to spatialize their faith in a way that helps them envision their world in time's double register: "We call this hill Delectable Mountain," Jo tells Laurie, who has joined the sisters on an outing, "for we can look far away and see the country where we hope to live sometime" (141). Jo's allusion to the country where they hope one day to live obscures the distinction between a neighboring village and the Celestial City, even as the term "sometime" conjures both historical and eternal time.

The March sisters' capacity to understand this bifurcation of time represented in their enactment of Bunyan's allegory—or for their readers to understand the repetition of that bifurcation in *Little Women*—is predicated on the homiletic novel's capacity to depict the story's action and characters both in a realist mode and as an allegory. Nineteenth-century homiletic writers blurred the line between allegory and novelized realism, illustrating why twentieth-century criticism that situates and defines literary realism against allegory—a tact increasingly followed after Ian Watt's influential study—generalizes too broadly from a very specific aesthetic paradigm.[7] While the allegorical nature of Christian in Bunyan's incremental narrative more clearly opens his story to every person's experience, the novel, as Catherine Gallagher has argued, similarly opens itself up to readerly participation and identification by being both everybody's and thus nobody's story.[8] What Gallagher's theory unintentionally describes is the everyman mechanism at the core of homiletic identification, indeed at the core of the *imitatio Christi*, in which the Christian story is at once universal and personal—everybody's and nobody's—disclosing, perhaps, the secular and homiletic novel's twinned origin in allegory. In particular, in the homiletic novel, the identity of protagonists had to resist a kind of ontological completeness. They had to be both a type—allegorical—and realistic. Homiletic authors struggled against a secular literary realism that sought to make material referents an end in themselves rather than the means to transcendent knowledge. If each of the March sisters can attach to the snares Christian encounters on the road to salvation their own spiritual stumbling blocks—occupying the hollow space of the allegorical with the specificity of realist detail—so can *Little Women*'s young readers find a type to which they can identify, for, as the narrative informs us, there are many "Beths in the world" and, by extrapolation, many Megs, Jos, and Amys.

In Christian board games, this combination of allegory and specificity is enacted through the game tokens and their movement across the board. As in Alcott's "Playing Pilgrim," where areas within and outside the house take on particular significance grounded in both individual experience and a typological framework, specific spaces in religious board games are filled with both individual and typological significance. Like Bunyan's allegorical everyman, the board game token enables the player to inhabit it through its initial emptiness, its interchangeability with other tokens, distinguished merely by shape or color, and their identical directional movement across the board. Yet a token increasingly takes on specificity. While the spinner seemingly simulates chance—one advances according to a random spin—it also stands in for Kairos, the classical concept that Christians transformed into the sweep of destiny that intersects diachronic or historical time. What from a secular standpoint might appear as chance, from a spiritual orientation might also stand in for providence or divine destiny. In this way, board games reflected and reinforced the theological shift away from Calvinism's strict determinism after the Civil War. As players' surrogates, tokens become individuated through the players' agency, the choices each player makes in response to the dictates of the space on which his or her token lands. In this way, tokens accumulate a range of specific details. They accrue a game history, an individualized narrative, determined as much by the game algorithm—the seemingly endless shuffle of space sequences—as by the spiritual experiences players bring to the game's journey paradigm and the level of their ability to engage the biblical typology signified by the board spaces as historical and sacred sites. The narrative is increasingly differentiated by a journey that gradually unfolds over the course of the game not only as tokens are prompted to move forward or backward in accordance with spiritual trials, moral failures, or virtues rewarded, but also as they accumulate unique histories by the sequence of spaces that comprise players' paths. As in homiletic novels, this individuation assists players to understand how the Christian pilgrimage is both typological and literal, universal among Christ's followers, and individualized to each disciple.

Aesthetics of Immediacy: Overcoming Anachronism

To an extent board games' flat surfaces could only crudely approximate religious experience, while novels could sustain the imaginative encounter with Christian history, utilizing the genre's techniques of extensive realistic description and intensified identification and participation with protagonists. The novel offered a technology more commensurate with a modern world, with an emphasis on time and realism. It provided templates for organizing action and agency in an increasingly material world. And it offered a way to live simultaneously in the particular and to render life allegorically. As with the March sisters, while each pilgrimage is deeply individual, keyed to the personal flaws and virtues of each, the novelistic pilgrimage achieves success to the degree it, like that of Bunyan's pilgrim, becomes representative of every Christian's path.

Theories and histories of the novel tend to emphasize its break—epistemic and literary—from older literary forms rather than its gradual adaptation of new and traditional discursive forms and strategies. One of the unrevised formulas of the novel's rise sees it resulting from a gradual shift away from allegory to a formal realism commensurate with the eighteenth century's emphasis on Baconian empiricism and the Enlightenment's reliance on an epistemology predicated on individual experience.[9] According to this formula, the shift in epistemology fostered a market for new literary modes that privileged a kind of formal realism, genres attuned to the discursive simulation of everyday middle-class life. What this story neglects is how religious literature adapted both to account for this new taste for vivid narratives of protagonists engaging daily life and to counter the increased attention on the details of the material world. Taxed by a shift toward an empirical epistemology and its persistent commitment to a bifurcated world, visible and invisible, religious pedagogy had the double task of accounting for a world increasingly perceived as a referent in and of itself and as a referent of an imperceptible domain beyond it. Religious novels had to split the difference between allegory and a new focus on the particularity of material details. From this perspective, what Catherine Gallagher's theory of the novel as everybody's and nobody's story suggests is that even the realist novel had not quite relinquished its formation in religious allegory, even if it jettisoned the eschatology that that allegorical structure once served.

One of the key challenges for religious writers of the nineteenth century was, in fact, to make the spiritual reality of the Bible real to their readers by making the material reality of the Bible real to them. Religious educators responded to the ever-widening gap between biblical reality and life in industrial America with increasingly vivid techniques for making the life of Christ real to believers. Believing that material details would verify the Bible's historical accuracy and thus its spiritual truth, John H. Vincent, the principal architect of the Chautauqua movement, for example, had experimented in the 1850s with interactive pedagogy steeped in realism. In his ministry in Camptown, New Jersey, he laid out a walk-through model of Palestine in the churchyard through which touring congregants experienced the world of Christ. So successful was the interactive experiment that he repeated it in his ministry in Galena, Illinois, in 1859. A decade after his own trip to Palestine during the Civil War, Vincent created an even more detailed virtual reality of Christ's world on a much larger scale, the "Park of Palestine." Part of the Chautauqua Center, this reproduction became a template not only for topographical re-creations across the nation, but also for a range of media forms, from public cycloramas and magic-lantern shows, to private stereopticon slide series and parlor board games. In an age popularizing primitive Christianity through the idealization of the first-century Church, the reproduction of these media forms with vivid realism assisted tens of thousands of Protestants to understand their heritage not in Roman Catholic cathedrals or medieval shrines, but in the ancient Roman world, allowing them to project themselves into the lives of fishermen disciples, low-born shepherds, or even foreign satraps guided to Judea to pay homage to a child king.

The nineteenth-century homiletic novel was one form this heuristic took. Against long-standing wariness toward the novel as a form, the novelist Josiah Gilbert Holland defended it in 1857 as incarnating the abstraction of spiritual truths in the same way that Christ incarnated the abstraction of the divine. After pointing out that "[t]he Author of the Christian system spake evermore in parables in the illustration of important practical truth," Holland argued that "the claims and power of legitimate fiction" rest on the "great principle in human nature which called Him into the world." Christ's incarnation was necessary in order "to exhibit truth in its relations to the feeling, thinking, acting soul," so "that the case should be imagined and the relations created."[10] Thus, just as Christ "came to embody abstract truth in human relations, and the naked, incomprehensible idea of God, in the human form ... to exhibit in human development the true nature of the divine life, and to demonstrate, in human experience, under the influence of legitimate human motives, the beauty of holiness," so the novel served to embody the abstract truths and incomprehensible ideas of the Christian faith so that "the case should be imagined and the relations created" by modern readers. By setting up a parallel between Christ's relation to God and the novel's relation to the Bible, Holland accords to the homiletic novel, among evangelicals like himself, something of the age's revivified commitment to biblical inerrancy and the Bible's "living-word" status, essentially making the homiletic novel the Bible's modernized surrogate, charged with illustrating Christ's teachings—biblical parables and allegories—in the visually oriented realism of modern life. Extrapolating from Holland's defense of the novel, we can recognize how its realistic form—with its focus on ordinary individuals, iteration in diachronic time, dramatization of cause and effect through character development and reflexively unfolding plots, and narrative length that mandated serialized reading—encouraged readers to bridge the difference between reality and representation by helping them cast their lives, their own spiritual development, within the frame of narrative time.

Perhaps no work better combines the emphasis on historical detail in Vincent's virtual tour of Palestine Park with Holland's schema for the novel's capacity to embody abstract spiritual truths than Lew Wallace's *Ben-Hur* (1880). Best known now for its many twentieth-century filmic adaptations, *Ben-Hur* was among the top best-selling novels of the nineteenth century. Subtitled "A Tale of the Christ," *Ben-Hur* follows its protagonist's life journey as it parallels the events in Jesus's life. Wallace identified his task as one that many religious writers confronted, to make Christ's life real, to make his life a pattern for the faithful, without reducing it to merely another man's story: "The Christian world would not tolerate a novel with Jesus Christ its hero, and I knew it. Nevertheless, writing of Him was imperative, and He must appear, speak, and act. Further, and worse as a tribulation, I was required to keep Him before the reader, the object of superior interest throughout."[11] In his autobiography, Wallace confesses to creating Judah Ben-Hur as an avatar of Christ, for he could not fill in the "unities" of Christ's life: "But the unities are inexorable. Because they run through every life they must be observed. And here in this story there was a lapse of eighteen or twenty years—being the interval between the remarkable appearance of the Holy Child in the Temple, what time He came up to the Passover, and His appearance a man with a mission" (931). Wallace's readers understand Christ's life because its "unities" are the same as those that unify the lives of all Christians. This is why a novel in which Christ appears only once, briefly, can still be subtitled "A Tale of the Christ." Just as the faithful are to mirror

the journey of Christ, so Ben-Hur stands in for religious readers in his parallel position to Christ, a type readers were meant to identify with and emulate.

The key to Wallace's task was to make the world of Jesus and Ben-Hur vitally
real to his readers. In this attempt, he followed the pattern established in Joseph
Hale Ingraham's 1855 novel, *Prince of the House of David*. Written in epistolary
form, thus highlighting the subjective, individualized nature of one's relationship
to Christ, this novel fleshed out the events of the Gospels in order to revivify their
spiritual meaning for modern readers. According to many ministers, it succeeded,
for the novel's "astonishing scenes and facts" bring Christ's ministry "nearer to our
human feelings, and certainly awaken afresh all our admiring wonder at the mysterious nature and work of the Redeemer of man." While some religious reviewers
still worried about the propriety of re-creating—from the fictional perspective of
a young woman, no less—what was already narrated in the Gospels, the Boston
Congregationalist averred that, like any one of us, "*Somebody* must have had just
such experience," and the vivid recording of that experience not only assists the
Christian "to a more vivid conception of the scenes on which he loves to meditate,
and so of the character which he adores" but also "excite[s] in ["the impenitent"] a
more life-like idea of realities which are too apt to be unreal to them." Like the religious board game's combination of empty token and freighted spaces, the novelistic
re-creation of Christ's story enables believer and nonbeliever alike to inhabit that
experience that *Somebody* must have had of viewing Christ's ministry firsthand. As
the Reverend Dr. Dowling of Philadelphia attested, through Ingraham's "graphic"
depiction of "the Saviour's life, and the scenes amid which these events occurred,"
the novel "pictured before the reader, almost transports one back for eighteen centuries, to the very time of the life of Christ on earth."

Dowling here attests to Ingraham's success in drawing readers into the frame of
the text, into an alternative world where they might imaginatively participate in the
events of Christ's life. Ingraham's novel thus belongs to a long homiletic tradition
that sought ways to simulate the wages of sin so that the faithful might experience
firsthand otherwise abstract concepts like eternal suffering. In its use of what I call
an "aesthetics of immediacy," a series of discursive strategies that seek to narrow the
epistemological gap between the reader and the text's imagined world, *The Prince
of the House of David* evokes a detailed tapestry of primitive Christian life in first-
century Judea in an effort to "transport" readers back in time that they might more
readily understand the way in which, for believers, the present moment simply
overlays the sacred past.[12] In so doing, Ingraham's novel is meant to illustrate how
one's actions in the historical moment have transhistorical agency in the struggle
between good and evil occurring in and outside time.

Ben-Hur similarly asks readers to enter the text in imagination, much as many
nineteenth-century sermons did, or as interactive video games do today. It illustrates this mode of reading when young Ben-Hur's mother prefaces the story of the
past by encouraging him to imagine that he is present in the moment, stepping outside the historical frame of his own time—first-century Judea—into a past rendered
present in the immediacy of the homiletic novel's capacity to tap into Christianity's

habits of anachronistic seeing. This virtual visualization of historical reality for spiritual ends echoes Reverend A. D. Gillette's call in his praise for *The Prince of the House of David* for novelists to bring "the events of Gospel History as vividly to view as if they were actually transpiring before us." In *Ben-Hur*, Judah's mother embodies a scene of the Hebrew past so vividly real that it produces auditory hallucination: "deeply stirred," Judah urges his mother, "Do not stop, I pray you.... You give me to hear the sound of timbrels. I wait for Miriam and the woman who went dancing after her" (104). In describing the first century in such vivid detail and instructing Judah how to engage with history as though standing in its midst, *Ben-Hur* illustrates the mode of its own reading: "If you can hear the timbrel of the prophetess," his mother responds, "you can do what I was about to ask; you can use your fancy, and stand with me, as if by the wayside, while the chosen of Israel pass us at the head of the procession." Wallace creates a remarkable scene by emblematically staging an intergenerational procession before Ben-Hur, in which individuals and their descendants and forebears—separated perhaps by centuries—proceed by, only the order of the progression marking historical time in the otherwise intersecting simultaneity of the temporal and eternal. Increasingly the narrative pulls Judah— and the reader—deeper into the almost cinematic realism: "Now they come—the patriarchs first; next the fathers of the tribes. I almost hear the bells of their camels and the lowing of their herds. Who is he that walks along between the companies?" (105). This scene thus depicts how for the religious, past, present, and future merge into a continuous temporal present, to reveal how the individual stands both in and outside time.

Ben-Hur repeatedly recurs to long description and specific allusions to connect physical reality with spiritually laden locations and events. The narrative pulls readers into the novel's historical frame, much as Ben-Hur had been drawn into the history his mother evoked, to "stand as by the wayside" as witnesses to the action before them. Like Ingraham's novel and board games such as *Journey to Bethlehem*, Wallace relies on biblical place-names familiar to nineteenth-century Christians to orient his readers to the first-century world. Wallace exploits older sermon strategies—he relies on an aesthetics of immediacy—to engage readers' analogical imagination. One such strategy is the narrator's use of direct address to foster greater textual intimacy. Ministers had long used the first-person plural and second-person forms of address in virtual-tour narratives that drew audiences into simulated scenes in which they stood by the wayside at Judgment or toured the sin-correlated rooms of hell. Such scenes required the reader's capacity to live in the historical moment, while projecting themselves into the future.

Early in the novel, for example, when Ben-Hur first appears, the narrator guides the reader through the "Vanity Fair" of Jerusalem, evoking the immediacy of the present moment in vivid detail: "A little mixing with the throng, however, a little familiarity with the business going on will make analysis possible" (32). Voice and tense here illustrate the reader's parallel position in simultaneous temporal registers: speaking to the reader in first person, the narrator is both within the text and without it—in the reader's localized historical moment and in the first-century world the scene embodies. In so doing, the narrator operates from the liminal gap between the figural and the literal, the threshold between allegory and realism that readers are themselves trained through typological exegesis to occupy: "The brutal look which goes with the gesture disgusts us," the narrator confides, evoking an intimacy that characterized the hellfire tradition of the eighteenth- and nineteenth-century sermon. "And we turn happily to something more pleasant. . . . Opposite us is a fruit stand" (45). Such historical detail is the stuff of historical romances such as Walter Scott's *Waverly* (1814), James Fenimore Cooper's *The Pioneers* (1823), and Edward Bulwer-Lytton's *Last Days of Pompeii* (1834). But unlike Scott and Cooper who attempt to re-create earlier worlds in order to develop their readers' sense of a national heritage, or Bulwer-Lytton's account of a desacralized Western genealogy, Wallace provides such detail as a strategy to strengthen the faithful's capacity to see themselves in the world and outside it, thus in and not of the world.

This tension between a secular focus on national history and a spiritual focus on redemptive history becomes central to the plot's development, as Ben-Hur oscillates between envisioning Christ as a Messiah come to release the Jewish people and Israel from their Roman yoke—furthering his revenge against his traitorous friend, the Roman Messala—and as the Savior, whose kingdom is not of this earth. Just as Ben-Hur must learn to read the details of biblical typology correctly in order to understand how he, like all Christians, is a Christ type, "we"—the readers whom the narrator addresses with pronominal intimacy—must learn how to identify with Ben-Hur through the novel's evocative temporal and visual immediacy in order to transcend that particularity through the typological mechanism that renders all Christians an everyman, like Ben-Hur, a type of Christ. Paradoxically, then, the transmutability of this scene to our own lives—from material to spiritual, from a discursive realism to the allegory—is only catalyzed through the specificity of historical detail that make the steps of Ben-Hur's journey real, that make them particular only to himself and to the context of the first-century Mediterranean world.

This journey returns us to the incrementalism the board game renders visible. Wallace's emphasis on historical detail brings the past alive that his readers might more readily inhabit the incremental pattern of Ben-Hur's parallel journey with Christ's. A failure to see how this detail works to foster an incremental sense of Ben-Hur's—and one's own—life as a journey to the cross has led critics to misread the novel as merely redacting late nineteenth-century cultural conditions through the primitive Christian world of first-century Rome. The novel's historical details, in fact, work in the other direction. Rather than using Ben-Hur's experience as a galley slave, for example, to comment on industrialism and postemancipation, Wallace attempts to draw his readers into this experience that they might connect their material trials with those of Ben-Hur and thus their spiritual transformation with his. Being enchained to the oar is meant to figure the reader's own enslavement to a range of moral vices, sins, work life, and otherworldly cares. Thus, in commenting on his own time as governor of the territory of New Mexico, Wallace referred to his challenges as his own path to Golgotha. Whereas historicist critics have tended to read novelistic depictions as commenting on contemporaneous political events,

Wallace actually asks his readers to see through the particular events of their time and lives by identifying with Ben-Hur and through him with Christ. Updating a traditional Christian paradigm of understanding one's life as an incremental journey unfolding in both a historical and transcendent register, homiletic novelists like Wallace reveal allegory's invisible role in enabling readers to find deeper significance in the narrative details of literary realism.

NOTES

1 While many critics have assumed that Mrs. March gives her daughters a New Testament, Elaine Showalter demonstrates that it is, in fact, a copy of Bunyan's *The Pilgrim's Progress*. For more on this argument, see Elaine Showalter, Introduction, *Little Women* iv-xl.

2 Brooks E. Holifield, *Theology in America: Christian Thought from the Age of the Puritans to the Civil War* (New Haven, CT: Yale University Press, 2003), 127–217.

3 For the importance of the subjunctive mood in nineteenth-century homiletic novels, see Gregory S. Jackson, *The Word and Its Witness: The Spiritualization of American Realism* (Chicago: University of Chicago Press, 2009), 157–214.

4 See Michael McKeon, *The Origins of the English Novel, 1600–1740* (Baltimore: Johns Hopkins University Press, 1987); see chap. 8, "Romance Transformations (II): Bunyan and the Literalization of Allegory," 295–314; and Leopold Damrosch Jr., *God's Plot and Man's Stories: Studies in Fictional Imagination from Milton to Fielding* (Chicago: University of Chicago Press, 1985); see chap. 4, "Experience and Allegory in Bunyan," 121–86.

5 For a study of *Little Women* that makes this argument in a different context, see Jackson, *The Word and Its Witness* 125–156.

6 Sally M. Promey, "Seeing the Self 'in Frame': Early New England Material Practice and Puritan Piety," *Material Religion* 1.1 (March 2005): 10–46; 25.

7 Ian P. Watt, *The Rise of the Novel: Studies in Defoe, Richardson, and Fielding* (London: Chatto and Windus, 1957).

8 Catherine Gallagher, *The Vanishing Acts of Women Writers in the Market Place, 1670–1820* (Berkeley: University of California Press, 1994).

9 In *The One vs. the Many: Minor Characters and the Space of the Protagonist in the Novel* (Princeton, NJ: Princeton University Press, 2003), Alex Woloch modifies the conventional wisdom on the novel's move away from allegory, by demonstrating that minor characters work allegorically in relation to the protagonist: "Secondary characters—representing delimited extremes *become* allegorical, and this allegory is directed toward a singular being, the protagonists, who stands at the center of the text's symbolic structure…" (18). With his focus on the canonical works of the great tradition, however, Woloch's emphasis remains on the individualized, nonallegorical psychological depth of the protagonist, a depth always in tension with the allegorizing tendency in the characterization of minor characters; see esp. 18–30.

10 Josiah Gilbert Holland, *The Bay-Path; A Tale of New England Colonial Life* (New York: G. P. Putnam, 1857), v–vii.

11 Lew Wallace, *An Autobiography* (New York: Harper and Brothers, 1906): 2:933.

12 For the development of the concept of an "aesthetics of immediacy," see Jackson, *Word and Its Witness* 31–35; and 255–259.

BIBLIOGRAPHY

Bunyan, John. *The Pilgrim's Progress*. Edited by Roger Sharrock. London: Penguin, 1987.

Damrosch, Leopold Jr. *God's Plot and Man's Stories: Studies in Fictional Imagination from Milton to Fielding*. Chicago: University of Chicago Press, 1985.

Finley, Martha. *Elsie Dinsmore*. New York: Dodd, Mead & Co., 1867.

——..... *Elsie's Childhood: A Sequel to "Elsie Dinsmore."* New York: Dodd, Mead, & Co., 1872.

——..... *Elsie's Girlhood: A Sequel to "Elsie's Childhood."* New York: Dodd, Mead, & Co., 1872.

——..... *Elsie's Motherhood: A Sequel to "Elsie's Womanhood."* New York: Dodd, Mead, & Co., 1876.

——..... *Elsie's Widowhood: A Sequel to "Elsie's Children."* New York: Dodd, Mead & Co., 1880.

——..... *Elsie's Womanhood: A Sequel to "Elsie's Girlhood."* New York: Dodd, Mead & Co., 1875.

Gallagher, Catherine. *The Vanishing Acts of Women Writers in the Market Place, 1670–1820*. Berkeley: University of California Press, 1994.

Holifield, E. Brooks. *Theology in America: Christian Thought from the Age of the Puritans to the Civil War*. New Haven, CT: Yale University Press, 2003.

Ingraham, J. H. *The Prince of the House of David; or, Three Years in the Holy City*. New York: Pudney & Russell, 1855.

Jackson, Gregory S. *The Word and Its Witness: The Spiritualization of American Realism*. Chicago: University of Chicago Press, 2009.

McKeon, Michael. *The Origins of the English Novel, 1600–1740*. Baltimore: Johns Hopkins University Press, 1987.

Promey, Sally M. "Seeing the Self 'in Frame': Early New England Material Practice and Puritan Piety." *Material Religion* 1.1 (March 2005): 10–46.

Showalter, Elaine. Introduction. Alcott, Louisa May. *Little Women*. Penguin Classics. New York: Penguin, 1989.

Wallace, Lew. *Ben-Hur: A Tale of the Christ*. New York: Harper, 1880.

Watt, Ian P. *The Rise of the Novel: Studies in Defoe, Richardson, and Fielding*. London: Chatto and Windus, 1957.

Woloch, Alex. *The One Vs. the Many: Minor Characters and the Space of the Protagonist in the Novel*. Princeton NJ: Princeton University Press, 2003.

CHAPTER 14

SKEPTICISM IN NINETEENTH-CENTURY AMERICAN LITERATURE AND PHILOSOPHY

MAURICE S. LEE

ALMOST as famous as Adam and Eve's expulsion from Eden is Plato's banishment of the poets from his utopian republic on the grounds that imaginative literature inflames the passions and provides no direct access to truth. Western philosophy has traditionally understood itself as a distinctively rational effort to establish the foundations of knowledge. By contrast, literature is often taken to concern emotion, beauty, and the messy experiences of life, while its methods—if one can call them such—are subjective and intuitive. Yet as Philip Sidney and Percy Shelley point out in their respective defenses of poetry, much philosophy, including Plato's *Republic*, is highly imaginative work. Literature may have no legitimate role in the philosophical quest for certainty, but historically the poet has proven to be like the eponymous character of Melville's "Bartleby, the Scrivener" (1853): alternately useful and maddening, familiar and unaccountable, logical and loony, literature can be evicted from the office of philosophy, but it continues to haunt the premises, unsettling systematic, rational claims to authoritative truths. Skepticism—generally speaking, the doubting of knowledge and the methods by which certainty is sought—is fundamental to philosophical inquiry, though nineteenth-century literature is especially active in challenging epistemological confidence. Can we trust our perceptions, feelings, and reason? Are there absolute moral and natural laws; and if so, how can we know them? Is the self a stable, transparent entity, and can we understand other minds? As the Enlightenment gave way to modernity, and as literature and philosophy became more established as disciplines, imaginative writers in the United States found skepticism threatening and inspiring.

For modern scholars working at the conjunction of literature and philosophy, overarching definitions of both discourses are elusive. Peter Lamarque and S. H. Olsen argue that literature has no integral commitments to the telling of truths, while John Searle discusses what he takes to be the special intentions and conventions of fiction. Martha Nussbaum shows how literature can mediate ethical questions that confound moral and political philosophies, as does Wai Chee Dimock, who pays sustained attention to nineteenth-century American texts. All of these scholars explicitly and implicitly differentiate literature and philosophy, and yet they often find analytic power in complicating distinctions, something that can also be said of Stanley Cavell, Anthony Cascardi, Charles Altieri, and any number of theoretically inclined critics who study texts that we have learned to call literary from perspectives we identify as philosophical. Interdisciplinary approaches in this vein have been immensely productive, though the further analysis strays from individual texts and authors, and the more it is removed from historical contexts, the more a literary critic might feel skeptical, if only because literature's commitments to subjectivity, historicity, and everyday experience resist (or at the very least, complicate) the urge for theoretical generalization.

Abstract attempts to distinguish literature and philosophy can be insightful or reductive but should ultimately serve as guidelines more than rules. Autobiography, drama, poetry, and fiction are quite capable of mounting rational arguments about the status of truth, while philosophers study (and stir) the emotions, examine (and aspire to) linguistic beauty, and address the complexities of ordinary life in ways that are not purely logical. Arthur Danto notes that philosophers across history express themselves in manifold genres; and the neopragmatist Richard Rorty has gone so far as to claim that philosophy is best regarded as a kind of writing—as a discipline defined, not by essential goals or methods, but as a rhetoric that has historically evolved. Such postmetaphysical thinking is roughly compatible with the stances of Wittgenstein, Heidegger, and Derrida, whose diverse attentions to the indeterminacies of language have powerfully shaped literary theory and criticism over the last half century. While much current philosophy has moved away from literature toward evolutionary and cognitive science, the linguistic turn of major twentieth-century philosophers aligns traditional epistemological interests with literary criticism's abiding dedication to ambiguity, language, and form.

If antifoundationalism and poststructuralism (as their critics sometimes charge) risk relativism, nihilism, solipsism, and other extreme types of skepticism, Rorty's point about the instability of philosophy has been difficult to unmake. It seems impossible to step outside of time to define literature and philosophy in universal terms that square with our historically, culturally conditioned sense of which texts belong to which discipline. Distinctions remain a necessary convenience for discussion and organization, and to challenge the separation of literature and philosophy is at some level to admit their differences as a premise of one's claims. But to believe too seriously that, say, Montaigne, Locke, and Freud sit together on one side of a divide that excludes Shakespeare, Pope, and Woolf is to use so blunt a categorizing tool as to miss fine distinctions and broader affinities within and between each grouping. The best that we can probably do is proceed with some measure of critical modesty by resisting the urge for absolute definitions and asking instead how specific philosophical traditions relate to specific congeries of texts such as nineteenth-century American literature.

The nineteenth century is an especially rich period for studying the shifting, contingent dynamics between philosophy and literature, in part because ongoing discipline formation made the two fields increasingly visible as such. Gerald Graff has shown that what we now call literary study occurred mainly in clubs and popular print culture of the early nineteenth century and was not institutionalized in American higher education until after the Civil War. More broadly, the relatively holistic humanism that governed early American thought gave way to intellectual and professional specialization over the course of the nineteenth century. From Plato forward, philosophers and literary writers have often eyed each other suspiciously; but only after the hardening of disciplinary boundaries could major thinkers such as Goethe, Coleridge, Emerson, Nietzsche, and William James begin to look positively, oddly interdisciplinary in their romantic conflations of philosophy and literature.

Another reason why the relationship between literature and philosophy is so compelling in nineteenth-century America is that both discourses participated in the ongoing emergence of modernity. A conventional overview sounds something like this: the nineteenth century signals the beginning of the end of traditional metaphysics insofar as systems of foundational knowledge, best represented in America by the Scottish Enlightenment, came under pressure from thinkers who doubted, not just our ability to know absolute truths, but the existence of such truths altogether. Skepticism, we are told, first flourished in America with the rise of romantic philosophy in the middle of the nineteenth century; and it reached new heights in what is frequently seen as the antifoundationalism of pragmatism. For historians of American philosophy such as Herbert Schneider and Bruce Kuklick, the narrative is generally redemptive in that an overreliance on staid British models gives way to the transcendentalists' inspired variations on European romanticism, which in turn leads to the exceptional, homegrown contributions of the American pragmatists.

Traditional accounts of United States literary history take a similar progressive shape. For F. O. Matthiessen and scholars working in his wake, early nineteenth-century American authors were as unimpressive as their philosophical countrymen until the middle of the century brought a renaissance of romantic writing, commencing an autochthonous literary tradition that continued after the Civil War in naturalist and modernist responses to romanticism. Formally innovative, intellectually daring, and coinciding with the expanding confidence of a nation becoming an empire, nineteenth-century American literature (the story goes) eventually broke with its Old World past and, like Natty Bumppo, Ishmael, and Huckleberry Finn, struck out on its own. As with American philosophy, imitation matured into independence, originality, and achievement, an arc suggested as early as Van Wyck Brooks's *America's Coming-of-Age* (1915).

There is some truth in these scholarly narratives, and the sections that follow share some of their claims as well as organizational concepts. What's different are two lines of argument that unsettle teleological accounts of intellectual, aesthetic, and national progress. The first is that American literature and philosophy do not advance in linear fashion from naive, derivative metaphysics toward more skeptical, more sophisticated epistemologies. American thought and culture did of course become more modern during the nineteenth century, but skepticism already had a powerful presence before the rise of romanticism. Moreover, as suggested by Whitman's Civil War poem, "A March in the Ranks Hard-Prest, and the Road Unknown" (1865), the erosion of philosophical certainty includes not only a loss of bearings but also a return to old sources of truth, including Enlightenment and Christian ideals that appear simultaneously familiar and changed under the flickering lights of modernity. In this sense, skepticism recommends that we doubt even the rise of skepticism itself.

A second point that this chapter will emphasize is the unavoidable impositions of its own parameters, for not only are literature and philosophy difficult to define in nineteenth-century America, neither can be cordoned off from social contexts or transnational influences. In 1909, James wrote of what he called "the multiverse": "[E]very part, tho it may not be in actual or immediate connexion, is nevertheless in some possible or mediated connexion, with every other part however remote, through the fact that each part hangs together with its very next neighbors in inextricable interfusion." James's insistence on both the particularity and contingency of truth-claims within complicated networks invites us to "read" reality like the sprawling plot of a novel or an unfolding, multivalent line of poetry. More meta-critically, James encourages a pluralistic approach to the study of nineteenth-century American literature and philosophy, a topic that has been largely defined by scholarly accounts of white male authors leading the charge (or the fall) toward modernity. Dwelling on inextricable interfusion will not render a neatly progressive narrative, but it may come closer to something like truth, unsettled and unsettling though it may be.

ENLIGHTENMENT, GOTHICISM, AND SENTIMENTALITY

The murder weapon in Poe's "The Imp of the Perverse" (1845) is a poisoned candle, conveniently symbolizing the struggle between Enlightenment reason and counter-Enlightenment forces, best represented in nineteenth-century American literature by the high emotionality of sentimentality and the terrors of the gothic. Poe famously indulges the latter, though "The Imp of the Perverse"—from its philosophical and scientific preamble, to the rational comportment of its murderous narrator, to the poisoned candle itself—suggests how difficult it is to disentangle reason and madness, thinking and passion, morality and nihilism, themselves Enlightenment dualisms that gothic and sentimental writings challenge in the nineteenth century. To appreciate fully the complex interplay between reason and irrationality in the period requires an understanding of how Scottish philosophy defined Enlightenment in early America.

When Thomas Jefferson wrote in 1776, "We hold these truths to be self-evident: that all men are created equal, that they are endowed by their Creator with certain unalienable rights," he aspired to found the new American nation on the dominant Enlightenment philosophy of the time. Scottish commonsense philosophers, also called Scottish realists, believed in Christianity, natural laws, and self-evident truths based not simply on the accuracy of the senses as in Locke, but also on the validating power of commonly experienced, innate intuitions. The Scottish Enlightenment was immensely influential in America in the late eighteenth and nineteenth centuries through the work of Francis Hutcheson, David Hume, Adam Smith, Thomas Reid, and their followers, whose thinking was disseminated through American textbooks and burgeoning transatlantic print culture. For many modern philosophers, Scottish common sense is simply too tautological: nothing can be said to be self-evident (truths, including the existence of God, must be proven); one cannot assume that all humans share the same rights, capacities, and feelings. That Americans fought a bloody civil war over the supposedly self-evident claim that all men are created equal suggests that Scottish common sense works no better in practice than theory. For literary scholars such as Terence Martin, Scottish realism has the additional disadvantage of being too constraining for the innovative spirit of American romanticism, though as Susan Manning and Theo Davis have more recently argued, Scottish Enlightenment thought played a generative role in American literature by vindicating the possibilities of intersubjectivity, national letters, and an aesthetic of experience.

The first step in rehabilitating Scottish common sense is to recognize that its realism is not naive. Fully cognizant of the skeptical point that we have no way to verify the accuracy of our sense impressions, Reid held that we still must trust in experience—that in the absence of fully demonstrable truths, we have no choice but to treat some convictions as self-evident or risk doubting what we have no warrant to doubt, a position that is strikingly modern in acknowledging the limits of reason. Hutcheson, Smith, and Hume (himself notoriously skeptical in some matters) also confronted the solipsistic potential of Lockean atomism, turning to affective connections between people as a basis for shared understanding. They argued that through God-given sympathy, moral sentiment, and moral sense individuals can imagine the subjectivity of others and thus agree on epistemological, ethical, and contractual claims. Smith used novels to exemplify such intersubjectivity; and Scottish realists such as Lord Kames, Hugh Blair, and Archibald Alison applied the associationist psychology of Scottish realism to aesthetics: because readers naturally react similarly to literary stimuli, writers and orators can create broadly shared artistic experiences. Accordingly, commonsense aesthetics privileged objectivity, formal unity, and conventional morality, even as some nineteenth-century American authors questioned this orthodoxy to the point of denial.

The American gothic tradition is typically placed in opposition to Enlightenment reason, though this dualism neglects the contested status of reason in nineteenth-century America. In Charles Brockden Brown's novel *Wieland* (1798), a utopian community is shattered when a villainous ventriloquist pretending to be the voice of God convinces the supposedly rational Wieland to kill his wife and child. The book begins with logical disputations in a neoclassical temple and ends with murder, suicide, sexual threats, and the inability of characters—and even readers—to trust their senses, fellow humans, or religious beliefs. In Brown's *Edgar Huntly* (1799), the narrator's semiconscious states also destabilize selfhood and perception, while the conflation of animals, whites, and American Indians hints that all men are created equally brutal. Writing during a period in which republican thinkers struggled to contain the imagined and very real passions of mobs, factions, religious enthusiasts, women, and nonwhites, Brown draws on counter-Enlightenment ideas from Hobbes, Christopher Wieland, and Friedrich Schiller, even as he offers ventriloquism and sleepwalking as rational solutions to the mysteries of America.

Brown's unsettling of the Scottish and American Enlightenment continues in later gothic-inflected writers. Like Poe and Hawthorne, Melville shows how socially organized violence punctures illusions of enlightened consensus, as when the lawyer of "Bartleby" fecklessly appeals to "common sense" before abandoning his scrivener to prison and death. James Fenimore Cooper shared with Scottish realists a belief in natural law, though his demonization of some Native American characters and his explorations of paradoxes in contractual logic simultaneously suggest that nature's truths are not always benevolent or legible. Similarly, slave narrators appeal to moral norms when descrying the terrible inhumanities of chattel bondage; but if they implicitly—or in the case of Frederick Douglass, explicitly—deploy commonsense arguments, their depictions of pervasive violence and irremediable sin threaten Enlightenment ideals. In moments and extended periods of doubt, American writers wonder whether common sense exists as a mental faculty, moral principle, and foundation for an empire of reason and right. Yet as disorderly as gothic texts can be, many assume or attempt to evoke consensus in their audience: surely the shared experience of a narrative world supports a realist epistemology; surely every reader can react to transgressions with a commonly experienced horror. Right?

Gothicism and the skeptical potential it entails are traditionally associated with male authors in America, while counter-Enlightenment writings from women are most often discussed in terms of sentimentality. Scottish realism helps debunk this false dualism in two ways: it shows that affect and intuition are fundamental, not anathema, to the American Enlightenment; and though Adam Smith's *Theory of*

Moral Sentiments (1759) claims that women are more sympathetic than men, Smith and his fellow Scots agreed that everyone possesses moral sense regardless of their sex. Male sentimentality is everywhere in the nineteenth century, while many female authors wrote in gothic modes. Indeed, as seriously as their male peers, women authors critically examined Scottish Enlightenment ideas, despite their culture's sense of philosophy as a masculine pursuit.

Beginning as early as Susanna Rowson's *Charlotte Temple* (1791), novels in America show the risks of trusting emotions that turn out to be passions, not moral sentiments. When Charlotte at the beginning of the book meets a man who celebrates wild swings of feeling, she concurs, "This is true philosophy"; but after she follows her own emotions into sin and death, the reader learns to be more circumspect. The challenge of identifying affective correctness is a major theme in sentimental writing, especially when young women must gain control of their hearts as in Hawthorne's *The Scarlet Letter* (1850) and Susan Warner's best-selling *The Wide, Wide World* (1850). In philosophical theory, common sense is universally recognized, but fictive practice raises epistemological problems; for if communal conventions, especially Christianity, often enable sentimental protagonists to know their moral sense as such, in other instances—contra Scottish realism—the feelings of the majority are wrong.

Women writers also complicate intersubjectivity as formulated by Scottish philosophy. Harriet Jacobs in *Incidents in the Life of a Slave Girl* (1861) denies that freeborn readers can understand the experiences of slaves, instantiating Hume's controversial point that sympathy struggles to bridge the gaps of cultural and racial difference. In novels such as *Dred* (1856) and *The Minister's Wooing* (1859), Harriet Beecher Stowe also questions sentimental philosophy, qualifying her prediction in *Uncle Tom's Cabin* (1852) that right feelings commonly understood can end slavery and unify the nation. As suggested by postbellum writers such as Charlotte Perkins Gilman and Kate Chopin, irreducible emotions and intuitions do not always bring people together. Instead, intensely affective subjects sometimes understand reality so differently than their peers that they cannot—or are not permitted to—participate in civic spheres, family life, or even linguistic norms. As Emily Dickinson writes in her poem, "Much Madness is divinest Sense" (1863), those who fail to "Assent" to "the Majority" are considered "straightway dangerous, / And handled with a Chain." Dickinson is speaking generally about the dangers of rebellion, but her emphasis on "Sense," "Majority," and the Scottish realist "Chain" of associationist psychology suggests a more poignant critique. The universalizing principles of Scottish common sense accorded women (and, in some cases, nonwhites) significant rational and political powers, and its respect for ordinary intuitions and feelings expanded philosophical authority beyond the masculine-coded logical forms of an educated elite. Yet as Dickinson hints, Scottish realism was popular because it encouraged conformity, sometimes sounding less like philosophy and more like, well, common sense. Like the Declaration of Independence, the ostensibly self-evident truths of the Scottish Enlightenment could be both liberating and limiting as presented in American literature.

ROMANTIC IMPROVISATIONS

When Kant complained in 1783 that Scottish realists based their concept of truth, not on reason, but on "the judgment of the multitude," he registered a philosophical departure from British empiricism: the mind is not a blank slate that passively receives impressions from the object world, nor should social norms be mistaken for intuitions that validate Lockean sensations. For Kant and those working under his influence, the individual subject participates in the construction of phenomena through the organizing powers of the mind; and the acquisition of knowledge is not marked by smooth consensus but rather by dialectical struggle, whether in the domain of sublime aesthetics, divided psyches, or Hegelian history. Whereas most scholars treat the Scottish Enlightenment as an important but not particularly inspiring context for early nineteenth-century American literature, the belated entry of romantic philosophy into the United States is taken to spark an extraordinary body of writings in the decades before the Civil War. Familiar figures of American romanticism include the transcendentalists Emerson, Margaret Fuller, Thoreau, and Whitman, as well as their supposedly more skeptical interlocutors Poe, Melville, and Dickinson. All of these authors address the skeptical potential of a post-Kantian radical subjectivity in which reality, untethered from Scottish realism and norms, becomes whatever is in the eye of the beholder. Yet as powerfully as they anticipate and even mark the advent of antifoundational modernity, romantics also look backward with some longing toward more grounded metaphysics.

As suggested by Poe's short story "Ligeia" (1838) in which an opium-addled transcendentalist emigrates from Germany to Britain, the transmission of German romantic philosophy to America was circuitous and not always trustworthy. Following M. H. Abrams's influential scholarship on the Continental contexts of British romanticism, historically minded critics such as Leon Chai and Barbara Packer trace the philosophical roots of American romanticism through Coleridge, Carlyle, De Quincey, and de Staël to Kant, Schelling, the Schlegels, and Goethe. If American writers did not fully comprehend the intricacies of romantic philosophy, and if some of their intellectual habits were more whimsical than systematic, many found in post-Kantian ideas inspiration for and confirmation of a set of related propositions: individuals can forge original relationships with the universe; ecstatic states of perception such as intuition most closely apprehend transcendental ideals; experience, the self, and nature enjoy open-ended growth; literature fulfills the truth-telling potential of philosophy when fragmentation, chaos, and irony progress toward syntheses associated with organic form and sublime oneness. These beliefs cohere with the religious freethinking and political radicalism of many American romantics. They also engendered serious doubts from outside and within the tradition. When does subjectivity slide into solipsism, atheism, and relativism? Are there (or should there be) limits to personal, political, and aesthetic freedoms? How does one simultaneously champion flux and higher law, personal experience and transcendental ideals? Though American romantics have more affinities with Scottish philosophy than is sometimes supposed, they usually subordinate common sense and consensus to sallies of the individual spirit, even as they acknowledge the skeptical dangers of romantic subjectivity.

If only from a philosophical point of view, Emerson is the unstable center of American transcendentalism (though how central transcendentalism is to American romanticism is another issue). Emerson is the only nineteenth-century thinker to figure prominently in both United States literary and philosophical history; and his influence, to borrow one of his tropes, forms an ever-expanding horizon. Emerson's philosophy famously resists paraphrase, in part because of its principled resistance to consistency, certitude, and facile clarity. His first major philosophical work, *Nature* (1836), offers a relatively systematic ascent from various aspects of materialism through idealism and finally to spirit, but it also becomes increasingly mystical in its efforts to encompass, rather than deny or resolve, long-standing philosophical quandaries. The dialectics that Emerson broaches in *Nature* govern his subsequent writings. "Self-Reliance" (1841) claims epistemological authority for the subject, while "Circles" (1841) unsettles the stability of the self. "The Poet" (1844) promises that literature will overcome skepticism, but "Experience" (1844) dwells on how debilitating doubt can be. "Power" (1860) and "Fate" (1860) respectively emphasize free will and determinism. And even these pairings are not as orderly as they can seem, for Emerson's warring philosophical impulses play out between *and within* individual texts, as when "The Transcendentalist" (1843) describes a double-consciousness alternating between Locke and Kant, materialism and idealism.

Even further, as Richard Poirier has shown, Emerson's epistemological open-endedness enacts itself at the level of language. Essays and paragraphs do not progress toward a single point but proliferate in superabundant theses that overwhelm linear logic and argumentative closure. Terminology slides between and within sentences as Emerson slips between various philosophical positions, thus unsettling all epistemological claims. Accordingly, some readers deny Emerson's status as a legitimate philosopher, though Stanley Cavell has most forcefully argued that Emerson's lubricity is a philosophical strength: systematic reasoning has limits; experience is not consistent; moral perfectionism demands impermanence; skepticism is a condition to live with, not a problem to be bemoaned or agonistically solved. If nothing else, Emerson's distinctive style dramatizes post-Kantian epistemology; for just as subjects dialectically constitute the world, readers of Emerson must continually participate in his unfolding efforts to live and write according to truths that may someday be possessed by all but are initially pursued individually.

Privileging Emerson should not diminish the philosophical work of fellow transcendentalists, including three erstwhile disciples. As Charles Capper has shown, Fuller studied German romanticism more rigorously than her mentor, while her many essays and reviews helped introduce romantic aesthetics to America. Fuller's political commitments were more intense than Emerson's, particularly her melding of transcendentalism and feminism in *Woman in the Nineteenth Century* (1845), as well as her participation in the Italian Revolution of 1848. Like Fuller, Thoreau in many ways grew beyond the influence of Emerson. Though often cast as a practitioner of

Emersonian theory, Thoreau explored Eastern philosophy more widely than his friend and competitor, and in *Walden* (1854) and his journals he explicates a philosophy of science that complicates easy distinctions between empiricism and transcendental art. Compared to Emerson, Whitman made more of Hegel and was a superior poet whose experiments in free verse and sexual expression more radically embody romantic poetics. Along various axes—political, scientific, somatic, and aesthetic—Fuller, Thoreau, and Whitman push Emerson's transcendentalism toward more sustained encounters with materiality. Yet as independent as each author is, none is entirely legible without the philosophical influence of Emerson, who does not have the last word on American transcendentalism but establishes the terms of engagement.

Philosophically considered, Poe, Melville, and Dickinson are often taken to react against the optimistic idealism of Emerson and his circle, though they also have more direct, original connections with transatlantic romantic philosophy, a discourse that does not enter the United States solely through the portals of Concord. Poe's romantic syntheses of subject and object, material and ideal, literature and philosophy are simultaneously attractive and terrible, even if his attacks on the transcendentalists (whom he calls the "Frogpondians") tend to be sophomoric. Melville's satires of transcendentalism in *Pierre* (1852) and *The Confidence-Man* (1857) are more incisive than Poe's, though *Mardi* (1849) and especially *Moby-Dick* (1851) more directly interrogate the philosophical ideas of Kant, Coleridge, Byron, and Carlyle. Poe and Melville ultimately trace the limits of philosophy rather than inhabit any single system; and a famous comment from Hawthorne about Melville's skepticism can also apply to Poe's: "He can neither believe, nor be comfortable in his unbelief."

The same can be said of Dickinson, whose skepticism is animated in part by romantic philosophy. Poems such as "The Outer—from the Inner" (1862) seem directed at Emerson, while others like "The Brain—is wider than the Sky" (1863) more generally examine problems of post-Kantian subjectivity, including the fallibility of the senses and the challenge of knowing other minds. Whereas the expansive multiplicities of Whitman's style embody the grand synthetic urges of romantic aesthetics, Dickinson's fragmented, ironic turnings represent in a different romantic mode what she calls the "Sweet skepticism of the Heart" (1877). A Dickinson poem from 1874 shows the power of her literary skepticism:

> Wonder—is not precisely knowing
> And not precisely knowing not—
> A beautiful but bleak condition
> He has not lived who has not felt—
> Suspense—is his maturer Sister—
> Whether Adult Delight is Pain
> Or of itself a new misgiving—
> This is the Gnat that mangles men— (#1347)

Neither knowing nor knowing not, this poem begins on a privative middle ground between Enlightenment confidence and utter doubt. Quickly, however, it moves beyond epistemology toward the complicated experience of how skepticism feels—beautiful and bleak, delightful and painful, overwhelming and small as a bug. Most important, the poem does not see skepticism as a terminal condition. Philosophical uncertainty can be wonderful and leads to a forward-looking Suspense that anticipates, not the fulfillment of absolute truths, but the discovery of new misgivings. In "An Answer to the Question: What Is Enlightenment?" (1784), Kant compared the age of reason to man's growth beyond immaturity. In "Wonder—is not precisely knowing," Dickinson describes how epistemological maturation is always incomplete, violent, and humanizing. To be mangled by the feeling of skepticism is to be made a man. The poem even *sounds* like skepticism in that its slant rhymes and halting meter intimate but do not consummate the possibilities of order, unity, and closure.

In comparison to American transcendentalists, Poe, Melville, and Dickinson focus more on the tragic potentials of romantic subjectivity: Poe's world-constructing individuals plunge into crime and madness; Melville's irresponsible idealists damage everyone around them; Dickinson repeatedly worries about solipsistic loneliness and the displacement of God. That said, all three writers found romantic philosophy invigorating, and we should not overlook the fact that the shadows of skepticism also fall over Emerson and his circle. Rather than divide American romantics into light and dark, optimistic and tragic, a better approach is to recognize that all worked in chiaroscuro.

Historicist scholarship tends to look backward in studying the philosophical sources of American romanticism, though as profoundly as any group in the American literary canon, romantics anticipate and even precipitate major philosophical developments of the twentieth century. Cavell and others read Emerson as a forerunner to Nietzsche, who carried a copy of Emerson's essays with him; and through Nietzsche, Emerson can be taken to influence postmetaphysical philosophy in general. Most powerfully represented in "Civil Disobedience" (1849), Thoreau's political philosophy shaped the thinking of Gandhi and Martin Luther King Jr. while philosophers of science take Thoreau to prefigure modern modes of environmental consciousness. Derrida and Jacques Lacan, despite their differences, approach Poe's "The Purloined Letter" (1844) as an exemplary poststructuralist work, as do Gilles Deleuze and Giorgio Agamben in their readings of "Bartleby, the Scrivener." For many modern philosophers, including the deconstructionist Paul de Man and (as we will see) neopragmatists, romanticism presages the end of a traditional metaphysics that seeks absolute, universal laws.

American romantics did indeed doubt the philosophical foundations of the Enlightenment, and many of their texts dwell on the problems and prospects of living in a world without certainty. At the same time, they often express a yearning, howsoever temporary or repressed, for more stable philosophical frameworks. When transcendentalists appeal to higher law, they indicate their residual and living religiosity; and their championing of intuition and experience is compatible with Scottish common sense, as are their claims that individuals share similar potentials and that human history progresses toward a consensus of beliefs. Melville and

Dickinson take Christianity (and especially Calvinism) seriously enough to resent it, while Poe—along with Emerson and Thoreau—considers the possibility that science might illuminate hard facts and natural laws. Viewed from a distance, Kant and his followers revolutionized philosophy and literature in nineteenth-century America. Looking more closely at individual authors and texts, one finds that it provoked, not a series of clean breaks, but rather a tumult of productive tensions, uncertainties, and experiments.

PRAGMATIST DEPARTURES AND RETURNS

Pragmatism may be the first philosophical tradition to originate in America, though it remains a loose confederation of thinkers and ideas with no founding document or moment. Begun around the late 1860s by figures such as William James, Charles Peirce, and Oliver Wendell Holmes Jr., pragmatism (as it came to be called) stretches from epistemology and psychology, to logic, mathematics, and semiotics, to political theory and law. Particularly as described by neopragmatists, pragmatism boldly abandons the philosophical quest for certainty, embracing instead indeterminacy, probability, fallibilism, and pluralism. Yet if pragmatists are in some senses skeptics, they are also realists who value experience and draw on materialist traditions such as utilitarianism and Darwinism. For pragmatists, the proper test of a truth-claim is not whether it is internally logical or coheres with posited theories but whether it is validated by consequences in the domain of experience. Louis Menand emphasizes that pragmatism is less a set of principles and more a method for approaching problems. If its romantically inflected hostility to metaphysics makes it hostile to much conventional philosophy, pragmatism over the last few decades has been quite useful in the study of nineteenth-century American literature, not only because pragmatists (especially James) find epistemological power in literature, but also because their attentions to the limits of reason accord with romantic and poststructural sensibilities.

As much as any critic, Poirier has helped bring pragmatism into conversation with literature by demonstrating how Emerson's unique style exemplifies a pragmatist comportment: the relations of language and reality are not static in their unending approaches to correspondence; skepticism inheres not only in arguments but also in literary form. Poirier's followers can overplay James's interest in language (and slight the more rigorous semiotics of Peirce), and they may reify nationalist narratives of American literary and intellectual history (by neglecting European influences). Yet Poirier's approach remains exemplary in combining epistemological seriousness and literary explication, thus opening the way for Elisa New, Joan Richardson, Susan Manning, and other scholars, who trace pragmatist tendencies in Emerson and other antebellum figures such as Thoreau, Whitman, Dickinson, and even Melville, Douglass, and Poe. We can think of such readings as back-formations in which pragmatists provide a logic and language with which to interpret earlier texts. Or we might invoke the explanatory power of culture insofar as antebellum literary writers along with the first generation of pragmatists recognized through broadly experienced phenomena (e.g., the American landscape, the slavery conflict, and the spread of technology and capitalism) that traditional metaphysical systems do not adequately explain the world.

Mechanisms of influence are not so conjectural when addressing two major literary figures of the later nineteenth century—Henry James and W. E. B. Du Bois, both of whom have direct links to pragmatism. Henry often claimed to be mystified by his brother William's philosophy, but he wrote to him after reading *Pragmatism* (1907) that he had "unconsciously pragmatized" all his life. In the novels that made his fame, Henry does indeed—as Ross Posnock has shown in *The Trial of Curiosity* (1991)—dramatize pragmatist concepts. His eye for rich physical detail, whether understood from an aesthetic or economic perspective, insists on the materiality of experience, while works such as *In the Cage* (1898) anticipate William's argument that intersubjectivity is imperfect but inescapably real. Henry's many portrayals of cultural pluralism join pragmatism in undermining moral absolutes without succumbing to utter skepticism, a point made by the philosopher Robert Pippin; and almost all of Henry's fiction turns on tragic moments in which characters realize that their imaginations and abstractions are incommensurate with lived life. Even Henry's line about being an unconscious pragmatist is apposite in that it acknowledges the pragmatist claim that experience teaches us without our knowledge and that pragmatism is a natural way of thinking.

Trained in philosophy by William James at Harvard and further educated at the University of Berlin (particularly in Hegelian thought), Du Bois demonstrates how pragmatist ideas can advance the cause of social justice, even if Cornel West and Walter Benn Michaels have shown that pragmatism has not always been useful in righting racial wrongs. In "The Conservation of Races" (1897), Du Bois advocates cultural pluralism, applying Jamesian notions of separate-but-connected subjectivities to races instead of individuals. In *The Philadelphia Negro* (1899), he turns to sociological facts in order to combat racist ideologies that he condemns as a priori abstractions. Yet just as James felt constrained by scientific positivism, Du Bois becomes increasingly attuned to epistemological limits. *The Souls of Black Folk* (1903) remains committed to studying the material conditions of African Americans, but the book also engages philosophical issues that occupied pragmatist thinkers—the inadequacies of intellection and positivism; the difficult necessity of understanding others; the importance of recognizing spiritual and aesthetic experience as part of the actual world. When Du Bois argues in *The Souls of Black Folk* that the problem of race is "a concrete test of the underlying principles of the great republic," he takes up the pragmatist position that ideas mean little until they are practically realized, a point indicating affinities between Du Bois's pragmatism and later Marxism. Among other African American texts of the time, Anna Julia Cooper's *A Voice from the South* (1892), Booker T. Washington's *Up from Slavery* (1901), and Pauline Hopkins's *Of One Blood: Or, the Hidden Self* (1903) can sound at times like pragmatism, though Du Bois more surely deploys the philosophy of William James and remains, as Shamoon Zamir has shown, a wide-ranging philosophical thinker who reveals the political power and limits of skepticism.

A less progressive aspect of pragmatism and literary skepticism is strenuously represented by Holmes, who saw life not as a rational realm governed by logic and moral absolutes, but as a bewildering, Darwinian struggle in which comprehensive knowledge is impossible. Literary realism and naturalism share a similar view, though they have not received as much attention from philosophers as has romantic literature, in part because their ostensibly positivist epistemology can seem philosophically inert. However, as Alan Trachtenberg, James Livingston, and Jane Thrailkill have shown, pragmatism can illuminate realist literature when it is taken less as a technical philosophy and more as a cultural discourse intertwined with social Darwinism, consumer capitalism, and scientific approaches to the emotions and body. In Frank Norris's writings, intellection is overpowered by atavism and overdetermined by material conditions. For Stephen Crane, subjectivities are ruled by primal instincts that make it impossible to know nature. If the characters of Theodore Dreiser's *Sister Carrie* (1900) have psychological depth, their self-reflections are often thin disguises for self-interested passions and appetites. In a long version of the manuscript, Dreiser offers the "speculative and idealistic" Ames as an intellectual counterbalance; but Ames's role is later severely reduced, as if in response to a question that neopragmatists sometimes ask: if pragmatist philosophers are right, is there much use for philosophy at all?

In his classic essay, "Edwards to Emerson" (1940), Perry Miller drew comparisons between the two greatest American philosophers before the Civil War, despite the fact that they were separated by a century of immense change. Puritanism is no longer so popular a subject; cultural studies have overtaken the history of ideas; and expanding canons and transnational approaches have challenged Miller's New England-centric paradigm. Yet continuities of American literature and philosophy cannot be entirely dismissed—even when considered across a rapidly modernizing nineteenth century, even if continuities are less linear and more characterized by networks of connections. As suggested by the subtitle of James's book, *Pragmatism: A New Name for Some Old Ways of Thinking*, pragmatists for all their iconoclasm do not divorce themselves from the past. Holmes once bragged in a letter that he could teach all of Kant in fifteen minutes over tea; but romantic philosophers, particularly Emerson, shaped pragmatist commitments to individual subjectivity, intuition, flux, and the legitimacy of faith. If pragmatism was once seen as a hard-nosed response to the flighty ideals of romanticism, the two traditions seem increasingly compatible in their encounters with skepticism.

Neither does pragmatism, as Robert Brandom argues, depart from Enlightenment traditions. Nineteenth-century pragmatists can be antifoundational, but Hilary Putnam notes that they also follow Scottish commonsense philosophy in relying on experience as a fallible but sufficient basis for action and belief. James holds that sentiments help determine rationality and that higher laws remain a living option, while pragmatist faith in the ameliorative power of reason accords with

Enlightenment ideals. Pragmatism and its associated literary texts form decidedly modern discourses animated by questions that Scottish realists and romantics also ask: How does one acknowledge the limits of reason without becoming a full-blown skeptic? How can one admit disparate subjectivities without abjuring communal responsibilities and beliefs? It is a long way from Charlotte Temple to Hester Prynne to Huck Finn and Carrie Meeber, but all suggest that feeling and experience have claims against logic and moral absolutes. Nature poses different unsolvable problems for Cooper, Thoreau, Dickinson, and Crane, but none can entirely repress the hope that we might better know natural laws. Brockden Brown, Melville, Henry James, and Du Bois all confront similar epistemological crises, despite their different styles, historical moments, subject positions, and philosophical influences. As if to frustrate desires for order, Emerson links Edwards and Nietzsche in an inextricable interfusion of literature and ideas. To insist on teleological narratives is to neglect multitudes of contingent relations and to fail to experience with the nineteenth century the risks and possibilities of skepticism.

BIBLIOGRAPHY

Abrams, M. H. *The Mirror and the Lamp: Romantic Theory and the Critical Tradition.* Oxford: Oxford University Press, 1953.

Brandom, Robert. "When Philosophy Paints Its Blue on Gray: Irony and the Pragmatist Enlightenment." *Boundary 2* 29.2 (Summer 2002): 1–28.

Capper, Charles. *Margaret Fuller: An American Romantic Life.* 2 vols. 1992. Oxford: Oxford University Press, 2007.

Cavell, Stanley. *Emerson's Transcendental Etudes.* Ed. David Justin Hodge. Stanford, CA: Stanford University Press, 2003.

Chai, Leon. *The Romantic Foundations of the American Renaissance.* Ithaca, NY: Cornell University Press, 1987.

Danto, Arthur C. "Philosophy as/and/of Literature." *Literature and the Question of Philosophy.* Ed. Anthony J. Cascardi. Baltimore, MD: Johns Hopkins University Press, 1987. 1–23.

Davis, Theo. *Formalism, Experience, and the Making of American Literature in the Nineteenth Century.* Cambridge: Cambridge University Press, 2007.

Deppman, Jed. *Trying to Think with Emily Dickinson.* Amherst, MA: University of Massachusetts Press, 2008.

Dickinson, Emily. *The Poems of Emily Dickinson: Reading Edition.* Ed. R. W. Franklin. Cambridge, MA: Belknap Press of Harvard University Press, 1998.

Dimock, Wai Chee. *Residues of Justice: Literature, Law, Philosophy.* Berkeley, CA: University of California Press, 1996.

Dooley, Patrick. *The Pluralistic Philosophy of Stephen Crane.* Champaign, IL: University of Illinois Press, 1994.

Dreiser, Theodore. *Sister Carrie: A Norton Critical Edition.* Ed. Donald Pizer. New York: Norton, 2006.

Du Bois, W. E. B. *Writings.* New York: Library of America, 1986.

Graff, Gerald. *Professing Literature: An Institutional History.* Chicago: University of Chicago Press, 1987.

Hawthorne, Nathaniel. *The English Notebooks by Nathaniel Hawthorne*. Ed. Randall
     Stewart. New York: Russell and Russell, 1962.
James, William. *The Collected Letters of William James: William and Henry*. 3 vols. Ed. Ignas
     K. Skrupselis and Elizabeth M. Berkeley. Charlottesville: University Press of Virginia,
     1992–1994.
———. *Writings, 1902–1910*. New York: Library of America, 1987.
Jefferson, Thomas. "The Declaration of Independence." *The Essential Jefferson*. Ed. Jean M.
     Yarbrough. Indianapolis, IN: Hackett, 2006. 23–26.
Kant, Immanuel. *Prolegomena to Any Future Metaphysics That Will Be Able to Come
     Forward as Science*. Ed. Gary Hatfield. New York: Cambridge University Press, 1997.
Kuklick, Bruce. *A History of American Philosophy, 1720–2000*. Oxford: Clarendon Press,
     2001.
———. *The Rise of American Philosophy, Cambridge, Massachusetts, 1860–1930*. New
     Haven, CT: Yale University Press, 1977.
Lamarque, Peter, and Stein Haugom Olsen. *Truth, Fiction, and Literature*. Oxford: Oxford
     University Press, 1994.
Livingston, James. *Pragmatism and the Political Economy of Cultural Revolution, 1850–1940*.
     Chapel Hill: University of North Carolina Press, 1994.
Manning, Susan. *Fragments of Union: Making Connections in Scottish and American Writing*.
     New York: Palgrave, 2002.
Martin, Terence. *The Instructed Vision: Scottish Common Sense Philosophy and the Origins
     of American Fiction*. Bloomington: Indiana University Press, 1961.
Melville, Herman. "Bartleby, the Scrivener." *Pierre, Israel Potter, The Piazza Tales, The
     Confidence-Man, Uncollected Prose, Billy Budd, Sailor*. New York: Library of America,
     1984. 635–672.
Menand, Louis. *The Metaphysical Club*. New York: Farrar, Straus and Giroux, 2001.
Michaels, Walter Benn. *Our America: Nativism, Modernism, and Pluralism*. Durham, NC:
     Duke University Press, 1995.
Nussbaum, Martha C. *Love's Knowledge: Essays on Philosophy and Literature*. Oxford:
     Oxford University Press, 1990.
Packer, Barbara. *The Transcendentalists*. Athens: University of Georgia Press, 2007.
Pippin, Robert. *Henry James and the Moral Life*. New York: Cambridge University Press,
     2000.
Poirier, Richard. *Poetry and Pragmatism*. Cambridge, MA: Harvard University Press,
     1992.
Posnock, Ross. *Color and Culture: Black Writers and the Making of the Modern Intellectual*.
     Cambridge, MA: Harvard University Press, 1998.
———. *The Trial of Curiosity: Henry James, William James, and the Challenge of Modernity*.
     New York: Oxford University Press, 1991.
Putnam, Hilary. "Pragmatism and Realism." *The Revival of Pragmatism: New Essays
     on Social Thought, Law, and Culture*. Ed. Morris Dickstein. Durham, NC: Duke
     University Press, 1998. 72–80.
Richardson, Joan. *A Natural History of Pragmatism: The Fact of Feeling from Jonathan
     Edwards to Gertrude Stein*. Cambridge: Cambridge University Press, 2007.
Rorty, Richard. *Consequences of Pragmatism (Essays: 1972–1980)*. Minneapolis, MN: University
     of Minnesota Press, 1982.
Rowson, Susanna. *Charlotte Temple; and, Lucy Temple*. Ed. Ann Douglas. New York:
     Penguin Classics, 1991.

Searle, John. *Expression and Meaning: Studies in the Theory of Speech Acts.* Cambridge: Cambridge University Press, 1985.

Schneider, Herbert. *A History of American Philosophy.* New York: Columbia University Press, 1963.

Thrailkill, Jane. *Affecting Fictions: Mind, Body, and Emotion in American Literary Realism.* Cambridge, MA: Harvard University Press, 2007.

Trachtenberg, Alan. *The Incorporation of America: Culture and Society in the Gilded Age.* New York: Hill and Wang, 1982.

West, Cornel. *The American Evasion of Philosophy: A Genealogy of Pragmatism.* Madison: University of Wisconsin Press, 1989.

Zamir, Shamoon. *Dark Voices: W. E. B. Du Bois and American Thought, 1888–1903.* Chicago: University of Chicago Press, 1995.

AQ1: Could you confirm whether the shortened RH was okay?

CHAPTER 15

ON THE REDUNDANCY OF "TRANSNATIONAL AMERICAN STUDIES"

JARED HICKMAN

My thesis is simple: "Transnational American Studies" is a logically incoherent formulation whose plausibility arises from its perpetuation of a hemispheric cultural-political project of a *very* long nineteenth century (1776–1939) that has distinguished "America" as more than yet another nation but rather "a teeming nation of nations." The essence, or promise, of "American" nationality, the argument goes, is precisely its transnationality. One can draw a line from Thomas Paine's 1776 trumpeting of "the cause of America" as "the cause of all mankind," which foresees in the nascent multicultural republic an enlightened cosmopolis in which petty national distinctions might dissolve, to Shelley Fisher Fishkin's 2004 celebration of the United States as "a transnational crossroads of culture" that has "itself generated a host of other crossroads of cultures as it has crossed borders"—for instance, Gandhi's Thoreauvian and then Martin Luther King's Gandhian education in civil disobedience. Both formulations belong to the same political meta-narrative: enlightened values—here, cosmopolitan fraternity and civil disobedience—are on a global march, and "America" is a primary base of operations. Even as transnational American studies attempts to elude American exceptionalism by proclaiming "the freedom of trans-nations" (Lott 201) over and against the hegemonic nationality of the United States, it reveals its rhetorical and conceptual indebtedness to Paine's elevation of "America" as precisely the first trans-nation.

Current critiques of transnational American studies are too presentist to unravel this genealogy whereby transnationality and Americanity became fundamentally linked. A familiar *materialist* critique reifies rather than unpacks the linkage of Americanity and transnationality by its too facile equation of global capital with the United States (see Pease, "Re-thinking"). A certain *disciplinary* critique likewise reasons from a contemporary moment in which American power seems especially ominous to urge American studies to "go back inside," resuming "the task and interpretive challenge for which it was created": "the analysis of the cultural sources of American power" (Fluck 28–30). Neither critique sufficiently comprehends that American studies' transnational turn is not merely mimetic of contemporary U.S. hegemony but a profound and predictable return to the very wellspring of American exceptionalism—the Enlightenment localization of the universal in "America." The cosmopolitan frame of *planetarity* to which many transnational American studies practitioners hopefully look for global justice is not only a "period concept…developed within the paradigm of global modernity" but quite literally contingent upon the European discovery of the Americas and the emergence of "Americanity as a concept" (Pease, "Literary Extraterritoriality" 20; Quijano and Wallerstein). Americanity, globality, planetarity, and modernity predicate each other. This historical circumstance has made "America" the projection screen of the modern radical imaginary—the site, actual and otherwise, of a utopian dreaming of collectivities that might transcend the limiting "claims of historicity" (Quijano and Wallerstein). "Transnational American studies" rather than simply "transnational studies" presupposes a special relationship between Americanity and transnationality that has historically been the basis of a robust brand of American exceptionalism. "Transnational American studies" is thus not so much "oddly oxymoronic" as it is unselfconsciously synonymizing (Brickhouse 696). This chapter investigates the profound *redundancy*—terminological and historical—of transnational American studies in hopes of tempering the field. By providing a much deeper historicization of the field, I aim, on the one hand, to dampen certain enthusiasms about having eluded American exceptionalism but, on the other, potentially to strengthen the field by pointing toward a new critical history of "Atlantic/world" modernity that frankly addresses the complex centrality of "America" to any imagination of the global.[1]

Republicanism, American
and Universal

"In the beginning, all the world was America," John Locke famously averred, and, by a certain principle of eschatological symmetry, so many philosophes thought it should be in the end (Locke 29). The American (and later the French) Revolution was taken as heralding the direction that all the world should go, pointing the way toward the universal republic invoked by Paine, Anacharsis Cloots, Immanuel Kant, and many others. Cosmopolitanism thus has a particular national(ist) "cradle."[2] Two Atlantic

cosmopolitans, J. Hector St. John de Crèvecoeur and Thomas Paine, derived cosmopolitanism from experiences of the multicultural transnationalism of revolutionary
North America, as registered in their seminal works, *Letters from an American Farmer*
(1782) and *Common Sense* (1776). Specifically, "America" furnished two enduring figures that at the time seemed to throw into dramatic relief the small-mindedness of
European-style nationalism: "continental" space and a new American "race."

The seemingly infinite expanse of North America is a crucial starting point for
Crèvecoeur and Paine. British cultural and political insularity reflects literal, geographical insularity ("the narrow limits of three hundred and sixty miles," as Paine
notes) and contrasts with an American cultural and political hospitality enabled
by spatial vastness. America's massive continentality becomes cosmopolitanism's
condition of possibility: because there is literally "room for everybody in America,"
Americans "know, properly speaking, no strangers" (Crèvecoeur 81, 80). To be
American is thus not to be American per se, but cosmopolitan: "When in England,
[the English emigrant to America] was a mere Englishman; here he stands on a
larger portion of the globe, not less than its fourth part, and may see the productions of the north, in iron and naval stores; the provisions of Ireland; the grain of
Egypt; the indigo, the rice of China" (Crèvecoeur 81). Once in America, the former
"mere Englishman" is organically transformed into a citizen of the world—call it
natural super*nationalism*.

Both Crèvecoeur and Paine rather literal-mindedly refer the moral universality of the American experiment to its greater geographical fraction of globality:
because it constitutes "a larger portion of the globe, not less than its fourth part"
(Crèvecoeur), because it is "a continent…at least one eighth part of the habitable
globe" (*Common Sense* 4, 28–29), America represents a "universal" "circumstance."
Crèvecoeur and Paine anticipate contemporary invocations of planetarity as the
basis for a new cosmopolitan humanism—just witness how cannily Paine couches
his universalist claim for the rights of man in a planetary metaphor: it is "a subject
that embraces with equatorial magnitude the whole region of humanity" (*Rights
of Man* 210). But what cannot be missed is the historical fact that Americanity was
perhaps the original vehicle whereby abstract universalist humanism was translated
into concrete planetary humanism, which of course is precisely the function it continues to serve in contemporary transnational American studies—take Wai Chee
Dimock's much celebrated recasting of American literature as a sort of transhistorical, transnational portal through which we might glimpse a better global future.

So the continental space of America creates uniquely cosmopolitan conditions,
bringing together diverse peoples in an environment wherein they can peace-
fully coexist—and, it turns out, cohabit. Transnational marriages and children
become the ultimate measure of the cosmopolitan, which gives way to a vision of
an American "race" that by its very mixed makeup underscores the enlightened
tenet of human equality. Insofar as the American race is here being leveraged as
a metonym of the human race, race is meant to operate as the most capacious of
categories, shaming the provincialism of nation. That said, it is essential to note
that "the scope of diversity" for both Paine and Crèvecoeur is extremely limited

by our standards—pan-Europeanism represents the extent of their fantasizing, although this should not be trivialized in light of substantial national and imperial conflicts (Hollinger, *Postethnic America* 90). "That race now called American," writes Crèvecoeur, is a "promiscuous breed" of "English, Scotch, Irish, French, Dutch, Germans, and Swedes," possessing "a strange mixture of blood, which you will find in no other country" (68, 70). Exceptionalism inheres in encyclopedism: "I could point out to you a family," Farmer James reports, "whose grandfather was an Englishman, whose wife was Dutch, whose son married a French woman, and whose present four sons have now four wives of different nations" (70–71). The American race is a race of *derácinés* whose multiple origins effectively cancel each other out, clearing the ground for the formation of an enlightened autonomous subject.

But intractable tensions and tautologies here begin to rear their heads. What does it mean to define Americanity as a subjective state of transnationality? At what point does the delineation of "America" as a special subject of universal history reduce the universal to a particularized subject of "American" history? Above all, what does it mean to racialize cosmopolitanism as an "American" birthright, the outcome of an organic process of development under uniquely "American" conditions?

The great liberator of South America, Simón Bolívar, was vexed by questions like these—by the alternately exemplary universality and insular particularity of the "America" he knew. Bolívar's "Jamaica Letter" (1815), written from exile at a nadir of the Latin American revolutions, translates the semantic ambiguity inherent in these various formulations of American universality into finely wrought affective ambivalence. On the one hand, Bolívar interprets events in his America as possessing universal moral import: "Generous souls are ever interested in the lot of a people to recover the rights with which the Creator, or nature, has endowed them, and one would have to be in the grip of error or passion to reject such a noble sentiment" (Bolívar 17). But the same features—continental space and a new American race—that afford Paine and Crèvecoeur the confidence to universalize make Bolívar less sanguine about the New World's power to renew humanity. For Bolívar, the specter of American "farmers, shepherds, nomads, lost in the middle of vast, thick forests, solitary plains, often isolated by lakes and torrential rivers" produces an epistemological anxiety that undermines any Enlightenment political meta-narrative: "Who could come up with complete and accurate statistical data for such regions.... Any idea relative to the future of this land seems to me purely speculative" (18). American expanse becomes a topos of hermetic sublimity rather than coextensive globality. Bolívar feels isolated and dwarfed rather than connected and aggrandized by the vastness: "We are a small segment of the human race," rather than its nifty shorthand version.

Bolívar's uncertainty is only deepened by the prospect of a new American race. Often cited as a founding statement of the Latin American cult of *mestizaje*, the "Jamaica Letter," like Crèvecoeur's *Letters*, understands ethnic mixture as a process of negation, a "melting" away of established identities that yields something new and unforeseen, "American." But Bolívar describes this process in decidedly more negative terms as producing painful in-betweenness rather than triumphant aboveness: we are "neither Indians nor Europeans, but a race halfway between the legitimate owners of the land and the Spanish usurpers—in short, being Americans by birth and endowed with rights from Europe—we find ourselves forced to defend these rights against the natives while maintain[ing] our position in the land against the intrusion of the invaders. Thus, we find ourselves in the most extraordinary and complicated situation" (18). American exceptionalism consists in a criollo political and cultural predicament wherein the "American" is indeed a self-sufficient subject, but in the most precarious sense—cut off from authorizing origins on either side, ineffectively legislating ex nihilo. The fruit of colonial interracialism and multiculturalism in Latin America is a historically bounded people ill equipped to morph into the idealized "people" of republican theory. Bolívar's comparative pessimism about "America" presents a useful point of contrast in probing the structuring paradoxes of a common Enlightenment discourse on Americanity.

POSTCOLONIAL AMERICAN CULTURAL NATIONALISMS: TURNING HISTORY INTO A NATURAL RESOURCE

Postcolonial American cultural nationalisms creatively extended Enlightenment environmentalism into the nineteenth century. Noteworthy articulations of American difference—Walter Channing's "Essay on American Language and Literature" (1815) and Argentine statesman Domingo Sarmiento's *Facundo: or, Civilization and Barbarism* (1845)—theorize national distinctiveness as a reflection of natural surroundings. Channing's thesis is that "the remotest germs of literature are the native peculiarities of the country in which it is to spring.... [And] the whole external character of our country [the United States] is totally unlike that of England" (308, 309). Sarmiento concurs: "If any form of national literature shall appear in these new American societies, it must result from the description of the mighty scenes of nature" (Sarmiento 28). And both likewise agree about the defining quality of formative American nature. Echoing Paine, Crèvecoeur, and Bolívar, Sarmiento identifies "immensity" as "the universal characteristic of the country" (9). An Argentine literature is ready-made, for "the disposition and nature of the Argentine people are poetic" as a result of the inherent sublimity of Argentina's soul-stretching vistas: "What impressions must be made upon the inhabitant of the Argentine Republic by the simple act of fixing his eyes upon the horizon, and seeing nothing.... Here is poetry already" (30–31). Channing reverts to the same topos of scale: "How tame will his language sound, who would describe Niagara in language fitted for the falls at London bridge, or attempt the majesty of the Mississippi in that which was made for the Thames?" (309). The particularity of the American scene seems unabashedly to be in the service of a romantic nationalist project. But in this case, natural peculiarity signifies beyond the end of establishing national distinctiveness insofar as the very peculiarity of American nature is located in its *sweeping representativity* (an argument only given fodder by—and perhaps providing fodder for—the spectacular U.S. land grabs of the nineteenth century). Geographical immensity and variety are enlisted to insinuate a greater universality at the very core of American nationality, which makes America more than merely national: America is "every person's country," because "the variety of our soils, situations, climates...and produce hath something which must please everybody" (Crèvecoeur 80). To be "Nature's nation" is to be a cosmopolitan trans-nation. What is particular about the American environment is precisely that it is *not* particular, so huge and topographically compendious as to be more seamlessly evocative of the planetary. What makes America unique is the fact that it is not a quaint place but something like pure space—Sarmiento's Argentine horizon of nothingness, which draws his mind to wander to "the wilds of Asia," "Arab tents," "the life of the Spartans and Romans" in an attempt to describe his native land (15, 20, 22). Dense locality vaporizes into airy translocality.

The point resonates with Paul Giles's recognition that nineteenth-century American cultural nationalists did not necessarily "mark [their] originality" through "mimetic reflection of locality" but rather through "intertextuality, through taking icons and ideas from classical European culture and spinning them round in a new way" (Giles 42). More precisely, the American writer's "mimetic reflection of locality" actually fuels this strategy of intertextuality insofar as infinitely various American nature is understood to afford the American writer much more than national self-understanding—namely, what Emerson called "an original relation to the universe," an opportunity to be not just an American but a "universal man" who surveys space and time, selecting from the smorgasbord of universal history the tastiest tidbits of world culture.[3] Emerson's transcendentalist comrade, Margaret Fuller, crystallizes the connection in her *Things and Thoughts in Europe*: the "thinking American recognize[s] the immense advantage of being born in a new world and on a virgin soil, yet does not wish one seed from the Past to be lost. He is anxious to gather and carry back with him all that will bear a new climate and new culture....He wishes to give them a fair trial in this new world" (Fuller 406–407). Fuller's America is quite literally the ground of the universal. It is a laboratory in which tests can be conducted on bits of world culture to determine their universal value. If they flourish under American conditions, that means they transcend the national. So America is not a nation but a clearinghouse of national cultures out of which emerges a universal one. American postcoloniality assumes a much grander form than mere cultural differentiation from the mother countries; it aims at the transcendence of the narrow notion of a national culture altogether, asserting originality through a "cannibalizing encyclopedism" that converts history into empowering resource rather than constraining source (Bersani 153).

A luminary of the first generation of U.S. cultural nationalists will further illustrate. Over several essays in his *Sketch Book of Geoffrey Crayon, Gent.* (1819–1820),

Washington Irving constructs a natural history of "bookmaking" that cleverly capitalizes on American coloniality—its cultural derivativeness and marginality. "Providence" has wisely "implanted in authors" a "pilfering disposition" that fosters the endless "mutability of literature," English in particular. English never has been and never will be "Spenser's 'well of pure English undefiled,' " but rather is "a mere confluence of various tongues, perpetually subject to changes and intermixtures" from the hollow, flatulent antiquarians Crayon encounters in the British Museum library, the literary greats among whose tombs he walks in Westminster Abbey, and, of course, American aspirants like himself (Irving 80–81, 132–134). This promiscuous proliferation enables the dissemination and (re)discovery of "family jewels" in the textual rough—"the beauties and fine thoughts of ancient and obsolete authors" (136, 81). Irving's analogical point of reference for this comprehensive process is nature, *American* nature specifically. Just as nature has provided "for the conveyance of seeds from clime to clime, in the maws of certain birds," so she has provided that "seeds of knowledge and wisdom shall be preserved from age to age," "caught up by [the] flights of predatory writers and cast forth again to flourish and bear fruit in a remote and distant tract of time," "spring[ing] up under new forms" in their new spatiotemporal locations (81; cf. 133). The particular "nature" upon which Irving's analogy depends is vast, various, and dynamic in precisely the ways that "English scenery"—"associated in the mind with ideas of order, of quiet, or sober, well-established principles, of hoary usage and reverent custom," Irving sums up in another essay—is *not* (70). Instead, any naturalist analogy of the sprawling vicissitudes of a transhistorical and transnational literary history must settle on/in America: "The clearing of our American woodlands; where we burn down a forest of stately pines, a progeny of dwarf oaks start up in their place, and we never see the prostrate trunk of a tree, but it gives birth to a whole tribe of fungi" (81).

Not only is the source of Irving's naturalist metaphor a postcolonial American imperative to decenter (English) literature, the particular source of the metaphor, in the technical sense of cognitive linguistics—"our American woodlands"—enacts a recentering of the very forces of "bookmaking" in the geographically and culturally wide-open spaces of the new American republic. The argument implicit in the metaphor is that the practice of ceaseless cosmopolitan *translation*—both linguistic cross-pollination and spatiotemporal reincarnation—that constitutes the literary as such comes more *naturally* to Americans. "American literature" deserves our attention not so much because it is *American* but because it is somehow more attuned to the universalist ontology of *literature*. The reason English critics don't appreciate American literature is because its themes are simply "too vast and elevated for their capacities," which have been formed of course by the provincial charms of their topographically and socioculturally manicured little island (57). It is not their particular nationalist resentments but an Old World principle of nationality itself that prevents them from comprehending the elementally trans- or supernational character of literature produced in the United States, which, as a "republic...opening...an asylum for strangers from every portion of the earth," is necessarily "destitute of national antipathies" (63). "What have we to do with national prejudices,"

Irving asks, doing his best Crèvecoeur imitation. "They are the inveterate diseases of old countries.... We, on the contrary, have sprung into national existence in an enlightened and philosophic age, when different parts of the habitable world and the various branches of the human family have been indefatigably studied and made known to each other" (63).

But this trope of the American trans-nation betrays itself, and perhaps with Irving's knowing wink. For the fortunate emergence of the United States in an "enlightened and philosophic age" is immediately cast in terms of hereditary nobility associated with the unenlightened political and cultural imperialism of England: "We forego *the advantages of our birth* if we do not shake off the national prejudices as we would the local superstitions of the old world" (63, my italics). Through Irving's chicanery, the upstart republic on the margins—"the infant giant"—is thus destined *by birthright* to supersede England and become global modernity's exemplary aristocracy (59). As the first and best local realization of Enlightenment cosmopolitanism, the American republic is king by a familiar principle of primogeniture that converts fugitive cosmopolitanism into triumphant American nationality. The finishing touch of this reverse cultural imperialism is a sanctimonious expression of cheek-turning liberality: although English writers have greeted American literature with disdain, American writers will demonstrate the moral superiority of their republican transnationalism by continuing to "place England before us as a perpetual volume of reference, wherein are recorded sound deductions from ages of experience... wherewith to strengthen and to embellish our national character" (64). Here the rhetoric of colonial receptivity—of Americans as a "young people, necessarily an imitative one"—is transmuted into a form of postcolonial cultural agency: no longer does England determine which books Americans read and write; rather England itself is now but a book—among many books—from which cosmopolitan America benevolently culls its universal culture.

Two Critiques of the Cosmopolitan-American

Herman Melville and Henry James both bought into such cosmopolitan-Americanism early in their careers but subsequently became two of its most sophisticated critics. Nationalist enthusiasm courses through Melville's early writings, most famously in a passage from *Redburn* (1849): "We are not a nation, so much as a world.... Our ancestry is lost in the Universal paternity; and Caesar and Alfred, St. Paul and Luther, and Homer and Shakespeare are as much ours as Washington.... We are heirs of all time, and with all nations we divide our inheritance. On this Western Hemisphere all tribes and people are forming into one federated whole; and there is a future which shall see the estranged children of Adam restored as to the old hearthstone in Eden" (*Redburn* 239). A generation later, James expressed similar sentiments in an 1867 letter to a compatriot: "We young Americans are (without cant) men of the future.... To be an American is an excellent preparation for culture. We have exquisite qualities as a race, and it seems to me we are ahead of the European races in the fact that more than either of them we can deal freely with forms of civilization other than our own, can pick and choose and assimilate and in short (aesthetically etc.) claim our property wherever we find it" (*Letters* 1:77). At the heart of the nineteenth century in the work of two of America's most trenchant cultural critics one finds the same distinctive mélange of Americanity, globality, cosmopolitanism, and racialism: Americans as the superrace of a global future that will somehow deliver on the promises of Enlightenment universalism by embodying it.

But Melville's *The Confidence-Man* (1857) and James's *The American* (1876) show both men taking a more skeptical view of the localization of the universal in cosmopolitan America. *The Confidence-Man* anticipates contemporary debates regarding the "trade-off" between the empirical and normative dimensions of cosmopolitanism: "To the extent that it seems to float outside or above social life…cosmopolitanism will always be vulnerable to charges like elitism and inefficacy.... But to the extent it is…grounded, becoming the possession of actual social groups, it takes on the less-than-ideal political characteristics of those groups, each of which can of course be seen as less than ideally cosmopolitan in its treatment of others" (Robbins 214). *The Confidence-Man* addresses cosmopolitanism as a *formal* problem—what authentic form, if any, can cosmopolitanism take—and it does so through the problem of its own novelistic form.

From its opening invocation of the "cosmopolitan and confident tide" of the Mississippi, Melville's novel establishes an equation between cosmopolitanism and the con that draws our attention not only to how cosmopolitanism may be the ultimate con but also to how cosmopolitanism itself is an unbalanced equation. For the novel's tipping point is none other than Frank Goodman, the Cosmopolitan. Once he appears on the scene in chapter 24, the serial performativity of the confidence man—seven disguises over the first twenty-three chapters—is transmuted into the performative simultaneity of the Cosmopolitan over the final twenty-two chapters. Purely in terms of the novel's formal arithmetic, the advent of the Cosmopolitan marks an incremental "increase in seriousness" that ushers the reader from episodic enjoyment of dramatic irony as we detect the confidence-man in each of his successive disguises to an apocalyptic eclipse, well suggested by the absence of a twenty-third chapter to make the novel perfectly equilateral—a darker version of *Tristram Shandy*'s black, blank page. The Cosmopolitan Frank Goodman skews the structure of the novel and, in so doing, draws our attention to how cosmopolitanism itself just never adds up.

Through the figure of the Cosmopolitan, Melville enacts a dilemma between a Kantian "empty" cosmopolitanism and a Hegelian "full" one (see Hollinger, "New Cosmopolitans"). On the one hand, Goodman's cosmopolitanism is empty: he climactically urges on the barber a patently Kantian moral position—"the experiment of trusting men" in toto. But this empty cosmopolitanism seems to correspond to the terrifying emptiness of Goodman's character. To the extent he can be called a character, he highlights the extent to which character is a matter of mere characters — words on a page, dramatis personae that constantly shift and blur due to Melville's grammatical and typographical tricks like deliberately removing quotation marks and deictic markers (162–164). Even as the novel seems to settle on and in the guise of the Cosmopolitan, even as the Cosmopolitan would seem to become a center of sorts, the narrative itself becomes more nonlinear—digressing even more wildly and even being entirely overtaken—at least momentarily—by the inset narratives of Colonel Moredock, the Indian-hater, and China Aster. We can read the characterological emptiness of the Cosmopolitan as a commentary on the impossibility of sustaining an entirely uncompromised, uncompromising—an empty—cosmopolitanism, of locating an integrity in the confidence-man's duplicity. Melville's Cosmopolitan is either mere assemblage without depth—the pure splendorous surface of his crazily stitched costume of "Highland plaid, Emir's robe, French blouse," etc. (136)—or a profound principle of apocalyptic negation (225, 233). In either case, he is empty. It seems one can be a "liberalist" only "in dress" or as demigod (136).

On the other hand, the Kantian moral position that Goodman urges on the barber, we should not forget, is circumscribed within an unfair bet, drawn up in snaky legalese, from which the Cosmopolitan stands to profit. Universalism is blatantly compromised by its interested articulation. Hence, the novel is also attuned to the liabilities of a "full" cosmopolitanism—the extent to which cosmopolitanism "is a discourse of the universal that is inherently local—a locality that is always surreptitiously imperial," as Timothy Brennan has put it (81). Even more so than Brennan and his cohort, Melville seems to appreciate that the problem of cosmopolitanism's locality is a problem of language—not only of enunciation, of the sitedness of the spoken—but of language itself, of something like Derridean *differánce*. Time and again in the novel, one traces universalism's descent in and through language. "Philanthropy"—in its original Greek root, abstract love of man—is colloquialized aboard the Mississippi steamer to mean any cranky humanitarian project, and then finally subliminalized as an especially effective form of capitalist enterprise—"the charity business" (47–48, 230). Along similar lines, "charity" lexically devolves from a Christian theological virtue into a hermeneutical practice suspiciously described in the terms of finance capital: to be charitable is to take things on "credit" (127). Cosmopolitanism is fundamentally a problem of representation—*linguistic* before *political*.

More than a "comedy of thought...[or] action" *The Confidence-Man* is, in its very form, a self-deconstructing tragicomedy of language that demonstrates how the synthetic rhetoric of a "full" cosmopolitanism is subsumed by the very particulars it attempts to subsume. Beginning with the initial comparison of "the man in cream-colors" to Manco Capac, the mythological founder of the Incan empire, *The Confidence-Man* follows "a pattern in which Melville superimposes geography and theology from other times and places onto the United States of the 1850s" (9 n. 2). This heavy-handed cosmopolitanism of reference unravels in striking ways. Take the Whitmanian catalogue with which Melville completes his initial description of the globally diverse "pilgrims" aboard his American ship of fools. "Natives of all sorts, and foreigners," from "English, German, Scotch, Danes" to "slaves, black, mulatto, quadroon; modish young Spanish Creoles, and old-fashioned French Jews," are breathlessly enumerated (16). American continentality and cosmopolitanism are yet again linked: the eclectic cultural landscape mirrors the "American wood-lands," which "interweave [the foliage]" of "pine, beech, birch, ash, hackmatack, hemlock," as well as "the Mississippi itself... uniting the streams of the most distant and opposite zones... in one cosmopolitan and confident tide" (17). But just when we think we're on familiar ground, Melville slyly settles this "dashing and all-fusing spirit of the West" under the sign of quaint ethnicity: the global tableau partakes of a "Tartar-like picturesqueness," he writes (17). The jarring effect (one cosmopolitan allusion too many?) makes the reader aware of the extent to which the catalogue as cosmopolitan device is bound by a synecdochal logic in which the final particu-lar of the catalogue may awkwardly stand in for the universalistic whole the trope is meant to evoke. Suddenly, the arbitrariness of the entire edifice is thrown into relief: how can the globe possibly be compressed into the United States and then further compressed into the Western frontier of the United States and still further compressed into a single Mississippi steamer? Language itself has been called into question—"the doctrine of analogies" that underwrites metaphor, allegory, and so many communicative modes is exposed in the novel as nothing more than a tau-tological means of "corroborat[ing]...cherished suspicions" (135). Sure, America is the world if your world is America.

The representational conundrum of cosmopolitanism thus comes to the fore, underscored by Melville's other esoteric reference in his opening catalogue to Anacharsis Cloots, the Prussian-born Parisian and self-appointed ambassador of the human race who brought a multiracial and multinational delegation before the French National Assembly in 1790 to agitate for universal human rights. In describ-ing his American shipload as an "Anacharsis Cloots congress of all kinds of that multiform pilgrim species, man," Melville draws attention to the dense historic-ity of cosmopolitanism, to the fact that it is a recent "age-of-revolution legacy," as Lawrence Buell has observed (Buell 142–146). In a profound sense, the allusion sug-gests, cosmopolitanism itself never was or is cosmopolitan—it is rather the idiosyn-cratic idiom of crackpots with silly names caught up in intensely localized struggles for national autonomy. Historically speaking, it has been of a piece with American and French national cults. Melville's bewildering satire thus leaves us with a sense of cosmopolitanism as intrinsically a con—a too-good-to-be-true ideal that can only tragicomically hypostatize the universal into the gross particulars of a fallen world.

Henry James's The American, centering on Christopher Newman's betrayal by the French aristocratic family of his fiancée, Madame de Cintré, is also a novel inter-ested in the confluence of cosmopolitanism and confidence. On multiple levels, The American severely qualifies James's youthful statement regarding Americanism as an "excellent preparation for culture." This is not to say that James paints his pro-totypical American protagonist as a hopelessly insular provincial; rather, the labor of the novel is to delineate a particular style of American cosmopolitanism and consider its limits. The novel is conscious of a tradition of routing cosmopolitanism through Americanism on the basis of the United States' sociopolitical codification of certain Enlightenment values. When Valentin de Bellegarde characterizes Newman in patently cosmopolitan terms as possessing "an air…of being thoroughly at home in the world," Newman attributes it to "the privilege of being an American citizen…That sets a man up" (95). James further ventures into familiar territory when he has Bellegarde chalk up the fact that the American has "fewer prejudices even than I" to Newman having "revolved to and fro over a whole continent as I walk up and down the Boulevard. You are a man of the world with a vengeance" (97). James not only particularizes but literalizes the trope of the "man of the world": the American is more cosmopolitan by virtue of having logged more planetary miles. So what exactly is the nature of this cosmopolitanism that accompanies "the great Western Barbarian's" "democratic instincts"? the novel asks (42, 52; see also 38, 152).

Two primary qualities of American cosmopolitanism emerge: its indiscriminate voracity and its acquisitive rather than inquisitive character. From the opening scene in the Louvre in which he proves himself unable to and uninterested in distinguishing original from copy, Newman is presented as someone with an insatiable "appetite for facts" rather than a discerning taste for culture: "Everything interests me," he declaims, and so he must rely on travel guides and tourist gossip to organize his sightseeing time, to provide him with a to-do list whose items he proudly checks off (66, 124, 17, 18, 75). It is no mistake that Newman is "fond of statistics," for it is precisely in the calibration of facticity that his cosmopolitanism consists (55).

Newman's calculating cosmopolitanism in relation to things, places, and people is a kind of consumerism, a worldliness purchased by purchasing the world around him. "The world, to his sense, was a great bazaar, where one might stroll about and purchase handsome things," and so with the "mania of the 'collector' " Newman sets out to "get the best out of [Europe] I can": "the biggest kind of entertainment…the tallest mountains, and the bluest lakes, and the finest pictures, and the handsomest churches, and the most celebrated men, and the most beautiful women" (66, 26, 33, 35). The desire of Newman's cosmopolitanism is to *have*—and relish the mere presence of—lots of things, rather than to *know* anything in depth: perfect self- and mutual understanding are not prerequisites for his friendship or love, a quality, it should be said, that is not treated unsympathetically in the novel (71).

Above all, as the last term in the above sequence suggests, Newman is interested in acquiring a wife who is "the best article on the market," and it is in his failed courtship with Madame de Cintré that James most clearly shows us the limits of his American cosmopolitanism (44). What we might call Newman's purely *affective* cosmopolitanism eventually leads to his downfall with the Bellegardes. Not only does his cosmopolitanism not need to know, it doesn't *want* to know, especially about particular things. In a particularly revealing moment, Newman tells the young Marquis de Bellegarde, his fiancée's oldest brother and head of the household, "I don't understand you at all.…But you needn't mind that. I don't care. In fact, I think I had better not understand you. I might not like it. That wouldn't suit me at all, you know. I want to marry your sister, that's all" (143). Here Newman's "natural and organic" "sense of human equality" is exposed as less than universal. His egalitarian sympathy is politically circumscribed, not straightforwardly by nationalism but by a cosmopolitanism historically particular to the Atlantic Age of Revolution that is closely identified with Americanism: it cannot extend to an anachronistic aristocrat of the ancien régime, a man whose "single political conviction" is "the divine right of Henry of Bourbon, Fifth of his name, to the throne of France" (152–153). Newman's implicitly (post)colonial cosmopolitanism clashes with Bellegarde's monarchist metropolitanism and so marks the peculiarly modern scope of his universalist sentiments.

Newman's inability or unwillingness to understand the Bellegardes even as he feels his way toward great affection for both Madame de Cintré and Valentin eventually entraps the American (as well as *The American*) in a story not of his own making. As in the case of *The Confidence-Man*, metafictionality becomes a measure of a critique so profound as to become reflexive. From the time of its publication, critics, including James himself, have lamented the extravagant contrivances of the last two-thirds of the novel, which include Valentin's purposeless duel to a pathetic death, Madame de Cintré being spirited off to a nunnery, the uncovering of the Marquise de Bellegarde's murder of her husband, and a secret document attesting to the crime. But might not the collapse of this novel about an exemplary New World man into a clichéd Old World romance be interpreted not (only) as artistic immaturity but also as a metafictional symptom of the unwitting recolonization of a confident, know-nothing American cosmopolitanism by Europe? To the extent cosmopolitanism is identified in the novel as a recent postcolonial American formation shot through with Enlightenment optimism, does its fragile historicity render it vulnerable to the much-longer-lived metropolitanism of the French time warp Newman enters?

The novel simply goes too far in its metafictional goofiness not to consider such a reading. One could summarize the moral of *The American* thusly: because Newman has "never read a novel," he is subjected to living through the bad "novel" that is the last two-thirds of the novel, *The American* (38). From the moment Newman enters the Bellegarde vortex, James compulsively characterizes the action as seeming weirdly like a novelistic or dramatic romance: "It is like something in a play," Newman says upon first hearing of Madame de Cintré's predicament, and when he meets her, sure enough, it is as though "he had opened a book and the first lines held his attention," a topos that becomes tiresome by novel's end not only to the reader but seemingly to Madame de Cintré herself, who recognizes that Newman apprehends her as an operatic character like Donna Elvira: "I am not a heroine," she warns him (80, 82, 200, 138; see also 98, 99, 102). Everyone in this premodern world seems to walk out of a romance: the Marquis de Bellegarde's mustache is like "a page in a romance" (90); the chatter of the marquis and novel-addicted "comical old duchess," "a bit of amusing dialogue in a play" (288–289, 190); Valentin's duel a "wretched theatrical affair," attended by a doctor who gives Newman "an old copy of 'Les Liaisons Dangereuses'" to keep him wakeful at his friend's dying side (211, 227).

Once the Bellegardes make their play to stonewall the marriage, Newman alternately finds himself "playing a part, mechanically, in a lugubrious comedy" and living "a page torn out of a romance" (231, 246). The narrative voice even has to bring him down to earth occasionally, as when it parenthetically interjects that the plaintive scene of Newman hearing Madame de Cintré chanting behind the convent wall is likely fiction "inasmuch as she had obviously not yet had time to become a member of the invisible sisterhood" (276–277). When the Bellegardes' English servant, Mrs. Bread, gives Newman the dirt on the Bellegardes, her "decent narrative" of secret murder, full of dramatic pauses fit for "the most artistic of romancers," plunges him and us back into "the page of a novel" within the novel (259, 262).

And so Newman momentarily becomes "a man with a plot in his head," as Mrs. Tristram observes: will he bring this romance to its glittering, gory end, black-mailing the Bellegardes and regaining from them the right to marry Madame de Cintré perhaps only to find that she has killed herself out of despair in the convent before the news has been conveyed or some other such grand climax? (307). No, Newman—and James—resolve to "close the book" on this romance and relent from pursuit (306). But James does not allow this abandonment of the Old World romance that has usurped the novel to stand for the New World's moral and literary ascendancy and autonomy (243). Instead, the uncanny Mrs. Tristram suggests, this American anticlimax—Newman's and the novel's final eschewal of the Old World literary plot—may have actually played into the plot of the Bellegardes, who all along had "confidence" that "[Newman's] remarkable good nature"—clearly a coyly encoded allusion to his Americanness, his "democratic confidingness"—would prevent him from insisting on the marriage (309, 25). This would-be moment of proud Americanism collapses into a moral critique of Newman's "loose," American-style cosmopolitanism, "unstiffened" by any content, which leaves him ever (a) Newman, the American, the selfsame despite his excursion into otherness (243, 70). The American's cosmopolitanism is caught in a loop that merely feeds back into his nationalized ego. A poor cosmopolitanism, to be sure.

Epilogue: "The Cosmic Race" and Other Americanizations of Universal History

Melville and James exposed the false cosmopolitanism of American culture and so steadfastly subordinated Americanity in relation to globality and universality, disabling any metonymic reflex. But cosmopolitan-Americanism found a new lease on life in the late nineteenth and early twentieth centuries. National, hemispheric, and global crises—the U.S. Civil War, Emancipation, the Spanish American War, World War I—occasioned ideological recommitments that attempted to (re)solidify various American exceptionalisms that often competed with and opposed one another. Given the rising stakes of U.S. imperialism for both its proponents and opponents, it is perhaps no surprise that one encounters in this period a new set of national and subnational cosmopolitanisms across the Americas that sought to establish themselves on the seeming bedrock of *race*.

Walt Whitman's nation-healing incantation, *Democratic Vistas* (1871), is a case in point. Its premise is the insufficiency of liberal contractualism to ground the nation. Political democracy—"popular superficial suffrage," as he dismissively calls it—is just too damn democratic: it has no telos and so permits disasters like civil war (932). Beneath—if not before—thin political liberalism one needs the thick cultural communitarianism of "feudalism, castes, and ecclesiastic institutions," and literature, of course, with its "irresistible power" (959, 957, 960). In a word, one needs the historically programmed automatisms, the motivating mysteries not of nationality, as Whitman might have said before, but of *race*. Whitman attempts to provide a literally more *compelling* account of democracy by transmuting civic into ethnic nationalism, by "convert[ing]" the political ideal of "democracy" into a racial teleology of "America" (954). The past, present, and future of democracy are thus contained in the story of America's ongoing messianic racial formation. Only with the emergence of what Whitman calls "the democratic ethnology of the future"— will his longed-for "imperial republican forms" emerge to benevolently "dominate the world," making the United States "the empire of empires" (987–988, 983, 954, 1014–1015).

This bastardized version of universal republicanism is predicated on a eugenic scheme whereby two vaguely adumbrated high castes—"new races of Teachers," presumably male, and "strong and sweet Female Race, a race of perfect Mothers"— are bred to "endow the birth-stock of a New World," eventually yielding "a copious race of superb American men and women," each of which is a perfect democratic "personality" (954, 964, 985). Whitman gives us a science fiction of a biologically and socially engineered master race of "sweet democratic despots" (998). Given his rather weak and vague rhetoric of inclusivism the American race draws on "the grand, common stock" of both North and South (clearly national reunion rather than multiracial democracy is the imperative)—Whitman's assertion that "parentage must consider itself in advance" sounds like a racist recipe for reproducing only "the best blood" (970, 987). *Democratic Vistas'* unabashed racialization of Enlightenment cosmopolitanism is ground zero of xenophobic U.S. imperialism.

By the same token, the essays written in the 1890s by one of Whitman's many Latin American admirers, Cuban activist-writer José Martí, are ground zero of an anti–U.S. imperialism out of which was born Latin American cosmopolitanisms. The cult of *mestizaje* from which Latin American exceptionalist claims to representative globality have typically been made largely originated in defiant self-distinction from the racist U.S. imperium. One sees this dialectic clearly in Martí's work, which time and again draws a fundamental contrast between the meaning and function of racial difference between the two Americas: "our America...must save herself through her Indians...and is going from less to more...North America...drowns its own Indians in blood and is going from more to less" (Martí 289). The source of Latin American ascendancy is its potential, based on what is perceived as a greater

degree of interracial contact, to embody Enlightenment universalism more perfectly. But, unlike Whitman, who lets his cultural-nationalist ideal of "adhesive-
ness" collapse into racial identity, Martí maintains that "an affinity of character is
more powerful than an affinity of color" (320). The cultural nation must remain the
primary category—people only "see their patria in the color of their skin or abjure
the land where they were born" if their patria affords them no "roots and a pillow
to sleep in," as is the case for African Americans in the United States (311–312). By
contrast, "in Cuba there is no fear whatsoever of a race war. 'Man' means more than
white, more than mulatto, more than Negro. 'Cuban' means more than white, more
than mulatto, more than Negro" (319).

So *Cubanidad*—as an avatar of multicultural and multiracial nationality—becomes the true measure of the cosmopolitan. Martí's cunning conflation of "Man"
with "Cuban" reroutes universal history through "our America," through those who,
"in heroic stages, are climbing the road that republics travel," rather than through
the decadent empire of North America. Performing the same gesture as Irving at the
end of "English Writers on America," Martí urges his compatriots at the end of "Our
America" to demonstrate their more authentic cosmopolitanism by refusing "out of a
villager's antipathy, [to] impute some lethal congenital wickedness to the continent's
light-skinned nation," even though, of course, the neocolonial United States "does
not think highly of quick-tempered, swarthy men" (296). Martí's strident antiracism
wins for his side the exceptionalist contest between the two Americas. However, it
must be emphasized it is an antiracism founded on the givenness of Latin American
mestizaje—cosmopolitan nationality presupposes a racial intermixture so profound
as to submerge race as a primary marker of identity. Hence, Martí's assertions arguably all come back to a sense of Latin America having produced a more bona fide
American race than the United States.

Some U.S. African American intellectuals similarly experimented with relocat-
ing cosmopolitanism at the sub/transnational level of African America. In his preface to *The Book of American Negro Poetry* (1922), James Weldon Johnson establishes
a tight circuit between the African American, the American, and the universal:
Negro literature and art, he argues, are the only "distinctive American products" that
have achieved "universal appeal" (Johnson vii). Johnson thus establishes African
American culture as the litmus test for the United States' metonymic globality. If the
United States wants to think itself the cosmopolis, then it will have to acknowledge
forms like ragtime as the quintessential expression of "our national spirit" (xv). The
price of fulfilling the national globalist fantasy is fully nationalizing the Negro. But
Johnson, not content with mere national recognition, assumes the globalist fantasy
for his race: "This power of the Negro to suck up the national spirit from the soil
and create something artistic and original, which, at the same time, possesses the
note of universal appeal, is due to a remarkable racial gift of adaptability; it is more
than adaptability, it is a transfusive quality. And the Negro has exercised this transfusive quality not only here in America, where the race lives in large numbers, but
in European countries, where the number has been almost infinitesimal" (xix). It is
a brilliant turn—the cosmopolitan inheres not in exceptional American conditions

but in the "creative genius of the Negro" wherever he finds himself. The diasporic African has something like a knack for universality, Hegel be damned.

The American racialization of the cosmopolitan reached its apotheosis in the work of two mystics from Latin and African America, Mexican philosopher José Vasconcelos and erstwhile African American avant-gardist, Jean Toomer. Vasconcelos's *The Cosmic Race* (1925) wrests universal history from the other America on the basis of Latin America's colonial history of *mestizaje*. In Vasconcelos's eschatological scheme, the age-defining "conflict of Latinism against Anglo-Saxonism" has until now seemed tilted in the latter's favor—"It seems as if God Himself guided the steps of the Anglo-Saxon cause, while we kill each other on account of dogma or call each other atheists"—but God is now poised to subordinate Anglo-America for "the sin of destroying those races" that Latin America "assimilated" (10, 17). In a now familiar move, Vasconcelos figures the cosmopolitan ideal as a millennial "mixing of all peoples" but one prophetically anticipated by Latin rather than Anglo-American "tradition," which exhibits "greater facility of sympathy towards strangers.... Our civilization, with all its defects, may be the chosen one to assimilate and to transform mankind into a new type; that within our civilization, the warp, the multiple and rich plasma of future humanity is thus being prepared" (9, 16–17). Latin American cosmopolitanism in the colonial past paves the way for a glorious Latin American global imperium in the future: because they have assimilated the most races, all races, including Anglo-Americans, will now be assimilated to them. The great "Universopolis will rise by the [Amazon] river" (25). The way for one America to get a leg up on the other—and everyone else—is always to declare itself more cosmopolitan, to consecrate *its* "American soil" as the gathering place, the end of "dispersion" (18). On the one hand, in the context of inter-American cultural politics, Vasconcelos's transmutation of a disparaging discourse of Latin American "mongrelization" into an oppositional cultural nationalism must be appreciated for its bravery and creativity. On the other hand, like any other variant of cosmopolitan-Americanism, it is bound to embarrass itself as a provincialism at the core. In Vasconcelos's case, this takes the forms of aesthetic racism—blacks "may" disappear in his "Fifth Age" due to the fact that its regnant "free instinct of beauty" may not select for them—and Christian triumphalism—because Christianity "contains universal, not national revelation," it will of course be "one of the fundamental dogmas of the fifth race" (35). It becomes hard to distinguish Vasconcelos's vision of a cosmic race from the oldest dreams of the Spanish Franciscans and Jesuits who saw in the New World a chance to realize a genuinely universal Catholic Church.

In his personal communications and writings of the 1930s, Jean Toomer took the idea of a new American race in less conventional directions. An African American who could pass for white and who had high literary ambitions, Toomer was eager for personal and professional reasons to identify himself as "simply an American" (106). But by "American" Toomer meant something infinitely greater than a national or even racial identity. He begins with a strong sense of a fundamentally mixed "American race" of which he is an exemplar, and he associates this race, à la Vasconcelos, with "the birth of a new order, a new vision, a new ideal of man" (105). This American race, he emphasizes, "is itself, a third thing, a different and unique substance with unique attributes" that cannot be reduced to the sum of its parts—the American represents the supersession of "the old divisions into white, black, brown, red" (109, 105). But, in the end, Toomer's point seems to be that the universality and profundity of race mixture effectively means "there is only one pure race—and this is the *human* race. We all belong to it—and this is the most and the least that can be said of any of us with accuracy" (109). Interracial mixture at any given time yields not a special fifth race but merely "other members of the human race" (110)

So whence the new American race?

> The real and main difference between this new American group and previous groups will be found, necessarily not in blood, but in *consciousness*....In America we have a new body. And, having recognized this, let [us] forget it...Let us be born above the body. The important thing is consciousness. Here, in this country, among the people I refer to, the human essence, *humanness*, is again to be realized and emphasized....We are waking up, we are nonidentifying from surfaces and from the preferences and prejudices associated with them, and we are realizing our basic human stock, our human essence, our humanness, our fundamental and universal humanity. Those who have or who are approaching this [sensing?], this realization—these are the ones I mean when I say Americans. These Americans are not of America only; they are of the earth. And, with various [titles?] in various countries they of course exist in other national groups. These are the [natural?] conscious internationalists. (110)

No longer is the American inherently—racially or otherwise—cosmopolitan; rather, the cosmopolitan is nominally "American." "American" signifies not the U.S. national but the "conscious internationalist" anywhere. Well, sort of. The slipperiness of cosmopolitan-Americanism is nowhere more evident than in the blockages, qualifications, and hedges of Toomer's rhetoric. Toomer allows America's globalist fantasy to quietly die when he finds himself forced to concede that there might be "[titles?]" other than "American" under which the cosmopolitan might travel, other "national groups" from which "conscious internationalists" might spring. Cosmopolitanism's condition of possibility might just be cosmopolitan, not primally, purely, or chiefly American. "Transnational American studies" would do well to learn from this language lesson and ask itself how its own cosmopolitan visions have been shaped by this long tradition, from Paine to Toomer.

NOTES

1 For "Atlantic/world" as a concept meant to emphasize the opening of the Atlantic to the global, see Coclanis.
2 The "cradle" metaphor is Cloots's, qtd. in Kristeva 211 n. 65: "France was the cradle and rallying point of the god-people."

3 "Nature," "History," and "The American Scholar" are the key texts here. See Emerson 7, 67, 237, 250.

BIBLIOGRAPHY

Bersani, Leo. "Incomparable America." *The Culture of Redemption.* Cambridge, MA: Harvard University Press, 1990.

Bolívar, Simón. *El Libertador: Writings of Simón Bolívar.* Ed. David Bushnell. Trans. Fred Fornoff. New York: Oxford University Press, 2003.

Brennan, Timothy. "Cosmopolitanism and Internationalism." *New Left Review* NS 11 (September/October 2001): 75–84.

Brickhouse, Anna. "Scholarship and the State: Robert Greenhow and Transnational American Studies 1848/2008." *American Literary History* 20.4 (Winter 2008): 695–722.

Buell, Lawrence. "The Unkillable Dream of the Great American Novel: *Moby-Dick* as Test Case." *American Literary History* 20.1–2 (2008): 132–155.

Channing, Walter. "Essay on American Literature and Language." *North American Review* 1.3 (September 1815): 307–314.

Coclanis, Peter A. "Atlantic World or Atlantic/World." *William and Mary Quarterly* 53.4 (October 2006): 725–742.

Crèvecoeur, J. Hector St. John de. *Letters from an American Farmer and Sketches of Eighteenth-Century America.* 1782. New York: Penguin, 1986.

Dimock, Wai Chee. *Through Other Continents: American Literature across Deep Time.* Princeton, NJ: Princeton University Press, 2006.

Emerson, Ralph Waldo. *Essays and Lectures.* New York: Library of America, 1996.

Fishkin, Shelley Fisher. "Crossroads of Cultures: The Transnational Turn in American Studies: Presidential Address to the American Studies Association, November 12, 2004." *American Quarterly* 57.1 (March 2005): 17–57.

Fluck, Winfried. "Inside and Outside: What Kind of Knowledge Do We Need? A Response to the Presidential Address." *American Quarterly* 59.1 (March 2007): 23–32.

Fuller, Margaret. *The Essential Margaret Fuller.* Ed. Jeffrey Steele. New Brunswick, NJ: Rutgers University Press, 1992.

Giles, Paul. "The Deterritorialization of American Literature." *Shades of the Planet: American Literature as World Literature.* Ed. Wai Chee Dimock and Lawrence Buell. Princeton, NJ: Princeton University Press, 2007.

Hollinger, David A. "Not Pluralists, Not Universalists, the New Cosmopolitans Find Their Own Way." *Constellations* (June 2001): 236–248.

———. *Postethnic America: Beyond Multiculturalism.* New York: Basic Books, 2000.

Irving, Washington. *The Legend of Sleepy Hollow and Other Stories in the Sketch Book.* 1819–1820. New York: Signet, 1961.

James, Henry. *The American.* 1876. Ed. James W. Tuttleton. New York: Norton Critical Editions, 1978.

———. *Henry James: Letters.* 4 vols. Ed. Leon Edel. Cambridge, MA: Belknap Press of Harvard University Press, 1974–1984.

Johnson, James Weldon. *The Book of American Negro Poetry: Chosen and Edited with an Essay on the Negro's Creative Genius.* New York: Harcourt Brace Jovanovich, 1922.

Kristeva, Julia. *Strangers to Ourselves.* Trans. Leon S. Roudiez. New York: Columbia University Press, 1991.

Locke, John. *Second Treatise of Government*. 1690. Ed. C. B. MacPherson. Indianapolis: Hackett, 1980.

Lott, Eric. *The Disappearing Liberal Intellectual*. New York: Basic Books, 2006.

Martí, José. *Selected Writings*. Ed. and trans. Esther Allen. New York: Penguin, 2002.

Melville, Herman. *The Confidence-Man: His Masquerade*. 1857. Ed. Hershel Parker and Mark Niemeyer. New York: Norton Critical Editions, 2006.

———. *Redburn*. 1849. New York: Penguin, 1976.

Paine, Thomas. *Common Sense*. 1776. New York: Penguin, 2005.

———. *The Rights of Man*. 1791–1792. New York: Penguin, 1984.

Pease, Donald. "From American Literary Studies to Planetary Literature: The Emergence of Literary Extraterritoriality." *REAL: Yearbook of Research in English and American Literature* 23 (2007): 9–36.

———. "Re-thinking 'American Studies' after US Exceptionalism." *American Literary History* 21.1 (March 2009): 19–27.

Quijano, Aníbal, and Immanuel Wallerstein. "Americanity as a Concept, or the Americas in the Modern World-System." *International Social Sciences Journal* 134 (1992): 549–557.

Robbins, Bruce. "Cosmopolitanism, America, and the Welfare State." *REAL: Yearbook of Research in English and American Literature* 19 (2003): 201–224.

Sarmiento, Domingo F. *Facundo: or, Civilization and Barbarism*. 1845. Trans. Mary Peabody Mann. 1868. New York: Penguin, 1998.

Toomer, Jean. *A Jean Toomer Reader: Selected Unpublished Writings*. Ed. Frederik L. Rusch. New York: Oxford University Press, 1993.

Vasconcelos, José. *The Cosmic Race/La raza cósmica: A Bilingual Edition*. Trans. Didier T. Jaén. Baltimore: Johns Hopkins University Press, 1997.

Whitman, Walt. *Poetry and Prose*. New York: Library of America, 1982.

PART III

IMPACTS

CHAPTER 16

HOW TO READ: REGIONALISM AND THE *LADIES' HOME JOURNAL*

TRAVIS M. FOSTER

THIS chapter reads the regionalist sketch by reading the *Ladies' Home Journal* (hereafter, the *Journal*). It examines the *Journal's* commentary on literature and literary culture during a period corresponding to regionalism's prominence, from the periodical's founding in 1883 through the turn of the century. It looks at reviews, recommendation lists, bits of advice, editorial comments, and informal criticism in order to renarrate the literary history of the regionalist sketch. It wagers, ultimately, that archives documenting reading and reception have as much to tell us about literature as do literary texts themselves. Exemplary in this regard, the *Journal* provided its subscribers with a carefully nuanced set of lessons in how to read literature, instructing them to turn engagement with fiction into a practice that would improve their social lives and interpersonal intimacies. As an archive, the *Journal* thus allows us not only to access contemporary critical response, but also to understand the reading of regionalism as a practice within the history and politics of friendship.

Largely ignored by literary critics, the *Ladies' Home Journal*—née the *Ladies' Home Journal and Practical Housekeeper*—shaped late nineteenth-century mass culture and became the world's first periodical to surpass a million in paid subscribers.[1] Inaugurating a genre of women's advice magazines, the *Journal* played a foundational role in the intimate public sphere Lauren Berlant has labeled "women's culture." It provided "a porous, affective scene of identification among strangers" and promised its subscribers "a better experience of social belonging" (viii). It taught readers how to fashion and recognize themselves as white American women, and it cathected that subject position with meaning and social cohesiveness. Proclaimed by its title as a group possession, the *Ladies' Home Journal* thus nurtured subscribers' "attachment to being generic, to being a member of a population that has been marked out as having collective qualities" (x). Magazines like the *Journal* encouraged subscribers to read themselves into the print and visual signifiers of women's culture; within their mediated mode of attachment, individual existence and social convention circled one another with centripetal force. But the *Journal* also did something more. Distinguishing literary from nonliterary reading, it instructed subscribers how to develop specialized skills for reading and evaluating literature and, moreover, how to apply those skills not only when engaging texts but also when engaging each other.

From the 1880s through the early twentieth century, the *Journal* explicitly and extensively advocated literature as an alternative to even its own fantasies of generic belonging. Alongside advice about caring for ferns over the winter, keeping infants content during hot summer months, instilling morality in teenage boys, and re-creating the latest dress fashions, the *Journal* provided specific recommendations about what to read, why to read, and how to read. More specifically, the *Journal* advised women that reading imaginative literature, particularly regionalist literature, would provide them and their children with the best possible apprenticeship for navigating the improvisations, experimentations, emotional sensitivities, and interpersonal contingencies of those rare relationships that rise to the name "friendship." The *Journal* thus engaged two tasks central to the discipline of "literary studies": the broad work of generic differentiation (separating the literary from the nonliterary, elaborating and specifying groups of aesthetic conventions, and assigning value) and the development of reading into a specialized skill (call it "critical reading" or "close reading") with a use value that extends far beyond immediate engagement with the printed page. Yet if today's English departments advertise these skills as quasi-utilitarian tools for critically engaging text-driven culture, the *Ladies' Home Journal* of the late 1800s associated them more narrowly with readers' ability to forge nongeneric modes of intimacy and interpersonal connection. Reading, subscribers were told, teaches us to construct accomplished and meaningful social lives. As a mass media genre that engaged both women's culture and literary culture, the *Journal* invited readers to navigate two parallel dialogues: between general reading and close reading, on the one hand, and generic social belonging and intimate friendship, on the other.

Already, I hope, this brief outline suggests a departure from prevalent literary historical narratives about the regionalist sketch, which associate the genre almost exclusively with a metro-centric literary elite. Looking to the regions from locations of urban prestige and condescension, we are told, readers in the 1880s and '90s turned regionalism into a vehicle for cultural homogenization and an auxiliary of the nation-state. This chapter's first task, then, is to suggest how the history of reading regionalism alters these scripts. If reading practices constitute the scene of impact through which literature transitions from text to meaning, then how we think men and women read regionalist sketches in the past changes not only how we might read and interpret the genre today, but also what kind of social, political, and aesthetic functions we assign to its history. A second section begins such reevaluation by tracing the *Ladies' Home Journal's* reading pedagogy. Over two decades, the *Journal* articulated a program for what I call "closer reading," a literary practice coupling specialized reading skills with the supple work of friendship, and it presented this program as a marked improvement over reading practices advocated by elite publications such as the *Atlantic Monthly*. Applying this evidence to the regionalist sketch, the next section argues that regionalism aligned itself generically and formally with the *Journal's* reading program, modeling both the substantive intimacies and meticulous attentions prescribed by closer reading practices. No reading practice is inherent to a particular genre or text, but the evidence of regionalism's generic and formal conventions dramatizes the strategies by which it facilitated and rewarded closer reading practices. A final section examines the historical and methodological implications of this approach to literary history, which merges the history of reading and genre criticism in order to make a new case about regionalism's socio-symbolic influence. Might the *Journal's* regionalism comprise a genre distinct from that we find in journals such as the *Atlantic Monthly*? If so, then how can we begin to account for the substantive effects of this distinction?

THE HISTORY OF READING REGIONALISM

Toward the end of his 1871 *Democratic Vistas*, Walt Whitman poses the reader as a problem for literary historiography. If, as he claims, "[n]ot the book needs so much to be the complete thing, but the reader of the book does," and if it is therefore the reader who "must himself or herself construct indeed the poem, argument, history," then how do literary historians, looking back across the decades, account for something so ephemeral as the productions and experiences of readers? (1017, 1016). Since New Criticism, scholars, including reader-response critics, have responded to this question by privileging meaning over function. We treat reading as an abstract process governed by immersion in textuality while simultaneously turning our own immersions in the text into a disciplinary sine qua non. We pay more attention to what we read than how we read or why we read—or to how and why texts have been read in the past. Analyzing how texts manifest what New Critic Cleanth Brooks calls "claims to be made upon the reader," critics delimit reading to how readers respond to textual features (154). The result is the remarkable durability of New Critical methods into the twenty-first century. As Thomas Augst puts it, even as we have rejected New Critics' esteem for the autonomy of the literary text, we "have nevertheless accomplished an analogous alienation of reading from the spaces and practices of everyday life" (3). In analyzing the *Journal's* preferred reading formation, this chapter aims to re-embed the reading of regionalism into white women's socio-literary culture in the late nineteenth-century United States. It reads the genre through those institutions and strategies that integrate literary texts into social practices and readers into collective patterns.

An ideal archive for this kind of literary history, the *Ladies' Home Journal* documents a set of values underlying reading for an entire generation of white, middle-class women. While the *Journal* fails to tell us how individual women read regionalist fiction (a failure it shares, to varying degrees, with all archives of reading), it succeeds in organizing a theoretically consistent program of reading that aspired toward—and perhaps even attained—normative status. In so doing, the *Journal* intervenes in the questions that have dominated regionalist fiction's critical history since its feminist revival during the 1970s: questions about how the genre negotiates between the subnational settings and unhurried temporalities of its rural subjects and the transnational fury of U.S. imperialism.

Attention to reading shifts the ground upon which critical histories are built and alters the assumptions we implicitly make about how literary texts act upon their worlds. To align a historical genre with a new history of reading is to invest it with new narratives, new social possibilities, new meanings. Within regionalism's critical history, the monolithic shadow of one single reader—William Dean Howells—has privileged a series of compelling yet also singular interpretations depicting the genre's political effects as reactionary and nationalist. Howells famously advocates for regionalist fiction not because it acquaints readers with rural existence or refines readers' skills of interpersonal relation, but because the genre reaffirms and archives ethnographic knowledge through the reliable depiction of rural types. Yet Howells's admiration of Mary Wilkins Freeman—that her sketches depict "just the expression of that vast average of Americans who do the hard work of the country, and live narrowly on their small earnings and savings" (156)—contrasts sharply with the kind of praise we're likely to find in the *Ladies' Home Journal.* There, for instance, Freeman is celebrated precisely because she avoids typography and enables a reading experience that cannot fall back on previously held knowledge: "She leaves us to meet her people very much as we should, if we went to visit…a friend who could give us the history and ancestry of her neighbors, but is forced to allow us to follow their lives, to find out their minds and characters for ourselves" (Ramsey, "New Books" 13). For most of regionalism's critics, past and present, Howells's ethnographic reading style synecdochically stands in for all of regionalism's readers, while the *Journal's* closer engagement with rural lives remains largely neglected. Thus in a foundational essay, "The Aesthetics of Regionalism," John Crowe Ransom reproduces both Howells's elite demographic and reading style when he derides regionalist fiction for disarming and flattening cultural difference: "The region is now 'made' in the vulgar sense…that the curious and eclectic populations of far-away capitals will mark it on their maps, collect its exhibits for their museums, and discuss it in their literary essays" (50). Wittingly or not, the critique turns all readers of regionalist fiction into Howellsian curators of rural idiosyncrasies.

Ransom's argument perfectly predicts a set of late twentieth-century theses claiming that regionalism aided in the cultures of white nationalist reunion. By dehistoricizing the recent past, so the narrative goes, regionalist fiction transformed regions into a series of timeless images that allowed white readers, alienated by an emergent modern industrial society, to reimagine their nation as a fraternity hailing from shared agrarian origins. In "Nation, Region, and Empire," Amy Kaplan argues that regionalist sketches share with tourists and anthropologists the perspective of a modern urban outsider who projects onto the native a pristine authentic space immune to historical changes shaping their own lives. Similarly, in *Cultures of Letters*, Richard Brodhead argues that regionalism is the product of a Howellsian literary establishment, more eager to tame regional difference than to consider it. Brodhead describes the reader of regionalism as a "sophisticate-vacationer" who grew fond of the genre because text and reader held so much in common: "[R]egional fiction…rehearsed a habit of mental acquisitiveness strongly allied with genteel reading" (133). These critics assume a reader who bypasses the complexity of regional characters' social relations in order to infuse the local with what Raymond Williams calls a "fly-in-amber quality" (61). This reader recognizes distinctive regional features, but he or she simultaneously consigns regions to a pettiness that removes them from the forces of history. In such hands, regionalist fiction serves to advance a compensatory ideological agenda that both incorporates and tames local strangeness; the reader of regionalist fiction isolates those aspects of regional idiosyncrasy that can provide usefully nostalgic fantasies of the national past and then folds these newly timeless regions facilely into an American national identity. In this sense, critics like Kaplan and Brodhead critique regionalist fiction not so much on the basis of its distinct formal or thematic aspects, but on the basis of its association with a reading practice that cultivated a certain type of centric, chauvinist person.

Two unexamined warrants support this critical narrative: that contemporary readers did indeed maintain a condescending detachment from regional subjects and characters, and that regionalist texts were exclusively read by bourgeois urban audiences. While this chapter will primarily analyze the former assumption about the interpretive and experiential practices that late nineteenth-century readers brought to regionalist fiction, let me first dwell briefly on the demographics of regionalism's audience. In his research on late nineteenth-century print culture, Charles Johanningsmeier documents a pattern wherein Mary Wilkins Freeman, Sarah Orne Jewett, Charles Chesnutt, and other writers sold their regionalist sketches to independent syndicates, which then dispersed the fiction to newspaper markets that transcended the boundaries of class and geography. Johanningsmeier's research severs regionalist fiction from any presumed monopolistic grasp of the *Atlantic Monthly, Century,* or *Harper's Monthly*. Syndication, he suggests, worked to undo the boundaries between rural subjects and urban readers, thereby enabling rural residents "to become consumers, and thus proprietors, of their own fictional currency" ("Sarah Orne Jewett and Mary E. Wilkins [Freeman]" 72).[2]

Johanningsmeier's evidence suggests that many regionalist sketches would have counted more nonurban readers than urban ones. The syndicated stories appeared, on average, in forty to fifty daily newspapers, which by the 1880s were selling throughout entire regions, and many may have additionally appeared in hundreds of weekly newspapers targeted specifically to rural audiences.[3] Moreover, Jewett, Wilkins, and other regionalist writers published frequently in magazines with less cultural capital but larger and more dispersed circulations than the *Atlantic*-style magazines, including the *Ladies' Home Journal*, as well as magazines like *Woman's Home Companion, Everybody's, Romance,* and *Pictorial Review.* Thus even though Jewett published over a dozen stories in the *Atlantic Monthly* between 1890 and 1900 (including the serialization of *The Country of the Pointed Firs* in 1896), the *Ladies' Home Journal's* publication of around just eight of her stories (depending on how you count them) reached hundreds of thousands more readers. Likewise, the *Atlantic* published none of Freeman's fiction during the century's last decade, while the *Journal* published over ten of her stories, including the serialization of *The Jamesons* between 1898 and 1899. We can make many generalizations about the demographics of regionalism's audience based upon this publication history—that it was largely white, female, middle class, and native born, for instance—but we cannot say that the dominant reading demographic was elite, urban, and geographically homogenous. More important for our purposes, we cannot say that regionalism had a dominant reading demographic at all.

Closer Reading

For that matter, nor did the *Ladies' Home Journal*, which I now offer as an alternative archive to Howellsian reading practices and demographic assumptions, remain entirely consistent in its approach to reading regionalism. On some notable occasions, its contributors replicate the reading style Richard Brodhead names acquisitive. In a 1902 column, for instance, Hamilton W. Mabie praises Freeman and Jewett for their "sharply defined types of American character" ("Literary Talks" 17). Assimilating the plural to the singular (types to character), Mabie values regionalism in precisely the fashion that recent critics denounce and implicitly prescribes a reading practice that petrifies regionalist content. So doing, Mabie replicates an approach to the genre first introduced to *Journal* readers by Conan Doyle seven years earlier. In an interview with Mabie, Doyle generously and unexpectedly calls Mary Wilkins Freeman's *Pembroke* (1894) the "greatest American novel since 'The Scarlet Letter,'" but he then singles out as his sole item of praise Freeman's depiction of "very strongly marked New England types" ("Literary Aspects of America" 6). Perhaps most strikingly, the *Journal* lent this taxonomic understanding of regionalist fiction its own institutional imprimatur when, between 1895 and 1896, it printed a series of six Freeman sketches under the heading, "Neighborhood Types." In distinguishing regionalism's characters as realistic, rural "types," Mabie, Doyle, and the *Journal's* mid-1890s editors follow Howells in presuming that regionalism requires a cognitively and epistemologically distinct practice of reading, one simultaneously distant and self-congratulatory. The genre becomes a way of getting to know the world through observation rather than participation and a way of knowing the world as always already fixed and familiar—always already the way one knew it before.

Yet the vast majority of the *Journal's* meta-discourse about literature offers itself as a distinct alternative to typological reading patterns. The evidence for this alternative is, to be sure, less explicit and systematic than it would be for a periodical like the *Atlantic Monthly*, which included regular, extensive, self-identified literary criticism. The first thing a literary scholar notices when reading multiple issues of the *Journal* is that it rarely packaged its ideas about literature in the form one contributor derides as "a studied essay of professional criticism and dictation" (Whitney, "Friendly Letter I" 14). Indeed, even its few attempts to feature a recurring column of new book reviews quickly dissipated. At the same time, recurrent emphasis on literature and literary culture emerges just as strikingly. The *Journal* returned systematically, regularly, and in multiple forms to the triumvirate of questions that govern any reading practice: What to read? Why read? And how to read? Over the course of the 1880s and '90s it developed a consistent set of responses to these questions—a coherent program of reading that it repeatedly suggested to its own readers. Through series of columns, lists of book recommendations, and open letters from reader to reader, the *Journal* suggested that its subscribers read widely, though avoiding overly photographic realism; read meticulously, developing a refined sense of irony and a philological appreciation for the subtlety of language; read passionately, emotionally engaging, befriending, and developing intense curiosity toward literary characters; and read with a social purpose in mind—to become better, more conscientious friends.[4]

I call this reading formation *closer reading*, a name I intend to call forth its close kinship to the professionalized critical reading that, as Mary Poovey writes, has become "the signature methodology" of literary studies, "its characteristic—and, thus, its characterizing—disciplinary feature" (337). Yet by distinguishing closer reading from close reading, I also intend to mark two key differences: first, the *Journal* unabashedly endorsed strong identification between reader and character, prescribing an affective investment that current disciplinary norms position against close reading along a critical-uncritical axis; and, second, the *Journal* hoped that closer reading would produce exceptional friendships, rather than critical perspective.[5]

The *Journal's* program of closer reading demanded a specific type of imaginative literature. More to the point, it precluded what one anonymous reviewer names "realism carried to the extreme" ("Mr. Howells's Latest Novel" 13).[6] As the *Journal* developed a more consistent approach to literature, it refined a system of generic differentiation and evaluation that derided overly literal realism for leaving readers stifled—cramped among too many details and too little characterization, denied entry points through which to develop experiential knowledge about fictional characters and worlds. An 1890 book review, comparing the latest novels by William

Dean Howells and Charles Dudley Warner, allows the *Journal* to articulate its aesthetic criteria while simultaneously positioning itself and its approach to literature as a distinct alternative to Howells and, by extension, the *Atlantic Monthly*. In it, Annie R. Ramsey contrasts Warner's imaginative realism to Howells's technical realism: "Mr. Howells photographs those who pass before his camera, and makes a study of their inconsistencies, being just as much interested in any one point, as in any other." Warner, on the other hand, brings to the same "studied details...a sentiment, a poetic feeling which Mr. Howells does not, will not, allow himself to believe in" ("An Hour with New Books" 11). Howells's camera fixes its representations into still images; he leaves the reader no possibility to interact with his subject because he presents her with an empirical and undistinguished "study" of reality rather than an aesthetic engagement with contemporary experience. The "sentiment" and "poetic feeling" Ramsey identifies in Warner's fiction, what our contemporary parlance might refer to as "style," enables a more fluidly interactive reading experience. Where we observe the way Howells's types "put on their hats," take note of their "certain trick of speech," and nod in recognition at their "habit of shrugging the shoulders," we join in with Warner's characters: "[W]e go with them through every phase and detail" of their daily lives (11). For Ramsey, Warner's fiction is not merely valuable for itself, for its expression of "poetic feeling," but also as a medium that enables reading to become a playful, engaged social experience. Howells's fiction, on the other hand, in offering itself as a positivist, photojournalistic record of the details that comprise contemporary existence, traps readers in a tautology that stifles their ability to interact with characters or fictional worlds. Ramsey's ambitions thus exceed any simple evaluation of Howells's fiction. She works to construct an alternative program for evaluating literature and reading, one that positions the *Ladies' Home Journal* against Howells, Howells's criteria for realist fiction, and the entire genre of *Atlantic*-style magazines through which Howells and his peers sought to influence American literary history.[7]

When the *Journal* turns to the question of why its subscribers should read literature, it reveals the stakes of Ramsey's generic distinctions. If, as the *Journal* suggests, we read in order to become more adept at producing and maintaining intimate social relationships, then literature needs to offer us more than an occasion to observe how characters "put on their hats." Consider the title to a series of open letters written by popular novelist Adeline D. T. Whitney. In November 1892, the *Journal*'s editor excitedly announced "The World of Reading" as "the general title" for a series of letters that will explore "the most interesting and entertaining authors and books" ("What Should Girls Read?" 22). Yet in December 1893, when the first letter finally appeared, "The World of Reading" had been replaced by "A Friendly Letter to Girl Friends" (Whitney, "Friendly Letter I" 14). This substitution of titles, left entirely unremarked, together with the doubled friendliness of the chosen title (friendship as both a quality and a subject position), signal a guiding principle held by a majority of the *Journal*'s contributors and, likely, editors: the distance between reading and friendship is at most negligible; the two entail practices of discernment and engagement that work synergistically and develop complementary proficiencies.

Through our reading, the *Journal* suggests, we develop skills required to relate and understand across interpersonal difference. Engaging with fictional worlds ushers us into the best possible affective apprenticeship for constructing meaningful—and, hence, also laborious—social intimacies.

Taken together, Whitney's letters constitute the *Journal's* most systematic articulation of closer reading. Expanding on Ramsey's generic differentiation, Whitney encourages her readers to put aside realist fiction that remains interested in "mere technicalities" and instead to seek out texts that "lift up our realism" ("Friendly Letter I" 14; "Friendly Letter VI" 8). Defending literary style and imaginative storytelling, she calls for fiction that is "an imaging of the true," sufficiently removed from its immediate, empirical context to open a deeper hermeneutic space in which the reader can interpret and engage ("Friendly Letter II" 10). For Whitney, texts that simultaneously refract and represent reality enable an ideal reading practice that, paradoxically, expands and regulates the self by "either confirming and developing, or checking and denying...proclivities," thereby exposing readers to the full range of "human possibilities" ("Friendly Letter I" 14). Fiction mediates between private and social life. It "fits" readers for interpersonal relationships, for, indeed, Whitney insists, "most of us do have to be fitted, in taking ourselves—if there is anything of us—out of our separate life into the world" ("Friendly Letter VI" 8). To be thus "fitted" is to cultivate the skills necessary to enter "genuine friendship," a relationship form she contrasts to the "little, frittering, life-exhausting etiquettes," the "show and pretense," and the fraternalism ("women nowadays are clubbing themselves to death") that characterize "artificial society" ("Friendly Letter VI" 8).

For Whitney and the *Journal*, closer reading therefore offers the best available solution to an ethical problem that has demanded substantial space in the pages of Western philosophy from Aristotle to Jacques Derrida: How do we maintain friendships marked by both constancy and renewal, while avoiding those marred by stasis and misrecognition? How do we, as Maurice Blanchot writes, maintain a relationship that "is brought into play and lost at each moment, a relation without relation or without relation other than the incommensurable?" (25). Put differently, how do we build friendships apart from the stability of a fraternal sameness into which friendship always threatens to lapse? It will not surprise readers of this volume that Ralph Waldo Emerson answers these questions by citing what, for him, remains ideal friendship's near impossibility. "We are armed all over with subtle antagonisms," he writes, "which, as soon as we meet, begin to play, and translate all poetry into stale prose. Almost all people descend to meet" (351). Where Emerson sees a phantom ideal that remains, except in the most utterly rare of occasions, too far-fetched to ever be realized, others see a laborious practice worth cultivating. Despite his insistence that friendship requires an underlying equality and, thus, political sameness, for instance, Aristotle maintains that sameness alone is insufficient to construct the type of "genuine friendship" Whitney values. To enter such a relationship, for Aristotle, friends must "live together and share conversation and thought," creating over time a fully realized consideration of incommensurable others "for their virtue and themselves" (261, 263). In *Politics of Friendship*, Jacques Derrida elaborates on Aristotle's claim that virtue, rather than nature, gives friendship its signature quality. At the same time, he picks up on Whitney's insistence that friendship not default into predetermined scripts: "[F]riendship does not—and above all must not—have the reliability of a natural thing or a machine;…its stability is not given by nature but is won, like constancy and 'fidence', through the endurance of a virtue" (23). Closer reading, for the *Ladies' Home Journal*, names the practice best suited to developing such endurance.

But, of course, not just any old reading would do. Meticulous reading of interpersonal difference requires an equally meticulous reading of literature's thick textures. Books, Whitney insists, "are for far more than amusement. They are for vital sympathies and understandings; human thought to human thought, hope to hope, motive to motive" ("Friendly Letter III" 15). Bridging these gaps between human thoughts, hopes, and motives requires a set of skills that correspond neatly to those required, in the words of another *Journal* contributor, to "enjoy books and gain their friendship" (Mabie, "World's Greatest University" 28). When the *Journal* details more precisely how one ought to read, it anticipates avant la lettre the practice we now associate not with popular readers, but with scholars and professional practice. Closer reading demands the close reading that, in New Critic F. R. Leavis's famous description, requires us to attend "sensitively and with precise discrimination to the words on the page" (228). A practice that allows scholars to achieve greater understanding of the work as an aesthetic production—or, more recently, of the text as the cause and effect of history—allows closer readers to achieve increasingly intricate familiarity with fictional characters and social spheres, while simultaneously acquiring the skills of friendship that Aristotle and Derrida associate with virtue. "Dear girl friends," Whitney writes as an opening for her second letter, "Do you know I dearly love a bit of philology—of word tracing?" ("Friendly Letter II" 10). In her open letters, she encourages her readers to share in this love. She models for them the archival work of etymology, needling at multiple meanings through the consideration of one word's past and present resonance. She asks them to consider the materiality of the signifier, heeding the shape their tongues require in order to pronounce certain sounds. She tells readers to observe the text on multiple levels, considering possible allegories, symbols, metaphors, and ironies. It is up to the readers of literature, she claims, "to unroll the details 'hidden in their foundation' " ("Friendly Letter I" 14). Though such punctilious practice, readers become closer readers (and slower readers), forging what Hamilton Mabie calls a "habit of mind" that turns them into more astute participants in both fictional and social spheres ("World's Greatest University" 28).

To put this argument anachronistically, Whitney combines Leavis's and Derrida's separate modes of close reading. While she adheres more closely to Leavis's search for hidden meaning than to the subtle pressure Derrida applies in his development of multichronic and mobile readings, she also divorces close reading from structural or autonomous meaning when she values it as a process more than a tool. Like Derrida, who insists that the virtuous work of friendship constitutes the antithesis of "essence" and falls always in the realm of the "perhaps," Whitney values the skills of close reading precisely because they help friends negotiate the always unfinished work of friendship and the ceaselessly shifting contingencies of relationships that refuse to collapse difference (Derrida 30).

In formulating its stringent program of reading, the *Journal* participated in a significant late-century trend. The 1870s and '80s witnessed a host of voices on both sides of the Atlantic calling upon readers to refine mere literacy into systematic practice. Prescribing, often explicitly, an Arnoldian project of self-improvement, texts like *Books and Reading: What Books Shall I Read and How Shall I Read Them*, *The Choice of Books*, and *Hints for Home Reading* asked their audiences to cultivate an "art of reading" (Richardson 5).[8] In language reminiscent of many an Introduction-to-the-Study-of-Literature syllabus, they advised readers to keep a sheet of paper handy for taking notes; to read a few books intensively and slowly rather than many books cursorily; to reflect and converse on what they've read; to keep a reading journal; to reread; to read from a range of genres, both fictional and not; and to persevere through difficult reading, for, their authors insist, worthwhile knowledge works in tandem with vigor and effort.[9] Alongside these advice books, we can see how the *Journal*'s program of reading may very well have merged public into private and work into leisure in order to give literature a function within the emergent middle-class "culture of professionalism" (Bledstein). Reading, in this schema, becomes just another technocratic effect of capitalist industrialization. In particular, closer reading becomes an exhaustive program for systematizing and assigning use value to all those effects of reading (emotional investment, distraction, sentimentality, and the like) that cannot be assimilated into programs of reading as self-help.

Yet even as it assigned usefulness to "critical" and "uncritical" modes of reading alike, the *Journal* simultaneously shifted the value of such reading to an affective realm that fit at best uneasily with bureaucratic calculation and predictability. Where reading advice books saw their project as an extension of the self-improving and self-regulating work Benjamin Franklin describes in his autobiography (a text one author references directly), the *Journal* at least partially disengaged reading from strict instrumentality (Porter 42). While it certainly exhorted a gendered audience of women and girls to expand their roles as consumers and become more efficient household managers, it also carved out the reading of literature as a coeval sphere that, ideally, enabled women to construct intimate relationships apart from capitalist efficiency. In short, the *Journal* channeled the benefits of reading from self-improvement to "genuine friendship." It shifted its emphases from products to processes. It suggested that reading creates opportunities to construct new forms of intimacy precisely insofar as that intimacy refuses to become a known quantity. The *Journal* aimed to refashion reading as a dynamic and experimental practice field for the nonce work of intimacy: through the critical hermeneutics and "uncritical" emotional identifications of reading, we acquire a way of being uniquely suited to negotiate shifting social, personal, and affective relationships.

READING REGIONALISM

The *Ladies' Home Journal* did not limit closer reading to regionalist fiction. In addition to Wilkins, Jewett, and other regionalist authors, Whitney's open letters recommend writers who span period, language, and genre—from Oliver Goldsmith to Fredrika Bremer to Susan Warner. Similarly broad in its scope, though limited almost exclusively to U.S. literature, Thomas Wentworth Higginson's suggestions for "A Young Girl's Library" include Nathaniel Hawthorne, James Fenimore Cooper, Washington Irving, Edward Bellamy, Henry David Thoreau, and Emily Dickinson, in addition to a bevy of regionalist fiction, such as Freeman's *A Humble Romance* (1887), M. N. Murfree's *In the Tennessee Mountains* (1884), Celia Thaxter's *Among the Isles of Shoals* (1873), Hamlind Garland's *Main-Traveled Roads* (1891), and Grace King's *Tales of a Time and Place* (1892).

Yet regionalism's prominence in this list is no accident. If, to recall the *Ladies' Home Journal's* review of Freeman, regionalist sketches force readers to engage literary subjects by finding out "their minds and characters for ourselves," then regionalism emerges as a privileged genre within closer reading practices. Its generic conventions emphasize the gradual unfolding of character knowledge, shirk any overly strict realism, and highlight the human social landscape, in particular downplaying family in favor of friendship. Its stories center on widows, widowers, lifelong bachelors, spinsters, and others whose primary affective connections typically link them into non-familial networks of affinity. Sarah Orne Jewett's narrator in "A White Heron" (1886) thus describes a typical regionalist setting when she names "home" a place where most "didn't hitch" (*Novels and Stories* 673). Moreover, even the regionalist sketch's family-bound characters cannot help but forge social links within their immediate localities; regionalism binds its inhabitants through what Freeman terms, in "A New England Nun" (1891), the "soft diurnal commotion" of local associations, as well as the geographic fixedness that results from poverty, duty, history, desire, old age, and disability (*New England Nun* 22). As such a list suggests, the regionalist sketch does not depict utopian or even quasi-utopian spheres of friendship free from the acrimony, contestation, and competition found in an otherwise "real" world, for, as Wai Chee Dimock puts it, "the commingling of lives is always a form of imposition" (259). Instead, regionalism acquires particular significance for the closer reader as a genre uniquely attuned to how one lives with and even values the imposition of proximate others. It suggests to readers a practice of friendship that hinges on immediate, local, and diurnal cohabitation—what Aristotle refers to as "liv[ing] together"—instead of abstracted, a priori, and assumed sameness (261). Regionalism invites readers to become familiar with social worlds that foreground the anti- or nonfraternal friendships that, according to Whitney, closer reading enables and desires.

The sketch form likewise reinforces closer reading's ideals. Writing sketches enabled regionalist authors to free themselves from novels' plot imperatives, which are so often inextricable from compulsory heterosexuality and, more to the point, compulsory marriage. As a character- rather than plot-centric form, the sketch isolates finer moments of interpersonal exchange, moments that, in their casual everydayness, signify the repetition and constancy through which intimacy is produced and enhanced over time.[10] We can, in this sense, read "A White Heron" as a meta-commentary on the sketch form itself. When the story's young heroine decides to rebut romantic attentions proffered by an intriguing and handsome outsider, she decides, as it were, to remain within the social world of the regionalist sketch while also fending off the romantic teleology that accompanies so many nineteenth-century novels. Opening the pages of the latest Freeman or Jewett or Murfree sketch, closer readers entered fictional worlds teeming with the forms and contents of friendly affinities; there they found an ideal imaginative setting in which to enhance their own skills and sensitivities as friends and neighbors.

Even readers unfamiliar with the *Ladies' Home Journal*'s program for closer reading may have become familiar with its practices and aims by reading regionalism. The framing devices typical to the regionalist sketch enable it to formally represent and model a closer reading practice that extends from fine observation to accomplished intimacy. Through hearing and interpreting stories—practices homologous, in the logic of the frame narrative, with reading—characters turn relationships of mere convenience or proximity into meaningful, "genuine" friendships. *The Country of the Pointed Firs*, for instance, comprises a sequence of framed narratives that incorporate the narrator, a traveling spinster from Boston, into Dunnet Landing's overlapping social networks. Each sketch tracks the narrator's keen skills as a reader of verbal and nonverbal communication as she collaborates with various residents to forge intimate ties across sometimes stark difference: she becomes "the best of friends" with Captain Littlepage, whose nostalgia has succumbed into an alienated disorientation; she wordlessly navigates a mutual, tender, and chaste affection with the socially phobic William Blackett; she moves from being "strangers" to being "warm friends" with the hopelessly melancholic Elijah Tilley; she becomes "sincere friends" with the imperial, imposing, inconsiderate, and "strange" traveler, Mrs. Fosdick; she expands upon an increasingly deeper intimacy with her host, Mrs. Todd; and she even enters into a paradoxical fellowship with the memory of Poor Joanna, "one of those whom sorrow made too lonely to brave the sight of men" (*Novels and Stories* 399, 486, 424, 421, 444). The novel's opening paragraph instructs its readers how to make sense of these dynamic and developing intimacies. Contrasting the fleetingness of romance with the more fluid and strenuous work of friendship, the narrator writes: "The process of falling in love at first sight is as final as it is swift ... but the growth of true friendship may be a lifelong affair" (377). Rather than minor episodes, the framed sketches of regionalist fiction constitute building blocks out of which intimacies resist stasis and fraternity. By representing friendship as a way of life, the genre itself labors to reward closer reading, even as it models the sensitive and careful consideration that closer reading demands.[11]

Regionalism's Historiographies

I have been arguing about regionalism and reading, but literary historiography and critical methodologies have never been far from my concerns. The archives of reading and reception are not merely relevant for ascertaining immediate historical context; they additionally change how texts resonate across time, across readers, across critical practices. Leah Price puts it this way: "[T]he history of books is centrally about ourselves. It asks how past readers have made meaning (and therefore, by extension, how others have read differently from us), but it also asks where the conditions of possibility for our own reading come from" (318). To enter into the archives of reading is to bring strangeness and variety into readers' roles and experiences; paradoxically, it is to come face-to-face with our own roles as readers, teachers, students, critics, and historians.

As one such archive, the *Ladies' Home Journal* enables two arguments—one methodological and one historical. In opening the contemporary literary critic to a radically different regionalism than that we find in the pages of the *Atlantic Monthly*, the *Journal* suggests that the history of reading is not merely a way of ascertaining how previous readers understood and interpreted literature. It is additionally a way of rethinking both genre and methodologies of genre criticism. Fredric Jameson claims to lay to rest the "typologizing abuses of traditional genre criticism" when he insists that "genre theory must always in one way or another project a model of the coexistence or tension between several generic modes or strands" (141). The history of reading productively shifts such a project beyond what even Jameson has in mind. It exposes how genres are in tension not only with their own intra- and intergeneric "modes and strands," but also their own multiple receptions. Ultimately, the history of reading and genre criticism are versions of one another. That is, the kind of work this chapter relies upon—archival research into the literary cultures that influenced how and why people read—constitutes a crucial mode of inquiry into the generic interconnections between texts and, indeed, between texts and readers. Histories of reading uncover sets of conventions that shape genres by, in turn, shaping the kinds of patterns that readers mark as generic. It is apparent that the *Ladies' Home Journal* and the *Atlantic Monthly* articulate different conceptions of regionalism because they brought to it such starkly different reading practices. Yet we can also push this claim a step further. Might not the *Journal's* regionalism and the *Atlantic's* regionalism comprise two separate genres entirely, made up in large part of the same texts, yet tracing starkly different sets of interconnection, isolating different sets of attributes, and calling for related yet unique literary histories?

Jewett points us in the right direction when, in a letter to her friend Alice Meyness, she suggests that friendship occupies its own "country" (*Letters* 200).[12] The twofold description most obviously refers to a geography that circumscribes the accumulation of those everyday interactions out of which intimacy develops, but it also marks this fluid intimacy as a distinct sociopolitical territory. Jewett thereby suggests a way of understanding one's intimate social life as superseding the loyalties of patriotic citizenship and the imagined communities of fraternal camaraderie.[13] The *Ladies' Home Journal* privileges this antinational geography of friendship precisely by associating it with the reading of Jewett's preferred literary genre, the regionalist sketch. Yoking reading to the philosophy of friendship, the *Journal* assigns new conventions to regionalist fiction. Its pages associate regionalism not merely with the depiction of rural lives and customs, but also with the careful representation of sociality apart from familial prescriptions; not only with the specificity of the local, but also with a meditation on how to transform friendship into a process, a way of life; not merely with the sketch form, but also with a roomy aesthetics that allows readers to find out "minds and characters for ourselves." We likely have no way of knowing the exact extent to which the *Journal's* mode of regionalism became a resource for antinational intimacies. Yet as a prominent and influential archive of regionalism's reception, the *Ladies' Home Journal* at the least helped to popularize Jewett's model for friendship. In advancing an ideal association between reading and intimacy, it aligned regionalism with social relationships that could never be subsumed into generic attachments—relationships, therefore, that ran afoul of the experiences of social belonging that undergirded "American" nationalism.

NOTES

1 The *Journal* spent its first three years as the *Ladies' Home Journal and Practical Housekeeper*. For more on the *Journal's* history and influence, see Damon-Moore and Scanlon.

2 For Chesnutt's work with syndications, see Johanningsmeier, *Fiction and the American Literary Marketplace* 4. I focus only briefly on Johanningsmeier's relevance to Kaplan and Brodhead because others, including Johanningsmeier himself, have already made clear the relevance of his findings for reconsidering their theses. See Johanningsmeier, "Sarah Orne Jewett and Mary E. Wilkins" 61; Howard; and Fetterley and Pryse.

3 Another way to gauge Sarah Orne Jewett's widespread readership is to look at Katherine Cole Aydelott's wonderfully exhaustive PhD dissertation, "Maine Stream: A Bibliographical Reception Study of Sarah Orne Jewett."

4 This meta-discourse includes Annie R. Ramsey's "Books and Bookmakers" (1889), "Some Books on My Table" (1890), and "An Hour with New Books" (1890); multiple columns by Edward W. Bok on subjects ranging from "Words for Young Authors" to "Is Literature a Trade?" (1889–1906); "In Literary Circles" (1890–1892); "Literary Women in Their Homes" (1892–1895); "Droch's Literary Talks" (1896–1897); and "Mr. Mabie's Literary Talks" (1902–1904).

5 On the disciplinary axis dividing critical from uncritical reading practices, see Warner.

6 See also a column written by the *Journal's* editor, Edward Bok, that admonishes "the most radical believers of realism in fiction" (12).

7 For an excellent history of realism and the *Atlantic*-group magazines, see Glazener.

8 See also Abbott, Porter, and Rees.

9 Although these recommendations recur throughout reading advice books of the 1870s and '80s, you can find them (and more) in a convenient eighteen-point list in Moore 11–13. For a recent history of "the reading habit" as a recurrent concern in the late nineteenth-century United States, see Hochman.

10 For a related argument, see Fetterley and Pryse 171–172.
11 For a separate examination of friendship in Jewett's text, see Shannon. For a related argument about the work of framing devices in regionalist fiction, see Pryse.
12 Elsewhere, I argue that F. O. Matthiessen provides us one surprising and prominent example of a reader who merges antinational affiliation with the closer reading of regionalism. Reading Jewett enabled Matthiessen to construct meaningful intimacies outside of the heteronormative limitations of U.S. national identity. See also Celia Thaxter's *Among the Isles of Shoals* for her representation of the region as an alternative form of political anticitizenship, in which residents "troubl[e] themselves but little about what State they belong to" (13).
13 See Anderson 7.

BIBLIOGRAPHY

Abbot, Lyman, ed. *Hints for Home Reading: A Series of Chapters on Books and Their Use.* New York: G. P. Putnam's Sons, 1880.

Anderson, Benedict. *Imagined Communities: Reflections on the Origin and Spread of Nationalism.* New York: Verso, 1991.

Aristotle. *Nicomachean Ethics.* Trans. Terence Irwin. Indianapolis: Hackett Publishing Company, 1985.

Augst, Thomas. Introduction. *Institutions of Reading: The Social Life of Libraries in the United States.* Ed. Thomas Augst and Kenneth Carpenter. Boston: University of Massachusetts Press, 2007. 1–23.

Aydelott, Katherine Cole. "Maine Stream: A Bibliographical Reception Study of Sarah Orne Jewett." PhD Thesis, University of Connecticut, 2005.

Berlant, Lauren. *The Female Complaint: The Unfinished Business of Sentimentality in American Culture.* Durham, NC: Duke University Press, 2008.

Blanchot, Maurice. *The Unavowable Community.* Trans. Pierre Joris. Barrytown, NY: Station Hill, 1988.

Bledstein, Burton J. *The Culture of Professionalism: The Middle Class and the Development of Higher Education in America.* New York: Norton, 1976.

Bok, Edward. "The Pen of a Mountaineer." *Ladies' Home Journal* 11 (July 1894): 12.

Brodhead, Richard H. *Cultures of Letters: Scenes of Reading and Writing in Nineteenth-Century America.* Chicago: University of Chicago Press, 1993.

Brooks, Cleanth. *The Well Wrought Urn: Studies in the Structure of Poetry.* New York: Harcourt, 1947.

Damon-Moore, Helen. *Magazines for the Millions: Gender and Commerce in the Ladies' Home Journal and the Saturday Evening Post, 1880–1910.* Albany: State University of New York Press, 1994.

Derrida, Jacques. *Politics of Friendship.* Trans. George Collins. New York: Verso, 1997.

Dimock, Wai Chee. "Rethinking Space, Rethinking Rights: Literature, Law, and Science." *Materializing Democracy: Toward a Revitalized Cultural Politics.* Ed. Russ Castronovo and Dana Nelson. Durham, NC: Duke University Press, 2002. 248–266.

Emerson, Ralph Waldo. "Friendship." *Essays and Lectures.* Ed. Joel Porte. New York: Library of America, 1983. 339–354.

Fetterley, Judith, and Marjorie Pryse. *Writing Out of Place: Regionalism, Women, and American Literary Culture.* Urbana: University of Illinois Press, 2003.

Foster, Travis M. "Matthiessen's Public Privates: Homosexual Expression and the Aesthetics of Sexual Inversion." *American Literature* 78 (June 2006): 235–262.

Freeman, Mary E. Wilkins. "Neighborhood Types; I—Timothy Sampson: The Wise Man." *Ladies' Home Journal* 13 (December 1895): 7.

———. "Neighborhood Types; II—Little Marg'ret Snell: The Village Runaway." *Ladies' Home Journal* 13 (January 1896): 5.

———. "Neighborhood Types; III—Cyrus Emmett: The Unlucky Man." *Ladies' Home Journal* 13 (February 1896): 3.

———. "Neighborhood Types; IV—Phebe Ann Little: The Neat Woman Drawings." *Ladies' Home Journal* 13 (March 1896): 5.

———. "Neighborhood Types; V—Amanda Todd: The Friend of Cats." *Ladies' Home Journal* 13 (April 1896): 5.

———. "Neighborhood Types; VI—Lydia Wheelock: The Good Woman." *Ladies' Home Journal* 13 (May 1896): 11.

———. *A New England Nun and Other Stories.* New York: Penguin Books, 2000.

Glazener, Nancy. *Reading for Realism: The History of a U.S. Literary Institution, 1850–1910.* Durham, NC: Duke University Press, 1997.

Higginson, Thomas Wentworth. "A Young Girl's Library." *Ladies' Home Journal* 12 (November 1895): 4.

Hochman, Barbara. "Highbrow/Lowbrow: Naturalist Writers and the 'Reading Habit.'" *Twisted from the Ordinary: Essays on American Literary Naturalism.* Ed. Mary E. Papke. Knoxville: University of Tennessee Press, 2003. 217–236.

Howard, June. "Unraveling Regions, Unsettling Periods: Sarah Orne Jewett and American Literary History." *American Literature* 68 (June 1996): 365–384.

Howells, William Dean. "Editor's Study." *Harper's New Monthly Magazine* 83 (June 1891): 152–156.

Jameson, Fredric. *The Political Unconscious: Narrative as a Socially Symbolic Act.* Ithaca, NY: Cornell University Press, 1981.

Jewett, Sarah Orne. *The Letters of Sarah Orne Jewett.* Ed. Annie Fields. Boston: Houghton Mifflin, 1911.

——— *Novels and Stories.* Washington, D.C.: Library of America, 1994.

Johanningsmeier, Charles. *Fiction and the American Literary Marketplace: The Role of Newspaper Syndicates, 1860–1900.* New York: Cambridge University Press, 1997.

———. "Sarah Orne Jewett and Mary E. Wilkins (Freeman): Two Shrewd Businesswomen in Search of New Markets." *New England Quarterly* 70.1 (1997): 57–82.

Kaplan, Amy. "Nation, Region, and Empire." *The Columbia History of the American Novel,* Ed. Emory Elliott. New York: Columbia University Press, 1991. 240–266.

Leavis, F. R. *Anna Karenina and Other Essays.* London: Chatto and Windus, 1967.

"Literary Aspects of America: An After Luncheon Talk Between Dr. A. Conan Doyle and Hamilton W. Mabie." *Ladies' Home Journal* 12 (March 1895): 6.

Long, Elizabeth. *Book Clubs: Women and the Uses of Reading in Everyday Life.* Chicago: University of Chicago Press, 2003.

Mabie, Hamilton W. "Mr. Mabie's Literary Talks." *Ladies' Home Journal* 19 (March 1902): 17.

———. "Mr. Mabie Tells of the World's Greatest University." *Ladies' Home Journal* 24 (November 1907): 28.

Moore, Charles H. *What to Read, and How to Read, Being Classified Lists of Choice Reading, with Appropriate Hints and Remarks, Adapted to the General Reader, to Subscribers to Libraries, and to Persons Intending to Form Collections of Books.* New York: D. Appleton, 1871.

"Mr. Howells's Latest Novel." *Ladies' Home Journal* 7 (March 1890): 13.

Poovey, Mary. *Genres of the Credit Economy: Mediating Value in Eighteenth- and Nineteenth-Century Britain.* Chicago: University of Chicago Press, 2008.

Porter, Noah. *Books and Reading: What Books Shall I Read and How Shall I Read Them.* New York: Charles Scribner, 1871.

Price, Leah. "Reading: The State of the Discipline." *Book History* 6 (2004): 303–320.

Pryse, Marjorie. "Reading Regionalism: The 'Difference' It Makes." *Regionalism Reconsidered: New Approaches to the Field.* Ed. David Jordan. New York: Garland, 1994. 47–63.

Ramsey, Annie R. "An Hour with New Books." *Ladies' Home Journal* 7 (April 1890): 11.

———. "New Books on My Table." *Ladies' Home Journal* 7 (May 1890): 13.

Ransom, John Crowe. "The Aesthetics of Regionalism." *Selected Essays of John Crowe Ransom.* Ed. Thomas Daniel Young and John Hindle. Baton Rouge: Louisiana State University Press, 1984. 45–58.

Rees, J. Rogers. *The Diversions of a Book-Worm.* London: Elliot Stock, 1886.

Richardson, Charles F. *The Choice of Books.* New York: American Book Exchange, 1881.

Scanlon, Jennifer. *Inarticulate Longings: The Ladies' Home Journal, Gender, and the Promises of Consumer Culture.* New York: Routledge, 1995.

Shannon, Laurie. "'The Country of Our Friendship': Jewett's Intimist Art." *American Literature* 71 (June 1999): 227–262.

Thaxter, Celia. *Among the Isles of Shoals.* Boston: Houghton, Mifflin, 1873.

Warner, Michael. "Uncritical Reading." *Polemic: Critical or Uncritical.* Ed. Jane Gallop. New York: Routledge, 2004. 13–38.

"What Should Girls Read? Mrs. Whitney to Travel with Girls in 'The World of Reading.'" *Ladies' Home Journal* 9 (November 1892): 22.

Whitman, Walt. *Poetry and Prose.* New York: Library of America, 1996.

Whitney, A. D. T. "A Friendly Letter to Girl Friends—I." *Ladies' Home Journal* 11 (December 1893): 14.

———. "A Friendly Letter to Girl Friends—II." *Ladies' Home Journal* 11 (March 1894): 10.

———. "A Friendly Letter to Girl Friends—III." *Ladies' Home Journal* 11 (August 1894): 15.

———. "A Friendly Letter to Girl Friends—VI." *Ladies' Home Journal* 13 (December 1895): 8.

Williams, Raymond. "Region and Class in the Novel." *The Uses of Fiction: Essays on the Modern Novel in Honour of Arnold Kettle.* Ed. Douglas Jefferson and Graham Martin. Milton Keynes, England: Open University Press, 1982. 59–68.

CHAPTER 17

....

LITERATURE AND
THE NEWS

....

ELISA TAMARKIN

In 1875 Henry James arranged to send correspondence from Paris to the *New York Tribune* but could not find anything to report. "I can think of nothing in life to put in the *Tribune*," he writes to his brother William, and later complains to his father that, in Paris, "there has been a painful dearth of topics to write about" (quoted in Edel 238). Of course, to say that there was no news in Paris is only to suggest that the ideas and impressions that it inspired for James were not "the right sort of thing for a newspaper" (James, *Parisian Sketches* 220). So while his editor asks for letters that are more "'newsy' in character," James keeps insisting that "subjects are woefully scarce," and as his biographer Leon Edel puts it, "We thus have the spectacle of a man of James's large imagination unable to imagine subjects for a newspaper—and in a city teeming with them" (James, *Parisian Sketches* 217; Edel 238). Years later, in *The American Scene*, James also fails to find anything newsworthy in Baltimore, which makes the "momentous proposition" that Baltimore is "interesting" hard for him to prove despite its atmosphere of "pleasant-playing reference and reflection" (James, *American Scene* 606–607). The more James likes the city, in other words, the more he realizes that the most telling evidence of how his "sensibility yielded so completely to Baltimore" is his surprising failure to have discovered any "features" or "items" in it worth reporting to his readers (James, *American Scene* 607–608). Like Paris, Baltimore's sources of interest "were too closely of the texture" and character of the city "to be snipped off…by any mere sharp shears of journalism" and since, unlike Paris, Baltimore may not exactly be *teeming* with subjects, "it would be 'no good' to a journalist—for *he* is nowhere, ever, without his items; but it would be everything, always, to the mere restless analyst" (James, *American Scene* 607, 608). The journalist cuts experience down to size, but the "restless analyst" indulges a more capacious and attentive model of perception than the expedience of the news requires. To the extent that James's writing, as critics suggest, turns on the cognitive and stylistic distinctions between information and more "nonconceptual" forms of knowledge, so does his sense that, by the end of the nineteenth century, literature was nowhere to be found amid the "'items' by the thousand" that journalists produce (Posnock 148; James, *American Scene* 608).

That James feels the need to distinguish between literature and the news is just one example of the extent to which authors asserted the prestige of their work as a function of its durability and complexity within an accelerating culture of print. "Men are divided broadly into journalists and eternalists," writes an author in the *Atlantic* in 1891 (Stillman 688). When Julian Hawthorne (son of Nathaniel Hawthorne) says in 1888 that authors did "not like the idea of appearing in newspapers" because "a copy of a newspaper is a thing of an hour," he insists that literary meaning is lost on readers who have come to expect the constant novelty of the daily news and the feeling of timeliness it delivers (quoted in Johanningsmeier 216). As *Harper's* observes in 1892, the sentiment toward books is "becoming like that towards newspapers— that they are to be rudely handled and cast aside when the news has been snatched out of them"; the newspaper thus comes to exemplify a rapidly modernizing culture of information, where journalistic prose is designed for obsolescence and where readers have no more patience for the form that content takes than "a hungry man for oysters, who scoops out the soft parts and chucks away the shells, perhaps with pearls in them" ("Editors" 966) The laments for literary value see the ephemerality of the news as a challenge not only to the material survival of the book, but also to the more layered and synthetic attitude toward time that literature sustains. Put differently, it is easy to imagine that James and others, faced with a distractible audience that had come to "love change for its own sake," would have approved of Ezra Pound's famous declaration that "literature is news that stays news" (Tocqueville 548; Pound 29).

James is making—at the expense of news—a familiar call for literature's own aesthetic and autonomy at a moment when increasingly impatient audiences seemed to demand that every text produce the same feeling of currency as the events that made the news. When James Gordon Bennett, founding editor of the *New York Herald*, calls the nineteenth century "the age of the Daily Press," he asserts the centrality of newspapers to the culture of his times, but also links the character of the times to a mode of writing whose significance endures no longer than the next edition (Pray 217). Thus the widespread popularity of newspapers reflects the growing demand for connection to a modern world in which the recency of knowledge is an essential index of its value: in America, writes Alexis de Tocqueville in 1835, the "idea of the new is coupled...with the idea of the better" (Tocqueville 466). For James, producers of literature have little to gain in trying to keep up with an age that changes utterly on a daily basis, but his disregard for the contingency and topicality of the news is only one variety of nineteenth-century response to the timely aesthetic of the newspaper. Indeed, many writers of the period are more receptive than James to journalistic practices and imperatives, and many in fact aspire to pattern their own texts on innovations derived from the forms of news itself.

If E. L. Godkin could write at the end of the century of the growing "segregation of the newspaper-reader from the book-reader," he at once confirms the divide between literature and the news that James tried turning to his favor, but also testifies to the fact that this was not always the case (Godkin 203). Literature in the nineteenth century was often indistinguishable from the news, appearing on the pages of newspapers alongside reports of recent events, and assuming many of the stylistic features that structured the daily experience of a print culture for which the disposability of newspapers as texts was just another way of registering the currency of their information. Even writers who did not publish in newspapers had to address—or, like James, strategically reject—the imperatives of recency and progress that made the news and that also transformed the ritual of reading itself into a daily event. Understanding literature in the age of news—when newspapers were at once a dominant media technology and a powerful institution in the literary marketplace—means keeping track of how writers adapted their aesthetics to the priorities of a period that was now so preoccupied with being informed that it left audiences with little time to reflect on their own hierarchies of knowledge. Readers placed a premium on works that not only promised to be "a window onto" the realities of modern life, but more important, embraced the temporality of a particular and fleeting present as the most meaningful horizon of historical experience.

Thus to the extent that we continue to discover that past literary texts possess the power to change the way we understand our own contemporary situation, we participate in a mode of presentism inherited from nineteenth-century audiences and authors who had to find a place for literature within a high-speed economy of information that could see no difference between newsworthiness and other forms of value. The idea, then, that literature should speak to its times—that it must inescapably refer to the immediacy of its contexts—brings with it a set of expectations about our reading practices that still shape how we believe that works of poetry and fiction can register the history that makes them. Revisiting the period when the modern newspaper emerges helps us understand how literary practices that we have inherited owe their currency to the information age of the nineteenth century, when literature itself first takes the measure of the news.

In Washington Irving's "Rip Van Winkle," the archaism of prerevolutionary society most reveals itself whenever the men of the village gather to debate an "old newspaper" (Irving 772). By the nineteenth century, old news had become a source of amusement that Thoreau, for example, can play on when he chooses to read the scraps of newspaper in which his "dinner of bread and butter" are wrapped; there are, as Thoreau says, things to "relish" in the fragments of the "Daily Times" that make their way to the woods but the absurdity of his "appetite" for them is also the sign of his distance from the world "in which the events that make the news transpire" (Thoreau, *Walden* 356; *A Week* 293, 251; "Life" 360). As media historians observe, the daily papers of the 1830s marked a turn away from the partisan and trade papers that provided weekly content to audiences of subscribers who shared political and public interests and whose discussion of their interests formed the basis of the deliberative public sphere that Jürgen Habermas famously ascribes to the late eighteenth century (Nerone). Now the dailies competed for a mass readership that demanded its information at accelerating speeds and shared, if nothing else, an investment in the commodity of news itself which became central like never before to both the business and culture of newspapers. For the first time the news, instead of political or editorial comment, became the primary object of the newspaper, so when Charles A. Dana, editor of the *New York Sun*, writes that "a newspaper without news is no newspaper" it is not self-evident because the news is what was new (Dana 60). "Newspapers bear us along with them," writes George Lunt in 1857, "abreast of the rapid flood of passing events" (Lunt 68). If in 1800 readers might find five to twenty items in a four-page paper—mostly long political essays that ran for more than a page and continued from one issue to the next—by midcentury, a typical four-page paper contained thirty-five to forty items about the day's events (Dicken-Garcia). Editors devoted their resources to extensive newsgathering operations, employing carrier pigeons, boats, competing rail lines, the pony express, and, after 1846, the telegraph, while readers measured the efficiency of papers by "[counting] the number of items they contained" (where "the newspaper with the most items was the best paper") (Park 108). Newspapers rivaled one another for timeliness with "extras" and "late editions"; the invention of the steam-powered cylinder press made multiple editions of daily papers cheaper and more profitable; and reporters specialized to provide comprehensive and expert coverage on a wide range of "beats" (Schudson; Blondheim). "There is," writes the editor of the *Springfield Republican* in 1851, "a great deal more news nowadays than there used to be," suggesting how the world itself seemed essentially more eventful as the horizon of what could be known expanded across networks of new transportation and communication technologies and as the telegraph and wire services especially intensified the timely transmission of news (quoted in Merriam 1:98).

As newspapers began to prioritize the coverage of events over the discussion of ideas, the competition for readers came to depend less on the deliberative public life that followed from their content, and more on the ability of the news itself to give shape and meaning to communities that emerged in response to the fact that something had happened somewhere and not very long ago. The cycles of such "simultaneous consumption," as Benedict Anderson writes, impart to reading newspapers in the nineteenth century the character of a "mass ceremony"; by recognizing the regularity with which the news was always changing, readers were "continually reassured" that their modern world was visibly rooted in habits that they could learn and make their own (Anderson 35). The diminishing time lag between distant events and their appearance in the newspaper came to pattern daily rituals of urban culture especially as "extras," hawked by newsboys on the streets, made it possible for crowds of readers to track unfolding stories with a sensation of real time while preserving the sequential flow of new developments (Henkin). Reading newspapers was a practice of historical engagement with the present moment as it emerged and then inevitably receded; thus what Anderson calls "the obsolescence of the newspaper on the morrow of its printing" is a crucial aspect of its power to keep readers coming back for more news when the old became irrelevant (Anderson 35). As early news gave way to breaking news, newspapers encouraged the belief that time itself is dynamic and superseding, and that our reading is significant to the degree that it keeps pace with the progress of the current moment. What happens latest matters most since news as a form of knowledge is perishable and can only exist in the present. "Where there were no news-boys," writes Thoreau, "I did not see what would they do for waste paper" (Thoreau, *Cape Cod* 946).

In America, Tocqueville says, where "everything seems to be in constant flux, and every change seems to mark an advance," there is "only a very limited time to devote to literature"; "the only recognizably American authors I know," he says, "are journalists. They are not great writers, but they speak the country's language" (Tocqueville 466, 542, 539). It is not surprising that Tocqueville's *Democracy in America* (1835) appeared the same year as the most successful of the early penny dailies, James Gordon Bennett's *New York Herald*, since the "constant need for novelty" that the newspaper satisfies is also, for Tocqueville, the "greatest defect" of a restless, democratic society that "seems to live from day to day" (544, 718, 237). After all, he says, "no one is less given to reverie than the citizens of a democracy" and newspapers are, what Thoreau calls, "easy reading" or "little reading": they yield up their contents to a commercial population whose "habitual inattention" (Tocqueville's phrase)—whose habit, that is, for being unhabituated to reflection—was more conducive to consuming or digesting than to thinking (Tocqueville 702, 718; Thoreau, *Walden* 406). The modern dailies in the United States, with their belief in faithfully registering events as they happen, precede by decades comparable developments in Britain and France; even by the end of the nineteenth century Dana suggests that Britain put less value on the newsworthiness of a newspaper since "people were willing to wait a week there to find out the news"; "the world might be revolutionized," he continues, but the English "would not know it until their weekly paper comes around" (Dana 9).

Dana may be overstating just how dramatically the number and scale of U.S. newspapers was a "feature of American civilization," but, like Tocqueville, he suggests how the temporal logic of the news had become linked to American ideas of revolution and continuous change. Impatient readers want "all the news, and nothing but the news" because they believe "that humanity is advancing," and that every day's paper ratifies that "there is progress in human life and human affairs" (Dana 9, 19–20). Thus when Ralph Waldo Emerson writes earlier in the century that "newspapers," are the proper literature of America," he too sees the news as a correlative to American narratives of progress in which independence itself is figured as freedom from historical memory and continuity (Emerson 195). Newspapers, we might say, assume the revolutionary break between today and yesterday and a faith in the primacy of the present that Henry James attributes to the naive innocence of Americans for whose "candid minds newspapers and all they contained were part of…the recurrent freshness of the universe, coming out like the sun in the morning or the stars at night" (James, *Reverberator* 166). Or put differently, the newspaper is the ideal medium for a culture of liberal individualism that depends on a pervasive disregard for precedent and prior attachments. If progress means abandoning the past, the newspaper offers an object lesson in, as Tocqueville calls it, the "universal movement" of democratic life and the American's daily determination to move on (Tocqueville 466). So when a character in William Dean Howells's *A Modern Instance* describes Americans who follow the news as never feeling "so prosperous as when [they] can't remember what happened last Monday," we hear a particularly mordant variation on a familiar sentiment: that Americans are most fully who they are when living in the self-sufficient present that the newspaper produces (Howells 552).

In James's novel, *The Reverberator*, an American newspaper man, George Flack, publishes gossip about an established Parisian family as it was reported to him by an American girl; though the family is scandalized by the story, the novel insists on the "innocence" of the girl since Flack, in gaining the facts from her, simply claims that a newspaper will record everything that occurs: "he wants everything," the girl says of Flack, "it's a very fine paper" (James, *Reverberator* 56, 146). James suggests that her transgressions are just a function of her national character ("you might explain—," she pleads, "I'm only an American girl") which makes her susceptible to the way that newspapers try to naturalize their intrusions into privacy as just another aspect of their impulse to completeness and transparency (James, *Reverberator* 150). French society is shocked by the exposure because, unlike the Americans in the novel, they do not understand that newspapers are now part "of the general fatality of things" and that it is as impossible to keep scandal out of them as it is for the "perfectly simple" girl not to report every item she hears (James, *Reverberator* 166, 78). "The journalist recording...the thing that has come to pass," writes the American critic James Parton in 1867, "is Providence addressing men" (Parton 265). The French aristocrats in James's novel can neither understand the rhetoric of newsworthiness that Flack attaches with such fervor to their family secrets, nor find any comfort in the fact that even the most salacious story will only matter for a moment since its pressing interest to the reading public is just a sign of its impending obsolescence within the progress of daily events. When Flack calls the newspaper "the great institution of our time," he means both that it is "the history of the age" and that it communicates the presence of an age that is now moving faster than any ancien régime can bear, so that refusing to keep up with the news is to resist being assimilated to the times the "Times" describes (James, *Reverberator* 124). This is why Lunt writes that "the newspapers bear us along with them"—"to resist," he continues "may seem to some little better than rank heresy to the spirit of the age and its main instruments of thought" (Lunt 80).

By the nineteenth century, newspapers—often called "The Spirit of the Age" or "The Spirit of the Times"—claimed to represent the free and impartial flow of information that put readers in relation to their world: a newspaper, writes Henry Ward Beecher in 1864, "is a window through which men look out on all that is going on in the world" (quoted in Hudson, Lee, and Mott xviii). Only when reading the newspaper became a practice of daily life could it become a reflection of the moment one was in, which is also to say that the nineteenth century saw its own progressive character reflected in the perpetual advance of the news. Newspapers increasingly allowed their readers to experience the events of future history—the events, that is, that would someday count as history—in the present moment as fully immanent to a contemporary world that could, for the first time, witness the results of all its collective energies and larger conflicts as they were happening. The newspaper, Parton says, "is that which connects each individual with the general life of mankind, and makes him part and parcel of the whole" (Parton 264). We might think of newspapers in the nineteenth century as the medium whose ambitions were most resonant with the period's own impulses to modernity, and especially to the philosophies of progress that sustained them.

For Hegel, historical change is not simply a consequence of transformative events, but follows from the way they are recorded and narrated to the world; that "history" means both events that happen and the form they take in writing is a profound coincidence for Hegel, who sees the progress of his times as depending, at least in part, on a self-conscious understanding of progress. Change is a recursive process that is intensified by reading stories of change, and the nineteenth century had faith that its newspapers were the expression of the "world spirit" that emerges, as Hegel would say, when the "writing of history and the actual deeds or events of history make their appearance simultaneously" (quoted in Houlgate 19). Hegel himself worked as a reporter and editor, and remained a lifelong reader of the news, following current events with almost religious devotion ("Reading the morning paper," he writes, "is the realist's morning prayer") (Pinkard 242). So perhaps he saw in newspapers—especially as their reporting of events became more direct and comprehensive—another means of communicating "the spirit of the age as the spirit of the present and aware of itself in thought" (quoted in Houlgate 9). Newspapers could now register the progress of the present for their readers, who could in turn understand their own acts of reading as "part and parcel" of, and relevant to, its progress. What nineteenth-century Americans learned from the newspaper, in other words, was that reading—indeed the act of reading it suggested as a daily practice—was nothing less (and perhaps nothing more) than a reflection of the moment they were in. To read was to keep up with the times, and to find their place within them.

The nineteenth-century newspaper, as John Nerone writes, "mark[s] the horizon at which the history of the book meets the enveloping history of communication," suggesting that for much of the century literature and the news were not, as Henry James would wish, discrete domains but mutually constitutive ones (Nerone 230). Newspapers not only reviewed and advertised fiction, but published and serialized it; book publishers, such as Harper and Brothers, produced newspapers (*Harper's Weekly*), while regional newspaper plants were often book printers too. At the same time, book publishers made efforts to market their fiction in the form of news. In the 1830s and 1840s, "mammoth newspapers" (up to ten feet long and over four feet wide) published pirated British novels in serial form that were hawked by newsboys on the streets for pennies or sent through the mail unbound and "subject to

Newspaper Postage only" (Lehuu 60). "Extra" editions, in which popular titles were reprinted in full and bound in paper covers, set a precedent for serialized novels in newspaper format and for cheap nickel-and-dime paperback books that were published weekly in parts long after the mammoth weeklies disappeared. Literary weeklies, or story papers, including Street and Smith's *New York Weekly Dispatch* (revived in 1855), Robert Bonner's *New York Ledger* (1856), Beadle and Adams's *Saturday Journal* (1870), and Norman Munro's *Family Story Paper* (1873), were also sold at newsstands and by subscription through the mails and reached a mass readership (the *Ledger* claimed a circulation of four hundred thousand per week in 1860). If, by 1889 the *Atlantic* hoped the time might arrive when "a work of art in literature" might be "quite independent of its mere mode of production," then the mammoth papers, story papers, and their "extras" and "supplements" already suggested that literature might not have an ontological relationship to the book as an object, but be measured by the forms of currency and circulation on which the fact of a newspaper depends (quoted in Lund 61). "A newspaper," writes Robert E. Park in "The Natural History of the Newspaper," "is not merely printed. It is circulated and read. Otherwise it is not a newspaper" (Park 97).

When literature was published in the form of news, it took its place within a larger print ecology that challenged both the temporality and material culture of reading books; as just another kind of content that newspapers delivered, literature might be judged less by its durability than by the reach of its audience which expanded with the number of newspapers. When one critic imagines in 1831 a coming moment when "journalism will be the whole Press—the whole human thought," his enthusiasm for a universal medium of communication that will let literature be written "with the rapidity of light" provocatively anticipates a contemporary rhetoric of information technologies and the practices of online reading that inform it; which is to say that the fantasy that all expression might be "*instantly conceived, instantly written, and instantly understood*" without the physical experience of books is as much a relic of the nineteenth century as newsboys on the street. Thought, the critic continues, will not have time to "accumulate in a book; the book will arrive too late. The only book possible from to-day is the newspaper" (quoted in Dicken-Garcia 116).

In the nineteenth-century United States, perhaps the greatest distributor of fiction, as Charles Johanningsmeier suggests, was the daily newspaper, a fact rarely discussed in literary histories of serialization that tend to focus on texts that appeared "in parts" (Charles Dickens's 1836 *Pickwick Papers* set the precedent for works by George Lippard, E.D.E.N. Southworth, and others) or in elite monthly magazines, with limited circulation, such as *Putnam's*, *Graham's*, *Harper's*, *Scribner's*, and the *Atlantic*. After 1860, news syndicates supplied literary material to the rapidly increasing number of metropolitan dailies and rural weeklies through stereotype plates, galley proofs, or ready-print sheets (with literary material on one side, to be printed with local news on the other) so that serialized novels and short stories especially could be published alongside reports of current and local events. Through the syndicates, a single written work might appear simultaneously in twenty to one thousand newspapers, all produced and read within the same region or else carried by special express trains from city centers to outlying regions, where the literature traveled at the rate, and with the expediency, of news. William Dean Howells, Mark Twain, Sarah Orne Jewett, Charles Chesnutt, Stephen Crane, Jack London, and even Henry James published syndicated work, which is maybe why James has Flack say, in *The Reverberator*, that "some of the finest books have come out first in the papers" (James, *Reverberator* 124).

If magazines and story papers separated fiction from nonfiction texts, and relegated advertisements to their back pages, a work of fiction in a newspaper was often visually indistinguishable from all the latest news that finally had become the "great thing" in a newspaper, and even from the ads which, like news, were resubmitted daily so that their copy changed (Dana 60). The serialization of fiction encouraged attention to the dramatic momentum of plot, presenting long narratives as discrete stories that advanced for readers with the same periodicity as breaking news, and could be discontinued when public interest ran thin. Authors, like journalists, were compared to "day laborers" who wrote methodically on deadlines and adapted literary works to the standardized demands of the syndicates (Halsey 7); Jack London's character Martin Eden, a syndicated author much as London had been, describes the formula as "fifteen hundred words maximum dose" (quoted in Johanningsmeier 108). Newspaper editors often controlled the visual form of literary texts, adding paragraph breaks and subtitles, like headlines, so that the content of novels might be as accessible as telegraphic dispatches. The editor of the syndicate that bought Stephen Crane's novel *The Red Badge of Courage* asked Crane to cut the manuscript by two-thirds to fit the length requirements of newspaper editors and to make it a more plot-driven work for newspaper readers. Syndicates also tried to emulate the timeliness of the wire services on which they were modeled by soliciting fictions that were topical and resonant with contemporary events, though this meant that literary works could become irrelevant and dated along with the news they referenced. (The regular headline for one newspaper's syndicated fiction section was "Fiction That Deals with Things That Are Up to Date.") There was often little to differentiate fiction from nonfiction items in the newspaper, and as Johanningsmeier points out, not only was the word "story" applied to both categories, but advertisements also took the visual form of reported news and used headlines to attract readers' attention to the products they promoted. Readers, then, were invited to understand the news and fiction as part of the same prolific flow of information about an eventful and changing world. But the integration of fiction within newspapers is peculiar to the nineteenth century since, by 1890, new and cheap mass-market magazines (*McClure's*, *Collier's*, and the *Saturday Evening Post*) began to pay authors more than the syndicates, and soon became far more profitable as forums for mixing fiction and nonfiction on the page; literature, when it appeared in newspapers at all, was relegated to special sections or the occasional Sunday edition, where it could be compartmentalized from current events.

In "the age of the Daily Press" when readers followed the events of daily life in print, and when literature became a part of daily life, books could also become the events that made the news. Books were given notices and reviews in newspapers that worked to "keep up" with cultural trends and fashionable authors or to mine the contents of other publications for, in Dana's words, the "sort of information which the people demand" (Dana 11). Newspapers digested recent books for impatient audiences and provided content for restless readers who, as one critic puts it, looked to notices "not so much for scholarly criticism as for information as to what books exist in current literature that can have any interest or value" (Halsey 54). Literary celebrity emerged in the nineteenth century (the term "celebrity" itself in the modern sense first appeared in 1829) through the publicity of newspapers that turned the personal lives of writers such as Dickens and Harriet Beecher Stowe into ongoing dramas for readers who may not have known their latest works but still wanted to watch the course of their careers as media events (Baker). Writers could now achieve unprecedented levels of fame by simply trading on their currency: to know about the period's most celebrated authors was itself a way of responding to the newsworthiness of current tastes without needing to return to the literature at their source. Authors, in other words, became fashionable as the press inspired a second-order interest among a larger audience of readers who, approaching literature exclusively from the perspective of news, increasingly assumed the transience and contingency of literary value. Books, as one critic of the period says, "are in fact fast becoming what many newspapers and magazines have been—publications whose term of life is ephemeral. They exist as the favorites of a month, or possibly a year; then having had their brief summer-time of success, they silently go their destined way" (Halsey 5).

What did it mean to stay current with culture? In Howells's novel about newspapers, *A Modern Instance*, Clara invites an author to a dinner party not because she had read and admired his book but because "it had made talk" (another guest is a "teacher of Italian, with whom she was pretending to read Dante") (Howells 379). Her social performances of reading derive from an age of news in which literary knowledge, and the fluctuating value of literary merit, had become vogue information. Newspapers not only acquainted readers with new books but also gave them enough of the experience of having read them that they might be, as Lunt suggests, "a substitute" for them (Lunt 94). The press, in other words, allowed for a new kind of cultural literacy that blurred the distinction between knowing a book and knowing *of* it: one might not be well read so much as culturally informed. Even nonreaders of books could register their interest by following newspapers, so that gaining literary knowledge was not so much a private pursuit as a social act, suggesting that books are a way of primarily engaging with the life around them. Clifford Siskin, following communications theorists David Kaufer and Kathleen Carley, calls this phenomenon "reverse vicariousness": if we usually think of reading literature as a vicarious experience for the world, here the reader finds in the newspaper—and all the communal forms of knowing and sharing the newspaper promotes—a way of experiencing literature vicariously (Siskin 216). The phenomenon allows for pretensions to literary knowledge that Lippard, for example, mocks when a dentist, and former bricklayer in *The Quaker City*, Jonas Pulp, asks his patient whether he thinks "Dickens excels in the quiet touches" or whether "the beauties of Shelley are appreciated by the mass"; outside, a ragged newsboy sells an "extra" with sensational accounts of an accident and the juxtaposition suggests for us that, at a moment when accounts of Dickens and Shelley are just more items on the page, all literature belongs to "Pulp" (Lippard 196–197).

Reverse vicariousness may point to the loss of "inward life" that for Thoreau is also the beginning of the end of close, reflective reading in a democratic society, but for others "keeping up" with "literary news" was a welcome form of participation in the progressive nature of the times (Thoreau, Life 359). For Walt Whitman, as editor of the *Brooklyn Daily Eagle*, the timely coverage of literature—which promotes, in turn, an understanding of literature as a timely source of information—is part of the responsibility of a newspaper to its readers. A newspaper, he writes, that does not provide literary notices is

> "behind the age;" for brief as those notices generally are, they enable a man to keep up with what is doing in the literary world, and to see the gradual steps made in the advancement of every thing.... The custom alluded to has another good effect also—it enables *editors* to keep up, in some sort, with the foremost [developments] of the age. For though it cannot be expected that they will study from top to bottom every book they have—that skimming tact which an editor gets after some experience, enables him to take out at a dash the meaning of a book—and his paper and his readers are invariably the gainers by it. An editor thus surrounded by the current literature of the age...*cannot lag behind*."
> (Whitman, *Journalism* 2:112)

Of course, Whitman also capitalized on these notices by including advertisements and reviews for *Leaves of Grass* in its 1856 edition, as well as, famously, a letter from Emerson to the author, which "[greeted him] at the beginning of a great career," but only after seeing his book "advertised in a newspaper" and verifying his identity there (quoted in Whitman, *Leaves of Grass* 637). In his reply to Emerson, Whitman describes his poem as part of a national literary movement that includes "the three thousand different newspapers, the nutriment of the imperfect ones coming in just as usefully as any—the story papers...the onecent and two-cent journals" and other forms of the "active ephemeral myriads" of print that, for him, link the urge toward currency in writing with the ceaseless democratic progress of America: "[A]ll are prophetic;" he writes, "all waft rapidly on. I see that they swell wide, for reasons. I am not troubled at the movement of them, but greatly pleased" (Whitman, *Leaves of Grass* 640). By the time Whitman wrote *Leaves of Grass* he had edited or coedited ten newspapers and contributed to over twenty, calling his early journalistic career the "gestation-years" on "which everything else rests" and "the period...out of which *Leaves of Grass* rose" (Whitman, *Journalism* 1: xxv–xxvi). The inventorial impulses of Whitman's poems, with their ecumenical mingling of events—street fights, suicides, sudden illness, riots, criminal arrests—resemble a newspaper page, where the principle of organization is just all that manages to occur at a moment in time (Fishkin; Trachtenberg). Whitman's inclusion of "these one and all" sounds, for example, much like Dana's claim that the *New York Sun* was "not too proud to report...whatever the

Divine Providence permitted to occur" (Dana 12). The preface to the first edition of
Leaves of Grass was set in columns like a newspaper, and one might say that Whitman's
famous decision to leave his name off the title page (leaving Emerson to confirm his
authorship in the ads) was also in sympathy with the newspapers, which published
largely without bylines. The cleaner title page, as Ed Folsom suggests, also speaks to
Whitman's training as a newspaper compositor who was deeply invested in visual
design (Folsom 16); indeed, in its wide spacing and modern typeface, the title page
visually recalls the changes Whitman made to simplify the look of the *Brooklyn Eagle*
which appeared, as he puts it, with "a clean face" ("as clean and neat as a newly washed
child") soon after he began to edit it (Whitman, *Journalism* 1:402). If there was, in
Whitman's words, an "incisive directness" to the 1855 edition, we might say that the
simplicity of a title page without an author's name on it aspires to the kind of accessible and unmediated transparency of the poet who claimed to do nothing but "flood
himself with the immediate age" or of the nineteenth-century newspaper that claimed
to be, in Whitman's words, "the mirror of the world" (quoted in Folsom 10; Whitman,
Leaves of Grass 633; quoted in Greenspan 24). Each of the eight editions of *Leaves
of Grass* absorbs and builds on prior editions, like the "extras" and "supplements"
Whitman says he bought throughout the Civil War and after ("we got every newspaper morning and evening, and the frequent extras of that period"), so that his poem
grew and unfolded dynamically over time. It may be no surprise that Whitman, who
saw the newspaper as a model of progress, also liked Hegel, for whom, in Whitman's
words, "the whole earth... with its infinite variety" was slowly becoming known to us
through "the endless process of Creative thought, which, amid numberless apparent
failures and contradictions, is held together by a central and never-broken unity—not
contradictions or failures at all, but radiations of one consistent and eternal purpose;
the whole mass of everything steadily, unerringly tending and flowing" (Whitman,
Specimen Days 896). "Do I contradict myself?" writes Whitman in "Song of Myself."
"Very well then I contradict myself" (Whitman, *Leaves of Grass* 77).

In *The Profession of Journalism* (1918), Willard Grosvenor Bleyer writes, "If from
the point of view of successful democracy the value of news is determined by the
extent to which it furnishes food for thought on current topics, we are at once given
an important criterion for defining news and measuring news-values. Thus, news
is anything timely which is significant to newspaper readers in their relation to
the community, the state, and the nation" (quoted in Mott 477). As the news event
became of paramount value, and timeliness became the measure of its worth, the
nineteenth century would learn from newspapers to read for relevance. By the 1840s,
newspapers not only made coverage of daily events their primary purpose, but also
began the practice of organizing their events for readers within a visual hierarchy
of information that suggested the most current items were the most significant to
know. Headlines were new to journalism and announced the latest items by making them increasingly visible on the page (critics note that several papers in 1837
still had no headlines, but by 1847 almost all did). The division of news content into
columns and digests grouped items together and prioritized some items over others
within an expanded field of information that changed each day. All items were now

sorted for relevance and their respective force was due to the visual impact of their headlines and subjects heads (arranged in decks and banks that often diminished in size and heaviness from the top to bottom bank). And while newspapers often continued the tradition of placing the latest news on page two (with less timely material on the outside pages in case ink smudged in delivery), by the end of the century the "front page" had become the icon and expression of the news itself. The headline that announced the top story increased in size and width until it migrated across columns and finally the whole of the front page, with the first banner headline appearing in the *New York World* in 1898 (Mahin; Barnhurst and Nerone). The headline in the American newspapers, writes one historian in 1923, "is deemed by [foreign travelers] the most striking feature of the American press" (Salmon 51). Newspaper writing comes to adapt its own techniques for producing the effect of relevancy, with stories now employing the "inverted pyramid" of the news "lead" to standardize the packaging of facts in descending order of importance. Where earlier reports proceeded inductively—often withholding the most pertinent details of events while supplying their context—journalists began to condense the most pertinent facts of their accounts into the lead of the story so that, by the last decades of the century, readers could know everything they needed to know without completing a story (Mindich).

In his Civil War poem "Donelson," Herman Melville tells the story of the Union victory at Fort Donelson through the "latest news" that appears as nothing but a succession of headlines and dispatches read to a crowd on the street; "events unfold" and each day's reports and late editions press forward new developments in the battle (Melville 45, 46). As a narrative poem, Melville's account about the news of war resembles a ballad and so makes a nod to the earliest form of news (before newspapers), which circulated as printed ballads. But "Donelson" is finally not a ballad so much as a series of modern headlines that keep pace with the progress of the news; ballads are organized around refrains and repetitions but Melville's narrative, pursuing the "vicissitudes of the war" as they unfold ("LATER AND LAST. / THE FORT IS OURS"), never looks back (Melville 53, 55). Derived from actual newspaper accounts of the war, the poem does not simply refer to the topics that make the headlines, so much as communicate—and test the limits of—an aesthetic of contemporaneity that makes reading literature itself feel as relevant as the news.

The newsiness of Melville's "Donelson" helps us better appreciate the efforts of other writers in the period who tried to assert the currency of their work by insisting on its relevance. Whitman's poems are filled with events from the daily papers; his 1865 "Year of Meteors" alone makes reference to the hanging of John Brown, the presidential race, the visit of the Prince of Wales, and the arrival of the British steamship, the *Great Eastern*. In his notebooks, poetic fragments share pages with news clips, and occasionally with drafts of his own reporting or editorials for the Brooklyn, New York, and New Jersey newspapers, and especially for the Brooklyn *Daily Times*, which he edited from 1857 to 1859 (Bowers 1955 xxvii–iii). Whitman was only one of many nineteenth-century authors, including George Lippard, Margaret Fuller, Fanny Fern, Frederick Douglass,

William Dean Howells, Stephen Crane, Mark Twain, and Ambrose Bierce who trained as journalists and whose work encouraged readers to think of fiction as another way of "[furnishing] food for thought on current topics" and of participating in a culture that had increasing faith in the promise of perpetual change it saw in the news (Fishkin; Robertson). Lippard, for example, who worked as a news reporter for a Philadelphia penny paper, the *Spirit of the Times*, saw his city novels—derived from accounts of crime, scandal, and corruption in the dailies and filled with references to them—as part of a larger project of social awareness and reform: "a literature," he writes, "which does not work practically for the advancement of social reform, or which is too good or too dignified to picture the wrongs of the great mass of humanity, is just good for nothing at all" (Lippard viii). Lippard's *The Quaker City* exposes the character and crimes of Philadelphia in a plot-driven novel, whose dizzying sequence of episodes and events, and nearly six hundred pages, nonetheless covers only three days of condensed action (since each day in the life of the news was essentially eventful). The final events of the novel, like the events in "Donelson," are narrated through the newspaper that reports them; "we will glance at the contents of a newspaper," says the narrator who also says that "we like to look at nature and the world, not only as they appear, but as they are!" (Lippard 305, 571).

"The newspaper," writes Charles Dudley Warner in 1881, "is not a willful creation nor an isolated phenomenon but the legitimate outcome of our age" (Warner 32). The literature of reform that Lippard helped introduce to America was both derived from the news and also, perhaps, the "legitimate outcome" of the same moment and impulse that made the daily news a defining medium of the nineteenth century. The belief that literature could be timely and relevant by participating in the contemporary world informed not only the sensationalist urban fiction of Lippard, George Thompson, Henri Foster, Ned Buntline, and others (some fifty novels of city life appeared between 1844 and 1860) but also all novels that took up reformist subject matter and the language of social purpose in and out of the papers, including antislavery and temperance literature. In the first installment of Harriet Beecher Stowe's serial novel, *My Wife and I*, the narrator suggests, "Hath anyone in our day, as in St. Paul's, a psalm, a doctrine, a tongue, a revelation, an interpretation—forthwith he wraps it up in a serial story, and presents it to the public. We have prison discipline, free-trade, labor and capital, women's rights, the temperance question, in serial stories" (Stowe ix). At the same time as news became the subject of literature, the press began to increase its readership and visibility by making literature out of news. After the Civil War, the "new journalism"—a phrase coined by Matthew Arnold in connection with *New York World* editor Joseph Pulitzer—vividly presented the news as entertaining "stories" with central characters, dialogue, descriptive details, dramatic tension, and points of view. The new journalism developed alongside a model of the news as pure and impartial information, blurring the line between literature and the news and rewriting current events as narratives that borrowed from the style and techniques of urban fiction, detective fiction, mysteries, travel adventures, and romance, to name a few of the literary genres. The news read a lot like fiction, but for Pulitzer, at least, the accessibility of the new journalism to an expanded and working-class readership was "truly democratic" for how the truth it delivered in literary form could promote social change while "[serving]...the people with earnest sincerity" (quoted in Roggenkamp 29). After all, as Stowe's narrator continues in *My Wife and I*, "In our modern days...it is not so much the story, as the things it gives the author a chance to say" (Stowe xii).

There were of course those who disagreed, and for every claim that literature should be sympathetic to the news, Thoreau or James, or someone else, might make the case for the "story" itself over the things it could say to a public that was increasingly accustomed to the news. *Scribner's Monthly*, which had argued for topical fiction in its "Topics of the Time" column, later laments novels that engage with "a question of the day" because contemporary relevance means future irrelevance and because "such novels are not likely to survive the discussion or disturbance that gave them birth" (quoted in Lund 96). In Edgar Allan Poe's story "The Mystery of Marie Rogêt," Auguste Dupin investigates a crime by following the comprehensive coverage of events as they appear in the daily newspapers and with "no other means of investigation than the newspapers afforded." Though he "seek[s] truth," as he says, in all the relevant "details" he transcribes for the reader from the press, it is not enough to solve the crime because the evidence he ultimately needs derives from a kind of "philosophical" truth and logic that resides outside the logic of the events: "I would divert," Dupin says, from the "unfruitful ground of the event itself" (Poe 445, 493, 473). Poe's detective reports the most "decisive information," only to tell us that there are things we will never discover when we "[confine our] discussion to the bounds of apparent relevancy" and that, in the end, the most productive forms of knowledge are precisely what the "facts" of the newspapers leave out (Poe 473). Sometimes it is possible to resist an age of news even while being consumed by its own progress. Poe suggests, in other words, that one way to make literature out of news is to take all the information it delivers with such timeliness and speed and render it irrelevant to a story about how we imagine a modern world we largely know by our own readings of it.

BIBLIOGRAPHY

Anderson, Benedict. *Imagined Communities: Reflections on the Origin and Spread of Nationalism*. Rev. ed. New York: Verso, 1991.

Baker, Thomas N. *Sentiment and Celebrity: Nathaniel Parker Willis and the Trials of Literary Fame*. New York: Oxford University Press, 1999.

Barnhurst, Kevin G., and John Nerone. *The Form of News: A History*. New York: Guilford Press, 2001.

Blondheim, Menaheim. *News over the Wires: The Telegraph and the Flow of Public Information in America, 1844–1897*. Cambridge, MA: Harvard University Press, 1994.

Bowers, Fredson. *Whitman's Manuscripts, Leaves of Grass (1860): A Parallel Text*. Chicago: University of Chicago Press, 1955.

Dana, Charles A. *The Art of Newspaper Making: Three Lectures.* New York: D. Appleton, 1895.

Dicken-Garcia, Hazel. *Journalistic Standards in Nineteenth-Century America.* Madison: University of Wisconsin Press, 1989.

Edel, Leon. *Henry James: The Conquest of London: 1870–1881.* New York: Avon Books, 1962.

"Editor's Study." *Harper's New Monthly Magazine* (November 1892): 962–967.

Emerson, Ralph Waldo. *The Journals and Miscellaneous Notebooks.* Vol. 2, *1822–1826.* Ed. William H. Gilman, Alfred R. Ferguson, and Merrell R. Davis. Cambridge, MA: Belknap Press of Harvard University Press, 1961.

Fishkin, Shelley Fisher. *From Fact to Fiction: Journalism and Imaginative Writing in America.* New York: Oxford University Press, 1985.

Folsom, Ed. "What We're Still Learning about the 1855 *Leaves of Grass* 150 Years Later." *Leaves of Grass: The Sesquicentennial Essays.* Ed. Susan Belasco, Ed Folsom, and Kenneth Price. Lincoln: University of Nebraska Press, 2007. 1–32.

Foster, George G. *New York by Gas-Light and Other Urban Sketches.* 1850. Ed. Stuart M. Blumin. Berkeley: University of California Press, 1990.

Godkin, E. L. "Newspapers Here and Abroad." *North American Review* 150 (February 1890): 197–204.

Greenspan, Ezra. *Whitman and the American Reader.* New York: Cambridge University Press, 1990.

Halsey, Francis Whiting. *Our Literary Deluge: And Some of Its Deeper Waters.* New York: Doubleday, Page, 1902.

Henkin, David M. *City Reading: Written Words and Public Spaces in Antebellum New York.* New York: Columbia University Press, 1998.

Houlgate, Stephen. *An Introduction to Hegel: Freedom, Truth and History.* Oxford: Blackwell, 1988.

Howells, William Dean. *A Modern Instance* in *Novels, 1875–1886.* 1882. Ed. Edwin H. Cady. New York: Library of America, 1977.

Hudson, Frederic, Alfred McClung Lee, and Frank Luther Mott, eds. *American Journalism, 1690–1940.* Vol. 1. New York: Routledge, 2000.

Irving, Washington. "Rip Van Winkle." 1819. *The Sketch Book of Geoffrey Crayon, Gent. History Tales Sketches.* Ed. James W. Tuttleton. New York: Library of America, 1983. 769–785.

James, Henry. *The American Scene* in *Collected Travel Writings.* 1907. Ed. Richard Howard. New York: Library of America, 1993.

———. *Parisian Sketches.* Ed. Leon Edel and Ilse Dusoir Lind. New York: New York University Press, 1957.

———. *The Reverberator.* New York: Charles Scribner's Sons, 1908.

Johanningsmeier, Charles. *Fiction and the American Literary Marketplace: The Role of Newspaper Syndicates, 1860–1900.* New York: Cambridge University Press, 1997.

Lehuu, Isabelle. *Carnival on the Page: Popular Print Media in Antebellum America.* Chapel Hill: University of North Carolina Press, 2000.

Lippard, George. *The Quaker City; or, The Monks of Monk Hall.* 1845. Ed. David S. Reynolds. Amherst: University of Massachusetts Press, 1995.

Lund, Michael. *America's Continuing Story: An Introduction to Serial Fiction, 1850–1900.* Detroit, MI: Wayne State University Press, 1993.

Lunt, George. "The Uses and Abuses of the Press." *Three Eras of New England and Other Address, with Papers Critical and Biographical.* Boston: Ticknor and Fields, 1857. 67–109.

Mahin, Helen Ogden. *The Development and Significance of the Newspaper Headline*. Ann Arbor, MI: George Wahr, 1924.

Melville, Herman. "Donelson." *Poems of Herman Melville*. 1862. Ed. Douglas Robillard. Albany, NY: New College and University Press, 1976. 49–56.

Merriam, George S. *The Life and Times of Samuel Bowles*. 2 vols. New York: Century, 1885.

Mindich, David T. Z. *Just the Facts: How "Objectivity" Came to Define American Journalism*. New York: New York University Press, 1998.

Mott, Frank Luther, ed. *Interpretations of Journalism: A Book of Readings*. New York: F. S. Crofts, 1937.

Nerone, John. "Newspapers and the Public Sphere." *A History of the Book in America*. Vol. 3, *The Industrial Book, 1840–1880*. Ed. Scott E. Casper, Jeffrey D. Groves, Stephen W. Nissenbaum, and Michael Winship. Chapel Hill: University of North Carolina Press, 2007. 203–248.

Park, Robert E. "The Natural History of the Newspaper." 1923. *On Social Control and Collective Behavior: Selected Papers*. Ed. Ralph H. Turner. Chicago: University of Chicago Press, 1967. 97–113.

Parton, James. "James Gordon Bennett and The New York Herald." *Famous Americans of Recent Times*. Boson: Ticknor and Fields, 1867. 259–305 .

Pinkard, Terry. *Hegel: A Biography*. New York: Cambridge University Press, 2000.

Poe, Edgar Allan. "The Mystery of Marie Rogêt." 1842–1843. *Tales of Mystery and Imagination*. Rutland, VT: Everyman, 1993. 445–493.

Posnock, Ross. *The Trial of Curiosity: Henry James, William James, and the Challenge of Modernity*. New York: Oxford University Press, 1991.

Pound, Ezra. *ABC of Reading*. New York: New Directions, 1934.

Pray, Isaac Clark. *Memoirs of James Gordon Bennett and His Times*. New York: Stringer and Townsend, 1855.

Robertson, Michael. *Stephen Crane. Journalism, and the Making of Modern American Literature*. New York: Columbia University Press, 1997.

Roggenkamp, Karen. *Narrating the News: New Journalism and Literary Genre in Late-Nineteenth Century American Newspapers and Fiction*. Kent, OH: Kent State University Press, 2005.

Salmon, Lucy Maynard. *The Newspaper and the Historian*. New York: Oxford University Press, 1923.

Schudson, Michael. *Discovering the News: A Social History of American Newspapers*. New York: Basic Books, 1973.

Siskin, Clifford. *The Work of Writing: Literature and Social Change in Britain, 1700–1830*. Baltimore: Johns Hopkins University Press, 1998.

Stillman, W. J. "Journalism and Literature." *Atlantic Monthly* 68 (November 1891): 687–695.

Stowe, Harriet Beecher. *My Wife and I; or, Harry Henderson's History*. Boston: Houghton, Mifflin, 1871.

Tocqueville, Alexis de. *Democracy in America*. 1835–1840. Trans. Arthur Goldhammer. New York: Library of America, 2004.

Thoreau, Henry David. *Cape Cod*. 1865. Ed. Robert F. Sayre. New York: Library of America, 1985.

———."Life without Principle." 1863.*Collected Essays and Poems*. Ed. Elizabeth Hall Witherell. New York: Library of America, 2001. 348–366.

———. *Walden; or, Life in the Woods*. 1854. Ed. Robert F. Sayre. New York: Library of America, 1985.

———. *A Week on the Concord and Merrimack Rivers.* 1849. Ed. Robert F. Sayre. New York: Library of America, 1985.

Trachtenberg, Alan. "Whitman's Lesson of the City." *Breaking Bounds: Whitman and American Cultural Studies.* Ed. Betsy Erkkila and Jay Grossman. New York: Oxford University Press, 1996. 163–173.

Warner, Charles Dudley. "The American Newspaper." 1902. *Fashions in Literature and Other Literary and Social Essays and Addresses.* Introduction by Hamilton Wright Mabie. New York: AMS Press, 1969.

Whitman, Walt. *The Journalism. The Collected Writings of Walt Whitman.* 2 vols. Ed. Herbert Bergman. New York: Peter Lang, 1998–2003.

———. *Leaves of Grass and Other Writings.* Ed. Michael Moon. New York: Norton, 2002.

———. *Specimen Days in Poetry and Prose.* Ed. Justin Kaplan. New York: Library of America, 1982.

CHAPTER 18

READING MINDS IN THE NINETEENTH CENTURY

PAUL GILMORE

TOWARD the end of Kate Chopin's *The Awakening* (1899), Dr. Mandelet responds to Edna Pontellier's disorientation at viewing Madame Ratignolle give birth by offering an account of the tension between nature and culture: "[Y]outh is given up to illusions. It seems to be a provision of Nature; a decoy to secure mothers for the race. And Nature takes no account of moral consequences, of arbitrary conditions which we create, and which we feel obliged to maintain at any cost" (134–135). Embodying the voice of a kind of late nineteenth-century Darwinian naturalism, Dr. Mandelet, who knows "his fellow-creatures better than most men...that inner life which so seldom unfolds itself to unanointed eyes" (93), potentially explains Edna's tragic story as well as the critical response to Chopin's novel. Stripped of moral consequences and arbitrary social and culture conditions, our lives are the product of nature, wherein the chief end lies in the reproduction of the species. To read another's "inner life," as both Dr. Mandelet and we the readers are called upon to do, we must see through those social and cultural illusions and seek the deeper biological explanations offered by scientific medicine.

Published a hundred years earlier, Charles Brockden Brown's *Edgar Huntly* somewhat similarly offers the medical opinions of Huntly's former mentor, Sarsefield, a surgeon, as a way of explaining Huntly's and Clithero's enigmatic behavior. In the preface to *Edgar Huntly*, Brown establishes his task as bringing the full attention of "the moral painter" to a country that has already "opened new views to the naturalist" (*Three Gothic Novels* 641). Through the recurrence of medical authorities in his works—Sarsefield as well as Thomas Campbell in *Wieland* (1798) and Dr. Stevens in *Arthur Mervyn* (1799, 1800)— who offer rationalistic, scientific explanations for the seemingly inexplicable, highly irrational behavior surrounding them, Brown hints that the moral painter needs the naturalist to help him elucidate "the moral constitution of man." Potentially, at least, as with Dr. Mandelet a century later, readers encounter individual, sometimes bizarre, cases, that we, like the observer physicians, must explicate by relying on the best scientific theories available.

Yet these texts, Brown's gothic oeuvre as well as Chopin's *Awakening*, remain resolutely noncommittal to whether we should fully trust the scientific explanations of the observing doctors to guide our own reading of the central characters and their behavior. Most prominently, through Edna's suicide and Sarsefield's inability to comprehend Edgar's motivations, these novels emphasize the potential of their characters' behavior to exceed the grasp of the most insightful readers of mind within the texts themselves. As such, the novels do not dismiss the scientific authorities and their analyses of the minds at work, but rather gesture to their ultimate insufficiency at fully accounting for individual behavior. I want to take this skeptical acceptance of the insights offered by the medical science of the day as a template for my own engagement with the competing claims of the contemporary sciences of the mind and for mediating the intersection of historicist literary criticism with cognitive neuroscience.

From a historicist approach, the key to reading the minds of these characters and their creators lies in recovering the contemporary scientific theories Chopin and Brown engage in eliciting readers' responses and placing that engagement within a broader social, cultural, and/or institutional context. The emerging field of cognitive literary studies, however, would emphasize the universal mental structures allowing such reading practices to be possible at all, the innate human desire to read the minds of others by constructing imaginative narratives about their inner lives. In what follows, I will offer an overview and critique of cognitive literary studies before moving on to suggest how recent developments within neuroscience and studies of embodied cognition can potentially offer a better model for an historicism grounded in brain science. Where cognitive literary studies has largely drawn on a cognitive science that posits the universal nature of seemingly disembodied human mental processes, embodied cognition and cognitive neuroscience have theorized how consciousness and higher-level cognitive processes are grounded in the human body's interaction with the world. In this way, embodied approaches to cognition treat the brain and its processes, creations, and functions as the product of both eons of evolutionary history and specific sociocultural conditions. As the examples of *The Awakening* and *Edgar Huntly* suggest, modern literature's attention to the idiosyncratic and the particular further complicates this picture by accentuating the indeterminate effects of history and environment on specific cases. Combining formal and historical analysis with the insights of embodied cognitive neuroscience, I conclude, provides the basis for a neural historicism that would illuminate some of the ways minds have been read and understood and how those minds have read texts and the world.

The Cognitive Turn

In *The German Ideology*, Marx declares that "[t]he first premise of all human history is, of course, the existence of living human individuals [and] [t]hus the first fact to be established is the physical organisation of these individuals and their consequent relation to the rest of nature" (149). Yet most of the ideological criticism—whether cultural studies, new historicism, or identity-based analyses—of the past decades has neglected the body's physical organization in favor of viewing it as the product of social practices. For all of the impressive insights into the material bases of literary practice amassed by the political, cultural, and historical turns in academic criticism, these critical methods have almost completely omitted the material space in which and through which literature, culture, and history are most directly experienced, embodied, and reiterated: the brain-body continuum. Cognitive literary studies, comprising a variety of approaches building on the insights of cognitive linguistics, cognitive psychology, evolutionary psychology, and philosophy of mind, has often based its claims on exactly this ground, arguing that attending to the mind and its functions is central to an examination of literature. Yet this work, to a great extent, has also failed to address the bodily nature of the mental experience of literature and culture.

In offering the most schematic of overviews, I will outline what I take to be some of the most important insights offered by this diverse field before returning to its shortcomings. Cognitive literary criticism has relied on the work of cognitive scientists from a variety of fields even as it argues for literary study's capacity to make unique contributions to the sciences of the mind. The central ground for this claim can be summed up by Mark Turner's thesis in *The Literary Mind*, that rather than being unique to literature, the cognitive structures underlying literature, notably metaphor and narrative, are essential to almost all higher-level mental processes. In terms of metaphor, Turner, working with the cognitive scientist Gilles Fauconnier, has elaborated a theory of conceptual blending, the human mind's prelinguistic capacity to combine mental patterns from two different frames in order to produce an altogether new, third conceptual frame. Using the research of paleoanthropologists, Turner and Fauconnier link this ability to the explosion in human creativity—and the emergence of language, art, and religion—some fifty thousand years ago. From this perspective, the underlying processes making metaphor—the sophisticated conceptual blend of linguistic elements—possible are not simply poetic but absolutely fundamental to any higher-level thinking.

Turner and cognitive narratologists have made similar claims about narrative or what Turner calls parable (see Herman). Turner extrapolates from what he calls "small spatial stories"—"The wind blows a cloud through the sky, a child throws a rock, a mother pours milk into a glass, a whale swims through the water" (13)—to argue that "Narrative imagining—story—is the fundamental instrument of thought.... It is a literary capacity indispensable to human cognition generally" (4–5). Other cognitive critics, most notably Lisa Zunshine in *Why*

We Read Fiction, have focused on a more specific kind of narrative in elaborating the idea of theory of mind from cognitive psychology (see also Boyd). Theory of mind specifically refers to the hypothesis that humans attempt to read the minds of other human actors, to deduce their thoughts and intentions, by creating theoretical explanations for their behavior based on universal ideas of human psychology. A sense of narrative structure seems implied by theory of mind, as to posit another's beliefs, ideas, drives, we must assume some schema of future activity. Literature is thus at the heart of our normal ways of thinking about the world and others as we rely on metaphorical structures, on basic narrative patterns, and on our identification with and theorization about other people, whether fictive or real.

Returning to Edna and Edgar can help highlight the strengths and weaknesses of this approach. Both novels are propelled by their desire to detail their main characters' minds. Where Edgar focuses less often on his own mental processes than on attempting to understand (and correct) Clithero's, the narrator of *The Awakening* takes great care to describe the mental processes Edna is undergoing. Despite the difference in narrative point of view (first person in *Huntly*, third in *The Awakening*), both novels stress, at the sentence level as well as through plot, the need for readers to bring their own inferences to bear. From the perspective of cognitive literary theory, we could understand these novels as working by engaging our theories of mind through the cues and clues, overt and subtle, scattered through the texts. Brown foregrounds this process via Huntly's narration of his failed attempts to read Clithero, from the first chapter onward. As it becomes clear that Huntly misreads Clithero, we are pushed to examine our own readings of both young men, just as in *The Awakening* the narrator guides us to revise our interpretations of Edna's inner life by offering us glimpses of her and other characters'—her husband's, Madame Ratignolle's, her father's—readings of her behavior.

These works function as novels, then, by allowing our theories of mind to play with imagined narrative constructions of social others, providing us pleasure by challenging our ability to make sense of them and their world, to devise and test theses about the characters and their "inner lives," in such a way as to grant us insight into "the moral constitution of man," as revealed by the scientific "known principles of human nature" (Brown, *Three Gothic Novels* 3). We are drawn to these texts because they engage deep-seated, evolutionarily adapted mental functions, our natural tendencies to want to understand processes, here, social, interpersonal, psychological ones, in terms of cause and effect, in terms of narrative structure. Further, cognitive literary studies would suggest that key organizing metaphors—such as awakening or sleepwalking—are based less in any contemporaneous ideas about consciousness than in fundamental human physical processes and the way we make sense of the world through our metaphoric translation of those processes to other realms. In pursuing this line of thought, we might, for example, draw on empirical studies on the nature of cognition upon first awakening from sleep to examine how the metaphor of Edna's transformation—her lack of full consciousness, her sense of renewal and of a new world, the suspension or occlusion of cultural and social norms and values—emerges directly from a universal human, embodied experience.

This account of these novels, it seems to me, offers some potential insights, but leaves many questions unanswered and largely fails to explain the textual particulars that make the works memorable. In fact, many of the readings produced by cognitive literary studies seem, as with other reductionist materialisms such as vulgar Marxism, simply to tell the same story over and over. Chopin's metaphors resonate universally due to their basis in shared human experiences; Brown's plot engages us all due to our desire to construct a complete, satisfying narrative. Yet Chopin's metaphors have not met with the same success with readers at different times, and Brown's convoluted plots have not equally engaged readers at different historical moments. Initial reviewers of Chopin's novel varied in their reactions to Edna's awakening, the more sympathetic equating it with her becoming "aware she is a human being," while the majority viewed her as never truly waking up, as she unconsciously sleepwalks into "the temptations she trumped up for herself" or "a merely animal instinct" (qtd. in Petry 55, 52, 53). Further, while both texts depend on evoking readers' desires to get inside the minds of their characters, their ability to motivate readers' mind-reading capacities have varied, depending on a number of social, cultural, and historical factors. One can imagine that neither text, focusing, as they do, on the close analysis of the motivations, desires, and actions of ordinary individuals living on the edge of the community as an adulterer and an orphan would hold much interest for readers expecting stories about supposedly universal prototypes of romantic heroes or exemplary actions. Reviewers of *The Awakening* repeatedly rejected it for providing a "detailed history of the manifold and contemporary love affairs of a wife and mother" (qtd. in Petry 52), and as Cathy Davidson's magisterial history of the novel in the early republic repeatedly emphasizes, critics of Brown's period regularly questioned the propriety of making lower class men like Huntly or Arthur Mervyn and fallen women like Charlotte Temple the focus of fictional imagination.

The kind of cognitive literary studies conducted by Turner, Zunshine, and many others can help us recognize the underlying evolved cognitive structures allowing for any basic narrative and for metaphoric language of all sorts; it can help us to recognize that Chopin's metaphor largely works, when it does, by engaging a shared framework grounded in universal human experience, that Brown's plot largely allures us, when it does, due to our innate need to form satisfying stories about the world and other humans. But, so far at least, cognitive literary studies has done little to help us understand why certain kinds of narratives, with distinctive formal and thematic features, might arise in particular periods in certain places appealing to specific groups of readers. Cognitive literary criticism's focus on universals derives, in part, from an attempt to use more scientific methods, for, as Patrick Colm Hogan puts it in *The Mind and Its Stories*, "One reason literature has played such a limited role in cognitive study is that science seeks generalities while literature seems to be tied to narrow particularity" (2). In this way, for many in cognitive literary studies, the universalism of science offers a tool to contest the canon-busting particularism and celebration of difference of identity politics and poststructuralist theory. But such a view relies on a somewhat narrow, almost positivist, notion of science, and many of the shortcomings of cognitive literary criticism can be traced not to its reliance on science per se but to its overreliance on a very distinct and debated form of cognitive science (see Kramnick for a similar argument about the use of evolutionary biology in literary studies). By broadening our understanding of cognitive science and the debates within it we can overcome the blind spots of cognitive literary studies while integrating its perspective into a revised sense of literary history.

Cognitive Science Is Not Brain Surgery (or Neuroscience)

One of the problems with building a literary criticism on the foundation of cognitive science is that cognitive science itself is a rather young and disparate field. Cognitive science casts its net widely, drawing on such disciplines as sociolinguistics, cognitive linguistics, evolutionary psychology, cognitive psychology, philosophy of mind, evolutionary anthropology, computer science, artificial intelligence, and neurobiology. These various disciplines do not always come together easily or well, and the field as a whole, while unified by certain core ideas, is riven by serious and deep disputes. One of the weaknesses of much cognitive literary criticism has been its failure to recognize or represent these divisions and debates very clearly, more often than not relying on one strain of cognitive science and citing it as offering *the* insights yielded by contemporary sciences of the mind.

At the risk of some simplification, we can distinguish two leading approaches in cognitive science according to their accounts of the mind and its relationship to the body, what I will refer to as cognitive science proper and embodied cognitive neuroscience. Cognitive science proper was initiated in the late 1950s by Noam Chomsky's critique of dominant behaviorist psychology. Over the succeeding decades, cognitive science developed in large part by viewing the mind in terms of computational functions and through what Alvin Goldman aptly describes as "the armchair method" of "observation and reflection on human behavior and discursive practices" (4). Broadly speaking, cognitive science of this sort (sometimes called first-generation cognitive science) embraces a top-down methodology—from observed cognitive processes we can deduce the necessary underlying mental structures—and has theorized an innatist, functional modularist model of the human mind. That is to say, according to most scholars within this mode of cognitive science, the human mind is universally the same, a highly structured organ with multiple modules largely devoted to particular evolutionarily adapted functions; the

mind, as the evolutionary psychologists Leda Cosmides and John Tooby have influentially described it, is like a Swiss army knife, an instrument with a set of highly
specialized, if somewhat flexible, tools. As formulated by Cosmides and Tooby, philosophers such as Jerry Fodor, linguists like Steven Pinker, and related thinkers in
cognitive psychology and other fields, this version of cognitive science has provided
the foundation for most cognitive literary studies.

From the 1970s onward, through work in artificial intelligence as well as in the
cognitive linguistics of George Lakoff and others, an alternative cognitive science
developed, emphasizing the brain's embodiment and its plasticity. This approach
and the functional modularity of first-generation cognitive science are sometimes
characterized, 1990s rap style, as East Coast (varieties of innatist functionalism
and modularity—Fodor, Pinker, and Chomsky at MIT) and West Coast (work
centered at Berkeley—Lakoff—and UC-San Diego). Where many in cognitive
science proper attempt to tie their theories to neurological studies, in its "strong
form," as Jerome Feldman delineates it, functionalism "claims that the way the
mind is physically embodied in the brain is irrelevant to the study of mind" (33),
a point emphasized by Chomsky's infamous rejection of the idea that neuroscience can really tell us anything conclusive about the cognitive functioning of the
human mind. Embodied cognitive neuroscience, on the other hand, attempts to
move upward from observations of neural activity and downward from cognitive
and linguistic research, often meeting in the middle with computer modeling of
neural networks (connectionism). Contra innatist functionalism, in which the
brain's architecture is genetically predetermined, connectionism theorizes that
neural circuitry largely emerges from the strengthening and weakening of syn-
aptic connections among neurons due to experience, that repeated stimulation or
repression of those connections leads to fundamental changes in the brain's wiring. Connectionists do not embrace a blank-slate view of the mind, but rather use
computer modeling to theorize how stimuli might transform the brain's underlying physiological structures to produce cognitive functions. In related fashion,
the body's constant interaction with the physical world provides the basis for
Lakoff and Mark Johnson's theory of embodied metaphor: "[T]he very properties
of concepts are created as a result of the way the brain and body are structured
and the way they function in interpersonal relations and in the physical world"
(37). This means that much, if not all, of our thought is built on a core group of
metaphorical schemas related to basic physical processes grounded in shared spatial human experience—walking erect, the placement of our sense organs, having
certain basic needs, including food, community, sex. Thus, humans "acquire a
large system of primary metaphors automatically and unconsciously simply by
functioning in the most ordinary of ways in the everyday world from our earliest
years. . . . Because of the way neural connections are formed during the period of
conflation, we all naturally think using hundreds of primary metaphors" (47). In
this way, like other cognitive scientists, Lakoff and Johnson emphasize a basic set
of neural and linguistic structures shared by all people, what Feldman calls "universal conceptual schemas" (189).

As this similar emphasis on universal structures hints, the East Coast–West Coast distinction never was as firm as the rhetoric sometimes indicated, and in the past couple of decades, the distinction has blurred, as advances in brain imaging and the maturing of the discipline have led to more nuanced and sophisticated theoretical blends as well as more radical theories (see Chemero for one recent attempt at taxonomy). Most cognitive literary criticism skims over these distinctions, however, only acknowledging them in order to render them seamless (see, for example, Hogan's *Cognitive Science, Literature, and the Arts*). At the same time, though, even as they cite research from embodied cognition and cognitive neuroscience, most cognitive literary critics maintain something akin to a first-generational cognitive science stance in positing the mind as largely disembodied and hardwired. Such a starting point leaves little room for intensive textual attention to suggest modifications to this model of the mind, and thus despite claims otherwise, much of cognitive literary criticism has not so much produced a cross-fertilization of scientific approaches and literary studies as simply reproduced the theories of cognitive science.

Conversely, embodied cognitive approaches tend to emphasize the role experience plays in structuring neural circuits, thus providing a better foundation for theorizing cultural and historical difference and at least the possibility of those differences significantly altering the way people think and act. Building on these and similar theories as well as recent research on the brain's plasticity and on the human genome, Bruce Wexler, a neurocognitive psychiatrist, has perhaps gone furthest in asserting the primacy of culture in understanding the brain: "[T]he specific patterns of all the intricate connections among neurons that constitute these functional systems are determined by sensory stimulation and other aspects of environmentally induced neuronal activity." And thus, "In the details of this neuronal 'wiring,' no two individuals are the same" (21–22). While most cognitive neuroscientists would not go as far as Wexler, his emphasis on individuality brings us back to what Hogan identifies as one of the problems for literature's attempt to engage with science: modern literature's focus on the particular and the individuated, if not the idiosyncratic or abnormal. But rather than being a problem, the attempt of postromantic literature to represent individuals provides a bridge between imaginative literature and cognitive neuroscience. While literature has relied on types and implicit laws of human behavior in attempting to convey the irreducible particularity of individuals, times, and places, cognitive neuroscience has reiterated the centrality of shared underlying neural structures, determined both by genetic and ontogenetic forces, while recognizing that the exact neural makeup of any one individual—and thus his or her neural functioning, thought processes, emotions, responses, and sense of self—will be unique in ways perhaps inaccessible to empirical study. The question then is to what extent and how does culture—individual experience within a social framework of historical time—affect and potentially transform the genetically originated structures of the human brain and how do we study those effects. It is in this respect that literature can truly and most fully contribute to cognitive studies as an equal partner.

Toward a Neural Historicism

The starting point for such a partnership, a neural historicism focused on the changes recorded in and taking place in the brain, is the neuroscientific truism Feldman articulates: *"learning does not add knowledge to an unchanging system—it changes the system"* (72). Contrasting the rejection of the concept of learning by many in cognitive science (see Tooby and Cosmides 122–123 and Pinker 35), this seemingly obvious thesis foregrounds the idea that any change in ideas, beliefs, linguistic understanding, or worldviews reflects some change in individual and group brain organization. To ground such an argument, a neural historicism first needs to acknowledge the underlying adaptive structures of the functioning brain and nervous system, to recognize that certain bodily experiences and needs—birth, movement, hunger, bodily space—further elaborate those structures in nearly universal ways, and to understand how the constraints of basic neuroanatomy and adaptive functions might lead brains to respond to specific cultural or historical problems or needs by constructing and utilizing similar neural connections. Yet a neural *historicism* must also investigate exactly how the specific experiences of a particular place over a certain period might fundamentally shape the brains of living individuals. This, in fact, is what lived history is, the temporally specific manifestation of the embodied brain, a brain structured by evolution but reconfigured by the stimuli it has encountered through the body, stimuli at times particular to a specific place and/or time. Over the past decade, a number of critics have advocated a kind of cognitive historicism. Yet their work, so far, either has offered fairly thin accounts of the interaction between brain and specific historical environment in attempting to contextualize unchanging, universal cognitive processes or has elaborated the ways that earlier authors and thinkers have anticipated the insights of the recent brain sciences. While illuminating and often provocative, these studies have tended to neglect (or reject) the historical transformation of cognitive structures. Cognitive historicism, to date, has largely failed to address the way history—experience—is inscribed in and transforms, at some level at least, the human brain-body continuum (for the best exception, see Richardson, *Neural Sublime*).

The idea of recovering how neural circuitry in the past worked, how individuals' brains in the same time and place, as well as across time and space, might have been organized similarly and differently due to genetic and experiential continuity and variation, is daunting, to say the least. There is, as far as I know, no conceivable scientific approach for determining the nature of such historical biological structures. We cannot yet map living individuals' changing beliefs and ideas through available technology, let alone dig up our ancestors and subject them to brain imaging studies. Yet, I want to propose, changes and differences in literary form, in literature's production and reception, both indicate some level of different neural organization and suggest a mode for accessing and conceptualizing those differences. As many historicist critics, most notably Fredric Jameson, have contended, one of the most sensitive markers to this kind of historical change is literature and, in particular, literary form. According to most accounts, modern written literature is distinguished most fundamentally by variety, by the development of multiple reading publics who react quite differently to the various forms, genres, and themes of the past few centuries. That literature, its production, and circulation point to the increasing varieties of reading minds, providing at least one index of the extent to which brains react dissimilarly to similar stimuli. The reception history of Chopin's *Awakening* and Brown's gothic oeuvre alone would strongly suggest that people do not read in the same way, even if they utilize some of the same underlying cognitive processes and neurological structures. To read minds, both those of characters and of readers, in the nineteenth century, to make sense of the brain and its functions, it follows, we must attend both to the distinct historical pressures—the stimuli consisting of the physical environment, social interactions, and cultural codes—and to a genetically shared substrate.

We can use the organizing metaphor of this chapter—"reading minds"—to sketch how we might conduct such research. For the metaphor of the mind as a book to gain widespread acceptance within a society, that society would have to be largely literate, and books would have to be at least familiar to many. While reading minds as a metaphor certainly has a longer history, one perhaps going back to the origins of written language itself, its viability as an organizing concept would only seem to emerge with the democratization of print. The *OED*, in fact, offers an 1840s commentary on Poe's "Murders in the Rue Morgue" as its earliest example of the phrase. In that story, of course, Poe's detective Dupin is able to perform a virtuosic feat of reading the narrator's mind by observing small clues and forming theses about what they reveal, a classic case of theory of mind. Cognitive science proper, in fact, has often conceived of the human mind as acting in Dupin-like fashion; Jerry Fodor, for example, quipped that Arthur Conan Doyle, the parent of Dupin's progeny, Sherlock Holmes, was "a far deeper psychologist—far closer to what is essential about the mental life—than, say James Joyce (or William James, for that matter)" (92). But Poe is certainly closer to Joyce and James (Henry or William, for that matter) than Fodor's Conan Doyle. For all the suggestions of the supernatural in his gothic fiction and poetry and the emphasis on rational analysis in his cryptography, criticism, and cosmology, Poe repeatedly questions contemporaneous scientific theories of the mind through his emphasis on the embodied mind's irrationality and indeterminacy. In "The Imp of the Perverse" (1845), for example, Poe's murderous narrator challenges both phrenologists and moralists who have failed to recognize the perverse desire for punishment due to their faith in deducing mental structures from necessity, a process akin to that of cognitivists. His characters, in fact, far more often misread the minds of others and themselves—think of the narrators of "The Tell-Tale Heart," "The Black Cat," or, to cite a ratiocinative tale, "The Gold-Bug"—than succeed as Dupin does. Even in "Murders in the Rue Morgue," Poe's narrator reflects on the apparent "incoherence between the starting-point and the goal" (403) of a line of thought. It is less analysis than identification—Dupin succeeds when he "throws himself into the spirit of his opponent, identifies himself therewith" (398)—that enables Poe's detective to reconstruct or predict another's thoughts.

In this way, Poe's account of his detective prefigures the debate over mind reading or mentalizing within cognitive science. Where literary critics have most often built on the idea of theory of mind from cognitive science, the discovery of mirror neurons has suggested that our understanding of others' behavior is both more immediate and more unconscious than the more rationalist theory of mind. First recognized in macaque monkeys, mirror neurons are neurons that fire both when the observer sees an action and when the observer undertakes the same action. Brain-imaging studies of humans strongly suggest similar neurons exist in the human brain, and, perhaps even more notably, have indicated a connection between these neurons and both the emotional and language centers of the brain. In other words, this work seems to evidence that when we see someone crying, some of the same neurons that fire when we cry fire in our brain and activate at least some of the circuits leading to our emotions when we cry. Even more recent work has indicated that the same mirror neurons fire when we just read about someone performing an action, hinting "that when we read a novel, our mirror neurons simulate the actions described in the novel, as if we were doing those actions ourselves" (Iacoboni 94–95). Building on these insights, Michael Arbib and other neuroscientists have hypothesized that mirror neurons are essential to the origins of human communication and human language in gesture. By enabling us to imitate not just the action but also the underlying emotional content of actions, mirror neurons would allow us to begin to feel as others do through the use of a kind of gestural prelanguage. From this perspective, language arises from the shared interpersonal experience enabled by our mirror neurons, allowing us to feel as others feel, through our ability to unconsciously and immediately simulate—neurally—what they are doing.

The existence of mirror neurons in humans remains controversial within neuroscience as does the exact role mirror neurons might play in the development of language, but the evidence for their existence provides a plausible model for literary critics to think through the mechanics of empathy and language as more embodied than in theory of mind accounts. Yet the scientific theorizing about mirror neurons also points to the need for literary studies to make its own contribution. Rather than revealing our innate, unconscious, and inevitable ability to intuit another's mental state as mirror neuron theory sometimes suggests, the novel—and much of modern literature and modern experience—consists of our conscious attempts to infer about others' minds and our frequent misconstruction and misidentification of the mental states underlying gestures, actions, or words. Within embodied cognitive neuroscience, Shaun Gallagher has made a convincing case that most of the time we need neither theory of mind nor simulation theory to make sense of other people, that we more immediately and physically respond to others without theorizing or empathizing their mental states. Modern literature, on the other hand, seems to foreground the occasions when such approaches become necessary. Unlike scientific studies which tend to emphasize how things work—the amazing capacity of humans to understand one another, to feel as others do—much of modern literature foregrounds the breakdown of these systems. Poe's ratiocinative narrator of "The Man of the Crowd" (1840) epitomizes this point in his conclusion about the man he has followed all night: "*er lasst sich nicht lesen*," which translates as he cannot be read (396). While the metaphor of mind reading may be misleading, it strongly suggests the subjective experience of attempting—and often failing—to decode, to interpret, the minds of others.

If this kind of misconstruction of others' intentions, beliefs, and feelings is, to some extent, inherent to the cognitive structures underlying human empathy and communication, it would be of no surprise that we could locate texts—oral, written, visual—reflecting on these possibilities of deception and misunderstanding from the earliest cultural record. The use of the specific reading-minds metaphor in *The Awakening*, Brown's gothic novels, and Poe's tales reveals how historical change is embodied in the brain's circuitry. The reading-minds metaphor highlights the cultural, learned nature of the process of gaining access to another's mind, revealing the central difficulty of interpretation and translation. Recent work on the neurophysiology of reading strengthens this point through its emphasis on the ways that reading changes the underlying genetically coded brain circuitry. (It is notable, in this respect, that with its tendency to define universal cognitive modules, cognitive literary criticism seldom addresses "reading" itself as a cognitive process.) Maryanne Wolf foregrounds that "[w]e were never born to read. Human beings invented reading only a few thousand years ago. And with this invention, we rearranged the very organization of our brain, which in turn expanded the ways we were able to think, which altered the intellectual evolution of our species... a process made possible by the brain's ability to be shaped by experience" (3). While other neuroscientists such as Stanislas Dehaene emphasize the extent to which all reading brains, no matter the language or symbolic system, seem to process characters in a similar fashion, they similarly reiterate Wolf's point that reading fundamentally alters the neural connections of the brain. As with so many questions in cognitive neuroscience, the exact extent of the changes to the brain rendered by reading is a point of some debate. The science simply cannot at this point—and perhaps never can—offer a conclusive resolution to the exact nature of all the ways reading transforms the brain.

Literature and literary history, on the other hand, provide a particularly fruitful register of the ways people conceived of and practice reading, conceptions and practices then materialized in their brain circuitry. Reading, as Wolf describes, "is a neuronally and intellectually circuitous act, enriched as much by the unpredictable indirections of a reader's inferences and thoughts, as by the direct message to the eye from the text." This "associative dimension" is not merely "negative," however, for it is "part of the generative quality at the heart of reading" (16). From hers and others' accounts, reading and writing originated in small groups for purposes of trade or sacred ritual or community bonding. But written language's fluidity and efficiency enabled it to spread more widely, outside a group with closely shared experiences (and thus more similar neural wiring). This especially becomes true with the explosion of print materials in the early modern era, with the expanding sense of different human communities and languages from European exploration and contact between previously distinct peoples, and with the increasing democratization of literacy. As new reading minds, with distinctly different experiential backgrounds, and, it would follow, more variegated circuits for making inferences from written language, emerge, the reading community itself fragments.

Returning to our metaphor, whether we approach the question from a theory of mind perspective or, what seems more productive and convincing, a simulation theory built on mirror neurons and a delayed theorization of the mind, the more the experience of the observer and the observed are dissimilar, the more likely for misreading. Dr. Mandelet's attempt to understand Edna, for example, following on the heels of her husband's confusion about her behavior, is contrasted with Adèle Ratignolle's clarity, whose "candor…every one might read" (35). In some cases, cases in which the individual seems simply to mirror cultural expectations, the mind appears, to continue the metaphor, as an open book. Brown's novels even more explicitly reiterate the difficulties of reading others' minds, recurring to the point Ormond makes in his challenge to Constantia: "Look at me; steadfastly. Can you read my thoughts?…What pity that you have not instruments for piercing into thoughts!" (*Ormond* 245). The novel and much modern literature, through its various formal techniques, obsessively attempt to provide just such instruments. But as Brown's novels emphasize and Poe's narrator in "The Man of the Crowd" succinctly concludes, modern literature just as consistently comes back to the impenetrable (and, perhaps, indeterminate) nature of others' minds.

In concluding, I will delve a bit more deeply into *Edgar Huntly* to outline how we might bring these various points together in producing a neural historicism. After Clithero's narrative reveals he had nothing to do with Waldegrave's murder, Huntly's mind "exists in a kind of chaos" (*Three Gothic Novels* 718). Only with time is he able "to reduce [his ideas] to distinct particulars, and subject them to a deliberate and methodical inspection" and thus produce an account of Clithero's actions as "the necessary result of a series of ideas mutually linked and connected" (719). As cognitive critics have demonstrated, humans innately desire to make sense of others by constructing narratives about their mental processes. In this way, Huntly's attempt—and our vicarious participation in it—potentially transcends any specific historical scale, making it possibly accessible or translatable to any individual Homo sapiens over the past one hundred thousand years. There may be a universal desire to reconstruct human actions as "the necessary result of a series of ideas mutually linked and connected." Yet Huntly's particular way of attempting to construct this story—by relying not only on his own experience but also on his having "communed with romancers and historians" (718) and heard the "moralizing narratives and synthetic reasonings" of Sarsefield (724)—places it within a much more specific cultural-temporal frame, not just a literate culture but a culture immersed in both the narrative strategies of history and romance and Enlightenment moral philosophy. Written language, as described by the neurocognitive research of Wolf and Dehaene, even further elaborates Huntly's and his readers' ability to imagine the complex factors leading to Clithero's behavior. Literary and intellectual history, then, functions primarily to reconstruct the mental patterns promoted by the philosophical thought, histories, and romances that would be most readily accessible to Huntly and his contemporaries.

What is most striking, though, is that Huntly—and the rest of the book that follows—fails to make Clithero and his story fit these various models. Despite his deep empathy for Clithero, Huntly still cannot accurately read Clithero's mind. Unlike some of the theorizing about mirror neurons, Huntly's mirroring of Clithero's behavior through his own sleepwalking does not grant him access to his inner mental states. Huntly can only expostulate, blind to his own lack of judgment, "How imperfect are the grounds of all our decisions!" (720). Such a conclusion returns us to the irreducible particularity of individual existence that is the starting point for so much of modern literature. But it also returns us to the broader context of modernity for understanding Huntly's reading mind and his attempt to read Clithero's mind. Clithero presents a mystery to Huntly because he is a "foreigner," "an emigrant from Ireland" (651) and because Waldegrave has been killed by an Indian seeking to recover his people's lost territory. Much of the difficulty of understanding the other's mind emerges through the distinct otherness of that person, his representing and, to some extent, embodying a different kind of experience. It is within the transnational contact zones of modernity, the discursive and material confrontation and translation of different cultures with one another, that reading minds becomes both such an imperative and such an impossibility. *Edgar Huntly* reveals both a mind wired in a particular way due to the confluence of evolutionary and historical factors and the impossibility of ever fully reconstructing the exact interaction of those factors.

Combining a historical formalist and an embodied neurocognitive approach to these texts, then, entails attending to multiple layers of historical causation, expanding our frame beyond the historical moment to the long evolutionary history of Homo sapiens and the long history of the literate brain. What I have provided is, admittedly but necessarily, a schematic historicization of the neural circuitry that might give rise to the production, circulation, and development of metaphors of reading minds in nineteenth-century American literature and in these texts in particular. What this analysis leaves out—necessarily so in a chapter of this sort—is both an account of how these representations of the mind's workings and failures are formally conveyed, through the texts' particular engagement with readers, and, relatedly, how they contend with and build on contemporaneous reflections on the mind. A more developed analysis of *The Awakening* would thus spend considerable time on its impressionistic elements, its stylistic, sentence-level engagement with and fostering of particular reading and comprehension processes, placing the implicit model of reading and cognition in conversation with the work of someone like William James, a favorite precursor for many cognitive neuroscientists (see Thrailkill for one move in this direction). More profound attention to Brown would attend much more fully to the narrative tangles he constructs, as well as exploring and offering explanations for his tedious (and often seemingly misguided) descriptions of characters' mental processes. In doing so, such research might investigate his relationship to the ideas of Erasmus Darwin and Benjamin Rush as well as to associationist psychology, a field scorned by many cognitive scientists but one offering parallels to recent connectionist neuroscience (see Sutton). What would emerge from such research would be both a more fluid and robust historicism; a more nimble account of how and why we attempt to understand others' minds, especially through literary works, in terms of our long evolutionary history, the development of reading and writing, and the particular social and cultural moment giving rise to these specific texts. It would offer a new kind of historical materialism, one based in, as Marx called for, the very "physical organization" of individual humans.

BIBLIOGRAPHY

Arbib, Michael A., ed. *Action to Language via the Mirror Neuron System*. Cambridge: Cambridge University Press, 2006.

Boyd, Brian. *On the Origin of Stories: Evolution, Cognition, and Fiction*. Cambridge, MA: Harvard University Press, 2009.

Brown, Charles Brockden. *Ormond; or The Secret Witness*. Ed. Mary Chapman. Peterborough, Ontario: Broadview, 1999.

———. *Three Gothic Novels*. New York: Library of America, 1998.

Chemero, Anthony. *Radical Embodied Cognitive Science*. Cambridge, MA: MIT Press, 2009.

Chopin, Kate. *The Awakening*. 2nd ed. Ed. Nancy A. Walker. Boston: Bedford, 2000.

Davidson, Cathy N. *Revolution and the Word: The Rise of the Novel in America*. New York: Oxford University Press, 1986.

Dehaene, Stanislas. *Reading in the Brain: The Science and Evolution of a Human Invention*. New York: Penguin, 2009.

Fauconnier, Gilles, and Mark Turner. *The Way We Think: Conceptual Blending and the Mind's Hidden Complexities*. New York: Basic Books, 2002.

Feldman, Jerome A. *From Molecule to Metaphor: A Neural Theory of Language*. Cambridge, MA: MIT Press, 2006.

Fodor, Jerry. "Fodor's Guide to Mental Representation: The Intelligent Auntie's Vade-Mecum." *Mind* 94 (1985): 76–100.

Gallagher, Shaun. *How the Body Shapes the Mind*. Oxford: Clarendon, 2005.

Goldman, Alvin I. *Simulating Minds: The Philosophy, Psychology, and Neuroscience of Mindreading*. New York: Oxford University Press, 2006.

Herman, David, ed. *Narrative Theory and the Cognitive Sciences*. Stanford, CA: Center for the Study of Language and Information, 2003.

Hogan, Patrick Colm. *Cognitive Science, Literature, and the Arts: A Guide for Humanists*. New York: Routledge, 2003.

———. *The Mind and Its Stories: Narrative Universals and Human Emotion*. Cambridge: Cambridge University Press, 2003.

Iacoboni, Marco. *Mirroring People: The Science of Empathy and How We Connect with Others*. New York: Picador, 2009.

Kramnick, Jonathan. "Against Literary Darwinism." *Critical Inquiry* 37 (2011): 315–347.

Lakoff, George, and Mark Johnson. *Philosophy in the Flesh: The Embodied Mind and Its Challenge to Western Thought*. New York: Basic Books, 1999.

Marx, Karl. *The German Ideology*. *The Marx-Engels Reader*. 2nd ed. Ed. Robert C. Tucker. New York: Norton, 1978. 146–200.

Palmer, Alan. *Fictional Minds*. Lincoln: University of Nebraska Press, 2004.

Petry, Alice Hall, ed. *Critical Essays on Kate Chopin*. New York: G. K. Hall, 1996.

Pinker, Steven. *The Blank Slate: The Modern Denial of Human Nature*. New York: Penguin, 2002.

Poe, Edgar Allan. *Poetry and Tales*. New York: Library of America, 1984.

Richardson, Alan. *The Neural Sublime: Cognitive Theories and Romantic Texts*. Baltimore: Johns Hopkins University Press, 2010.

———. "Studies in Literature and Cognition: A Field Map." *The Work of Fiction: Cognition, Culture, and Complexity*. Ed. Alan Richardson and Ellen Spolsky. Burlington: VT: Ashgate, 2004. 1–29.

Richardson, Alan, and Francis F. Steen. "Literature and the Cognitive Revolution: An Introduction." *Poetics Today* 23 (2002): 1–8.

Slingerland, Edward. *What Science Offers the Humanities*. Cambridge: Cambridge University Press, 2008.

Spolsky, Ellen. *Gaps in Nature: Literary Interpretation and the Modular Mind*. Albany: State University of New York Press, 1993.

Sutton, John. *Philosophy and Memory Traces: Descartes to Connectionism*. Cambridge: Cambridge University Press, 1998.

Thrailkill, Jane F. *Affecting Fictions: Mind, Body, and Emotion in American Literary Realism*. Cambridge, MA: Harvard University Press, 2007.

Tooby, John, and Leda Cosmides. "The Psychological Foundations of Culture." *The Adapted Mind: Evolutionary Psychology and the Generation of Culture*. Ed. Jerome H. Barkow, Leda Cosmides, and John Tooby. New York: Oxford University Press, 1992. 19–136.

Turner, Mark. *The Literary Mind*. New York: Oxford University Press, 1996.

Wexler, Bruce E. *Brain and Culture: Neurobiology, Ideology, and Social Change*. Cambridge, MA: MIT Press, 2006.

Wolf, Maryanne. *Proust and the Squid: The Story and Science of the Reading Brain*. New York: Harper, 2007.

Zunshine, Lisa. *Introduction to Cognitive Cultural Studies*. Baltimore: Johns Hopkins University Press, 2010.

———, ed. *Why We Read Fiction: Theory of Mind and the Novel*. Columbus: Ohio State University Press, 2006.

CHAPTER 19

MAKING AN EXAMPLE: AMERICAN LITERATURE AS PHILOSOPHY

ELIZABETH DUQUETTE

It is easy to take examples for granted. Not only are they ubiquitous, their utility is undeniable. Even a reader who thrives on complexity and difficulty, like Paul de Man, can admit to experiencing "relief" when a "concrete example" "interrupt[s]" an abstract argument (276). A short narrative or anecdote, an example tells a story that helps to make a difficult point understandable and specific. Even when the example is just a brief gesture, as in the above reference to de Man, it nonetheless implies a narrative that repeats an abstract or general idea in a concrete manner. We imagine de Man struggling through a text, sighing with "relief" when an example appears, a quick tale that clarifies how examples work and why readers like them; if my example works, it does so because de Man's experience is one that many readers can understand. Unlike figures that generate ambiguity, like metaphor or irony, the successful example is dutifully redundant in its replacement of convolution with clarity, opacity with transparency.

But to nineteenth-century writers and scholars, the figure we take for granted was fraught with complications. In politics and ethics, epistemology and economics, nineteenth-century thinkers repeatedly worried about how to conceptualize the relationship of a single person or thing to a larger community or group, some fretting about the rise of "individualism," others celebrating the new possibilities for creativity and innovation such changes heralded (see G. Brown, *Domestic Individualism*).

As existing ways of understanding the connections between the individual and the group became uncertain, so too did norms and assumptions about the selection and use of examples. In the previous paragraph, Paul de Man provides an effective example because the readers of this chapter are likely to recognize de Man as a difficult literary theorist; if de Man is not recognizable, my example loses much of its force. This was the problem facing many nineteenth-century writers and thinkers. The spread of political liberalism and representative democracy, the romantic celebration of genius, and the increasing importance of economic markets putatively controlled by regulative interests all complicated ideas about who or what could be an example. In the United States, national uncertainty about identity (personal and political) and a culture increasingly split over who could count as a person contributed to the evolution of multiple, often contradictory, modes of exemplification. Even the most cursory comparison of two dominant antebellum intellectual traditions—transcendentalism and sentimentality—reveals widely disparate assumptions about who should be celebrated as exemplary, how to understand the parameters of personhood given a pervasive investment in the explanatory power of race, and what the moral response to others, and to slavery, might entail.

With uncertainties about identity and the nature of representation—political, moral, and aesthetic—came broad concerns about the example. Across the nineteenth century, in multiple national traditions, thinkers questioned the figure's didactic utility, clarity, and transparency. What, they asked, makes a good example? In Henry James's *The Tragic Muse* (1890), the main character, Nick Dormer, says to a friend, "[Y]ou've converted me from a representative into an example—that's a shade better" (404). Yet what is "better" about being an example? How might we understand the distinction being drawn between different particularizing structures, between representatives and examples? At the beginning of *Discipline and Punish*, Michel Foucault juxtaposes two models for correcting criminal deviance: the exemplary figure on the late eighteenth-century scaffold and the anonymous nineteenth-century prisoner subjected to a form of discipline focused on the soul. These punitive modes correlate to alternate ways of thinking about the distribution of power associated with what an example can do and who should be held up as exemplary. Although Foucault's discussion is focused on penal structures, like coordinates of force and coercion are evident when we take people and their stories as examples; in such cases, what lessons can or should we reasonably be able to draw, if we do not want to draw and quarter the subject? What are the consequences, intended and not, of the example's disciplinary potency? The concrete example is intimately connected with, indeed dependent upon, the abstract ideas that precede it, ideas that structure its parameters and force: how does focused attention on the example complicate our current critical investment in the particular? This chapter engages these questions in an effort to problematize established hierarchical relationship norms between theory and example.

As he complains bitterly about being used as an example for abolitionist ideas in *My Bondage and My Freedom* (1855), Frederick Douglass pointedly challenges antebellum assumptions about the example's place, role, and force. In an oft-cited section of this autobiography, Douglass details his growing distress at the increasing constriction of his assignment. "During the first three or four months, my speeches were almost exclusively made up of narrations of my own personal experience as a slave," Douglass explains, a task he soon found tedious. Although he longed to shape his presentation differently, moving beyond the merely personal, his white advisers deplored the idea of change, worried that audiences would not accept a revised account as authentic. "'Tell your story, Frederick,' would whisper my then revered friend, William Lloyd Garrison, as I stepped upon the platform." "People won't believe you ever was a slave, Frederick, if you keep on this way," George Foster observed while trying "to pin [him] down to [a] simple narrative." John Collins was even more direct: "Give us the facts, we will take care of the philosophy." "I could not always obey," Douglass wryly notes:

> It was impossible for me to repeat the same old story month after month, and to keep up my interest in it. It was new to the people, it is true, but it was an old story to me; and to go through with it night after night, was a task altogether mechanical for my nature. (367)

The mindless similitude of his subordinate status is captured in the marked redundancy of the passage ("month after month," "night after night," "old story" after "old story"). Seeking to escape the rote repetition of his role, represented as a kind of rhetorical bondage, Douglass decides to "take care" of the philosophy himself, a move that contributes to his eventual rupture with Garrison. If the center of Douglass's 1845 *Narrative of the Life of Frederick Douglass, an American Slave* depicts the conversion of the slave into a man, *My Bondage and My Freedom* associates some (although assuredly not all) of the same narrative force with the conversion of *example* into *philosophy*. In the episode, Douglass begins this process by using the white abolitionists as examples of *his* claim that there is a hierarchy between theory and example in which the example is forced to serve mechanically the system it (or he) represents.

What we see in the above passage, and throughout *My Bondage and My Freedom*, is Douglass's incisive reading of the ethics and politics of examples. Douglass shows that the example's force is not only a function of its content, but is also dependent on its formal relationship with specific abstract principles or ideals. To make an example of someone is to subordinate and erase that person's particularity, as Douglass forcefully establishes with the harrowing tale of the death of a slave named Denby. This "powerful young man" is murdered by a white overseer because he "set a dangerous example" to other slaves, Douglass recalls, threatening the entire edifice upon which chattel slavery depended (201–202). As shocking as this scene is, however, Douglass encourages the reader not to be distracted by its horror. "It was slavery—not its mere *incidents*—that I hated," he pointedly explains (228). Across his writings, Douglass consistently engages with the fallacies and failures that result when examples prove so arresting that they prevent the reader's recognition of the larger interests these "*incidents*" serve. That is to say, Douglass maintains that when the particular is taken for the universal, it becomes nearly impossible to counter or challenge abstractions, like those justifying slavery, that the specific example simultaneously instantiates—and obscures.

This chapter explores how Frederick Douglass navigates concerns about the relationship between theory and example in "Self-Made Men," his most popular lecture. The choice of "Self-Made Men" brackets the complex question of Douglass's own status as a representative, making it easier to chart his thinking about examples and their complicated servitude. Methodologically, the chapter draws upon the careful scrutiny of philosophical reading; as a practice, philosophical reading requires committed engagement with a text's terms, claims, structure, and conclusions. Finding key critical concepts, theoretical problems, or structural paradigms *within* texts, rather than importing them from elsewhere, is its signature procedure. That there is a necessary, although not sufficient, connection between what a text says and what it means is this chapter's primary methodological premise. While some might complain that this presupposition is either obvious or naive, pointing out a similitude with the apolitical stance of New Criticism or deconstruction, I would maintain, to the contrary, that it is precisely in the apparent embrace of superficiality that a revived—and fundamentally political—critical practice may be found, one that resists the cynicism that has evolved in part from the assumption that texts seldom mean what they say (or say what they mean). Far from being opposed to identarian or political concerns, in other words, philosophical reading of the kind this chapter models complicates our responses to texts by challenging readers to resist and question critical hierarchies that often seem fixed and final.

The example provides one indication of how philosophical reading might prove beneficial by putting assumptions about the relationship between abstraction and particularity under examination. According to David Lyons, example is "the figure that is most intimately bound to a representation of the world and that most serves as a veil for the mechanics of that representation" (ix). As scholars working with Lyons in sixteenth- and seventeenth-century studies have established, differences in the "representation of the world" are closely correlated to changing norms for examples. Pointing to a crisis of Renaissance exemplarity, these scholars compellingly show that changes to thought (like that captured in the Cartesian cogito) and shifts in social organization were mirrored by basic modifications in who or what could function as an example; the concept of exemplarity was redefined to accommodate changing definitions of personhood and agency. Despite sweeping intellectual shifts across the nineteenth century associated with the new idea of the individual,[1] persistent engagement with Foucault's arguments about the social forces brought to bear on persons, and broad scholarly interest in the politics of representation, little attention has been specifically paid to the exemplifying structures deployed to negotiate or narrate the relationship of the individual to the social.

Given the extensive social changes across the nineteenth century, we should ask why the example has not received more critical attention. A partial answer may be found in the declining importance of rhetoric, which was central to Renaissance culture but had been marginalized by the middle of the nineteenth century. The oversight is more comprehensively explained, however, by the broad shifts in critical priorities associated with forms of analysis dependent on ideology critique. The benefits of this work have been undeniable and far-reaching. Yet there have also been consequences, most surely unintended, associated with the assumption that a text's manifest content, including the philosophical ideas it might articulate, is less important to its meaning than material pressures or latent political traces. At the same time, a pervasive critical conviction that abstraction and its discursive formations are necessarily repressive encourages a tendency to limit analysis to the seemingly particular in a way that impoverishes our ability to appreciate the manifold forces being brought to bear on persons.

Returning philosophy to the way we approach and read American literature requires not only being willing to reexamine assumptions about abstraction, and what we do when we read a literary text, but also a reconsideration of the practice and place of philosophy in nineteenth-century American literature. While it might seem perverse to make this claim while calling for a reconsideration of the concrete example, our habit of dismissing the abstract as hopelessly associated with a devaluation of the particular may well disable us from appreciating the nuances of texts that find philosophy on whale ships or rafts, by ponds or in ballrooms. It also has prevented us from seeing the ways in which ideology critique can yield a representation that is as totalizing as the older philosophical systems it supplanted. *For example*, it is an understatement to say that the scholarship on the evolution of American identity in the nineteenth century is vast; that these concerns are part of a transnational philosophical discussion about structures of individuation has been of markedly less interest to scholars, a critical orientation that reinscribes a commitment to exceptionalism even when it seems to be under examination. For American literary scholars questioning entrenched assumptions about identity or exploring the possibilities and parameters of postnational critical practices, philosophical reading, as well as a renewed investigation of the example, promises to yield broad insights, especially about two persistent and pernicious myths of U.S. culture—the ideal of the self made man and the belief in exceptionalism, individual and national.

My reading of "Self-Made Men" reveals the sophistication of Douglass's thinking about exemplary representation and demonstrates the extent to which even concerns that seem local to American culture are better understood as participating in transnational conversations.[2] In this lecture, first delivered in 1859 and repeated more than fifty times before its 1893 publication, Douglass details an ethical philosophy predicated on three basic ideas: that abstract thought about the human condition is both necessary and natural; that an elementary kinship exists between people; and, finally, that labor, broadly construed, is the basis of our moral relations.[3] As part of its exposition, the lecture also posits a theory of the example, taking both racial prejudice and the specifics of Douglass's position into consideration. "Self-Made Men" is thus a critical component of the rigorous thinking about examples, heroism, and individuality that Douglass undertakes across his career, most famously in "The Heroic Slave" (1853) and *My Bondage and My Freedom*.

"Self-Made Men" posits that the impulse for abstract or philosophical thought provides the basis of our shared humanity. Instead of being the property of one race or class, speculative inquiry is "universal," "natural," even "all controlling" (546). Whereas Douglass complains in *My Bondage and My Freedom* that repeating his life story quickly became "mechanical," there is no danger in "Self-Made Men" that abstract thought will become "tarnished by repetition." Because such thinking "contains a great truth and a truth alike for every age and generation of men,"

> [it] is always new and can never grow old. It is neither dimmed by time nor tarnished by repetition; for man, both in respect of himself and of his species, is now, and evermore will be, the center of unsatisfied human curiosity. (546)

Thanks to the nature of the topic, particularly its ability to correlate the individual with the species, Douglass maintains that "curiosity" will prevent repetition from becoming dull; satisfaction, not the tedium of numbing redundancy, will be its product. When coupled with "a wise and vigorous cultivation of [the] faculties," abstract thought "leads irresistibly" to the best that is possible in and for humankind (546).

For Douglass, problems arise when people fail to recognize one of the central paradoxes of the human condition: we have a close relation to what is "Infinite" but our powers of comprehension are finite. "Man is too closely related to the Infinite to be divided, weighed, measured and reduced to fixed standards, and thus adjusted to finite comprehension," he explains. Rendering what is, or should be, "Infinite" into something suitable for "comprehension" ignores a basic fact, namely that "[n]o two of anything are exactly alike." That is to say, attempts to delineate common standards obscure a more important truth—the "distinctive qualities" of humankind "are inherent" and eternal—by stressing what is merely trivially true ("what is true of man in one generation may lack some degree of truth in another"). "Rushed" standards prevent us from drawing the right kinds of conclusions about humankind, a concern clearly associated with racial prejudice even though Douglass lets the obvious conclusion linger unspoken. Humankind comes closer to fulfilling its promise when we recognize that as powerful as "progress" might seem, it can neither "overtake" nor "make known…the limits of [our] marvellous powers and possibilities" (547–548). The "earnest desire for the fullest knowledge of human nature" distinguishes humans from other species and, more important, enables the greatest human "happiness" (570).

What does Douglass's investment in the importance of abstract thought for human happiness indicate for those who seek to follow an example? Given the ease with which shared norms become dangerous, what is appropriate in the selection and use of an example? Douglass addresses these questions in multiple ways. He defers specific examples of self-made men to the final third of the lecture; when he does name individuals, he stresses that they have been selected from an "abundance" of alternatives in all walks of life: Hugh Miller, Louis Kossuth, Benjamin Banneker, Abraham Lincoln, and Toussaint-Louverture. What unites these disparate persons is not the fact of their particular achievements, but their shared commitment to work as the means of reaching their goals. Even as he points to specific persons, however, Douglass quickly shifts to images that establish a fundamental connection between part and whole. "Such men as these," Douglass continues, "whether found in one position or another, whether in the college or in the factory; whether professors or plowmen; whether Caucasian or Indian; whether Anglo-Saxon or Anglo-African, are self-made men" and, in each case, "there is genuine heroism in his struggle and something of sublimity and glory in his triumph" (550). Douglass uses this strategy throughout the lecture, as when he describes the differences between "a thousand arrows shot from the same point and aimed at the same object" (551); the relationship between waves and the ocean (549); and an apple "carelessly flung into a crowd" (552). These images underscore Douglass's central claim, that individual identity is composed of difference and dependence. For Douglass, there is no such thing as "absolute independence." "I believe in individuality," he explains,

> but individuals are, to the mass, like waves to the ocean. The highest order of genius is as dependent as is the lowest. It, like the loftiest waves of the sea, derives its power and greatness from the grandeur and vastness of the ocean of which it forms a part. We differ as the waves, but are one as the sea. (549)

Just as there is no wave without a larger body of water, so there can be no individual without other people. Identity is in constant tension with the universal, in other words, a position Douglass admits might "not accord well" with American assumptions about "self-conscious individuality and self-conceit." We have all "begged, borrowed or stolen" what we assume, with time and pride, makes us unique. Our success may be dependent on our labor but, even though the effort must proceed from each person, he or she is doomed to fail without help "either from our contemporaries or from those who have preceded us in the field of thought and discovery" (549). Forgetting to recognize the ways we are dependent on the larger group is, in other words, as mistaken as is the abdication of initiative in imitation. A proper balance between the individual and the larger group, throughout the lecture demonstrated by Douglass's examples, is the only way that either can flourish.

The care Douglass takes with his own examples circles back to the dangers he identifies as resulting from the human tendency to develop our abstract ideas from wrongly conceived evidence. When so perverted, what should lead to our happiness yields instead the most extreme "misery" (570). Douglass flags two signal dangers. First, we must recognize that our "natural reverence" for what is "great in man" has "shown itself far otherwise than wise. It has often given us a wicked ruler for a righteous one, a false prophet for a true one, a corrupt preacher for a pure one, a man of war for a man of peace, and a distorted and vengeful image of God for an image of justice and mercy" (548). Douglass chooses not to pursue the problem that our tendencies seem to make the world unjust and corrupt, but it is the core of the argument's engagement with the difficulties and confusions arising from the simultaneous need for, and danger from, examples in ethical thinking and decision making. Closely linked to our worrisome tendencies is the second danger: the ease with which we slip into "dogmatiz[ing]." Doctrinaire and rigid, the dogmatic impulse—everywhere evident in Douglass's concern with measurement—is opposed to the more ethical methodology he seeks to model, one that "define[s], explain[s] and demonstrate[s]" flexibly. The principles according to which human society is best organized "seem to be equal and are equal," and only a philosophical practice that navigates carefully between "the subjects" of these "natural laws" and the "inequalities, discords and contrasts" that impede their fullest observance can yield a social world that is genuinely equal (551).

As a counter to dogma, Douglass again gestures to the paramount importance of "physical, mental, moral, or spiritual" labor (555). In its myriad forms, labor provides the means of achieving personal success and the best way to determine if the purportedly great are worthy of our "reverence." In both our abstract thought and our more mundane endeavors, in both "temporal and spiritual affairs," "patient, enduring, honest, unremitting and indefatigable work" is the only way to reach the goals we set (556). Neither a "royal road to perfection" nor a guarantee of success, Douglass nonetheless argues that labor offers the surest path to future achievement. For Douglass, then, "examples of successful self-culture and self-help" are a comfort but cannot replace "WORK! WORK!! WORK!!! WORK!!!!" (565, 556). While profitably employed, we learn the paramount importance of self-dependence, a "virtue" that "cannot be bestowed" (557). Because they import standards that are neither natural to human nature nor predicated upon principles that are usually "wise, just and beneficent," models of social organization that do not emphasize work result in "chaos," while various kinds of idle chatter erode ethical standards and norms (557).

"Self-Made Men" can be easily located in American discussions about self-making or race, but that the lecture also participates in a transnational conversation about the relationship between the exemplary individual and his or her community has been harder to see. The issues it examines overlap importantly, however, with those explored in Thomas Carlyle's *On Heroes and Hero-Worship* (1841), Søren Kierkegaard's *Fear and Trembling* (1843), and Ralph Waldo Emerson's *Representative Men* (1850). Like Douglass, these thinkers ask what it means that we take other people as examples and consider how such choices determine conceptions of success and failure, broadly understood. Although Waldo Martin has pointed to crucial links between Douglass's lecture and Emerson's "Uses of Great Men," the introductory essay in *Representative Men*, it is worth noting that there are points of marked divergence between the two thinkers, especially on the idea of instrumentality, that gesture to the importance of Douglass's contribution to the larger philosophical debate.

There are "two kinds of use or service" we receive from great men, Emerson writes, the direct and the indirect. "Direct giving" benefits us in material or metaphysical ways, but it is the indirect service they render that is more interesting to Emerson (6). Because men "have a pictorial or representative quality," they serve us intellectually by making us clearer to ourselves; great men are "a collyrium to clear our eyes" (7, 18). What "great men" do, in other words, is provide the conditions of possibility for identifying what is great in the "observer" himself (8). Put more simply, what is most striking about Emerson's essay is its comfort with using people as means to an end, rather than as ends in themselves. Emerson's coercive understanding of "use" stands in marked contrast to Douglass's insistence that only through labor can an individual find him- or herself. The rhetoric of servitude and utility evident in Emerson's "Uses of Great Men" is absent from Douglass's "Self-Made Men," a measure of the vast disparity in privilege associated with the racialized subject positions of nineteenth-century America. While Emerson is cavalier in advising readers to make others into examples, Douglass is more reticent, intimately aware of the murderous force that can attend such decisions. Explaining the qualities associated with self-made men, Douglass writes that "[t]hey are in a peculiar sense, indebted to themselves for themselves" (550). Having been used himself as an example, Douglass seems unwilling to relegate others to a like servitude, stressing instead how examples help us in the work we must do.

Even as he distinguishes between help and use, Douglass acknowledges that examples are "better than any mere assertion," especially when they "enabl[e] man to take hold of the roughest and flintiest hardships incident to the battle of life, with a lighter heart, with higher hopes and a larger courage" (551). "We imitate those we revere and admire," Douglass admits (553). But it is a mistake to be misled by examples into wrong conclusions, as when we suggest that "accident theory" or divine assistance, both of which are "made to explain too much," account for an individual's success (553). "Faith, in the absence of work," Douglass observes, "seems to be worth little, if anything":

> The preacher who finds it easier to pray for knowledge than to tax his brain with study and application will find his congregation growing beautifully less and his flock looking elsewhere for their spiritual and mental food. (555)

While previously we considered his concerns with dogmatism, here Douglass warns auditors about another danger—pleasure—particularly as it encourages us to confuse effort and entertainment. In Douglass's own case, the problem of pleasure was immediate and pressing. As Robert Fanuzzi notes, Douglass's physical presence—the fact of his body—was a substantial part of what auditors "embraced" with abolition, some even going so far as to see in it "an irresistible logic" (83). The assumption that a particular body could stand in *for* an argument is precisely the kind of category mistake "Self-Made Men" seeks to combat because such thinking replaces work with stimulation, thought with *mere* example.

While it is tempting to view the pleasure associated with Douglass's presence on the abolitionist stage as an exceptional disruption to the efficacy of examples, Paul de Man explains that all feelings of "relief" at the example's interruption undermine our ability to "understand" abstract arguments:

> [A]t that very moment, when we think at last that we understand, we are further from comprehension than ever; all we have done is substitute idle talk for serious discourse. Instead of inscribing the particular in the general, which is the purpose of any cognition, one has reversed the process and replaced the understanding of a proposition by the perception of a particular, forgetting that the possibility of such a transaction is precisely the burden of the proposition in the first place. (276)

De Man's worry—that examples *prevent* readers from recognizing the abstract claims they are supposed to make clear—succinctly presents a concern Douglass considers at length. Instead of producing conceptual clarity, the example provides momentary pleasure. For this reason, de Man finds in the example's particularity "a betrayal" of the "general truth it is supposed to support and convey" (276). The analogy upon which the example relies is "illusory" in that the similitude too often fails; either the example does not demonstrate the principle or, more important, the "perception of a particular" prevents a move to the abstract. Examples obscure the rules by which they function, and this is why de Man likens their actual function to supplanting thought with sensation. The danger of this inversion—evident in our communal "relief" at the appearance of the example—is that we forget to *make* the move from the particular to the general, dooming ourselves to pleasurable misunderstanding and incomprehension. That an exclusive focus on the particular example (or body), divorced from a nuanced understanding of the possibilities associated with abstraction, can perpetuate is a concern both de Man and Douglass engage. If it brings too much pleasure, in other words, the example makes us lazy, unwilling (and, for de Man, unable) to undertake serious intellectual work.

"Self-Made Men" consistently counters the problem of the example's pleasure, but we can also see Douglass working against the problem in *My Bondage and My Freedom* when he complains about "mere *incidents*" and at the beginning of "The Heroic Slave," which delays the reader's experience of the slave leader's "manly form" until the ideals for which he fights have been introduced. In this fictional account of the life of Madison Washington, leader of the 1841 revolt aboard the *Creole*, Douglass presents Washington to the reader in stages: first, in the context of established traditions of Virginia heroism; second, through a "soliloquy" on the idea of freedom; and, finally, as physically exceptional ("tall, symmetrical, round, and strong" [178–179]). The pleasure that might result from Washington's "manly form" thus underscores, rather than replaces, the argument presented in his "soliloquy." In the response of a white traveler, converted to abolitionism by Washington's address, the reader is carefully instructed how to understand the kind of example Washington presents: "I have seen enough and heard enough, and I shall go to my home in Ohio resolved to atone for my past indifference to this ill-starred race, by making such exertions as I shall be able to do, for the speedy emancipation of every slave in the land," the traveler asserts (182). Here, as in "Self-Made Men," we see the stakes associated with the correct application of examples; properly deployed, they may be able to influence the fate of millions.

A brief look at the first African American novel—William Wells Brown's *Clotel: or, The President's Daughter* (1853)—provides a complementary indication of the value of putting both examples and abstractions under examination. Like Douglass, Brown lauded Toussaint-Louverture, whose example he compared favorably with both Napoleon and Washington; yet, in *Clotel*, Brown does not deliver the exemplary narrative seemingly promised by the novel's title. The tale of Clotel's sad fate is simply one of many brought together in the novel as multiple accounts of cruelty and suffering establish Brown's main point: chattel slavery is unjust, immoral, and arbitrary. Pointing to the different kinds gathered together in *Clotel*, Lee Schweninger wonders about the author's aim: "[H]ow," he asks, "does Brown...wish these documents to function?" (23). Schweninger replies that the materials should be understood as anecdotes that mediate "between the literary and the real," a process that "authenticates" his representation of American slavery. If we recognize that what Schweninger calls an anecdote could also be called an example, we can also see that the novel itself explains what it means to attend fully to their lessons. The redundancy that Douglass found personally intolerable is deployed by Brown to indicate the utter pervasiveness of slavery's horrors. The examples assembled in *Clotel* "lay bare" the "institution" of slavery itself; their accumulated force strips away the myths of benevolence and "exposes" the conditions of American slaves to "the gaze of the world," work that Brown explains in the preface to the 1853 edition is incumbent on all "true friends of the slave" (46). For Brown, as for Douglass, the relationship between example and theory is a matter of life and death.

Clotel begins with the sale of Currer, Thomas Jefferson's former housekeeper and mistress, and their two beautiful daughters, Clotel and Althesa; the fates of these women and their children provide the loose link between the novel's episodes. Currer is purchased by a Methodist minister, who is the father of a beautiful and religious daughter, Georgiana. A better Christian than her professional parent, Georgiana is the moral center of the novel, much in the manner of Eva from Stowe's *Uncle Tom's Cabin*. Like Eva, Georgiana dies well before the end of the novel but, where Stowe's child cannot free her slaves, Brown's older heroine is able to complete the necessary legal steps for manumission. As she informs the gathered crowd of the peculiar challenges facing them as they exit the peculiar institution, Georgiana urges the group to

> [r]emember what a singular relation you sustain to society. The necessities of the case require not only that you should behave as well as the whites, but better than the whites; and for this reason: if you behave no better than they, your example will lose a great portion of its influence. Make the Lord Jesus Christ your refuge and exemplar. His is the only standard around which you can successfully rally. (182)

Parsing how race structures the "relation" to the larger community, Georgiana explains to her former slaves the importance of paying attention to the kind of example they can (and will) be taken to offer. On this account, each of them will be used as an example of the possibilities or limitations of all African Americans, a kind of exemplary servitude from which whites are exempted. Their example will either ratify existing prejudices or encourage whites to reconsider racist presuppositions. For this reason, they should strive to emulate an unimpeachable exemplar, someone whose "standard" is far above the social norm; only in this way can they even hope that their behavior will have a positive "influence" on white perceptions. Drawing a distinction between an example, any one from the group of freed slaves, and the exemplar, an individual who is absolutely not part of society, Georgiana points to the multiple ways in which examples can construct both our notions of particular cases and the abstract rules or principles they instantiate. Not only do these different uses of example rely on alternate modes of constructing knowledge, they also gesture to the critical importance of understanding the various purposes for which we use examples.

Georgiana's precept accounts, as well, for the narrative organization of Brown's novel as a whole. Sometimes the good escape and sometimes they do not, and it is dangerous to make judgments about merit or effort from the success or failure of these attempts. Despite Clotel's importance to the novel, her sufferings consistently give way to the equally dreadful experiences of other slaves. The effect of this proliferation of narrative examples is to establish the regularity—the normalcy—of such horrors for black Americans. Because there are so many examples—and because they bring horror not enjoyment—Brown's text avoids the pleasure problem indicated by de Man and Douglass. Instead, the accumulation of examples drives the reader to recognize the larger claim being inductively established, namely that slavery is a moral evil. This remapping of the example's corrective force avoids the violence of making someone into an example, while establishing the moral and political point that those persons lucky enough to survive or escape slavery's influence are exceptions to a general rule.

In this chapter, I have read a popular lecture for the abstract claims it seeks to make rather than tracing the philosophical influences that might have shaped the author's arguments; I have also briefly indicated how these claims might enable us to approach other works in a new manner.[4] That is to say, I have read the lecture *as* philosophy, rather than *through* philosophy. Because one of the organizing principles of philosophical methodology is the interrogation and clarification of assumptions and presupposition, it is ideally poised to expose the false necessities and faulty conclusions that can creep into thought and argument. As the practice of Socrates long ago made clear, the obvious and the subtle can come together in philosophy in unique and exciting ways. Reading literary texts philosophically demonstrates that speculative thought can be, indeed already is, part of our everyday experience of the world.

Despite the above benefits, however, philosophy has not been as important to the recent evolution of American literary criticism as the abstract ambitions of many nineteenth-century texts would seem to encourage. Although critics point selectively to portions of Adam Smith's *The Theory of Moral Sentiments* or John Locke's *Second Treatise on Government*, there has been little sustained engagement with philosophical writing or reasoning as part of the field's general embrace of multi- or transdisciplinary approaches.[5] When compared to anthropology or sociology, philosophy does not seem quite interdisciplinary enough to constitute a fresh way of engaging with literary texts. Complaints about the "totalizing power of universal reason" and its repressive or coercive effects have rightly given critics pause (Gilroy 69).

The critiques launched by structuralists, poststructuralists, and new historicists against the atemporal and ahistorical presumption of both the continental and the analytic philosophical traditions have been, in the main, incisive and accurate.

Throughout the centuries, philosophers have sought to provide authoritative and final definitions for concepts like justice or reality, too often blind to how history and circumstance shape both the problems that draw their attention and the answers they craft. Complacency about theoretical totality, as well as what does (or does not) constitute the proper subject of philosophy, drew reasonable complaints about the racial violence of Enlightenment thought, to rely on a familiar example (see Gates). Recent work on Georg Wilhelm Friedrich Hegel and Haiti by Susan Buck-Morss demonstrates that there is still much to be done to recognize how philosophy's biases contributed to unjust conceptions of the world and our places in it. This is work we should not continue to ignore. As Douglass and Brown make clear, the particular can be equally repressive for those permanently deemed little more than a body or a thing. By failing to challenge either our own assumptions or the intellectual traditions that shaped our pasts, we run the risk of installing a new orthodoxy with its own blindness and intolerance.

As scholars work in increasingly transnational ways—asking questions about periodization and the transmission of ideas—the cosmopolitan nature of philosophical speculation can provide useful models for thinking beyond and around the nation. Intellectual debate evolves over time and across national boundaries, even as increasingly rigid territoriality shaped the conception of the literary more locally. Immanuel Kant wrote with Jean-Jacques Rousseau and David Hume in mind, while Søren Kierkegaard draws on the thought of René Descartes and Hegel. That is to say, once philosophy is replaced in the historical context that, in the eyes of many, it has often resisted and denied, much can be learned from the method of philosophical inquiry.

Philosophical speculation is organized around sets of problems or puzzles. Epistemologists study what we know and how we know it, while ethicists consider the challenges associated with the pressing reality of other people. It is fair to say, in fact, that philosophy is better at posing questions than answering them. Philosophy is thus useful to literary critics as a way of establishing the premises or stakes of arguments, framing debates, or understanding the implications of claims, more than it is in providing guides or keys for interpretation. The best way to close, then, is with a question. This chapter has sought to present a reading of Douglass's thinking on examples and the philosophical freight they carry, while remaining constantly mindful of the coercion that choosing an example entails. I may argue that I have skirted the danger of, yet again, taking Douglass as an unwilling example, but this remains, as it should, for readers to decide. Just as Douglass urges his auditors to resist the tendency to dogmatize, so too should literary critics, including this one, be careful to avoid the doctrinaire application of all philosophical ideas and theoretical models.

NOTES

1 See Bérubé 204.
2 For arguments that locate Douglass in a transnational context, see Levine; and Wilson.

3 While the published text of the lecture undoubtedly differs from the version presented in 1859, Douglass explains in *Life and Times of Frederick Douglass* (1893) that he "adhered pretty closely" to its original form over the years, merely "retouching it and shading it a little from time to time" (814).

4 For an example, see Lee.

5 There are notable exceptions to this sweeping claim. In addition to the invaluable work of Stanley Cavell, see Menand; Arsic; Evans; and Szendy. For readings of Douglass by philosophers, see Lawson and Kirkland.

BIBLIOGRAPHY

Arsic, Branka. *Passive Constitutions or 7 1/2 Times Bartleby.* Stanford, CA: Stanford University Press, 2007.

Bérubé, Michael. *Public Access: Literary Theory and American Cultural Politics.* New York: Verso, 1994.

Best, Stephen, and Sharon Marcus. "Surface Reading: An Introduction." *Representations* 108 (Fall 2009): 1–21.

Brown, Gillian. *Domestic Individualism: Imagining Self in Nineteenth-Century America.* Berkeley: University of California Press, 1990.

Brown, William Wells. *Clotel: or, The President's Daughter.* Ed. Robert S. Levine. New York: Bedford/St. Martin's, 2000.

Buck-Morss, Susan. *Hegel, Haiti, and Universal History.* Pittsburgh: University of Pittsburgh Press, 2009.

de Man, Paul. *The Rhetoric of Romanticism.* New York: Columbia University Press, 1984.

Douglass, Frederick. *Autobiographies.* Ed. Henry Louis Gates Jr. New York: Library of America, 1994.

———. "The Heroic Slave." *Autographs for Freedom.* Ed. Julia Griffiths. Boston: John P. Jewett, 1853. 174–239.

———. "'Self-Made Men' An Address Delivered in Carlisle, Pennsylvania, in March 1893." *The Frederick Douglass Papers: Series One: Speeches, Debates, and Interviews. Volume 5: 1881–1895.* Ed. John W. Blassingame and John R. McKivigan. New Haven, CT: Yale University Press, 1979–1992.

Emerson, Ralph Waldo. *Representative Men.* Ed. Pamela Schirmeister. New York: Marsilio, 1995.

Evans, K. L. *Whale!* Minneapolis: University of Minnesota Press, 2003.

Fanuzzi, Robert. *Abolition's Public Sphere.* Minneapolis: University of Minnesota Press, 2003.

Foucault, Michel. *Discipline and Punish: The Birth of the Prison.* Trans. Alan Sheridan. New York: Vintage Books, 1979.

Gates, Henry Louis Jr., ed. *"Race," Writing, and Difference.* Chicago: University of Chicago Press, 1985.

Gelley, Alexander, ed. *Unruly Examples: On the Rhetoric of Exemplarity.* Stanford, CA: Stanford University Press, 1995.

Gilroy, Paul. *The Black Atlantic: Modernity and Double-Consciousness.* Cambridge, MA: Harvard University Press, 1993.

James, Henry. *The Tragic Muse.* New York: Charles Scribner's Sons, 1908.

Lawson, Bill E., and Frank M. Kirkland, eds. *Frederick Douglass: A Critical Reader*. Malden, MA: Blackwell Publishers, 1999.

Lee, Maurice. *Slavery, Philosophy, and American Literature, 1830–1860*. Cambridge: Cambridge University Press, 2005.

Levine, Robert S. *Dislocating Race and Nation: Episodes in Nineteenth-Century American Literary Nationalism*. Chapel Hill: University of North Carolina, 2008.

Lyons, David. *Exemplum*. Princeton, NJ: Princeton University Press, 1989.

Martin, Waldo E. Jr. *The Mind of Frederick Douglass*. Chapel Hill: University of North Carolina Press, 1984.

Menand, Louis. *The Metaphysical Club: A Story of Ideas in American Culture*. New York: Farrar, Straus and Giroux, 2002.

Schweninger, Lee. "Brown's *Clotel* and the Historicity of the Anecdote." *MELUS* 24.1 (1999): 21–36.

Szendy, Peter. *Prophecies of Leviathan: Reading Past Melville*. New York: Fordham University Press, 2010.

Wilson, Ivy G. "On Native Ground: Transnationalism, Frederick Douglass, and 'The Heroic Slave.' " *PMLA* 121.2 (2006): 453–468.

CHAPTER 20

....

ABOLITION AND ACTIVISM: THE PRESENT USES OF LITERARY CRITICISM

....

JAMES DAWES

When I was in graduate school, my favorite teacher explained that one of the primary pleasures of criticism for the Vietnam generation was the pleasure of unmasking, of revealing the lie. This remains a dominant feature in literary studies in the twenty-first century, and promises to endure for some time. It is, in fact, one of the primary modes available to literary critics wishing to practice ethical or engaged criticism: we are gadflies, more practiced at revealing the failures of social narratives and constructs promoting human dignity than understanding what about their interior structures works and might be portable to other contexts. Of course, some important work on ethics and American literature has been done in a different vein, treating ethical systems as internally coherent rather than contradictory, consistent with rather than covertly opposed to human welfare and rights. But such studies are the exception. The majority of ethically valenced works (works fundamentally about our responsibility to others) are instead fugue-like developments on the now familiar theme of exposing, of discovering the coercion behind particular conceptions of the ethical, the cruelty that twines into benign human practices. Ethical systems are, familiarly, extensions of ideology, subjective desires disguised as objective imperatives, and internally self-defeating.

It is precisely the undeniable potency and repetitive success of unmasking studies—rediscovering hegemony, the containment of subversion, and the infiltration of the ethical by the instrumental—that makes this an opportune moment for seeking new ways of understanding and framing the function of cultural artifacts. But even though unmasking faces the disadvantages of familiarity and repetition, it nonetheless promises to remain for a long time a deeply resonant mode for literary criticism, if only because its existential terror feels so much like *mattering*. Sympathy and empathy, as an example, have long been and continue to be sites of special interrogation for unmasking work in literary studies—precisely because they are so fundamental to our capacity to live in community and with dignity, so fundamental to the changes we seek to effect in the world and the meaning this gives our lives. They are recurrent targets because their centrality to being means we can, each time, be freshly jolted by their convincing deconstructions. The feeling of urgency this generates has, in nineteenth-century studies, been part of the sustaining energy in the long-running debate over sentimental literature, usefully if crudely summarized as a classic subversion-containment debate—one that extends back to James Baldwin's claim about *Uncle Tom's Cabin* that its sentiment "is the mark of dishonesty...the signal of a secret and violent inhumanity, the mask of cruelty" (14). More recently, this frisson has been essential to reconsiderations of abolition as the first and most sacred grassroots human rights movement of modern times. Saidiya Hartman's *Scenes of Subjection*, for instance, reveals the ways empathy in nineteenth-century American abolitionism became an extension rather than reversal of dehumanization. Anita Patterson likewise finds in her study of Ralph Waldo Emerson that "his defense of rights and his racism are intimately and deliberately connected" (4); Karen Sánchez-Eppler notes that abolitionism's "moral and emotional standards" are "implicated in the values and structures of authority and profit they seek to criticize" (49); and Matthew Frye Jacobson argues that racism has not been "anomalous to the working of American democracy, but fundamental to it" (12). In *Specters of the Atlantic*, finally, Ian Baucom extends the history of this clustering of theses, tracking in a case study of abolition and the slave trade the internal links between racism and the defense of rights in order to mount a critique of human rights and the Enlightenment more generally. A universal rights regime, he argues, is a regulatory regime not unlike, or rather sharing the same epistemological grounds as, a globally ambitious, militarized state sovereignty, and is tied into the state's threatening capacity to define the very nature of the human.

From Hannah Arendt to Slavoj Zizek, scholars have argued that the production of the concept of the human, through human rights, depends upon, coordinates with, or even produces a series of devastating exclusions. I'll consider variations on this insight in more depth later. For now, the relevant core question behind such studies is: are the crimes that occur within particular institutionalizations of conceptions of ethical responsibility (democracy, radical abolitionism, human rights, humanitarianism) the inevitable if shameful limitations of complex systems struggling forward to their more full and ideal realization, or are these crimes essential components of their stable functioning? Are such justice movements imperfect because they are in process, or are they fundamentally a paradox, built upon the principles of exclusion that their neutral universalities deny? The latter, more jolting answer is the one favored in the studies I've designated as unmasking. For such critical work to remain fresh, it must do two things. First, it must always rigorously question whether the discovery of analogic resemblance or partial overlap between two sites of analysis justifies a strong characterization of their functional congruence, whether the shudder of counterintuitive conflation might in some examples come at the cost of a nuanced understanding of enduring distinctions. Second, it must theorize beyond negation—as the best work is already doing—to detail how the crosscutting cleavages and fissures in such complex systems have functioned or have been appropriated to open genuine opportunities for liberation. As Joseph Slaughter writes of the human rights movement, "the projection of the normative egalitarian imaginary not only sets the terms and limits of universality's constituency, it makes possible nonhegemonic rearticulations of universality's compass" (5).

If unmasking is to remain a productive mode in ethically engaged criticism of the U.S. nineteenth century, what might be a useful theoretical frame? In the rest of this chapter I will offer up examples of what might be called a rigorous presentism, of the sort surging in contemporary Shakespeare studies (self-identified as a rejection of the new historicism that has so thoroughly defined the field since Stephen Greenblatt's first essays). Evelyn Gajowski, explaining the rise of presentism in Renaissance studies, urgently underscores her view of the ethical obligations of criticism by insisting that to write historical criticism is "to write the future," and that "the ethical implications of our actions in the present [must] enter into the equation in a way not possible under the regime of those theoretical approaches that privilege the past at the expense of the present" (7). Her colleagues Hugh Grady and Terence Hawkes add that presentist criticism must "seek out salient aspects of the present as a crucial trigger for investigations...[and] deliberately begin with the material present and allow that to set its interrogative agenda" (4).

Saidiya Hartman's work is an exemplary Americanist counterpart of this approach; as she commented in an interview about *Scenes of Subjection*, discussing the problem of the sympathetic ally who is blind to his own racism: "I think of the book as an allegory; its argument is a history of the present" ("Interview" 190). Paul Downes is perhaps more explicit about his presentism: he turns to Melville specifically for his "pertinence for contemporary discussions of humanitarian intervention," using *Benito Cereno* in a delightfully nervy way to conclude that *The Responsibility to Protect* (the presiding policy declaration of international humanitarian norms) "might also be the name for an international protection racket" (484). An even more explicit example can be found in the unpublished but widely circulated (especially outside of academia) current work of the preeminent scholar of U.S. abolitionism, James Brewer Stewart, who uses his rigorous studies of abolitionism as a framework for creating a practical template for organizing a grassroots twenty-first-century neoabolitionist movement, directed at ending contemporary slavery and human trafficking.

What might a research agenda in a presentist frame look like for younger nineteenth-century Americanists? It might, perhaps, begin with questions like this: How can

we draw lessons from the social and organizational features of the radical abolitionist movement to better understand the human rights movement in the twenty-first
century? How can our understanding of texts and issues today be informed by our
analysis and understanding of the myths and metaphors of who we are that we have
inherited from earlier literatures and movements? Here are a few ideas for essays
that such questions could generate, frames for readings of and arguments about the
literary and cultural artifacts of the time—in other words, not the "how" of ethical
or engaged close reading, but the "to what end," not ornamented samples of textual
analysis (which strike me as low utility in this context), but rather examples of goals
that our familiar analytic methods might serve.

Consciousness Raising versus Organizational Change

Many of the decisions about strategies and goals in contemporary activism come
down to this binary: Do you change the world by targeting the consciences of
individuals, or through organized participation in established institutional proce-
dures? Where do you stand on the 1960s countercultural spectrum, from Diggers
and hippies to yippies and politicos? Do you model your organization on Amnesty
International, changing people's hearts one at a time, or Human Rights Watch, lob-
bying the U.S. Congress in a complicated balancing of political interests? A study of
abolitionism can contribute to our understanding of these questions.

The question of the place of individual consciousness in political action was
never staged more dramatically than in radical abolition. Unitarians of the time
tended to believe that reform achieved through legislation was doomed to failure,
"since such action would do nothing to change the hearts of the individuals most
affected" (Gougeon 561). For years Emerson largely concurred, criticizing abolitionist efforts to seek political changes without first reforming the consciousness of
individuals. Radical abolitionists, of course, railed against this depoliticizing philosophy. Maria Chapman complained of Emerson that "hundreds of young persons
have made him their excuse for avoiding the Anti Slavery battle & talking about the
clear light; just as thousands have refused to aid the cause because Dr. Channing
wrote essays against associations" (Gougeon 572, 563). Abolitionists wanted people
to act. Quaker editor Benjamin Lundy worked to convince individuals to eman-
cipate slaves; William Lloyd Garrison worked to persuade a nation of individuals
to separate from slaveholders (Mayer 74). But even early abolitionists committed
to organizing remained suspicious of moving beyond individual moral suasion to
political action (as historians have characterized the Garrisonian/non-Garrisonian
split). R. Laurence Moore writes that Garrison retained an "aversion to the use of
laws, institutions, and force as instruments to make people better" (Castronovo
159). He refused to vote and dismissed third-party politics as an attempt "to propel

a locomotive engine without steam," worrying that participation in the legislative process—for instance, by way of the Liberty Party—would dilute the purity of the abolitionist movement, making it another cynical tool of party politics (Mayer 298, 272). Garrisonian abolitionists believed in something like "consciousness raising" or "naming and shaming": "the destruction of error by the potency of truth—the overthrow of prejudice by the power of love—the abolition of slavery by the spirit of repentance" (Stewart, *Abolitionist* 12). This view would, however, change over the decades, as abolitionists became increasingly frustrated by their perceived failure to make a difference. As Elizabeth Cady Stanton wrote: "Sympathy as a civil agent is vague and powerless until caught and chained in logical . . . propositions, and coined into state law" (Clark 490). Summing up the conflict, Garrison biographer Henry Mayer writes: "If the abolitionists had learned anything from their third-party misadventures, it was that issues should not be pushed to premature defeat at the ballot box. Nor should an admirable moral stance be considered an effective substitute for practical political organization" (570).

Sensationalism

How, then, do you change hearts and minds? Contemporary community organizers and international human rights activists are in a continual process of creating what amount to political laboratories for testing the effectiveness of various techniques for moving people to action. What is the best way to heighten public awareness of a crisis or structural injustice? From those working in communications and fundraising for human rights and humanitarian organizations you will often hear the same thing: vivid, sensational, and simplifying depictions of victimization are in the short term the most effective way of bringing in the largest infusions of cash—but this comes at a long-term cost. As former Médecins Sans Frontières (MSF; Doctors without Borders) president Rony Brauman once put it: "He to whom humanitarian action is addressed is not defined by his skills or potential, but above all, by his deficiencies and disempowerment. It is his fundamental vulnerability and dependency, rather than his agency and ability to surmount difficulty, that is foregrounded by humanitarianism" (Downes 469). Hartman may very well have been writing about contemporary humanitarianism when she wrote that "protection was an exemplary dissimulation for it savagely truncated the dimensions of existence, inasmuch as the effort to safeguard slave life recognized the slave as subject only as he violated the law or was violated (wounded flesh or pained body)" (*Scenes* 94). Over the long term, such representations produce what is sometimes called donor fatigue. Some have argued, for instance, that it was precisely the success of previous, sensational campaigns to generate sympathy in the West for crises in Africa that led to U.S. and European apathy and disengagement during the Rwandan genocide. As François Mitterrand is reported to have said: "In those countries, genocide is not very important" (Pfaff 6). For long-term commitment to regions facing durable challenges, then, many insist that issues must be framed differently. MSF, for one, has committed to advancing fuller, more complex representations of the nature of crises and to agentic representations of those surviving them.

How can our study of abolitionism contribute to these experiments in social movements? Early white abolitionists believed deeply in the strategic, even trans-formative effectiveness of sympathy because they had experienced it. The anti-slavery congressman from Ohio, Joshua Giddings, was radicalized during his first weeks as a representative by the experience of seeing a slave coffle in the shadow of the Capitol and, shortly after, the brutal beating of a slave (Stewart, *Abolitionist* 120–121). Historian Elizabeth Clark describes how many abolitionists practiced at victim-sympathy as if it were a kind of moral exercise, forcing themselves, as John Rankin did, to imagine their own families being whipped as slaves (Clark 479). Offering up a sketch of a slave coffle, Quaker editor Benjamin Lundy commanded readers of his newspaper: "LOOK AT IT, *again* and *again!*" (Mayer 53). As the Boston *Chronotype* put it in a review of *The Narrative of the Life and Adventures of Henry Bibb, an American Slave* (1849): "Argument provokes argument, reason is met by sophistry. But narratives of slaves go right to the hearts of men" (DeLombard 105). Girded by this belief in the power of narratives of suffering, abolitionists like Theodore Dwight Weld contributed to the development of the genre of the modern human rights report, producing a dramatic "catalog of atrocities" supplemented by copious evidence of authenticity and accuracy entitled *American Slavery As It Is* (1839), which Clark notes was the single best-selling antislavery tract until the pub-lication of *Uncle Tom's Cabin* in 1852 (467).

Frederick Douglass's relationship to the dramatic display of suffering was, per-haps unsurprisingly, more complicated. His only published fiction, "The Heroic Slave," is a sentimental story designed to change the hearts of the reading public that begins with a scene of a sentimental story changing an individual heart. When Mr. Listwell (listens well) overhears the slave Madison Washington delivering a dramatic monologue on his misery and his desire for freedom, Listwell declares: "From this hour I am an abolitionist" (476–477). But as Julie Ellison notes, the lit-erature of victimization and sentiment is not simply "a taste for pathos"; it can be keenly aware of the troubled "market for pain" that it relies upon (7). Douglass cer-tainly was. He once commented that he was "willing to be regarded as a curiosity, if I may thereby aid the high and holy cause of the slave's emancipation" (McFeely 114). In "The Heroic Slave," however, such curiosity becomes suffocating, a matter of intrusive, exploitative pleasure. Listwell encounters Madison Washington first as a slave, then as a fugitive. Each time he presses for a moving anecdote: "[H]e had long desired to sound the mysterious depths of the thoughts and feelings of a slave"; "do tell us something…we are deeply interested in everything…we could hear you talk all night." Later, when Listwell finds Madison recaptured and in chains again, he is "pleased" and "eager" because he is assured that he will be told all that has hap-pened: "Now do tell me all about the matter" (476, 483, 494–495). Scenes of such sympathetic overhearing metastasize in the story until, by the end, it is difficult to distinguish ostensibly proper abolitionist curiosity from that of racist Southerners anxious to hear news of slave revolts from survivors.

Clark argues that abolitionists continually worked to stabilize the reception of their messages because they were well aware that victimization imagery might become the object of voyeuristic, even sadistic curiosity (486). The range of worries then and now is extensive. Philip Fisher acknowledges sentimentality as a "crucial tactic of politically radical representation throughout Western culture"—a power modeled in *Uncle Tom's Cabin*, where sympathetic stories literally kill Little Eva—but ultimately concludes that it invokes "tears rather than revolt," and that in sentimental literature "the feeling of suffering becomes more important than actions against suffering" (92, 107, 108, 110). Sánchez-Eppler links the moral "profit" children gained from hearing antislavery stories with "the material profits reaped by the slaveowners" (47). Ian Baucom notes in his study of the slave trade that sympathy leads to a sense of the "self's enrichment," a narcissistic satisfaction with the idea of the sympathetic self (249, 263, 293), and Catherine Gallagher's study of David Hume emphasizes the way sympathy both takes the victim as a kind of property and renders the victim irrelevant (*Nobody's* 168–173). Taking a different tack from analyses that focus on the interior states of the spectator, Christopher Castiglia argues that sympathy negatively affects the psyche of the survivor: "Sympathy was a form of surveillant discipline—what we might call sympathetic discipline—in which the black sufferer must imagine himself or herself always in the eyes of whites, becoming a body shaped by an idea of a body" (37). The range of concerns continues, including the fear that: victimization narratives may have solidified the notion of blacks as a separate category of persons; focus on extreme abuse of the body thinned out efforts to imagine broader programs of social and economic justice; image saturation was as likely to produce "cathartic complacency" as action; and, as one critic writes, "the position of victim, like that of the criminal, was a precarious one from which to assert civic agency, much less autonomous legal personhood" (DeLombard 110–111). A rights regime philosophically founded on the idea of our mutual capacity to suffer pain is separated only by a thin line from a rights regime that understands survivors exclusively through their experience of pain. It is for this reason that critics like Dwight McBride and Gregg Crane qualify the criticism often directed at Emerson for his abstract, decontextualized approach to slavery. Whatever his many failings, Emerson may be thanked for not "parading the image of the pitiful and pitiable slave onto the rhetorical stage in order to defend against the Fugitive Slave Law" (McBride 74; Crane 100).

Victimization narration, or what Jeannine Marie DeLombard calls the abolitionist "fetishization of black corporal suffering," was, no doubt, a powerful and risky strategy. DeLombard argues that Garrison and his colleagues borrowed from the "grisly sensationalism of the penny press," hoping that the morbid desires producing financial profit for others could be effectively managed to generate social reform for them. Could they control it, or did antislavery tracts and images function as a kind of cryptopornography? William MacCreary's proslavery novel, *White Acre vs. Black Acre* (1857), insisted on the latter with its satire of an abolitionist meeting that devolves into group fondling of a slave's body (DeLombard 186, 56, 10, 190, 188). Contemporary critics are equally suspicious. James Brewer Stewart emphasizes the "dynamics of race and sexuality inherent in white abolitionism," pointing to the breathless response to the striking, light-skinned fugitive Ellen Craft. Garrisonian Samuel May Jr. found himself appalled imagining her as a piece of property (although, he noted in a parenthetical aside, her subjugation was "in reality no worse than when done to the blackest woman that ever was" [*Holy* 141]— making her something like a real-life version of the "tragic quadroon" dynamic of sentimental literature [Nelson 79] or the "innocent victim" dynamic of AIDS representation). Critics like Sánchez-Eppler, however, have argued that the "allure of bondage" and fantasy of domination not only appalled but also fascinated consumers of abolitionist representation (3). Indeed, Hartman suggests that John Rankin's moral exercises, praised above by Clark, involved a "pleasure" that, in the U.S. culture of human bondage, was "inseparable from subjection" (*Scenes* 21, 33).

FRAMING

What happens when past successes become current failures? When well-proven strategies find their limits or reveal the ways they have become counterproductive? When issues need reframing? The way abolitionists adapted and expanded their strategies over the years might provide some insights to reformers today, who face the very same sorts of questions. As community organizers will often say among themselves, the politics of the poor is poor politics. Attempting to organize local and regional coalitions around justice or empathy for racial or economic subgroups has become extremely difficult; arguing for the right of equality even more so. The latter gets mired in ideological divisions between those advocating equality of result and those advocating equality of opportunity, while the former is vulnerable to reactionary strategies of pitting subgroup against subgroup—a strategy Frederick Douglass noted himself when describing how poor whites in Baltimore, afraid that "educating the slaves as mechanics may . . . give slave-masters power to dispense with the services of the poor white man altogether," organized to force the firing of free black carpenters and hazed and tormented slaves working as day laborers (McFeely 60). Many organizations have responded to such challenges by changing the frame, emphasizing the rhetoric of opportunity, for instance, or characterizing civil rights issues not as a matter of injuries done to subgroups but rather as a matter of collective self-interest. As one regionalist organizer put it, concentration of poverty in urban centers may be a collective moral failure, but the suburbs won't do anything about it until you can show how it materially affects them—a local expression of the strategy for international human rights advocated by William Schulz, former executive director of Amnesty International USA, in his illuminatingly titled book, *In Our Own Best Interests*.

Radical abolitionists exploited the violent defensiveness of the South by changing the frame of the slavery debate, shifting it over the years from an argument over the rights of slaves to those of white Northerners: abolition was, they insisted, in our own best interests. In the early 1830s antislavery print tactics were judged incendiary even in the North, treated, as DeLombard describes it, as "criminal behavior by both government authorities and violent mobs" (40–41). When proslavery thugs murdered antislavery editor and Presbyterian minister Elijah Lovejoy in Illinois in 1837, however, a change began. Theodore Weld raged: "FREE! The word and the sounds are omnipresent masks and mockers. An impious lie unless they stand for free Lynch Law, and free murder; for they are free" (Stewart, *Holy* 77–78). Weld was not alone in his view that white freedoms were being challenged. The next month a crowd of five thousand gathered in Faneuil Hall to protest. Notably, the organizer, William Ellery Channing, insisted that the demonstration be framed as a defense of free speech, warning Garrison not to "mix up the meeting with Abolition." But abolitionism's golden trumpet, Wendell Phillips, won the day by giving a speech that wedded free speech with abolition, portraying Lovejoy as a "martyr to liberty" (Mayer 238). As DeLombard writes of abolitionism's effective frame change: "Early abolitionists repositioned themselves vis-à-vis American public opinion by identifying the Slave Power with a corrupt judiciary and the suppression of free speech and, at the same time, cultivating the association of their movement with cherished civil liberties" (41).

Antislavery activists cannily turned the racism and self-interest of many Northerners into a force supporting abolitionism. Highlighting disruption of abolitionist meetings, Garrison filled the columns of the *Liberator* with defenses of free speech and, in response to a reward of $5,000 offered by the Georgia legislature for his arrest, thundered: "A bribe to kidnappers. . . . A price set upon the head of the citizen from Massachusetts! . . . Where are the immunities secured to us by our Bill of Rights?" (Mayer 402, 123) The free speech frame did not only generate ambient support outside the core movement, however; it served as an entry point *into* the movement for many who would have otherwise shunned it. Emerson's first public address on slavery in 1837, for instance, focused primarily on free speech (Gougeon 560). Historian Richard Newman details the way two newspapers, the *Salem Gazette* and the *Plymouth We, the People*, moved in the early 1830s from protesting the refusal of Southern postmasters to forward abolitionist mail as important only as infringements on white rights ("We must be careful not to let our regard for our southern brethren carry us to the extreme of surrendering our own rights") to eventually becoming "ardent" supporters of the abolitionist movement (165). James Brewer Stewart notes likewise that, in a dramatic amplification of the "free speech" conflict, Northerners who had before abjured immediatism leaped into the breach with the passage of the Fugitive Slave Law, supporting escaped slaves "as a way to express their own growing worries over the political impact of slavery in the nation's affairs" (*Abolitionist* 25). When authorities wrapped chains around the Boston courthouse holding fugitive Thomas Sims, hoping to prevent a rescue, and Chief Justice Lemuel Shaw was forced to kneel and crawl beneath to enter, the frame change was complete: slavery threatened civil liberties in the North (DeLombard 59–64).

A few other frame changes are worth noting, if only because they draw attention to the important risks of such strategies. Reframing slavery as a threat to the Northern political economy of free labor, abolitionists like Joshua Leavitt helped consolidate resistance to slavery among racist Free Soilers and others uninterested in the rights of blacks. Just so, as Stewart notes, the abolitionist effort to convert the Civil War into a war of emancipation involved arguing that it was strategically useful: slaves were doing work to support Southern troops; emancipation made good military (not moral) sense. Finally, the passage of the Fourteenth and Fifteenth Amendments owed something to the strategies of Republicans who argued that assuring black freedom in the South would prevent a massive, unwanted migration north (*Holy* 80, 103, 173, 189, 202). Goals were achieved, but at what cost? Moral purity was sacrificed and moral battles were sometimes veiled, de-escalated, or avoided. Are we still paying the price today?

RADICAL VERSUS CONSERVATIVE TACTICS

Abolitionists, caricatured sometimes as inflexible ideologues, adapted their strategies in creative and supple ways over the years of the movement: amelioration competed with abolition, gradualism with immediatism, nonviolence with calls for insurrection, and party politics with political nonparticipation. Robust and sometimes bitter arguments over these different approaches centered on the question of the place of radicalism: Was it more or less effective? More or less morally grounded? Were British abolitionists brilliantly strategic or essentially counterrevolutionary in choosing to attack the slave trade rather than slavery itself (McBride 28)? Was President Lincoln, who revoked General John C. Frémont's emancipation of slaves held by rebels in Missouri, "a dwarf in mind" despite being "six foot four inches high," as Garrison claimed (Stewart, *Holy* 184)? Did Joshua Giddings help or hurt the cause by deliberately baiting Southern senators to violence on the floor of Congress (Stewart, *Abolitionist* 158–159, 128–136)? Did John Brown advance or retard the progress of liberty? Was the Northern black community overcautious in voting down a proposal to adopt a motto of resistance to slavery at the 1843 National Convention of Colored Citizens (McFeely 106)? Was Douglass, who had voted against the motto, justified later in publicly promoting the "the fear of death" among slaveholders (Blight 95–96)? Was Garrison's expanding vision of universal emancipation—holy governments, world peace—a radical implosion, a diversion, or a "means of maintaining the ethical imperatives of the movement" (Mayer 238, 250–251)?

Richard Newman's history of first-wave abolitionism in Pennsylvania and second-wave abolitionism coming out of Massachusetts is an instructive opening case study. The Pennsylvania Abolition Society (PAS) emphasized the power of white elites and wealthy benefactors to lobby Congress and to press legal claims for emancipation of individual African Americans (in just two years they took fifty-three cases, winning in over half). They shunned emotion, sensational representation, and religious fervor. They urged fellow abolitionists to be "careful to join moderation to your zeal," argued that revolutionary action of any kind (from the Haitian Rebellion to Denmark Vesey) was counterproductive, reaffirmed slaveholders' rights to their "property," discouraged politicizing fugitive slave cases or criticizing racist colonization schemes, and insisted on "reasonable limits" in petitions to Congress lest they alienate moderate representatives.

Was this shrewd caution or moral cowardice? The maximization of practical effectiveness in a constrained environment, or the fear of taking the difficult steps necessary to make a *real* difference? Second-wave abolitionists of the early 1830s believed the latter. The New England Anti-Slavery Society modeled itself upon black abolitionism's "strategy of moral confrontation," demanding immediate abolition rather than amelioration or gradual emancipation and emphasizing impassioned moral appeal. As Amos Phelps thundered: slavery was "a robbery of human rights! A ROBBERY OF THE WORST KIND!" (Newman 104, 129). The new radical abolitionists made a revolutionary, even utopian demand, one that would seem a kind of fanaticism until mainstreamed two decades later by *Uncle Tom's Cabin*: turn "hundreds of millions of dollars' worth of slaves into millions of black citizens, eradicating two centuries of American racism" (Stewart, *Holy* 48). They also revolutionized human rights organizing:

> Whereas the "dignified" PAS worked diligently and deferentially among legal and political elites, the new abolitionists made the cause a noisy public affair among "thousands" and "thousands" of ordinary supporters....Second-wave abolitionists [proceeded] by focusing less on working strictly through formal institutional structures and more on mobilizing the people (especially *new* groups of people) to fight slavery. It was, quite simply, the difference between working the courts and working the streets. (Newman 174–175)

Radical abolitionists escalated conflict with the South and increased political instability. They deliberately alienated potential allies, bitterly attacking all half-way measures and schemes of slow transition to freedom. The audacity of the mission and the bold public face of the movement attracted and energized a generation of new activists, who could now envision "themselves involved in a cosmic drama, a righteous war to redeem a fallen nation (Stewart, *Holy* 46). These "Christian combatants" rejected past incrementalism with extreme prejudice. "*Expediency!*" Garrison declaimed, was "the deadliest word in our language." Here he echoed the English Quaker Elizabeth Heyrick, who (describing British abolitionism) had called "gradualism in politics...the very masterpiece of Satanic policy." "The fear of losing everything by asking too much intimidated reformers into prolonging sinfulness by asking too little," one scholar characterizes the position (Mayer 129, 70).

But there's more than one way to see the relationship between these two modes of political action and their effects in the culture at large. In a study of slavery in the courts, Robert Cover underscores the way radicalism's tactic of conflict escalation can backfire: "[T]he threat of serious damage to the fabric of civilized interaction grows more credible and produces a tendency to question whether the moral values of liberty for an oppressed group are indeed worth the price" (221). Radical politics, moreover, can energize not only the base but also the opposition, pushing them into more intense martial defensiveness—some argued thus in the time of abolitionism just as they have today with the International Criminal Court's indictment in 2009 of Sudanese president Omar al-Bashir for war crimes in Darfur.

By contrast, some have argued for a kind of synergy between radical tactics and conservative aims. Donald Mathews claims that "the existence of a radical element pulled some Americans into more liberal positions. Professing that they were not so extremist as abolitionists, they nevertheless felt that they should be against slavery" (Bennett 42). Garrison himself seemed to confirm such a view, acknowledging that " 'It will, alas! be gradual abolition in the end.' Yet even if slavery would not be overthrown by a single blow, he reasoned, shouldn't abolitionists always contend for what 'ought to be'?" (Mayer 129). Even as radical abolitionists attacked conservatism in all its forms, however, they served and were served by it. Many radical abolitionists came, for instance, from the American Colonization Society. Garrison later called the ACS a *conspiracy against human rights*," but as James Brewer Stewart argues: "For these white radicals-in-the-making, colonization functioned as respectable outlet for misgivings about slavery in an era which demanded ideological conservatism." The conservative ACS thus functioned as "an important transition for abolitionists-to-be"; it "foreshadowed radical abolitionism while at the same time affirming the status quo" (*Holy* 56–57, 31).

If the first great break in white abolitionism occurred with immediatism in 1831, the second great break occurred not ten years later. It was, as before, a break generated by the tension between radical and conservative tactical visions: Is it more effective to work inside or outside the system? Inside or outside the cultural mainstream? By 1840 the abolitionist movement had splintered into three factions, each representing a different approach to the question of how to relate to established institutions and background cultural values: Garrisonians, anti-Garrisonians (represented by the American and Foreign Anti-Slavery Society), and the Liberty Party. The founders of the Liberty Party believed Garrison's stance of nonvoting and nonparticipation meant effective tools were not being used on behalf of the slave. They believed Garrison's utopian purity consigned him and his followers to the margins. Garrison contended, against those who conceived the Liberty Party, that changes in people's souls needed to precede changes at the ballot box, and that participating in party politics would involve moral dilution. But while abolitionists like Garrison were criticizing the Liberty Party for being too pragmatic, others were condemning it for not being pragmatic enough. Joshua Giddings, in an argument familiar to those living through Ralph Nader's presidential campaigns, argued that every vote for Liberty candidate Birney was a vote taken away from Harrison, who favored antislavery measures, thereby aiding the servant of the South, Van Buren. Some historians, meanwhile, have countered that the Liberty Party succeeded in the sense that it forced major parties to "adopt more emphatic antislavery repositions" (Stewart, *Holy* 149, 99, 104, 100).

Advocates of the American and Foreign Anti-Slavery Society attacked Garrison and his followers for a different set of reasons: they felt he had simply moved too far out of the mainstream of cultural values. They were, at least in their diagnosis of his position, correct. Radicalism tends to self-amplify. The antiauthoritarianism of activists attracted to exclusive causes inevitably draws them to a range of others, and attention to a single injustice heightens the salience of others. Garrison's development toward a vision of universal justice pushed him, for instance, to radical nonparticipation and nonresistance. It was, for some, a very threatening stance. The Reverend Joseph Tracy charged that it challenged "the right of a nation to govern its individual members," a position that was "the very foundation principle of Jacobinism" (Fanuzzi 2). Even worse than this, however, radical abolition had led women in the movement to discover, as Abby Kelley put it, that "*we* were manacled *ourselves.*" Garrison supported women like Angelina Grimké, Lucretia Mott, Abby Kelley, Maria Weston Chapman, and Elizabeth Cady Stanton, who all believed that the "woman question" could not be postponed, that abolitionists must take (as Kelley insisted) "a decided stand for *all truths*, under the conviction that the whole are necessary to the permanent establishment of any *single* one." "*Human* rights," Garrison proclaimed, "*that* is the great question which agitates the age" (Mayer 265, 234–235, 296). But promiscuous assembly with assertive, highly visible women was too much for many abolitionists. Men shouted, stormed out of meetings; clergy forced conventions out of their churches (McFeely 99; Mayer 247). As Elizur Wright Jr. insisted: the "Tom turkeys"—not the hens—"ought to do the gobbling" (Stewart, *Holy* 92).

Abolitionist men believed that the "woman question" would injure the cause of the slave, that it was "a tactical disaster" to associate abolitionism with "extraneous" causes (Mayer 247; Stewart, *Holy* 267). But the abolitionist movement simply could not have functioned without the participation of activated women and, as James Brewer Stewart argues, women's rights functioned as a powerfully effective means of productively escalating conflict with the South. The women's movement benefited from codevelopment as well: it received invaluable boosts from male allies in the movement and from its access to abolitionist media outlets like the *Liberator* (Stewart, *Holy* 122). Frederick Douglass, by contrast, frequently experienced the way radical movements can work at cross-purposes. When John Collins, a Fourierist and the white general agent of the American Anti-Slavery Society, shifted the focus of an antislavery meeting in Syracuse to what he saw as the broader evils of private property, Douglass, Abby Kelley, and their African American colleague, Charles Lenox Redmond, were infuriated. A bitter public dispute ensued; the Boston headquarters was forced to intervene. Collins stood his ground, however, and refused to restrict his focus to slavery at future meetings, taking what he might have insisted to Kelley was a "decided stand for *all truths*" (McFeely 104–107, 135). The dispute was representative of the disagreements that fractured the abolitionist movement, and a case study in radical schism more generally. Collins reveals not just the challenge of radicalism, but the challenge of radical personalities. The very qualities that make activists indispensable to movements can also make them liabilities. How, after all, do you manage workers whose very self-concept is built upon antiauthoritarianism, the enjoyment of notoriety, and a taste for the pleasure of righteous indignation? How do you organize individuals who not only have a robust capacity to resist group pressures but who also have a tendency to experience exclusion as a kind of meaning?

In movement after movement over the generations, tactical centrists have charged that the pursuit of utopia can kill reform, that holy personalities disrupt stable organizational function, and that the contagious quality of justice is self-defeating rather than empowering, because liberation movements compete with rather than complement each other. But if radicalism is indeed strategically incompetent in these ways, it is because such incompetence is also a value—in fact, a necessity—in the reimagination of cultures. Radicalism, in other words, is for better and worse the rejection of the constraints of the perceived "possible."

A range of other issues and questions might be pursued linking past and present. Let me conclude by briefly running through a few—again, identifying in broad brushstrokes the cultural, political, or philosophical issues and debates that might be investigated and developed by literary scholars through readings of the key texts in the period. While the following may seem prompts for unmasking (in brief preview: justice depends on injustice, self-sacrificing saints are self-absorbed narcissists, and the deep philosophy of human rights is an opportunistic and trend-driven brand), the most productive work around such questions would resist the lure of the counterintuitive—or rather, acknowledge that at this point the counterintuitive is easy. The best work might start with alluring double-binds and insurmountable paradox, but it will remain there only briefly. It will move beyond showing how things can't work, and start showing how things might.

- Do rights movements work against, or collaborate with, injustice? Can unjust social arrangements function to promote equality, and rights movements inequality? Does the contemporary regime of human rights reorganize power in new and liberating ways, or make inequality just bearable enough to be sustainable? Debates about globalization, for instance, focus on the relationship between neoliberal economic policies and the global immiseration of the poor: is market liberalization an efficient creation of wealth that lifts millions out of poverty, or a brutal exploitation that exacerbates inequality? The history of the former argument, what might be called the corporate resistance to human rights, is long and, in its self-justifying rhetoric of economic necessity, astonishingly unchanging. In the early 1800s British planters argued that they could not remain globally competitive if forced to work with free laborers rather than slaves (McBride 33). Nearly a century later, Jane Addams wrote of the passage of child labor laws in Illinois that "the bitterest opposition" came from "the large glass companies, who were so accustomed to use the labor of children that they were convinced the manufacture of glass could not be carried on without it" (153). Similar arguments are made today about different sectors of the global economy. But despite the pernicious effects of these and other claims, many scholars have argued for a relationship of qualified, antagonistic, but nonetheless very real support between amoral market economies and humanitarian movements. Studying abolition, scholars including Eric Williams, David Brion Davis, Thomas Haskell, and John Ashworth have argued for a link between the rise of abolition and the development of modern capitalism, revealing the way antislavery militancy, codeveloping with the "market economy and its shifting class interests," helped "to reinforce and legitimize the interests of the developing economic elite, with its concomitant embrace of free labor principles" (McCarthy and Stauffer xviii). How might studying this contested thesis about abolition contribute to our understanding of the human rights movement and its links to globalization today?

- Whether it was abolitionists inspecting the bodies of former slaves for sensational evidence of abuse, white colleagues exhorting Frederick Douglass to speak less like himself and more like what Northerners expected of plantation slaves, or aid workers today making mass spectacles out of the private suffering of Africans, the position of white humanitarians has always been complicated by a narcissism that promotes the treatment of survivors as means rather than ends in themselves. How might understanding this narcissism, which has been so essential to past rights movements, help us to better understand the psychological blind spots of contemporary humanitarianism? As Wendell Phillips once proclaimed, describing the way abolition altered his experience of the "dull and rotting weeds" of life: "My friends, if we never free a slave, at least we have freed ourselves in our efforts to free our brother man" (Stewart, *Abolitionist* 108–109). What does it mean for survivors of atrocities to have men like this speaking for them? What are the complications of enfranchised advocacy for the disenfranchised? Few would deny the utility and necessity of proxy advocacy, but just as few would deny the risks. "Too long have others spoken for us," John Russwurm and Samuel Cornish wrote in the first issue of *Freedom's Journal*, the country's first black-edited newspaper. "Too long has the public been deceived by misrepresentations, in things which concern us dearly" (McCarthy 115).

- In what ways can human rights movements become brands or styles that allow people to replace action with gesture and commitment with a signature on a petition? One of the key anxieties about the contemporary human rights movement is the way successes can become the greatest failures. Among some activists and scholars, there is significant concern that human rights has become something of a brand or lifestyle badge, that precisely because of its ascendance as the lingua franca of global moral thought it has been thinned of content or has developed into an alternative to substantive action among citizens. C. Duncan Rice, for instance, writes that in Britain abolition eventually became "the one harmless reform cause," "an anodyne commitment which carried no ideological risk" (McCarthy 14). What can we learn today about how organizers addressed this challenge in the past? For instance, abolitionists were deeply committed to the dissemination of commodities imprinted with images of the kneeling slave. Michael Bennett argues that the National Anti-Slavery Bazaar, by circulating "objects produced by nonslave labor," created a "resistant consumerism that contributed to the antislavery cause" (24). But contemporary political activists like Naomi Klein have mounted persuasive critiques of such consumerist ethics, portraying it not only as a form of conscience-duping nonintervention, but also as the final transformation of citizen into consumer, a solidification of the idea that we are nothing more than shoppers, even in our interior ethical lives. What can the pious consumption practices of nineteenth-century abolition teach us about consumer boycotts and green or fair trade consumption today?

As numerous shorthand histories of the discipline have argued, the turn away from formalism to historicism, from aesthetic appreciation to ideology critique, was all about wanting to be relevant. To scholars who came of age during the Vietnam War, the New Criticism seemed increasingly disconnected from the values and aspirations of the time. The new literary historians were those who desired connection to "the lives real men and women actually live," to "the everyday, the place where things are actually done"— or, as Gallagher and Greenblatt write with characteristic grace: "We wanted the touch of the real in the way that in an earlier period people wanted a touch of the transcendent" (Gallagher and Greenblatt 20, 21, 48, 31). But where new historicists wished to speak to the dead, to understand the reality of an exoticized past, scholarship post-2001 wishes to speak to the living.[1] It seeks to reply to the rhetorical question Stanley Fish posed, "What use are the humanities?" with the assertion that as scholars of the past we can seek to better understand why and how we do what we do as global citizens in the present.

NOTE

1 I borrow this phrasing from Grady and Hawkes 4.

BIBLIOGRAPHY

Addams, Jane. *Twenty Years at Hull-House.* New York: Signet, 1910.
Baldwin, James. "Everybody's Protest Novel." *Notes of a Native Son.* Boston: Beacon Press, 1955.
Baucom, Ian. *Specters of the Atlantic: Finance Capital, Slavery, and the Philosophy of History.* Durham, NC: Duke University Press, 2005

Bennett, Michael. *Democrat Discourses: The Radical Abolition Movement and Antebellum American Literature*. New Brunswick, NJ: Rutgers University Press, 2005.

Blight, David. *Frederick Douglass' Civil War: Keeping Faith in Jubilee*. Baton Rouge: Louisiana State University Press, 1989.

Castiglia, Christopher. "Abolition's Racial Interiors and the Making of White Civic Depth." *American Literary History* 14.1 (2002): 32–59.

Castronovo, Russ. *Necro Citizenship: Death, Eroticism, and the Public Sphere in the Nineteenth-Century United States*. Durham, NC: Duke University Press, 2001.

Clark, Elizabeth. "'The Sacred Rights of the Weak': Pain, Sympathy, and the Culture of Individual Rights in Antebellum America." *Journal of American History* 82.2 (September 1995): 463–493.

Cover, Robert. *Justice Accused: Antislavery and the Judicial Process*. New Haven, CT: Yale University Press, 1975.

Crane, Gregg. *Race, Citizenship, and Law in American Literature*. Cambridge: Cambridge University Press, 2002.

DeLombard, Jeannine Marie. *Slavery on Trial: Law, Abolitionism, and Print Culture*. Chapel Hill: University of North Carolina Press, 2007.

Douglass, Frederick. *The Heroic Slave*, in *The Life and Writings of Frederick Douglass*. Vol. 5. Ed. Eric Foner. New York: International Publishers, 1975.

Downes, Paul. "Melville's Benito Cereno and the Politics of Humanitarian Intervention." *South Atlantic Quarterly* 103.2–3 (Spring/Summer 2004): 465–488.

Ellison, Julie. *Cato's Tears and the Making of Anglo-American Emotion*. Chicago: University of Chicago Press, 1999.

Fanuzzi, Robert. *Abolition's Public Sphere*. Minneapolis: University of Minnesota Press, 2003.

Fish, Stanley. "Will the Humanities Save Us? *New York Times*, January 6, 2008, http://opinionator.blogs.nytimes.com/2008/01/06/will-the-humanities-save-us/.

Fisher, Philip. *Hard Facts: Setting and Form in the American Novel*. Oxford: Oxford University Press, 1985.

Gajowski, Evelyn. *Presentism, Gender, and Sexuality in Shakespeare*. London: Palgrave, 2009.

Gallagher, Catherine. *Nobody's Story: the Vanishing Acts of Women Writers in the Marketplace, 1670–1820*. Berkeley: University of California Press, 1994.

Gallagher, Catherine, and Stephen Greenblatt. *Practicing New Historicism*. Chicago: University of Chicago Press, 2000.

Gougeon, Len. "Emerson and Abolition: the Silent Years, 1837–1844." *American Literature* 54.4 (December 1982): 560–575.

Grady, Hugh, and Terence Hawkes, eds. *Presentist Shakespeares*. London: Routledge, 2007.

Hartman, Saidiya. "The Position of the Unthought: An Interview by Frank B. Wilderson, III." *Qui Parle* 13.2 (2003): 183–201.

———. *Scenes of Subjection: Terror, Slavery, and Self-Making in Nineteenth-Century America*. Oxford: Oxford University Press, 1997.

Jacobson, Matthew Frye. *Whiteness of a Different Color: European Immigrants and the Alchemy of Race*. Cambridge, MA: Harvard University Press, 1999.

Mayer, Henry. *All on Fire: William Lloyd Garrison and the Abolition of Slavery*. New York: St. Martin's, 1998.

McBride, Dwight. *Impossible Witnesses: Truth, Abolitionism, and Slave Testimony*. New York: New York University Press, 2001.

McCarthy, Timothy, and John Stauffer. *Prophets of Protest: Reconsidering the History of American Abolitionism*. New York: New Press, 2006.

McFeely, William. *Frederick Douglass*. New York: Norton, 1991.

Nelson, Dana. *The Word in Black and White*. Oxford: Oxford University Press, 1992.

Newman, Richard. *The Transformation of American Abolitionism: Fighting Slavery in the Early Republic*. Chapel Hill: University of North Carolina Press, 2002.

Patterson, Anita. *From Emerson to King: Democracy, Race, and the Politics of Protest*. Oxford: Oxford University Press, 1997.

Pfaff, William. "An Active French Role in the 1994 Genocide in Rwanda." *International Herald Tribune*, January 17, 1998 (Opinion).

Sánchez-Eppler, Karen. "Bodily Bonds: The Intersecting Rhetorics of Feminism and Abolition." *Representations* 24 (Autumn 1988): 28–59.

Slaughter, Joseph. *Human Rights, Inc.: The World Novel, Narrative Form, and International Law*. New York: Fordham University Press, 2007.

Stewart, James Brewer. *Abolitionist Politics and the Coming of the Civil War*. Amherst: University of Massachusetts Press, 2008.

———. *Holy Warriors: The Abolitionists and American Slavery*. New York: Hill and Wang, 1976.

CHAPTER 21

WHOSE PROTEST NOVEL? *RAMONA*, THE *UNCLE TOM'S CABIN* OF THE INDIAN

SUSAN GILLMAN

HARRIET Beecher Stowe is infamous as the little lady who started the big war and author of what James Baldwin decried as "everybody's protest novel." Helen Hunt Jackson, defender of Native American rights and critic of federal Indian policy (*A Century of Dishonor*, 1881) is famous for her novel *Ramona* (1884), itself known as the *Uncle Tom's Cabin* of the Indian. Not only does Jackson thus live on in Stowe's shadow, but also the twin fame of their novels as cornerstones of American social protest fiction is enshrined in the many popular versions on stage and screen. Both works have strikingly long adaptation histories, encompassing multiple editions and translations, feature articles and travelogues, as well as dramatic scripts, films, and all the accompanying program, publicity, and visual materials. Blockbusters with extraordinary abilities to translate and be translated, *Ramona* and *Uncle Tom's Cabin* would thus seem to provide an almost unparalleled opportunity to study a pair of authors and texts known for and through their adaptations. Yet it has proven difficult to do much more than register the fact of their comparability.

Jackson herself perhaps inadvertently contributed to the problem when she said that she did not dare to think she had written a second *Uncle Tom's Cabin*. Who could miss the assumption of inferiority in the presumed equivalence? Maybe the problem is with the formulation itself. We'd all recognize *as* a backhanded compliment another familiar formula for comparison: X is the George Washington of his country. Or, in Stowe's own version of the formula: "A portrait of General Washington hangs on the wall of Uncle Tom's cabin, drawn and colored in a manner which would certainly have astonished that hero, if ever he had happened to meet with its like" (68). It is not necessary, or perhaps neither possible nor accurate, to say that this is a "black" George Washington. The most proximate term, given the nineteenth-century cultural context, would be "blackface" but the explicit minstrel connotations are missing from this enigmatic portrait. Elsewhere in the novel, Stowe willingly exploits minstrelsy in what she brands the "ludicrous imitations" of her comic black characters, and the famous anti-Tom adaptations of the novel reflect the overt uses of blackface in nineteenth-century popular culture. It's not even clear that the Stowe portrait is in fact black, so unspoken is its racial idiom.

In much the same ambiguous terms as this "other" George Washington, Jackson always plays second to Stowe's first lady, much as *Uncle Tom's Cabin* is the gold standard, the first term in the many comparisons that follow in its wake. Comparison both generates and reflects the fame of the "original," and continually draws critical attention back to it. Following the author's lead, many *Ramona* readers, including one of Jackson's best-known translators, José Martí and his "otra *Cabaña*" ["another *Uncle Tom's Cabin*"], likewise make the comparison but few follow up on the gesture. Given how strikingly often the old saw "a second *Uncle Tom's Cabin*" is invoked and just as quickly passed by, it's as though the initial comparative gesture is both unavoidable and insufficient, the fact of comparison assumed and then abandoned.

In light of these problems, how do we compare? How can we avoid the pitfalls of juxtaposition without analysis or, perhaps worse, the unspoken hierarchy of birth order that gives one object implicit priority over the other? Alternatively, in lieu of assuming equivalence between the objects of comparison, how do we incorporate the historical unevenness and asymmetry that are either denied or poorly accommodated by pairings of objects, eras, or nations (especially the two-country pairings that are endemic to comparative studies)?

In the Stowe-Jackson case, the basis of the comparison itself has not been questioned or reflected on. While both novels have individually produced their own substantial performance and adaptation histories as well as critical studies of them, the two have not been systematically or consciously compared. Instead, while the extensive performance history, across media and languages, of the globetrotting *Uncle Tom's Cabin* is well known, in contrast, the *Ramona* archive, smaller in scale, is studied more locally as a Southern California phenomenon. The adaptation history of *Uncle Tom's Cabin* dominates, most recently in the form of a "transatlantic Stowe" (tracking her travel in "European culture," but focusing mainly on the nineteenth-century stage adaptations in English, with a nod to Continental versions).[1] In short, no comprehensive critical comparison of the self-conscious kind invited by Jackson-Stowe and Co., thinking about how their print and performance cultures and histories develop, diverge, and intersect across time in relation to national and linguistic traditions, has yet been done. Neither has a meta-critical view been taken of the limits and possibilities of comparison itself.

In part the problem is that we have a fairly narrow conception of adaptation. Literary and film studies, understandably oriented toward their own genres, concentrate on traditional intermedial translation, and Jackson-Stowe studies are dominated by performance studies of the stage and film versions. (Translations get relatively short shrift in all this.) What if we think more broadly, so that we include among the adaptations, and *as* a kind of adaptation, less conventional and obvious forms, such as the relationship between the novels themselves or even the different authenticating materials spawned by both works? As factual fictions, both *Ramona* and *Uncle Tom's Cabin* are especially subject to the litmus test of authenticity, holding social protest fiction accountable for how and to what extent it *adapts* the sources, textual and contextual. This would bring in both new evidence and a new conception of what forms count under the rubric of adaptation.

Almost from the moment of publication, each novel has set in motion a search to authenticate its sources and thus via comparison with the factual to establish the credentials of the fiction. Stowe takes primary responsibility herself for documenting the truth-value of her work—largely but not entirely in response to challenges by proslavery critics—with the "Keys" to *Uncle Tom's Cabin* published in several editions in the United States and England (with translations in French and German) between 1853 and 1856. The title articulates the ideology of authentication: *A Key to Uncle Tom's Cabin: presenting the original facts and documents upon which the story is founded/Together with corroborative statements verifying the truth of the work.* Jackson, on the other hand, was barely in her grave by the time that the search for the "original" Ramonas was on, almost overshadowing the novel with documentary, photographic and testimonial evidence devoted to establishing the identity of "Ramona's Home," "Ramona's Marriage Place," and the "real Ramona." Identifying the people and especially the places on which the novel was based started as a turn-of-the-century "Ramona promotion of fantastic proportions" that persisted throughout various boom periods of California tourism, 1885–1955 (McWilliams 73). The invention of "Ramonaland" or "Ramona's Country" was recognized almost immediately as a phenomenon in its own right, as often with skepticism as celebration. Whether claimed as the "real," decried as touristic inventions that become a "fantasy heritage," or studied as "memory places,"[2] together these sites have produced and become living adaptations of the novel—and I would argue the most important and enduring of all the *Ramona* adaptations. Only two of the four films survive, the 1910 D. W. Griffith short starring Mary Pickford and Henry King's 1936 Loretta Young hit, whereas there are many Ramona place-names throughout California today, not to mention all the Ramonas and Alessandros in the handbooks of California place-names, the many guides to the origin, meanings, and etymology of geographical names. In contrast, *A Key to Uncle Tom's Cabin*, generally treated as a footnote to the main event, never dominated the novel's afterlife in the way that the real Ramonas have.[3]

One response to "whose protest novel?" then would be to turn to the mini-fact-checking industries that have grown around both novels, reflecting the expectation that social protest fiction, like adaptations, be judged by fidelity to the original. In their case the original is the "real," and the comparison is to the social, political, and economic contexts that they represent. "Everybody's protest novel," James Baldwin said of *Uncle Tom's Cabin*, was not intended to do more than "prove" that slavery was wrong, was in fact "perfectly horrible," and to that end it had to be "a catalogue of violence." What "forced her to so depend on the description of brutality" and produced "her determination to flinch from nothing in presenting the complete picture" ("an explanation which falters only if we pause to ask whether or not her picture is indeed complete") was the very "nature of Mrs. Stowe's subject matter." Less a novelist than an "impassioned pamphleteer," Mrs. Stowe writes for "the good of society" at the expense of novelistic "truth." Truth here, Baldwin concludes, is meant to imply "a devotion to the human being," "not to be confused with a devotion to Humanity which is too easily equated with devotion to a Cause" (and "Causes are notoriously bloodthirsty") (14–15).

Baldwin defines one end of the authentication spectrum that has meant different things for each novelist. Stowe adapts the historical contexts of slavery to establish her antislavery credentials in both the novel and the *Key*, while Jackson is an oddly double adapter, anchoring her authority as a social protest novelist in the precedent of Stowe's antislavery novel by saying, ironically, that she can't have hoped to write a second *Uncle Tom's Cabin*. Both writers make their points by comparing themselves, Stowe to the real, and Jackson to Stowe. What cultural work is done, for them and us, then and now, by pairing the two blockbusters? Why compare/pair any two texts, not to mention their contexts? What does one get out of comparison? These questions lead to the why, when, and how of the work of "(com)pairing."

Some preliminary answers. When Jackson compares herself to Stowe, she gets the benefits (and disadvantages) of a very well-known and highly successful model. The advantage of invoking such an extraordinary best seller (already measured through the checklist of "translated into X languages and adapted into Y plays") is as obvious as the risk of failing to live up to the model—or even simply of being permanently shadowed by what Benedict Anderson calls the "specter of comparison." Anderson takes this term from José Rizal (celebrated Filipino novelist and nationalist), who coins it in his famous novel *Noli Me Tangere* (1887), to convey the subtle haunting when the young mestizo hero views the botanical gardens in colonial Manila and sees the shadow of their European sister gardens. When Rizal is lauded as the Filipino George Washington, as he so often was by the Americans who "liberated" the Philippines from Spain at the end of the Spanish-American War, the same specter of comparisons (or in Spanish, *el demonio de las comparaciones*, at first interestingly mistranslated by Anderson as "the demon of comparisons") is right there on the surface, transparent if not visible (Anderson, *Spectre* 2; *Under* 32). Both Rizal and his hero are dogged by the double vision that lurks behind Jackson's own comparative formula, *Ramona* as a second, another *Uncle Tom's Cabin*, an image that has itself cast a long shadow ever since.

Beyond such obeisance to the past, with obvious motives of self-aggrandizement and/or self-deprecation, why has Jackson's foundational statement had such a long afterlife? The formula conveys several different senses of the comparative relation, most prominently defining the object of comparison, as model, analogy, and parallel. Operationally and spatially, these concepts all require measurement, calculations of similarity and difference, comparison and contrast. How much does Y live up to or fall from the standard of the model X; how close is the analogy, how faithful to the model, how straight the parallel between them? Temporally, these uses of comparison navigate the weight of the prior and the burden of coming later.

Yet another quite different sense of the comparative that's also part of the picture is the counterfactual and speculative. To wit: the "portrait of General Washington [that] hangs on the wall of Uncle Tom's cabin, drawn and colored in a manner which would certainly have astonished that hero, if ever he had happened to meet with its like" (68). What a cryptic line. Written in the conditional tense that describes hypothetical scenarios, this statement is the conditional of might-have-beens: the past perfect (as past as tenses get) grammatically links a scenario that didn't happen in the past to the hypothetical outcome of conditions that are untrue in the present or unlikely in the future, but not impossible. Just so, *Uncle Tom's Cabin* ends, controversially, with its mulatto spokesman George Harris gesturing toward a separatist racial nationalism in the future: "I want a country, a nation, of my own" (610), he writes in a letter near the end. The novel's many references to the revolutionary legacy of the founding fathers, and how it might be extended to the slave, end abruptly, foreclosed in the vexed image of Liberia, where he announces he will take himself and his family (and thus Stowe engages the contemporary debate over colonization as a solution to black freedom). If George Harris is George Washington's unnamed black alter ego, the colored liberator, a figure who would have astonished that hero if ever he met with its like, then the portrait is a maladaptation with a counterfactual energy, a projection of alternative histories into possible futures. So comparatively minded thinking like Jackson's spans different relations, oriented toward the past and the future, from the most conventional form of the model against which one is compared and contrasted, to the speculative counterfactual.

All of these comparisons stem from and do the work of adaptation, and thus from my perspective account for the long shelf life of Jackson's statement. More than simply an intertextual comparison of *Ramona* and *Uncle Tom's Cabin* or of the relations between the novels and their stage-and-screen versions, adaptation in this broad sense follows the multidimensional life cycle of a literary work across texts and contexts, media, languages, cultures, and histories. How do we delimit and define the object of study, when the objects not only include the multiple editions, translations, authenticating documents, dramatic scripts, films, and publicity materials for both Stowe's and Jackson blockbusters, but also extend to the histories, languages, and cultures of the contexts in which they circulate?

The model that I propose follows on and extends the "text-network" of poet-patriot José Martí, whose role as translator of Jackson's *Ramona*—one of his favorite books in English, translated and published at his own expense in 1888 during his longtime exile from his native Cuba in New York City, where he also wrote his most famous essay "Our America" [*Nuestra América*] (1891)—makes him a perfect emblem for the project of adaptation. When Martí called his *Ramona* (1887) "otra

Cabaña" ["another *Uncle Tom's Cabin*"], speaking out in favor of the Indians as "la Beecher" did for the Negroes, he signaled that it is more than a literal translation: rather a *transculturation* (anticipating Cuban anthropologist Fernando Ortiz's 1940s term, about which more later), the product of more than one author, belonging to more than a single national literary tradition, that elevates the role of translation to active participant in, rather than mere footnote to, the production of literary and cultural meaning. "Text-network" is one term for this kind of circulation, borrowed from studies of the ancient novel, where it refers to a characteristic and central type of Hellenistic world literature, such as the "Alexander Romance," bodies of prose composition with no definitive origin and no telos in their dissemination, no known "author" and no definitive form; rather they exist only as a multiplicity of different versions, in a wide variety of different languages, retailored to fit a host of different cultural contexts, diffused (always in a multiplicity of directions) over much of the Asian-African-European land mass. One way to describe them would be as translations without an original.[4]

Moving through literary assemblage to national histories, we can see how Martí's *Ramona* maps a text-network through connections among language, nations, and empires, with different roles played by Spanish and English in drawing imperial and national boundaries. Martí's translation of Stowe-Jackson also makes visible the idiom of race and allows us to follow how representations of racially charged scenes have transmuted over time, across media within and among different linguistic and national boundaries. Within the texts the translatability of keywords for race, place, and ethnicity provide a laboratory for observing across time and space the vagaries of mistranslation and the cultural work that it can do, positively and negatively. Thinking in this way through adaptation can thus account for a spectrum of modes and genres, across print and performance, in which national histories are translated and compared as models of other nations' histories. Martí's image of *Ramona* as "otra Cabaña" allows us to follow adaptation not just across national borders, across time, across languages and media but also across gender— and thus to comment on the debates surrounding Stowe that have been central to American studies for so long.

RAMONA: THE SECOND, ANOTHER *UNCLE TOM'S CABIN*

My concept of the Stowe-Jackson text-network builds on and, I hope, goes beyond the comparison that Jackson herself initiated with her "second '*Uncle Tom's Cabin*.'" This is a formulation that I will rely on and return to throughout the rest of this chapter, working with, not despite, the limits it imposes. The question of firsts and seconds, of originals and copies, and their unexamined assumptions and potential uses, is key to any study of adaptation and translation. These questions would lead, in the realm of language studies, to such critical issues as the "inequality of languages" (Asad 156). Jackson started something big when she said that she did not dare to think she had written "a second 'Uncle Tom's Cabin.'" The comparison circulates as freely as it is unexamined, a famous line that's carelessly quoted and attributed. The 2005 Modern Library edition of *Ramona* prints the Jackson line on the back cover, and on the front, Martí's version from his 1888 preface (translated by Esther Allen as "*Romana* is a second *Uncle Tom's Cabin*"). As it turns out, Jackson used the line not once but three times, each one slightly different, in letters to three different recipients. Each time she speaks with the self-deprecating modesty of the nineteenth-century American woman writer, and each time she uses a different numerical quantifier to make the comparison that measures her failure to live up to it. The three letters were written at different stages in the composition of the novel, and the three lines reflect her thinking at these moments, ranging from aspiration, as she is engaged with the work of writing, to resignation, expressed in the past tense, once she is finished. The three iterations in Jackson's letters tell us that comparison is always being reevaluated, sliding even from esteem to mortification. As such, the threesome is a good test case for the outer limits and possibilities of comparison.

Writing in 1883–1884 during the most intense period of extended work on the novel, Jackson wrote first in a letter to Thomas Bailey Aldrich, literary confidant and editor of the *Atlantic Monthly*, "[I]f I could write a story that would do for the Indian a thousandth part what Uncle Tom's Cabin did for the Negro, I would be thankful the rest of my life" (May 4, 1883) (Mathes, *Indian Reform* 258–259); second, to William Hayes Ward, superintending editor of the *New York Independent*, with whom she corresponded on the "Indian question," "[I]f I can do one-hundredth part for the Indian that Mrs. Stowe did for the Negro I will be thankful" (January 1, 1884) (307); and, last to longtime president of the Women's National Indian Association Amelia Stone Quinton, "I do not dare to think I've written a second Uncle Tom's Cabin—but I do think I have written a story which will be a good stroke for the Indian cause" (April 2, 1884) (319).

A thousandth, one-hundredth, and the second: Jackson undermines the comparison even as she makes it, measuring how little the fractional proportion with which she meets the Stowe standard. "If I could," "if I can": Jackson consigns the comparison to the grammatical realm of the conditional if-clause and the possible future of the will-or-would main clause. With these ambivalent nods to a famous predecessor, Jackson raised the specter of comparison that has become a virtual *Ramona* cliché. She speaks in both the language of measurement and the conditional mode that would frame the relations between the two works and dictate the comparative possibilities that are raised. There's evidence of more comparative thinking in the first two letters, those written in the present tense, before the novel was completed, when Jackson tries to gauge the right proportion of "Mexican life" that will keep readers reading "before they suspect anything Indian." Comparing the proportion of "Indian" to "Mexican" in the novel, Jackson was clearly energized by the implied comparability between the two groups, but it is unclear how and why she meant to use historical Indian-Mexican relations, whether as parallels or substitutes, masking or displacing one another. Hers is an intuitive and unexamined process of comparing, a "curious mixing up" of the fates of the Indians and Californios that is signaled by the line on *Ramona* as another, second *Uncle Tom's Cabin* (McWilliams 76). All those comments suggest how fertile are the uses of comparison both for Jackson and, later, for the historians of race relations in California and the Southwest, who work on the uneven racialization of Mexicans and Indians, both subject to different degrees and kinds of discrimination in legal and land rights after 1848 (Almaguer; Haas).

Jackson herself set in motion an equally ambivalent and ambiguous beginning to her own critical legacy with her comparative statements. Excerpts from these letters were published in 1909 in James's *Ramona's Country*, fostering the circulation of the Jackson-Stowe comparison in the criticism. We can use her threesome to set out some parameters of comparative thinking by tracing the afterlives of her statements, closely reading a small sample of critical comments made by well-known *Ramona* interpreters in the first twenty-five years after the novel was published. My sample comes from a group of literary guidebooks that Carey McWilliams calls the "husky volumes of Ramonana" that appeared in Southern California between 1887 and 1914, the years when "the chambers of commerce of the Southland kept this fantastic [*Ramona*] promotion alive and flourishing" (73–75). All are *Ramona* promoters and some Southern California boosters, who speak from the same starting point (not chronological but ideological) but don't necessarily end up in the same place. I will begin with the chronologically latest of the reviews and work backward, in the multidirectional spirit of adaptation, ending before the novel was completed by briefly reconsidering Jackson's own comparative statements. Finally, I'll return to the question of "why compare?" and offer a few more provisional answers to what they got then and what we get now out of it.

The latest of my sample, Carlyle C. Davis and William A. Alderson's *The True Story of "Ramona,"* advertises its boosterism upfront (1914). The dedication reads "To the Memory of Helen Hunt Jackson, The Most Brilliant, Impetuous and Thoroughly Individual Woman of American Literature," and the book is in all ways typical of the *Ramona* promotion that McWilliams recognized. (Like so many tourists, one of the authors makes a pilgrimage to Rancho Camulos, which Jackson is known to have visited, and attests that it is still there, "just as Mrs. Jackson saw and described it" [Davis and Alderson 198].) Jackson's fame, we are told, culminated with

> "Ramona," the influence of which has been second to the production of but one
> other American purpose writer. The inspiration of "Uncle Tom's Cabin" and of
> "Ramona" was identical—the wrongs inflicted by a superior upon an inferior
> race. The chief aim of each was ultimately achieved; the one through . . . sacrifices
> of blood . . . , the other through the peaceful evolution of public sentiment. (15)

The confident assertion of equivalence here, somewhat undermined by the "second only to," is not sustained throughout the two hundred pages establishing the novel's factual basis. A few chapters later an extended analysis of the comparison questions its validity:

> Numerous writers have undertaken to compare the work of Mrs. Jackson with that of Harriet Beecher Stowe, with indifferent success. The works of the two gifted authors possibly may be contrasted but not well compared. For "Uncle Tom's Cabin," as all well informed persons must be well aware, there was a ready-made public sentiment. For nearly a century human slavery had been a living and a burning issue.... So successful had the book been that Mrs. Stowe at once set herself the task of writing "The Key to Uncle Tom's Cabin," followed by "Dred," all upon the same theme, and all of these several works were translated...and widely read.... But a far different sentiment awaited the coming of "Ramona." It was unlooked for and unwanted. It was most indifferently received. Nowhere was there sympathy for "H.H." or "her Indians." (78–79)

For the *True Story* authors, the specter of the failed comparison is a source of regret and lament; for us it offers a means of contextualizing the novels and their respective reform movements. On the one hand, Jackson failed to take into account social and political changes in the postemancipation context that might make the climate less friendly to her cause than the earlier moment for Stowe. On the other, the idea of the historical parallel itself, between the institution of slavery and the treatment of the Indian, between the struggles for abolitionism and Indian reform, may itself fail to hold up. Kevin Starr comments in his multivolume history of California that among Jackson's set in New England the Indian cause had replaced abolitionism as a "fashionable concern"; other historians closer to the *Ramona* context question whether American society at the time viewed the situation of the Indians and the slaves as comparable.[5] Finally, there is a meta-historical problem of causality: because the statement that "*Uncle Tom's Cabin* caused the Civil War" is not subject to proof, it has all the speculative force of a perceived, high-stakes effect—often imitated, never duplicated. The very notion of a "second," "another" *Uncle Tom's Cabin* is in this sense a counterfactual. Just so, the status of the parallel between the texts and their contexts can break down and undermine the basis for comparison.

My second example moves back to 1909, when George Wharton James includes in *Through Ramona's Country* excerpts from Jackson and others, in a move typical of the palimpsest of adaptation, crowded with the shadows of earlier and later works and versions. James (English-born author, lecturer on the Southwest, advocate for Indian lifeways), known for quoting others, included a long passage from his rival and fellow traveler in Ramonaland, Charles F. Lummis ("the virile editor of *Out West*"), one of the most tireless promoters and preservationists of California's Spanish legacies as well as advocate for Native American causes, known for his multiple roles as magazine editor, first city editor of *Los Angeles Times*, librarian of the Los Angeles Public Library, founder of the Southwest Museum in 1903 and author of his own Ramonana (*The Home of Ramona. Photographs of Camulos, the Fine Old Spanish Estate Described by Mrs. Helen Hunt Jackson as the Home of "Ramona,"* 1888). In a chapter on the staging of "Ramona," James quotes verbatim Lummis's foreword to the 1905 dramatization by Virginia Calhoun, a five-hour stage adaptation of the novel with a limited run and limited success (James 349–353).[6] We can see the multilayered adaptation history (facing backward and forward) already emerging in the lengthy review James also reprints from the *Los Angeles Times* (February 28, 1905) that mentions the actor Lawrence Griffith, who played the Indian hero Alessandro opposite Calhoun's Ramona and, later, as film director D. W. Griffith, produced the first screen version of the novel, starring Mary Pickford and shot on location in Southern California for Biograph in 1910.

In the Lummis piece inset in James's *Ramona's Country*, Lummis addresses at some length the pros and cons of the Stowe-Jackson comparison. "It was a happy critic," Lummis says, "who first called *Ramona* the *Uncle Tom's Cabin* of the Indian."

> The California classic has less of humor than Mrs. Stowe's masterpiece; it has greater truthfulness to fact, and a considerably higher literary quality. But despite their differences, the two books form a class by themselves. Each is the flower of a crusade.... It is not too much to call both these novels epochmaking. Slavery had, sometime, to cease; but it could not possibly have ceased so soon...if *Uncle Tom's Cabin* had not been read in almost every home, in almost every language.... The appeal of *Ramona* is to a narrower constituency, perhaps—perhaps it is of less imperishable quality.... But...*Ramona* has become beyond question one of the World Books, and beyond comparison *the* California book.... *Ramona* is pure fiction. Not one of its characters lived. Among all the falsehoods told to tourists perhaps none are more petty than those of people who "knew Ramona," who "knew Alessandro," and so forth. All the characters were suggested by actual people; and all of them are truthful, though not real. This is the enduring beauty of the book; that it is not a newspaper report of actual occurrences, nor a photograph of an event. It is in the high sense a work of art, an absolutely truthful painting of conditions and of characteristics. There *could* be a "Ramona" and an "Alessandro"—in fact there have been many who have gone to make this composite photograph...one of the most surprising *tours de forces* that I know of in literature. (James 350–352)

The overall movement of the passage is strikingly oscillating: alternating between similarities and differences, all the time thinking comparatively and taking measurements with more or less self-consciousness. Lummis also draws distinctions that generate more and finer distinctions (work of art versus photograph; not a photograph of an event but a composite photograph). The overt comparative terms here of less than/greater than (*Ramona* is more factual and literary than *Uncle Tom's Cabin*, with less humor, narrower appeal, perhaps less lasting quality) underwrite the less examined, more unspoken distinction that Lummis wants to make between the regional and the national, or even something "beyond." He celebrates Jackson as the writer of a "California classic," "*the* California book." By implication Stowe is a national figure, whose "masterpiece" may even have the, again implicit, permanence and transcendence of a universal work of art. But in this light, what is *Ramona*? World Book, California book—both, or neither, just "beyond" (beyond question, beyond comparison). Lummis finally throws up his hands: comparison is a conversation stopper. It appears to be most difficult for him to negotiate the spatial scale, the local-national-world location of *Ramona* in comparison with the assumed status of "Mrs. Stowe's masterpiece." It's as though comparative thinking feeds on itself (perhaps especially when unexamined), producing multiple superlatives and categoricals, distinctions and further distinctions, ending in an impasse, the "beyond." As such, comparative thinking is also self-undermining, or at least self-critical, raising questions about the calibration and nature of the scale itself. Most revealing is the way Lummis manages to get back to the issue of *Ramona's* facticity, through the springboard of comparison. (There, too, the passage ends up embroiled in distinctions so fine as to be almost but not quite self-canceling: truthful versus real, as in Baldwin.) Lummis runs the whole interpretive gamut of the comparative perspective, and in so doing he clarifies both its limits (hierarchical, static, determinist) and possibilities (speculative, open-ended, futurist).

And now, for something quite different, another *Ramona* promoter, but this one not identified either with the region or the nation of the others: José Martí, writing in the late 1880s in New York for a Spanish-speaking audience in the United States and throughout the Caribbean and Latin America. Martí's translation of Jackson's subtitle—*A Story*—suggests the sweeping nature of the adaptation: his is *Ramona: Novela Americana*. If Martí's view of translation is capacious—"*traducer es transpensar*" [to translate is to think through/across], he wrote—his *Ramona* is clearly something more than the Stowe-Jackson comparison that was in the air at the time. Jackson, Martí says in his prologue, using the familiar greater/less-than formula to unfamiliar ends, "with more art than Harriet Beecher Stowe spoke out in favor of the Indians as she did on behalf of the blacks with her *Uncle Tom's Cabin* [*Cabaña del tio Tom*]. *Ramona*, according to the North American verdict, is save only the weaknesses of la Beecher's book—another Uncle Tom's Cabin" [otra "*Cabaña*"] (204).

For Martí, the point of pairing Stowe with Jackson is not so much to compare who is the "better" writer or more effective advocate but rather to bring together the two subjugated groups for whom the authors speak. Likewise Martí is less interested in ranking the relative merits of the two reformist writers than in transcending the divide between them (and between what are in the United States historically separate causes, against slavery and for indigenous rights). Comparison for Martí is not simply an exercise, neither perfunctory nor invidious, as it so often is in the Jackson-Stowe context, but rather becomes the means of thinking in terms of composite forms and collective identifications.

The grammatical sign of his comparative thinking is the Martíean signature pronoun "our," the *nuestra* that Martí uses so distinctively and idiosyncratically. Anticipating his essay "Our America [*nuestra América*]"—dedicated to imagining a collective "American" identity, reflecting the intertwined hemispheric histories, aboriginal, slave, European, of the New World—his introduction repeatedly presents *Ramona* as "*nuestra novela*": "a work that in our countries of America could be a true resurrection;" and Helen Hunt Jackson as an author, who "in her famous *A Century of Dishonor* was as passionate as our eloquence and piercing as our prickly pears; who in her solemn verses has the serene clarity of our nights and the purple and blue of our ipomeas,—she paints with American light our panorama, drama, and temperament" (203). "As [*Como*] Ticknor wrote the history of Spanish literature," Martí even speculates, toward the end of the introduction, "Helen Hunt Jackson, with more fire and knowledge, has perhaps written in *Ramona* our novel" (204). Six "ours" and two "Americas" in the short course of a few sentences join with the comparative "as" (as passionate, as piercing) to link theirs with ours. The total is greater than the sum of the parts: a conditional and speculative vision of *Ramona* in nuestra América, a work that *could be* a true resurrection.

So it is, counterfactually, Jackson's North American novel that may be ours, *nuestra novela*. Martí's stress on the plural possessive "our" gestures toward a hemispheric genealogy that is, paradoxically, grounded not only in North America (alluding to George Ticknor's three-volume *History of Spanish Literature*, published in New York and London in 1849, soon translated into Spanish as well as French and German) but also in a feminist-sentimentalist tradition, based as it is on both Jackson and Stowe. "*Nuestra novela*," like "*nuestra América*," is a composite, a volatile and unstable product of ethnically and culturally mixed cultures. Rather than a geographically or culturally specific term, Our America is a rhetorical phrase dependent on the shifting referent "our." As the reference changes from one context to another, a multidimensional, multidirectional comparativism develops. Martí's is both a conditional and prophetic vision of *Ramona*, a work, he says, that "could be" [*pudiera*] and is "perhaps" [*quizas*] ours.

Martí's *Ramona: Novela Americana* is thus less a novel translated from English to Spanish and more a novel transculturated, to use Fernando Ortiz's term for the multidirectional relations, colony-to-metropole, core-to-periphery, of the contact zone—in effect anticipating a concept that would not be developed until 1947— from the United States back to its origins in Latin America. When Martí presented us with his transculturated *Ramona*, he was looking both backward and forward, anticipating a view of the contact zone that wouldn't emerge until the new waves of decolonization in the late 1940s. As an example of what I call the strategic anachronisms that are common in many adapted works—the disjunctive presence either of time past or future in the work's present, ranging from the modernized settings of Shakespeare's plays to the black-white slave buddies in more than one gladiator film—Martí's transculturated novel suggests that the process of adaptation reveals a similarly disjunctive relation of space, location, and origin. If the process of adapting is what makes Ramona "our novel," Martí's translation actually returns the novel to its original culture. It takes the circuitous route of adaptation to complete the process of repatriation.

Understood, then, as repatriated rather than exported, the transculturated novel and its composite author together break out of the various local critical categories and domestic debates—sentimental versus political, artist versus propagandist, antislavery versus Indian reform—that have heretofore isolated its and her component parts. Martí's Stowe-Jackson is herself greater than the sum of her parts: as a writer both of the abolitionist novel and the romance of Indian reform, she becomes an interethnic, international figure capable of speaking to both the limits and possibilities of the multiple racial and national aspirations of "Our America." Likewise, Martí's *Ramona* is not the "*Uncle Tom's Cabin* of the Indian" that it is for Jackson and others, writing in English in the United States, but rather the story of what he calls *la mestiza arrogante*, "the arrogant *mestiza* who through persecution and death is knit to her Indian…until the conquering blond race casts them out" (204).

Martí's *mestiza arrogante* represents a real departure from Jackson's Ramona, "the unsuspecting young girl with a taint of Indian blood in her veins," as Albion Tourgée (Reconstruction lawyer and author of the brief on behalf of Homer Plessy) aptly describes her in his 1886 *North American Review* essay on Ramona and Hubert Howe Bancroft's *History of the Pacific States* (250). Tourgée's aptness may be gauged by the terms used in Jackson's novel to refer to Ramona, where most prominently she is called a "half-breed" with "alien and mongrel blood" (30, 234). Instead, Martí's *mestiza arrogante*, the product of mixed Indian and white heritage, is the implied ideal subject and physical embodiment of the revolutionary interracial collectivity he calls *nuestra América mestiza*.

As such, Martí's Ramona owes her mixed heritage to the Latin American conception of *mestizaje*—a term, long identified with the notion of racial mixture, for which there is, tellingly, no literal English equivalent and which is sometimes pejoratively translated as "miscegenation." The racial valence of the term is critical to the rich and troubled story of *mestizaje* in the Americas, where it is associated with the double legacy of colonial histories of conquest and slavery and their aftermath (the erasure of blackness and disappearance of the Indian, through outright genocide or a process of temporally subsuming the Indian as "heroic past" to the mestizo as "heroic present," as well as the drive toward "new and often utopian possibilities of aggregation").[7] So, too, with the related adjective *mestizo*, a word important to Martí and one that has always been especially problematic for his English translators, sometimes translated as "half breed," sometimes left in the original Spanish, as in "our *mestizo* America." "It is telling," Benedict Anderson remarks, "that English has had to borrow 'mestizo' from Spanish" (*Imagined* 203).

Both terms are left untranslated in a key passage in the 1971 English translation of "Caliban," Roberto Fernández Retamar's famous essay where he credits Martí with originating a radical Calibanesque tradition of cultural criticism: "[I]n the colonial world there exists a case unique to the entire planet: a vast zone for which *mestizaje* is not an accident but rather the essence, the central line, ourselves, 'our *mestizo* America.'" Fernandez Retamar fixes on "*mestizo*" and says that "Martí, with his excellent knowledge of the language, employed this specific adjective as the distinctive sign of our culture—a culture of descendants, both ethnically and culturally speaking, of aborigines, Africans, and Europeans."[8] To leave terms untranslated in this way reflects a foreignizing strategy designed by translators to retain key elements of the source text, but the limits of that strategy appear in the gender of the masculine ending of *mestizo*. The net effect is to truncate Martí's central conceit of the feminine "*nuestra América mestiza*" under siege, sexual and otherwise, by the predatory America which is not ours. The subtleties of the Martíean *nuestra* are lost in translation. Given the limits of translation, only when *Ramona* is transculturated and counterfactually "returned," repatriated to what become, after the fact, its linguistic and cultural origins, might it truly become "*nuestra novela.*"

What draws Martí into the circuitous route of adaptation, then, is the potential for collective identification across the hemisphere's languages and borders in the name of "race." When Martí called his *Ramona* "otra *Cabaña*," he used the machinery of comparison to recognize a composite author figure, Stowe-Jackson, whose work is the product of more than one language and national culture. His own translation, Martí's *Ramona*, becomes yet another piece of the text-network. And when Martí called Ramona "*la mestiza arrogante*," she tapped into what would later become the vexed discourse of *mestizaje*. Tensions between race and culture, biology and ideology, and the uneven presence and absence of the primary "racial" groups—absorption of the Indian, disappearance of blackness—reflect the conflicted past of *mestizaje* as well as the debates over its uses in Chicano, Latin American, and indigenous contexts and studies. The "elision of *mestizo* with the Indian body" that was part of the broader nineteenth-century racial logic used to dispossess Mexicans in the United States would one hundred years later, Pérez-Torres says, provide Chicano activists with a strategic argument for inclusion in the twentieth century, a means of laying "postnational claims for identity and place" (9). As a writer in both English and Spanish, Martí's Stowe-Jackson raises these kinds of questions about linguistic and cultural translation, mistranslation and untranslatability. In Martí's hands comparison evolves into a composite form, a collective identification grounded in the mestizo/a body, and a collective cultural production signaled by the complexities of the pronoun "our." Composite texts, like the composite identity of *mestizaje*, offer an important multidimensional and multidirectional alternative to the conventional uses of comparison.

WHAT'S THE USE OF COMPARISON?

If the Stowe-Jackson text-network shows anything at all, it is that the comparative impulse is unavoidable, ubiquitous even when dysfunctional. The Martíean "our" leads back to the questions of "why compare?" and "whose protest novel?" The latter question refers at once to the subject, the author, and the audience of the text. What subject-group is the object of protest in the novels? Who is the author of Martí's *Ramona*? And does the "everybody" (Baldwin's dehumanized human subject of protest) also include the audience, not only the many readers of both novels but also the many more consumers of their popular-cultural spinoffs? When Jackson hitched her wagon to Stowe's star, she set in motion a machinery of comparison that took off in some surprising directions. While it's no surprise that Jackson should have made *Uncle Tom's Cabin* her model, nor that she would in her own estimation fail to live up to the Stowe standard, the Jackson-Stowe pairing also gives her a certain unexpected freedom to speculate and push back against the available forms of the protest novel. Seeking an alternative to the "Indian story" that might not have popular appeal, Jackson imagined instead a setting, mid-nineteenth-century Southern California, that would, simply by virtue of location, implicitly compare Indian and Mexican histories of the United States. Translating this novel into Spanish, Martí went further in the direction of speculative comparison, as befits a translator, who deals regularly with issues of linguistic and cultural (un)translatability, imagining Jackson's *Ramona* as "perhaps our novel." In presiding over these kinds of open-ended, futurist configurations that are dependent on subterranean streams running through the past, the composite figure of Stowe-Jackson suggests a way for the comparatively minded, us and them, past, present and future, to think both within and beyond compare.

NOTES

....

1 See Kohn et al.; Meer.
2 On the "fantasy heritage," see McWilliams 70–83; on the "vast literature on Ramona land," see Allen 12; James; on "memory places," see Kropp 5.
3 Cindy Weinstein's "Uncle Tom's Cabin and the South" is an exception (39–57).
4 For the concept of the text-network, I am indebted to my colleague Dan Selden in the Literature Department at UC Santa Cruz.
5 Starr 58; Mathes, *Helen Hunt* 158.
6 Lummis. For the Lummis foreword to *San Gabriel Mission*, see the Huntington Library Rare Books collection.
7 See Pérez-Torres xiii; Saldana-Portillo 12, 220–226.
8 Retamar 4.

BIBLIOGRAPHY

....

Allen, Margaret V. *Ramona's Homeland*. Chula Vista, CA: Denrich Press, 1914.
Almaguer, Tomás. *Racial Fault Lines: The Historical Origins of White Supremacy in California*. Berkeley: University of California Press, 1994.
Anderson, Benedict. *Imagined Communities: Reflections on the Origins and Spread of Nationalism*. 1983. London: Verso, 2006.
———. *The Spectre of Comparisons: Nationalism, Southeast Asia, and the World*. London: Verso, 1998.
———. *Under Three Flags: Anarchism and the Anti-Colonial Imagination*. London: Verso, 2005.
Asad, Talal. "The Concept of Cultural Translation in British Social Anthropology." *Writing Culture: The Poetics and Politics of Ethnography*. Ed. James Clifford and George E. Marcus. Berkeley: University of California Press, 1986. 141–164.
Baldwin, James. "Everybody's Protest Novel." 1955. 1957. *Notes of a Native Son*. Boston: Beacon Press, 1984.
Davis, Carlyle C., and William A. Alderson. *The True Story of "Ramona": Its Facts and Fictions, Inspiration and Purpose*. New York: Dodge, 1914.

Haas, Lizbeth. *Conquests and Historical Identities in California, 1769–1936*. Berkeley: University of California Press, 1995.

Jackson, Helen Hunt. *Ramona*. 1884. Introduction by Denise Chavez. New York: Modern Library, 2005.

James, George Wharton. *Through Ramona's Country*. Boston: Little, Brown, 1909.

Kohn, Denise, Sarah Meer, and Emily B. Todd, eds. *Transatlantic Stowe: Harriet Beecher Stowe and European Culture*. Iowa City: University of Iowa Press, 2006.

Lummis, Charles Fletcher. *San Gabriel Mission, The Birthplace of Ramona and Fifth Station on El Camino Real*. Los Angeles: Edward Hilton, 1905.

Martí, José. *Obras Completas*. Vol. 24. Havana: Editorial Nacional de Cuba, 1965.

Mathes, Valerie Sherer. *Helen Hunt Jackson and Her Indian Reform Legacy*. Austin: University of Texas Press, 1990.

——, ed. *The Indian Reform Letters of Helen Hunt Jackson, 1879–1885*. Norman: University of Oklahoma Press, 1998.

McWilliams, Carey. *Southern California: An Island on the Land*. 1946. Santa Barbara, CA: Peregrine Smith, 1973.

Meer, Sarah. *Uncle Tom Mania: Slavery, Minstrelsy and Transatlantic Culture in the 1850s*. Athens: University of Georgia Press, 2005.

Pérez-Torres, Rafael. *Mestizaje: Critical Uses of Race in Chicano Culture*. Minneapolis: University of Minnesota Press, 2006.

Retamar, Roberto Fernández. *Caliban and Other Essays*. Trans. Edward Baker Minneapolis: University of Minnesota Press, 1989.

Saldana-Portillo, Maria Josefina. *The Revolutionary Imagination in the Americas and the Age of Development*. Durham, NC: Duke University Press, 2003.

Starr, Kevin. *Inventing the Dream: California through the Progressive Era*. New York: Oxford University Press, 1985.

Stowe, Harriet Beecher. *Uncle Tom's Cabin or, Life among the Lowly*. 1852. Ed. with Introduction by Ann Douglas. New York: Penguin, 1987.

Tourgée, Albion W. "A Study in Civilization." *North American Review* (September 1886): 246–261.

Weinstein, Cindy, ed. *The Cambridge Companion to Harriet Beecher Stowe*. Cambridge: Cambridge University Press, 2004.

CHAPTER 22

NINETEENTH-CENTURY AMERICAN LITERATURE WITHOUT NATURE? RETHINKING ENVIRONMENTAL CRITICISM

STEPHANIE LE MENAGER

I⊤ has been some time now since the verdict came in on Nature. As a concept, a heuristic, a trope, and as a matter of fact, it has become passé. Environmental critics find themselves faced with a reevaluation of the American nineteenth century, whose rhetorics of Nature once spoke to the field's core concerns. We no longer have the leisure to consider Nature as a *locus amoenus* or place apart from human constructs, nor to play out a nature-human dialectic that reaffirms a generative energy greater than, and distinct from, our own. The convergence of global climate change or GCC, peak oil production, and food and water scarcity upon the twenty-first-century planet produces a new order of criticism. Worries about anthropocentrism that gripped first-wave environmental critics have been replaced by a revivification of the human and the ironically anthropocentric category of the posthuman. Criticism responds to what feels like an urgent need to explore human survival and the extension of the human through lifelike media ecologies. Environmentalism 2.0, a U.S. movement which grew up with anxieties about GCC, calls for the Internet to be conceived as a complement to the human mind—the digital mind more capable of grasping crises unfolding at multiple sites and scales.

Epistemological questions treating how we know Nature are largely irrelevant to a twenty-first-century environmentalism that embraces digital "thinking." The pragmatic Emerson of "Experience" (1842) may be more useful to us now than the romantic Emerson of *Nature* (1837), the "transparent Eyeball" who exalted in the near-eclipse of human mind by Being. Yet even the Emerson of "Experience" was tormented by the elusiveness of presence, the fall of objects into subjects, our inability to see "but mediately." In the critical and frankly political turn toward ecology and its pursuit of life in the era of GCC, doubts press upon the literary historian. For example, what is to be done with nineteenth-century American literature? More pointedly, what might nineteenth-century American literature do to Nature and ecology?

When read without suppositions about Nature, nineteenth-century American literature wreaks havoc upon twentieth-century environmental truisms. It is a literature for the twenty-first century in that it offers an unfinished, lively engagement with the Nature idea. In the nineteenth-century United States, Nature had yet to be fully formed as the agent of a broad spectrum of modern ideologies, from the genocidal programs of eugenics to the populist preservationism instantiated in national parks. Nineteenth-century American authors queried and activated Nature, pursuing objects of concern to contemporary humanists, such as the problem of where the human *ends,* and ecological practices based in ordinary interactions with the nonhuman that have been forgotten or caricatured in a postindustrial, largely urban America. The most celebrated defenders of Nature for twentieth-century critics, including Henry David Thoreau, John Muir, George Perkins Marsh, and Walt Whitman, recognized Nature as a fragile alternative to more philosophically and scientifically complex notions of life, and life as a representational problem larger than the Nature idea.

The choice to defend Nature, insofar as it was made by nineteenth-century American authors, often involved considerations of what the U.S. Civil War taught the nation about the value of humanity, political geographies, and narrative itself as a means of species survival. The shadow of Civil War that flickered across the nation from the 1830s through the 1890s and the pursuit of a sociality that might be antithetical to this cataclysmic war birthed an American ecological imagination that was pragmatic and aesthetically keen. As witnesses to mortality rates unknown to late twentieth-century environmentalists and to the degradation of humanity in U.S. slavery, the Civil War, and post-Reconstruction racial violence, nineteenth-century American authors crafted Nature as an ideal image of history. Yet they knew better than their self-proclaimed heirs that Nature was distinct from life. The alternate genealogies of ecological imagination embedded in nineteenth-century American literature are worth considering in the GCC era, when the banishment of Nature complements a rising panic that, without Nature as we have known it, we can no longer tell the human story. If the narrative arts can grapple with the ecological complexity of GCC, clues to survival reside in nineteenth-century U.S. literature. It is an archive that enables potent metaphors for the persistence of life.

SUSTAINABLE TASTES

Henry David Thoreau outlasts twentieth-century U.S. environmentalism because he is not bound by its theories of value, particularly its preference for the apartness of Nature. In Lawrence Buell's foundational *The Environmental Imagination* (1995), Thoreau's *Walden; or Life in the Woods* (1854) centers the archive of environmental literature that Buell canonized for the field. *Walden* elaborates upon "season" and "place," which Buell recognizes as primary figurations (along with "catastrophe") that creative writers have used to perceive "nature's structure" (144). Moreover, *Walden* serves as the template for the epic of voluntary simplicity, a genre of nature writing wherein the trappings of industrial modernity are relinquished for pastoral *otium,* a studied leisure that opens up "the experience of place, of self as continuous with place" (154). The imbrication of self in place that Buell describes could, and has, led critics to question where anthropocentrism begins and biocentrism ends, raising epistemological concerns that reiterate a romantic melancholy. Yet Buell's keywords "season," "place," and "catastrophe" have also given birth to ecocritical emphases upon social justice and disaster, as in Buell's own theorization of "toxic discourse" and Ursula Heise's readings of risk theory against nuclear accident in *Sense of Place and Sense of Planet.*

Thoreau himself, an avatar for first-wave environmental critics, deserves some credit for the flexibility that environmental criticism has shown in regard to shifting concepts of "environment" and "catastrophe." The project Thoreau hones in *Walden* and brings to a radical anticonclusion in his late writings, some of which are published as *Wild Fruits,* indicates the tough pragmatism of his essentially aesthetic program. The writings of *Wild Fruits* begin to elaborate an aesthetics of sustainability. In this late work, Thoreau's interest in apparently nonhuman structures such as the seasons gets distilled into a theory of taste that incites ecological self-knowledge.

Sustainability, summed up as a credo of conservative use, is not easily allied to pleasure. Thoreau's interest in frugal tastes appears as puritanical dicta in *Walden,* where we are warned to curb "gross appetites," while in the later writings of *Wild Fruits* human appetite is encouraged, though from within a context of ecological relationship. *Wild Fruits* is about gleaning and eating, the ways in which these activities sustain each other and, at least implicitly, promote the renewal of local resources. Thoreau's late work offers an agile reading of the intersection of sustainability with desire. Kathryn Dolan places Thoreau within a larger discourse of U.S. consumption, recognizing his sustainable appetites as explicitly anti-imperialist. In addition, Denise Gigante's study of taste suggests how Thoreau develops Anglo-American romanticism, which allowed the senses of taste, smell, and touch—once conceived as lower-order bodily appetites unworthy of distinction—into the larger project of aesthetic judgment (11). As concept and practice, "taste" refines what it means to be human. Thoreau's treatment of taste in *Wild Fruits* finds the category of the human in the sharp sensory pleasures of huckleberries, blueberries, service berries, crab apples—eminently local foods. These fruits express themselves synesthetically; they "blue" the ground, they emit fragrance, they pucker the mouth, they place pressure upon the teeth. The multidimensionality of the experience of the fruits is precisely what makes them "wild," a term Thoreau uses to indicate that which cannot be purchased. "The value of these wild fruits is not in the mere possession or eating of them, but in the sight and enjoyment of them.…If it were not so, then going a-berrying and going to market would be nearly synonymous experiences" (4).

Thoreauvian taste is interactive, implying effort in time, "a-berrying" or more strenuous practice. Ken Hiltner has argued quite ingeniously that "wildness," for Thoreau, indicates a mode of temporality, a practice of attention to earth's own cycles of ripening. Thoreau asks of wild apples, "Was there one that hung so high and sheltered by the tangled branches that our sticks could not dislodge it?" (91) The answer he elicits from us is clearly, "No, we will go to any effort to dislodge it!" In case the reader needs more evidence of how effortful pursuit sweetens the flavor of crab apples, Thoreau writes of the pleasures of wading into "sphagneous" swamps in pursuit of fruit-plunder (32). Wild fruit acts as immersive and interactive media, stimulating all of the human senses in and through time. As media, the fruit competes with the literary, which falls from the realm of representation toward the realm of practice. In sum, both fruits and literature become, for Thoreau, at once media and life. Thoreau's frequent querying and inciting of the reader in *Wild Fruits*, *Walden*, and his essays indicate a theory of reading as, like fruit collecting, strenuous engagement with an environment that pleases because it yields only grudgingly. The various writings that comprise *Wild Fruits* aspire, as does *Walden*, to make time felt through strong claims on the senses, image-rich or vehicular metaphors, to paraphrase Barbara Johnson (55), that defy the mimetic transparency of what Thoreau called "little reading" (*Walden* 96).

Thoreau's seasonal fruit calendar offers an "accounting" of time more rigorous in its attention to histories of both human and nonhuman agents than the narratives of Thoreau's neighbors and predecessors in natural history (*Wild Fruits*, 38). Recently, Thoreau's seasonal accounts have been conceived as archival evidence that might be used to trace the effects of anthropogenic climate change from the early industrial era in the United States, the 1850s. Given that Thoreau understands the seasons as coproduced by human activity or at the least meaningless without it, anthropogenic climate is a relevant subject within his late work. Thoreau's seasons are already anthropogenic, to an extent, and thus not identical to Bill McKibben's twentieth-century seasons, which represent a nonhuman time called Nature that McKibben believes to be ending. What wild fruits have to say to Thoreau about time is that time is a "tangled object," in Bruno Latour's words, an ongoing relationship among human and nonhuman partners (*Politics* 21). The seasons are essentially figures or even stories of ecological relationship, indicating at which points in time and space human and nonhuman lives (farmers, gleaners, fruits) might habitually touch one another. Ecological loss is imaginable within *Wild Fruits,* yet it is conceived not as "the end of Nature" but as the loss of a specific human/nonhuman "sociality" (52). Thoreau laments that the "education" developed through gleaning will be destroyed when fences begin to appear around local huckleberry fields (58).

A taste for wild berries is a taste for ecology, for the thickness of a life that develops through self-conscious entanglement with other beings obeying their distinct schedules of mortality. Again, I invoke Hiltner's temporality of ripening. Early June figures for Thoreau as the "ante-huckleberry season." Thoreau informs us that July, in the Abenaki language, means "when the blueberries are ripe," with the Abenaki dragged in to authenticate his own reimagination of time in terms of ecological interactions like harvesting (21, 48). Thoreau seizes onto the enmeshment of human and nonhuman behaviors, for example, the accidental work of fruit cultivators like cows and fire: "We have all heard of the numerous varieties of fruit invented by Van Mons and Knight. This is the system of Van Cow, and she has invented far more and more memorable varieties" (82). A lengthy history of domestic agriculture qualifies and interrupts the Thoreauvian "wild."

What envelops the human in *Wild Fruits* is not the seasons, not place, not structures of nature per se—in fact, there is no envelope. Humans are in the mix of the so-called natural, and eating becomes a happy figure for the interpenetration of human and nonhuman bodies. Thoreau goes so far as to equate eating berries with human cognition, and though his point may be to refine eating as an attribute of mind, he also refigures thinking as a physiological function of the brain: "You eat these berries in the dry pastures where they grow not to gratify an appetite, but as simply and naturally as thoughts come into your mind, as if they were the food of thought, dry as itself, and surely they nourish the brain there" (53). Wild fruits act as proof that matter extends human presence, and that human presence extends matter. "I believe almost in the personality of such planetary matter," Thoreau acknowledges within a discussion of the European cranberry. "We are so different we admire each other" (168). Here difference lacks the fallenness of Emerson's lost objects in "Experience," and it assumes, instead, the quality of tense proximity that both Thoreau and Emerson attribute to friendship.

While it is tempting to read Thoreau's fruit diaries as a simple endorsement of a contemporary program of sustainability such as locavorism—and to a certain extent this is valid—the notion of taste that Thoreau cultivates includes, as do all ideas of taste, a program of consumption, criteria for aesthetic judgment, and a way of being social. Taken in its full complexity, Thoreau's ecological taste could furnish the erotics of sustainability that the philosopher Kate Soper has called for as an affective complement to sustainable development, including economic relocalization. Still, it is worth remembering, with caution, how contemporary critics tend to mine literary history for politically productive affects. As Thoreau avers of his own discovery of alternatives to the stymied thinking he calls "pretended life," "it was not with such blasting expectations as these that I entered the swamp" (WF, 166).

Thoreau's own gleaning, rather than mining, offers a textually sensitive, low-impact model for reading nineteenth-century American literature, all over again in the face of GCC, as a means toward feeling ecological. Thoreau sets a famous trap for literary "miners" in *Walden*, where he laments a series of lost objects, "a hound, a bay horse, and a turtle dove," which are conspicuously figures without ground (Johnson, 50–51). These figures that defy the practice of reading for presence that Timothy Morton associates with ecomimesis, or the fallacy of representing Nature, suggest a tenuous relationship between deconstruction, as reading practice, and ecological practice. Gleaners, unlike miners, look for what has fallen to the ground by chance or for what hangs within the living system and can be taken without damage. As a mode of reading, gleaning respects the resiliency of figures, their nontransparency and vitality. Thoreau rewards literary gleaners, setting his figural fruits in such a way as to continually nettle our received ideas of the natural and the human, of literature and life.

FORGETTING THE SOUTH

When in the aftermath of Hurricane Katrina mainstream U.S. media referred to residents of New Orleans's lower Ninth Ward as "refugees," national attention alighted upon a key problem for scholars and advocates of environmental justice. For the sake of economy, let us call this problem "forgetting the South," where the South refers to the global South, which can be seen as including parts of the southern United States, particularly the Gulf Coast. Forgetting the South means, for scholar-activists such as Vandana Shiva, the plundering of seed stocks and medicinal plants by pharmaceutical corporations headquartered in wealthy nations. Forgetting the South also means the expectation that Southern countries will remain low emitters of fossil fuels, or that they will allow intervention into their economies by foreign energy developers. These are two of many examples that might be offered in a discussion of how the global South has been denied environmental benefits and saddled with burdens. To pursue the history of "forgetting the South" within U.S. environmental writing, I turn to the one figure who, after Thoreau, most clearly represents nineteenth-century America's defense of Nature. John Muir, born in Scotland and a citizen of the "Earth-planet, Universe," as he describes himself in an 1867 notebook, offers a valuable perspective on how forgetting the South became a feature of U.S. environmentalism that complements the valorization of Nature over life.

The environmental historian Aaron Sachs suggests that Muir stopped thinking in 1892, when he became a founder of the Sierra Club and an official "defender of Nature." "The Muir of the Sierra Club rarely talked about *living in nature,*" Sachs notes, offering a comparison between "the complex realism" of Muir's early articles about his Arctic explorations and his "propaganda" for the national parks (314). While Sachs argues that the extreme environments of the Arctic challenged Muir to ecological thinking, Muir also weighs Nature against a complex set of ecological propositions in the notebooks of 1867–1868, which have been published as *A Thousand-Mile Walk to the Gulf*. In these journals, which were revised at least once before Muir embarked on the early twentieth-century trip to South America that he first had hoped to take in 1867, Muir describes his "long march" through the U.S. South in terms deliberately suggestive of General William T. Sherman's March to the Sea of 1864 (6, 28, 34). Of course, Sherman's March is now an emblem of the doctrine of total war. In its time, it was a hugely destructive assault upon Southern environments, infrastructures, and persons.

Describing Georgians as his "favorite" Southerners and himself as a "botanist" in explicit contrast to the soldier, Muir laments the "traces of war" upon the landscapes he encounters, "the broken fields, burnt fences, mills, and woods ruthlessly slaughtered" (36). The countenances of Southern people, particularly the generation of parents, "bear in sad measure the ineffaceable marks of the farthest-reaching and most infernal of all civilized calamities" (36). Muir may joke that "my 'marching through Georgia' terminated handsomely in a jubilee of bread" (34) upon purchasing gingerbread from an African American woman in the Savannah market, but he understands the severity of war, and the particular humiliation of Southerners in the U.S. Civil War. The connotations of *jubilee,* the long-prophesied freeing of the slaves that was partially delivered by the Emancipation Proclamation of 1863 and, again, partially delivered by the conclusion of the Civil War, may have been more difficult for Muir to access. Paul Outka suggests that Muir's Southern notebooks perform the ideological project of constructing a "modern white subjectivity," allied with the Nature idea, to supplant the traumatic experience of Reconstruction-era blackness (Outka, *Race and Nature*, 162).[1] For as Muir walks through the war-torn South, he expands the definition of "life" to include plants and inorganic matter; he expands the definition of the South such that the United States figures as part of a global region inclusive of Cuba and the Caribbean.[2] He also awkwardly, inconsistently refuses to include certain human types, often "negroes" and poor whites, within the *bios,* as Giorgio Agamben in *Homo Sacer* defines the good life, life possessed of rights and protected by a corporate body, such as the state or, in Muir's case, the state of Nature.

Muir's visit to the still-famous Bonaventure cemetery in Savannah marks the pivot point in these Southern notebooks where an idealization of life called Nature becomes more appealing than actively living within a community or habitat. Muir arrives in the cemetery at a moment of extreme vulnerability, hungry and exhausted, missing an expected letter from his brother that would compensate his dwindling funds. The "tillandsia-draped oaks of Bonaventure," which were planted to border the driveway of the crumbling Bonaventure plantation, strike Muir as the most "impressive…company of trees" that he has seen "since I was allowed to walk the woods" (30). Trees are of particular interest to Muir, being the item he most frequently notes, after human "natives," in his readings of the *Personal Narrative* of his naturalist hero, Alexander von Humboldt (Sachs 329). In Florida, the palmetto will speak to Muir of "grander things than I ever got from human priest" (38). Muir advocates for the personhood of trees throughout these journals, and his point is not anthropomorphization, making trees like humans, but rather expanding the definition of *bios*, the good life, to include trees: "They tell us that plants are perishable, soulless creatures, that only man is immortal, etc.: but this, I think, is something that we know very nearly nothing about" (38).

Muir, who was nicknamed "Botany" by the Canadians who housed him from 1864 to 1866, just prior to his Southern rambles, understands science as a means of troubling statuses that often stand for what we know very nearly nothing about. Science offers the possibility of rethinking cultural statuses in such a way as to extend privileges and rights, to extend "life." Muir's most affirmative interactions with Southerners are scientific conversations, as in his discussion of botany versus "e-lec-tricity" with Mr. Cameron, a Georgia planter who recognizes Muir as "a decent man"—not one of "Sherman's bummers"—when he realizes that they share the scientific hobby (27). In this conversation and another with a Mr. Munford of Munfordville, Kentucky, who regales Muir with rock and plant specimens, the dream of a democracy built upon public science comes momentarily into focus, a dream that Ulrich Beck suggests has been destroyed by modern scientific professionalism and the privatization of research. Mr. Cameron, who impresses Muir with his foresight ("nearly all that he foresaw has been accomplished") and Mr. Munford, who bores Muir to tears, both recognize Muir as a brother rather than a Yankee—their community comes about through reflective interaction with nonhuman beings and matter (10, 28).

When questioned by a Tennessee blacksmith about why "a strong-minded man" such as himself might be strolling around "picking up blossoms" at a time, after the war, when "real work is required of every man," Muir sketches the lay scientist as a type of redeemer. "Now whose advice am I to take, yours or Christ's? Christ says, 'Consider the lilies.' You say, 'Don't consider them' " (15). Somewhat befuddled, the blacksmith concludes that Muir "was fully justified in picking up blossoms" and then goes on to warn him that "although the war was over," small bands of guerillas still roam the Cumberland mountains (16). Botany figures as an antidote to war, a "picking up" of beauty and its spur to sociability in a region defined by keen distrust of human agency and intention.

By the time that Muir reaches Savannah and the Bonaventure cemetery, his connection with the human communities of the South has diminished, although his regard for plants as virtual persons has not. The irony that Muir should develop a strong impulse to redefine life as "Nature" within a cemetery is not entirely lost upon him. "The whole place seems like a center of life," he notes, adding that "the few graves are powerless in such a depth of life": "Bonaventure is one of the most impressive assemblages of animal and plant creatures I have ever met" (30). That this rich ecosystem comes about through design, a Southern variant of the rural cemetery movement begun in the northeastern United States of the 1830s, does not detract from the authenticity of the place. Muir sees "[l]ife at work everywhere, obliterating all memory of the confusion of man" (31). In this raw contrast between "life" and "man," Muir makes the case for Nature, and for the dismissal of humanity to a separate category. Muir's romantic conceit that Nature binds "life and death" in a "friendly union" in the cemetery pushes toward a more radical assumption that humans fulfill their potential *as* life only in death (30). Echoes of another Union, recently forged at the expense of over six hundred thousand human lives, pursue the benevolent union that Muir remarks in the cemetery. "Almost any sensible person would choose to dwell here with the dead rather than with the lazy, disorderly living" (29). Muir sleeps soundly on a gravestone but experiences night terrors in reaction to the "jarring hallos of negroes far away in Savannah" (32). He admits that "idle negroes were prowling everywhere, and I was afraid" (31). Anxiety about such refugees, symptoms of the South's devastated postwar economy, drives Muir to the cemetery. Among the graves, he believes he will be protected from superstitious "mischief maker[s]" who are fearful of "ghosts" (31).

Ironically, it is Muir who is haunted, having endowed his fears with an improbable ubiquity—"prowling everywhere." Muir's Southern ghosts are not only the aforementioned blacks, whose poverty offers an uncomfortable residuum to his effort to redo Sherman's March for the cause of botany and life. Muir encounters *himself* as a ghost in these Savannah scenes, due to the severe hunger, thirst, and penuriousness that leave him at the mercy of his own body, hallucinating such that "the ground ahead seemed to be rising up in front of me, and the little streams in the ditches on the sides of the road seemed to be flowing up hill" (33). Biographer Steven J. Holmes speculates that Muir may have revised the Bonaventure scenes while feverish (Holmes 263). With the "negroes" and the other "disorderly living" of Savannah, Muir recognizes himself wavering between *bios* and *zoe*, the good life and bare life. Bare life suggests "life not worthy of being lived," in Agamben's analysis; it is politically irrelevant life, without rights or protection (*Homo Sacer* 142). Throughout his thousand-mile walk from the southern tip of Indiana through Florida, Muir will be narrowly questioned and taken for a spy, carpetbagger, thief—essentially, a refugee like those who inspire his nighttime fears. Muir's fall outside of the *bios* and into *zoe* makes up the core experience of becoming Southern, for him as for others. His dis-acculturation into bare life culminates in Florida's Cedar Keys, where he passes out unconscious from malarial fever. The watchman of Muir's lodging house finds him sprawled on the ground but refuses him help because he takes Muir for a drunken worker (51). Muir will be rescued, but he remains sick, and his fever, he admits, causes him "morbidity," anxiety, and fear—much of which he directs toward theorizing Nature (40).

It is from a state of self-described "melancholia" that Muir produces, in these Southern journals of the 1860s, two crucial ideas for twentieth-century U.S. environmentalism: (1) that human life is worth less than any nonhuman being, including predators of humanity such as alligators and bears; and (2) that the location of Nature, a realm of being apart from the "disorderly" human, is the American West—not the South. Muir's march to the Gulf ends not at the edge of the Caribbean Sea but in California's Sierra Nevada, where he exclaims: "Here, here is Florida!" in reference to the meaning of "Florida" as a "land of flowers" (72). Outka recognizes Muir's discovery of the sublime in the mountains of California as an explicitly racial project, one that naturalizes whiteness through his own loss of self-consciousness in a landscape distant from the histories of slavery and Civil War (*Race and Nature*, 170). In a profound sense, Nature, which Latour wittily conceives as a "blend of Greek politics, French Cartesianism, and American parks" (Latour, *Politics* 5), grows out of an American effort to forget the South and to ensure that to be American *never* comes to mean being Southern. Being Southern, in turn, implies a profound and complex humanity, a vulnerability to sickness, to poverty, and to violence, an ecological enmeshment in the world which Muir strives to disassociate from Nature and from the transcendental humanity that it validates.

Nature, as a trope enduring into the twentieth century, might be regarded historically as a byproduct of the failure of Reconstruction, or, alternately, as a successful reconstruction of national identity and unity in the permanent elsewhere of the Far West, explicitly the ancient scenery of the Yosemite Valley. Yosemite had been consecrated a "public resort," "inalienable for all time," by the wartime Thirty-Eighth Congress. The Yosemite Park Act of 1864, providing for the transfer of the Yosemite Valley and the Mariposa Grove of giant sequoias to the state of California, created a precedent for the later establishment of Yellowstone National Park. As historian Alfred Runte attests, "the national park idea was already in place by 1864" (26) at Yosemite. Yosemite offered an American landscape of wonders, including the giant trees, which the British had maligned as a fraud when specimens of them were brought to the World's Fair in London. Union politicians recognized the sequoias in situ as evidence of U.S. potency and a timely retort to Britain's Confederate sympathizers. The year that debates about preserving Yosemite were launched, 1863, marked a time for protecting an American passion as innocent as wonder; this was the bloodiest year of the U.S. Civil War.

ENDURANCE AS ECOLOGICAL AGENCY

The U.S. Civil War was ongoing when George Perkins Marsh composed *Man and Nature* (1864), the first U.S. environmental history to attempt global-scale analysis. As Marsh finished the book, he was writing hundreds of dispatches on the Civil War from his post as a Union government agent in Turin, Italy. War figures in *Man and Nature* as a means of understanding humans as environmental actors whose agency is predicated upon the imagination of their own extinction. In his thinking about human self-destruction in war, Marsh suggests the "historicist paradox" that Dipesh Chakrabarty identifies with the era of global climate change—the problem of making history from an anxious present in which we anticipate a future where we cease to exist (197). The temporal continuity from past to present to future that Chakrabarty recognizes as necessary to historical imagination and threatened by climate crisis is compromised, too, in wartime. While nuclear war may be the only current threat commensurate with the world-destroying potentiality of GCC, Marsh recognized war in his own time as exemplary of humans' capacity to interfere with biological and even geological process. From the 1860s, modern U.S. environmentalism develops alongside questions about the supposed division between "human" and "natural" histories, a division institutionalized through monuments to Nature such as the national parks. The Civil War–era writings of Marsh and Walt Whitman offer an alternate genealogy of environmental imagination that begins in war and the biophysical character of "endurance," the perseverance of life through the possibility of its extinction.

In a characteristically lengthy footnote near the conclusion of *Man and Nature*, Marsh remarks with irony that "man's highest ingenuity has been shown...in the contrivance of engines of destruction of his fellow man" (286). A "partial view" of the relationship of war and ingenuity might lead one to believe "the human race [is]...destined to become its own executioner" (286). However, Marsh continues, "war...[also] brings into action a degree and kind of physical energy that seldom fails to awaken new intellectual life"—"heroism, endurance and perseverance" (286). The technophilia that in the twentieth century created what Barbara Adam calls the fallacy of reversibility, the belief that damage caused by modern technologies can be reversed by newer technologies, shows itself in Marsh's faith that the same machines that were designed for extermination might actually extend human survival. Use of DDT as a chemical pesticide and other aspects of the twentieth century's green revolution would complicate Marsh's hopes, betraying the dire consequences of applying war technologies to peacetime pursuits. To his credit, Marsh predicts unexpected and irreversible harms, stating that "the collateral and unsought consequences of human action [are] often more momentous than the direct and desired results" and may cause "comprehensive mutations...in earth, sea, and sky" (456, 19). The idea of the present as the Anthropocene, a geologic age in which humans are changing the most basic physical processes of earth, is already available in Marsh: "It is certain that man has done much to mould the form of the earth's surface, though we cannot always distinguish between the results of his action and the effects of purely geological causes." Marsh's presciently global vision includes not only a grasp of environmental conditions in various world regions but also a sense of deep history, wherein human history is recognized as cocreating the only apparently repetitive time of geology.

If human history collapses into geologic time, both history and the human become problematic concepts. Marsh indicates the problem of losing the human within deep, geologic time in two ways. First, he awkwardly forces the question of "whether man is of nature or above her" as the telos of his environmental project (465). Secondly, he writes almost unreadable history in *Man and Nature*, which progresses, insofar as it does, as an accretion of observations, anecdotes, scientific theories, allusions, and interpolations by a variety of international voices, some scientific authorities and others testifying for what we might call phenomenological experience. The copious footnotes that form a parallel text to *Man and Nature* indicate its overall form—this is literature for vertical as well as horizontal scanning, virtual hypertext, a book demanding interaction and without center in the persona of "the historian" or the delimited narrator. It is antinarrative history, predictive of twentieth- and twenty-first-century representational experiments (like Google Earth) intended to capture spatial realities as lived time that consists of networked, performing agents. The reader must do a great deal of work to construct the global environment as an object of analysis in *Man and Nature* and to distinguish in it the human and nonhuman copartners involved in an ongoing cause-and-effect relationship where, as Marsh concludes, *primary* agency is nearly impossible to sort out.

While it is "within the power of man irreparably to derange the combinations of inorganic matter and organic life," Marsh attributes a resilient "equilibrium" to inorganic and organic life. He follows now outdated ecological theories that emphasize the harmonious cooperation of nonhumans (36). Moreover, Marsh recognizes the "reckless destructiveness" of humanity as not only "collateral" damage but also as subject to misrepresentation. Marsh's commitment to thinking through the "extinction of the [human] species" (43) that he envisions as a real possibility includes his attempt to find a better means of representing humans within ecological process. In brief, human ecological endurance, for Marsh, includes the perseverance of human cognition in the form of literature, even when relations of cause and effect have become unsure, or when spatial and temporal scales exceed the small frame of story. Marsh's strenuous effort to write *Man and Nature* in the midst of the U.S. Civil War attests to what his biographer David Lowenthal calls his "pragmatic optimism"—about the survival of humanity and the survival of history, with literary art as its vehicle ("Introduction" to *Man and Nature,* xxx). That *Man and Nature* turns out to be a nearly unreadable book is perhaps less important than Marsh's effort to write such a book. His courage if not success as a writer testifies to the crucial role of story as an ecological actor in both his and our own time, where political paralysis in the face of GCC is compounded by fears that we can no longer describe what is happening to us.

Though not a proto-environmentalist like Marsh, Walt Whitman has been read as a defender of Nature, akin to Muir and Thoreau. Whitman also takes the Civil War as an opportunity to ask whether historical and narrative agency is still viable. He comes to these questions through a realization of the collapse of the human into matter and a concomitant collapse of historical into natural time. Whitman's *Memoranda during the War* (1875–1876), the limited publication of his war journals that was folded into the autobiographical *Specimen Days* (1892), concludes with a set of questions about the viability of history and Nature as enduring ideas. "Is there not such a thing as the Philosophy of American History and Politics? And if so—what is it?" (129). These questions, though not unprecedented for Whitman, arise from "the dangers and defections of the present," the Civil War that has generated an almost hopeless present tense from which to imagine national futures (129). Thinking through "cataclysm" requires faith in "deep, hidden, unsuspected" forces, which Whitman refers to somewhat more specifically as the second "will" of a people, the "divine, eternal scheme," and "the general laws of Nature" (131–132). Whitman's call for a recognition of natural time in order to reinvigorate national history as a fulfillment of eternal design rather than what it appears to be at present—"a series of *accidents*"—attests to the role of Nature as a model of continuity from which to imagine human history as continuous and meaningful (128). As an external frame for history, Nature confers value upon a human experience that does not, in itself, suggest progressive, generative development.

To some extent, Whitman courts romanticism; one might also say that he instrumentally employs Nature to the same purpose as does Muir, to forget the South, or at least what it meant to the war. Yet Whitman's call to Nature as a means of making history and narrative possible again happens in the war *Memoranda* in the subjunctive mood: "Let us hope there is…this great, unconscious and abysmic second will" (129). He defers the writing of American futures to the future itself: it "is only to be written at the remove of hundreds, perhaps a thousand, years hence" (133). Whitman recognizes his service in war hospitals as a retreat from narrative history and its ally, Nature. Hospital service introduces him to "Humanity, laid bare in its inmost recesses, of actual life and death," which proves to be "better than the finest, most labor'd narratives, histories, poems" (101). This "Humanity, laid bare," another iteration of *zoe*, indicates a challenge to ideas of Nature and a separate human nature. In the war, humanity performs itself, before Whitman's eyes, as "trans-corporeal," in Stacy Alaimo's apt term for bodies constituted by and in continual relation to other bodies. From the typhus microbes present in the Armory Hospital that Whitman frequents to the deep mud, rain, and burning trees that he witnesses as agents in the killing fields, life presents itself to Whitman as what James Dawes describes as "an uncanny figurative blending, or mutual substitution, of organic and inorganic matter" (50). For Dawes, Whitman's confrontation with war, what I call his confrontation with bare life, results in a rejection of narrative as a therapeutic technology of closure in favor of more discontinuous descriptions that encourage "statistical empathy," empathy for suffering in the aggregate (54). Moreover, Whitman's gestures away from the narrative continuities that he also believed necessary to national meaning indicate his groping toward the tangled objects of ecology.

The idea of statistical empathy present in Whitman's war prose might be of use to contemporary environmental writers struggling to generate affect as well as activism in regard to global crises. Whitman's panning out to conceive the larger frames of battle, "from 500 to 600 poor fellows" in a burning wood at Chancellorsville, for instance, and his focused narrative interludes of "typic" persons like the unnamed soldier who "crawls aside to some bush-clump, or ferny tuft, on receiving his death-shot," model a multiply scaled and sited prose that pushes compassion beyond its conventional definitions in regard to proximity (24, 27). But Whitman's retreats from narrative as a means of conveying sequence, catharsis, and the logic of cause and effect come at a cost. We can count the cost in his keen nostalgia for Nature. Figuring Nature as the moon throughout the *Memoranda*, Whitman imagines a literalized transcendental signified, "round, maternal queen, looking from heaven at intervals so placid—the sky so heavenly—the clear-obscure up there, those buoyant upper oceans" (25). As Paul Fussell notes in regard to the importance of the skies as a symptom of the eternal life of Beauty for British soldiers schooled in Ruskin and in the trenches during World War I, Whitman's wartime skies convey an aspiration to eternity and to art. But life, in its "minutia of deeds and passions," overtakes the moon, the skies, this Nature (7). War teaches Whitman to conceive Nature as sub-junctive, a wish structure, and to disarticulate life from Nature and from art when it is understood as Beauty. These are, again, impulses toward ecological thinking, even if such thinking per se does not occur in *Memoranda during the War*.

Consider the following figure of endurance, titled by Whitman simply "An Incident," as the seed of an ecological vision:

> In one of the fights before Atlanta, a rebel soldier, of large size, evidently a young man, was mortally wounded in the top of the head, so that the brains partially exuded. He lived three days, lying on his back on the spot where he first dropt. He dug with his heel in the ground during that time a hole big enough to put in a couple of ordinary knapsacks. He just lay there in the open air, and with little intermission kept his heel going night and day. Some of our soldiers then moved him to a house, but he died in a few minutes. (58)

Brain matter mingling with earth matter, the physiological brain replaces think-ing in this image of human persistence, through and essentially beyond death. The soldier's digging of a hole in earth makes for an accomplishment that Whitman can neither ignore nor fathom as a symbol of soul or eternity in the manner that, say, Thoreau fathoms Walden Pond. The digging is most likely a reflexive act, conveying no intention; it means nothing, yet it is something, an insistence that is readable as time passing and held by entangled bodies—brains, foot, dirt. What the dying soldier does, in essence, is to write life, and the human, without reference to the validating structure of Nature. Whitman's transcription of this act memorializes a monumental absence (literally a hole) where the human used to be, an absence that nonetheless indicates the significance and even poignancy of *mere* bodies.

Coda: Sympathy

Sympathy, the ineffable community among human selves that Adam Smith elabo-rated in his *Theory of Moral Sentiments* (1759) and that served as a foundation for the sentimental novel, has played a strong role in U.S. environmentalism. Modern nature writing from its inception in Muir through more current iterations in the work of Aldo Leopold and Annie Dillard, has drawn upon the nineteenth-century project of sentimental fiction, including its valorization of sympathetic response as a symptom of social refinement and middle-class status, its figuration of suffering as moral vic-tory, and its theory of bodily knowledge, sense experience, as the basis of democratic equality. Sympathy as a means of knowledge and action is at the bottom of the vexed quest for presence and "ecomimesis" lamented by critics, following Morton, who pursue theories of ecology without Nature. Sympathy, though unnamed as such, has also contributed to arguments against the validity of anthropogenic climate change by evangelicals and others who embrace a populist science based in testimony. Like Nature, sympathy seems to suggest the growing irrelevance of nineteenth-century American cultural forms in the GCC era. Yet, I would argue, American sympathy, as it was worked out in the nineteenth-century sentimental novel, cannot be disregarded; its premises continue to be popular and to challenge the scientific foundations of global ecological crises.

The work of sympathy in sentimental fiction is most famously attributed to Harriet Beecher Stowe, whose *Uncle Tom's Cabin* (1852) revised American reality, to paraphrase Philip Fisher, by eliciting sympathy for slaves in order to establish them as sentient, human beings, thus legitimating black humanity. Of course, Stowe's success in using the novel to naturalize cultural statuses (black/white, male/female) as eternal essences, though laudable insofar as she linked her project to U.S. abolitionism and racial equity, elicited reasonable charges of essentialism and even moral cruelty from twentieth-century readers. Stowe's elaboration of racial and gendered "natures" also suggests the abjection of human being in a broader sense, for it assumes that the human is outside the realm of life and in need of rebranding under the category of "human nature." Latour, for one, finds this translation of human life into human nature inauthentic and antiecological, a means of separating our species from vital networks to which we properly belong. Stowe certainly cannot shoulder the blame for the generation of "human nature" as an enduring concept, since its making has been a central goal of Western culture. However, what Stowe does with Nature and the human tells us something more particular about U.S. modernity in relation to ecological thought.

In *The Pearl of Orr's Island* (1869), a novel of the Maine coast that prefigures the environmentally sensitive regionalism of Sarah Orne Jewett, Stowe renders a maritime community where women are (proto) environmentalists and men work the sea for a living—to riff upon the perceived split between environmentalism and labor that has been elaborated by the environmental historian Richard White. Stowe's gendering of environmentalism as feminine has to do with two factors: (1) what Stowe famously perceives as the heightened sensibilities of women, their perceptual and spiritual acuity; and (2) Stowe's assumption that the woman of sensibility, the true woman, is more distant than man from "life." In a complex comparison of her female and male protagonists, Mara and Moses Pennel, Stowe's narrator remarks that "surveying man merely as an animal, these sensitively-organized beings [women, artists, seers, and poets], with their feebler physical powers, are imperfect specimens of life" (178). What Stowe means by "life" is not entirely clear, but it is allied to biophysical strength and mass.

When she is dying of consumption, Mara, somewhat like the malarial Muir in Florida, becomes most able to define Nature—the concept figures, again, as a byproduct of human disease. "Mara had been all her days a child of the woods"—and in fact vivid descriptions of Maine's coastal forests and rocky inlets enliven Stowe's novel—"her delicate life had grown up in them like one of their own cool shaded flowers" (371). It is important to Stowe that the reader recognize Mara's imbrication in nonhuman life. However, of equal importance is Mara's exile from this forest, an exile that in an explicit Judeo-Christian sense limits Nature to that which cannot answer the human with responding sympathy: "[S]he looked out into the old mossy woods…with a yearning pain, as if she wanted help or sympathy to come from their silent recesses" (371). Finally mute, Nature has trained Mara's perceptions so that she might recognize, at last, its and her own apartness. The translation from living within life to living without it, and the Christian-romantic reinvention of Nature at a conceptual distance from humanity, allows Mara to know, through her very senses, that she *is* saved.

Stowe defines the Christian specifically as one not made "for life." Nature, as a concept, facilitates that definition, and the proof of faith by the body. Stowe's paradox and a central Christian paradox is that to know that one is not made for life one must be able to testify on behalf of life, its ongoingness and apartness from oneself, with one's senses. Sympathy is a theory of knowledge whereby the body is utilized to determine the limits of what can be known and then to feel itself beyond those limits, toward God or what the romantics conceived as an ideal Nature usurping the place of anthropomorphic deity. What sympathy and specifically Stowe's use of it teaches is that we cannot altogether do away with the body and its feelings in the pursuit of hypotheses that address imperceptible realities. Faith, whether in the acidification of the oceans or in Christ, relies upon the possibility of testimony. Testimony, in turn, indicates democratic access to knowledge, insofar as it entails embodiment rather than expertise. Popular denials of anthropogenic climate change have been in part a protest against what is perceived as an attempt to eradicate the validity of human sense experience and "feelings."

As Brian McCammack suggests of evangelicals in relation to global climate change, the admission of testimony in regard to unusual weather events such as Hurricane Katrina has made, for some, the difference in favor of belief—which has quite a lot to do with an ability to participate in the process of knowledge formation. Even in earlier days of climate and weather science, personal testimony and the significance of feeling helped legitimate the professionalization of what had once been the popular and eminently social habit of weather-wising (Golinski 5). An amateur weather observer for the Smithsonian Meteorological Project ends her 1873 letter to Joseph Henry, the project's chief meteorologist, with a stark plea: "[A]nd believe me." What precedes this plea is the woman's account of placing herself in bodily harm so that she might deliver reliable testimony to a daytime electrical "shower" that she thinks is a variant of aurora borealis. Using her body as an instrument of scientific knowledge, this amateur, Harriet Greenough, relies upon a type of sympathy, her ability to feel her way toward hypothesis.

Mrs. Greenough argues that her experience, if improbable, be taken up by Dr. Henry as a contribution to meteorological science. She asks for his validation of her sensibility. Her wish indicates a nascent defense of the human as a tangled ecological object. The wish is also a reminder that no ecological project can incite political will without considering popular sentiment and offering venues for participation, embodied interaction—virtual or actual. As environmental scientists cross campuses and disciplines in search of narrative means for expressing impending ecological crises, the narrative innovations made available by digital media might be productively considered alongside experiments from the cultural moment in which modern Nature was born. The American nineteenth century offers a complex thinking through of Nature itself as a product of modernity that may or may not endure as the primary theory of what it means to be human.

NOTES

1 Outka first introduced Muir's *A Thousand-Mile Walk to the Gulf* as a counternarrative to more established visions of Muir as an advocate, if not inventor, of the American Nature idea.

2 My sense of Muir's imagination of a hemispheric if not global South grows from my transcription of Muir's Panama notebook of 1868, now published as *Crossing the Panama Isthmus*, John Muir Newsletter, Spring/Summer 2011, pp. 1, 4–7.

BIBLIOGRAPHY

Adam, Barbara. *Timescapes of Modernity: The Environment and Invisible Hazards.* New York: Routledge, 1998.

Adamson, Joni, Mei Mei Evans, and Rachel Stein, ed. *The Environmental Justice Reader: Politics, Poetics, and Pedagogy.* Tucson: University of Arizona Press, 2002.

Agamben, Giorgio. *Homo Sacer: Sovereign Power and Bare Life.* Trans. Daniel Heller-Roazen. Stanford, CA: Stanford University Press, 1998.

———. *The Open: Man and Animal.* Trans. Kevin Attel. Stanford, CA: Stanford University Press, 2004.

Alaimo, Stacy. "MCS Matters: Material Agency in the Science and Practices of Environmental Illness." *Topia* 21 (Spring 2009): 7–25.

"Animal Studies." *PMLA* 124.2 (March 2009): 472–576.

Beck, Ulrich. *Ecological Enlightenment: Essay on the Politics of the Risk Society.* Trans. Mark A. Ritter. Atlantic Highlands, NJ: Humanity Books, 1995.

Buell, Lawrence. "Ecoglobalist Affects: The Emergence of U.S. Environmental Imagination on a Planetary Scale." *Shades of the Planet: American Literature as World Literature.* Ed. Wai Chee Dimock and Lawrence Buell. Princeton, NJ: Princeton University Press, 2007. 227–248.

———. *The Environmental Imagination: Thoreau, Nature Writing, and the Formation of American Culture.* Cambridge, MA: Harvard University Press, 1995.

———. *The Future of Environmental Criticism: Environmental Crisis and Literary Imagination.* Oxford: Blackwell, 2005.

———. "Toxic Discourse." *Critical Inquiry* 24 (Spring 1998): 639–665.

———. *Writing for an Endangered World: Literature, Culture, and Environment in the U.S. and Beyond.* Cambridge, MA: Harvard University Press, 2001.

Chakrabarty, Dipesh. "The Climate of History: Four Theses," *Critical Inquiry* 35 (Winter 2009): 197–222.

Cronon, William. "The Trouble with Wilderness; or, Getting Back to the Wrong Nature." *Uncommon Ground: Rethinking the Human Place in Nature.* Ed. William Cronon. New York: Norton, 1995. 69–90.

Dawes, James. *The Language of War: Literature and Culture in the U.S. from the Civil War through World War II*. Cambridge, MA: Harvard University Press, 2002.

Dolan, Kathryn. "Thoreau's 'Grossest Groceries': Dietary Reform in *Walden* and *Wild Fruits*." *ESQ* 56 (Spring 2010): 162–191.

Fisher, Philip. *Hard Facts: Setting and Form in the American Novel*. New York: Oxford University Press, 1987.

Fussell, Paul. *The Great War and Modern Memory*. New York: Oxford University Press, 1975.

Garrard, Greg. *Ecocriticism*. London: Routledge, 2004.

Gigante, Denise. *Taste: A Literary History*. New Haven, CT: Yale University Press, 2005.

Glotfelty, Cheryll, and Harold Fromm, eds. *The Ecocriticism Reader*. Athens: University of Georgia Press, 1996.

Golinksi, Jan. *British Weather and the Climate of Enlightenment*. Chicago: University of Chicago Press, 2007.

Guha, Ramachandra, and Juan Martinez-Alier. *Varieties of Environmentalism: Essays North and South*. London: Earthscan, 1997.

Haraway, Donna. *The Haraway Reader*. New York: Routledge, 2004.

Heise, Ursula K. "The Hitchhiker's Guide to Ecocriticism." *PMLA* 121.2 (2006): 503–516.

———. *Sense of Place and Sense of Planet: The Environmental Imagination of the Global*. New York: Oxford University Press, 2008.

Hiltner, Ken. "Ripeness: Thoreau's Critique of Technological Modernity." *Concord Saunterer* 12–13 (2004/2005): 322–338.

Holmes, Steven J. *The Young John Muir: An Environmental Biography*. Madison: University of Wisconsin Press, 1999.

Johnson, Barbara. "A Hound, a Bay Horse, and a Turtle Dove: Obscurity in *Walden*." *A World of Difference*. Baltimore: The Johns Hopkins University Press, 1987. 49–56.

Latour, Bruno. *Politics of Nature: How to Bring the Sciences into Democracy*. Trans. Catherine Porter. Cambridge, MA: Harvard University Press, 2004.

———. *We Have Never Been Modern*. Trans. Catherine Porter. Cambridge, MA: Harvard University Press, 1993.

Levine, Robert S. "American Studies in the Age of Extinction." *States of Emergency: The Object of American Studies*. Ed. Russ Castronovo and Susan Gillman. Chapel Hill: University of North Carolina Press, 2009. 161–182.

Marsh, George Perkins. *Man and Nature*. 1864. Reprint edited and introduced by David Lowenthal. Seattle: University of Washington Press, 2003.

McCammack, Brian. "Hot Damned America: Evangelicalism and the Climate Change Policy Debate." *American Quarterly* 59 (September 2007): 645–668.

McKibben, Bill. *The End of Nature*. New York: Anchor Books, 1989.

Morton, Timothy. *Ecology without Nature*. Cambridge, MA: Harvard University Press, 2007.

Muir, John. *A Thousand-Mile Walk to the Gulf*. 1916. Danvers, MA: General Books, 2009.

Outka, Paul. "Posthuman/Postnatural: Ecocriticsm and the Sublime in Mary Shelley's *Frankenstein*." *Environmental Criticism for the Twenty-First Century*. Ed. Stephanie LeMenager, Teresa Shewry, and Ken Hiltner. New York: Routledge, 2011. 31–49.

———. *Race and Nature from Transcendentalism to the Harlem Renaissance*. London: Palgrave Macmillan, 2008.

Phillips, Dana. *The Truth of Ecology: Nature, Culture, and Literature in America*. New York: Oxford University Press, 2003.

Runte, Alfred. *Yosemite: The Embattled Wilderness*. Lincoln: University of Nebraska Press, 1990.

Sachs, Aaron. *The Humboldt Current: Nineteenth-Century Exploration and the Roots of American Environmentalism*. New York: Viking/Penguin, 2006.

Shiva, Vandana. *Earth Democracy: Justice, Sustainability, and Peace*. Cambridge, MA: South End Press, 2005.

Smithsonian Institution Archives, Washington, D.C., RU 60, Meteorological Project Records, Incoming Correspondence, Miscellaneous Correspondence.

Stowe, Harriet Beecher. *The Pearl of Orr's Island: A Story of the Coast of Maine*. 1869. Charleston, SC: Bibliobazaar, 2000.

Thoreau, Henry David. *Walden; or Life in the Woods*. 1854. Oxford: Oxford University Press, 2008.

———. *Wild Fruits*. Ed. Bradley P. Dean. New York: Norton, 2000.

White, Richard. "'Are You an Environmentalist or Do You Work for a Living?': Work and Nature." *Uncommon Ground: Rethinking the Human Place in Nature*. Ed. William Cronon. New York: Norton, 1995. 171–185.

Whitman, Walt. *Walt Whitman's Memoranda during the War*. 1875–1876. Ed. Peter Coviello. New York: Oxford University Press, 2004.

Ziser, Michael, and Julie Sze. "Climate Change, Environmental Aesthetics, and Global Environmental Justice Cultural Studies." *Discourse* 29.2–3 (Fall 2007): 384–410.

CHAPTER 23

"ACTION, ACTION, ACTION": NINETEENTH-CENTURY LITERATURE FOR TWENTY-FIRST-CENTURY CITIZENSHIP?

RUSS CASTRONOVO AND DANA D. NELSON

As humanist academics, we operate in a world where deliberation is more habitual than action, and, indeed, our intellectual habits seem often to necessitate the deferral of engagement, which threatens always to compromise the purity of our critical standards *for* action. The tension between intellectual work, political deliberation, and action has long been taken for granted in U.S. culture, and even our most notable thinkers have tended to reinforce, not question it. Ralph Waldo Emerson tried revaluing the relationship between critique and action on March 7, 1854, when he delivered an address on the Fugitive Slave Law. "I do not often speak to public

questions," the most widely known American intellectual of his day began, acknowledging a momentous shift in perspective that prompted him to overcome his reluctance to take a stand on one of the most pressing political questions confronting the
nation. Anxious that "intellectual persons" misstep when they trick themselves into
forgetting "their own task," Emerson's comments then still speak to the dilemma
faced by academics perplexed by the relationship of intellectual work to political
critique and action.

How might the intellectual project of reading and interpreting American literature prepare us for the deliberative work of democracy? And what does American
literature tell us about this difficult relationship? Our chapter takes up this challenge by exploring how literature can be read politically, and how it can be put
together with historical artifacts to provide lessons about the fundamental importance of individual and shared interpretation to political action. In this way, our task
becomes not only to explain *how* to read literature politically but to examine *why* we
need to do so. U.S. intellectual culture, as Emerson perceived in his address on the
Fugitive Slave Law, often evades these difficult questions. Like so many of his day, he
had been content to sidestep slavery until he experienced its effects closer to home
in the shape of a law requiring him to recognize that slaveholders had a right to their
"property," that is, men and women claimed as slaves, even in Northern states. By
extending Southern interests into Massachusetts, "the New Bill…required me to
hunt slaves," Emerson protests. He feels jolted out of his privacy to make an intellectual address on a political issue, or rather, he feels forced to turn the intellectual's
position into a political issue. Even though Emerson on this occasion achieved only
moderate success in balancing thought and action, his struggle remains instructive
for thinking about the ambivalent relationship between literary interpretation and
politics. U.S. literary history has often felt the legacy of this ambivalence.

As the inheritors of Emerson's scholarly endeavor, we would do well to wonder about the political and ethical efficacy of critique, which, despite what we may
tell ourselves, can often easily appear as a disincentive for action, substituting an
all-knowing but nevertheless dead-ending and self-defeating cynicism for practical
action. And though this problem of prioritizing democratic deliberation over and
against democratic action is often seen as the particular burden of intellectuals and
academics, it turns out that it's endemic to U.S. culture more generally, as political scientists Elizabeth Theiss-Morse and John Hibbing detail in their book, *Stealth
Democracy*. Political psychologist Diana Mutz even makes the case in her book,
Hearing the Other Side, that the two are necessarily opposed. Of her empirical studies, she concludes that "it is doubtful that an extremely activist political culture can
also be a heavily deliberative one" (3). People can, she insists, either participate or
talk: deliberation among politically mixed groups is inversely related to their level
of political participation.

We offer a countervailing view: the tension between deliberation and action is a
false opposition, one that enervates the work we do in studying literature by seeing
interpretation, on the one hand, as removed and quietist and political action, on the
other, as unreasoned and anti-intellectual. This false opposition renders literary and

cultural critique a caricature of itself, an avocation that bemoans its egghead tendencies all the while professing skittishness toward what it casts as the unreflective, indeed crude, nature of action-oriented politics. Here, we might remember the dismissals of "vulgar Marxism," "ideological political correctness," and "the holy trinity of race-class-gender" that have been made out of supposed concerns to uphold traditional academic rigor in the face of fashion. Instead, we seek a more nuanced portrait that links argumentation and deliberation with citizen involvement.

Lest it seem that we are tilting at windmills, we want to make clear that we are not trying to reinvent the "wheel" of either literary criticism or political commitment. Such "wheels" already exist, but their history—which includes a history of their use as well their failure—has fallen into disrepair. Recent historical scholarship shows high levels of democratic action and expectations for citizen involvement in the early nation—expectations and actions that the framers, as historians like Christian Fritz, Woody Holton, and Terry Bouton argue, consciously designed the Constitution to squash. The interrelation of deliberation and action is a long and durable problem in U.S. history and, as we will argue, in literature, and turning to some earlier writers grappling with the seeming necessities of this founding false opposition might help us open up more fruitful ways of reevaluating and imagining that relationship. The road we will travel is hardly a smooth one, careening from Emerson's careful explorations to the savage freedom imagined by Harriet Beecher Stowe to the uncompromising violence practiced by John Brown. Starting with nineteenth-century literature, we hope to end up with some thoughts about the prospects for reading and social change in the twenty-first century.

BE YOURSELVES DECLARATIONS OF INDEPENDENCE

It's oft-repeated political wisdom that average people don't like to involve themselves in the political work of self-governance and that "democracy" can be safely left to expert representatives. The historical record of the early nation puts the lie to this old saw of political realism. Well before American resistance to British colonial rule emerged as a full-blown revolt, common folk acting on the principle of popular sovereignty had defied government officials who seemed to be overstepping the bounds of their authority. Nathaniel Hawthorne's short story, "My Kinsman, Major Molineux," famously depicts the rough unseating of one particularly unpopular colonial governor at the hands of a mob, but it would be a mistake to see crowd action only in Hawthorne's terms, as unrestrained and lawless. In historian Ronald Formisano's summary, "Though common, crowds and mob action showed remarkable restraint and sought to avoid violence, especially bloodshed, whenever possible. After 1765, the conflict with British officials called into play an extraordinary outburst of crowd activity, and popular protests, inside and outside the law, gained further legitimacy. The patriot cause entrenched a template for later movements that would attempt, in the name of 'the people,' to end social injustice or the corrupt sway of powerful elites" (19).

It was this template that the Constitution's framers sought to overturn by building what elites referred to as "barriers against democracy" (see Bouton 8). In their political counterformulation, soon enforced during the so-called Whiskey Rebellion, such long-standing traditions of active protest to new federal policies were depicted as prepolitical, even *anti*political, and certainly unlawful. The so-called rebels in this instance opposed an onerous tax on whiskey, which they had successfully worked to defeat in the *state* legislature just three years prior. These were not lawless vigilantes, but rather, men and women willing to question and check elected government officials and policy in the name of self-government, and, following democratic tradition, they called themselves "Regulators." To portray them as a mob of rebels is only to accept the terms of history's victors: careful historians of that episode observe that before the outbreak of violence, the whiskey tax Regulators drew on and honored democratic and republican ideals, as well as the new Constitution in staging their opposition. But dialogue was seemingly not the federal administration's aim: to put down this political "crisis" in western Pennsylvania, President Washington first forced the rebellion and then called out more troops (thirteen thousand) than he had commanded during the revolution.

The Sedition Act, passed just four years later (1798), made explicit the new political template:

> That if any persons shall unlawfully combine or conspire together, with intent to oppose any measure or measures of the government of the United States...or to impede the operation of any law of the United States, or to intimidate or prevent any person holding a place or office in or under the government of the United States, from...performing his trust or duty, and if any person or persons...shall counsel, advise or attempt to procure any insurrection, riot, unlawful assembly or combination, whether such conspiracy, threatening, counsel, advice or attempt shall have the proposed effect or not, he or they shall be deemed guilty of a high misdemeanor. ("An Act for the Punishment of Certain Crimes against the United States," *Statutes at Large*, Fifth Congress, second section, chpt. 74, II Statute, 596)

The statute recast active, democratically invested, sovereign citizens of the early nation as criminals. This Federalist attempt to outlaw citizen dissent would soon be redressed. But even as suffrage began its celebrated expansion in the 1820s to white men without property, citizens were accepting a diminished role in self-government, redirecting their energies accordingly. The 1830s and '40s highlight this transition. Reform efforts were roiling and the targets were diverse. Increasingly, however, the aim for reform was not government: citizens began turning their regulatory aims onto themselves.[1]

Emerson simultaneously rejects and fulfills this tendency toward privatizing self-discipline in his speech on the Fugitive Slave Law in 1854. Even though he declares the necessity of the intellectual's participation in public debates, he personalizes public questions to such an extreme that the horizon of collective political action emerges as a mirage. Emerson initially discovers his opposition to the Fugitive Slave Law via popular print culture, specifically the newspaper, which appeals to "all classes" and makes its way into "shops, counting-rooms, work-yards, and warehouses" (74). Conveying news from afar, the newspaper is the popular vehicle that brings an awareness of Daniel Webster's compromise to Emerson's doorstep. It is without a doubt a mixed blessing since it communicates all sorts of sordid affairs, but ultimately it is to be commended for bringing readers closer to "fact and thought and wisdom...from all regions of the world" (74). But uncertainty remains whether knowledge, no matter how expansive, can or will promote action. Is it too risky for the intellectual to wade through political currents? Emerson's address registers how news of public deliberation creates a sea change in his thinking, encouraging him to venture beyond the local intellectual shores he knows so well.

Soon, though, Emerson begins to worry that he is adrift in a world of sharks: politicians like Webster who privilege eloquence over morality; judges, who despite their charge to protect the lambs, prefer "a wolfish interpretation" of the law; Christians who contort the Bible into justifications of slavery. He craves his former solitude, and so buoys himself with his central tenet: in this world, we have only ourselves to rely on: "To make good the cause of Freedom you must draw off from all these foolish trusts on others. You must be citadels and warriors, yourselves Declarations of Independence" (83). This preference for the Declaration over the Constitution hardly makes Emerson a democratic populist; quite differently, his solution individualizes political critique, retracting the significance of that document's revolutionary creation of a new polity to the limits of the sovereign self. Rather than solicit a crowd for the Declaration, he encourages a response that effectively abrogates the popular public power that radical democratic republicans associated with that founding document. Each of us should be a Declaration of Independence in miniature, internalizing the challenges of a community engaged in realizing its difficult promises of equality. Emerson insists that our civic energy finds its strength not in public, together with others, but in isolation where our political principles are parceled out separately. "He only who is able to stand alone is qualified for society," declared Emerson. He liked this phrase so much that he recycled it two years later when he weighed in on the face-off between Free Soilers and proslavers in Kansas: "He only who is able to stand alone is qualified to be a citizen." This small change from "society" to "citizen" registers the hardening of Emerson's thinking, as the potentially plural body of society gives way to the abstract, singularized marker of legal personhood. Yes, he encourages strenuous resistance in his military language of "warriors" and "citadels," but the result of such heroic self-discipline is civic inaction: he encourages his auditors to cooperate by waiting for the avenging spasms of nature—Divine and Providential Justice—which comes slowly ("centuries and ages")—but, he promises, surely.

SAVAGE FREEDOM

Harriet Beecher Stowe has long been apocryphally known as the "little lady who started this Great War." In our critical generation, she has been as famously castigated for popularizing Emerson's ideas about the transcendent civic good of self-disciplined citizen inaction. In Lauren Berlant's famous formulation, Stowe's *Uncle Tom's Cabin* (1852) promotes the anorexic politics of sentimentalism, teaching readers to substitute a craving for world-changing power with the simpler, more private, and sweeter satisfactions of a changed *heart*. This may be true of *Uncle Tom's Cabin*, but it might not be fair to attribute these politics to the entirety of Stowe's career or her oeuvre. A careful reading of her less-popular novel, *Dred* (1856), shows her offering a different plot about the relation of deliberation and dissent to public action. As Robert Levine has shown, Frederick Douglass's reaction to *Uncle Tom's Cabin* led Stowe to explore different possibilities or racial protest in *Dred*. Stowe's ambivalence in this novel is less about political action per se than about collective action. Throughout this novel, the possibility of mass political action looms promisingly and ominously; Stowe utilizes the terms of the Federalists and Emerson, even as she struggles against them.

In this novel, we meet the young Nina Gordon, a captivating spendthrift flibbertigibbet in the midst of settling into a serious courtship with the idealistic young lawyer Edward Clayton. Nina shares the responsibilities of running the family plantation with her malcontented and scheming brother Tom, who nurses bottles along with grudges. It is actually their unacknowledged half brother, the passionate, intelligent, and enslaved Harry, who looks after the finances and management of the plantation, even as he works to buy freedom for himself and his beautiful young wife. Harry is ridiculed for his diligent obligation to the terms of his enslavement by the charismatic and mysterious leader of the maroon community, Dred. This character, who lives in the shadowy recesses of the Dismal Swamp, turns out to be the son of Denmark Vesey, a former slave living free in Charleston, who planned what would have been one of the largest slave revolts in U.S. history, timed to have taken place on Bastille Day in 1822. As Vesey's heir, Dred is working to fulfill his father's revolutionary aims.

Stowe's historical romance plots a dangerous confluence of careful reading, political critique, and action. Alarmed that Clayton's sister, Ann, keeps a school for their plantation's slaves, white neighbors send a delegate to remind her that it is "a notorious fact that the worst insurrections have arisen from the reading of the Bible by these ignorant fellows: That was the case with Nat Turner, in Virginia. That was the case with Denmark Vesey, and his crew, in South Carolina" (196). Dred inherits a hermeneutic tradition in which the Bible figures not simply as the foundation for commentary, discussion, and moral self-reflection, but as the wellspring for active resistance to injustice. The slaveholder's nod to the Bible's capacity to spur collective action conveys the true dimensions of this threat. But, Stowe worries, such action may not in the end be righteous. The gesture to Vesey and his comrades also alludes to Milton's Comus, who "with his crew," as the dramatic instructions to the masque specify, seeks to overthrow a social order based on faith and chastity. Much more than cleverness is involved here since in Stowe's world—where slaves cite the Bible along with the Declaration of Independence—reading and action are not separate spheres. In *Dred*, textual traditions as far-flung as seventeenth-century English literature and eighteenth-century American revolutionary rhetoric segue to crowds and conflict. Such confluences may or may not be auspicious.

Every bit as charismatic as Milton's tempter, Dred seduces others into a whirlwind of violence. As Harry implores this forest tempter, "Don't talk that way!—don't!... You are raising the very devil in me!" Differently from Comus's devotion to moral anarchy, though, Dred feels called by the Lord to lead an interracial revolution against slavery. Throughout the novel, readers encounter Dred deliberating the morality of rising against slavery, rescuing escaping slaves from the men and dogs tracking them, coaxing his community toward violent revolt, and preaching the necessity of armed resistance. Reading is central to this deliberative process toward social change: the novel joins collective textual interpretation with collective action. In addition to Vesey's and Dred's use of the Bible to inspire others with liberation theology, the novel's white characters showcase scenes of communal literary criticism. Nina and her set debate the virtues of "novel-reading" and decide for "a good historical romance" over "dull history" any day of the week—except Sunday (147). More than a validation of Stowe's chosen genre, these readerly deliberations complement debates about the ethics of action. When readers first encounter Edward Clayton, in a library, he is questioning the difficulty of bringing "the theory" to "the practice" of law (21). Prompted by his friend to throw his hat into the political ring, Clayton demurs, saying that his models of Roman virtue would be sorely out of place in Washington, D.C. Clayton objects to the competitive parceling of individual interest, the obligation of lawyers to represent private interests and advocate only partial truths in a contest over "Truth." Clayton wrests a concession from his interlocutor that "the style of political action has altered somewhat since those days" (21) of the Roman republic, but Stowe's point is more forward-looking: namely, that new circuits of reading, deliberation, and action have to be imagined if the American republic is to live up to its founding promises.

A series of interlinking story lines suggest that social mixing and political deliberation might result in group action that benefits rather than destroys the larger whole. The novel's conceptual task is thus to align competing private interest with larger visions of the public good. Nina and her suitor Clayton find in each other a suitable reflection of their contrarian temperament, a disposition that will lead each of them—both slaveholders—to abolitionist sympathy and, in Edward's case, action. In one of their early courting scenes, as Edward and his sister pay a visit to Nina, the Gordon family decides to attend a camp meeting in a clearing in the woods. All classes of people attend: poor whites, Yankee traders, minister, slave hunters, enslaved blacks and the elite whites who own them. This extended scene—like the scenes in Dred's swamp encampment—cultivates an anxious fascination about how promiscuous social exchange might lead to collective action. The revival swings into full gear, and the prayers, hymns, and mounting excitement begin to blend the diversity of the crowd into a single ecstatic body. The narrator observes that

> [t]here is always something awful in the voice of the multitude. It would seem as if the breath that a crowd breathed out together, in moments of enthusiasm, carried with it a portion of the dread and mystery of their own immortal natures. The whole area before the pulpit, and in the distant aisles of the forest, became one vast, surging sea of sound, as negroes and whites, slaves and freemen, saints and sinners, slave-holders, slave-hunters, slave traders, ministers, elders, and laymen, alike joined in the pulse of that mighty song. A flood of electrical excitement seemed to rise with it, as, with a voice of many waters, the rude chant went on. (250)

The Gordons and their visitors regain affective distance by exploring their various critical reactions to the scene. When Edward's sister Anne exclaims: "I think we might teach them to be decent. These things ought not to be allowed!" he defends the cacophony of charismatic screams, shouts, and trances, invoking the variety and abundance of nature as both an explanation for human diversity and justification for honoring multiple pathways toward religious conversion (245). Ann protests: "[T]here is so much in the wild freedom of these meetings that shocks my taste and sense of propriety" (254). But it is this freedom that her brother treasures. Calling her a "conventionalist," he counters:

> You would have well-trimmed trees and velvet turf. But I love briers, dead limbs and all, for their very savage freedom....Just so it is with men. Unite any assembly of common men in a great enthusiasm—work them up into an abandon, and let everyone "let go" and speak as nature prompts—and you will have brush, underwood, briers and all grotesque growths; but now and then, some thought or sentiment will be struck out with a freedom or power such as you cannot get in any other way. You cultivated people are much mistaken when you despise the enthusiasms of the masses....I reverence the people, as I do the woods, for the wild, grand freedom with which their humanity develops itself. (254–255)

Edward Clayton accepts the Federalist legacy that frames democratic action as "primitive" and "savage" and yet he revalues it as a positive good. So, too, he revalues the unruly wooded terrain that harbors Dred, viewing it as the setting that might transform the anarchic Comus into a freedom fighter. Rejecting "conventional" understandings of the need to barricade the polity against the common people, Edward insists that such "wild, grand freedom" can enhance the good of the larger whole. In the same breath he counters Emerson's privatizing and individualizing aesthetic, insisting that the moral beauty of human sentiment shines precisely through such mass expression.

Stowe thus takes her central metaphor for describing the political possibility *and* dangers of acting in concert from the verdant over- and undergrowth of the Great Dismal Swamp. Elsewhere, the narrator reverses the terms of Edward's speech to analogize Dred's mental construction:

> It is difficult to fathom the dark recesses of a mind so powerful and active as his, placed under a pressure of ignorance and social disability so tremendous.

> In those desolate regions which he made his habitation…trees often, from the
> singularly unnatural and wildly stimulating properties of the slimy depths from
> which they spring, assume a goblin growth, entirely different from their normal
> habit. All sorts of vegetable monsters stretch their weird, fantastic forms among
> its shadows. There is no principle so awful through all of nature as the principle of
> *growth*. It is a mysterious and dread condition of existence. (496)

The very human and vegetable growth that Clayton so admires turns now "mysterious and *dread*." Stowe's narrator loads her eponymous character with Emerson's
and the Federalists' contempt for democratic grassroots action, even while she has
him stand alongside Clayton as the character most true to the nation's revolutionary
principles.

 Dred embodies the novel's ambivalence about group action: the freedom he
heralds is always overloaded with the dark potential of collective savagery. Stowe
notably analogizes her revolutionary, rabble-rousing Dred to a wrathful Christ—
right before she kills him off. But readers have already been signaled that his revolution won't achieve fruition in a pivotal swamp scene, one that echoes the earlier
camp revival. Portently denominated "the camp of the Lord's judgment," this meeting takes place in Dred's swamp redoubt, what he calls the "stronghold of Engedi."
Participants read and debate the Bible alongside the Declaration of Independence.
They share their stories and experiences, progressing, like the camp revival participants, toward a rapturous and revolutionary union of belief and action. They
ecstatically wait, under Dred's guidance, for the proper sign from the Lord to begin
the work of smiting their oppressors. His lieutenant, Hannibal, thinks the time for
heavenly retribution is at hand, and his scriptural rhetoric of revenge urges a swift
response. Dred, however, is not so sure that the moment for smiting has arrived.
But before he can sort out this question in consultation with his crew, the Gordons'
loyal house-servant, Milly, interrupts the scene, preaching Christlike humility. She
appeals to the crowd. "If the Lord could bear all dat and love us yet, shan't we? O
brethren, there's a better way…love yer enemies!" Her interruption forestalls the
revolution, as Dred confirms: "Woman, thy prayers have prevailed for this time!"
(461–462). The transcendent nature of her plea leaves no space for deliberation: as
the narrator reports, "A dead silence followed this appeal. The key-note of another
harmony had been struck." Whereas Milly seeks mellifluous arrangement with no
room for either discussion or dissent, the counterharmony of Dred and his cocon-
spirators has the potential to embody spirited difference, clashing views, and passionate debate.

 At the same moment in the novel, Tom Gordon is organizing a mob to ter-
rorize any who support emancipation. From this point, it seems, the novel stops
equivocating about collective action, which is now reframed entirely as unlawful,
"foolish," and destructive. Instead, redemption comes through the individual and
more private actions of the Claytons, who leave North Carolina with their slaves to
establish them in a free and enterprising model community in Canada, and through
Milly, who escapes to New York and founds a tenement home for street children in
New York City.

In this reading, Stowe flirts with, more than she embraces, an alternative to the negative casting that the Federalists and Emerson reserve for public action. And so we're left again disappointed in Stowe, who seemingly cannot find an alternative to the impasse between critique and action in the nation's critical debate over slavery.

BUT WAIT!

But is that right? Or are *we* being too categorical? In *Home Fronts*, Lora Romero warns against our field's critical disdain for compromise, our misplaced insistence that the novels we study either liberate us from culture or enslave us to it. She calls for a more critically nuanced approach, one that refuses both idealization and demonization, and her caution might be worth applying here. Our reading may, in other words, be creating the very false opposition we warned against in our introduction.

Turning briefly to another novel about violent action against slavery can help us highlight the contour of our critical mistake. Russell Banks's acclaimed *Cloudsplitter* (1998), a fictionalized biography of the radical abolitionist John Brown penned by his son Owen, foregrounds this opposition between citizen critique and action. While *Cloudsplitter* is surely an artifact of late twentieth-century American literature, it hearkens back to nineteenth-century debates over the perceived antagonism between intellectual discussion and social change. In other words, Banks's text is both a novel and a critical commentary on the tense, uncertain relationship between impassioned belief and political action. It is also a methodological gambit that seeks lessons about contemporary citizenship in the literary and historical archive of the United States.

In *Cloudsplitter*, Owen recollects a father who insistently demands "Action, action, action!" while impatiently dismissing New England's radical abolitionists (he calls them the "Boston ladies") and Garrisonians, who offer only "talk, talk, talk" (246, 320). At one point Owen and John Brown travel to Boston and attend a lecture by Emerson. Owen is enraptured by the reformer's discourse, asking his father, "[D]idn't you admire his [Emerson's] language?" Brown only scoffs that Emerson, a literary figure canonized in just about every anthology of nineteenth-century American literature, is "truly a *boob*," a judgment he soon repeats. Owen, however, is less dismissive and sees the problem as a symptom of the apparently unbridgeable gulf between Emerson's heroic language and his father's heroic action. Owen's memoir monumentalizes the father, who fearlessly pursues action instead of debate. But in the novel's denouement, structured around the raid at Harper's Ferry, readers learn something different. In Owen's recollection, the raid fails because of the lack of deliberation. As John Brown moves his loyal cohort toward decisive action, he squelches dissent. Summarizes Owen:

> [A]ll of the men, wear on their faces a single expression.... it is the hungry look of a follower, of a true believer. There is no Thomas the Doubter in this room, no sober skeptic, no ironist, no dark materialist. We have all been confined here

in this isolated place for too many weeks and months to have any mentality left
that is not a piece of a single mind, and that mind is shaped and filled by Father
alone. (706)

As Owen details, his father's suppression of critique, his insistence on loyalty to his
vision for action, dooms the mission at Harper's Ferry. It disables the conspirators
from thinking through key challenges to their plan, most notably whether local
slaves will rally to Brown's cause and begin a revolution that will sweep the South.
In *Cloudsplitter*, Frederick Douglass tries without success to convince Brown of
this point, but so consumed is Brown with action at the expense of talk that he
seems unable to process Douglass's warning. In Banks's rendition of this actual historic meeting, Brown appeals to Douglass, "'When I strike, the bees will begin to
swarm, and I will need you to help hive them.' It was a trope that he had used many
times, and he spoke it mechanically" (736). Brown is no longer seeking dialogue;
instead, we might say that he employs a tired sound bite that cuts off deliberation.

Associating Brown with the opposition of talk and action is hardly Banks's
twentieth-century invention. This antithesis appears in two key allusions in *Dred*,
allusions that are all the more remarkable because they predate Brown's fateful
raid on Harper's Ferry by three years. The first comes when Harry learns that his
comrade Hark has been murdered by Tom Gordon in an attempt to uncover evidence of a "slave conspiracy." Stowe analogizes his grief by drawing a comparison
to "Bleeding Kansas": "Let the associates of Brown ask themselves if they cannot
understand the midnight anguish of Harry!" (499). Here, Harry is on the brink of
violent reprisal and remains in this heated state until Clayton sends him letters urging patience and restraint. Stowe's fiction anticipates a momentous event that will
occur in three years when Brown and Douglass have their legendary meeting at a
quarry outside of Rochester—but with the important difference that *Dred* depicts a
white man advising a black man against any precipitous action while *Cloudsplitter*
shows Douglass urging a white radical to plan more carefully before taking the fight
into the heart of the slavocracy.

The second allusion appears in a very different context, as Tom Gordon stokes
the passions of the mob. His speech, vulgar and profane, is something that Stowe
struggles to convey. She again turns to recent events associated with Brown's activities on the front lines against the expansion of slavery. In May 1856, after proslavery
forces raided the Free-Soil town of Lawrence, Kansas, Brown and his sons sought
retaliation by killing five proslavery settlers with broadswords. Stowe never mentions Brown's violence; instead she focuses on rhetoric, comparing Tom's speech to
proslavery demagoguery: "Any one who has read the speeches of the leaders who
presided over the sacking of Lawrence will get an idea of some features in this style
of eloquence, which our pen cannot represent" (506). The collective action that *Dred*
ends up demonizing begins in the misuse of speech. It's not that Stowe prefers talk
over action; rather she prefers a certain style of talk—seemingly Clayton's measured
lawyerly counsel, a type of discourse we might associate not only with Emerson but
with current academic style—in which an intellectual tells a would-be activist what
to do, how to behave, and how not to act.

Here again, Banks offers a notable contrast. In *Cloudsplitter*, Brown's insistence on "action" and impatience with "talk" comes after hearing Emerson lecture, a scene that more or less corresponds with the historical record that has Brown commenting after the New England antislavery convention of May 1859, "These men are all talk. What is needed is action—action."² Banks embellishes these sentences, refusing to condense history into a sound bite—after all, *Cloudsplitter* is a novel so it is unlikely that its author wants to get rid of words altogether as if both readers and characters could live in some sphere of pure action. And at 758 pages long, Banks's novel does not scrimp on discourse, discussion, or debate. Accordingly, *Cloudsplitter* contextualizes Brown's belittlement of talk not as an out-and-out rejection of speech but of words that go nowhere because they are trapped within an insular community that is dangerously fixated on its internal politics: antislavery people "waste their time…squabbling amongst themselves, while our Negro brethren languish in slavery" (320).

Banks reminds us of a wisdom receiving new critical scrutiny. As business analyst James Surowiecki reports in his book *The Wisdom of Crowds*, groups—in wiki pages, in predictions markets, in aggregated and averaged form—are impressively good under the right circumstances at providing correct solutions to a range of problems. As he puts it: "With most things, the average is mediocrity. With decision making, it's often excellence. You could say it's as if we've been programmed to be collectively smart." But not just any group is smart. Some are terrible: groups of "experts," like-minded groups, groups that are bound by strong social ties, and individuals all tend to produce less healthy decisions than properly diversified crowds of loosely linked individuals. The expert, like-thinking, and socially connected groups do so because they tend toward an unhealthy homogeneity making them susceptible to group polarization, a phenomenon legal scholar Cass Sunstein has described at length in his book *Why Societies Need Dissent*. In settings where a group shares basic leanings or opinions, deliberation tends to intensify the opinion of the group and individuals within it, polarizing rather than moderating or informing opinion. Study after experiment has shown that no individual is as smart or as good at problem solving as a diverse and informed group of individuals. Surowiecki highlights the work of political scientist Chandra Nemeth, who establishes that "the presence of a minority viewpoint, all by itself, makes a group's decisions more nuanced and its decision-making process more rigorous. This is true even when the minority viewpoint turns out to be ill-conceived" (183–184). Thus the fundamental importance for any deliberation leading to action of diverse opinion, differing expertise, and norms that support dissent.

This is the fictional Owen Brown's insight, and, as it turns out, this may be Stowe's at least partial insight too. Let's step back from our previous analysis and recollect that *Dred*'s awful portentousness is not "natural," as Stowe's swamp metaphors seemingly signal, but rather the "natural" byproduct of sociopolitical oppression: the "dread" she attaches to her eponymous character and his "portentous and astonishing" maroon cohort is man-made—by the white republic (496). Dred assumes the heroic stature of a prophet in this novel less because of his charismatic leadership, and more because of what the narrator calls the "perfectness of his own religious enthusiasm." Such religious enthusiasm manifests itself in his self-critical, Christlike openness to others who suffer and to their opinions, which he brings to bear on his plans for action. Millie's exhortation may have silenced the crowd and halted its plans, but chapters later, we find Dred ruminating over her "pre-sentation...[on] the eternal principle of intercession and atonement." "[D]eeply affected" by Milly's message, Dred struggles to align it with his own "habitual and overmastering sense of oppression and wrong" (497). In this pivotal chapter, Harry, having spent the night grieving over the murder of his friend Hark, wakes up ready for "an immediate insurrection" to indulge "the fearful craving of his own soul for justice." But Dred, "true to the enthusiastic impulses which guided him, persisted in waiting for that sign from heaven which was to indicate when the day of grace was closed and the day of judgment was to begin" (499).

Dred dies before we can know how his struggle might have played out. But what he represents does not die with him. As the narrator underscores at the conclusion of one of Dred's last passionate prayers, "[W]e who live in ceiled houses would do well to listen to that sound, lest it be *to us* that inarticulate moaning which goes before the earthquake" (498, our emphasis). She warns against ignoring such forms as merely "natural," insisting that we must anticipate the consequences of social actions and bad institutions. Dred's openness to Milly's disruptive message offers a key for interracial social justice: white readers' political behaviors should be guided by attention to and even dialogue with Dred and those like him, whose abilities grow though "placed under a pressure of ignorance and social disability so tremen-dous" (496).

The opposition between Stowe's depiction of the "savage" Dred and "civilized" Clayton is destabilized in precisely this way. As it turns out, Clayton's conversations with Dred and his interactions with the maroon community intensify his willing-ness to act on his abolitionist commitments. Rescued from Tom Gordon's lynch mob by Dred and Harry, Clayton spends days in Engedi before returning to con-sciousness, nursed and watched over by members of the fugitive community. Once conscious, he stays there to gather strength, spending hours in conversation with Dred. Though he cannot always fathom the logic of Dred's charismatic ramblings, he finds himself strangely impressed and inspired by his prophesying. When Dred is killed, Clayton mourns with the community and persuades them not to rise up against the whites but rather to avail themselves of an escape route to the North. This is no cowards' path: Stowe is clear that in this counsel, Clayton becomes an enemy to the "laws and customs of the social state under which he was born." The camp members go—taking numerous slaves from adjacent plantations with them. And Clayton returns to his plantation, energetically attempting to persuade his neigh-bors to allow him to follow the course of his conscience with his own slaves before deciding with his sister to move to Canada. His actions, in other words, are not simply private, and they affect far more than his individual destiny, just as Milly's tenement house translates her values into action, impacting the lives of dozens of children, white, black, and foreign.

In *Storming the Gates of Paradise*, environmental and social justice activist Rebecca Solnit reminds us that "change is not always by revolution...any step toward connection and communion is a step toward paradise" (8). It is a mistake, she insists, to discount the power of the big changes that can come through small actions toward a better world. As she puts it elsewhere:

> [I]t's always too soon to calculate effect.... Cause and effect assume history marches forward, but history is not an army. It is a crab scuttling sideways, a drip of soft water wearing away stone, an earthquake breaking centuries of tension. Sometimes one person inspires a movement, or her words do decades later; sometimes a few passionate people change the world; sometimes they start a mass movement and millions do; sometimes those millions are stirred by the same outrage or the same ideal and change comes upon us like a change of weather. All these transformations have in common is that they begin in the imagination. (*Hope in the Dark*, 4)

In *Dred*, before Civil War and Emancipation, Stowe shows us change that begins in the imaginations of oppressed *and* privileged men and women, in conversation with each other and in critical engagement with their biblical and national predecessors. These small, but important public and group actions are crafted out of critical reading, intellectual deliberation, and sympathetic exchange. Readings, conversations, disagreements, compromises, and practical courses of action can make significant contributions to a changed world, engendering actors who change the way they and others live in their shared world.

These novels urge us to remember how important an archive literary history is for our current dilemmas: indeed, it is a commonwealth resource for our own deliberations and actions. It's worth thinking about how contemporary contexts summoning deliberation and action can guide and open new windows on literature and events nearly a century and a half past. The challenge of this kind of reading lies in remembering that these actors could not foresee the events that have so fundamentally shaped our understanding of this period. In order fully to engage the dilemmas informing the deliberations of the characters in Stowe's and Banks's novels, we must engage them in terms of what literary critic Myra Jehlen terms "history before the fact." Stowe challenged her readers to deliberate and act without any certain knowledge of the Emancipation Proclamation and Civil War on the horizon. Taking away the shattering solution of civil war puts Stowe and her readers into a context much like our own. In a world of uncertain outcomes, where political, social, ethical, and economic disagreements are so fierce and unrelenting, Stowe and Banks offer crucial advice about the necessity of difference of opinion to both fruitful deliberation and plans for action. They remind us that those wishing to engage in action must start by deliberating in order to implement large or small actions toward a better world. They insist on the central importance of dissent to deliberation. They challenge readers to understand that creating such a basis for deliberation is action itself, and yet is not itself a substitute for acting for a more just democratic polity.

NOTES

1 See Fritz, who argues that the notion of the people's sovereignty as existing independently of government—the notion enshrined in the state constitutions of the revolutionary era, began to dissipate in the 1830s, replaced by a strong cultural emphasis on the Constitution as an embodiment of an imperative toward perpetual union: "If created by the sovereign people, government could not be beyond the control of the people. Yet the idea of an irrevocable union repudiated this underlying authority of the people. The strength of the notion of a permanent union grew as the revolutionary generation passed away" (234). See also Castiglia, who theorizes the conditions by which "Federal affect" redirects citizens' energies toward regulating government toward self-regulation in the early nation.

2 See Rhodes 341.

BIBLIOGRAPHY

Banks, Russell. *Cloudsplitter*. New York: Harper Flamingo, 1998.

Berlant, Lauren. "Poor Eliza." In "No More Separate Spheres!" *American Literature* 70.3 (1998): 635–668.

Bouton, Terry. *Taming Democracy: "The People," The Founders and the Troubled Ending of the American Revolution*. New York: Oxford University Press, 2007.

Castiglia, Chris. *Interior States: Institutional Consciousness and the Inner Life of Democracy in the Antebellum United States*. Durham, NC: Duke University Press, 2008.

Emerson, Ralph Waldo. "The Fugitive Slave Law." *Emerson's Antisalvery Writings*. Ed. Len Gougeoin and Joel Myerson. New Haven, CT: Yale University Press, 1995. 73–89.

Formisano, Ronald. *For the People: American Populist Movements from the Revolution to the 1850s*. Chapel Hill: University of North Carolina Press, 2008.

Fritz, Christian. *American Sovereigns: The People and America's Constitutional Tradition before the Civil War*. New York: Cambridge University Press, 2008.

Hawthorne, Nathaniel. "My Kinsman, Major Molineux." *Nathaniel Hawthorne: Tales and Sketches*. 4th ed. New York: Library of America, 1982. 68–87.

Hibbing, John R., and Elizabeth Theiss-Morse. *Stealth Democracy: Americans' Beliefs about How Government Should Work*. New York: Cambridge University Press, 2002.

Holton, Woody. *Unruly Americans and the Origins of the Constitution*. New York: Hill and Wang, 2007.

Jehlen, Myra. "History before the Fact: Or, Captain John Smith's Unfinished Symphony." *Critical Inquiry* 19.4 (1993): 677–692.

Levine, Robert S. *Martin Delany, Frederick Douglass, and the Politics of Representative Identity*. Chapel Hill: University of North Carolina Press, 1997.

Milton, John. "A Mask (Comus)." *John Milton, Complete Poems and Major Prose*. Ed. Merritt Y. Hughes. Indianapolis: Hackett, 2003. 86–114.

Mutz, Diana. *Hearing the Other Side: Deliberative versus Participatory Democracy*. New York: Cambridge University Press, 2006.

Rhodes, James Ford. *History of the United States from the Compromise of 1850 to the McKinley-Bryan Campaign of 1896*. Vol. 2. New York: Harper, 1899.

Romero, Laura. *Home Fronts: Domesticity and Its Critics in the Antebellum United States*. Durham, NC: Duke University Press, 1997.

Solnit, Rebecca. *Hope in the Dark: Untold Histories, Wild Possibilities.* New York: Nation Books, 2004.

———. *Storming the Gates of Paradise: Landscapes for Politics.* Berkeley: University of California Press, 2007.

Stowe, Harriet Beecher. *Dred: A Tale of the Great Dismal Swamp.* Ed. Robert S. Levine. Chapel Hill: University of North Carolina Press, 2000.

Sunstein, Cass. *Why Societies Need Dissent.* Cambridge, MA: Harvard University Press, 2003.

Surowiecki, James. *The Wisdom of the Crowds: Why the Many Are Smarter Than the Few and How Collective Wisdom Shapes Business, Economies, Societies and Nations.* New York: Doubleday, 2004.

INDEX

....

Emboldened page ranges refer to chapters; italicized locators refer to figures; 'n' following a locator refers to a Note. Individuals referenced are writers or critics unless otherwise noted. Character names are alphabetized by first name.